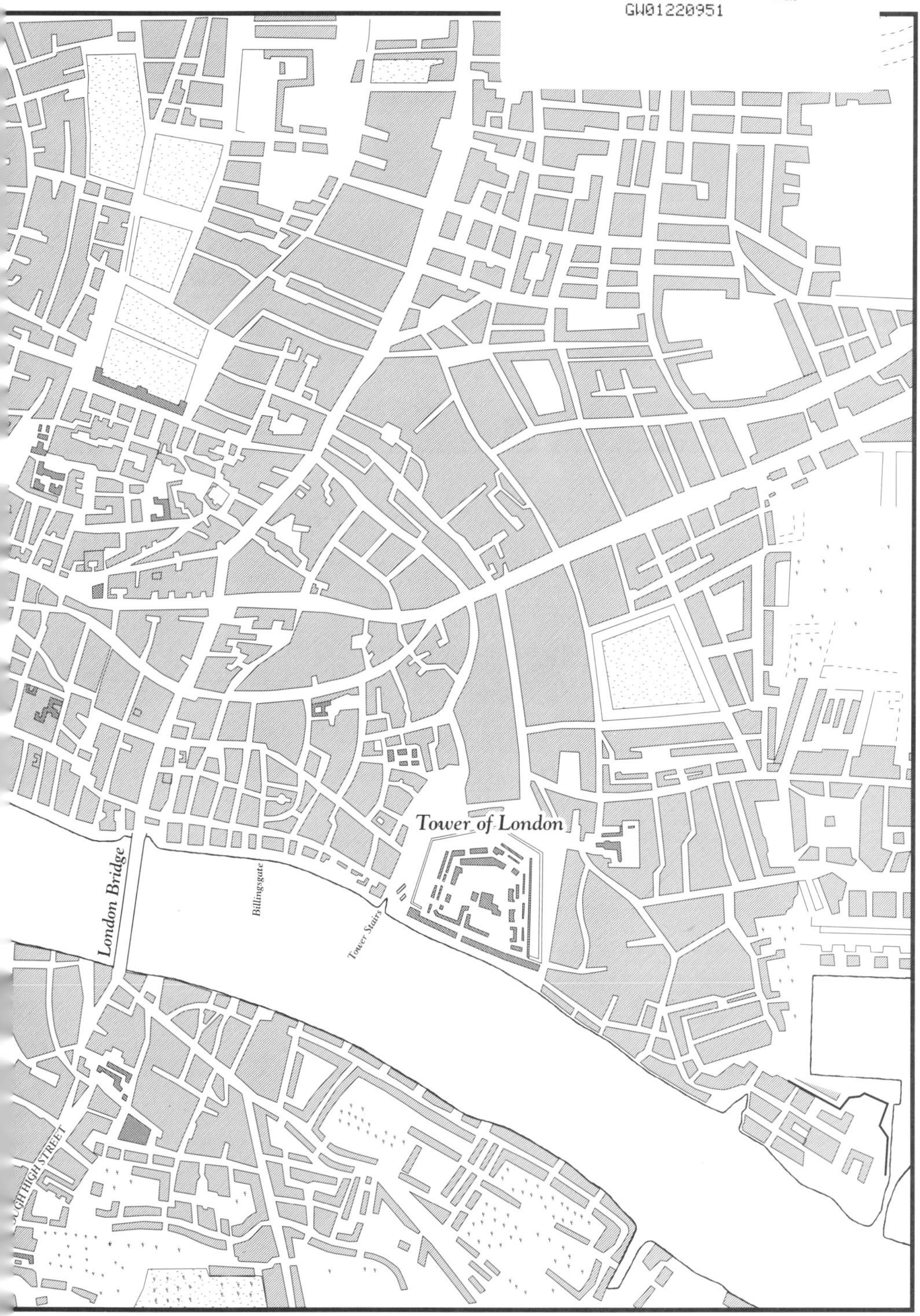
Tower of London
London Bridge
Billingsgate
Tower Stairs

THE DICKENS COMPANIONS

Series Editors: Susan Shatto and David Paroissien

The Companion to *Great Expectations*

THE DICKENS COMPANIONS

[1]
The Companion to *Our Mutual Friend*
MICHAEL COTSELL

[2]
The Companion to *The Mystery of Edwin Drood*
WENDY S. JACOBSON

[3]
The Companion to *Bleak House*
SUSAN SHATTO

[4]
The Companion to *A Tale of Two Cities*
ANDREW SANDERS

[5]
The Companion to *Oliver Twist*
DAVID PAROISSIEN

[6]
The Companion to *Hard Times*
MARGARET SIMPSON

[7]
The Companion to *Great Expectations*
DAVID PAROISSIEN

THE COMPANION TO
Great Expectations

DAVID PAROISSIEN

HELM INFORMATION LTD

© David Paroissien, 2000

A CIP catalogue record for this book
is available from the British Library.

All rights reserved: No reproduction, copy or
transmission of this publication may be made
without written permission.

No paragraph of this publication may be
reproduced, copied or transmitted save
with the written permission or in accordance
with the provisions of the Copyright Act 1956
(as amended), or under the terms of any licence
permitting limited copying issued by the
Copyright Licensing Agency, 7 Ridgmount
Street, London WC1E 7AE.

Any person who does any unauthorised act in
relation to this publication may be liable to
criminal prosecution and civil claims for
damages.

Published in Great Britain in 2000 by
Helm Information Ltd.
The Banks, Mountfield,
near Robertsbridge,
East Sussex TN32 5JY
U.K.

ISBN 1-873403-57-7

Printed on acid-free paper and bound by
Guinti Grafiche Industrie, Italy.

Affectionately inscribed to Keelan

CONTENTS

	page
List of Illustrations	ix
General Preface by the Editors	xi
Acknowledgements	xiii
Abbreviations for Dickens's Works and Related Material	xv
Bibliographical Symbols and Abbreviations	xvi
Introduction	1
A Note on the Text	15
How to Use the Notes	17
The Notes	19
Appendix One: The Sequence of Events in Pip's Narrative	423
Appendix Two: The Hoo Peninsula and Rochester	435
Appendix Three: The Temple, Little Britain and the River Thames	438
Appendix Four: Maps	441
Appendix Five: Serial Instalments in *All the Year Round*	453
Select Bibliography	456
Index	481

LIST OF ILLUSTRATIONS

		page
1	The first serialized page of *Great Expectations* in volume 4, number 84, of *All the Year Round* (1 December 1860)	20
2	Pip's 'little stone lozenges'	31
3	St Mary's Higham, 4 miles north-west of Rochester	32
4	St James's Cooling, 6 miles north-west of Rochester	32
5	The Comport and Baker gravestones, St James's Cooling	57
6	Elevated pulpit, Trottiscliffe church	58
7	Prison hulk at Woolwich	69
8	Coastguard hulk, Lower Hope	70
9	Restoration House, Rochester, Kent	91
10	Satis House	92
11	Restoration House, ground plan	92
12	Rochester Guildhall	129
13	Interior: the Court Hall 'with some shining black portraits on the walls'	130
14	Rochester Castle, Cathedral and bridge over the Medway, *c*.1800	161
15	Barnard's Inn, *c*.1800	195
16	The Temple, 1720	303
17	Staircase leading to a set of chambers	304
18	Old London Bridge, *c*.1800	353
19	The Custom House	354

20	Steamers at London Bridge wharf	359
21	Gravesend	360
22	Plan of Middle Temple	441
23	Mr Jaggers's Little Britain	442
24	The Thames and Kent Road from London to Rochester	444
25	Map of the Hoo Peninsula	449
26	Map of Dickens's Rochester	450
27	Miss Havisham's Uptown	451
28	Hole Haven Creek	452

GENERAL PREFACE
BY THE EDITORS

The Dickens Companions series provides the most comprehensive annotation of the works of Dickens ever undertaken. Separate volumes are devoted to each of Dickens's fifteen novels, to *Sketches by Boz* and to *The Uncommercial Traveller*; the five Christmas books are treated together in one volume. The series will be completed by a General Index, making nineteen volumes in all.

The nature of the annotation is factual rather than critical. The series undertakes what the general editors of the Clarendon Dickens have called 'the immense task of explanatory annotation' of Dickens's works. Each Companion will elucidate obscurities and allusions which were doubtless intelligible to the nineteenth-century reader but which have changed or lost their meaning in a later age. The 'world' of Dickens passed away more than a century ago, and our perceptions and interpretations of his works can be sharpened by our having recalled for us a precise context or piece of information.

The annotation identifies allusions to current events and intellectual and religious issues, and supplies information on topography, social customs, costume, furniture, transportation, and so on. Identifications are provided for allusions to plays, poems, songs, the Bible, the Book of Common Prayer and other literary sources. Elements of Dickens's plots, characterization and style which are influenced by the works of other writers are also identified. When an aspect of the text can be shown to have been influenced by Dickens's own experience this is indicated. The work of Dickens's illustrators is also discussed. Finally, although the Companions do not attempt the work of a modern scholarly edition, material from Dickens's manuscripts and proofs is included when it is of major significance.

The main part of the information in each Companion is arranged in the form of notes presented for convenient use with any edition of Dickens's works. The information is thus placed where it is most relevant, enabling the notes to be used to elucidate a local difficulty, or to pursue the use of a certain kind of material or the development of a particular idea. To facilitate the last purpose, the notes are cross-referenced, and each Companion contains a comprehensive index. The introduction to each Companion traces the major influences and concerns revealed by the annotation and, where appropriate, demonstrates their place in the genesis and composition of the text.

Dickens's vital and imaginative response to his culture is a familiar fact, but the Dickens Companions demonstrate and explore this response more fully and in far greater detail than has ever been attempted. Hitherto, Dickens's works have been annotated only on a modest scale. Many modern editions of the novels contain some notes, but there is not space in one volume for both the text of a novel and a comprehensive annotation of the text. Because most volumes of the Dickens Companions are devoted to a single work, the series can provide the full-scale, thoroughgoing annotation which the works of Dickens require. The completed series will compose a uniquely comprehensive archive of information about Dickens's world, affording the modern reader an unparalleled record of Dickens's concerns and the sources of his artistry. For many kinds of scholar, not merely Dickensians, the Dickens Companions will provide a fundamental tool for future critical and historical scholarship on various aspects of nineteenth-century British culture.

To undertake the 'immense task' of annotation, the Editors have assembled a team of Dickens scholars who work closely together and with the Editors in order to enhance the depth and scope of each Companion. The series is not a variorum commentary on Dickens: it does not consist of a survey or a selection of comments by other annotators and scholars. Previous scholarship is, in general, cited only when it is considered to identify an important piece of information about the historical, literary and biographical influences on Dickens's works.

The annotation in the Dickens Companions is based on original research which derives for the most part from the writing of Dickens's own time, the reading available to him and the books he is known to have read. The annotation is not perfunctorily minimal: a large number of notes are substantial essays and all are written in a readable style. Nor does the annotation consist of narrow definitions of what the reader (in the opinion of another reader) 'needs to know' in order to 'understand' the text. Rather, the annotation attempts to open up the actual and imaginative worlds which provided the sources and the backgrounds of Dickens's works in the belief that what interested, engaged and amused Dickens can hardly fail to interest, engage and amuse his readers. Our largest hope for the Dickens Companions is that the volumes will be read with a pleasure akin to that with which Dickens's own writings are read, and that they will be genuine Companions to both his works and his readers.

The idea of providing each of Dickens's major works with a companion volume of annotation originated with the late Professor T. J. B. Spencer. It is to his memory that the series is gratefully and affectionately dedicated.

1980–95   SUSAN SHATTO
                                              MICHAEL COTSELL

After the publication of five volumes, Michael Cotsell retired from the series as Associate Editor. David Paroissien replaces him as co-editor, pledged to continue with Susan Shatto an annotative enterprise devoted to recovering and illuminating the allusive worlds of Dickens's novels and the culture which gave rise to them.

1997   SUSAN SHATTO
                                              DAVID PAROISSIEN

ACKNOWLEDGEMENTS

The seven years I have spent researching and writing this study have left me heavily indebted to many people. Most particularly, I wish to acknowledge Susan Shatto's assistance, encouragement and judicious editorial eye as she read various drafts and responded generously and frequently to my many questions. I am also most grateful to Michael Cotsell for his help during an early draft and for generously turning over to me notes and references he had compiled, intending originally to undertake the study himself. In addition, Robert E. Bagg and Vincent J. DiMarco, both former English Department chairmen at the University of Massachusetts, Amherst, lent significant support to my work. Two fruitful summers working at Oxford University's Bodleian Library with assistance from the English Department's Oxford Summer Seminar helped me launch my research and get the project well under way.

A study of this kind inevitably draws on the efforts of other scholars. In this respect, I have been well served by Edgar Rosenberg, who, with Carol Stiles Beamis, his last Norton editor, generously made available the proofs of his invaluable edition of *Great Expectations* and agreed to my using the Norton Critical Edition as my copy-text. An excellent bibliographical study of the novel by George J. Worth and Anny Sadrin's fine critical study of *Great Expectations* saved me many hours of library searching and stimulated my own scrutiny of the text. To both I am most grateful.

Help from reference librarians at the University of Massachusetts' W. E. B. Du Bois Library and Oxford University's Bodleian Library has been unstinted and continuous. In particular, I wish to thank Reference Librarians Elizabeth B. Fitzpatrick, Paula F. Mark, Barbara L. Morgan and Jeffery M. Tenenbaum; Christine Mason in the Upper Reading of the Bodleian Library, William H. Clennell, and Julie Anne Lambert, Supervisor of the John Johnson Collection of printed ephemera. Karen V. Kukil, Assistant Curator of Rare Books, made my work in the Neilson Library of Smith College most pleasurable. Graeme Powell, Manuscript Librarian at the National Library of Australia, promptly helped me obtain a copy of John Ward's 'Diary'. Charlotte Brown, Archivist of Special Collections at UCLA, and Russell Johnson were also prompt in responding to questions. Of equal importance and equally generous has been the response from my university's Interlibrary Loan Office; I am especially indebted to Edla K. Holm, former Head of the University's Interlibrary Loan Office, and her able staff.

For permission to reproduce certain illustrations, I wish to thank the Bodleian Library (plates 19 and 21, G.A. Fol. A. 13), the Guildhall Library, Corporation of London (plates 7 and 20), and the National Maritime Museum London (plate 8).

In Rochester and in London I profited considerably from the help of librarians, archivists and people I met by chance. It is a pleasure therefore to thank the following: Mr M. I. Moad of the Guildhall Museum, who answered many questions and shared his knowledge of the city with me, both in person and in correspondence; Kate Woollacott and Pat Salter, respectively Manager and Public Services Supervisor at the Rochester upon Medway Studies Centre; Rita Bryon, Assistant Librarian at the

Maritime Information Centre of the National Maritime Museum, Greenwich; Ralph Hyde, former Keeper of Prints and Maps of London's Guildhall Library; and Lesley Whitelaw, Archivist at Middle Temple Library, London. To Barbara Mackey and Robert Tucker, who stimulated my local research in Rochester, I owe special thanks.

I am indebted to many friends and colleagues whose patience I have tried with arcane and frequently obscure questions. It gives me pleasure to list them as follows: Hon. Michael J. Beloff, QC, David P. Borbeau, Joel J. Brattin, Joseph Donohue, David Fairer, Kenneth J. Fearn, James F. Freeman, Robin Gilmour, Robert R. Googins, Margaret R. Hunt, Jan Martin, Walter Karcheski, Curator of the Higgins Armory Museum, Worcester, MA, Fred Levit, Nancy Aycock Metz, John R. Nelson, Howard Nenner, Steven Parissien, Paul and Agnes Paroissien for their hospitality, Trey Philpotts, Eric Quackenbush, former Brewmaster of Northampton Brewery, Catherine Stevenson, Karen Kurt Teal, William Wall, Garry Wilson, Richard Witt and John Wright.

Throughout Amanda Helm and Stanley Radosh, respectively publisher and production editor, have shown considerable patience as this project matured, and I wish to acknowledge their generous support. I am indebted to Marc Dando for the expertise he lent to the preparation of the maps; Edward Leeson copy-edited the typescript with meticulous care and prepared the index. My family and especially my wife, Miriam, have exercised great tolerance throughout the years as I have worked to shake off this obsession with the details of a novel I admire all the more after this long immersion. It is therefore my hope that I have served well a cause I believe in and that these pages, despite inevitable flaws, will enhance the pleasure of future readers of *Great Expectations*.

The General Editors express their gratitude to the Dickens Society for a generous contribution to help defray the cost of preparing the final version of the typescript for publication.

ABBREVIATIONS FOR DICKENS'S WORKS AND RELATED MATERIAL

1. Works: Major

AN	*American Notes*
BH	*Bleak House*
BL	*The Battle of Life*
BR	*Barnaby Rudge*
C	*The Chimes*
CC	*A Christmas Carol*
CH	*The Cricket on the Hearth*
CHE	*A Child's History of England*
DC	*David Copperfield*
DS	*Dombey and Son*
GE	*Great Expectations*
HM	*The Haunted Man*
HT	*Hard Times*
LD	*Little Dorrit*
MC	*Martin Chuzzlewit*
MED	*The Mystery of Edwin Drood*
MHC	*Master Humphrey's Clock*
NN	*Nicholas Nickleby*
OCS	*The Old Curiosity Shop*
OMF	*Our Mutual Friend*
OT	*Oliver Twist*
PI	*Pictures from Italy*
PP	*The Pickwick Papers*
SB	*Sketches by Boz*
TTC	*A Tale of Two Cities*
UT	*The Uncommercial Traveller*

2. Works: Miscellaneous Writings

Bentley's	*Bentley's Miscellany*
CP	*Collected Papers*
MP	*Miscellaneous Papers*
RP	*Reprinted Pieces*
AYR	*All the Year Round*
HW	*Household Words*

HN	*The Household Narrative of Current Events*
CD	Charles Dickens Edition, 21 vols (1867–[74])

3. Related Material: Basic Sources

BCP	*The Book of Common Prayer*
BPP	*British Parliamentary Papers*
Forster	John Forster, *The Life of Charles Dickens*, 3 vols (1872–4)
HO	*Home Office Papers* (Public Record Office)
Letters	*The Letters of Charles Dickens*, ed. Madeline House and others, Pilgrim Edition. 8 vols to date (1965–)
Letters: Coutts	*Letters from Charles Dickens to Angela Burdett-Coutts, 1841–1865*, ed. Edgar Johnson (1953)
Letters: MDGH	*The Letters of Charles Dickens*, edited by his Sister-in-law and his Eldest Daughter. Vol 1. 1833–1856 (1880)
Memoranda	*Charles Dickens' Book of Memoranda*, ed. Fred Kaplan (New York: New York Public Library, 1981)
Nonesuch	*The Letters of Charles Dickens*, ed. Walter Dexter, Nonesuch Edition, 3 vols (1938)
Speeches	*The Speeches of Charles Dickens*, ed. K. J. Fielding (1960, 2nd edn 1988)

BIBLIOGRAPHICAL SYMBOLS AND ABBREVIATIONS

MS	Manuscript
CP	Corrected proofs
< >	Deletion in MS or proof
∧ or ∧	Addition or substitution in MS
∧ OR ∧	Addition or substitution in proof
illegible word	Signifies an unreadable word in MS

INTRODUCTION

Surveying his literary affairs in the summer of 1860, Charles Dickens had reason to feel composed. Looking back, he could point to the successful course he had charted for *All the Year Round*. The journal's weekly sales had reached 100,000 copies during the thirty-one instalments of his own serial, *A Tale of Two Cities* (30 April 1859 to 26 November 1859), and similar momentum had been maintained by Wilkie Collins's *The Woman in White*, scheduled to conclude in two final numbers in mid-August 1860. Looking forward, he saw Collins's successor, the popular Irish novelist, Charles Lever, ready to receive the baton and run with his *A Day's Ride: A Life's Romance*. Further down the road, Bulwer Lytton, another proven bestseller, warmed up for his leg in the relay – a prospect Dickens, like any editor anxious about sales and contributions, surely contemplated with satisfaction.[1]

All the Year Round – his 'valuable' property as Dickens referred to the weekly periodical he 'Conducted' (*Letters* 9.320) – owed its literary capital to a shrewd reshaping of *Household Words*, the journal's predecessor, which Dickens began not long after announcing his intention on 15 November 1858 to withdraw as its editor.[2] In format and price (twenty-four double-column pages at twopence an issue), *All the Year Round* resembled *Household Words*. But in significant ways Dickens had built in important differences. 'We propose always reserving the first place in these pages for a continuous original work of fiction, occupying about the same amount of time in its serial publication, as that which is just completed,' Dickens informed *Household Words* readers when he published the concluding instalment of *A Tale of Two Cities* on 26 November 1859. A greater emphasis on serial fiction at the expense of essays treating social and political topics, he continued, set the new journal

---

[1] *The Woman in White* (serially in AYR for forty weeks from 26 November 1859 to 25 August 1860); *A Day's Ride: A Life's Romance* (thirty-two weeks from 18 August 1860 to 23 March 1861); and *A Strange Story* (thirty-one weeks from 10 August 1861 to 8 March 1862).

[2] Dickens broke with Bradbury & Evans, his former publishers and the publishers of *Household Words*, on account of their unwillingness to include in *Punch*, which they also owned, a personal statement Dickens had published on the front page of *Household Words* for 12 June 1858. Under the title 'Personal', Dickens made enigmatic reference to his 'domestic troubles' and castigated his in-laws (without referring to them in this capacity) for what he saw as their role in spreading malicious rumours about a young person with whom his name had been connected. Bradbury & Evans declined the explanation Dickens offered, arguing that 'statements on a domestic and painful subject' remained wholly inappropriate in the 'columns of a comic miscellany' ('Mr. Charles Dickens and His Late Publishers', *Once a Week* 1 (1859): 3). In retaliation, Dickens – who co-owned, with his subeditor, W. H. Wills, three-quarters of the shares of *Household Words* – withdrew from conducting the journal, which was auctioned off. Its publication ceased, but following a legal settlement Dickens retained the copyright of the name 'Household Words', which he incorporated into the title of its successor, *All the Year Round*. To distinguish the latter from the former, Dickens reduced the emphasis on social and political matters, increased the coverage of foreign affairs and, most importantly, reserved the main space for a serial novel by a major writer. Ella Ann Oppenlander provides a succinct account of the chronology of events leading to the publication of *All the Year Round* in her *Dickens' All the Year Round: Descriptive Index and Contributor List* (Troy: New York, 1984), 3–17.

apart from the old. It 'is our hope and aim', he wrote, speaking on behalf of *All the Year Round*, that 'while we work hard at every other department of our journal, to produce, in this one, some sustained works of imagination that may become a part of English Literature' (*AYR*, 2.26 November 1859, 95). The readership he had won with *A Tale of Two Cities* proved his point, achieving spectacular immediate weekly sales and, in due course, permanent literary recognition. Few might grant the same lasting status to *A Woman in White*, but Collins's work, as the next novel to anchor the journal, fulfilled its destined role for the duration of its serial publication from late November 1859 to mid-August 1860. The sensational story, told by a succession of different narrators, served as an effective page-turner; its characters succeeded because Collins managed to 'fix the people in the beginning', while the mysterious events exercised a hold over readers because they rested securely on 'some one strong ground of suspended interest' (*Letters* 9.328, 327).

Meanwhile, starting on 28 January 1860, the journal's 'Conductor' had launched a series of essays under the name of the 'Uncommercial Traveller', a meditative, reflective persona who wandered around London and north Kent, reporting to readers on behalf of the firm of 'Human Interest Brothers'. Written in the first person and mixing both the autobiographical and the imaginary, the sixteen pieces which followed formed an imaginative landscape against which Dickens began to project a more extended work of fiction. 'I am prowling about, meditating a new book,' he wrote on 8 August 1860, saying something similar to another correspondent and repeating to Mrs Richard Watson, an old friend: 'I . . . am on the restless eve of beginning a new book' (*Letters* 9.284, 294, 309).

We lack conclusive proof that those words refer to the novel we know as *Great Expectations*. However, comments on childhood in some of the Uncommercial essays and the narrator's probing of scenes connected with Dickens's own past give some indication of the drift of his thought at the time. More certainly, had Dickens's plans for *All the Year Round* taken the course he projected, the novel that succeeded *A Tale of Two Cities* would have come down to us as a book published in twenty monthly parts. Instead, a crisis forced a dramatic adjustment and precipitated a work that, born of external circumstances, paradoxically represents perhaps Dickens's most nearly perfect artistic achievement.

The explanation for the departure from a battle plan drawn up months before is simple: Dickens's weekly readers of *All the Year Round* required no more than three instalments of Lever's novel to express their displeasure. 'Our fall is not large,' Dickens explained to Forster on 6 October 1860, perhaps trying to put the best face on things, before offering a more pessimistic assessment of the implications of the drop in circulation that accompanied the publication of *A Day's Ride*. But 'we have a considerable advance in hand of the story we are now publishing [*A Day's Ride*], and there is no vitality in it, and no chance whatever of stopping the fall' (*Letters* 9.320). Harder to understand are the reasons for Dickens's misplaced confidence in Lever, from whom he had solicited a full-length serial to serve as the journal's front runner as soon as Collins's novel concluded. Let me have 'any thing in the way of fiction – any thing in the way of actual observation and the reflection suggested by it – any thing about Italy – any thing grave or gay about any thing in the wide world, that has filtered through the mind of a man who sees the world with bright and keen eyes such as yours. "Say what will suit you," say you. "*That* is what will suit me," say I,' he had written to Lever in October 1859 (*Letters* 9.134).

Enticed by an offer he could not refuse, Lever nevertheless failed to deliver, proving incapable of supplying a story suitable for the weekly serial format essential to success in *All the Year Round*. Whether the introspective ruminations of Algernon Sydney Potts, the young Dublin apothecary, proved 'too detached and discursive' for the audience and form of publication, Dickens declined to say. But the narrative 'does not *take hold*', he informed Lever in a tactfully worded letter of explanation written on 6 October 1860. 'The consequence is, that the circulation [of the journal] becomes affected, and that subscribers complain. I have waited week after week, for these three or four weeks, watching for any sign of encouragement'. In the face of none, only one course remained, a step Dickens decided on before communicating the news to Lever. Shortly before writing, he had called a 'council of war' with the staff of *All the Year Round* on 2 October 1860 to consider the state and prospects of the journal. 'It was perfectly clear that the one thing to be done was, for me to strike in,' he wrote in a letter to Forster, summarizing the outcome of the meeting (*Letters* 9.319).

Dickens offered a similar rationale to Lever, before outlining how the failure of *A Day's Ride* required a serious counter-measure. He would have to abandon the design of the novel he had intended for one of his 'long twenty number serials', forgo its profit, and shape the story instead for the pages of *All the Year Round*. Resolving to act quickly, Dickens designated 1 December 1860 as the date to begin, commenting to Lever: 'For as long a time as you continue afterwards, we must go on together' (*Letters* 9.321).[3] By way of consolation, Dickens assured his friend that what had happened with his novel 'might have happened with any writer'. Even the success Collins had achieved 'was a toss-up' at first. 'But he strung [his story] on the needful strong thread of interest, and made a great success' – something Lever had totally failed to do (9.321).

Born, then, of an emergency, a hastily devised means of arresting *All the Year Round*'s free-falling readership, the novel Dickens shaped bears no trace of improvisation, haste or even hesitation (save his last-minute alteration of the ending). Within days of deciding to step in, Dickens had announced the title – 'The name is GREAT EXPECTATIONS. I think a good name?' – and got in 'the pivot on which the story will turn too' (*Letters* 9.320, 325). Both were crucial steps, preliminaries he usually had to decide before proceeding. In this instance he settled each without fuss: no pages of trial titles proved necessary for his thirteenth novel, no pacing the midnight streets of London in search of a controlling idea. Rather the 'pivot' – a 'very fine, new, and grotesque idea' – opened upon him in the course of writing 'a little piece' he initially intended for publication in his Uncommercial series. That 'notion', by consensus, refers to what Forster describes as 'the germ of Pip and Magwitch' and the convict's resolution 'to make his little friend a gentleman' after he had come to the convict's assistance on the marshes. 'I can see the whole of a serial revolving on

---

[3] When *A Day's Ride* terminated on 23 March 1861, Lever's novel had run for seventeen issues concurrently with *Great Expectations*.

it, in a most singular and comic manner' (*Letters* 9.310). Dickens spoke equally decisively on two other points: the book would not lack for humour and the story would be written throughout in the first person, beginning with the hero as 'a boy-child' and 'Then he will be an apprentice' (*Letters* 9.325).

From this point onwards, the composition of the three stages that constitute Pip's 'Expectations' unfolded with an ease that prompts puzzlement about the novel from nowhere: Where *did* the story come from? What was 'the new book' he alluded to in letters sent to various correspondents in the summer of 1860? And how did Dickens manage, with so little apparent preparation, to write a novel most critics place among the great works in the English language? Commentators in search of clues find little to scrutinize beyond brief hints.

The letters Dickens wrote while at work on *Great Expectations*, for example, reveal some details about the chronology of composition. It seems that by mid-October he had finished the first four chapters up through the Christmas dinner. Writing to Collins on the 24th, he noted that 'Four weekly numbers have been ground off the wheel', and that he intended to complete one more before the end of the month (*Letters* 9.330), presumably chapter 8, a single long episode introducing Satis House, Miss Havisham and Estella. Making good use of the available time mattered because Dickens and Collins had agreed to travel to Devon and Cornwall for five working days at the beginning of November in search of material they could use in *A Message from the Sea*. The title refers to the story for the extra Christmas Number scheduled to appear in *All the Year Round* on 13 December. Work on the annual Christmas book consumed much of November, although *Great Expectations* continued to occupy him, too. 'Before Christmas, my story and what I had to do for Christmas kept me in actual bondage for weeks together,' Dickens wrote to Edmund Yates early in the following year (*Letters* 9.387).

The months after Christmas provide tantalizing glimpses of the novel's progress as Dickens proceeded with the story towards the end of February 1861 amidst personal distractions and other professional pursuits. On 4 February, Dickens left Gad's Hill for temporary quarters in a furnished flat in London, an arrangement he made to be easily available for the six public readings he had scheduled at St James's Hall, Piccadilly, between 14 March and 18 April. In April he sent Forster the chapters 'which open the third division of the tale', and estimated that 'Two months more will see me through it' (*Letters* 9.403). The forecast proved accurate: after hiring a Thames steamer on 22 May to research details for chapter 54 (see p. 383), he took a brief working holiday in Dover, informing Collins from there on the 24th that he expected to finish the book 'about the 12th of June'. On the 11th, he announced to his old friend William Charles Macready: 'I have just finished my book . . . and am the worse for wear. Neuralgic pains in the face have troubled me a good deal, and the work has been pretty close. But I hope that the book is a good book, and I have no doubt of very soon throwing off the little damage it has done me' (*Letters* 9.424).

At this late stage, events relating to the novel took an unexpected turn when Dickens paid a visit to Bulwer Lytton at his estate in Hertfordshire. Lytton criticized the ending of the novel, and Dickens responded by going back to Gad's Hill to unwind the end and then put it back together again (see p. 418). The 'extreme end, I mean', Dickens explained to Collins on 23 June, 'after Biddy and Joe are done with', adding that Bulwer's reasons for rejecting the original conclusion had been expressed so clearly 'that I have resumed the wheel, and taken another turn at it. Upon the whole, I think it is for the better' (*Letters* 9.428).[4] Accordingly, Dickens sent this revised version to the printers, made further slight adjustments to the proofs (see p. 421) and published the final instalment of *Great Expectations* in *All the Year Round* on 3 August 1861. This is the so-called 'happy' reunion of Pip and Estella, now an eligible widow, in the grounds of Satis House, instead of the brief exchange that served as the original conclusion, in which Pip hears of Estella's remarrying, subsequently meets her by chance in London and never sees her again.[5]

Two other sources supplement the scattered comments retrievable from Dickens's letters: the *Book of Memoranda* Dickens kept from 1855 onwards and the Working Plans he devised while writing the novel. Both are useful but far from comprehensive, and in their paucity of detail help to preserve the aura of elusive reticence surrounding *Great Expectations*. The list of names Dickens recorded in his memorandum book includes several he adopted; of the 117 entries or jottings the *Book of Memoranda* contains, I can identify only 8 as relevant to the novel.[6] Similarly, Dickens's Working Plans – notes he drafted on loose sheets of paper to serve as memoranda as he worked on a novel – are, in this case, of minimal use. Because the main action of the novel seems to have been so clear from the start, Dickens evidently dispensed with these 'Mems.', as he referred to them, save for two half-sheets marked 'Dates', two of the same called 'General Mems.' and a single brief set of notes headed 'Tide'. For further details, see pp. 344–8.

The remaining sources that bear on *Great Expectations* in some slight way or other can be found among earlier contributions Dickens made to *Household Words* and *All the Year Round*. Each is noted in its appropriate place in the present volume save one recent discovery by Edgar Rosenberg, who points out some curious but interesting echoes of *Great Expectations* in the first and third chapters Dickens contributed to the Christmas number of *Household Words* published in 1857. *The Perils of Certain English Prisoners* tells the story of an ignorant but sterling private in a detachment of Royal Marines sent to protect a small English outpost on an island off the east coast of Central America, where silver extracted from a silver mine on the

---

[4] The meeting was very much a working weekend in which Bulwer read the proofs of the final chapters of *Great Expectations* and discussed his own serial, *A Strange Story*, scheduled to begin on the front page of *All the Year Round* on 10 August at the conclusion of Dickens's novel. Anticipating Forster's surprise about the change to the ending that came about as a result of this meeting, Dickens explained that he made the alteration because Bulwer 'supported his views with such good reasons' (*Letters* 9.433). Scholars are tantalized by the fact that no record of those reasons exists, although the absence of precise information has encouraged rather than dampened speculation. Rosenberg's authoritative discussion, 'Putting an End to Great Expectations', *Norton*, 491–527, provides the best introduction to this interestingly vexed issue. See especially pp. 491–500.

[5] The revised ending appears in all subsequent editions of the novel published during Dickens's lifetime and represents his final choice. No public knowledge of the original ending existed until Forster included it in the third volume of his *Life*, thereby initiating a seemingly limitless critical debate about the respective merits of the two endings. See also, pp. 11–14.

[6] Throughout, I follow identifications originally made by Kaplan with four exceptions. See pp. 23, 99, 102 and 200.

mainland was stored. Gill Davis, the private, falls hopelessly in love with Marion Maryon, a woman far above his station engaged to a captain of one of the British vessels stationed in the area. Long after the events that compose the story, the illiterate Gill dictates to Marion his part in the rescue of the English prisoners. In his opening lines (compare those of Pip), he relates how 'the name given to me in the baptism . . . was Gilbert . . . [but] I always understood my christian-name to be Gill' (*Christmas Stories* 163). Later, continuing his narrative, he recounts how, after his warm praise for her brother's bravery, she touched his arm, saying, 'I know it. Heaven bless you!':

> "She took my hand – my rough, coarse hand – and put it to her lips." (185) . . .
> After I left [Miss Maryon] I laid myself down on my face on the beach, and cried for the first time since I had frightened birds as a boy at Snorridge Bottom [a corruption of Snowledge Bottom, not far from Chatham; again, compare Pip's employment in chapter 6], to think what a poor, ignorant, low-placed, private soldier I was. (181)

Equally intriguing in relation to the subject matter of *Great Expectations* is the last 'singular confession' Gill makes to his amanuensis:

> I well knew what an immense and hopeless distance there was between me and Miss Maryon; I well knew that I was no fitter company for her than I was for the angels; I well knew that she was as high above my reach as the sky over my head; and yet I loved her. What put it in my low heart to be so daring, or whether such a thing ever happened before or since . . . I am unable to say; still, the suffering to me was just as great as if I had been a gentleman. I suffered agony – agony. I suffered hard, and I suffered long. . . . If it had not been for [her] dear words, I think I should have lost myself in despair and recklessness. (207)

The setting and events, a lightly disguised response to two recent massacres of British women and children in India, could not be further from the imaginative world Dickens creates in the novel. But Gill's love for Miss Maryon, as Rosenberg points out, 'remains strikingly similar' to Pip's for Estella in the emphasis on the gulf between the private and the lady and the intensity of the soldier's unrequited passion.

Details like these – a phrase, a situation, a passing resemblance – occur elsewhere in Dickens's fiction, connecting *Great Expectations* with several other earlier pieces. Nowhere are these verbal links more apparent than in the sixteen essays Dickens published in *All the Year Round* prior to his beginning work on the novel; each is duly recorded in an appropriate annotation and may be sought via the index.

Let us move from small to larger quarry. If we step back to consider how the factual annotations provided in the following pages serve a greater purpose, what salient points emerge? Do the novel's various contexts shed light on its composition and on Dickens's working methods? By paying attention to details of travel, topography and time, can we further our understanding of the voice of the narrator, of the distinctiveness of his retrospective stance as he surveys his past and talks about the great love of his life? By assembling information pertaining to Australia, convicts, currency and clothing, together with facts about brewing, social mobility and the mid-century conviction that, in the words of Samuel Smiles, 'Riches and rank have no necessary connection with genuine gentlemanly qualities', can we gain insight into the continuing debate about the two endings? To put the question bluntly in the manner of Mr Jaggers: what can the annotator usefully contribute to any novel as secure in its status as *Great Expectations*?

We might begin with the work of Dickens's many topographers whose earnest investigations have often earned ridicule rather than respect, due primarily to the insistent literalism that dogs even the best of them like W. Laurence Gadd, whose studies I have liberally incorporated. In defence of Gadd and others, one might say that the novel nevertheless invites this kind of curiosity because the descriptive writing evokes so powerfully a sense of place. More significantly, documenting the compelling topographical verisimilitude helps us understand the extraordinary speed with which the whole narrative fell into place, once Dickens had invented his 'pivot' and settled on the title. One reason why the writing moved so rapidly, so faultlessly and with such surety and momentum is that Dickens grounded *Great Expectations* in a world he really knew.[7] Better perhaps to say *worlds*: the regional world of the Hoo peninsula of north-east Kent, the city of Rochester and its immediate environs, and the various London locales that appear in the novel. Several of these stand out: the legal London of Little Britain, where Dickens locates Jaggers's office; nearby Newgate Prison and the Old Bailey; the two adjacent Inns of Court, the Inner and Middle Temple, home to Pip and Herbert after they leave their chambers in Barnard's Inn; and the Thames, the backdrop for important scenes west towards Hammersmith and east towards the lower reaches of Greenwich and beyond, whose dreary and deserted estuary vistas enhance the sinister atmosphere of the opening chapters.

An esoteric piece of information about Rochester and brewing supports my contention that *Great Expectations* comes as close to a definition of the regional

---

[7] Let me emphasize that this attempt to offer a partial answer for the rapidity of Dickens's progress with *Great Expectations* should not be confused with once-fashionable explanations of his earlier novels as the spontaneous effusions of a great comic writer who took up his pen and wrote effortlessly. My point is that the sixteen essays Dickens contributed to *AYR* under the title of 'The Uncommercial Traveller' constitute a kind of pre-writing in that the reflective, introspective voice of the narrator, the geographical territory he surveys, and the combination of personal detail and distanced irony anticipate, in some respects, the distinctive narrative voice Dickens develops for Pip. Suggesting a link between the novel and the essays, several of which explore scenes laden with memories Dickens clearly associated with the Medway region and with Chatham, 'the birthplace of his fancy' (Forster 1.1), together with the intense immersion Dickens experienced once he invented the 'pivot' and settled on the title, is about as far as we can go in any attempt to access his creative process. That Dickens recognized the distinctiveness of Pip's narrative voice is perhaps best substantiated by his comment to Forster that, anxious to make sure he had fallen into 'no unconscious repetitions' of *David Copperfield*, he read that novel quickly to ensure that he hadn't (*Letters* 9.325). Although Pip and David are Dickens's most obviously autobiographical figures, each maintains a distinctive voice; retrospects in the earlier novel remain confined to specific chapters, while in *Great Expectations* the point-of-view shifts almost constantly, moving between past and present.

novel as any of the fifteen Dickens wrote. Topographers have long known how Dickens borrowed the name of one real manor, Satis House on Boley Hill near Rochester castle, and attached it to Restoration House, another handsome residence in Crow Lane south-east of the cathedral, and invented an appropriate home for the reclusive daughter of a wealthy brewer. The location of Mr Havisham's enterprise, indisputably a commercial operation on account of details Dickens supplies in chapter 8, has remained a matter of speculation: it was or it was not to one side of 'Satis House', it did or it did not exist, no such defunct brewery can be traced in Rochester, and so on.

Further inquiry reveals, however, that in Dickens's lifetime (and for many years later) a perfectly suitable model for a brewery existed nearby on the corner of Victoria Street and East Row, to the south-west of Restoration House. No inveterate pedestrian with an observant eye as powerful as Dickens's, who regularly walked down Crow Lane and past Restoration House, could fail to spot the tower-shaped brewhouse, adjacent buildings and wooden beer-casks of Woodham's working brewery. Even a blind man would have known of it, by the smells associated with the production of beer, if by no other clue. Much harder to achieve, of course, was the imaginative transformation of reality: a *defunct* actual brewery moved to the *side* of the fictional house now inhabited by the half-mad daughter of the deceased owner, an eccentric recluse who wants to take revenge on the male sex because she was jilted twenty-five years ago at twenty minutes to nine.

Alterations of this kind appear throughout the novel as topographical details are captured and 'fixed', in the language of photography, and then *fancifully* transformed by the author's mind's eye when they appear on the page.[8] Nowhere are these skills in more extended use than in the chapter Dickens devotes to the attempted escape of Pip and Magwitch down the Thames by boat. Hiring a steamer to make sure that he would get their down-river course 'right' in such circumstances, Dickens managed both to enjoy the company of friends and, at the same time, to employ that 'sleepless observation' so much in evidence both in this episode and throughout the book (see p. 383).

His concern with detail in preparation for writing chapter 54 and describing the flight down the Thames is all the more impressive when we recall Dickens's description of his earlier self as 'a rower on that river'. Writing to W. F. de Cerjat some three months before hiring a steamer, Dickens made reference to his former

---

[8] Compare the analogy Dickens himself uses to describe his creative process. Walking in the pit country of Durham during his first reading tour in 1858, he noted to Wills how, as he worked his way north, he made 'a little fanciful photograph' in his mind of the area, thinking he could use it one day in *Household Words*. 'I couldn't help looking upon my mind as I was doing it, as a sort of capitally prepared and highly sensitive plate. And I said, without the least conceit . . . "it really is a pleasure to work with you, and receive the impression so nicely" ' (*Letters* 8.669). Earlier, writing in the preface to *Bleak House*, Dickens explained how, in that novel, 'I have purposely dwelt on the romantic side of familiar things'. Put in different terms, this states, comments K. J. Fielding: 'Dickens means to have it both ways: to root his action in reality, but to treat it romantically. That is to say, to make it wonderful and strange, to play with it linguistically, to involve it in a plot of striking coincidences, and yet avoid harsh unpleasantness' ('*Bleak House* and Dickens' Originals', *Dickens Studies Annual* 24: 1996: 130).

recreation in connection with a walk he took one winter afternoon, having left the office of *All the Year Round* with the intention of going down to the Houses of Parliament. Finding the day bright and warm, he carried straight on '*for three miles* on a splendid broad esplanade overhanging the Thames'. This section of the embankment – Millbank Road, a continuation of Millbank Row to Vauxhall Bridge, 2° miles from the Houses of Parliament – and the adjacent 'immense factories, railway work, and what not, erected on it', impressed on Dickens the changes that had occurred since his earlier familiarity with the river, when 'it was all broken ground and ditch, with here and there a public house or two, an old mill, and a tall chimney'. He had never seen it 'in any state of transition', he added, 'though I suppose myself to know this rather large city as well as any one in it' (*Letters* 9.383).[9]

Unquestionably, Dickens did, even perhaps to the point of obsessively wanting to update his knowledge of the changes along the shore that had occurred without his being aware of them. Further 'proof', should any be needed, of the unfailing accuracy of Dickens's eye, is evident in the very few topographical errors that slipped into the novel. One of the very few, and certainly one of no serious artistic consequence, is the description of Mucking Flats Lighthouse whose erection in 1851 postdates the action carefully set about thirty years earlier.[10]

The information relating to the sequence of events in Pip's narrative and the embedded histories of Miss Havisham and Magwitch assembled in Appendix 1 reveal a similar quest for accuracy. To serve the first-person retrospective narration, Dickens had to maintain a dual focus: Pip looks *back* to those events of his life set in Regency England but tells them from a present he belongs to, the *now* of the relating time. To appreciate how distinctly Dickens sets off the past from the present, we must be attentive to the temporal nuances that inform Pip's account of his life. In this respect, the book probably worked more easily for Victorian readers than

---

[9] For comments on Dickens as an excellent observer of the river, see William Addison, *In the Steps of Charles Dickens* (London: Rich & Cowan, 1955), pp. 95–108.

[10] Similar chronological mismatches are remarkably infrequent. Occasionally, fictional events (Estella's schooling in Paris, for example) clash with the historical setting I propose in Appendix 1. Compare also other educational issues such as the 'evening school' Pip attends as a boy (chapter 7) and Biddy's future employment as a teacher in a 'new school' (chapter 35). Lapses of a different kind occur when Pip describes Orlick using a match (chapter 53) or when he fancifully considers emigrating to America and hunting buffalo to make his fortune (chapter 34). Terms and expressions sometimes post-date the early setting: Wemmick's reference to 'Greenwich time' would not have been current before 1833; similarly, his 'proud as Punch' occurs earlier than instances of that expression cited in the *OED*. Magwitch's reference to 'Lock-Ups' seems to be equally out of context in his mouth (chapter 42), but Pip's memorable comparison of Wemmick's mouth to a mail slot, though clearly based on developments that occurred long after his initial meeting with Jaggers's clerk, raises no problems when we recall the double perspective of a narrator who looks back on the past through eyes shaped by subsequent history and events. The late telling-time (nearly forty years after the conclusion of the main events) also accounts for those of Pip's allusions which help define the telling-time of the early 1860s: 'a Medium of the present day' (chapter 5), Herbert's 'business' abroad (chapter 39), interest in 'going up the Nile' (chapter 52), 'Alterations' subsequently made in the vicinity of the Temple (chapter 39) and the references to Darwin's *Origin of Species* and Smiles's *Self-help*. The literary references in particular are wholly congruent with the character Dickens invented, an inveterate reader and self-improver from his earliest days, before he became a gentleman of fortune.

for many of us today. Among his contemporaries, Dickens could assume some shared knowledge about the late-Georgian world Pip describes. While we require notes, nineteenth-century readers would have been sensitive to the implications of references to matches, repeater watches, wax and tallow candles, rush lights, the sudden flare of gas-lights in the streets, the appearance of letter-slots in front doors, and many other historical and temporal markers. Fully annotating the novel therefore helps restore some sense of how it might have been read in Dickens's time.

And just how precise *is* Dickens about the dating of the events of Pip's narrative and the presumed time when he decides to compose his memoirs? We might start with the latter point since readers have complained about Dickens's unwarranted vagueness on this issue. Anny Sadrin, one of the best of recent writers on the novel, voices a typical comment when she notes that the text never says when the hero made up his mind to write his memoirs. Keenly aware of the existing gap between the 'then' when things happened to Pip and the 'now' as he writes, Sadrin argues that the narrator remains obstinately vague as to what 'then' and 'now' actually correspond to.

That 'vagueness' soon vanishes when we integrate the dating of the novel's internal chronology with the telling-time as it would have revealed itself to alert Victorians readers familiar with important literary and topographical landmarks embedded in Pip's narrative, readerly allusions in keeping with the bookish character Dickens created. Take the 'Alterations' Pip refers to in chapter 39, the changes made in that part of the Temple to which he and Herbert moved many years ago when they left Barnard's Inn. Quite specifically, Pip refers to the extensive work begun 'down by the river' in 1860 when the Metropolitan Board of Works undertook the systematic embankment of the north shore of the Thames in three sections. Equally in the news and even more closely tied to a recent event was the trouble which had broken out at Chatham convict prison on 12 February 1861. Reference to the full-scale riot that erupted (widely reported in the press at the time) makes its way into the twentieth weekly issue of the novel (published on 13 April 1861) when Pip accepts Wemmick's invitation to visit Newgate and offers, from the perspective of his later years, some rather biting commentary on the consequences of exposing old public wrongdoing. One result, Pip reflects, looking back in 1860 from his perspective of nearly forty years, is to encourage an 'exaggerated reaction' among overzealous reformers, who create conditions that allow convicts 'to set fire to their prisons with the excusable object of improving the flavour of their soup'.

Two further points to support my contention about the way Dickens establishes the late telling-time of Pip's narration. The allusions to Darwin's *Origin of Species* (1859) in chapters 1 and 28, together with the more pervasive presence of the language and ideology of Samuel Smiles's best-selling *Self-help* (1859) suggest how Mr Pirrip, an inveterate reader himself, sought to appeal to his audience by addressing them in terms many would recognize. Thus, if we grant that these references, taken cumulatively, establish a telling-time almost simultaneous with the novel's serial publication in 1860–1, what significance does that dating hold for the principal events in Pip's life, which (as I argue in Appendix 1) begin with his birth in 1797, follow his history closely until about 1821 and then in broad outline to 1833, after which time we hear nothing from the narrator until he decides at about 60 to tell his life's story?

Let us begin by recognizing that the novel contains two distinct chronologies: (1) the diegetic sequence of events (see Appendix 1) which belongs to the primary narrative, opens in 1803 and runs continuously until it closes in 1821; (2) the extradiegetic events containing the interlocking histories of Miss Havisham, her half-brother Arthur Havisham, Compeyson and Magwitch. This secondary narrative extends over a greater period of time – say, from 1760 to 1803 – and is revealed through the stories of different participants and witnesses. To (1) above, we also need to add a corollary sequence: after the close of the main events in 1821 – signalled by Magwitch's death, Pip's breakdown and recovery, the marriage of Joe and Biddy, and Pip's decision to go abroad and join Herbert in Cairo – 'Many a year' goes round as Pip returns to England and then much later begins to write his memoirs.

This post-1821 sequence of events requires careful scrutiny. In the original 'unhappy' ending Dickens decided not to publish, the main developments can be summarized as follows: Joe and Biddy marry in June 1821; 'Within a month' Pip quits England and by September or October becomes 'clerk to Clarriker and Co.' in Cairo. His 'first undivided responsibility' follows about four months later, as he is left in charge of the business when Herbert returns to England to marry Clara and then take her back to Cairo. Time passes, carrying us forward another eleven years, to the occasion of Pip's first return to England and visit to the forge, which occurs one evening 'in December'. The following day, Pip takes his little nephew to the churchyard; questioned by Biddy after dinner about Estella, he answers that he is sure and certain he doesn't fret for her. Two years later, no month specified, Pip records how he saw Estella when he was in England again. Then follows his description of their final encounter in Piccadilly, after which the novel ends (see pp. 416–17).

The sequence of events in the published ending follows a similar chronology, although Dickens moves forward by two years the date of Pip's second return to England. Visiting the forge in December, Pip has the same conversation with Biddy; but, while assuring Biddy that his poor dreams of Estella have all gone, he confides to the reader his secret intention to revisit the site of the old house *that evening*, 'alone', for her sake. 'Yes even so. For Estella's sake'. The meeting with Estella then follows on the same day; they talk and then take their leave of the old house – a departure Dickens worked hard to get 'right':

MS reading: 'I saw the shadow of no parting from her, but one'.

Corrected proof: 'I saw the shadow of no parting from her, <but one>'.

Serial and 1st. edition: 'I saw the shadow of no parting from her'.

1868 CD edition: 'I saw no shadow of another parting from her'.

Let us set aside the verbal ambiguity each text presents and forgo speculation about the reason for the cancellation in proof of the last phrase, 'but one'. Whichever final line critics prefer, one problem with them all is the gap in the novel's chronology Dickens created when, acting on Bulwer's advice, he rewrote the original ending. If so much time has elapsed (almost three decades), how can Pip, at 60 or so, teasingly pretend not to know: whether he and Estella remained friends (as *he* affirms, rising and bending over her); whether they will remain 'friends apart', as *she* immediately adds; whether they will remain together until the shadow of death parted them; or whether there was no parting at all?

I see no point in debating the merits of the different versions of Pip's final words in the revised ending, but offer instead an argument for the aesthetic and thematic superiority of the novel's close before Dickens altered it at the suggestion of Bulwer Lytton (see pp. 4–5 and n.). The case I put rests on two principal considerations. First, the original conclusion leaves readers in no doubt about the implied relationship between Pip and Estella. Clearly, she remains central to the memory of the 60-year-old narrator as he looks back on his childhood and youth; but during the course of Pip's later years he has learned to accept with dignity facts he can't change. He works hard for a modest living and does well; she has remarried and started her life again with the Shropshire doctor.

Time, we must remember, continued to run on for Pip after their chance meeting in London in 1834 and short but poignant exchange. Pip grew further into his self-described bachelorhood, while Clarriker & Co. continued to flourish, thanks in part to his industry and honest efforts to help the firm achieve commercial success. Living abroad and returning occasionally to England, would Pip have known if Estella had died? What about Joe and Biddy? And how do his nephew and niece fare as young adults? How many children had Lady Macbeth?[11] Better simply to say that reticences remain and assume that questions like these have no relevance to the story Pip chooses to tell. We can, however, infer from the original ending that at some point Pip made the decision to record the 'poor dreams' of his youth. Re-examining them as an adult in the light of experience and maturity, he also records his moral and intellectual growth, the fruit of a life of hard work and intellectual self-improvement derived from reflection and reading. That *something* good came of his expectations, Pip tells us twice, surely a sign of indicating the importance of this point, one Dickens also set down among the few recorded memoranda for the novel.[12]

The ensuing and unbroken elegiac voice constitutes, I think, the second reason for the superiority of the original ending; for Pip's narrative remains, above all, a moving lament for love lost, for lost hopes, dreams and aspirations. In this less conventional ending, Dickens clearly affirms the continuity of Pip's elegiac voice implicit in the recorded observations of a man who has lost the love of a lifetime not

---

[11] The question refers to the title of L. C. Knights's classic essay, *How Many Children Had Lady Macbeth?* (1931), which cautions Shakespearian scholars against some of the pitfalls of treating characters as if they were real people.

[12] Compare the observation of Humphry House: 'The very emphasis that Dickens gives this note [the final entry in the 'General Mems.'], by placing it as his last comment on the whole plan, gives it almost the status of a leading "moral" ' ('G.B.S. on *Great Expectations*', *Dickensian* 54 (1948), 184). Writing to Forster about 'the third portion' of the novel, Dickens observed regretfully that it could not be read all at once, 'because its purpose would be much more apparent; and the pity is the greater, because the general turn and tone of the working out and winding up, will be away from all such things as they conventionally go' (April 1861).

once but twice, initially to Bentley Drummle (the hateful 'Spider'), and then later to the kindly Shropshire doctor. Added to this loss is the poignancy of knowing that the suffering caused by Estella's first marriage had corrected Miss Havisham's cruel teaching and given her adopted daughter a heart that allowed her to sympathize with how Pip's heart used to feel. In the touch, the voice and the face Pip reads when he and Estella meet, and most importantly in the kiss she gives to the pretty child accompanying him, Pip learns that Estella can and does love, and that (presumably), had they met before she married the doctor, she would have married him.[13]

As far as love is concerned, Pip remains one of literature's great losers, a man deeply saddened but not embittered by loss, a man whose outlook and personality, as Dickens imagines them, place him in the tradition of earlier fictional characters. For example, the novel's ironic title echoes two earlier works familiar to Dickens: Sir Philip Sidney's sonnet sequence, *Astrophil and Stella* (1591), recounting the speaker's hopeless love for a cold, disdainful lady; and Milton's epic *Paradise Lost*. Sidney's sonnet 21 culminates with reference to 'that friendly foe,/Great Expectation'; and, in *Paradise Lost*, Adam, having heard God's plan for the future, comforts himself:

> . . . now clear I understand
> What oft my steddiest thoughts have searcht in vain,
> Why our great expectation should be call'd
> The seed of Woman: Virgin Mother, Hail,
> High in the love of Heav'n' . . . (book 12, 376–80)

For Astrophil and Pip – respectively 'the lover of a star' and the lover of Estella – the future calls for great fortitude: both lack the spiritual consolation Adam draws from the words of the Angel Michael. Thus, Pip recounts his bleak annals in a voice not unlike that of the narrator of Thomas Gray's 'Elegy Written

---

[13] Pip's exchange of emotional intimacies with Biddy on his first return to England prepares for the meeting with Estella as originally planned in significant ways. Talking with Biddy, a woman whom Pip could have married, had he bothered to ask her, and whom he assumes would have accepted, had she been given the chance, he notes her non-verbal communication of sorrow at the thought of Pip's not marrying, when he affirms how he has become already 'quite an old bachelor'. Biddy looks first at her child, kisses the child's hand and then puts 'the good matronly hand with which she had touched it, into mine'. Reflects Pip: 'There was something in the action and in the light pressure of Biddy's wedding ring, that had a very pretty eloquence in it'. Hardly the touch of an adulterous passion, one might add, but a touch freighted with meaning in a novel in which hands and touches of hand convey so much. The reference to the wedding ring in particular points simultaneously in two directions: backwards to the harsh ridgy effect of his sister's as it passed unsympathetically over his face as a young boy and forwards to the 'touch' of Estella's hand, in which Pip detects Estella's change of heart. And, in both cases, women to whom Pip is emotionally attached and who, presumably, reciprocate some feeling for him offer indirect kisses via a child named after Pip, Biddy in the first instance and Estella in the second, during the Piccadilly encounter Dickens subsequently discarded.

In this respect, the ending Dickens originally drafted, and which some argue he unconsciously borrowed from Lever's *A Day's Ride*, differs sharply in its emotional warmth and gestural communication. Whereas Lever's Catinka dismisses Potts with 'a cold smile and a haughty bow', seeing only 'riddles' in his reference to their past relationship, Estella reacts with emotional warmth and a clear wish to make amends for her past behaviour. See p. 418.

in A Country Church-yard', whom Pip also resembles – two men of humble birth, each marked by melancholy and fully aware in maturity how the paths of glory lead but to the grave.[14]

The likelihood of unqualified happiness in a world of reduced hope and graveyard shadows remains slight. But is there not some solace for one who has come to terms with the chain of iron and thorns he once mistook for gold and flowers? Shackled by links not wholly of his own making, Pip nevertheless settles for a realistic sense of his amatory losses, for self-esteem from his modest financial success abroad and for the satisfaction he draws from books and learning throughout his life. Is this not implicit in what Dickens called 'the general turn and tone of the working out and winding up' of the novel (*Letters* 9.403) and in what John Forster alluded to when he proclaimed the first ending more consistent with the book's drift, 'as well as natural working out, of the tale'?

June 1999

---

[14] The first-person voice Dickens adopted for the persona of his Uncommercial Traveller perhaps owes something to Addison's Mr Spectator, a figure, in turn, who shares some characteristics with Philip Pirrip, who, presumably retired from life when he comes to compose his memoirs, looks out on the world as a spectator of men and manners, above all maintaining the poise of a 'silent man' rather than a tatler. Further resemblances include the fact that both have travelled (France and the Grand Cairo); both have experienced disappointments in love; both are self-described bachelors of retired habits; and both prefer writing to speaking as a means of communication. Notes Addison's Mr Spectator: I hoped 'to Print my self out, if possible, before I Die'.

A NOTE ON THE TEXT

The text of *Great Expectations* cited throughout is that of the Norton Critical Edition, edited by Edgar Rosenberg (1999) 'Norton'). The annotations in this volume include only a small selection of the variant readings of Dickens's heavily revised manuscript. Readers interested in a systematic study of the manuscript and the revisions Dickens undertook while writing *Great Expectations* and seeing the Charles Dickens Edition of the novel through the press in 1868 should consult Rosenberg's detailed Textual Notes (pp. 367–88).

HOW TO USE THE NOTES

To help the reader locate in the novel the word or phrase quoted in an entry, the notes are presented in this way: the opening phrase of the paragraph which includes the entry is quoted as a guide and printed in italics; the entry itself appears in boldface type. This system should also help the reader who turns from the novel in search of a note on a particular word or phrase.

Documentation within the notes is kept to a minimum by the use of an abbreviated form of referencing. Works of literature are referred to by their parts: *Vanity Fair* 12; *Past and Present* 3.2; *The Faerie Queene* 2.12.17.14–16; 'The Idiot Boy' 8–10. Frequently cited works of criticism and other secondary sources are referred to by author, part (where relevant) and page: '(Collins 171–2)', '(Mayhew 3.106–7)'. References to infrequently cited sources add the date of publication: '(Sala, 1859, 23)'. Complete details are given in the Select Bibliography.

The articles quoted from *Household Words* and *All the Year Round* always antedate or are contemporary with the composition of the novel unless the reference indicates otherwise.

The notes indicate the divisions of the novel in its first published form as a serial in thirty-six weekly parts published in *All the Year Round* from 1 December 1860 to 3 August 1861.

Dickens's Working Plans

The notes include a typographic transcription of the five half sheets Dickens wrote evidently to guide him while composing the final chapters of the novel. The notes – referred to as Mems. – written in blue ink on pale blue laid paper – are briefer and more fragmentary than any that belong to any other novel. The notes are bound with the manuscript, which is owned by the Wisbech and Fenland Museum.

The Notes

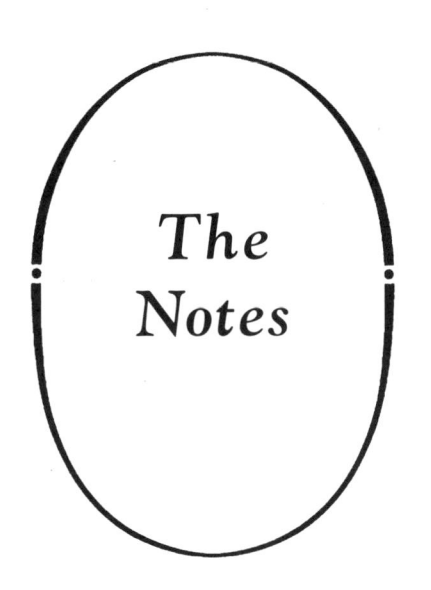

"THE STORY OF OUR LIVES FROM YEAR TO YEAR."—SHAKESPEARE.

ALL THE YEAR ROUND.
A WEEKLY JOURNAL.
CONDUCTED BY CHARLES DICKENS.
WITH WHICH IS INCORPORATED HOUSEHOLD WORDS.

N°. 84.]   SATURDAY, DECEMBER 1, 1860.   [PRICE 2*d*.*

GREAT EXPECTATIONS.
BY CHARLES DICKENS.

CHAPTER I.

My father's family name being Pirrip, and my christian name Philip, my infant tongue could make of both names nothing longer or more explicit than Pip. So, I called myself Pip, and came to be called Pip.

I give Pirrip as my father's family name, on the authority of his tombstone and my sister—Mrs. Joe Gargery, who married the blacksmith. As I never saw my father or my mother, and never saw any likeness of either of them (for their days were long before the days of photographs), my first fancies regarding what they were like, were unreasonably derived from their tombstones. The shape of the letters on my father's, gave me an odd idea that he was a square, stout, dark man with curly black hair. From the character and turn of the inscription, "*Also Georgiana Wife of the Above*," I drew a childish conclusion that my mother was freckled and sickly. To five little stone lozenges, each about a foot and a half long, which were arranged in a neat row beside their grave, and were sacred to the memory of five little brothers of mine—who gave up trying to get a living, exceedingly early in that universal struggle—I am indebted for a belief I religiously entertained that they had all been born on their backs with their hands in their trousers-pockets, and had never taken them out in this state of existence.

Ours was the marsh country, down by the river, within, as the river wound, twenty miles of the sea. My first most vivid and broad impression of the identity of things, seems to me to have been gained on a memorable raw afternoon towards evening. At such a time I found out for certain, that this bleak place overgrown with nettles was the churchyard; and that Philip Pirrip, late of this parish, and also Georgiana wife of the above, were dead and buried; and that Alexander, Bartholomew, Abraham, Tobias, and Roger, infant children of the aforesaid, were also dead and buried; and that the dark flat wilderness beyond the churchyard, intersected with dykes and mounds and gates, with scattered cattle feeding on it, was the marshes; and that the low leaden line beyond, was the river; and that the distant savage lair from which the wind was rushing, was the sea; and that the small bundle of shivers growing afraid of it all and beginning to cry, was Pip.

"Hold your noise!" cried a terrible voice, as a man started up from among the graves at the side of the church porch. "Keep still, you little devil, or I'll cut your throat!"

A fearful man, all in coarse grey, with a great iron on his leg. A man with no hat, and with broken shoes, and with an old rag tied round his head. A man who had been soaked in water, and smothered in mud, and lamed by stones, and cut by flints, and stung by nettles, and torn by briars; who limped, and shivered, and glared and growled; and whose teeth chattered in his head as he seized me by the chin.

"O! Don't cut my throat, sir," I pleaded in terror. "Pray don't do it, sir."

"Tell us your name!" said the man. "Quick!"

"Pip, sir."

"Once more," said the man, staring at me. "Give it mouth!"

"Pip. Pip, sir."

"Show us where you live," said the man. "Pint out the place!"

I pointed to where our village lay, on the flat in-shore among the alder-trees and pollards, a mile or more from the church.

The man, after looking at me for a moment, turned me upside-down, and emptied my pockets. There was nothing in them but a piece of bread. When the church came to itself—for he was so sudden and strong that he made it go head over heels before me, and I saw the steeple under my legs—when the church came to itself, I say, I was seated on a high tombstone, trembling, while he ate the bread ravenously.

"You young dog," said the man, licking his lips, "what fat cheeks you ha' got."

I believe they were fat, though I was at that time undersized for my years, and not strong.

"Darn Me if I couldn't eat 'em," said the man, with a threatening shake of his head, "and if I han't half a mind to 't!"

I earnestly expressed my hope that he wouldn't, and held tighter to the tombstone on which he had put me; partly, to keep myself upon it; partly, to keep myself from crying.

"Now then, lookee here!" said the man. "Where's your mother?"

1   The first serialized page of *Great Expectations* in volume 4, number 84, of *All the Year Round* (1 December 1860)

GREAT EXPECTATIONS

Dickens decided on the title of his thirteenth novel with few apparent preliminaries. His extant letters contain no evidence of hesitancy or indecision. Neither are there variants, afterthoughts or subtitles recorded in his *Book of Memoranda* or in the few working notes to the novel that remain. Within a week after deciding he must 'strike in' to arrest the rapid drop in sales due to Charles Lever's *A Day's Ride*, which had taken over as the lead serial in *AYR* on 18 August 1860, Dickens told John Forster he had got to work 'on a new story' (4 October 1860) and set a date for its commencement (1 December 1860; Plate 1). Expecting to visit Forster shortly, Dickens promised to bring 'the first two or three weekly parts'. The name, he added, with assurance, 'is GREAT EXPECTATIONS. I think a good name?' (*Letters* 9.302).

The inverted, ironic meaning implicit in the title appears to originate in the works of two earlier writers familiar to Dickens. In sonnet 21 of Sir Philip Sidney's *Astrophil and Stella*, lines 7–8 culminate with a reference to 'that friendly foe,/Great expectation'; and, in *Paradise Lost*, Adam responds to God's plan unveiled to him by the Angel Michael saying:

> . . . . now clear I understand
> What oft my steddiest thoughts have searcht in vain,
> Why our great expectation should be call'd
> The seed of Woman: Virgin Mother, Hail,
> High in the love of Heav'n'. . . . (12.376–80)

For Pip, concluding his story as Dickens originally planned it, there were no consolatory words of 'great deliverance' by woman and prophecy of a Saviour sent to earth to prepare man for God's second coming. Instead, he was left alone and 'greatly instructed', but without a partner as he continued on his solitary way, having learned of Estella's remarriage and also having seen for himself when they met by chance in London how 'her suffering had been stronger than Miss Havisham's [wrongful] teaching'.

Use of the phrase to signify a favourable change in one's fortunes occasioned by the inheritance of money or property, however, seems to derive from Sheridan's *School for Scandal* (1777): 'I have a devilish rich Uncle . . . from whom I have the greatest expectations' (3.3.149–50). See also the opening chapter of *MC* and young Martin Chuzzlewit's comment to Tom Pinch: 'I have been bred up from childhood with great expectations, and have always been taught to believe that I should be, one day, very rich' (*MC* 6; cf. also *MC* 10). Similarly, Uriah Heep comments on his change in station by saying to David Copperfield, 'You have heard something, I des-say, of a change in my expectations, Master Copperfield, – I should say, Mister Copperfield?' (*DC* 25). Compare also Mrs Gowan, who says of her son: 'You must remember that my poor fellow has always been accustomed to expectations' (*LD* 2.8).

Instances in other novels include Charles Kingsley's gentleman-hero Lancelot Smith, who exchanges his material expectations for 'an expectation, amid infinite falsehoods and confusions, of some nobler, more chivalrous, more godlike state!' (*Yeast*,

July–December 1848, ch. 17), and Charles Lever's dreaming hero, Algernon Sydney Potts. Within days of Dickens's deciding that he and Lever must 'go on together' in *AYR*, subscribers in diminishing numbers read how Lever's hero invented a dying relative who had vaguely hinted 'at great expectations and so on' as cover for his abrupt departure from friends in Ireland (*AYR* 3.578). Compare also the Mayhew brothers' 'Mr. Sertingley', a young man related to Lord Fortiwinx, who had 'very good expectations at his Lordship's death' (*Whom to Marry*, 1848, 106).

Variations of the phrase occur in *BH*, which contains a warning of founding one's life on 'expectation' (24, 35) and in *TTC*. Commenting on Charles Darnay's outlook, the narrator writes: 'he had expected neither to walk on pavements of gold, nor to lie on beds of roses: if he had had any such exalted expectation, he would not have prospered. He had expected labour, and he found it, and did it, and made the best of it. In this, his prosperity consisted' (*TTC* 2.10).

[DEDICATION]

AFFECTIONATELY INSCRIBED TO **CHAUNCY HARE TOWNSHEND**

Less than two years after meeting Chauncy Hare Townshend (1798–1868), Dickens described him in February 1842 as 'a gentleman of Independent fortune and station in Society, and of very high and varied attainments' (*Letters* 3.45–6). Townshend, who had been educated at Eton and at Cambridge, took holy orders but was disabled by illness from an active role as a minister. He drew, painted with skill, collected pictures, jewels and precious stones, took up poetry (*Poems*, 1821), travelled and spent considerable time abroad. Townshend was also the author of *Facts in Mesmerism, with Reasons for a Dispassionate Inquiry into it* (1840) and, in Dickens's opinion, 'an accomplished man, who has written better of Mesmerism than any one else' (*Letters* 7.342).

An interest in mesmerism led to their meeting in March 1840 and to a friendship that lasted until Townshend's death on 25 February 1868. In his will Townshend named Dickens his 'literary executor', with instructions to publish 'as much of my notes and reflections as may make known my opinions on religious matters' (*Nonesuch* 3.689 n.). The fragmentary nature of the material he had left made this a difficult task. To publish his religious views without alteration 'is absolutely impossible', Dickens declared. They are distributed 'in the strangest fragments through the strangest note-books, pocket-books, slips of paper and what not, and produced a most incoherent and tautological result' (*Nonesuch* 3.698). But Dickens set to, with characteristic industry, and made a book out of them, *Religious Opinions* (1868), to which he contributed a preface.

Chapter 1

First weekly number
1 December 1860

My father's family name being Pirrip

Philip,] Philip is derived from the Greek *philippos*, 'lover of horses', possibly an embedded reference to Pip's original destiny as a blacksmith. Compare, however, Sir Philip Sidney's *Astrophil and Stella* (1581–3), in which Astrophil (literally, the lover of a star, Stella, with a play on Sidney's own first name) recounts his love as a young courtier for an unobtainable woman. Stella, though not blind to his devotion, refuses to return it because she is married, albeit unhappily to a rich aristocrat. Sidney's work (108 sonnets and 11 songs) forms a series of conversations or monologues, many of which are openly autobiographical. In them Astrophil recounts his concerns, the torture he feels of unrequited love, the thought that love is 'vaine' and responsible for bringing him 'shame', until finally, by an act of will, he relinquishes his pursuit of Stella, knowing that he does not and cannot cease to love her. Other plausible links between the novel and the sonnet sequence include Sidney's use of the diminutive 'Phip' in sonnet 83 and the phrase 'Great expectation' in sonnet 21 (Endicott 158–9; LeVay 6–7). For connections between Stella and Estella, see chapter 8, note on p. 98; and see chapter 22, note on p. 196, for Herbert Pocket's negative associations with Philip. See also below.

I called myself Pip,] Pip's self-naming (corroborated by Joe in chapter 10), his benefactor's insistence that he keep the name, and Pip's willingness to accept the alternative proposed by Herbert Pocket (chapter 22) have occasioned extensive critical debate. Pip and Phil are common abbreviations. 'Pip' is richly allusive. The name connotes seeds, birth (or rebirth) and growth; the idea of a seed is also relevant to questions the novel raises about what Pip owes to heredity and what he owes to environment. See also chapter 9, note on p. 107.

A notation in the 'General Mems.' suggests how Dickens conceived of Pip's moral growth. Anticipating Pip's decision to use his fortune to help Herbert to a partnership, Dickens wrote: 'The one good thing' Pip did in his prosperity, 'the only thing that endures and bears good fruit' (see chapter 37, note on p. 297). A passage of dialogue transcribed in Dickens's *Book of Memoranda* in 1855 explores similar metaphors related to maturation and development:

> "There is some virtue in him too."
> "Virtue! Yes. So there is in any grain of seed in a seedsman's shop – but you must put it in the ground, before you can get any good out of it."
> "Do you mean that *he* must be put in the ground before any good comes of *him?*"
> "Indeed I do. You may call it burying him, or you may call it sowing him, <but> ∧as you like. ∧ <y> YOU must set him in the earth, before you get any good of him." (*Memoranda* 17)

The name or abbreviation appears elsewhere in Dickens's writings. There is a 'Mr. Pip' in MC (28) and a 'Mr. Pips' of Camberwell in 'It is Not Generally Known', published on 2 September 1854 in *HW* (10.49). In 'The Parish Clerk: A Tale of True Love', Nathaniel P*ip*kin adores a Maria Lobbs and suffers from her indifference (*PP* 17).

A link between Pip and Pippo in *The Maid and the Magpie; or, The Fatal Spoon* (1858), a burletta about a guiltless maid blamed for a magpie's theft, has also been suggested (Kaplan, 1986, 409). Dickens saw this travesty by Henry James Byron (1834–84) at the Strand theatre on 16 December 1858, not long after it opened (*Letters* 8.722). Pippo, 'a remarkably odd boy', played by an actress, is attached to the establishment of an Italian farmer. Berated by his employer's shrewish wife and badly paid, he aspires 'to tread the boards' and dreams of playing Hamlet and other tragic roles. Byron's version was taken from a French melodrama, *The Maid and the Magpie; or, The Fallacy of Circumstantial Evidence*, which was first performed at the Theatre Royal, Covent Garden, on 15 September 1815. See also below.

I give Pirrip as my father's family name

the blacksmith.]   The ability to combine strength and manual skill with artistry and knowledge of metals and their properties raised nineteenth-century blacksmiths above mere artisans and put them in a class comparable with instrument-makers, opticians, dyers, chemists and engineers. Essential tools include files, hammers, an anvil, benches for working in iron and in wood, and a forge fire for heating metal preparatory to shaping and working it (M. T. Richardson, 1890).

Originally, the trade offered opportunities to specialize, included shoeing horses, making agricultural implements and machinery or fitting iron tyres to wheels for coach-builders. Orders for gridirons, pot-hooks, ecclesiastical gates and grilles, hinges, locks and door-chains provided additional business. The mass production of iron and steel goods later in the century reduced blacksmiths mainly to shoeing horses. A country blacksmith, however, had to retain his versatility to survive and adapt to local demands (*Complete Book of Trades* 406).

(for their days were long before the days of photographs),]   Photography remained a recent development, as Henry Morley and W. H. Wills reminded readers of the 'external facts' in *HW* on 19 March 1853. Progress had begun with the *camera obscura* of the fifteenth century, an 'old friend' which had worked by fixing chemically the illuminated inverted images formed in the camera by light. Little forward movement occurred, however, until Nicéphore Niépce and Louis Jacques Mandé Daguerre (1789–1851) turned to the problem of stabilizing images early in the nineteenth century:

> In 1827 M. Niépce produced before the Royal Society what he then called heliographs, sun-pictures, formed and fixed upon glass, copper plated with silver, and well-polished tin. But, as he kept the secret of his process, no scientific use was made of the discovery. M. Daguerre, working at the same problem, succeeded about the same time in fixing sun-pictures on pages impregnated with nitrate of silver.

Just over a decade later in 1839, the French government bought 'for the free use of the world' the details of the discovery, and Niépce and Daguerre both received life pensions. Six months before the French government disclosed the process, William Henry Fox Talbot (1800–77) in England 'had discovered a process leading to a like result – the fixing of sun-pictures upon paper' ('Photography', *HW* 7.56–7).

Subsequent refinements and developments made possible the widespread introduction of photography, a term most mid-Victorian readers associated primarily with individual portraits and family albums. From the 1840s onwards, photography began to replace silhouettes and miniatures, the principal forms of likeness commonly available unless one could afford to employ portrait-painters.

The phrase 'long before' reinforces the case for dating the novel's opening shortly after the turn of the century. Similar adverbial expressions of distancing occur frequently throughout the novel. Compare 'Since that time, which is far enough away now' (chapter 2). For a hypothetical construction of the novel's chronology, see Appendix 1.

my first fancies regarding what they were like, were unreasonably derived from their tombstones.] Mary Lamb's 'Elizabeth Villiers' opens by describing the predicament of a child whose knowledge of her mother is confined to what she can infer from the carved letters on the tombstone that stands at the head of her mother's grave (Merchant). False tombstone inscriptions also played an important role in *The Woman in White*, the weekly serial by Wilkie Collins which preceded Lever's *A Day's Ride* in *AYR*.

"Also Georgiana Wife of the Above,"] Georgiana, an elaborated Latinate form of 'Georgia' or 'Georgina', a given name popular during the long reign of the Hanoverian kings (George I to George IV) from 1714 to 1830.

five little stone lozenges, each about a foot and a half long, which were arranged in a neat row beside their grave,] Small tombstones like these are relatively common on the Hoo peninsula in north Kent, and examples can be found in churchyards at High Halstow, All Hallows and Lower Higham. However, the accepted model is the headstones at Cooling – these are the smallest and most picturesque of any in the area (Plate 2; see Appendix 4, map p. 449). Forster wrote that Dickens 'often took friends to show them the dozen small tombstones of various sizes adapted to the respective ages of a dozen small children of one family which he made part of his story of *Great Expectations*'. Forster adds: 'About the whole of this Cooling churchyard, indeed ... there was a weird strangeness that made it one of his attractive walks in the late year or winter, when from Higham he could get to it across country over the stubble fields' (Forster 8.3.216). See also Dolby (1885, 423), Charles Dickens, Jr (1896, 347–9), and Sir Henry Fielding Dickens *et al.* (1925, 13).

Thirteen such small rectilinear tombstones lie on the south side of St James's Cooling, near the porch door. The 'lozenges' are in two sets grouped around a single headstone with three winged cherubs at the top. Three stones west of the headstone mark the graves of the infant children of John Rose Baker and his wife, Sarah Anne, née Comport. The second set of stones east of the headstone commemorates children born to the Comports of Cooling Court, Cooling Castle and Decoy House,

High Halstow. Coffin-like in shape, each is wider at the shoulders, lying horizontally in the ground with a curved surface upwards. The stones of the three Baker infants are approximately three and a half feet long; the ten Comport stones, identical in shape, are about six inches smaller.

The Comports were a long-established Kent family whose ancestors date from the twelfth century. Most of the markers date from the turn of the eighteenth century and appear to range from 1767 to 1854 (Gadd, 1929, 25–6; Smetham 2.201–2, 3.215–17; Plate 5). No explanation for these multiple deaths exists. Several children died between one and four months; none lived longer than seventeen months. Possibly the local 'marsh fever' (see chapter 3, note on p. 51) claimed the lives of some of them.

Unqualified emphasis on Cooling, however, overlooks Dickens's freedom to adapt features from other localities also suited to his imaginative purpose. The best case for a composite picture, one which emphasizes how Dickens fused details drawn from the churchyards of Cooling and Lower Higham, has been made by W. Laurence Gadd (1929). Discrepancies between Cooling and Higham are noted below when they occur.

The death of Dickens's brother Alfred Lamert Dickens (b.1822) on 27 July 1860, 'to which there are five little witnesses' (*Letters* 9.280), might have influenced Dickens's choice of 'five'. Alternatively, the association of the number five with dead infants may be connected with Dickens's visit to Bologna in November 1844. Touring the city's 'pleasant Cemetery', he came across an Italian tour guide looking wistfully 'at a certain plot of grass'. When Dickens asked who was buried there, the cicerone commented: 'The poor people, Signore. . . . Only the poor . . . there are five of my little children buried there' (*PI* 109). Equally plausible is the possibility that Dickens saw no reason to call attention to the thirteen gravestones of his supposed source.

sacred to the memory of] A phrase commonly used on tombstones. Simple and dignified wording came to be admired as a reaction to fanciful epitaphs developed later in the century: 'Neither our tombstones nor the inscription on them should be of a fantastic sort' ('Sacred to the Memory', 30 June 1866, *AYR* 15.594). For an example of the excesses found 'objectionable', see 'Curious Epitaph' taken from a churchyard in Pewsey, Dorsetshire (*HW* 1.168).

in that universal struggle] Compare 'Struggle for Existence', the title of chapter 3 of Charles Darwin's *Origin of Species* (1859). In the third paragraph Darwin draws attention to 'the truth of the universal struggle for life' and comments on his use of the phrase 'Struggle for Existence' in a 'large and metaphysical sense, including dependence of one being on another, and including (which is more important) not only the life of the individual, but success in leaving progeny' (62). Dickens's library contained a second edition (*Catalogue* 26; K. J. Fielding, 1996, 204). Two anonymous reviews of the *Origin* appeared in *AYR* before *GE* began on 1 December 1860. See 'Species', 2 June 1860 (3.174–8), and 'Natural Selection', 7 July 1860 (3.293–9). A third, 'Transmutation of Species', published concurrently with chapters 23 and 24 of the novel (9 March 1861), publicized further the content and implications of Darwin's work (*AYR* 4.519–21).

Dickens declared himself an evolutionist as early as December 1848 in his review of Robert Hunt's *Poetry of Science* in the *Examiner* (9 December 1848). Dickens also owned a copy of Robert Chambers's *Vestiges* (1844), whose Lamarckian theory of evolution he supported (based on K. J. Fielding, 1996, 201–3). Pip's use of Darwinian terminology has important implications for calculating his age when he decides to recount his life in the early 1860s. See Appendix 1.

they had all been born on their backs with their hands in their trouser-pockets,] This description appears to owe something to a childhood memory Dickens recounts in 'Dullborough Town' (30 June 1860) of being taken by his nurse to visit a lady whose five infants all died at birth. Seeing the house again, the narrator recalls the sight, etched in his mind, of the five 'deceased young people'. Each lay 'side by side on a clean cloth on a chest of drawers', displayed as pigs' feet usually are 'at a neat tripe-shop' (*AYR* 3.275). Compare also the description of a row of elm boards cut to serve as coffin lids which remind Oliver of 'high-shouldered ghosts with their hands in their breeches-pockets' (*OT* 5).

Ours was the marsh country, down by the river

Ours was the marsh country, down by the river, within, as the river wound, twenty miles of the sea . . . the dark flat wilderness beyond the churchyard, intersected with dykes and mounds and gates . . . and that the low leaden line beyond, was the river;] This is an accurate description of the Hoo peninsula, a triangular-shaped spur of land that forms the most northerly section of Kent. The peninsula lies north of a line drawn between Gravesend and Rochester. The estuaries of the Thames and the Medway form boundaries to the west and to the east (see Appendix 4, map p. 449).

Three distinctive traits define the topography of the region: uplands, marshes and saltings. The predominant vista even as late as the 1860s was bleak and windswept. Remote villages (eight in all), scattered churches, cattle grazing, chalk pits, smouldering lime-kilns and few roads gave the Hoo peninsula a lonely, unvisited atmosphere. Industrial development in the twentieth century has altered but not entirely destroyed this strange and haunting landscape.

Wide tracts of saltings, or tidal flats, and marshes begin east of Gravesend. From there they follow the course of the Thames through three reaches to the sea. East of Gantlet Creek and the Isle of Grain, the land curves round to form the northern shore of the Medway, which joins the Thames estuary approximately three miles east of London Stone on the north side of Grain. An imaginary line from this point to Southend Pier on the northern shore of the Thames marks the limit of the jurisdiction of the Port of London Authority (see Appendix 4, map p. 448).

Dickens's removal to Gad's Hill Place in August 1860 intensified his relationship with the whole lower Medway region. Excursions to Chatham, where he lived as a boy from 1817 to 1822, and to the adjoining city of Rochester, regularly featured in his daily walks. The opening descriptions of the tidal flats and dikes surrounding Pip's village, and later references to the nearby 'market town', convey an affinity with the environment characteristic of a regional novel. Additional local references are noted as they appear in this and subsequent chapters. Later, Dickens uses the Thames with equal effectiveness. See especially chapter 54.

My first most vivid and broad impression of the identity of things,]   The language of this statement raises philosophical questions in the tradition of the classical philosophers of the seventeenth and eighteenth centuries. Despite differences of doctrine between Descartes, Locke and Berkeley, each addressed a broad agenda concerned with issues of personal identity, the existence of an enduring, substantial self, and the extent to which identity is based on the experience of the senses or on ideas and thoughts derived from other contexts.

on a memorable raw afternoon towards evening.]   The initial chapters of the novel detail two 'memorable' days in Pip's early life. The first day opens late in the afternoon of Christmas Eve. Thereafter follows a sequence of events precipitated by the encounter with the convict which lasts for just over twenty-four hours. The second 'memorable' day occurs 'a full year after our hunt upon the marshes' when, with frost 'hard' on the ground, Pip first visits Satis House (chapter 8). Later chapters alternate between precisely narrated and detailed sequences and summaries covering months (or sometimes years) of routine during which no remarkable incidents occur. Generally, but not exclusively, single chapters which comprise a whole weekly issue (chs 5, 8, 11, 18, 19, 22, 29, 39, 40, 53, 54 and 57) serve to slow the pace by providing greatest scope for detailed narration. Further significant references to the novel's time-scheme are noted as they occur. See also Appendix 1.

Philip Pirrip,]   Originally, Tobias Philip.

dead and buried;]   Compare the phrase in the Apostles' Creed: 'I believe . . . in Jesus Christ . . . Who . . . Was crucified, dead, and buried . . .' (*BCP*).

Alexander, Bartholomew, Abraham, Tobias, and Roger,]   None of these names appears on the stones of the Comport and Baker infants (see above). All five were common Christian names throughout the eighteenth and nineteenth centuries. Three are of biblical origin (Abraham, Tobias and Bartholomew), one the Latinate form of a Greek name (Alexandros), and one (Roger) an English, French and Germanic name introduced to Britain by the Normans. In MS, Tobias and Roger were originally George and Robert.

intersected with dykes and mounds and gates . . . was the marshes;]   Dikes and run-off channels intersected land reclaimed over the centuries from the sea and prevented flooding. Rich deposits of alluvial soil made the area suitable for grazing.

the small bundle of shivers growing afraid of it all and beginning to cry, was Pip.]   Compare Carlyle's *Sartor Resartus* (1833–4): 'Wherefore, like a coward, doest thou forever pip and whimper and go cowering and trembling?' ('The Everlasting No', 2.7).

"Hold your noise!" cried a terrible voice

"Hold your noise!" cried a terrible voice, as a man started up from among the graves at the side of the church porch.] Biographical and literary elements appear to underlie this encounter. In 'Lying Awake' (30 October 1852), Dickens narrates an incident, apparently from his own childhood, when he once saw, 'just after dark', a figure 'chalked upon a door in a little back lane near a country church':

> How young a child I may have been at the time, I don't know, but it horrified me so intensely – in connection with the churchyard, I suppose, for it smokes a pipe, and has a big hat with each of its ears sticking out in a horizontal line under the brim, . . . that it is still vaguely alarming to me to recall (as I have often done before, lying awake) the running home, the looking behind, the horror of its following me; though whether disconnected from the door, or door and all, I can't say, and perhaps never could. It lays a disagreeable train.
> (*HW* 6.146)

In another childhood event sketched in 1859, Dickens describes in *HW*, from the perspective of a small boy, how he played a role in sheltering a man with a wooden leg in a coal-cellar. This man was unknown 'in the circle of my acknowledged and lawful relations and friends' and he may have 'robbed the house, before or afterwards, or otherwise nefariously distinguished himself' ('New Year's Day', 98; see also Carolan 28–9). Other instances of a character pursued by a coffin, corpse, ghost or similar terror appear elsewhere in Dickens's fiction (Winters).

A more obvious literary influence shaping this encounter between Pip and the convict is the folk-lore motif of an old man, under mysterious circumstances, bestowing a gift on a young boy. A 'little piece' based on this notion had suggested itself for a paper in the *UT* series. But in the midst of writing it 'such a very fine, new, and grotesque idea . . . opened' that Dickens decided to cancel 'the little paper' and reserve the idea 'for a new book'. This was, as Forster notes, 'the germ of Pip and Magwitch' and the convict's resolution 'to make his little friend a gentleman'. The meeting in the churchyard thus serves as the foundation for the novel's pivotal climax at the end of book 2, chapter 39, in which Pip describes Magwitch's return from Australia and the collapse of all his hopes (Forster 8.3.284–6). The 'new, and grotesque idea' presumably refers to Pip's overpowering realization that Miss Havisham's intentions towards him were 'all a mere dream' and that in fact he owes his gentlemanly status and wealth to a 'terrible patron' whose various felonies rendered him liable to 'the extreme penalty of the law'.

A fearful man, all in coarse grey

all in coarse grey, with a great iron on his leg.] Describing practices which prevailed in the 1820s, journalist and historian John Wade (1788–1875) noted:

> On their arrival at the hulks, from different gaols, [convicts] are immediately stripped and washed, clothed in coarse grey jackets and breeches, and two irons placed on one of their legs, to which degradation every one must submit, let his previous rank have been what it may. They are then sent out in gangs of a certain number to work on shore, guarded by soldiers. (A *Treatise on the Police and Crime of the Metropolis*, 1829, 365, quoted in Tobias, 1972, 141)

The idea of keeping convicts in chains and distinguishing them from other workers by special dress so that they would serve as 'visible and lasting Examples of Justice' appears to date from a bill introduced in 1752 'to change the Punishment of Felony in certain Cases . . . to Confinement, and hard Labour, in his Majesty's Dock Yards' (cited in Beattie, 1986, 522–3). Although the Lords rejected the resolution to engage convicts, uniformed and shackled, in laborious work at home instead of sending them to America, the main features of the bill were reintroduced in 1776 to provide the foundation of England's hulks system (see note on chapter 2, pp. 44–6). Convicts also wore numbers on their clothing 'at the back and the breast' (see chapter 28), to make them 'distinguishable at a distance' (*BPP, Crime and Punishment. Transportation*, 1. 'Second Report . . . Laws Relating to Penitentiary Houses', 10 June 1811, 126).

'Ironing' prisoners served the obvious purpose of ensuring security on board the hulks and making flight from a working party difficult; requiring convicts to undertake hard labour in public wearing chains also reinforced notions of humiliation and punishment implicit for generations in all forms of servitude stipulated by the authorities. With considerable understatement, one felon noted that irons 'were not desirable companions in bed'. However, good behaviour and co-operation earned convicts the privilege of 'half-irons', a weight 'about seven [pounds]' (Ward, 'Diary', 1841, 44, 49, 56). Felons were also ironed when they were removed from local gaols and taken to the dockyards. Upon the removal of irons after wearing them for some months, prisoners found their right leg jerking uncontrollably when they walked (R. Hughes, 1987, 140–1). Leg sores and inflammation were additional afflictions. See chapter 28, note on p. 248.

"Once more," said the man, staring at me.

"Give it mouth!"]   'Speak up!' or express it with vehemence.

I pointed to where our village lay

where our village lay, on the flat in-shore among the alder-trees and pollards, a mile or more from the church.]   The 'originals' of the village and the church remain a matter of conjecture. Most probably, they are composites based on more than one village and on combined features taken from St James's at Cooling and St Mary's at Lower Higham, a second church about three miles to the east of St James's (Plates 3, 4; see Appendix 4, map p. 449).

2 Pip's 'little stone lozenges'

3　St Mary's Higham, 4 miles north-west of Rochester

4　St James's Cooling, 6 miles north-west of Rochester

The case against Cooling and its churchyard alone rests on several facts. The village does not lie 'on the flat in-shore' and is only half a mile away from the church as opposed to the 'mile or more' stated in the novel. St James's churchyard also lacked remoteness. It was partially surrounded by a road. The ruins of Cooling Castle stand within a hundred feet to the west, and there were houses nearby in the nineteenth century. In addition, Cooling lacked a forge (see chapter 2, note on p. 40), a wheelwright's (see chapter 4, note on p. 56), a tavern and a general shop. Lower Higham had all four, although Dickens evidently incorporated details drawn from other villages as well.

The position of St Mary's at Lower Higham, by contrast, better fits the text in some respects. The churchyard is further from the village of Lower Higham (a mile) and has some of the outlying quality suggested by the novel. The churchyard practically stands on the marsh itself, which stretches away from a low wall of brick, chalk and flints. The village, unlike Cooling, also stands 'on the flat in-shore', a short distance from Higham and Gravesend marshes (Gadd, 1909, 68–9; 1924, 131–6; 1929, passim). For sceptical assessments of this preference, see Dexter (214) and Henry Fielding Dickens *et al.*, who assert that 'Lower Higham is quite out of the question' (13).

Alder trees grow well in wet, marshy conditions. Their wood resists decay and is not subject to rot, despite immersion in water for indefinite periods of time; pollards are trees polled or cut back, at some height from the ground, so as to produce at that point a rounded head or mass of young branches.

The man, after looking at me for a moment

turned me upside-down,] Inverting commonly accepted notions and turning the world upside down is an old rhetorical trope: the *mundus inversus*. The motif is common in Dickens's fiction, and aspects of it have been widely discussed, including a possible link between this scene and the visual depiction of reversals in eighteenth-century chapbooks like *The World Upside Down* and the extent to which GE repeats and inverts material Dickens used in *DC* (Campbell 153–65; Pearlman 190–202).

I saw the steeple under my legs] Lower Higham church has a steeple standing about twenty feet above the ridge of the roof; Cooling church has a rectangular tower whose stair turret projects above the parapet. Within the parapet there is a small, slated spirelet.

"Darn Me if I couldn't eat 'em," said the man

"Darn Me if I couldn't eat 'em,"] Dickens characteristically modified this oath, changing 'Damned Me' to 'Darn Me'. Compare also Wemmick's 'D–n it!' changed to 'Deuce take me' in chapter 48. Other modifications to the convict's speech between manuscript and print include the addition of the final 'g' to the original sub-standard versions of words such as 'keepin', 'harmin', 'perishin' and 'firin' and reversion to 'was' and 'what' for 'wos' and 'wot' (Cardwell xx, xxxv). For the most extended and helpful discussion of MS additions, cancellations and interlineations throughout the whole novel, see Rosenberg's essay (*Norton*, 427–68).

The terror inspired by the convict's threats against Pip's cheeks – and quickly extended to his heart and liver – seems to point to one of the 'dark corners' of Dickens's mind nurtured by various sources. Specifically, there are the gruesome tales about Captain Murderer, a cat that sucks the breath of an infant and rats that gnaw corpses told to him as a boy by his nurse ('Nurse's Stories'), together with traditional fairy tales about ogres and witches, many of which trade on children's primal fears of bogey men, like 'the young man' hidden with the convict, who snatches the young from the security of warm beds. Dickens also learned of cannibalism through the sensational materials he read as a schoolboy in the pages of the *Terrific Register* and the *Portfolio*. In these twopenny weeklies, he came across stories of the shipwrecked survivors of the *Medusa*, who, driven to extremity in their efforts to survive, ate human flesh, and accounts of similar deeds by an escaped convict in Tasmania (see below). Repeated references to cannibalism in Dickens's fiction, together with his admission on 20 November 1854 to W. H. Wills that he was 'rather strong on Voyages and Cannibalism' (*Letters* 7.470), suggest a fascination with the topic (based on Stone, 1962; 1979; and 1994, 3–77).

An additional contemporaneous source relevant to *GE* is the Molesworth 'Report' of 3 August 1838, which Dickens is known to have read within two years of its publication (*Letters* 7.818). This lengthy document details the findings of a parliamentary Select Committee responsible for advising the government whether or not to continue the practice of exiling felons to Australia and Tasmania. Amidst the copious documentation are two appendices that appear to have caught Dickens's eye. Labelled items 'C' and 'D', both recount events surrounding the escape of Alexander Pearce (1790–1824) and seven other convicts from a penal settlement at Macquarie Harbour, Van Diemen's Land, as Tasmania was known until 1856.

Questioned by committee members on 12 February 1838, John Barnes, a government witness, refers to two items in his possession: one is the confession of Pearce, taken down 'in his own language', of his escape; the second, a brief official account, provides particulars of Pearce's life following his capture, return to Macquarie Harbour, second escape, and subsequent recapture and execution.

Barnes elaborates sufficiently when testifying to provide the gist of Pearce's story. On the first occasion, in September 1822, Pearce fled with seven other convicts, 'five of whom were eaten by their companions' before his eventual capture. A year later, Pearce absconded a second time 'with another convict [Cox], whom he likewise murdered and ate'.

The account of the first escape relates how Pearce and his seven companions were pushed to extreme forms of behaviour. After enduring hunger and cold for several days, one of them confessed that he was so weak 'I could eat a piece of a man'. Human flesh, he added, 'eat much like a little pork'. This remark initiated a round of killing and eating that began with Pearce and another convict devouring the victim's partially roasted heart and liver.

Next morning the fleshy remains of their former companion were cut up and divided among the others. This gruesome ritual was re-enacted four times during the following seven weeks as the weaker members of the party were murdered, cooked and eaten. There were only three survivors: two who fled for their lives and Pearce himself. Sustained by the flesh of his former companions, Pearce eventually sought help from convict shepherds tending their flocks. He remained with them for several weeks before he was arrested and removed to the gaol at Macquarie Harbour. He then resumed work because prison authorities refused to believe his confession. Shortly after, he made plans for another escape.

Pearce fled a second time with a single partner, Cox, whom he murdered after a quarrel and then began to eat. On this occasion, he was captured with the evidence the authorities previously lacked. Pursuing soldiers located Cox's body 'in a dreadfully mangled state', and, finding bread, pork and fish in Pearce's pockets, surmised that 'he could not have done it for hunger'. Pearce confessed to the accusation and explained that he had developed a taste for human flesh. Members of the search party found none of the intestines; they had been thrown away, Pearce explained, after he had 'roasted and devoured the heart and part of the liver'. Cox's body, the report notes, was 'very nicely, washed and cleaned ... and suspended [from] the trunk to a tree'(*BPP, Crime and Punishment, Transportation*, 3, 'Documents relative to the Absconding of Pierce [sic] and Cox from Macquarie Harbour', 313–16).

Stories about cannibalism received a further boost in the mid-century. This occurred when hearsay evidence circulated in the British press about Sir John Franklin, who, with 129 officers and men and supplies for three years, set out for the Arctic on 19 May 1845 and soon afterwards disappeared. Members of this ill-fated expedition, it was later suggested, had taken to 'the last resource' in an attempt to survive. These allegations, first made in 1854, prompted a considerable debate, one which Dickens followed closely (Marlow 654–5), printing seven articles in *HW* between 1854 and 1857 defending Franklin and encouraging a final search to ascertain what had happened.

Other cannibalistic references in the novel sustain the mood of childhood terror the opening chapters evoke. These include Pumblechook's reference to young Pip's conjectural fate as 'a four-footed Squeaker' who would have been disposed of 'for so many shillings', laid in straw and had his blood shed by the local butcher, had Mrs Joe not brought him up by hand (chapter 4), Orlick's mouth 'water[ing]' for Pip (chapter 53), and Miss Havisham's vision of herself laid out on the table as a 'feast' for all the relatives she hates and despises (chapter 11). Eating human flesh serves as a metaphor for legal greed in *BH* (39); *OMF* (4.17) preserves the idea, which Dickens expressed in the *Examiner* ('The Niger Expedition'), where he noted that, in real life, such activities can be found only in darkest Africa (19 August 1848; *MP* 1.133–4).

"My sister, sir – Mrs. Joe Gargery – wife of Joe Gargery

Joe Gargery, the blacksmith,] Joe's original name, 'George Thunder', connects him with the Roman Vulcan, the god of the forge, guardian of the fire, and manufacturer of thunderbolts. The switch to the more euphonious 'Gargery', whose soft 'rge' is picked up in 'forge', was settled on by the beginning of chapter two. The name 'Gargery' appears in a list of names in the *Book of Memoranda*, as 'Gannery-Gargery' (14). This same source supplied ten other names: see subsequent chapters.

"And you know what wittles is?"

wittles] 'Victuals' – the cockney dialect substitutes *w* for *v*.

"You get me a file."

"Or I'll have your heart and liver out."] Good Mrs Brown in *DS* similarly warns Florence that she won't be safe in bed (6); compare also the words of the tinker who accosts David Copperfield just outside Chatham: 'Come here, when you're called . . . or I'll rip your young body open' (*DC* 13).

"You bring me, to-morrow morning early

that old Battery over yonder.] Remains of two different fortified works or mounds in the vicinity may have suggested the idea of the 'old Battery'. There was an old earthwork near Lower Hope Point, which inhabitants of Cliffe remembered in 1926 as a few mounds of grass-grown earth inside the sea-wall and surrounded by a moat (Gadd, 1926, 111). This battery was approximately three miles from both Lower Higham church and St James's, Cooling (see Appendix 4, map p. 449).

Traces also existed of a second bulwark built at Higham Creek in 1539 by Henry VIII which housed guns and mortars. This site was on the level of the sea-wall and commanded a wide view of the river. It was about three and a half miles west of Cooling and less than two miles north of Lower Higham church (see Appendix 4, map p. 449). Both fortifications served as part of a regional defence system which evolved from the fourteenth century to protect London and the south-east coast against raids by the French and later the Dutch.

"Say Lord strike you dead if you don't!" said the man.

Lord strike you dead] A favourite oath of the convict's (see chapter 40). The utterance appears to vary Old Testament expressions about the Lord's threatening to strike in retaliation for wrongdoing.

At the same time, he hugged his shuddering body

the low church wall.] This detail suggests the church at Higham, which looks directly over the marshes, rather than Cooling church, where the Comport grave-markers are located (see above). The wall is only about three feet high and is actually on the edge of the marsh. Today, the land is not waterlogged as it was in Dickens's time.

the green mounds,] These appear to be unmarked graves, as opposed to the mounds that belong to 'the dark flat wilderness beyond the churchyard'.

When he came to the low church wall

But presently I . . . saw him going on again towards the river . . . and picking his way . . . among the great stones dropped into the marshes here and there, for stepping-places when the rains were heavy, or the tide was in.] In Dickens's time wet marsh came no closer to Cooling churchyard than half a mile. 'On the other hand, the wet marsh, with its stepping stones in the form of great lumps of chalk reached right up to the wall of Lower Higham churchyard within living memory, before the railway embankment was built in 1881' (Gadd, 1924, 135). See also chapter 5, note on p. 66

The marshes were just a long black horizontal line then

The marshes were just a long black horizontal line then . . . and the river was just another horizontal line, not nearly so broad nor yet so black; and the sky was just a row of long angry red lines and dense black lines intermixed.] Looking west towards the Thames from Lower Higham churchyard, one sees marshland stretching out on either side of Cliffe Creek. Beyond Higham and Cliffe marshes lies the river, about a mile wide at this point. The visual quality of this and earlier descriptions of 'the dark flat wilderness' and 'the low leaden line' of the river beyond the marshes suggests an affinity with J. W. M. Turner, whose paintings of estuaries and shorelines have a similar evocative quality.

the beacon by which the sailors steered – like an unhooped cask upon a pole] Beacons were simple contrivances designed as alarm signals before they were displaced by the use of gunpowder to ignite rockets (*Complete Book of Trades* 208). The kind described here was an old-fashioned cresset, an iron basket or cage which held pitched rope, wood or coal. They were first put up on the Thames in the fourteenth century at the command of Richard II, who directed the sheriffs of Kent and Essex to erect '*certain beacons*' and keep them prepared so they could be fired 'on the first approach of . . . enemy vessels' (Hasted, 1778, 1.450). Beacons later came under the management of Trinity House, the agency responsible for setting up sea-marks, lighthouses and navigation aids to warn ships of shoals, sandbanks and other coastal hazards. Several beacons on the lower reaches of the Thames survived into Dickens's day.

a gibbet with some chains hanging to it which had once held a pirate.] Gibbeting, or hanging in chains, the bodies of executed offenders 'was a coarse custom very generally prevalent in medieval England' (J. Charles Cox, 1890, 2.43; cited in Radzinowicz 1.213 n.). Dickens more specifically ascribes the tradition to Richard II who, following the rebellion led by Wat Tyler in 1381, hanged the rioters and ordered some of the bodies to be chained up (*CHE* 19). Gibbeting continued through the centuries but did not acquire full legal status until 1752, by which statute judges could order the penalty for murderers (25 Geo. II, c. 37). The last gibbeting in England took place in Leicester in August 1832. Gibbeting was abolished in 1834 (4 & 5 Will. IV, c. 26, ss. 1 & 2).

Various steps were taken to intensify this form of aggravated punishment. The gibbet – an upright post with a projecting arm from which the body hung in a specially constructed iron frame – was often erected near the place of the crime or within sight of the offender's own house. Efforts were made to preserve the chained body as long as possible, usually by saturating it in tar before suspending it. Authorities also studded gibbet posts with thousands of nails in order to make it difficult to remove the body for burial. Gibbeting was usually reserved for notorious thieves or highwaymen.

Its deterrent value is hard to assess. But the gibbet attracted unhealthy interest and remained a feature of the English landscape during the first quarter of the nineteenth century. Although 'the bleached skulls and blackened quarters of political offenders' were no longer displayed on city gates, writes one observer, 'many a strip of green waste by the roadside, and many a gorse-covered common had its gibbet, from which swung in the breeze the clanking and creaking iron hoops encasing the grim and ghastly remains of what had been a man' (Frost, 1892, 194). Other witnesses recall the sight of bodies dangling in chains on Wimbledon Common, Bagshot Heath and Hounslow Heath, and on the Thames opposite Blackwall, early in the nineteenth century (T. Cross 1.14; Southey, 1807, 45; Timbs, 1867, 686).

There was no gibbet on the Cliffe or Cooling marshes. Possibly Dickens may have remembered from childhood the gibbet that stood opposite Chatham dockyard on the north bank of the Medway. Other gibbets in the area included one at Upnor Castle, one between Northfleet and Gravesend, and one on the marshes at Woolwich (Gadd, 'The Beacon and the Gibbet', 1926, 110). Riverside gibbets used for the execution of pirates (a capital offence since 1536) also stood at Execution Dock, Wapping, on the Thames until they were taken down in 1827.

Chapter 2

My sister, Mrs. Joe Gargery

more than twenty years older than I,]   Pip's age at the opening is never precisely stated. Asked later by Herbert how old he was upon first meeting Magwitch, he replies: 'I think [I was] in my seventh year' (chapter 50). Since his birthday occurs in November (chs 36 and 39), Pip could have just turned 6 when the novel opens on Christmas Eve in the churchyard. But notes made after the earlier chapters were written indicate that Dickens added a year to his age, making Pip 'about 7 at the opening of the story' (Harry Stone, 1987, 321). The calculations in the memoranda marked '<u>Dates</u>' evidently served to verify information about ages supplied in Stages I and II before Dickens completed Stage III and those parts of the narrative disclosing the interlocking histories of Miss Havisham and Compeyson, and Compeyson and Magwitch. For the text of the memoranda, see pp. 344–5.

and had established a great reputation with herself and the neighbours because she had brought me up "by hand."]   To the young boy, 'by hand' meant constant blows and corporal punishment; to the neighbours the term signified feeding infants a mixture of pap or semi-soft food. Crumbs of bread softened in water or milk and mixed with a little sugar typically formed the ingredients (Chavasse, 1839, 29).

Feeding by hand, or 'dry-nursing', led to a high infant mortality rate because there was no safe alternative to breast milk. Substitute ingredients were unsuited to infant stomachs, and pap and other mixtures were prepared and administered in ignorance of even elementary sanitary measures. Dry-nursing developed in the eighteenth century as an alternative to the 'wet nurses' popular among middle-class women, who often hired lactating mothers to nurse their own children. Raising infants by hand was common in workhouses and among poor women, many of whom worked long hours in factories (Fildes 191).

The first recorded usage of the phrase 'by hand' to mean dry-nursed occurs in Steele, *Tatler*, no. 89, 1709: 'I was bred by hand'. Medical authorities writing for the middle class generally took a firm stand against this practice. One author of a popular home medical guide argued that it was 'preposterous' for a mother to think it was beneath her to take care of her own child: 'If we search Nature throughout, we cannot find a parallel to this' (Buchan 2). Compare also *The Advice to Mothers on the Management of Their Offspring*, a firm advocate of breast feeding: 'The interest of the mother and the child demand it' (Chavasse, 1839, 27). Oliver Twist was also 'brought up by hand' (OT 2).

She was not a good-looking woman, my sister

He was a mild, good-natured, sweet-tempered, easy-going, foolish, dear fellow]   Dickens described the opening of the novel to Forster as 'exceedingly droll'. To create this effect, he explained, 'I have put a child and a good-natured foolish man, in relations that seem to me very funny' (Forster, 8.3.284–5). John Cayford, a mild, easy-going London blacksmith known to Dickens, claimed credit as the inspiration behind this portrait, and for the scene between Joe and Orlick in chapter 15 (Richards 464–7).

a sort of Hercules in strength, and also in weakness.] The mythic Greek hero celebrated for his strength and daring. Hercules performed twelve labours on behalf of his father, who wanted to appease Juno, whom he had deserted for Alcmena, mother of Hercules (*Lempriere's Classical Dictionary*, 274–6, 238).

Joe's forge adjoined our house

Joe's forge adjoined our house,] This may have been a detail drawn from the village of Chalk, nearly five miles west of Cooling. The blacksmith's forge stood on the corner where a lane leading towards Singlewell and Cobham intersected the old Dover Road. Dickens often passed by on walks and knew the smith, Mr Mullender, quite well. The forge adjoined the wooden house, and the kitchen door led to the forge, whose roof at the back reached down to within four feet of the ground (Gadd, 'The Forge', 1926, 234–6). See Pumblechook's speculation about how the forge was supposedly entered (chapter 6). The forge at Chalk also had red tiles and a small garden by the side of the lane. For the garden, see chapter 19, note on p. 165.

a wooden house, as many of the dwellings in our country were – most of them, at that time.] Brick began to replace timber as the main building material in Kent in the eighteenth century. Existing wooden houses fall into two main categories: some have exposed beams and half-timbered upper storeys erected before builders exhausted supplies of native oak; others are timber dwellings built after the introduction of Dutch weather-boarding about 1620. Houses built with weather-boarding – overlapping horizontal boards nailed in place – predominated in the villages and towns of Kent in the early part of the nineteenth century (Cox, 1935, 336). Several of the older timber houses with exposed beams survive in nearby Rochester and Maidstone. Many other examples can be found elsewhere throughout Kent.

At this dismal intelligence

intelligence,] News, information or tidings. The term was widely used in newspapers, where sections were headed 'Foreign Intelligence', 'Domestic Intelligence', etc.

a wax-ended piece of cane,] Binding the end with cobbler's thread (wax-end) added to the cane's effectiveness by forming a raised or corrugated surface all the more unpleasant to exposed or lightly protected flesh.

"She sot down," said Joe

and she Ram-paged out. That's what she did . . . she Ram-paged out . . . . "Well," said Joe . . . "she's been on the Ram-page,] 'Rampage' is an eighteenth-century term indicating a state of excitement or violent passion. Pip later records how his sister 'went on the Rampage' (chapter 12), and elsewhere uses the expression (chapter 15). OED cites GE as the earliest example of '[to go] on the rampage'.

"Well," said Joe, glancing up

the Dutch clock,] Import duties on foreign goods were reduced in 1823, opening up colonial trade to competition. One result was the increase of German, or 'Dutch' (a corruption of Deutsch), clocks whose popularity rose in the 1820s. The German clock industry dates from the mid-seventeenth century. Peasant craftsmen in the Black Forest area specialized in making clocks with a painted dial and a wooden casing. Many also had wooden figures that darted inside and shut a door when the hour struck (OCS 48). The clocks, either free-standing or wall-mounted, were about twelve inches high and eight inches wide. Their presence, according to one commentator, often served to indicate 'prosperity and personal respectability on the part of the working man' (Porter, 1847, 533).

the jack-towel] A long towel with the ends sewed together and suspended from a roller and frequently mounted behind a door. Mr Jaggers also uses one (chapter 26); references to them appear elsewhere in Dickens's fiction (PP 25 and OCS 13).

"I don't!" said my sister.

It's bad enough to be a blacksmith's wife (and him a Gargery), without being your mother."] Marriage to an illiterate blacksmith represented 'a drop' to a woman who considered her own background superior. Other signs of Mrs Joe's false gentility appear in her friendship with the prosperous corn-merchant Pumblechook and her eagerness to advance what she sees as Pip's prospects at Satis House.

My thoughts strayed from that question

a larceny] Formerly, English law distinguished between 'petty' larceny and 'grand' larceny (theft of goods whose value exceeded twelve pence), a capital offence since the time of Henry I. In 1827 the distinction was abolished (7 & 8 Geo. IV, c. 28, s. 2) in recognition of the progressive removal of capital punishment from all kinds of stealing during the second half of the nineteenth century.

in the avenging coals.] The phrase, with its suggestion of hell fire, possibly combines 'Hot coals of vengeance' (2 Henry VI 5.2.36) and the biblical injunction to

My sister had a trenchant way

she took some butter . . . on a knife and spread it on the loaf, in an apothecary kind of way as if she were making a plaister]   In the preparation of a plaister, or poultice, the poultice mixture was first warmed by the fire and made soft so it could be spread easily with a knife on soft cotton cloth. Blistering or suppurative poultices, made from a mixture of oatmeal, strong beer grounds and camphor dissolved in turpentine, were used to promote 'the maturation of indolent tumours or boils'. 'Emollient poultices', a mixture of water and white breadcrumbs, were applied to the surface of the skin to allay inflammation (Henry H. Gregory, 1837, 56).

Apothecaries dispensed drugs from prescriptions supplied by physicians and administered routine medical treatments. The Apothecaries Company was formed in 1617, when apothecaries were separated from grocers (*Complete Book of Trades* 5–6).

The effort of resolution necessary to the achievement of this purpose

freemasonry as fellow-sufferers,]   Pip uses 'freemasonry' figuratively to convey a sense of secret brotherhood. By the late seventeenth century, Freemasonry had spread to England from Scotland; subsequently it became a worldwide movement with a constitution (1723) endorsed by all official lodges. The movement's emphasis on secrecy and exclusion still creates suspicion among outsiders.

mug of tea]   Tea was introduced to Europe by the Dutch in 1606; it was first brought to England from the orient in the 1650s and 1660s, became fashionable at court and in time replaced the custom of drinking ale at breakfast. By Victoria's reign, tea was considered an indispensable article of diet 'among all classes of society' (Keith Imray, 1842, 823). Some doctors, however, warned that tea-drinking too soon after meals had the effect of 'distending the stomach, and impeding digestion'. In general, 'it should be drunk with cream or milk, which, to a certain extent, counteract its astringent quality' (825).

"Now, perhaps you'll mention what's the matter," said my sister

staring great stuck pig."]   A proverbial phrase originating from the expression of a pig whose throat has been slit. The butcher's art called for severing a vein so that the animal died slowly. A long bleeding of eight to ten minutes ensured that the meat would not be red and bloody. The blood was collected to make blood-pudding, 'those strings of black-puddings, with tempting little bits of fat in them, which stare us in the faces in some shops' (Simmonds, 1859, 21).

Some medical beast had revived Tar-water

Some medical beast had revived Tar-water in those days as a fine medicine,] Tar-water owed its popularity to George Berkeley (1685–1753), the Anglo-Irish philosopher and clergyman, whose *Siris, A Chain of Philosophical Reflections Concerning the Virtues of Tar-Water* (1744) did much to promote its use. Berkeley's tract went through three editions between 1744 and 1748 but lost its popularity before the end of the eighteenth century (Chance 4.454). Berkeley touted tar-water as an appetite-enhancer and as a cure for indigestion, smallpox, dysentery, eruptions, ulcers, ulceration of the bowels and lungs, consumptive cough, pleurisy, dropsy, gravel, gout, and sundry inflammatory disorders and fevers. Tar-water was made by mixing a gallon of cold water with a quart of tar taken from pine trees and allowing the tar to settle after a period of three days and three nights. Water infused with tar was kept in a tightly stoppered bottle and administered to those in need at the dose of half a pint twice a day. Attempts to revive bogus medicines evidently occurred with some frequency: ' "There is always," observed an unnamed writer cited in 'Infallible Physic,' "some one arch quackery that carries the bell in England. If it is not tar water, it is something else" ' (*AYR* 2.448).

It was Christmas Eve

It was Christmas Eve,] The novel's opening and the second 'memorable day' in Pip's life a year later both take place in December, coinciding with the issue of the first four serial instalments published between 1 and 22 December 1860. Frequently in Dickens's fiction, serial numbers correspond with the seasons in which they appear, although the cheerful sentiments he usually associates with Christmas are singularly absent in *GE*.

I had to stir the pudding for next day, with a copper-stick, from seven to eight] Plum-pudding (or Christmas pudding in its earliest form) came into vogue at the beginning of the eighteenth century. Originally it was served with the first course of a Christmas dinner. Plum-pudding was made by boiling beef or mutton and thickening the broth with brown bread. Additional ingredients included raisins, currents, prunes, cloves, mace and ginger. Later recipes for plum or Christmas pudding called for milk, eggs and brandy or sherry, and for a sweet white sauce to accompany the dish. Puddings required between three and five hours of boiling or steaming to cook, hence the need to prepare the dish ahead of time (Bishop 262–4). The copper-stick, so called because servants used a stick to stir clothes boiling in the copper, or tub, on wash day, evidently doubled as a stirring-spoon on occasions.

"Hark!" said I

"was that great guns, Joe?"] After signalling an escape by firing a cannon, captains of each hulk (see below) were under orders 'to make strict inquiry into the cause thereof, and to leave no means untried to recover' fugitives. Names and descriptions of escapees were also sent forward immediately to the local magistrate and to the stipendiary magistrates at all of London's police-courts (*BPP*, *Crime and Punishment, Transportation* 1, 'Second Report . . . 10 June 1811', 'Appendix B', 158).

Data collected by a Parliamentary Select Committee for the years 1804 to 1811 indicate that escapes during this period were relatively common, averaging twenty a year from six convict-ships stationed in naval ports in the south of England (*BPP*, *Crime and Punishment, Transportation* 1, 'Appendix B', 'Third Report . . . 27 June 1812', 165). Crowded conditions, the inadequate supervision of working parties ashore and perhaps a shortage of personnel accounted for this rate. Stories about escapes were also augmented by local lore arising from an earlier period when hulks stationed at Chatham were used to hold prisoners captured during the Napoleonic wars against France from 1803 to 1815 (Coombe, 1979, passim). Later in the century, escapes became rare (Mayhew, 1866, 217, 223).

"There was a conwict off last night," said Joe

"after sun-set gun.]   In the Navy guns were fired twice – at day-break and in the evening – to signal, respectively, reveille and retreat (Smyth). After the sunset or 'evening gun' had been fired, sentries would challenge anyone who approached (*BPP*, *Crime and Punishment, Transportation* 1, 'A Select Committee Report', 1831, 45).

"Drat that boy," interposed my sister

Ask no questions, and you'll be told no lies."]   Conduct manuals counselled both children and adults against asking questions:

> Never ask a question under any circumstances. In the first place, it may be very inconvenient or very awkward to give a reply. A lady inquired of what branch of medical practice a certain gentleman was a professor. He held the chair of *midwifery*! (*Etiquette for Gentlemen*, 1838, 48)

Compare also Tony Lumpkin's riposte: 'Ask me no questions, and you'll be told no lies' (Goldsmith, *She Stoops to Conquer*, 3.1).

"And please what's Hulks?" said I.

"And please what's Hulks?"]   Literally, hulks were old, out-of-commission, mastless line-of-battle ships or frigates moored in rivers and harbours around the south-east coast of England. Although unfit for sea service, wooden vessels like these were retained by the government to store naval supplies, provide temporary housing for crews and quarantine infected sailors. Ships known as 'shear hulks' were often specially built, fitted with two sloping poles (shears) and hoisting tackle used to raise masts and other heavy equipment.

From the late eighteenth century onwards, however, 'hulks' more frequently referred to the floating prisons first introduced on the Thames at Woolwich in August 1776 under the provisions of the Hulks Act (16 Geo. III, c. 43), large vessels without masts 'moored near a dock-yard, or arsenal, so that the labour of the convicts may be applied to public service'. John Wade, writing in 1829, refers to ten vessels stationed at Deptford, Woolwich, Chatham, Sheerness and Portsmouth holding three to four thousand convicts between 1826 and 1827. Most of those on board had been sentenced to short terms; those given fourteen years or life were usually sent on to New South Wales (*A Treatise on the Police and Crimes of the Metropolis*, 1829, 365, cited in Tobias, 1972, 141). (Plates 7, 8) See also below.

"That's the way with this boy!"

right 'cross th' meshes."] The preposition suggests proximity, making the prison-ships much closer to Pip's village than the distant Upnor reach of the Medway, where three hulks were moored during the 1820s when Dickens lived at Chatham (see Appendix 4, map p. 449). This imaginary location is also reinforced by the careful description of the journey along the Thames taken by the soldiers and their two captives in chapter 5. A hulk moored at Egypt Bay on the Thames, less than three miles across the marshes from Cooling, remains compatible with topographical details suggested in the text. This vessel, however, served as a coastguard station and did not house convicts (Gadd, 1926, 182). Evidence for the more distant (and conflicting) location at Upnor on the Medway is given in chapter 28, note on p. 250. See also below.

It was too much for Mrs. Joe

People are put in the Hulks because they murder, and because they rob, and forge, and do all sorts of bad;] The hulks existed, in the language of the Penitentiary Act of 1779, for 'the more severe and effectual punishment of atrocious and daring offenders'. Individuals convicted of 'Grand Larceny, or any other Crime, except Petty Larceny', were kept aboard and employed 'in Hard Labour in the raising of Sand, Soil, and Gravel from, and cleansing the River Thames, or any other River Navigable for Ships of Burthen' (19 Geo. III, c. 74). Even prisoners accepted the common view of themselves as hardened, incorrigible offenders. Commenting on the months he had spent aboard the hulk *York* in Portsmouth harbour, John Ward described his companions as 'the sweepings of the whole country' crammed into close proximity ('Diary', 1841, 49).

Those confined on board fell into two main categories: offenders sentenced to periods of hard labour, and, following the foundation in 1787 of a penal colony at Botany Bay in New South Wales, those for whom a period of hard labour preceded transportation to Australia (see chapter 40, note on pp. 319–20). All who were sentenced to the hulks, it was thought, were individuals who would never 'become useful Members of Society'. Indeed, observers feared, 'whenever [prisoners] shall be again discharged on the Public, they will come more expert in Fraud, and more hardened in guilt'. Appearing before the Select Committee on Finance which issued these conclusions in 1798, Patrick Colquhoun, an experienced magistrate and observer of prison life, was reported as saying:

> That he had seldom or ever known an Instance of an Individual discharged from the Hulks, who had ever returned to honest Industry; but that the indiscriminate Mixture of Criminals, which takes place in those Establishments, renders them a complete Seminary of Vice and Wickedness. (BPP, *Crime and Punishment, Transportation* 1, '28th Report . . . 26 June 1798', 17–18)

The statutory background that created this situation originated in 1717 when Britain began the practice of emptying its gaols by sending convicted felons to work in one of the thirteen American colonies as indentured servants. Routine sentences increased substantially after the Piracy Act of 1717–18 (4 Geo. I, c. 11) and its sequel in 1719–20 (6 Geo. I, c. 23). Both Acts allowed courts discretionary power to order felons to be transported to the American plantations for seven or fourteen years (Colquhoun, 1806, 436–7). Some 40,000 men, women and children were shipped abroad at the average rate of over 600 a year until 1776. That year 'the disturbances which had broken out in America . . . interrupted the transportation of Convicts to His Majesty's Colonies and Plantations in that quarter', and compelled the government to find another way to handle the surfeit of criminals the Hanoverian legal system created. This pressure brought the hulks system into existence.

Prominent figures like John Howard, Jeremy Bentham and Sir William Blackstone questioned so expedient a solution. Accommodation aboard was cramped and provided no separation of prisoners. Young and old were thrown together and often mixed with 'brutal companions'. Their assigned tasks, whether on the river or in the dockyards, were of the worst kind. No pretence was made of 'reformatory discipline', and these dank, evil-smelling and rotting structures quickly earned notoriety among reformers and prisoners alike. Yet their cheapness and convenience encouraged the government to postpone building new prisons and allowed hulks to continue as a part of England's incarceratory machinery until their use to house felons awaiting transportation to Australia decreased substantially. As late as 1843, the hulks housed 70 per cent of the felons imprisoned in England and Wales; by 1847 the number had dropped to 30 per cent (Harding *et al.*, 1985, 156).

In 1838 the Molesworth Committee recommended the abolition of the system of transportation, in agreement with many Australian colonists who also began to object. Further opposition on the grounds of cost, the opening of Pentonville Prison in 1843, and reports criticizing the disease, immorality and lax discipline prevalent in many hulks finally forced them out of service in 1857 (20 & 21 Vict., c. 3). Under the Penal Servitude Act of 1857, however, the Home Office retained the power to order the transportation of convicts; the system was finally abolished in 1867. For 'A Narrative of Daily Proceeding on Board a Convict Ship in Portsmouth Harbour', see John Henry Clapper's testimony before a Parliamentary Select Committee in 1828 (BPP, *Crime and Punishment, Police*, 4).

I was never allowed a candle

a candle to light me to bed,]   Candles were an important source of artificial light in households for much of the nineteenth century.

I felt fearfully sensible of the great convenience that the Hulks were handy for me. I was clearly on my way there.]   This was a plausible sentiment consistent with judicial practices which made few allowances for children. Youthful and adult offenders were given identical sentences, and young and old were often mixed when confined. 'In such a motley assemblage of crimes, ages and characters, I ask if any rational being can expect but that the bad should become worse, and youth and comparative innocence ripen into the finished and hardened offender?' (Bennett, 1819, 33). No significant change in English legislation occurred until the state recognized Reformatory and Industrial Schools in 1854 and 1857 as alternatives to prison for juveniles (17 & 18 Vict., c. 86; 20 & 21 Vict., c. 48).

In 1824 a separate hulk was 'exclusively appropriated for boys under 16 years of age'. Aboard *Euryalus*, which was moored on the Medway across from Chatham dockyard, boys learned to read and write, and were taught a trade in conditions regulated by strict naval discipline. Their day began at 5.30 a.m. and followed a regimen of work, exercise, meals and school – 'reading, writing, catechism and hymns' – succeeded by more chores, supper, prayers, and bed at eight o'clock. No games were allowed; birching and confinement to one 'solitary dark cell' were administered to 'any one very incorrigible'. According to testimony given to a Select Committee in 1831, the youngest boy was 9 years old. Two-thirds of those confined, the witness added, 'are either natural children, or discarded so completely that there is no place to send them to' (BPP, *Crime and Punishment. Transportation* 1, 'Report . . . on Secondary Punishments', 27 September 1831, 51–2).

Since that time, which is far enough away now

Since that time, which is far enough away now,]   This and similar adverbial phrases of time make it clear that Pip writes his memoirs many years after the events he records (see chs 25, 32, 39). Taken together , the phrases impart an elegiac note.

I have often thought that few people know what secrecy there is in the young, under terror. No matter how unreasonable the terror, so that it be terror. I was in mortal terror. . . . I am afraid to think of what I might have done, on requirement, in the secrecy of my terror.]   Popular religious books like Richard Allestree's *The Whole Duty of Man* (1658) and Henry Venn's *The Complete Duty of Man* (1763) promoted a belief, common among Evangelicals, in the fundamental depravity of children. Supernatural tales and horror-stories told to young children often added to their imaginary fears. Dickens recounts in 'Nurse's Stories' on 8 September 1860 how, as a child in Chatham at night, his nurse forced him before he was six years old to go back to 'without at all wanting to go' to 'the dark corners' of his mind by introducing to him, in story form, a series of 'diabolical' characters. The name of this 'female bard' was Mercy, but she had none on her vulnerable charge. She took 'a fiendish enjoyment [in] my terrors', Dickens recalls, as she told 'hundreds of times' the story of a cannibalistic Captain Murderer with an insatiable appetite for his 'tender brides' whom he chopped up and ate cooked in a huge pie. Other tales included one about a supernatural cat fond of sucking the breath of infants at night, and one about a shipwright named Chips who sold his soul to the devil for 'a bushel of tenpenny nails . . . half a ton of copper . . . and a rat that could speak' (AYR 3.517–19).

The reflections about secrecy resemble Dickens's own capacity for silence. In the Autobiographical Fragment which Dickens began in the 1840s, he recounts how he never, until imparting it 'to this paper, in any burst of confidence with anyone, my own wife not excepted', spoke of the intense humiliation and shame he experienced as a boy when he was sent to work in Warren's blacking factory in 1824. See also chapter 16, note on p. 148.

If I slept at all that night

a speaking-trumpet,] A trumpet-like device (chiefly used at sea) designed to carry one's voice over a distance or amplify it so that the speaker could be heard above loud noise. A similar apparatus, in the form of a straight or convoluted conoidal tube, was used by those with a hearing loss to enable them to hear more distinctly (OED).

There was no doing it in the night, for there was no getting a light by easy friction then; to have got one, I must have struck it out of flint and steel,] Matches ignited by friction were invented in 1827 by John Walker and then imitated by Samuel Jones and sold as 'Lucifers' from 1829 onwards (Thorpe and Whiteley 7.529). Prior to that date, people relied on tinder-boxes, which contained a dry inflammable substance ignited by a spark struck from a flint and steel (see chapter 53). By the mid-century, German-made 'lucifer-matches' dominated the trade on account of their reliability and cheapness:

> In the article of lucifer-matches, the Germans beat the London makers hollow, and no end of them are imported into this country, where they meet a ready sale: we have just lighted candles with one from a German box, containing 1000 matches, each perfectly cylindrical in shape, and lighting without noise; said box being sold retail for a penny. (C. M. Smith, 1857, 307)

As soon as the great black velvet pall

the pantry,] Here, a small apartment where a variety of cooked and uncooked foods were stored. In larger houses with rooms designated specifically for pastry, bread, game and fish, the pantry was reserved primarily for 'cold meats and what accords therewith' and not for uncooked meat or game. While practice differed between small and large establishments, the primary considerations for a pantry were common to each: cool temperatures, dryness and fresh ventilation (Kerr 47).

a hare hanging up by the heels,] Culinary practice called for hanging hares for several days, even before disembowelling them. 'A hare is nothing if not well hung and well cooked; a hare must be hung very long indeed to be hung too long'. Paunching (removing the stomach) was recommended only when the weather was hot and muggy; and 'in no case is it advisable to paunch it when first killed' (Bishop 146).

some brandy from a stone bottle] Brandy, a spirit distilled from wine or from the husks of grapes, was imported mainly from France in stone bottles not exceeding one quart and in casks of forty gallons. Stone bottles made from baked clay were brittle but cheaper than glass bottles. Small wooden casks in household sizes ranging from one to three gallons were also common, but their popularity declined during the course of the nineteenth century.

that intoxicating fluid, Spanish-liquorice-water,] Liquorice water is made by mixing water with black strips of liquorice, a saccharine product obtained from juice extracted from the roots of liquorice plants, boiled down and set in moulds. Spanish liquorice, so called because supplies came from Spain before the introduction of the plant into England in 1562, had several uses. Children drank liquorice water in hot summer weather (Simmonds, 1858), brewers employed it for flavouring and colouring stout and porter, and druggists as an emollient to treat colds and fevers. The drink has no alcoholic content.

There was a door in the kitchen

There was a door in the kitchen, communicating with the forge;] This detail also corresponds closely with the forge at Chalk, whose interior Dickens appears to have known, according to local legend. Other points of resemblance include the little garden, mentioned twice by Pip (chapter 19), on the side of the lane, and an old open fireplace in the kitchen complete with seats in the chimney corner.

Chapter 3   Second weekly number
8 December 1860

It was a rimy morning

It was a rimy morning,] The action follows consecutively, making this Christmas Day.

the wooden finger on the post] Guide-posts often terminated in the shape of a finger.

The mist was heavier yet when I got out upon the marshes

something of a clerical air] The comparison is with the white cravat and black cassock worn by Anglican clergymen.

All this time

when I was 'prentice to him regularly bound,] That is, bound by a legal agreement to serve Joe in return for instruction as opposed to learning the trade informally as an 'odd-boy about the forge' (chapter 7). See also chapters 7, 12 and 13, notes on pages 73, 124 and 131. Changing economic and manufacturing conditions associated with industrialization took a toll on the apprenticeship system. The new, freer economic climate of the 1780s encouraged employers to look for bright lads who were anxious to get on, as both masters and men challenged arrangements that stipulated the period of service required for training and set wages and rates of pay. 'I believe that *Free Trade in Ability* has a much closer relation to national prosperity than even Free Trade in Commodities,' wrote James Nasmyth (1809–90), the inventor of the steam-hammer. Like other enterprising and able men of the period, Nasmyth hated the apprenticeship system because it interfered with promotions based on merit. The arrangement 'which we greatly preferred was to employ intelligent, well-conducted young lads, the sons of labourers or mechanics, and advance them by degrees according to their merits' (Nasmyth, 1883, 218, 227).

And yet this man was dressed in coarse grey, too

a flat broad-brimmed low-crowned felt hat] See chapter 10, note on p. 111.

"I think you have got the ague," said I.

the ague,"] Violent shivers and quaking were the most striking external characteristics of ague, or 'intermittent fever'. Other symptoms include languor, discomfort, hot and dry skin, a severe headache, thirst, and profuse sweating caused by the fever. Physicians recommended wrapping patients in warm blankets and administering frequent warm drinks.

"It's bad about here," I told him.

"It's bad about here . . . "You've been lying out on the meshes, and they're dreadful aguish. Rheumatic, too."] Marshes and low-lying districts were notorious for ague and malaria. Raw air and bitter sleet, brought on by the 'east wind' in December, together with fatigue and a poor diet, would have increased the convict's susceptibility to 'the ague' (Keith Imray, 1842, 10).

Victorian physicians, ignorant of the anopheles mosquito, the means by which malarial fever was spread, incorrectly ascribed the disease to 'the exhalations from decaying vegetable matter'. Infections seem 'to arise from the effluvia proceeding from stagnant water or marshy ground, impregnated with vegetable matter, in a state of putrefactive decomposition' (Henry H. Gregory, 1837, 65). Physicians also linked rheumatic pains, inflammation and catarrhal afflictions with this part of Kent, reputed among historians to be as 'unhealthy as it is unpleasant' on account of 'the unwholesome air from the neighbouring marshes' (Hasted, 1797, 1.557). Public health on the peninsula did not improve significantly until early in the twentieth century, the result of better sanitation and the systematic drainage of surface water (Smetham 1.2–4).

"Nor giv' no one the office

giv' . . . the office] A slang expression meaning to give a private notice or signal to another person.

"Well," said he, "I believe you.

hunted as near death and dunghill] The slang phrase evidently means to be hunted to the point of capitulation or surrender. To 'die dunghill' meant to die without spirit or a fight and was used of those who repented at the gallows (Partridge; *OED*).

Something clicked in his throat

Something clicked in his throat, as if he had works in him like a clock,] This is the first of four occasions when Magwitch makes this sound (see also chs 5, 39 and 54). Dickens connects these non-verbal utterances with the convict's flow of tears, making both the 'clicks' and the tears instances of a spontaneous overflow of feeling. Despite the perverse social conditioning Magwitch had endured as a young boy (see chapter 42), he retains an innate sense of feeling and generosity. See also chapter 19, note on pp. 171–2.

I had often watched a large dog of ours eating his food

a large dog of ours]   The animal never appears, although later Joe admits to keeping a dog (chapter 18).

"Why, see now!" said he.

soldiers, with their red coats lighted up by the torches]   Red coats were first adopted by British soldiers in 1645 when Parliament raised an army for permanent service. Field uniforms allowed for some variation to distinguish among regiments, but red coats of varying lengths and grey or blue trousers remained standard until the introduction of khaki field uniforms among British soldiers in India in the mid-nineteenth century. The torches evidently consisted of twisted hemp or rope soaked with pitch or some other inflammable substance.

his number called,]   Identifying convicts by number rather than by name began late in the eighteenth century. The practice belonged to an attempt to standardize prison discipline, isolate prisoners and prevent communication among inmates.

coming up in order,]   That is, approaching 'in a pretty wide line, with an interval between man and man', as they later close in on the two convicts struggling at the bottom of a ditch (chapter 5).

Chapter 4

I fully expected to find a Constable

a Constable] A local officer employed by a town or parish to keep the peace; constables had no professional training and were notoriously incompetent. The office was abolished in 1872, when a mandatory county police system was established (35 & 36 Vict., c. 92), superseding an earlier statute in 1839 (2 & 3 Vict., c. 93) permitting but not compelling counties to introduce constables on the model of the Metropolitan Police. The Metropolitan Police Act of 1829 (10 Geo. IV, c. 44) introduced the first professional police force in Britain.

I said I had been down to hear the Carols.

the Carols.] Carols originated as folk-songs of a joyful nature on a religious theme. They almost disappeared under the Puritans but were revived in the nineteenth century and introduced into divine services, confined mainly to Christmas time.

Joe, who had ventured into the kitchen

Joe and I would often . . . be, as to our fingers, like monumental Crusaders as to their legs.] The comparison of crossed fingers to the crossed legs of medieval knights draws on a popular and erroneous belief. Many thought that the position of the legs on stone monuments indicated knights who had taken part in the Crusades of the eleventh and twelfth centuries. Guidebooks and other commentaries kept alive the notion that 'sepulchral effigies' with their hands 'folded piously over their breasts, and legs crossed' signified those who had made a pilgrimage 'to the Holy City' (*Summer Excursions in the County of Kent* 14). In fact, the convention served practical and aesthetic purposes. Crossed knees provided support for the legs when effigies were carved in the round; the recumbent posture also created a greater sense of ease than the stiff formalism of the earlier, upright figures (Brieger 102–5; Laurence Stone 115).

We were to have a superb dinner

a leg of pickled pork . . . and a pair of roast stuffed fowls.] Pork was pickled or cured by being rubbed with salt and stored, weighted down, in a mixture of salt, brown sugar, saltpetre and salt prunel. Covered with a coarse cloth to exclude the air, pickled meat could be kept for nearly two years. Prior to cooking, the meat was scraped, rinsed and soaked in fresh water for two hours, brought to the boil and simmered until the meat was tender. Pickled pork was often served with poultry or roast veal (Bishop 116; Beeton 655, 658). Fowl, dressed and trussed, was commonly sprinkled with flour, stuffed with various ingredients, herbs and seasonings, and roasted 'according to size'.

Breakfast;] Bread, butter, toast, muffins or meat and tea or coffee were standard items for breakfast.

So, we had our slices served out

a forced march] A march in which 'the marching power of the troops is forced or exerted beyond the ordinary limit' (*OED*). Troops under these orders received little to eat or drink.

a new flowered-flounce across the wide chimney] Laying a long strip of material across the flat surface of the mantel used to be a common way 'to hide an ugly fireplace or to give an air of comfort to a bare or cold-looking room'. The flounce was cut so that the material hung down about a foot or so at either end and in front across the mantel (Humphry, 1914, 1.224, 89). Shopkeepers stocked flounces in worsteds of various colours and 'ever varying patterns'. Articles like this were sold 'to meet the taste or the evanescent whims of female minds' (*Complete Book of Trades* 251).

parlour] 'Parlour' originally designated a room for conversation. Later, with the introduction of 'drawing room' for the reception of visitors, 'parlour' applied instead to a room for the family. Pip's usage is correct. In a modest house like the forge, the kitchen was the main family room, leaving the parlour as the one room in which to receive guests and entertain.

silver paper,] Fine white tissue-paper.

Cleanliness is next to Godliness,] Compare ' "Cleanliness is indeed next to godliness" ' (John Wesley, 'On Dress', Sermon 88, 1786). Bartlett (309) credits Wesley with the adage, explaining that he derived it from 'the Hebrew fathers', but in fact the expression had passed into proverbial form before Wesley (Outler 3.249). Victorian commentators spared no efforts to preach this message:

> Cleanliness, whether household or personal, may be considered as one of the unalloyed advantages derived from civilization. If it may not be ranked as a virtue, it is at least the parent of virtue, and not unadvisedly was the old saying first pronounced, "Cleanliness is next to Godliness". (Webster, 1844, 342)

My sister having so much to do

In his working clothes,] Blacksmiths wore a leather apron with a substantial bib to protect themselves from sparks as they hammered red-hot metal. Generally they worked with their sleeves rolled up. Trousers replaced breeches by the 1840s; a small, round cap was also common (Cunnington and Lucas 101).

everything that he wore then, grazed him.]   A reference to the stiff and pointed shirt- and coat-collars common during the period. See chapter 27, note on p. 242.

an Accoucheur-Policeman]   The description of Pip as an offender from birth possibly derives from steps taken by midwives known as 'guarding the bed'. Accoucheurs were male midwives, men with no formal training but experienced in assisting women at childbirth. Until the 1850s, the term *accoucheur* was applied to both women and men midwives, after which *accoucheuse* became increasingly popular. In preparation for a home birth, the mattress was covered with a large skin of red leather which was sold specifically for the purpose and came complete with tapes attached to each corner for fastening to the bedposts. Dirty, folded blankets and sheets were then placed on top of the leather. 'The above plan', medical authorities asserted, 'will effectually protect the bed from injury' (Chavasse, 1843, 56).

like a kind of Reformatory,]   The year 1837 had the first recorded use of 'reformatory' to mean an institution which took in juvenile offenders in an attempt to correct or change their behaviour (*OED*).

Joe and I going to church

I conceived the idea that the time when the banns were read and when the clergyman said, "Ye are now to declare it!" would be the time for me to rise and propose a private conference in the vestry. . . . I am far from being sure that I might not have astonished our small congregation by resorting to this extreme measure, but for its being Christmas Day and no Sunday.]   The *Book of Common Prayer* requires that the banns of 'all that are to be married together must be published in the church three several Sundays at the times when the greatest number of people may hear them'. Three times the curate must make the announcement and three times must ask his congregation 'If any of you know cause or just impediment, why these two persons should not be joined together in Holy Matrimony, ye are to declare it' ('Solemnization of Matrimony'). Under the provisions of the Marriage Act of 1823 (4 Geo. IV, c. 67) banns had to be published in an audible manner on three Sundays preceding the marriage. Since, as Pip states, Christmas Day on this occasion did not fall on a Sunday, he was spared an audience in the church vestry, a room in which clergy and choir robe for divine service.

Mr. Wopsle . . . was to dine with us; and Mr. Hubble . . . and Uncle Pumblechook

Mr. Wopsle . . . was to dine with us; and Mr. Hubble . . . and Uncle Pumblechook]   All three names appear in Dickens's *Book of Memoranda*. He considered but did not use 'Wopsell' as a variant spelling (14). Possibly wordplay determined Mr Hubble's occupation.

the clerk at church,]   A church official, usually a layman of some education, who, in the Anglican church, assists the priest. The clerk's duties include: making the responses of the congregation in the services, reading the epistle, and helping with the general care and maintenance of the church. The only payment parish clerks receive comes from the standard fees for marriages and burials.

the wheelwright]   Bad roads, the popularity of 'the pack-saddle mode of carriage', and the use of solid wooden wheels for waggons and carts into the seventeenth century account for the relative scarcity of wheelwrights and their late incorporation in 1670. From this date, the number of wheelwrights rose steadily. Improved roads, and the increase of private and public carriages, led to a growing demand for their services.

The construction of carriage wheels required skill. Equidistant spokes had to be let into four wooden felloes, which formed the outer rim or wheel. A hot iron tyre was then placed on the wood. As the iron contracted upon cooling, it caused 'the pieces which form the felloe to draw closer together, end to end' (*Complete Book of Trades* 476–7). Large coach-builders employed their own wheel makers; a rural wheelwright operated on a smaller scale, supplying and repairing wheels and also constructing carts. Growing reliance on railways in the 1840s led to the decline of wheelwrights later in the century.

corn-chandler in the nearest town,]   The reputed original of Pumblechook's premises is that of a real corn-chandler's in Rochester, a market and cathedral town on the Medway four miles from the village of Chalk (Gadd, 1929, 56). The population of Rochester was listed in 1842 as 9,891; Chatham, the adjoining town, was larger with some 17,430 inhabitants (*Miniature Road-Book of Kent*, 1842). See also chapter 8, note on p. 86.

chaise-cart.]   A general term for a light carriage, with two or four wheels, widely used for pleasure or local travel, the exact application of which varied during the eighteenth and nineteenth centuries. Some versions were open; others had a removable folding hood. A chaise-cart could carry one or two people; most were drawn by a single horse, although some versions required two horses abreast. Owning a 'chaise' (derived from the French *chaise* and subsequently mispronounced 'shay-cart' by Joe in chapter 27 and by Pumblechook in chapter 58) conferred status on the owner. See 'The Tuggs of Ramsgate' (*SB*).

The dinner hour was half-past one.]   Dinner, the principal meal of the day, was generally eaten between two o'clock and three o'clock, although in the higher ranks of society the late hour of the meal and its copiousness rendered dinner 'nothing less than a hearty supper' (Keith Imray, 1842, 830).

5   Comport and Baker Gravestones, St James's Cooling

Row of three stones (west side of headstone):
   1. Ellen Elizabeth Baker, d. 11 Aug., 1854, aged 5 months.
   2. Sarah Anne Baker, d. 2 July, 1837, aged 3 months.
   3. John Rose Baker, d. 9 June, 1837, aged 1 month.

All were the children of John Rose Baker and his wife, née Sarah Anne Comport, daughter of Michael Comport, of Decoy House, High Halstow

Row of ten stones (east side of headstone):
   1. William Comport, d. 12 May, 1771, aged 8 months.
   2. William Comport, d. 7 June, 1773, aged 7 months.
   3. James Comport, d. 15 Oct., 1777, aged 4 months.
   4. Frances Comport, d. 7 June, 1775, aged 17 months.
   5. William Comport, d. 9 Mar., 1779, aged 8 months.
   6. Elizabeth Comport, d. 5 Oct., 1779, aged 3 months.

The above were the children of Michael and Jane Comport, of Cooling Court and Cooling Castle

   1. Sarah Elizabeth, d. July 1799, aged 3 months, daughter of George Comport
   2. Thomas, d. Nov. 1800, aged 3 months, son of Michael Comport of Decoy House
   3. Elizabeth, d. Aug. 1797, aged 1 year, daughter of Michael Comport of Decoy House
   4. Not identified; thought to be Mary, eldest daughter of Michael and Jane

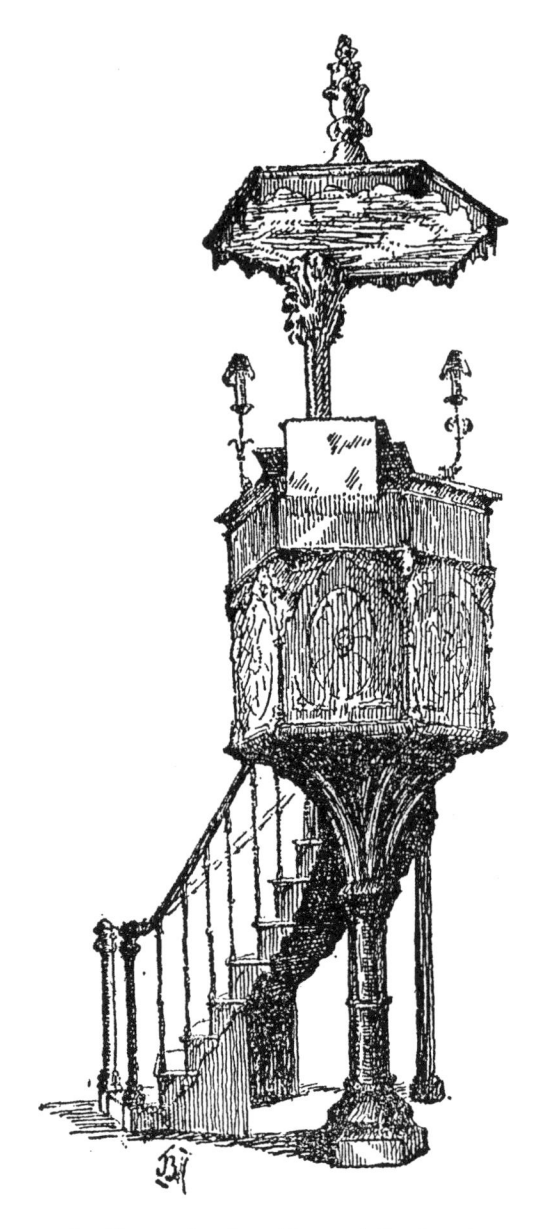

6   Elevated pulpit, Trottiscliffe church

The time came, without bringing with it any relief

a Roman nose] That is, a nose with a prominent upper part or bridge (*OED*). 'What style of nose? – What order of architecture', asks Mrs Nickleby, with reference to Frank Cheeryble as a possible son-in-law. 'I am not very learned in noses. Do you call it a Roman or a Grecian?' (*NN* 55).

if the Church was "thrown open," meaning to competition, he would not despair of making his mark in it. The Church not being "thrown open," he was . . . our clerk.] The use of competitions or examinations to determine a candidate's qualifications for holding office was a new concept in a society where connection and patronage determined most appointments. Competitive examinations were introduced in 1856 when entrance to the Indian Civil Service was first decided on the basis of ability. The phrase, 'to throw open', meaning to make something accessible to the public, came into general use in the 1840s. Entrance into the Church of England, however, remained tightly controlled. To join the ministry, one had to be a baptized and confirmed male. Candidates also had to be of good moral character, convinced they had a divine call ('vocation') to the office, willing to subscribe to the Thirty-Nine Articles and to the *Book of Common Prayer*, and ready to swear an oath of allegiance to the sovereign and an oath of canonical obedience to the bishop.

he punished the Amens tremendously;] Pugilistic slang: 'to punish' meant to inflict severe blows on one's opponent.

our friend overhead] The minister might be 'overhead' as he delivers his sermon from a wooden or stone pulpit, many of which stand several feet above the floor to allow the preacher's voice to carry and make him visible to the congregation. Alternatively, this might be a literal reference to a three-storeyed pulpit – a tower-like arrangement including a desk for the parish clerk, the reading-desk, and the pulpit proper, each storey arranged above the other. 'Three-deckers', as they were nicknamed, were common in many churches built or rebuilt between about 1700 and 1830 (Cox, 1915, 94–6).

Although there are no three-decker pulpits in the churches on the Hoo peninsula, Trottiscliffe parish church, about nine miles west of Rochester, has an elevated wooden pulpit which was installed about 1824. Complete with a canopy, it stands almost six feet from the ground, with a curving staircase providing access to the minister's platform (Plate 6; Smetham 1.129).

"Mrs. Joe," said Uncle Pumblechook

a bottle of sherry wine . . . a bottle of port wine."] Sherry and port, fortified wines imported from Spain, were popular in Britain, especially for entertaining. They were appropriate for use in small quantities and retained their freshness: 'Even in humble houses, there was a decanter of sherry with a few biscuits waiting for whosoever might call' (Jeffs 77). English sherry-drinkers favoured wines with a rich, nutty flavour;

according to Spanish producers, 'The English palate' did not like pale sherries preferred in Spain. Sherries for English consumption were 'doctored' by the addition of boiled wine, a 'rich, treacly-looking liquid' which sweetened and gave body to the naturally pale wine (G. W. Thornbury, *HW* 18.510).

Every Christmas Day he presented himself

And now are you all bobbish, and how's Sixpennorth of halfpence?"] 'Bobbish', a slang or dialectical expression meaning well or in good spirits. In this instance, Pumblechook puns on the expression since 'bob' also refers to the shilling, which, prior to the decimalization of the currency in 1971, was a silver coin representing one twentieth of a pound. The shilling, in turn, was worth twelve copper pennies, making the penny, for many people, the central coin of their currency, as in expressions like 'penn'orth' (i.e. a penny worth) of something: 'I'll take a penn'orth of tobacco'; and also as in 'it's a good penn'orth, sir', meaning it's good value for your penny. The penny was also accompanied by the halfpenny (pronounced *hape-nee* and sometimes written 'ha'penny', and the farthing, worth a quarter of a penny (Lewis). Literally, six penny worth of halfpennies would amount only to threepence (usually pronounced and sometimes spelt 'thruppence'). See also chapter 9, note on p. 105.

Among this good company

I was regaled with the scaly tips of the drumsticks of the fowls,] The breast, wings and portion of the bird when carved that contains the wish-bone were among the more highly esteemed parts of a fowl. Thighs could be served to gentlemen, but 'the drumsticks should be put aside, and used afterwards in some way that necessitated the flesh being minced' (Beeton 1270).

an unfortunate little bull in a Spanish arena . . . touched up by these moral goads.] The analogy is to the beechwood sticks, each about two feet long and decorated with coloured paper and fitted with one-inch steel barbs, placed in the hide of the bull to the rear of the upper loin by the banderillos following the capework of the matador. Their ostensible purpose serves to aggravate rather than wound the bull in preparation for the final stage of a classic Spanish contest during which the animal is mastered then ceremoniously killed with the sword (Arlott).

It began the moment we sat down to dinner.

a religious cross of the Ghost in Hamlet with Richard the Third] The ghost of Hamlet's dead father appears urging Hamlet to revenge his father's 'foul and most unnatural murder' (*Hamlet* 1.5.25); on the night before the battle at Bosworth, the ghosts of those whom Richard III has killed appear before him and foretell his defeat (*Richard III* 5.3).

Mrs. Hubble shook her head

"Naterally wicious."]   Evangelicals frequently represented children in terms that suggested an innate depravity in the young. Dickens habitually attacks adults who believe in this 'gloomy theology': the Murdstones (*DC*), Miss Barbary (*BH*) and Mrs Clennam (*LD*). As David Copperfield notes, it was a child who was 'once set in the midst of the Disciples' to show them the way, not a fierce or vengeful adult dedicated to reforming children by firmness (*DC* 4).

Joe's station and influence were something feebler

Joe's station . . . pint.]   This paragraph conveying Joe's affectionate support for Pip appears as an addition written on the verso MS page and marked for insertion.

"True again," said Uncle Pumblechook.

to put salt upon their tails.]   The expression signifies an attempt to catch an animal or person by foolish methods: 'It is . . . a foolish bird that staieth the laying salt on hir taile' (Lyly, *Euphues*, 1580).

A little later on in the dinner

Mr. Wopsle . . . remarked that he considered the subject of the day's homily ill-chosen . . . when there were so many subjects 'going about'.]   The criticism appears to fault the minister for his strict adherence to religious topics and evident indifference to issues of the day.

"Swine," pursued Mr. Wopsle

"Swine were the companions of the prodigal. The gluttony of Swine is put before us, as an example to the young."]   In this parable from Luke, the prodigal son, after wasting 'his substance with riotous living', is reduced to looking after pigs and envying 'the husks that the swine did eat' (15.11–32).

In the popular mind, pigs embodied gluttony and laziness – attributes that moralists claimed as one of the 'lessons' of 'Natural History'. One influential pedagogue, whose *English Spelling-Book* went through multiple editions, wrote:

> A hog is a disgusting animal; he is filthy, greedy, stubborn, and dis-a-gree-able, whilst alive, but very useful after his death. Hogs are vo-ra-ci-ous; yet where they find plentyful and de-lic-ious food, they are very nice in their choice, will refuse unsound fruit, and want the fare of the fresh; but hunger will force them to eat rotten putrid substances. (Mavor, 1819, 83)

To combat gluttony, medical authorities advocated the need to inculcate restraint, especially among the young. 'Children may be hurt by too little as well as too much food. . . . Children thrive best with small quantities of food frequently given. This neither overloads the stomach, nor hurts the digestion, and is certainly most agreeable to nature' (Buchan 21).

"Besides," said Mr. Pumblechook

a Squeaker"]   A colloquial term for a young pig.

"But I don't mean in that form, sir," returned Mr. Pumblechook

shillings]   Formerly, a shilling was a silver coin, one twentieth of a pound and equal to twelve copper pennies. Other silver coins were a crown (five shillings), a half-crown (two shillings and six pence) and a sixpenny piece. For copper coins, see chapter 9, note on p. 105.

Dunstable the butcher would have come up to you as you lay in your straw . . . and had your life.]   Butchers in country and in market-towns typically purchased their animals from local farmers and killed them where they had been raised. Afterwards they took the carcass to town, dressed the meat and displayed it for sale in shops (*Complete Book of Trades* 82). For pig-killing, see chapter 2, note on p. 42.

"Trouble?" echoed my sister; "trouble?"

a fearful catalogue of all the illnesses I had been guilty of,]   '[Trifling] ailments of infants' might include any of the following: chafings, costiveness, flatulence, hiccups, looseness of the bowels, red gum, 'snuffles', sickness and thrush. More serious and life-threatening were water on the brain, croup, mumps, measles, sore throats, colds and smallpox (Chavasse, 1839, 55).

I think the Romans must have aggravated

restless people]   Restless perhaps on account of the Roman empire. Its boundaries, under Augustus, extended over the whole Mediterranean region and north as far as Scotland.

I had filled up the bottle from the tar-water jug.

I had filled up the bottle from the tar-water jug.]   Pip's unintentional mixing of brandy and tar-water may owe something to the practical joke Smollett's Peregrine

Pickle plays on Mrs Trunion, his aunt, when he deliberately infuses 'a good quantity of powdered jalap', a purgative, into one of her bottles of brandy *Peregrine Pickle*, 1751 (14). For tar-water, see chapter 2, note on p. 43.

I moved the table, like a Medium of the present day, by the vigour of my unseen hold upon it.] Writing in November 1860, Sir William Hardman noted how the 'absurd delusion about spirits and their rapping powers' had gripped public attention and provided extensive copy for magazines and daily journals (Sir William Hardman 13–15). Dickens's likely target was Daniel Dunglas Home (1833–86), a renowned medium who claimed he could summon spirits, move objects, levitate, shrink or elongate his body, put his head into fire without injury and perform other dubious feats.

Dickens denounced spirit-rappers of Home's variety: the 'conditions under which such inquiries take place', he wrote to Mrs Lynn Linton on 16 September 1860, 'are preposterously wanting in the common securities against deceit or mistake':

> Mr. Hume, or Home (I rather think he has gone by both names) I take the liberty of regarding as an impostor. If he appeared on his own behalf in any controversy with me, I should take the further liberty of letting him publicly know why. But be assured if he were demonstrated a Humbug in every microscopic cell of his skin and globule of his blood, the disciples would still believe and worship. (*Letters* 9.311)

For a campaign against the spiritualists in *HW*, see essays by Henry Morley (1852) and by Dickens (1853 and 1858) listed in the bibliography. Three phases of this 'struggle with the spiritualists' have been charted (Peyrouton, 1959). Topical satire against clairvoyants and mediums also featured widely in other periodicals and publications: see *Punch*, July, August and September 1860, and Browning's 'Mr Sludge, the Medium', in his *Dramatis Personae* (1864).

But, Uncle Pumblechook, who was omnipotent in that kitchen

the gin, the hot water, the sugar, and the lemon-peel,] These are the principal ingredients of a classic version of punch. The drink (derived from *Punjab*, Hindustani for 'five') usually included spice as the fifth ingredient, hence the name. It was introduced to England in the seventeenth century by naval officers engaged in the East India trade. Variations included the substitution of hot green tea or cold soda water and ice in the summer (Bishop 390).

But, I ran no further than the house door

muskets:] The term was applied generally to the firearm of the infantry soldier from about 1550 up to and even beyond the adoption of rifled small arms around 1850–60. Its firing mechanism, the 'fusil' or flintlock, displaced the matchlock around 1690 and remained supreme until the introduction of a practicable percussion lock about 1830–40.

Chapter 5 Third weekly number
15 December 1860

The apparition of a file of soldiers

a file of soldiers]   When prisoners escaped from the hulks, troops were called in because military authorities were responsible for maintaining order aboard the vessels and because no professional civilian police force existed in England before 1829.

ringing down the butt-ends of their loaded muskets on our door-step,]   In a swivel motion, the soldiers unshoulder their muskets; once inside, they pile their arms 'in a corner'. Executing these steps with machine-like precision represented one of the results of military training: at drill or on parade, soldiers were taught 'habits of regularity' essential to the maintenance of military discipline and conformity.

to rise from table]   For this usage, see chapter 11, note on p. 121.

"Excuse me, ladies and gentlemen," said the sergeant

in the name of the King,]   Locutions like this one, articles in the soldier's kit bearing the monarch's cipher, and the fact that all weapons and other equipment were normally stamped with the crown served as constant reminders of royal authority and helped underline a personal connection between the king and his troops (Myerly, 1996, 100–1). In this case the monarch would have been George III (1760–1820), the commander-in-chief of all British military and naval forces.

"Missis," returned the gallant sergeant

speaking for the King, I answer, a little job done."]   The sergeant's elegantly turned sentence masks the obligation implicit in his request. Formerly, monarchs had the right to billet troops on their subjects, a practice which was ended in 1679 (31 Ch. II, c. 1). Henceforth, billeting was only by consent, and every subject, '[o]f any degree, quality, or profession could refuse to sojourn or quarter any soldier, notwithstanding any command, order, warrant or billeting request' (Adolphus, 1818, 2.289–90). At the same time, the sergeant had the authority to enlist Joe's help regardless of the holiday.

Joe threw his eye over them

piled their arms]   'Piling arms' is a military term for stacking weapons.

to spit stiffly over their high stocks,]   Stocks, 'the most hated article of the soldier's necessaries', were collars made of thick leather, usually four inches high, which showed at the neck. They fastened at the back with ties, buckles or hooks-and-eyes and were worn over the shirt but under the coat. Military authorities adopted neck stocks early in the eighteenth century: they kept the wearer's head erect in the correct martial posture and were always worn with the uniform in peacetime. Referred to variously as 'Calcraft's cord' – the hangman's noose – and as 'an almost iron neck-band', stocks permanently scarred the necks of soldiers and even inflicted serious injuries. A more pliant variety was introduced after 1845 when the Duke of Wellington was ' "grudgingly" ' won over to it (Myerly, 1996, 26, 78). Stocks spread to civilians, who adopted a full-dress stock of black velvet with a satin bow named after George IV (Lister, 1972, 16). In *AN* (1842) and in the letters Dickens wrote home during his travels, he expressed disgust with the tolerance for public spitting in America.

"Would you give me the Time?" said the sergeant

"Would you give me the Time?" said the sergeant,] This question and the next about the distance of the forge from the marshes indicate how precisely Dickens worked out the sequence of events which occur on Christmas Day. Pip leaves the forge at first light shortly before seven o'clock, runs with the stolen file and food to the old Battery, about four miles away, and returns home around nine o'clock to find his sister busy preparing for the day's festivities. The dinner, served at 1.30 p.m., was well under way when the soldiers arrived nearly an hour later. After a two-hour wait, they leave the forge just after four o'clock, 'A little before dusk', in accordance with the sergeant's orders, and walk briskly to the church, just a mile away, before setting off for the marshes. Once out on 'the dismal wilderness', Pip reflects how some 'eight or nine hours' earlier he had seen both men hiding. This thought seems to occur about five o'clock, making the chronology consistent if we assume that Pip delivered the food about eight o'clock in the morning.

"Well!" said the sergeant

"they'll find themselves trapped in a circle,] The sergeant evidently plans to keep the convicts on the open marshes and seal off the roads and villages to the west, which would have offered better cover. Forced towards the shoreline, the fugitives would have little chance of escape. Even if they managed to cross the Thames, soldiers on the Essex shore had been alerted.

Joe had got his coat and waistcoat and cravat off

wooden windows,] Wooden shutters. The forge at Chalk was closed this way when work stopped for the day (Gadd, 1929, 9).

The interest of the impending pursuit

a pitcher of beer . . . for the soldiers, and invited the sergeant to take a glass of brandy.]   Mrs Joe readily accepts the army's clearly defined difference in rank by offering beer, probably brewed at home, to the privates and expensive brandy to the noncommissioned officer.

"With you. Hob and nob," returned the sergeant.

Hob and nob,"]   Used as a verb, 'Hob and nob' meant to drink together or to each other's health; as a noun, the expression meant simply a toast. Both sayings were common in south-east England and derived from the Saxon *hab and nab* ('to have and to have not').

We were joined by no stragglers from the village

the way dreary, the footing bad. . . . We passed the finger-post, and held straight on to the churchyard. There, we were stopped a few minutes . . . while two or three . . . men dispersed themselves among the graves, and also examined the porch. They came in again without finding anything, and then we struck out on the open marshes, through the gate at the side of the churchyard.]   See Appendix 2 and the map on p. 449 for a hypothetical reconstruction of their route based on local topography.

It was of no use asking myself this question now.

We were taking the course I had begun with, and from which I had diverged in the mist.]   Earlier that morning, Pip struck out 'too far to the right' (i.e. to the east) and had to trace his way back to the Battery by following the bank of the Thames (see chapter 3 and Appendix 4, map p. 449).

Under the low red glare of sunset, the beacon, and the gibbet, and the mound of the Battery, and the opposite shore of the river, were plain,]   See Appendix 2.

The soldiers were moving on

It was at a distance towards the east,]   That is, along the shore towards Cliffe Creek and Cliffe marshes.

Chapter Five

It was a run indeed now

"a Winder."] MS reads 'buster', slang for taking away one's breath (*OED*).

"Tried to murder him?" said my convict

I dragged him here – dragged him this far on his way back.] Magwitch returns in the direction of the river and the prison-ship quite deliberately. Freed of his leg iron earlier in the morning, he could have got off 'these death-cold flats' had he chosen not to pursue Compeyson and hunt him down.

"Lookee here!" said my convict to the sergeant.

If I had died at the bottom there . . . I'd have held to him with that grip, that you should have been safe to find him in my hold."] Dickens refers elsewhere to the supposed ability of drowned men to hold on to their victims (Cotsell 277).

The two were kept apart,

There was a reasonably good path now, mostly on the edge of the river, with a divergence here and there where a dyke came, with a miniature windmill on it and a muddy sluice-gate.] For a conjectural route based on local topography, see Appendix 2. Post mills, which date from the medieval period, were usually quite small and simply arranged, consisting of a wooden body (the buck), which carries the sails, the wind-shaft, the gears and the millstone. These mills were so-called because they were pivoted about the top of a king post, allowing them to be turned by hand into the wind. In this instance, the mill appears to be a variant of the post mill with a water-raising scoop-wheel instead of a millstone, an application developed by the Dutch to drain water-logged, low-lying land. Drainage schemes based on this method were introduced into England during the reign of James I (McNeil, 1990, 246–50). By the late seventeenth century, extensive tracts of marshes in Cambridgeshire, Lincolnshire, Norfolk, Somerset and Kent, including land bordering the Thames, had been reclaimed and put to use as pasture or arable land suitable for grains and fruit trees (Dugdale, 1772, vii–ix). Windmills of various shapes and sizes were also used for grinding corn and for supplying power for other purposes (Singer et al., 1958, 3.89).

After an hour or so of this travelling

After an hour or so of this travelling, we came to a rough wooden hut and a landing-place.] These details may have been suggested by the coastguard station at Egypt Bay (see Appendix 4, map p. 449). The distance from Cliffe Creek to Egypt

Bay is about five miles. In Dickens's time, the coastguard station consisted of a hut, a landing-place and a floating hulk. See also below.

whitewash,] Most likely the walls had been treated with a mixture of hot water and slaked lime. Limewash, similar to whitewash, was applied to the walls of outbuildings, stables, sculleries and pantries. The mixture was valued on account of its antiseptic qualities and often used in cottages after an infectious disease had broken out (Humphry, 1914, 1.73).

a low wooden bedstead, like an overgrown mangle without the machinery, capable of holding about a dozen soldiers all at once.] The bedstead resembles the heavy, cumbersome box mangle, an eighteenth-century version of a machine to press linen and intended primarily for use in large houses or in communal laundries, where there was a quantity of linen to be pressed. This mangle was a large wooden box, almost seven feet long and three feet each wide and deep, filled with stones, standing on the floor. Damp, clean linen was wrapped round wooden rollers which were then placed under the box by means of a lifting device and a crank handle was then turned to make the heavy box trundle back and forth over the rollers. A flywheel helped to overcome the inertia of starting the box in motion; a system of stops prevented the box running off its bed and on to the floor. By about 1850, a standing design, smaller and easier to use, began to replace the box mangle; evolving further it became, by the end of the century, a handier instrument with smaller, rubber rollers used expel water from clothes rather than press linen in what was almost a completely dry process in the case of the prototype (McNeil 932).

Accommodation for twelve may be an exaggeration, although severe overcrowding and squalid conditions characterized barrack life. Until 1827, soldiers slept four together in cribs. Barracks seldom provided sufficient air for healthy respiration, and soldiers often had to make do with 200 to 300 cubic feet of air per man when 600 cubic feet were considered the minimum essential in British prisons (Myerly, 1996, 4; Chandler, 1994, 171).

great-coats,] Soldiers wore large, heavy top-coats as part of their uniform.

"I know, but this is another pint

up at the willage over yonder – where the church stands a'most out on the marshes."] The reference appears to combine details based on the villages of Cooling and Lower Higham and St Mary's church in Higham.

The something that I had noticed before

we followed him to the landing-place made of rough stakes and stones,] See Appendix 2 and chapter 28, note on p. 250, for contradictory information about this embarkation point.

7 Prison Hulk at Woolwich

8 Coast guard hulk, Lower Hope

we saw the black Hulk . . . like a wicked Noah's ark.] The description reverses typical associations of the ark with delivery from corruption and an opportunity to start life again. The biblical ark was built to dimensions specified by God and designed to protect one pair of every species from the flood sent by God to purge the earth (Genesis 6.15). Other writers also compared the outline of hulks to Noah's ark. In 'A Sail down the Medway, from Maidstone to Rochester, and from Rochester to the Nore', in July 1811, John Evans described the '*vast ponderous Hulks*' he saw as '*Noah's Ark*[s] in form and size'. The resemblance was apt, he noted, since the ark was little larger than 'a first rate man of war' (Evans 467). Lacking masts and riding high in the water, the hulks assumed an even greater resemblance to their biblical prototype.

Cribbed and barred] Compare Macbeth's 'But now I am cabined, cribbed, confined . . .' (*Macbeth* 3.4.24) and Keats's 'barred clouds' ('To Autumn', l. 25).

Chapter 6 Fourth weekly number
22 December 1860

Chapter 6]   Chapters 6 and 7 appear as a single chapter in the MS (*Norton* 38).

I do not recall that I felt any tenderness

his beer was flat or thick,]   The uneven quality suggests beer brewed at home. Beer was a household drink kept on hand for Joe and his journeyman to have with their meals every day.

Tar]   That is, tar-water. See chapter 2, note on p. 43.

As I was sleepy before we were far away from the prison-ship

knocked up]   A slang term for exhausted or spent (Hotten). 'To knock up' also means to awaken someone.

Chapter 7

At the time when I stood in the churchyard

Neither, were my notions of the theological positions to which my Catechism bound me, at all accurate; for, I have a lively remembrance that I supposed my declaration that I was to "walk in the same all the days of my life," laid me under an obligation always to go through the village from our house in one particular direction, and never to vary it by turning down by the wheelwright's or up by the mill.]   *The Book of Common Prayer* contains a series of questions and answers 'to be learned of every person before he be brought to be confirmed by the Bishop' and 'bound' to a body of teaching. The principal points of doctrine include: an explanation of Baptism, the Apostles' Creed, the doctrine of the Trinity, an explanation of a man's duty to God and to his neighbour, of the Lord's Prayer and of the Ten Commandments. The catechumen also vows to 'keep God's holy will ... and walk in the same all the days' of his life ('A Catechism').

The joke about always approaching the house from one direction possibly reflects the topography of Lower Higham, whose features supply some of the details Dickens used in the composite picture of Pip's 'village'. Since the wheelwright's workshop was 'formerly in the by-lane [running] from Gore Green to the church road', one could easily 'go through the village' repeatedly without passing it. Lower Higham, however, had no mill. But an old one existed up the hill towards Higham Upshire which remained in use into the twentieth century (Gadd, 1929, 15–16).

The comment also owes something to an incident related about Dickens as a child. On one occasion, when his nurse reported how he persisted in always going the same way on walks around Chatham, he explained to his mother: ' "Why, mamma ... does not the Bible say we must walk in the same path all the days of our life?" ' (Davey, June 1874, 774).

When I was old enough, I was to be apprenticed to Joe

When I was old enough, I was to be apprenticed to Joe,]   The word 'apprentice' derives from 'the Latin *Apprehendere*, which signifies to *apprehend* or to *learn*, which is the Duty of the young Man entering into an Engagement to *learn* or *apprehend* the Art or Mystery to which he is bound Apprentice' (S. Richardson 2). Apprenticeships usually began around 14 (although some boys began as early as 7 or 8) and lasted for a term of years, usually seven, making these engagements a common route to adulthood for many youths in pre-industrial and early industrial Britain. In return, masters received a premium. Opposition to child labour, one consequence of early industrialization, led to legislation in the 1830s designed to protect young children and remove them from the workforce.

if any neighbour happened to want an extra boy to frighten birds, or pick up stones ... I was favoured with the employment.]   Bird-scaring was a common occupation for poor, rural children. The Assistant Commissioners noted in their 1858 Report on Education that the task frequently encroached on such instructional opportunities as existed in the country, especially in the autumn (*BPP, Education General* 3).

the National Debt,]   John Capper, writing in *HW* in 1854, noted that England's 'enormous National Debt' dated back 'no further than the reign of William the Third'. But the habit of getting the state into debt did not originate with that monarch. Citing Macaulay, Capper added: 'from a period of immemorial antiquity it had been the practice of every English government to contract debts. What the revolution [of 1688] introduced was the practice of honourably paying them' by bringing the administration of finances under parliamentary control. William III left the debt at 16 million sterling in 1702; on the accession of William IV in 1830 it had reached 'the enormous amount of upwards of eight hundred millions, the yearly charge on which for interest was double the amount of the original debt of the country' ('Bulls and Bears', *HW* 8.518–19). The wars against Revolutionary France and Napoleon were primarily responsible for this rise. A single year of hostilities against France added 'not less than ninety-three millions' to the funded debt of the country in 1814. At the beginning of 1900 this debt had been substantially reduced to £621 million by applying surplus revenue to the national debt (Charles Knight, 1851, 641; and *Encyclopaedia Britannica*, 11th edn).

Mr. Wopsle's great-aunt kept an evening school

Mr. Wopsle's great-aunt kept an evening school in the village; that is to say, she was a ridiculous old woman . . . who used to go to sleep from six to seven every evening, in the society of youth who paid twopence per week each,]   Rosenberg speculates that the change from Mr Wopsle's 'aunt', which Dickens had originally written, to 'great-aunt' represents an attempt to underline further her lack of qualifications (*Norton* 427). The term 'evening school' as it is initially described here fits the definition of schools first suggested by members of the government in 1839. These institutions were established to offer an hour's instruction to poor children between 12 and 16 who were already at work or in service (*BPP, Education General* 3, 39). Taken literally, such schools would constitute an anachronism since they clearly postdate the novel's historical setting.

An alternative suggestion is that Dickens bases his description of the school on an earlier variety known as dame schools. These institutions were invariably run by an elderly woman, hence the term. They provided limited education, either in 'dwelling rooms' or in the women's homes, for children of the poor. The schools flourished because the state was slow to implement a national system of education, content to leave schooling to religious and philanthropic groups. Growing state intervention beginning in 1833 and culminating with the Education Act of 1870 supplanted these small-scale local efforts to educate children. See also chapter 10, note on p. 108.

There was a fiction that Mr. Wopsle "examined" the scholars,] Oral examination was a traditional way to evaluate knowledge. Its application to the young encouraged rote learning and recitation. Wopsle's standing in the community as parish clerk makes him an appropriate amateur examiner.

Mark Antony's oration over the body of Caesar . . . always followed by Collins's Ode on the Passions, wherein I particularly venerated Mr. Wopsle as Revenge, throwing his blood-stain'd sword in thunder down, and taking the War denouncing trumpet with a withering look.] Pupils memorized these and other 'Pathetic Pieces' from books like Enfield's *Speaker* (1820), copies of which were used to teach elocution and rhetoric. Mark Antony's is the well-known speech beginning, 'Friends, Romans, countrymen, lend me your ears' (*Julius Caesar* 3.2.73–107); in William Collins's 'The Passions, An Ode for Music' (1747), 'Revenge' and eleven other 'Passions' speak, each exhibiting its 'own expressive Pow'r', before the poem ends with an invocation to Music. Dickens retains Collins's syntax and cites part of the stanza on Revenge almost verbatim:

> And longer had She [Hope] sung – but with a Frown,
> Revenge impatient rose,
> He threw his blood-stained Sword in Thunder down,
> And with a with'ring Look,
> The War-denouncing Trumpet took . . . (39–42)

Collins's stanza on Fear reads:

> First Fear his Hand, its Skill to try,
> Amid the Chords bewilder'd laid,
> And back recoil'd he knew not why,
> Ev'n at the Sound himself had made.

After 'look', MS reads 'Fear, whistling to keep his courage up'.

Representation of 'the passions' on the English stage had become one of the staples of 'many of our modern plays' by the mid-century. Gilbert A. à Beckett parodies this tendency in his 'The Stage Passions. An Ode for Melodramatic Music': 'Ranting, stamping, screaming, fainting', the passions appear. First Fear, followed by Anger, Despair, Hope, Revenge drawing 'his blood-stained sword', Jealousy, Melancholy, Cheerfulness and finally Joy (1846, 1–4). Collins's poem was commonly learned for recitation.

Mr. Wopsle's great-aunt

a little general shop.] General shops sold a wide range of manufactured or dry goods but no food.

Biddy] A common abbreviation for Bridget; also an abbreviated form of Chick-a-biddy, a chicken and, figuratively, a young wench (Grosse).

Much of my unassisted self, and more by the help of Biddy

I struggled through the alphabet as if it had been a bramble-bush; getting considerably worried and scratched by every letter.] Dickens remembered his own puzzlement as a child learning the alphabet with his mother, but without the strife described here. Possibly the description recalls memories Dickens associated with his battle to learn shorthand, recorded in *DC*. After David bought 'an approved scheme of the noble art and mystery of stenography', he plunged into 'a sea of perplexity' and groped blindly towards the 'arbitrary characters, the most despotic characters I have ever known' (*DC* 38).

I fell among those thieves] Compare the man who 'fell among thieves' in the parable of the good Samaritan (Luke 10.30–6).

One night, I was sitting in the chimney corner

my slate] Slate tablets, a cheap and popular writing medium, were used throughout the century in shops, businesses and schools. They had the advantage of an erasable surface and were preferable to quill pens, which required constant sharpening with a penknife.

I think it must have been a full year after our hunt upon the marshes, for it was a long time after, and it was winter and a hard frost.] The episode therefore occurs either towards the end of December or early in January. By this time Pip would have had either his seventh or his eighth birthday in the preceding November.

i opE . . . I opE . . . B haBeLL] The phonetic spelling signifies Pip's local (and therefore) lowly social origins. Dropping the 'h' and overcompensating by adding it incorrectly elsewhere remained a linguistic habit among poorly educated people throughout the century. See, for example, Joe's 'HOUT' inscribed in chalk on the forge door on the rare occasions when he was not at work (chapter 13). Pip later flaunts his correctness when he affects incomprehension at Joe's regionalized pronunciation of Miss Havisham's name in chapter 27. (Based on Mugglestone, *passim*.) The letter's close – 'IN F xN PiP' – transcribes phonetically 'in affection, Pip'.

"I say, Pip, old chap!" cried Joe

"what a scholar you are! . . . "I should like to be," said I,] Working-class children in fiction often expressed this aspiration, shared by Dickens himself when his schooling was cut short at the age of 12 and he was sent out to work. In later years Dickens wrote how he felt his 'early hopes of growing up to be a learned and distinguished man crushed in my breast' (Forster 1.1.22).

I had never heard Joe read aloud

I had never heard Joe read aloud to any greater extent than this monosyllable, and I had observed at church last Sunday when I accidentally held our Prayer-Book upside down, that it seemed to suit his convenience quite as well as if it had been all right.] The absence of statistical evidence makes difficult projections of literacy rates among craftsmen and others. What is known is that the ability to read was always in advance of the ability to write and that reading was generally taught before writing. Some historians estimate the literacy rate among the working class in the 1840s extended to about two-thirds of the population (West 38–41).

Prayer-Book] The official service book of the Church of England, *The Book of Common Prayer* includes the daily offices of Morning and Evening Prayer, the forms for administration of the Sacraments and other public and private rites, the Psalter and the Ordinal. It was compiled to simplify and condense the Latin services of the medieval church and issued as a comprehensive single volume in English in 1549. The nineteenth-century Anglican church used the authorized version of 1662.

I derived from this

I derived . . . that Joe's education, like Steam, was yet in its infancy.] Steam power originated in eighteenth-century France, but important practical applications occurred in Britain, first among engineers in the mining industry. The Scottish inventor James Watt (1736–1819) led the way in 1776 by using steam to drive a static pump to remove water from coalmines. Later developments included the application of steam power to the manufacture of cotton (1785) and to locomotives, and the work of George Stephenson (1781–1848), through whose efforts the Stockton and Darlington railway opened in 1824. Attempts to use steam to drive boats and ships occurred at the same time. See chapter 54, note on p. 385.

Steam's versatility as a source of power encouraged enthusiastic estimates of its potential. By the 1830s, Pip's image had achieved sufficient currency for Dickens to satirize it as a popular cliché:

> "Wonderful thing, steam, sir." "Ah! (a deep drawn sigh) it is indeed, sir." "Great power, sir." "Immense – immense!" "Great deal done by steam, sir". "Ah! (another sigh at the immensity of the subject and a knowing shake of the head) you may say that, sir". "Still in its infancy, they say, sir." ('The River', *SB*)

"Well, Pip," said Joe, taking up the poker

and when he were overtook with drink, he hammered away at my mother, most onmerciful. . . . So, he'd come with a most tremenjous crowd and make such a row at the doors of the houses where we was, that they used to be obléeged to have no more to do with us and to give us up to him.] From the mid-century onwards, a chorus of writers spoke out against wife-beating, characterizing it as a predominantly working-class trait. Incidents such as the one invented here were not uncommon; possibly Dickens's work as a freelance reporter attached to Doctors' Commons (1829–30) increased his awareness of the problem. Two of the five courts (the Court of Arches and the Consistory Court of the Bishop of London) heard divorce cases and matrimonial disputes, many of which involved accounts of marital cruelty and violence not unlike the incident Joe describes.

A verbatim report from the period 1711–13 provided by one Mary Alderman describes how she was verbally and physically attacked by her husband, John Alderman, in the streets. She left the scene but later met up with him in Aldersgate Street, whereupon Alderman 'Raised the mob upon her and called out a whore a whore and a Thief she is run from her Baile[,] which occasioned the mobb to lay hold on her and [tear] almost all her Cloathes off of her back' (cited in Hunt 13). The comments of a later, anonymous writer, who observed a stout Welshman hit his wife in a London street, corroborate the apparent acceptance of such metropolitan spectacles. In this case the wife suffered blows about the face in full view of the couple's fellow lodgers until she exhibited 'both blood and marks'. Such behaviour was regarded as an 'old right' and, though repudiated in other parts of society 'in this refined age', 'in these walks of life, this ancient custom still holds good. Here a man is considered perfectly in the right to match his strength of arm against his wife's strength of tongue' (*Sinks of London Laid Open*, 1848, 73).

Frequent references to wife-beating occur in Dickens's fiction. See 'The Hospital Patient' (*SB*), Sikes's savage murder of Nancy (*OT*), the abused wives of brickmakers (*BH*), and Horne and Dickens's 'Cain in the Fields', *HW* 3.147–51. Several other writers also document the problem: see the journalists John Wight (*Mornings at Bow Street*, 1824, and *More Mornings at Bow Street*, 1827) and Henry Mayhew (*London Labour and London Poor* 3.281); 'Plain Speaking' and 'One Word More', in an anonymous mid-century collection of poems, *Songs of the Present*, two poems condemning working men who beat their wives; Wilkie Collins (*Man and Wife*, 1870); and John Stuart Mill (*Essay on the Subjection of Women*, 1869), who began a campaign against wife-beating in the 1820s and attacked the failure of courts to prosecute the culprits.

"Though mind you, Pip," said Joe

"rendering unto all their doo,] See Romans 13.7: 'Render therefore to all their dues'.

and maintaining equal justice betwixt man and man,] Compare Thomas Jefferson: 'Equal and exact justice to all men, of whatever state or persuasion, religion or political . . .' (First Inaugural Address, 1801; Dumbould 44).

"Well!" Joe pursued

keep the pot a biling,]   Literally, the expression referred to the family cooking-pot; figuratively, to the need for constant activity or movement, such as when Sam Weller urges Mr Pickwick not to balk on the slide and 'keep the pot a-bilin', Sir" (*PP* 30).

" 'Consequence, my father didn't make objections

in a purple leptic fit.]   An apoplectic fit.

Whatsume'er the failings on his part, Remember reader he were that good in his hart."]   Homely couplets like this existed, the object of scorn by those campaigning for a plain, unadorned style. Among some 'choice epithets' reported in various sources, Sir William Hardman noted an example recorded in 1862 from a churchyard in Walworth, London:

> Here lies the wife of Roger Martin,
> She was a good wife for Roger, that's sartin. (1923, 99)

The trend towards simplicity began in the 1840s, encouraging writers to attack 'vulgar extravagances' and sentimental clichés of the kind Dickens satirizes here and in Mr Sapsea's ostentatious tribute to his wife, Ethelinda (Jacobson 64–5).

"I made it," said Joe

it were my intentions to have had it cut over him; but poetry costs money . . . and it were not done. Not to mention bearers,]   Edwin Chadwick, the sanitary reformer, opposed the growth of expensive funerals requiring elaborate tombstones and the use of pallbearers and other attendants, a practice that began to spread even to the working class early in the century. One consequence was a threat to public health in crowded cities when people kept corpses at home for a week or more while trying to raise money for burials. Dickens held undertakers responsible for the many costly solemnities standard at Victorian funerals. See also chapter 35.

"But I did mind you, Pip," he returned

"When I offered to your sister to keep company,]   The conventions of a formal courtship required the man to request permission to 'keep company' with a woman. A proposal of marriage followed, after which the wedding banns were read.

"Your sister is given to government."

given to government."]   Possibly a trace of Joe's domestic situation occurs in the following entry in Dickens's *Book of Memoranda*: 'The man who is governed by his wife, and is heartily despised in consequence by all other wives – who still want to govern *their* husbands notwithstanding' (33). Compare also the description in 'Dullborough Town' of an acquaintance's father, who 'was greatly connected', as a man 'being under Government' (AYR 3.275).

"Given to government, Joe?"

I had some shadowy idea . . . that Joe had divorced her in favour of the Lords of the Admiralty, or Treasury.]   Possibly Pip's assumption that these office holders granted divorces originated in a confused notion that jurisdiction in divorce cases lay with the House of Lords and the ecclesiastical courts. Opportunity for divorce increased substantially in 1857 when the Divorce and Matrimonial Causes Act (20 & 21 Vict. c. 85) created a civil divorce court in London, with authority to grant judicial separations and divorce decrees.

The Lords of the Admiralty were a board of seven men, 'Commissioners for Executing the Office of Lord High Admiral'. Of these seven, three were usually naval officers, called 'professional' Lords, and four civilians, or 'civil' Lords. This board evolved early in the eighteenth century as a replacement for the office of the Lord High Admiral, a single individual in whom the Crown vested all the powers and functions of the Admiralty. The Admiralty Office is on the west side of Whitehall; responsibilities of the Admiralty Board included preparing the fleet for war, selecting its commanders and making officer assignments. Other offices managing naval affairs included the Navy Board at Somerset House (accountable for the material condition of the fleet and expenditures, including the payment of all salaries), the Ordnance Board at the Tower of London and the Warren, near Woolwich Dockyard. The creation of a unified ministry of defence in 1964 ended the Board's existence.

The modern version of the Treasury (formerly the private office of the Lord High Treasurer of England) originated as a place of deposit for treasure and coin. The Treasurer also presided in the Exchequer, which comprised an office of receipt and an office of audit. Under James I a set of commissioners replaced the single Lord Treasurer, whose office lapsed in 1714. Thereafter the Lords Commissioners assumed a permanent role at the Treasury Board. After the abolition of the ancient official structure of the Exchequer in 1833, the Treasury emerged as a ministerial department whose presiding officer, the Chancellor of the Exchequer, became a figure of cabinet rank. The name of the former office, however, survives in the title of the Chancellor of the Exchequer.

"And she an't over partial to having scholars on the premises," Joe continued

for fear as I might rise.]   Resistance to schooling on the grounds that it might encourage rebellion was not uncommon among opponents of public education. In 1807, Davies Giddy led opposition to Samuel Whitbread's bill to fund two years of schooling for the children of the poor from the poor rate by arguing that education would teach the poor 'to despise their lot in life . . . to which their rank in society had destined them' (1 *Hansard*, 9 (1807), 798, 802, 1174–8; Paz 5–6).

"Stay a bit.

your sister comes the Mo-gul over us,]   That is, she acts overbearingly like a great personage or an autocratic ruler.

throw us back-falls,]   A wrestling term for throwing one's opponent on his back.

a Buster."]   A slang version of a 'burster', one who bursts or explodes like gunpowder.

Mrs. Joe made occasional trips with Uncle Pumblechook

on market-days,]   Markets held at fixed times and places were a regular feature of English country life. Rochester market, the likely model in this instance, offered a wide variety of goods every Tuesday and Friday. Typical products included butter, cheese, eggs, fowls, fruit and 'other wares or merchandize' sold from a collection of stalls erected in an enclosed paved area under the city's Guildhall (*Miniature Road-Book of Kent*, 1842; Moad [1-5]). Pip's first visit to Satis House (chapter 8) occurs on a Wednesday, the day immediately following Pumblechook's excursion to the market with Mrs Joe.

The sound of her iron shoes upon the hard road

We got a chair out, ready for Mrs. Joe's alighting,]   Using a chair made stepping down from a chaise easier, especially for a woman in long skirts. A typical chaise, high-mounted on iron axles, stood over four feet from the ground (Loudon, 1857, 428).

I had heard of Miss Havisham up town

I had heard of Miss Havisham up town – everybody for miles round, had heard of Miss Havisham up town – as an immensely rich and grim lady who lived in a large and dismal house barricaded against robbers, and who led a life of seclusion.]   The character of Miss Havisham (Dickens wrote 'Miss Havish' several times before he added 'am') evidently derives from a range of actual and fictional prototypes. In an essay published in 1853 called 'Where We Stopped Growing', Dickens readily acknowledged how 'real people and real places' made a profound impression on his youthful imagination:

> There was a poor demented woman who used to roam about the City, dressed all in black with cheeks staringly painted, and thence popularly known as Rouge et Noire. . . . The story went that her only brother, a Bank-clerk, was left for death for forgery; and that she, broken-hearted creature, lost her wits on the morning of his execution, and ever afterwards . . . flitted thus among the busy money-changers. . . .
>
> Another very different person . . . we associate with Berners Street, Oxford Street. . . . The White Woman is her name. She is dressed entirely in white, with a ghastly white plaiting round her head and face, inside her white bonnet. She even carries . . . a white umbrella. . . . She is a conceited old creature, cold and formal in manner, and evidently went simpering mad on personal grounds alone – no doubt because a wealthy Quaker wouldn't marry her. This is her bridal dress. She is always walking up here, on her way to church to marry the false Quaker.(*HW* 6.362–3)

Stage impersonations of both figures conceivably offered further details from which Dickens may have drawn (see below). In January 1852 a paragraph about another London eccentric had appeared in the *Household Narrative of Current Events*, a short-lived supplement to *HW*. The section headed 'Narrative of Law and Crime' contained an account of a woman with some attributes resembling Miss Havisham's:

> An inquest was held on the 29th, on Martha Joachim, a *Wealthy and Eccentric Lady*, late of York buildings, Marylebone, aged 62. . . . In 1825, a suitor of the deceased, whom her mother rejected, shot himself while sitting on the sofa with her, and she was covered with his brains. From that instant she lost her reason. Since her mother's death, eighteen years ago, she had led the life of a recluse, dressed in white, and never going out. A charwoman occasionally brought her what supplied her wants. (10)

Six years later, in April 1856, Dickens wrote to Forster from Paris with details of the murder of a French duchess 'over the way' on the Champs Élysées. The investigation, Dickens added, 'seems to disclose the strangest state of things':

> The Duchess who is murdered lived alone in a great house which was always shut up, and passed her time entirely in the dark. In a little lodge outside lived a coachman (the murderer), and there had been a long succession of coachmen who had been unable to stay there, and upon whom, whenever they asked for their wages, she plunged out with an immense knife, by way of an immediate settlement. The coachman never had anything to do, for the coach hadn't been driven out for years; neither would she ever allow the horses to be taken out for exercise. Between the lodge and the house, is a miserable bit of garden, all overgrown with long rank

grass, weeds, and nettles; and in this, the horses used to be taken out to swim – in a dead green vegetable sea, up to their haunches. (*Letters* 8.101)

Forster appends to this letter a second anecdote Dickens sent from Paris around the same time. This one involved some local gossip from Kent about a dissipated squire who had married 'a woman of the town'. The two had a child before they eventually separated, but the daughter was brought up by the mother to spite the father and 'bred . . . in every conceivable vice'. Evidently in sexual frustration the woman's anger turned inwards on herself, prompting her to seek revenge through a perversely educated child (Sucksmith 177–88).

Tantalizing echoes of this story reappear in 1857 in the chapter Dickens contributed to 'The Lazy Tour of Two Idle Apprentices', whose fourth chapter, 'The Bride's Story', recounts in crude form the actions of a man who, jilted by the woman he loves, gains control of her child. Bringing up the young girl after the death of her two parents, he confines her to a gloomy house with a neglected garden, jealously keeping her from light and air as he wills her to die. The girl, reduced ultimately to 'a white wreck of hair and dress, and wild eyes', is so thoroughly under his spell that the young man who secretly sees her and falls in love with her fails to break her guardian's influence (chapter 4; Cardwell xv).

Other instances of real people driven into seclusion by the disappointment of a broken engagement have been proposed as models for Miss Havisham. Among them are a recluse from the Isle of Wight, another woman who lived near Hyde Park and who was burned to death (compare Miss Havisham's fate in chapter 49), and an Australian woman in Sydney (Hutchings; Kitton, 1897; Plummer; Ryan; Stow; but cf. Dilnot). Possibly of significance is the account in June 1778 of 'a maiden lady of genteel fortune' who shut herself off from society after meeting with 'a disappointment as to matrimony'. Dickens may have come across this entry in the *Annual Register*, a complete edition of which he kept in his library at Gad's Hill (Friedman, 1971, 24–5). William Allingham's 'The Dirty Old Man. A Lay of Leadenhall' may also have lodged in Dickens's memory. Allingham's verses, published in 1853 (*HW* 6.396–7), recount the history of one Nathaniel Bentley, a recluse who kept a hardware shop in Leadenhall Street, London. Bentley lived in broken-hearted gloom after his sweetheart failed to arrive on the day appointed for their wedding. In an upstairs room a former glorious hall housed the rat-eaten remains of a wedding breakfast set for guests who never arrived; elsewhere, spiders infested the property and mildewy grass sprouted from the windows. Another male recluse, perhaps known to Dickens through Edmund Yates, the journalist, lived in St John's Wood (Staples; see also Kitton,1897; Wright; and Fraser).

Interest in the aberrant behaviour of the mentally unstable may have provided additional material. When Dickens visited St Luke's Hospital for the Insane on 26 December 1851, a female patient among a group of quadrille dancers caught his attention. 'Weird-gentility', as he named her, was

> the old-young woman, with the dishevelled long light hair, spare figure and weird gentility . . . and there was no straiter waistcoat in company than the polka-garment of the old-young woman with the weird gentility, which was

of a faded black satin, and languished through the dance with a lovelorn affability and condescension to the force of circumstances, in itself a faint reflection of all Bedlam. ('A Curious Dance Round a Curious Tree', *HW* 4.387–8)

Like Miss Havisham in her bridal dress, this 'old-young woman' wears the clothes of her youth. Her spare figure, disembodied appearance and air of disappointed hope also shadow forth aspects of Miss Havisham's psychosis (Shatto, 1985, 45).

Ten years later, Dickens came face to face with one James Lucas, an encounter he subsequently fictionalized as the interview between Mr Traveller and Mr Mopes in 'Tom Tiddler's Ground' (*AYR*, Christmas 1861). 'Mad Lucas', as he was popularly known, lived alone at Elmwood House in Hertfordshire, a figure whose bizarre behaviour as 'the Hermit of Hertfordshire' had received coverage for over a decade by both country and London newspapers. Either familiar with some of the press accounts or perhaps informed of the hermit's eccentricities by Bulwer Lytton, Lucas's neighbour, Dickens also appears to have used this actual recluse as a source for Miss Havisham's aberrant behaviour more extensively than 'any one of her real-life originals already established'. 'Both inherit wealth and both live in big houses. Both are catapulted into a life of self-inflicted seclusion by the loss of a loved one', Miss Havisham by her fiancé and Lucas by his mother, whose death in 1849 precipitated his extreme grief and decision to turn Elmwood House into a stronghold. Terrified of imaginary attacks, he took to living in semi-naked squalor in the kitchen until he died in 1874 aged 61 (Shatto, 1985, 47, 46).

Theatrical productions may have provided additional useful details. Portraits of women wounded in love date back to the Elizabethan stage, particularly to Shakespeare's Ophelia. By tradition she often appeared disordered, dressed in tattered white and fantastically garlanded with straw or flowers in her hair. This same figure later became popular with Victorian artists and writers, for whom Ophelia represented, by consent, 'the very type of a class of cases by no means uncommon' (Bucknill, 1859, 110). Harriet Smithson's Ophelia, first performed in Paris during the English season of 1827–8, added to the currency of a woman young in years yet the embodiment of faded beauty and suffering. Elements of Ophelia entered the imagination of Tennyson ('Mariana', 'The Lady of Shalott' and 'Maud'); they also passed into the culture at large so that Ophelia 'became the prototype not only of the deranged woman in Victorian literature and art but also of the young female asylum patient' (Showalter, 1985, 90 and passim).

Two sketches by Charles Mathews (1776–1835) and Frederick Yates (1797–1842) deserve specific comment. 'The Next Door Neighbours' (Nos 26 and 27 in a series of 'At Homes' popularized by Mathews) came remarkably close to Dickens's later conception of Miss Havisham. In quick succession Mathews and Yates performed a series of parts, shifting immediately from one to the other as they swapped roles and entertained the audience with occasional help from dummies and silhouettes.

The slight plot of the two sketches centres around the observations of a clerk, who occupies a ground-floor office called 'the London Expectation Office'. Among the clients who call on the clerk's master are 'the old Lady in white Miss Mildew –

and the old Lady in black, Mrs. Bankington Bombasin'. The former is later described as 'the old eccentric Lady in White' who

> has lost her first love Forty years before, on the day which was to be appropriated to her wedding, & she has worn the same clothes – Bonnet &c &c ever since – faded virgin white – She apostrophises her lover . . . states that she is followed in the street, but that it is in admiration of her figure – She goes to the Expectation Office in the hopes of learning what has become of her first Love.
>
> . . . Enter immediately Mrs. Bankington Bombasin . . . the eccentric old Lady in black – She is also on her way to the office – She fancies that she is the heiress of vast wealth, describes it in all sorts of fictitious shares &c states how her money is employed, & is come now to the Expectation Office, to endeavour to make enquiry after a person, supposed to have gone to the West Indies 40 years before. . . . ('Diapololgue', Vol. 46, foll. 87–93, BM Add. MS 42910; quoted in Meisel 278–9)

Popular objections inspired by sympathy for the two figures, however, compelled Mathews and Yates to withdraw the sketches after only one performance at the Adelphi on 18 April 1831. The surviving manuscript 'presents a remarkable confluence of Miss Havisham': it contains elements of her history, hints of her decay, and points to a preoccupation with money and a vanishing treasure, unified by the concept of 'illusory expectations' (Meisel 279).

Poetic and novelistic prototypes for Miss Havisham have also been proposed. Among them are Tennyson's 'Mariana', whose jilted heroine living in a lonely house amidst an atmosphere of desolation Dickens transforms 'into the terms of . . . [his] own art' (Gilmour, 1979, 140); Charlotte Smith's Mrs Ryland in *The Old Manor House*, 1793, whose Ryland Hall partially resembles Satis House (Bartolomeo); and Wilkie Collins's Anne Catherick in *The Woman in White*, which concluded its serial publication in *AYR* three months before Dickens issued the first instalment of *GE* on 1 December 1860 (Meckier, 1987, 127; Currie 18). For the question of Miss Havisham's 'madness' within the context of mid-century debates about incarceration or the non-restraint of the mentally ill, see chapter 49, note on pp. 369–70.

"No, Joseph," said my sister, still in a reproachful manner

Mooncalfs,] A mooncalf was a dolt or an idiot, someone affected by the moon's reputedly malign influence.

With that, she pounced upon me

my face was squeezed into wooden bowls in sinks, and my head was put under taps of water-butts,] This arrangement was typical of poorer households in the country, where indoor plumbing remained unavailable until later in the nineteenth century. Water for domestic use – washing, cooking and drinking – came variously from wells, from outdoor pumps supplying water from rivers, and from large puncheons, or casks, which stored rainwater. Rainwater collected in the open country was regarded as pure, 'but in large towns it is more or less contaminated by the smokey atmosphere through which it falls, and by the impurities lodged on the roof of houses from which it drops' (Keith Imray, 1842, 822).

I suppose myself to be better acquainted than any living authority, with the ridgy effect of a wedding-ring, passing unsympathetically over the human countenance.)] Dickens refers elsewhere to 'the detestable ordeal' young boys endured of washing and combing and 'being made straight' ('First Fruits', *HW* 5.190). Elaborating later in an essay published as part of the *UT* series, Dickens wrote:

> On summer evenings, when every flower, and tree, and bird, might have better addressed my soft young heart, I have in my day been caught in the palm of a female hand by the crown, have been violently scrubbed from the neck to the roots of the hair as a purification for the Temple, and have then been carried off highly charged with saponaceous electricity. . . . ('City of London Churches', *AYR* 3.85)

George Eliot makes a similar point about the painful effect of 'a gold ring on the third finger' when one's face is washed 'the wrong way by a pitiless hand' ('Mr. Gilfil's Love-Story', *Scenes of Clerical Life*, ch. 3, 1857).

When my ablutions were completed

the Sheriff,] The office of sheriff dates from the eleventh century when earls delegated to 'shire-reeves' control of the shires. The Normans retained the office, but a century later sheriffs were generally chosen annually by the crown to counter their gaining power locally. Gradually, other officials like coroners and justices of the peace took over many of their duties. However, sheriffs continued to execute writs, prepare panels of jurors for the visiting assize judges and supervise prisoners taken into custody. Sheriffs also controlled shire elections up to the nineteenth century.

Chapter 8 Fifth weekly number
29 December 1860

MR. PUMBLECHOOK'S premises in the High-street

MR. PUMBLECHOOK'S premises in the High-street of the market town were of a peppercorny and farinaceous character, as the premises of a corn-chandler and seedsman should be. It appeared to me that he must be a very happy man indeed, to have so many little drawers in his shop;] Rochester, the model for Dickens's fictional 'market town', consisted principally of a single well-paved street 'of considerable length [approximately one mile] called the High-Street, having several bye-lanes on each side of it'. The Medway river and bridge to the west and the neighbouring town of Chatham to the east formed the extreme boundaries of the High Street (see Appendix 4, map p. 450). Most of the city's 9,000 inhabitants, according to a census taken in 1810, were engaged in 'trade and maritime occupations'. The intercourse of local tradesmen with the navy victualling office and with other branches of the shipping industry proves 'a continual source of wealth and employment to them, many of whom are induced to reside here on these accounts' (Hasted, 1778, 2.8; Denne, 1817, 312, 315).

Pumblechook's premises are reputedly those of John Bye Fairbairn, a corn-chandler and seedsman in Rochester High Street in the 1860s. He lived in one of three gabled houses (originally they formed a single mansion) that stand in a row in the High Street opposite Eastgate House. According to Gadd, several people living in Rochester in the 1920s 'perfectly remember the rows of little seed drawers' in Fairbairn's shop just as Dickens describes them (1929, 56).

Corn-chandlers typically engaged in a diversified retail trade. They sold hay, straw and corn; as seedsmen, they stocked split peas, various kinds of hulled grains, bird-seed and garden products for the nurseryman or gardener:

> This is a clean, profitable, and healthy business; but as it consists in merely buying and selling, the success of the Corn-chandler depends chiefly on his judgment of the quality of the article he deals in, and in making calculations upon the rise and fall of the markets. (*Complete Book of Trades* 164)

It was in the early morning

in an attic with a sloping roof, which was so low in the corner where the bedstead was, that I calculated the tiles as being within a foot of my eyebrows.] Attic rooms under the tiles exist in some of the older houses in Rochester. Rooms with sloping roofs that reached down to about a foot from the floor were also common. Gadd argues that Dickens 'must have been acquainted with the actual interiors [of houses and rooms in Rochester] because his descriptions are almost exact, in nearly all cases' (1929, 59). Descriptions of 'the ancient little city of Rochester in Kent' with its High Street 'full of gables' appear in *The Seven Poor Travellers* (Christmas Number, 1854, 1).

corduroys.]   Corduroys, a colloquial term for a pair of trousers, were generally worn by labourers or persons engaged in rough work (*OED*).

Mr. Pumblechook appeared to conduct his business by looking across the street at the saddler,]   The width of Rochester High Street (approximately thirty feet) makes it easy for one tradesman to watch another. As a child, Dickens thought the street 'at least as wide' as London's Regent Street 'or the Italian Boulevard at Paris'. Returning to Rochester as a man, 'I found it little better than a lane' ('Dullborough Town', *AYR* 3.276).

the saddler,]   This was an important trade early in the nineteenth century. It took skill to adapt particular saddles to 'awkward backs: as the roach-back, hollow-back, close-ribbed horse, long washy flanked animal, deep-chested, high-mounted, narrow-withered, and other contraries in *make*, shape, and consequent mode of *going*'. A saddler began by constructing a wooden foundation called a saddle-tree. Leather was then added as the saddler worked, like a tailor, with an awl and waxed thread to create a seat. Saddlers also built pack-saddles, which were made 'wholly of wood, iron-braces, and a stuffing of wool in a woollen lining' (*Complete Book of Trades* 395). In addition, saddlers were expected to fit buckles, studs, bars and brasses. They also made bridles, stirrups, girths, surcingles, holster cases and caps.

the coachmaker,]   The introduction of better roads and improvements in coach design account for coach-making as a flourishing occupation. Demand for four- and two-wheeled vehicles among the middle class also contributed to the business, as orders for coaches, chariots, post-chaises, gigs, tilburies and landaus increased early in the century. Related branches of the trade included coach-founders, painters, curriers and harness-makers, who were responsible for fitting up and adjusting 'the variety of articles that the several branches produce, particularly if [they made] the wood-work or frame of the carriage'.

When a customer commissioned a coach and approved the proposed design, the coach-maker began work on the exterior, assembling and painting the panels. Work on the interior followed, as the coach-maker lined the inside and added cushions and cloth and leather trimmings. Deal flooring, brass handles and glass windows gave coaches an attractive finish. Thereafter he concentrated on the upper and under carriage, as the body was hung and the front and back wheels attached. Upon the fitting of springs by a coach-smith, the vehicle was ready for the road (*Complete Book of Trades* 150; W. B. Adams, 1837, 42–8).

Towns the size of Rochester had at least one local coach-builder. *Wright's Topography of Rochester, Chatham* . . . for 1838 lists J. & T. Butcher in the High Street and a second coach-maker in Eastgate. Typically, coach-builders' customers included members of the local gentry, clergymen, professional men and substantial tradesmen like Pumblechook. Young Pip refers repeatedly to Pumblechook's driving 'his own chaise-cart', evidence of his status among those who looked up to the 'well-to-do corn-chandler' (*GE* 4 and 6).

the grocer,] A grocer (literally one who sold in gross or in large quantities) originally dealt in spices and foreign produce. After grocers were incorporated by this name in 1344, their retail trade gradually expanded. Sugar, tea, cocoa and coffee were added in the eighteenth century when Britain began to import these commodities from her colonies. Greengrocers, who sold greens, vegetables and some fruits, and fruiterers, who dealt solely in domestic and foreign fruit, represent further developments in the trade.

the chemist.] Retail chemists and druggists supplied patent medicines and made up prescriptions written by physicians and apothecaries. They also sold drugs to the public and gave medical advice to those who could not afford doctors' fees, according both to custom and to an act of Parliament early in the nineteenth century. Efforts by the Pharmaceutical Society (founded 1841) led to the imposition of some controls under the Pharmacy Act of 1852 (15 & 16 Vict., c. 56), which gave the society power to compile a register of chemists and druggists and to examine persons for registration. The move towards the professionalization of pharmacists continued throughout the century.

The watchmaker,] Watch-makers generally assembled the several parts of a watch previously made by allied specialists: movement-makers, cutters, watchspring-makers and case-makers. Watch-making, an offshoot of the clock industry, developed in the seventeenth century, after the invention of the spiral spring in watches by Robert Hooke (1635–1703) in 1658. Thomas Tompion (1639?–1713), reputedly Europe's 'best Watchmaker', gave England an early lead until the production of watches by Dutch, French, Swiss and German rivals shifted the centre of watch production to Europe in the nineteenth century. Wright's 1838 *Topography* lists one watch-maker in Rochester High Street together with two saddlers, one corn-factor, one seedsman, five chemists and two grocers.

smock-frocks] A loose-fitting, knee-length garment of rough linen worn by countrymen and farm labourers as protective clothing.

Mr. Pumblechook and I breakfasted at eight o'clock

hunch of bread-and-butter] A provincial term for a thick, clumsily cut piece of bread.

a sack of peas] Peas stored in a sack were dry and were used for soups, puddings and other culinary purposes (Loudon, 1857, 835–7).

For such reasons, I was very glad when ten o'clock came

Within a quarter of an hour we came to Miss Havisham's house, which was of old brick, and dismal, and had a great many iron bars to it.] Dickens based Miss

Havisham's home on Restoration House just off Rochester High Street and across from the Vines (Forster 8.3.215). This residence in Crow Lane (formerly Maidstone Road) is in fact only minutes away from the supposed 'original' of Pumblechook's premises in Rochester High Street (Plate 8; see Appendix 4, map p. 450).

The oldest portion of Restoration House, built entirely of brick, dates from about 1580. Former occupants subsequently added two wings, making it loosely conform to the classic Elizabethan 'E' plan. The name dates from 1660 and commemorates the night Charles II spent in the house on 28 May when he returned to England from exile in France to reclaim the throne (Hasted, 2.4). Later owners – among them prominent citizens and former mayors of Rochester – added iron bars to some of the windows as a protective measure. A heavy growth of ivy, its tall chimneys, gabled ends and the irregular arrangement of windows gave the house a gloomy and mysterious appearance. Its apparent hold on Dickens's imagination continued long after the completion of GE (see chapter 29, note on p. 235–4). Further similarities between Satis House and Restoration House will be noted as they appear.

Some of the windows had been walled up; of those that remained, all the lower were rustily barred.] After 'Some' MS reads 'Many'. Evidence of walled-up windows at Restoration House remains today, an economy measure common among homeowners during the eighteenth century. Stephen Aveling, who bought Restoration House in December 1875, found thirty windows 'closed against the light of day' and counted fifty-two windows in the front of the house alone (Aveling 459).

The practice of blocking up windows began after the government introduced a tax on windows in 1697 to compensate for money lost by clipping and defacing silver coins; between 1747 and 1808, the window tax increased sixfold before its eventual abolition in 1851.

a court-yard in front, and that was barred; so, we had to wait, after ringing the bell, until some one should come to open it.] A paved courtyard approximately thirteen by ten yards separates the main entrance to Restoration House from Crow Lane and leads to an open porch surrounding a heavy, iron-studded oak door. The door, about eight yards from the street, is flanked by fixed oak settles, above which are leaded windows and Delft tiles. Railings mounted on a low brick wall and a large wrought-iron gate convey the atmosphere of seclusion and enclosure Pip describes.

at the side of the house there was a large brewery;] Maps and other extant historical records reveal no trace of a commercial brewery at the side of Restoration House. One, however, did exist on the corner of Victoria Street and East Row to the south-west of the property (see Appendix 4, map p. 451). A stone marker mounted above the pavement on the high corner wall at the intersection names 'Woodham' as the original brewer and gives 1750 as the foundation date. In Dickens's day the brewery was a thriving concern which continued, under successive proprietors, to brew and bottle beer until the 1920s. Many of the original buildings remain, although the tower and outbuildings (see below) have long since been adapted to the needs of later businesses.

9 Restoration House, Rochester, Kent

10 Satis House

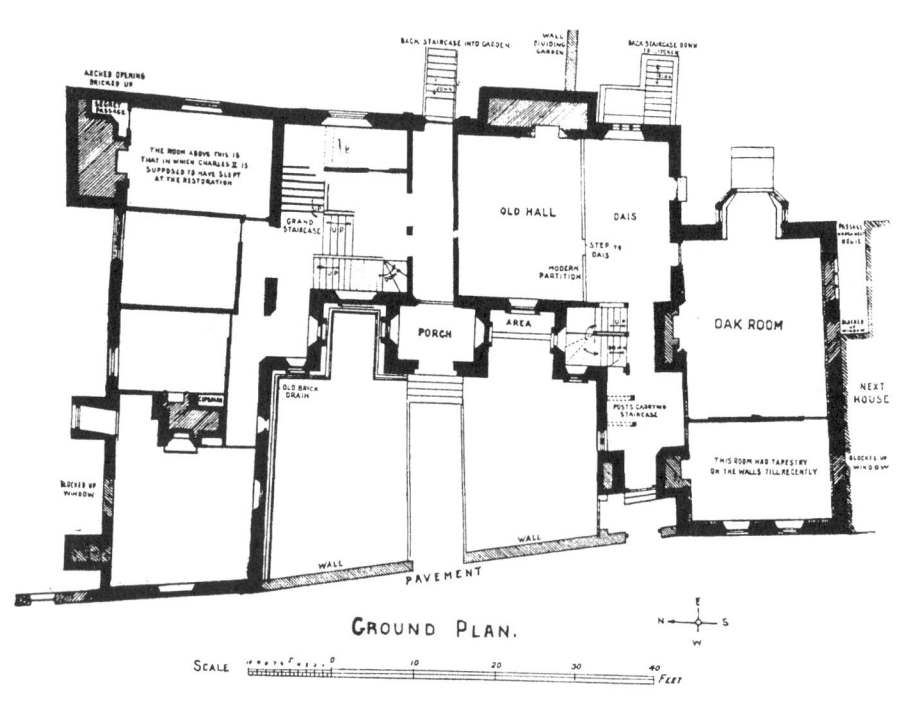

11 Restoration House, ground plan

A literal insistence on the location *at the side* has led to speculation that Dickens used as his prototype some abandoned buildings on the north side of Restoration House before they were razed to make way for a kitchen garden and the erection of a chapel in 1853 (see below) adjacent to Restoration House (Gadd, 1929, 67). Possibly these 'abandoned buildings' originally served as a small brewhouse where beer for domestic consumption in Restoration House was brewed. But subsequent descriptions of the defunct brewery in the text reveal a scale of operation compatible only with a commercial brewery, the existence of which Herbert confirms later in his account of the Havisham family's history and wealth. Local and national developments in the brewing industry also reinforce the plausibility of a Rochester brewer who achieved wealth and prominence during the eighteenth century (see chapter 22, note on pp. 199–200). There was also a second brewery in the vicinity operating in the nearby High Street, whose yard backed towards Restoration House, which may have provided details from which Dickens drew a composite description (*A Dickens Pilgrimage*, 1914, 19).

for a long long time.] For at least twenty-five years. See chapter 22 and Appendix 1.

A window was raised

the window was shut again, and a young lady came across the court-yard,] After 'young lady' MS reads '<pretty young woman> young <girl> lady'. The same hesitation is apparent in the next reference to Estella as 'a young lady'. Several windows in the front of Restoration House afford a view of the courtyard and would allow one to observe visitors. Estella appears to approach from an entrance in the south wing, to the right of the main gate (see below).

"Ah!" said the girl; "but you see she don't."

she don't] Standard usage in the nineteenth century.

My young conductress locked the gate

locked the gate, and we went across the court-yard.] The gate appears to be the front entrance. After crossing the courtyard, Estella evidently leads Pip in by a side-door.

The brewery buildings had a little lane of communication with it,] The 'little lane of communication' may have been suggested by an existing narrow passageway to the north of Restoration House created in 1853 by the construction of a Congregational church adjacent to the north wing of Restoration House on land purchased from a former owner for that purpose. This passage still exists and runs between Crow Lane and Victoria Street (see Appendix 4, map p. 451).

all the brewery beyond stood open, away to the high enclosing wall, and all was empty and disused.] The proximity of the brewery in Victoria Street to Crow Lane indicates that it might have been built by one of the previous occupants of Restoration House on land belonging to the former manor-house (see below). But the absence of comprehensive local records for either the house or Woodham's makes it difficult to ascertain the relationship (if any) between the two. Descriptions of the architectural features of the disused brewery in the novel, however, suggest a commercial structure built in the eighteenth century. Quite possibly, therefore, Woodham's served as Dickens's model, suitably disguised by its removal and changed status.

Breweries built during the eighteenth century, for example, had a tower-shaped brewhouse (see note below for further details). The brewing process began here at the top, where water for the beer was housed in tanks. Drawn from this source by pipes, water descended to the mash-tun located on a floor below, where it was heated, mixed with coarsely ground malt and then stirred with a long wooden pole resembling an oar to promote 'mashing' as the starches were converted to sugar. The mash-tub, or -tun, was then covered to prevent further loss of heat; later the sweetish brown liquid (wort) was drawn off and run into a large copper boiler. Hops (the dried blossoms of the hop plant) were then added to counter the beer's sweetness by providing a characteristic bitter taste and sharp aroma.

This mixture was boiled for several hours before it was directed into shallow vats to cool. From the coolers the liquid was piped into the working-tun, where fermentation occurred upon the addition of yeast. This stage takes several hours as the yeast multiplies considerably in volume, producing rising bubbles of gas. When the fermentation was complete about two days later, the beer was drained into casks or barrels, ready for consumption. Brewers followed the same steps for ale, except ale in the traditional sense was made only from water, malt and yeast before the introduction of hops by Dutch and German brewers in the fourteenth century. British brewers later accepted hops when Flemish growers settled in Kent in the sixteenth century.

Other buildings surrounded the tower or were located nearby, often forming the kind of 'L'-shaped structure visible today on the corner of Victoria Street. Outbuildings typically housed sacks of hops, malt storage bins, a malt mill and a weighing machine. Brewers needed a covered space to store the wooden casks in which beer was sold and distributed. Stables for horses to draw the carts for delivering the casked beer were also common. In addition, brewers required a boiler house to supply hot water to the mash-tub, where the first stage of beer-making began. Other uses of hot water included washing the casks, cleaning all surfaces and rinsing essential pieces of equipment.

Additional space may have been devoted to the storage of water in tanks. Breweries drew their water either from running streams or from artesian wells bored deeply into the ground. Water for Woodham's brewery came from a nearby well. In addition, many breweries had a malting, a complex of buildings where harvested barley is immersed in large tanks of water to promote germination and then dried and transferred to a kiln. Inside the kiln barley is heated with hot air to about 140° to stop its growth and then roasted further, depending on the degree of darkness sought by the maltster (based on *Brewing: A Book of Reference*, pts 1 and 2; *Complete Book of Trades* 68–72).

CHAPTER EIGHT

"Better not try to brew beer there now

"Better not try to brew beer there now, or it would turn out sour, boy;] Fresh, drinkable beer could not be brewed in a dilapidated brewery like the one described here. The state of the casks, too, would make the beer sour. See below.

"Not that anybody means to try," she added

As to strong beer, there's enough of it in the cellars already, to drown the Manor House."] Beer strength can be measured in two ways: by its original gravity as a measure of the amount of fermented material added to water to make beer and by the measurement of alcohol based on volume. Strong beers have an alcoholic content of above 10 per cent. Average beers contain between 3 and 4 per cent alcohol, the weakest around 2 per cent. Most commercial brewers in the nineteenth century would have produced a variety of strong and average beers and ales. 'Small' or weak beer, a mild table beverage usually brewed at home, had a low alcohol level because it was made from wort whose sugar content had been nearly exhausted by repeated additions of water during the brewing process.

Any strong beer in the house would have been recently purchased. Even in optimum conditions – steady temperatures between 47° and 50° – beer, strong or weak, cannot keep indefinitely, making it unlikely that beer had been left over from the time of Mr Havisham's death.

The reference to Satis House as 'the Manor House' appears to reflect local history: the land on which Restoration House was built formerly belonged to the Manor of Ambree, which centuries ago had been the property of St. Andrew's Priory (Marsh, 1974, 24).

"One more. Its other name was Satis

Satis; which is Greek, or Latin, or Hebrew . . . for enough."] *Satis* is Latin for 'enough'. Satis House in Rochester formerly belonged to Richard Watts (1529–79) (Plate 10). Bagshaw describes it in 1847 as 'an ancient mansion, now occupied as several dwellings, a little west of Boley Hill, near the river [Medway] and on the edge of the cliff' (Bagshaw 103).

Satis House owes its name to Elizabeth I, who spent one night there in 1573. When Watts, her host, apologized for the smallness of his residence, noting that it was 'but ill-suited for the reception of so great a Princess', Elizabeth graciously replied with a single word, '*satis*', indicating that 'she was very well contented with it' (Hasted, 1782, 2.51; James Dugdale, 1819, 3.233). By transferring the name of one house and combining it with features of a second (see Appendix 4, map p. 451), Dickens makes a composite portrait.

Though she called me "boy" so often

she was of about my own age] After 'age' MS reads 'age – very little older'. Further confirmation of Pip and Estella's similarity in age appears in the calculations Dickens made before he wrote the novel's third part. For the text of the memoranda about dates, see pp. 344–5.

We went into the house by a side door

by a side door] A single entrance to a house was considered unrefined since it forced the inhabitants to 'rub shoulders with the tradespeople' (Kerr, 1864, 75). A side-door off the main courtyard of Restoration House leads into the south wing.

the great front entrance had two chains across it outside] Shortly after acquiring the house in 1875, Aveling noted: 'Great precautions had been taken by some previous occupant of the house for protection against robbers; bars, bolts, chains, and locks almost defied admission' (459).

the first thing I noticed was, that the passages were all dark . . . we went through more passages and up a staircase,] Emphasis on the passages and their lack of light seems to combine details taken from Restoration House. A staircase in the south wing leads to the first floor and to the rooms customarily regarded as Miss Havisham's. See the house plan (Plate 11) and below.

This was very uncomfortable

in a pretty large room,] Reference to the room's size and then to the panelling, high chimney-piece and spacious landing across from a second large room opposite suggests knowledge of the interior of Restoration House. See also below.

well lighted with wax candles.] Wax candles signify wealth and refinement to someone used to tallow candles, which were made from melted-down animal fat and which smoked when in use. Wax candles provided better illumination, required less trimming and burned without a strong odour. Even as late as 1844, candles (wax or tallow) were judged 'the most convenient and the most general mode of obtaining artificial light for domestic purposes' (Thomas Webster, 1844, 133).

It was a dressing-room, as I supposed from the furniture,] An ordinary dressing-room was generally 'a comparatively small private room attached to a Bedroom for the purposes of the toilet' (Kerr, 1864, 149). Dressing-rooms for ladies – always bigger than those for gentlemen – typically contained a dressing-table, a washstand, a wardrobe, and a side-table and chairs. Closets, cabinets and even 'a small bedstead in one corner for occasional use' were also common, especially if a lady made the room a private sitting-room or boudoir (Kerr).

a gilded looking-glass,] Ornamental frames and gold-leaf mirrors were in demand early in the century. The mirror would have been a free-standing swing-glass, 'moveable to any angle in a frame'. One explanation for their popularity is that 'All ladies "study the glass" ' (*Complete Book of Trades* 314–15).

a fine lady's dressing-table.] Elegant versions existed, often with marble tops decorated with brass ornaments. Inlaid marquetry was also popular among the wealthy (Thomas Webster, 1844, 274).

She was dressed in rich materials

her watch and chain] Evidently an ornamental lady's watch or fob watch, suspended from a short chain or strap attached either to a brooch or to a lapel.

It was not in the first moments

some ghastly wax-work at the Fair, representing I know not what impossible personage lying in state.] Travelling exhibitions of waxworks were common at rural fairs in the nineteenth century. Collections included an array of costumed and decorated figures of monarchs, emperors, military leaders, murderers and assassins. Madame Tussaud, the most famous proprietor of waxworks, travelled widely throughout the country after arriving from France in 1802. She later settled permanently in London and opened her exhibition in Baker Street in 1835. Joe Smith, another exhibitor, recalls the first night when he began his career in 1840:

> I knew perfectly well that the [wax] figures were all made up, but when I saw their faces gleam in the moonlight which came through the tent . . . they all looked to be living and stared directly at me. I felt sure they were living ghosts. (quoted in Bill Smith, 1896, 95)

one of our old marsh churches] There are six 'marsh' churches on the Hoo peninsula, one in each of the following villages: Cooling, Cliffe, Lower Higham, Upnor, Hoo and Stoke. All date from either the twelfth or thirteenth century. Churches located at Chalk, Grain, St Mary's, All Hallows and High Halstow on the uplands are not considered as 'marsh' churches.

a skeleton in the ashes of a rich dress,] See below.

"I am tired," said Miss Havisham.

Play."] The order to 'play', given like a command to a servant, may have been read ironically by those of Dickens's readers familiar with the theories of Friedrich Froebel (1782–1852), the German educator who stressed the importance of freedom and spontaneity to the child's natural development. The adaptation of Froebel's system 'to the character and habits of the English nation', the opening of an Infant Garden in September 1851, and talks and tracts by John and Bertha Ronge helped promote his ideas (1855, ix). Froebel's pioneering work was favourably reviewed by Morley in his 'Infant Gardens' (*HW* 11.577–82).

"No, ma'am, I am very sorry for you

melancholy—"] Pip's use of 'melancholy' ignores earlier humorial implications and signifies a general mental depression some physicians now label 'the Miss Havisham syndrome': a condition confined to wealthy and beautiful women who, at some climactic point in their personal history, react to catastrophic disappointment by willing themselves into seclusion and acting as if time stood still (Critchely). For a comparable general use of melancholy, see the description of Coketown as a place where 'the piston of a steam-engine worked monotonously up and down like the head of an elephant in a state of melancholy madness' (*HT* 1.5).

"So new to him," she muttered

Estella."] The significance of 'Estella' has been variously interpreted. Etymologically, the link with 'star' (French *étoile*; Latin *stella*) and with Sidney's fictional Stella (see p. 21) are persuasive. Stella and Estella are equally distant, aloof and unobtainable female characters both sought with equal intensity by their respective lovers (Endicott 158). Estella's frigid indifference, petulance and spoiled proud behaviour (the result of Miss Havisham's teaching) have also been attributed to Ellen Lawless Ternan (1839–1914), the 18-year-old actress Dickens met in August 1857 when she joined the cast of *The Frozen Deep* and *Uncle John*, two plays Dickens directed and acted in to raise funds for the Jerrold family. The disparity in age between the two has led some to argue that Ellen's teasing, frigid and tormenting behaviour supplied Dickens with a model for Estella, whose name, comments Edgar Johnson, 'seems a kind of lawless anagram upon some of the syllables and initials of Ellen's name' (2.991). The supposed connection between Estella and Ellen Ternan has been challenged by Tomalin and Slater on biographical grounds. For Tomalin, there are crucial differences between Dickens's character and the real Nelly, whose warmth, nervousness and responsiveness to Dickens's charm bear no resemblance to Estella; Slater, on the other hand, argues that Estella the tormentor and heartless ice maiden hearkens back to Dickens's first love, Maria Sarah Beadnell (1810–68). For Dickens's positive use of star imagery, see 'A Child's Dream of a Star', where he refers to 'one clear shining star . . . larger and more beautiful . . . than all the others' (*HW* 1.25). 'Estella' remains one of the less commonly used given names in England (Withycombe 101).

Chapter Eight

"Nothing but beggar my neighbour, miss."'

beggar my neighbour,] A children's game in which players turn over cards in an attempt to 'beggar' opponents by forcing them to surrender cards by following suit or by playing a matching number. The game can be played by two and is well suited to young players.

It was then I began to understand

It was then I began to understand that everything in the room had stopped, like the watch and the clock, a long time ago.] Dickens labelled the entry in his *Book of Memoranda* about the woman who had remained bedridden or room-ridden *'Done in Mrs Clennam'*(13). The portrait of Miss Havisham nevertheless repeats (with important variants) elements used earlier in *LD*:

> Bedridden (or room-ridden) twenty – five and twenty – years; any length of time. As to most things, kept at a standstill all the while. Thinking of altered streets as the old streets – changed things as the unchanged things – the youth or girl I quarrelled with all those years ago, as the same youth or girl now . . .

The chronology sketched by Herbert Pocket in chapter 22 supports the claim made in Appendix 1 that Miss Havisham's self-destructive willed seclusion dates from 1792–3, a date that fits the non-specific 'a long time ago'. Only a small discrepancy in the years appears if we assume that Pip's first visit to Satis House occurs in 1804, some twelve years *after* she was jilted on the morning of her wedding but about eleven *before* Herbert reveals in 1815 the reason for Miss Havisham's eccentric behaviour.

could have looked so like grave-clothes, or the long veil so like a shroud.] Nineteenth-century grave-clothes for women were often quite elaborate, resembling the 'rich dress' Pip speaks of when he first mentions Miss Havisham's faded white bridal gown. Grave-clothes were made from white brushed cotton and decorated with panels of matching brushed cotton with floral designs and white satin scalloped ribbon with a satin bar at the neck. The sleeves were slit open and the dresses backless (John Morley pl. 51). The veil that resembles a shroud refers to the winding sheet in which corpses were wrapped; those used for the rich were often fine fabrics painted or soaked with wax or some other adhesive substance.

So she sat, corpse-like, as we played at cards

I knew nothing then, of the discoveries that are occasionally made of bodies buried in ancient times, which fall to powder in the moment of being distinctly seen; but, I have often thought since, that she must have looked as if the admission of the natural light of day would have struck her to dust.] This phenomenon evidently fascinated Dickens; references to the rapid disintegration of long-interred corpses on their exposure to air also appear in *BH* (29), *TTC* (1.3) and *MED* (4). See also Edmund Ollier's 'Eternal Lamps', which relates the story of how a woman's body, buried in Roman times and found in the sixteenth century, 'fell into a heap of formless dust' when the tomb was discovered (*HW* 8.185). Additional sources include Victor Hugo's *Hunchback of Notre Dame* (41, 1831) and Tennyson's 'Aylmer's Field' (1864).

"He calls the knaves, Jacks, this boy!"

"He calls the knaves, Jacks,]   'Knave' was obviously correct and 'Jack' the vulgar term. Originally, the Jack signified only the knave of trumps in the game of All-Fours as distinguished from knaves in the other suits.

I was beginning to remind her that

to-day was Wednesday,]   See Appendix 1.

She came back, with some bread and meat

a little mug of beer.]   'Small' beer (see above) was served to family members and servants. Medical authorities tolerated the practice of serving weak beer to boys but thought water or tea preferable. Beer was suitable for youths who took unusual exercise, 'but strong ale should never be allowed'. Wine was considered even more harmful. A youth's 'young blood does not want to be set on fire with wine' (Chavasse, 1839, 123–4). Pip nevertheless refers to the 'warming and tingling' effect he feels from the beer and an improvement in his spirits. Dickens, only two or three years Pip's senior, often drank beer with the meals he bought when he worked at Warren's blacking factory (Forster 1.2.29).

I was so humiliated, hurt, spurned, offended, angry, sorry – I cannot hit upon the right name for the smart – God knows what its name was – that tears started to my eyes.]   Dickens spoke with similar intensity when he recounted how he started menial work in 1824 among 'common men and boys' at Warren's. 'No words can express the secret agony of my soul . . . and [I] felt my early hopes of growing up to be a learned and distinguished man crushed in my breast. The deep remembrance of . . . the shame I felt in my position . . . cannot be written' (Forster 1.2.22).

Feelings of inadequacy continued into Dickens's adult life, despite his obvious literary, social and financial success. Possible sources of self-doubt include his lack of formal education, his parents' humble origins and the knowledge that both paternal grandparents had earned their living as servants employed by Lord Crewe (Allen, 1988, 11–12; *Dickens Quarterly*, 1988, 175–85). Later in life, sneers by snobbish associates may have added to Dickens's sense of social inadequacy. Gossip circulated in some quarters about his 'vulgar' taste in clothes. He was also criticized for naming six of his sons after famous contemporaries and for sending Charley, his eldest, to Eton. Painful talk like this may have taken a toll on Dickens's sense of self-worth and deepened with personal feelings the exposure of the painful effects of humiliation Dickens describes in Pip's narrative.

But, when she was gone, I looked about me

one of the gates in the brewery-lane,]   The lane, evidently adjacent to Satis House, led to various outbuildings connected with the brewery. See above.

My sister's bringing up had made me sensitive.

My sister's bringing up had made me sensitive. In the little world in which children have their existence whosoever brings them up, there is nothing so finely perceived and so finely felt, as injustice. It may be only small injustice that the child can be exposed to; but the child is small, and its world is small,]   Compare 'Travelling Abroad' (7 April 1860), one of several reflective and partially autobiographical essays published some months before GE began in AYR as part of the UT series. Commenting on the impressionable nature of young children and their tendency to remember instances of cruelty and injustice, Dickens wrote:

> It would be difficult to overstate the intensity and accuracy of an intelligent child's observation. At that impressionable time of life, it must sometimes produce a fixed impression. If the fixed impression be of an object terrible to the child, it will be (for want of reasoning upon) inseparable from great fear. Force the child at such a time, be Spartan with it, send it into the dark against its will, leave it in a lonely bedroom against its will, and you had better murder it. (AYR 2.559)

At work on DS while living in Switzerland, Dickens had written to Forster in October 1846: 'We should be devilish sharp in what we do to children. I thought of that passage in my life at Geneva,' he reflected, recalling the period when his mother and the younger children joined John Dickens in the Marshalsea and handed Dickens over as a lodger to 'a reduced old lady' in Camden Town (*Letters* 4.653). Reflecting on his more recent sufferings of the last five years, Dickens wrote to Forster in June 1862: 'The never-to-be-forgotten misery of that old time bred a certain shrinking sensitiveness in a certain ill-clad, ill-fed child, that I have found come back in the never-to-be-forgotten misery of this later time' (*Life* 1.3.35).

a big-boned Irish hunter.]   A large, dense-boned horse, part thoroughbred and part Irish draught horse, popular with huntsmen on account of its long stride and stamina.

To be sure, it was a deserted place

To be sure, it was a deserted place, down to the pigeon-house in the brewery-yard. . . . But, there were no pigeons in the dovecot, no horses in the stable, no pigs in the sty,] Compare an idea Dickens recorded in 1855 for beginning a novel with the description of a house 'abandoned by a family fallen into reduced circumstances'. What remain are 'the numberless tokens' of the family's 'old comforts':

> Great gardens trimly kept, to attract a tenant – but no one in them – a landscape without figures. Billiard Room; table covered up, like a body. Great stables without horses, and great coach-houses without carriages. Grass growing in the chinks of the stone paving, this bright cold winter day. (*Memoranda* 7)

Dovecots were built to breed doves for food; the stables may have housed draught horses for beer-carts or horses for riding and for drawing a carriage.

no malt in the storehouse,] For the storage of malt, see note above.

no smells of grains] See below.

beer in the copper or the vat.] Copper vats were used for 'mashing': see note above.

All the uses and scents of the brewery might have evaporated with its last reek of smoke.] A working brewery gives off a variety of aromas in which grainy smells from the malted barley mingle with warm, sweet odours arising from the boiling wort. Hops when added to the wort would impart an additional overlay of bitter and sweet fragrances. The smoke Pip refers to would have come from coal or wood fires in the boiler-house (see above).

there was a wilderness of empty casks,] Brewers required an extensive stock of hand-made wooden casks in which to store and transport beer and ale to local pubs. Casks came in different sizes, ranging from pins (about five gallons) to hogsheads (about fifty-five gallons), and offered publicans as many as five choices. When empties were returned they had to be washed and inspected. New casks required curing and seasoning, and old ones service and repair.

Strong oak casks with stout iron hoops lasted for as long as thirty years, if they were carefully maintained. Beer drawn from wooden casks remained the custom for several hundred years until a growing demand for bottled beers late in the nineteenth century prompted changes. Several factors account for this, including the introduction of filtration, pasteurization and pressurization, all of which altered the production of beer and undermined traditional methods of brewing. Recent challenges to these developments in England have prompted several brewers to return to former practices, including the reintroduction of wooden barrels. These allow the natural yeasts in the beer to ferment and produce only a moderate degree of carbonation, unlike beer stored in and served from metal containers, whose greater gaseous quality arises from artificially introduced carbonation, added to compensate for the natural yeasts destroyed by pasteurization.

a certain sour remembrance of better days lingering about them;] Possibly an echo of *As You Like It*: 'If ever you have look'd on better days' and 'We have seen better days' (2.7.113, 120). In a literal sense, disused and unsealed casks, perhaps partially filled with rainwater, give off a sour, acidic smell, the product of wild yeasts and other bacteria. Such casks in the brewing trade were referred to as 'stinkers'. If neglected for too long, mouldy and acidic casks had to be broken up and used for firewood since they would spoil good beer. Cask maintenance among brewers represented an essential aspect of their business. An experienced foreman or supervisor counted sniffing the casks as one of his duties.

– and in this respect I remember those recluses as being like most others.] Presumably with contempt: 'What *is* a Hermit?' asks the narrator of the 1861 Christmas story and answers:

> A slothful unsavoury nasty reversal of the laws of human nature . . . and for the sake of GOD'S working world and its wholesomeness, both moral and physical, I would put the thing on a treadmill (if I had my way) wherever I found it'. (*AYR*, *Tom Tiddler's Ground*, 1–5)

Behind the furthest end of the brewery

the rank garden was the garden of the house,] Compare the description of the Warren, the residence of the reclusive Mr Haredale in *BR* (13), and the decaying, untended garden in Tennyson's 'Mariana' (1842). The image of the rank garden may also owe something to Hamlet's sense of the world as 'an unweeded garden/That grows to seed; things rank and gross in nature/Possess it merely' (*Hamlet* 1.2.135–7). The gardens of Restoration House are located immediately behind the house and not beyond the brewery, as they are in the novel.

in the brewery itself – by which I mean the large paved lofty place in which they used to make the beer,] Architects favoured lofty, tower-like buildings to take advantage of gravitation in the production of beer (see above). The tower attached to the former brewery on Victoria Street is about thirty-six feet high. Paved rather than wooden floors were equally functional: they were easier to maintain and permitted the use of water to hose and wash machinery and keep surfaces clear of the sugary residue from spilt wort and beer. In addition, they afforded partial protection from fire, a hazard architects sought to reduce (*Brewing: A Book of Reference* 1.10).

and where the brewing utensils still were.] Commercial brewers required several essential pieces of equipment: a wooden or metal mash-tub, or -tun, which was a large circular vessel with a false bottom pierced with small holes on which the malt rests, a copper boiler housed in a conical brick structure, where the wort was heated, coolers or vats, pumps and the working-tun, where fermentation occurs. Other utensils might include long poles or mashing-oars to stir the wort in the mash-tub.

the extinguished fires,]   Fires heated the water that was pumped into the mash-tub; a furnace below the copper boiler boiled the wort and hops. Fires in the boiler-house heated water to wash casks and supply hot water for cleaning. Additional fires may have been used to supply heat to kilns in order to roast the barley.

ascend some light iron stairs, and go out by a gallery high overhead,]   Brewers were advised by architects to avoid wooden stairs and stairways to minimize the risk of fire. The gallery evidently led outside to a flat roof, allowing access to the various water-cisterns and -tanks where 'liquor', the brewer's term for water, was stored for use in making beer.

It was in this place, and at this moment

I thought it a strange thing then, and I thought it a stranger thing long afterwards.]   Dickens added this sentence to the proofs, presumably anticipating two later scenes: the occasion in chapter 29 when Pip walks in the garden with Estella and is startled by the ghost of a connection that eludes him at the time, and the momentary reappearance of the illusory figure 'all in yellow white' suspended from the beam while walking there a third time that prompts him to return upstairs to assure himself that Miss Havisham was 'as safe and well' (chapter 49). The comment also adds to the retrospective voice of the narrative.

a great wooden beam in a low nook of the building near me on my right hand,]   The wooden beam may refer to part of the equipment used to lift sacks of malt. Alternatively, it may have supported either an archimedean screw to convey malt to a central hopper or an automatic weigher, a device with a weighing-box and counterweight, which operated a lever to close the feed as soon as the weighing-box was full.

Nothing less than the frosty light of the cheerful sky

the sight of people passing beyond the bars of the court-yard gate,]   Passers-by in Crow Lane are easily visible from the courtyard as one looks towards the street.

She laughed contemptuously

the four-mile walk to our forge;]   See Appendix 4, map p. 449.

Chapter 9 Sixth weekly number
5 January 1861

The worst of it was that that bullying old Pumblechook

heaving with windy arithmetic,]   Teachers expected children to develop the ability to calculate sums rapidly in their head. Accordingly, arithmetic – 'the art of computing by numbers' and mastering 'four separate operations, Addition, Subtraction, Multiplication, and Division' – was taught to children as *mental* arithmetic (Mavor 150–1). Putting a series of rapid questions to children thus became standard pedagogical practice. The approach required rote learning, constant drilling, and rapid response to problems posed orally by the teacher.

Pedagogues justified the need for proficiency in this skill on practical grounds. England's pre-decimal coinage required the mastery of one's money tables and the aliquot parts of the pound sterling, Britain's central unit of money, which, prior to decimalization in 1971, was divided into twenty shillings, and each shilling, in turn, was divided into twelve pennies or pence (see also below). Although this system seems odd, the division of a pound into 240 equal parts made the pound capable of division into halves, thirds, quarters, fifths, sixths, eighths, tenths, twelfths, fifteenths, sixteenths, twentieths, twenty-fourths, thirtieths, fortieths, forty-eighths, sixtieths, eightieths, and one-hundred-and-twentieths. A decimal system allows only halves, quarters, fifths, tenths, twentieths, twenty-fifths, and fiftieths (Lewis). Irregular weights (avoirdupois, apothecaries' weights and troy weight) and liquid measures added further difficulties.

Dickens's opposition to Pumblechook's mode of instruction, in which 'the bright childish imagination is utterly discouraged' as pupils are turned into 'little parrots and small calculating machines', is well known. Compare also his parody of the practice in the harrowing 'lessons' Mr Murdstone gives David, demanding the cost of 'five thousand double-Gloucester cheeses at fourpence-halfpenny each' (*DC* 4). See also *Speeches* (241) and Shatto, 1974.

"First (to get our thoughts in order)

Forty-three pence?"]   The answer requires the rapid division of the numerator (43) by twelve to determine the number of shillings and express the remainder in pennies. In this case, there are three shillings (12 x 3=36) and seven pennies left over. The sum could have been written in one of two ways: as 3s 7d, in which the shilling is represented by 's' and the penny by a 'd' (for 'denarius', a Roman silver coin which was also used as the name for the English silver penny), or more simply as '3/7'.

Mr. Pumblechook worked his head like a screw

fardens,]   'Farden', a dialectical variant of the now extinct farthing, worth one

106   THE COMPANION TO GREAT EXPECTATIONS

quarter of a penny. Pennies, half pennies and farthings were all copper coins; each remained in existence until 1971.

"I'll tell you, Mum," said Mr. Pumblechook.

a sedan-chair.]   Sedan chairs – closed vehicles seating one person and carried on two poles by two bearers, one in front, the other behind – were introduced into England, possibly from Italy, in the sixteenth century. They remained fashionable until the early part of the nineteenth century.

If they had asked me any more questions

a balloon in the yard,]   Interest in balloons dates from the reading of papers at the Royal Society in 1782 on the property of hydrogen; experiments by the brothers Étienne and Joseph Montgolfier between 1782 and 1783, first in Annonay and then in Paris, demonstrated in public the principle of inflating hot-air balloons with gases lighter than common air. Further experiments with model balloons using both hot air and hydrogen led quickly to manned flights, the first of which carried the Montgolfier brothers across Paris on 21 November 1783. A surge of enthusiasm for ballooning followed and quickly spread throughout Europe, before ceasing abruptly during the period of the French Revolutionary wars (1792–1802). The French pioneered the use of balloons for the purpose of military observation in 1794, but neglected the application, leaving ballooning in the nineteenth century mainly to showmen for public amusement and to scientists for meteorological investigation (McNeil 609–12). Descriptions of balloon ascents appear in 'Vauxhall Gardens by Day' (*SB*) and in 'Lying Awake'(*HW* 6.146–7).

a bear]   Bears in captivity were generally kept for bear-baiting, a form of public entertainment that lingered to the end of the eighteenth century.

Now, when I saw Joe open his blue eyes

a young monster,]   For Mary Shelley's *Frankenstein*, see chapter 27, note on p. 237.

some genteel trade – say, the corn and seed trade]   The description of his own business as 'genteel' underlines Pumblechook's false airs and graces, although selective exceptions to the stigma of trade led to confusion. See chapter 22, note on pp. 198–9.

As I fixed my eyes hopelessly on Joe

Where do you expect to go to?"]   Children who attended Sunday school were taught to tell the truth always. Since lies came from 'the father of lies', those who told them would inevitably go to Hell. See below.

"There's one thing you may be sure of, Pip," said Joe

the father of lies,] A common epithet for the Devil. The phrase originates when Jesus challenges the claim his critics made to have descended from Abraham. On the contrary, he replies, 'Ye are of *your* father the devil. . . . When he speaketh a lie, he speaketh of his own: for he is a liar, and the father of it' (John 8.44). Compare also Prince Hal's comment to Falstaff: 'these lies are like their father that begets them – gross as a mountain, open, palpable' (*1 Henry IV* 2.4.214–15).

That was a memorable day to me

Pause you who read this,] Compare the Roman inscription, 'Siste, Viator' ('Stop, Traveller'). For a slight variation, see Mr Sapsea's epitaph in *MED* (4) and Jacobson (66). The thought Pip considers returns to issues the novel raises about the existence of patterns of cause and effect working to shape one's life and the individual's ability or failure to make choices of his own. Further treatment of this idea occurs when Pip records his 'impression' that Magwitch, too, may have pondered 'over the question whether he might have been a better man under better circumstances'. To Magwitch's credit, Pip adds, he never tried to excuse himself by hinting that his lot had been hard, or by trying 'to bend the past out of its eternal shape' (chapter 56), a verdict which applies equally to the narrator.

the long chain of iron or gold, of thorns or flowers] Compare the imagery used to invoke the differences and contradictions defining the world we live in with Milton's observation in *Areopagitica*. Recalling how the temple of Solomon was built in ancient times out of many different materials, including cedar and stone as well as gold and silver, he reminds us that 'it is not possible for man to sever the wheat from the tares, the good fish from the other frie; that must be the Angels Ministery at the end of mortal things'. Perfection, rather, consists not in flawless unity and uniformity but in many different materials and arises out of 'many moderat varieties and brotherly dissimilitudes' (*Works* 4.342–9).

Chapter 10

The felicitous idea occurred to me a morning or two later

The felicitous idea occurred to me]   Originally chapter 10 opened at what is now the fourth paragraph beginning 'Of course, there was a public-house in the village' (*Norton* 427).

a morning or two later]   See Appendix 1.

The Educational scheme or Course

The Educational scheme or Course established by Mr. Wopsle's great-aunt may be resolved into the following synopsis.]   Dickens's 'synopsis' resembles conditions that prevailed earlier in the century and those which members of the 1858 Royal Commission on Education reported as still existing in many parts of the country. Dame schools were 'little more than nurseries'. Women were always the teachers; invariably they were 'advanced in life, and their school is usually their kitchen, sitting and bed-room'. The little instruction that went on was given in a close, crowded and oppressive atmosphere. 'The children sit round the room, often so thickly stowed as to occupy every available corner.' Most of the time was spent in knitting and sewing until they were called up individually to be taught the alphabet and some easy words (*BPP, Education, General* 29). Dickens himself briefly attended one such school in Chatham, brief recollections of which appear in 'Our School' (*HW* 4.49).

a birch-rod.]   A tightly bound bundle of birch twigs was commonly used to chastise children. The practice originated in the fifteenth century and extended beyond schools to workhouses and even police stations, where refractory boys could be birched by a constable in the presence of a superior officer and at the request of a parent or guardian. Recalling memories of the dame school he attended in Rome Lane, Chatham, Dickens spoke of his first days there 'under the dominion of an old lady, who to my mind ruled the world with the birch' (*Speeches* 323).

the pupils formed in line and . . . passed a ragged book from hand to hand. . . . As soon as this volume began to circulate, Mr. Wopsle's great-aunt fell into a state of coma;]   Reading primers in dame schools were in notoriously short supply. Children, noted one government inspector, 'frequently spend a great part of the school hours sitting on forms round the kitchen, with dog-eared pages of spelling books in their hands, from which they are supposed to be learning, while the "schoolmistress" is engaged in sewing, washing or cooking' (quoted in Horn, 1974, 26).

speckled all over with ironmould,]   The detail suggests that the books were old: yellow or brown specks or spots point to machine-made paper of the late eighteenth century. The causes of this discoloration are not completely understood. Some book conservators suggest that airborne fungi cause yellowish-brown stains in the leaves of books; others propose that minute particles of iron from either mineral deposits in the water used during the production of paper or from the beaters of the pulp early in the process of paper-making account for the stains. The term 'ironmould', which suggests that the blotches are fungoid in origin, has been replaced by 'foxing', or 'foxed', and refers in the art world to (fox) colour.

one low-spirited dip-candle] Dip-candles made from tallow or left-over cooking fat provided poor illumination. Such candles 'blaze unsteady at every movement in the atmosphere, gutter, and run down in channels, and soon consume'. The candles were so-called because of the way they were made:

> To make the dips, the cotton wicks are disposed in numerous rows upon sticks, suspended aloft over the *vat*. The dipper then bends down several broaches of sticks into the liquid fat below, gently raises these up, and proceeds with others, alternately, until the *making* assumes the required size and weight.
> (*Complete Book of Trades* 435–6)

Candles cast in a mould, an invention ascribed to a French manufacturer early in the eighteenth century, provided an option for the more affluent (see chapter 8).

snuffers.] Snuffers, a scissor-like device, were used to 'snuff' or trim the wick to prevent it from falling over and melting what remained of the candle below. Snuffers were so contrived 'that they do not snuff the candle too low, or snuff it out, unless so designed; nor drop the snuff on the candle' (Anderson 4.708).

It appeared to me that it would take time,

moist sugar,] Unrefined or partially refined sugar.

a large old English D . . . from the heading of some newspaper, and which I supposed . . . to be a design for a buckle.] Old English (or English) is a black-letter font with an angular emphasis derived from Fraktur, a gothic type believed to have originated in Germany c.1510. Old English was often used for the masthead of newspapers, as in The$\mathfrak{D}$aily —. Dickens spoke of his own pre-literate associations with certain letters dating from the time when his mother taught him the rudiments not only of English but also of Latin. Explaining how the associations he formed then still existed, Dickens told Forster: 'when I look upon the fat black letters in the primer, the puzzling novelty of their shapes, the easy good nature of O and S always seem to present themselves before me as they used to' (Forster 1.1.6).

Of course there was a public-house in our village

Three Jolly Bargemen,] An old weatherboarded tavern in Lower Higham perhaps served as the 'original' of the fictional public house. The Chequers Inn in Chequers Street was 'a picturesque wooden hostelry, with a red-tiled roof, tall chimneys, and an old-fashioned interior, full of narrow passages and low-ceilinged rooms lighted by little small-paved lattices' (Gadd, 1929, 17). Dickens invented the name but may have been influenced by several local examples. The partiality for three was common. There was an inn called the Three Boys near Lower Higham (Frank S. Johnson, 1924), the Three Merry Boys, a tavern below Chattenden Woods, nearby, the Three Gardeners at Strood, the Three Daws at Gravesend, and the Three Crutches in Watling Street, not far from Gad's Hill Place (Gadd, 1929, 18). Pub signs also appealed to the occupations of working men: brickmakers, watermen, butchers, etc.

There was a bar at the Jolly Bargemen

long chalk scores . . . on the wall]   The use of chalk scores by publicans to keep track of customers' accounts dates back to the sixteenth century. 'On tick', or writing up with chalk a 'score', represented an account of credit given; when debts were settled, the chalk score could be erased. The bar at the Chequers had several long scores (Gadd, 1929, 17).

a quantity of chalk about our country,]   Chalk was (and is) found in abundance in the region of the Hoo peninsula. Its presence accounts for the lime industry of northeast Kent (see chapter 53) and the development, later in the century, of several cement works around the Medway estuary.

It being Saturday night

It being Saturday night, I found the landlord looking rather grimly at these records,]   Saturday, the traditional workman's payday, was also the time for settling accounts.

He was a secret-looking man

His head was all on one side, and one of his eyes was half shut up, as if he were taking aim at something with an invisible gun.]   Dickens ascribes a similar mannerism to Henry Thomas Buckle (1821–62), the empirical historian to whom he alluded earlier in his description of Mr Gradgrind (Simpson 15). Engaged to dine with Buckle on Saturday, 30 May 1854, Dickens confided to a friend that Buckle was a man who had read every book that was ever written 'and was a perfect Gulf of information':

> Before exploding a mine of knowledge he has a habit of closing one eye and wrinkling up his nose, so that he seems to be perpetually taking aim at you and knocking you over with a terrific charge. Then he loads again,

and takes another aim. So you are always on your back, with your legs in the air. (*Letters* 7.343)

"I wouldn't wish to be stiff company," said Joe.

"Rum."]   Rum was the next-cheapest spirit to gin.

The stranger, with a comfortable kind of grunt

a flapping broad-brimmed traveller's hat, and under it a handkerchief tied over his head in the manner of a cap;]   Hats with low flat crowns and wide curving brims were worn mainly in the country (Sichel 24). The Gothic Mr Rudge is similarly attired when he arrives at the Maypole Inn on a dark, stormy night (*BR* 1).

"No doubt, no doubt.

Do you find any gipsies, now, or tramps, or vagrants of any sort out there?"]   Vagrants, tramps and gypsies evidently passed west of Chalk and kept to the Dover road, which ran through Chatham and Rochester, on its way from London to the coast. So many 'tramps and wayfarers of a singularly undesirable description' walked by Dickens's house on Gad's Hill, he kept two large dogs partially for protection (Forster 8.3.214). In 'Tramps' (16 June 1860), Dickens comments on members of 'that numerous fraternity' encountered on 'the hot dusty roads near seaport towns and great rivers' (*AYR* 3.230, 234).

"What the Blue Blazes is he?"

"What the Blue Blazes is he?"]   A slang expression, often used as a curse. The phrase may derive from an idiom used by blacksmiths to designate the readiness of metal for hammering. Common terms included 'blood-red heat', 'white heat', 'welding heat' and 'blue heat'. The last phrase is used to indicate the temperature required for hammering articles in cast steel, which is lower than that for either cast iron or for joining two pieces of iron.

Mr Wopsle struck in upon that

having professional occasion to bear in mind what female relations a man might not marry;]   *The Book of Common Prayer* provides 'A Table of Kindred and Affinity Wherein Whosoever are Related are Forbidden in Scripture and our Laws to Marry Together'. The table, based on a list drawn up by Archbishop Parker in 1563, specifies thirty relations a man may not marry. Parish clerks would have known this information.

The choice of one's marriage partner was further narrowed in 1835 by Lord Lyndhurst's Act (5 & 6 Will. 4, c. 54), which made marriages of affinity as well as of consanguinity absolutely void rather than merely voidable. Attempts to modify this act by allowing marriage with a deceased wife's sister did not succeed until 1907 (7 Edw. 7, c. 47).

a most terrifically snarling passage from Richard the Third,]   Probably the scene in Act 1 in which old Queen Margaret overhears Richard wooing his sister-in-law, Lady Anne, whose husband he had recently killed. Margaret calls the two 'wrangling pirates' and asks:

> What? were you snarling all before I came,
> Ready to catch each other by the throat,
> And turn you all your hatred now on me?
> 						(*Richard III* 1.3.187 ff.)

the same inflammatory process]   That is, one that produces ophthalmia, inflammation of the eyes.

He did this so that nobody but I saw the file;

I knew it to be Joe's file, and I knew that he knew my convict, the moment I saw the instrument.]   Dickens offers no explanation for the transfer of the file, unlike the two one-pound notes (see below), which are clearly accounted for in chapter 28.

"Stop half a moment, Mr. Gargery," said the strange man.

"I think I've got a bright new shilling somewhere in my pocket, and if I have, the boy shall have it."]   A coin of this denomination – one twentieth of a pound – would indeed have been a treat. At the beginning of the century, 'The condition of the country in regard to the coined money in circulation . . . was exceedingly unsatisfactory'. The mint issued scarcely any silver coins: 'The shillings and sixpences that passed from hand to hand by common consent were almost all of them blank pieces of silver, intrinsically worth less than half the sums at which they were current' (Porter, 1836, 2.238).

I took it out of the paper

out of the paper,]   One-pound notes issued by the Bank of England measured 7° by 4° inches. Each note was numbered, first on the words 'I promise,' and second on the words 'for bearer' (Wills and Dickens, 'Two Chapters on Bank Note Forgeries', *HW* 1.618–19). The letterpress on the notes – black copperplate writing on a light-coloured background – typically read, depending on the year in which they were issued: 'Please pay to [blank] on Demand the sum of One pound. Date 1819 August 18 London. For the Governor and Comptroller of the Bank of England' (Johnson Collection, 'Bank Notes English A–F'). See also below.

Nothing less than two fat sweltering one-pound notes

two fat sweltering one-pound notes] This was a generous gift, a larger sum than many working-class men or women earned during a sixty-hour week, for whom a typical income in 1857 was estimated at 24 shillings a week or £60 a year. Compare also the five (later six) guineas a week Wilkie Collins received for his work on HW. Data from the Bank of England shows that prices (not wages) have risen roughly forty-fold since Victorian times, which would make the windfall the equivalent of about £80 (based on Lewis). See also chapters 13, 18, 24 and 37 for other references to specific sums and the note about Pip's annual income when he comes of age (chapter 36, note on p. 292).

The two one-pound notes belong to what Dickens termed 'the small-note era'. The period began when cash payments in gold were suspended by the Bank of England on 25 February 1797 and continued until the end of 1817. Prior to 1797, no notes were issued for small sums, and even five-pound notes did not exist until 1793 (Wills and Dickens, HW 1.615). The Bank of England introduced this measure to ease the demand for gold during the war against France from 1793 to 1815. During these years the market-price of gold remained high, driven by the Continental blockade, which kept British goods from almost every port in Europe and created obstacles to foreign trade (Porter, 1836, 2.238–40). Silver coinage, too, remained in short supply, and no silver coins were issued by the government until 1816.

One-pound notes remained in circulation and supplied the place of guineas until payment in specie was gradually resumed in 1817. Continued efforts by forgers to circulate counterfeit notes prompted their withdrawal in 1821. See also chapter 39, note on p. 309.

that seemed to have been on terms of the warmest intimacy with all the cattle markets in the county.] A variant of this image of dirty money occurs in MC when Dickens describes banknotes handled by farmers attending a county market as 'greasy wealth' which they tuck into their 'bulky pocket-books' (5).

Prior to 1797, the use of notes was limited mainly to 'the affluent and the educated', making banknotes 'a rarity and a "sight" ' to 'a vast number of the humbler orders'. The suspension of cash payments by the Bank of England and introduction of one- and two-pound notes ushered in a new era. Notes inevitably became ' "common and popular" ' since many who had never seen them were now called on 'to take one or two pound notes in exchange for small merchandise, or their own labour'. As a result, bills turned loose into 'fairs and markets' quickly assumed a dirty appearance after circulating among the less fastidious members of society (HW 1.615–16).

In The Book of Snobs (1846–7), Thackeray notes how some members of the upper class reacted to the widespread circulation of coins. It used to be the custom 'of some very old-fashioned clubs' in the City of London that, when a gentleman 'asked for change for a guinea, always to bring it to him in *washed silver*: that which had passed immediately out of the hands of the vulgar being considered "as too coarse to soil a gentleman's fingers" '. Following his analysis of the broader implications of washing, Thackeray comments how, during a generation or so, the City Snob's money 'washes' into estates, woods, castles and town-mansions, and passes eventually as 'real aristocratic coin':

> Old Pump sweeps a shop, runs of messages, becomes a confidential clerk and partner. Pump the Second becomes chief of the house, spins more and more money, marries his son to an Earl's daughter. Pump Tertius goes on with the bank; but his chief business in life is to become father of Pump Quartus, who comes out a full-blown aristocrat, and takes his seat as Baron Pumpington, and his race rules hereditarily over this nation of Snobs. ('Great City Snobs', *Works* 9.42–3)

GE documents a comparable tale of social fluidity, showing how new money (from brewing and from sheep-farming in Australia) pursues old status and creates heightened expectations whose ill effects the novel exposes.

I had sadly broken sleep when I got to bed

I saw the file coming at me out of a door, without seeing who held it, and I screamed myself awake.] Compare Macbeth's guilt-ridden vision of the 'fatal dagger' in the air as he steels himself to murder Duncan: 'Is this a dagger which I see before me, /The handle toward my hand: Come, let me clutch thee!' (*Macbeth* 2.1.34–48).

Chapter 11 Seventh weekly number
 12 January 1861

AT the appointed time I returned to Miss Havisham's

AT the appointed time] Cf. Job: 'Is there not an appointed time to man upon earth?' (7.1). Literally, another week appears to have elapsed. This scene occurs on a Wednesday early in January.

"You are to come this way to-day," and took me to quite another part of the house.] This other part may refer to the south wing of Restoration House. Clearly, Pip and Estella don't take the stairs from the side-entrance that lead to the first floor and to Miss Havisham's rooms. The 'small paved court-yard' into which they exit appears to have separated the south wing from the 'detached dwelling-house' to the side. See below.

The passage was a long one

the whole square basement] Basement, in this context, evidently refers to the whole lower part of Satis House.

I found myself in a small paved court-yard, the opposite side of which was formed by a detached dwelling-house, that looked as if it had once belonged to the manager or head clerk of the extinct brewery. There was a clock in the outer wall of this house.] 'This detached dwelling-house still stands behind the high enclosing wall of Restoration House, with its gable end towards the road. It is now called "Vines Cottage", but it stands on part of the land belonging to Restoration House, such a place attached to the Satis House of the story, exactly as [Dickens] said' (Gadd, 1929, 68).

It opened to the ground

It opened to the ground, and looked into a most miserable corner of the neglected garden,] One can look into the garden of Restoration House from the Vines Cottage.

one box-tree that had been clipped round long ago, like a pudding,] The art of clipping trees into ornamental or fantastic shapes dates from the sixteenth century. Box-trees were favoured on account of their thickness and density.

There were three ladies in the room

they were all toadies and humbugs, but . . . each of them pretended not to know that the others were toadies and humbugs: because the admission that he or she

did know it, would have made him or her out to be a toady and humbug.] Reflections on toadies and humbugs, tentatively dated 1858–60 by Kaplan, occur in Dickens's *Book of Memoranda*:

> The House-full of Toadies and Humbugs.
> They all know and despise one another; but
> – partly to keep their hands in, and partly
> to make out their own individual cases – pretend
> not to detect one another. (79)

'Toady' and 'humbug' have lost currency as terms of contempt. A toady, or toad-eater, derives from the attendant of a charlatan, who was employed to eat, or pretend to eat, toads (held to be poisonous) to enable his master to show his skill in expelling poison (*OED*). 'Humbug', a cant word which came into vogue about 1750, signified an impostor, fraud or deceiver.

Fawning and parasitic relatives were one of Dickens's peeves. Dependants surrounded him to such an extent that he remarked on one occasion that 'I never had anything left to me but [needy] relations'. Amongst these were his own and his wife's parents, and his brother Alfred Lamert Dickens, who died 'worth nothing' on 27 July 1860 and left 'a widow and five children – you may suppose to whom' (*Letters* 9.287).

They all had a listless and dreary air

Camilla,] An English and Italian name. According to tradition, Camilla was the name of a warrior maiden, Queen of the Volscians, who fought in the army of Aeneas (*Aeneid* 7.803–17).

"Poor dear soul!" said this lady

"Nobody's enemy but his own!"] Compare 'It smarts not halfe so ill as the phrase Euery body's friend but his owne' (Cornwallis, *Essays*, 1600, no. 7) and also Fielding's *Tom Jones* (1749): 'Tom, tho' an idle, thoughtless, rattling Rascal, was no-body's Enemy but his own' (*Tom Jones* 4.5). Estella also uses the same expression (chapter 33).

"Cousin Raymond," observed another lady

"Cousin Raymond,"] In the MS, proofs and text of *AYR*, Cousin Raymond began as 'Cousin John', before Dickens switched to Raymond later in the chapter when the Pockets, led in by Estella, come to watch Pip walk Miss Havisham round the room containing her decayed bridal feast.

"we are to love our neighbour."]   Compare the response of Jesus to the man who asks what one should do to have 'eternal life': 'Honour thy father and thy mother: and Thou shalt love thy neighbour as thyself' (Matthew 19.19; see also Leviticus 19.18).

"Sarah Pocket," returned Cousin Raymond

Pocket,"]   Mr Pockett was the name of the landlord of the George Hotel in Nailsworth, Gloucestershire, where Dickens stayed in January 1858 (Brian Davis, 1989, cited in Clarendon xvi).

"Poor soul!" Camilla presently went on

when Tom's wife died, he actually could not be induced to see the importance of the children's having the deepest of trimmings to their mourning? 'Good Lord!' said he, 'Camilla, what can it signify so long as the poor bereaved little things are in black?']   Victorian funeral practices recognized degrees of mourning, each of which was signalled by the appropriate use of colours and trimmings. The 'deepest of trimmings' (required when one's wife or husband died) would have included the addition of black lace, ribbons, buttons and other useless accessories to the children's dresses. Disregard for funeral rites encouraged outsiders to conclude that one took lightly the death of a spouse or close relative.

"You know I was obliged," said Camilla

with a D,]   This is an instance of 'demi-swearing', a tendency towards 'super-refinement' in language some arbiters of good manners regarded as a form of vulgarity. The rule for the use of euphemisms was simple. 'If it be indelicate to mention a thing, let it never be mentioned by any name whatever, if it be not indelicate to mention it, it cannot be so to use its ordinary proper name'. To illustrate, the writer noted how if legs are 'naughty' let us never speak of them; 'if not naughty, why blush to call them legs', adding that if legs be 'a naughty idea, then no recourse to "limbs" will save you' (*The Habits of Good Society*, 1860, 53).

As we were going with our candle

along the dark passage,]   Frequent reference to the dark passageways in Satis House appears to have some basis in fact. Possibly knowledge of local traditions about underground passages in the house also influenced Dickens's portrait of Satis House.

"Well! Behave yourself.

Now mind!" said he,] After 'he' MS reads 'threatening me with his great forefinger'.

With those words, he released me

scented soap] Scented soap and fine white soap were generally imported from Spain, Portugal, France, Italy or Tunis, where olive oil, from which these soaps were made, was plentiful. Common household soap and soft soap, both a mixture of potash and fish oil, were the two other kinds of soap widely available.

I crossed the staircase landing

I crossed the staircase landing, and entered the room she indicated.] The room opposite Miss Havisham's living room measures approximately thirty-two feet by nineteen feet. Panelled walls and a large fireplace with an Adam-style carved mantelpiece add to the room's elegance and handsome proportions. Stairs with treads up to 5 feet 6 inches wide and a generous landing contribute to the overall spaciousness of this part of the house.

an épergne or centre-piece] Épergnes (derived from the French *épergner*, 'to save') became popular in Europe and Britain from about 1730 and were designed to save guests the trouble of passing dishes at the dining-table. A basic design included two or three branches radiating from a stem with baskets for bread, cake, fruit, or containers for condiments. These centrepieces – silver or silver-plated – stood about a foot or more high and could extend to almost six feet from one side to the other.

I heard the mice too

I heard the mice too, rattling behind the panels] Compare: 'the mouse/Behind the mouldering wainscot shrieked,/Or from the crevice peered about' (Tennyson, 'Mariana', ll. 63–5; Gilmour, 1979, 140).

These crawling things had fascinated my attention

the Witch of the place.] Possibly an embedded allusion to one of the Weird Sisters in *Macbeth*; see chapter 38, note on p. 299.

If only Estella had come to be a spectator of our proceedings

we posted on] That is, they travelled like a courier delivering letters, who hired horses from inns along the road for use over a designated stage. Messengers or post-boys carrying important letters of state travelled considerable distances in the shortest possible time this way.

"Very easily said," remarked Camilla

ginger and sal volatile] Doctors commonly prescribed both ingredients as antidotes to indigestion and 'languors and flatulent cholic' (Henry H. Gregory, 1837, 5.46–7). Ginger was administered either in powdered form or as syrup of ginger; *sal volatile* (ammonium carbonate) was taken in small quantities either on a lump of sugar or mixed with peppermint or plain water. The salt's aromatic property was also widely utilized in solution as a stimulant or restorative in cases of fainting and hysterical fits.

nervous jerkings . . . in my legs.] Victorian doctors attributed these symptoms to a combination of indigestion and mild hysteria common among women between the ages of 15 and 30. Designated as especially vulnerable were women who combined 'a highly nervous temperament with spare habit of body'. Other causes of nervous pains reported by female patients were said to originate from 'disappointed love, jealousy, undue excitement, ungratified desires, and all powerful mental emotions, which act strongly on the nervous system, and tend to induce disorders or menstruation' (Keith Imray, 1842, 367). Sir Benjamin Brodie, the foremost Victorian authority on diseases of the joints, went so far as to say that 'at least four-fifths of the females among the higher classes of society, who are supposed to labour under diseases of the joints, labour under Hysteria and nothing else' (quoted in Imray 367).

Hysteria, viewed this way by doctors, reflects a moral judgement: many disapproved of the extent to which women were alternately pampered and encouraged to do little and then stimulated by a life of late nights, balls, parties and amusements. Going to bed early, rising early and exercising regularly on foot or on horseback in 'pure air' were prescribed as preferable and likely to promote a healthy life. Such a regimen, combined with an endeavour 'to acquire a degree of self-control, sufficient to enable [women] to prevent their tempers being ruffled by various sources of irritation to which every one must be subject' would benefit those who suffered from the symptoms Dickens describes. Meanwhile, applications of cold water or aromatic vinegar to the head and neck or doses of *sal volatile* offered temporary relief.

The Raymond referred to, I understood to be the gentleman present

Mr. Camilla.] Pip's fatuous reference underlines how the couple are given no surname by Dickens and claim kinship with Miss Havisham through Camilla, a Pocket before she married and, like her brother Matthew, a cousin of Miss Havisham. 'Cousin' was frequently used to refer to any distant relation, hence Sarah Pocket's use of the term.

"There's Matthew!" said Camilla.

I have taken to the sofa with my staylace cut, and have lain there hours, insensible, with my head over the side, and my hair all down, and my feet I don't know where"]   Laced two-pieced underbodices with metal, wood or whalebone inserts embracing the chest and designed to compress the waist, were popular throughout much of the century; cutting the tightly drawn laces was an emergency measure undertaken to allow the wearer to breathe. Can we wonder, asked Dr E. J. Tilt in 1853, 'that the sex suffers from shortness of breath, palpitation, indigestion, hysteria, and a host of maladies . . . incompatible with sound health?' (196). 'To be shaped like a wasp was . . . the object of female ambition; and so tight did [women] lace themselves, or rather so tightly were they laced, for it required assistant strength to fasten their girths, that women have frequently fainted from the pressure, and some actually perished by this monstrous kind of suicide' (Southey, 1807, 291).

Concern about the harm caused by wearing stays mounted during the century. An entry in the 'Chronicle' (26 April 1831) records how the jury returned a verdict that 'the deceased died of apoplexy, produced by her stays being too tightly laced'; later in the century, the Registrar General stated bluntly: 'To wear tight stays is in many cases to wither, to waste, to die' (*Annual Register; Nineteenth Annual Report*, 1858, 194–5). The long-term effects on women were equally pernicious, leading to physical distortion and the harmful compression of the soft boneless area of the waist. Fragile and airy forms might result, one doctor conceded. But sylph-like waists were often accompanied by paleness and melancholy, sure symptoms '*of feeble health*' (Combe, 1860, 104–5). Others noted that tight-lacing caused many illnesses, induced a 'general sense of languor and fatigue' (Flinn, 1886, 23), and reduced women to 'a sort of dull, negative suffering, the result of low vitality' (Ballin 7). In 'Malvern Water', Harriet Martineau speaks out against tight-lacing (*HW* 4.70).

'Without expecting any thanks

the pianoforte-tuner's across the street]   Piano-tuning represents a relatively late occupation as pianos (ascribed to B. Cristofori c.1710) replaced harpsichords following their introduction into England during the eighteenth century.

"I suppose there's nothing to be done," exclaimed Camilla

to feast on one's relations – as if one was a Giant]   In myths and in folk-lore giants and ogres feast on their children. See, for example, the cannibalistic giant in 'Jack and the Beanstalk'.

"On this day of the year, long before you were born

sharper teeth than teeth of mice have gnawed at me."]   *King Lear* 1.4.312: 'How

When I had exhausted the garden

a fallen-down grape-vine] Grapes had been introduced into Rochester by Bishop Gundulf when he founded a Benedictine priory there in 1082. The site of a former vineyard operated by the monks directly across from Restoration House still remains as a piece of open ground, now called 'The Vines'. For Dickens's walks through the Vines and past Restoration House, see chapter 29, note on pp. 253–4.

looked out of window.] Victorian usage omitted the definite article. Compare with an entry in the *Book of Memoranda*: 'The office-boy for ever looking out of window' (19).

"Halloa!" said he, "young fellow!"

fellow!"] 'Fellow' implies condescension, an appropriate address for a servant or person of humble rank. Pip ignores the insult, noting that he 'politely' omitted the phrase when he answered.

"Laws of the game!" said he.

"Laws of the game! . . . Regular rules!" Here, he skipped from his right leg on to his left. "Come to the ground, and go through the preliminaries!" Here, he dodged backwards and forwards, and did all sorts of things while I looked helplessly at him.] Many sons of gentlemen were exposed to boxing in the course of their education (*DC* 21). By the 1790s the sport had begun to gain wider acceptance, owing largely to the efforts of two men, Jack Broughton (1705–89) and John Jackson (1769–1845). Broughton drew up rules for the conduct of fights and helped separate boxing from bare-fisted pugilism by introducing padded gloves for sparring. Jackson, who exploited the use of padded gloves, was a superb all-round athlete and England's greatest teacher of boxing. His gymnasium in Old Bond Street, London, made him one of the best-known figures of the Regency era.

One result of these developments, which coincided with growing aristocratic patronage of the sport, was that boxing came to be regarded as a 'manly' amusement that taught boys to admire true courage, 'applaud generosity; to acquire notions of honour, nobleness of disposition, and greatness of mind' (Egan, 1828, 5.736). Egan also maintained that prizefighting taught English boys that 'fair play is the cry, and victory falls to the lot of him who has the greatest science, or the greatest strength'.

Rules governing prize-fights nevertheless remained minimal until the introduction of the Queensberry Rules in 1867. This code, the work of Sir John Sholto Douglas (1844–1900), 8th Marquis of Queensberry, required the use of padded gloves and introduced limits to the number and length of rounds. Earlier fighters often duelled for as many as forty or fifty rounds in contests which lasted from sixty to ninety minutes.

I was secretly afraid of him when I saw him so dexterous

a bottle of water and a sponge dipped in vinegar.]   A piece of linen or sponge soaked in vinegar and water and applied to the forehead, temples and around the nose was a popular remedy to stop nasal bleeding. Prize-fighters also made use of bottles filled with water and brandy to clean the bloodied hero 'or to revive his exhausted spirits, with that most essential article the *sponge*' (Egan, 1812, 3.18).

His spirit inspired me with great respect.

seconding himself according to form,]   Under the rules introduced by Broughton, seconds brought their respective contestants into the middle of the square stage where they fought. Seconds also interceded to declare their man beaten if he was unable to rise after he was knocked down. Herbert, anxious to put his superior knowledge to good use, has to act as his own second in the absence of an assistant.

went on his knees to his sponge and threw it up:]   A conventional gesture to indicate the defeat of one contestant.

Chapter 12 Eighth weekly number
19 January 1861

My mind grew very uneasy

the County Jail]   County gaols held accused prisoners awaiting trial at the assizes. See also chapter 57, note on p. 411.

When the day came round for my return

When the day came round for my return]   See Appendix 1.

myrmidons of Justice, specially sent down from London,]   A scornful reference to the Bow Street Runners from London's Bow Street police station (see chapter 16, note on pp. 148–9). Myrmidons were originally legendary Greek warriors from a warlike tribe in Thessaly; later usage broadened the meaning to a faithful follower who executed orders without question.

On the broad landing between Miss Havisham's own room

I entered, that same day, on a regular occupation of pushing Miss Havisham in this chair . . . round her own room, and across the landing, and round the other room. Over and over and over again, we would make these journeys, and sometimes they would last as long as three hours at a stretch.]   The dimensions of Restoration House lend plausibility to the time 'these journeys' apparently absorbed. A circuit of the two largest rooms – one measuring 32 feet by 18 feet and a second 21 feet by 17 feet – together with the landing, 16 feet by 5 feet, comes to around two hundred yards. In the course of a day's employment, Pip would have covered several miles.

I insensibly fall into a general mention of these journeys as numerous, because it was at once settled that I should return every alternate day at noon for these purposes, and because I am now going to sum up a period of at least eight or ten months.]   See Appendix 1.

There was a song Joe used to hum fragments of at the forge

There was a song Joe used to hum . . . Old Clem. This was not a very ceremonious way of rendering homage to a patron saint;]   Dickens's knowledge of the song possibly dates from one of his visits to 'the Yard' as a child ('Chatham Dockyard', *AYR*, 29 August 1863, 12–13), where blacksmiths employed by the navy could be heard singing 'Old Clem' as they beat out metal in the course of their work. St Clement I (fourth Pope, died AD 97) is the patron saint of tanners; St Dunstan (909–

Perhaps I might have told Joe

I did not know then, though I think I know now.]   MS reads 'Shade of Poor Biddy, forgive me!' Dickens deleted this elegiac intrusion from the proofs.

Meanwhile, councils went on in the kitchen at home

with respections]   More commonly the singular form, 're'spection' or 'respection', was used, as in 'Then sayd Christ, goe thou and do likewise, that is, without difference or respection of persons' (Tindale, *Works*, 1573, 78/2, cited in the *OED*). The phrase is now obsolete.

In these discussions, Joe bore no part.

I was fully old enough now, to be apprenticed to Joe;]   That is, about 14 (see chapter 7). In the time-scheme of the novel, six or more years have now passed, making the phrase 'a long time' much longer than the 'period of at least eight or ten months' mentioned earlier in the chapter. Critics have pointed out that the representation of time in this chapter remains confusing. Equally unspecific is the ambiguous 'We went on in this way for a long time' in the next paragraph, an obvious contrast with the careful presentation of chronological details elsewhere in the novel. See also Appendix 1.

She said no more at the time

On the next day of my attendance]   That is, the next day but one, according to the arrangement by which Pip returned 'every alternate day' at noon. See above.

"You had better be apprenticed at once.

indentures,]   'Indenture' derives from the French *endenter*, to 'jag' or 'notch', 'and signifies a Writing, which contains an Agreement between different Persons, whereof there are two Copies, which being cut, *waved* or *notched*, tally to one another when put together, and prove the Genuineness of both' (S. Richardson 1–2).

CHAPTER TWELVE   125

When I got home at night

my sister "went on the Rampage,"]   See note in chapter 2, p. 41.

a Negress Slave]   Britain's involvement with the African slave trade dates from the seventeenth century. Following the growth of plantation economies in the New World, Britain acquired a virtual monopoly on the transatlantic traffic in people. A legal decision in 1772 held that English courts refused to view slavery as an enforceable contractual agreement; the British slave trade was abolished in 1807. Emancipation throughout the British Empire followed when Parliament passed the Abolition Act of 1833 (3 & 4 Will. IV, c. 73).

Chapter 13

It was a trial to my feelings

court-suit]   Pip refers jokingly to the attire Joe selects for the ceremony as his court-dress, a suit worn by men at a royal court consisting of a cut-away jacket with tails, knee breeches, white stockings, black pumps and a light sword.

he pulled up his shirt-collar so very high behind,]   This appears to be a sign of respectability: to show little or no linen was judged 'seedy'. Ninette's father in Henry James Byron's 1858 burletta makes a similar gesture in response to criticism by pulling up an enormous shirt-collar (*The Maid and the Magpie* 1.1).

We walked to town

We walked to town,]   Walking was the accepted way to travel both long and short distances. Only the affluent travelled either by private coach or on horseback.

beaver bonnet,]   Bonnets made from beaver fur were fashionable in the nineteenth century. Women liked beaver on account of its glossy quality and the fur's ability to take a rich black dye without impairing its sheen. Beaver fur also wore well and repelled water. A combination of domestic and foreign skins from British settlements in Canada and Hudson's Bay supplied the demand for beaver fur, most of which went to hat-makers.

carrying . . . the Great Seal of England in plaited straw,]   The Great Seal is the main and original seal of authentication used by British monarchs to make wax impressions on state documents. On ceremonial occasions the Great Seal is carried in processions in 'a magnificently embroidered case'. The Lord Chancellor, the highest-ranking judge in England, is the usual custodian of the Great Seal (Bentley *et al.*).

a pair of pattens,]   Pattens, pieces of wood adapted to the shape of the sole of women's shoes, had 'fastening ears, or *patten ties*, to each side of the instep'. Pattens bore an obvious resemblance to clogs but they differed principally on account of the iron ring by which they were attached to the bottom of the wearer's shoe. In rural districts, unpaved roads and the lack of adequate drains made pattens popular among women and girls. In towns, clogs began to supersede pattens during the nineteenth century, but pattens were frequently worn by servants when doing such jobs as mopping floors (*Complete Book of Trades* 371–2).

whether these articles were carried penitentially or ostentatiously;]   By the third century the Christian church had developed a system of public penance as a means of atoning for post-baptismal sin. Punishments included fasts, continence, pilgrimages, floggings and imprisonment. Later these lengthy ordeals were replaced by a system of commutation which, in turn, led to the introduction of penitential books. These were codifications of the elaborate network of laws and disciplinary penalties associated with various mortal sins.

much as Cleopatra . . . might exhibit her wealth in a pageant or procession.] The judicious allusion is to the well-known description by Enobarbus of Cleopatra's procession on the river of Cydnus to meet Mark Antony:

> The barge she sat in, like a burnish'd throne,
> Burn'd on the water. The poop was beaten gold;
> Purple the sails, and so perfumed that
> The winds were love-sick with them; the oars were silver,
> Which to the tune of flutes kept stroke, and made
> The water which they beat to follow faster,
> As amorous of their strokes. For her own person,
> It beggar'd all description. She did lie
> In her pavilion, cloth-of-gold, of tissue,
> O'erpicturing that Venus where we see
> The fancy out-work nature. On each side her
> Stood pretty dimpled boys, like smiling Cupids,
> With divers-colour'd fans, whose wind did seem
> To glow the delicate cheeks which they did cool. . . .
> (*Antony and Cleopatra* 2.2.195–205)

"You expected," said Miss Havisham

premium] A fee paid to the master in return for board and instruction. In the case of young apprentices, premiums were generally paid by either a parent or a guardian.

"Pip has earned a premium here," she said

five-and-twenty guineas] A guinea was twenty-one shillings (£1 1s 0d), making the actual sum £26 5s. Subsequently reported by Joe, followed by Pumblechook, as 'five-and-twenty pound', the change appears to indicate a shift in the social register: the guinea was considered a more gentlemanly amount than £1. You paid tradesmen, such as blacksmiths or carpenters, in pounds but gentlemen, such as artists, in guineas, a unit always specified for the rate of pay to the contributors of *HW* (Lewis). The sum was a handsome gesture on two counts: (1) by 1837, when premiums paid to blacksmiths were recorded as being 'very low', £20 for the full term of an apprentice's indentures was considered a relatively high fee (*Complete Book of Trades*, 408); (2) payment in gold was particularly valuable since the scarcity value of coins during this period (see chapter 10, note on p. 112) meant that guineas were worth even more. The equivalent sum today would be about £1,040.

"Well!," cried my sister, with a mollified glance at Mr. Pumblechook.

Rantipole]   In the eighteenth and early nineteenth century, 'rantipole' was used to describe a wild, ill-behaved or reckless person. Compare also Grose: 'A rude romping boy or girl' (1811). From the mid-century onwards, the term was applied to Louis Napoleon, who assumed dictatorial powers in 1851 and reigned as Napoleon III, Emperor of France (1852–70).

The Justices were sitting in the Town Hall near at hand

The Justices]   Civic officials, including the city magistrates, the Mayor and the City Recorder. Presiding over the binding of apprentices was one of their regular duties.

Town Hall near at hand,]   Rochester Town Hall (also known as the Guildhall), 'a handsome brick structure supported by coupled columns, of stone, in the Doric order, the under part of which is open to the street' (Hasted, 1778, 2.8; Denne, 1817, 240–1), in the High Street. See also below.

picked a pocket]   Individuals charged with any crime first appeared before a local magistrate. Pick-pockets flourished in London and other cities. For the penalties imposed on young boys, see Paroissien (1992, 249).

fired a rick;]   Rick-burning was a rural crime associated with agricultural unrest in the 1820s and 1830s. The disturbances were most pronounced in southern England, where men marched, burned hayricks and smashed agricultural machinery as a protest against low wages and the high cost of bread. Incendiarist activity peaked in 1830–1 in Kent, Surrey, Berkshire, Hampshire, Oxfordshire and Dorset, prompting harsh and decisive penalties. Of the 2,000 or more insurgents tried that year, nineteen were hanged and 481 transported to Australia for terms of seven or fourteen years.

One person of mild and benevolent aspect]   A derisive allusion to reformers who were often criticized for overlooking the imposition of harsh penalties as a means of discouraging crime. Quakers and Evangelicals were in the forefront of those pressing for the repeal of England's 'ancient killing system' as it operated at its height during the years 1770–1830 (Gatrell 9). Thomas Carlyle condemned those who spoke 'beautiful whitewash and humanity and prison-discipline; and such blubbering and whimpering, and soft Litany to divine and also to quite other sorts of Pity, as we have had for a century now' (*Latter-Day Pamphlets*, 'No. II Model Prisons', 1850).

a tract ornamented with a woodcut of a malevolent young man fitted up with a perfect sausage-shop of fetters, and entitled To be read in my Cell.]   Publications like this, usually printed on a single sheet with a woodcut and decorative borders, were widely distributed as part of the flood of printed material that was poured out on the lower classes by those 'anxious to improve their minds and souls'. The practice

12 Rochester Guildhall

13 Interior: the Court Hall 'with some shining black portraits on the walls'

was pioneered by John Wesley and taken up by various religious and educational movements which flourished between 1830 and 1850 (James 135–8).

The Hall was a queer place, I thought

The Hall was a queer place, I thought, with higher pews in it than a church] Rochester Guildhall stands on the north side of the High Street on the site of the city's old corn exchange. The present building, built in 1687, originally consisted of a Court Hall, Council Chamber, city gaol and accommodation for the gaoler. The Hall and Council Chamber are still used today for meetings of the city council. (see Plate 12).

The Guildhall served several functions in the nineteenth century. The city Recorder conducted quarterly sessions there for the borough. Apprentices were also bound in the Court Hall, a lofty room, 47 feet by 28 feet, supported by a series of stone columns beneath which a covered area served as the main city market (see chapter 7, note on p. 81). A richly ornamented ceiling, which displayed the arms of the city and those of Admiral Sir Cloudsley Shovel, at whose expense the ceiling was installed (Dugdale, 1819, 3.234) and the carved wooden staircase leading to the Hall created an impressive effect which the interior of the building still retains. The 'pews' no longer exist. (see Plate 13)

and with mighty Justices (one with a powdered head) leaning back in chairs, with folded arms, or taking snuff, or going to sleep, or writing, or reading the newspapers] Local magistrates depicted in *OT* are similarly invigilant (3). The habits of powdering hair (see chapter 40, note on p. 320) and taking snuff retained their popularity among older gentlemen in the nineteenth century. Snuff is ground tobacco which has been moistened with a solution of common salt, then placed in heaps and allowed to ferment, and dried and supplemented with flavourings. By the eighteenth century, snuff-taking surpassed all other ways of using tobacco, but lost ground to cigar- and pipe-smoking early in the nineteenth century. Snuff-taking required a snuff-box or container and a handkerchief to sneeze into after an application.

with some shining black portraits on the walls, which my unartistic eye regarded as a composition of hardbake and sticking-plaister.] Sixteen large oil paintings now hang in the Court Hall, including portraits of William III and Queen Mary attributed to Sir Godfrey Kneller, and a collection of Rochester MPs, aldermen and former city mayors. Among the local dignitaries are Richard Watts, MP for Rochester in 1563 and owner of Satis House (see p. 95), and Alderman Thomas Stevens, Mayor of Rochester in 1787 and 1801, the original owner of Gad's Hill Place, Higham, the house Dickens purchased in 1856. In 1819, Dugdale listed the two full-length portraits of William III and Queen Anne at the upper end of the hall, portraits of Sir Joseph Williamson and Richard Watts at the lower end, and at the sides Sir John Jennings, Sir Thomas Colby, Sir John Leake, Sir Thomas Palmer and Sir Stafford Fairborne (Dugdale, 1819, 3.323) For a complete list, see Moad, App. I. The blackness of the paintings prompted several amateur attempts at cleaning and restoration, the first of which occurred in 1834.

Discoloration and ageing in the coats of varnish applied to oil paintings result in the darkening and cracking of the surface. Hardbake was a common name for almond toffee made from boiled sugar or treacle and blanched almonds. Sticking plasters, used to close cuts, consisted of a solution of isinglass and tincture of benzoin laid upon a piece of fabric spread with an adhesive.

When we had come out again

the boys who had been put into great spirits by the expectation of seeing me publicly tortured,] Hanging, whipping, sentencing malefactors to time in the stocks were all public rituals, enacted before onlookers of all ages and both sexes. In theory, such displays served both to deter potential offenders and to punish the body with degrees of severity calibrated to fit the seriousness of the crime, in accordance with old notions of punishment. Efforts by penal reformers begun in the 1770s gradually eliminated all forms of public torture, including public executions, which, after 1868, were conducted in virtual secrecy behind prison walls until Britain abolished capital punishment in 1964.

my friends were merely rallying round me,] Pip speaks ironically: 'to rally round' meant to assist or support someone. It was a current political expression which Dickens elsewhere used facetiously – for example, of Little Swills in *BH* (11): 'his friends will rally round him'; and of Mr Veneering in *OMF* (2.3), when he contemplates standing for Parliament 'but requires breathing time to ascertain "whether his friends will rally round him" '.

the Blue Boar,] The choice of inn sign (the Blue Boar) reflects a common one found throughout England. The sign derives from 'a blewe Bore with his tuskis and his cleis and his membres of gold', originally a 'Badge of Cognizance' worn by Richard Duke of York, father of Edward IV (Larwood and Hotten, 342). See also Appendix 2.

However, they were grown up and had their own way

on my being liable to imprisonment if I played at cards, drank strong liquors, kept late hours or bad company, or indulged in other vagaries which the form of my indentures appeared to contemplate as next to inevitable,] Injunctions to young apprentices were explicit. They were commanded, 'chearfully and willingly, without Hesitation, Murmuring or Reluctance', not to do damage to their masters, not to 'commit Fornication, nor contract Matrimony within the said Term' of their service, and not to sell their own goods, without licence from their masters. Apprentices were also instructed not to 'play at Cards, Dice, Tables, or any other unlawful games'; taverns, playhouses and other 'powerful Incentives to Mischief' were equally off limits (Richardson 3–13).

My only other remembrances

Collins's Ode, and threw his blood-stain'd sword in thunder down,]   See chapter 7, note on p. 75.

"The Commercials underneath sent up their compliments]   Inns commonly reserved rooms for private gatherings and for the meetings or functions of recognized groups. Rochester's Bull set aside one room specifically for commercial travellers and their customers on the opposite side of the archway leading to the inn's central courtyard, above which was an apartment reserved for private parties (Gadd, 1929, 49). A detailed description of the 'commercial room' of the fictitious Peacock Inn of Eatanswill (based on Sudbury in Suffolk) appears in *PP* (14).

'Commercials', agents for manufacturers or wholesale traders, travelled widely to show samples and solicit orders. A significant number of them were linen drapers, many of whom came from Scotland, Lancashire, Somerset and Devon (Charles Manby Smith, 1857, 309). Commercial travellers flourished in the days before rail and journeyed from district to district by horse and gig. Distaste for them was common. Commercials had a reputation for loud and uncouth behaviour, including whistling, standing in front of the fire 'with their back to it and their hats on', and pulling off their boots in public (Albert Smith, 1855, 23).

the Tumbler's Arms."]   Possibly the name contains an allusion to Wopsle's noisy rendition of Collins's 'Ode' (see chapter 7), which, acted out with props, may have sounded like a group of tumblers executing vaults, somersaults, leaps and other gymnastic feats. This suggestion was supplied by Margaret Simpson.

they were all in excellent spirits . . . and sang O Lady Fair! Mr. Wopsle taking the bass, and asserting . . . that *he* was the man . . . and that he was upon the whole the weakest pilgrim going.]   Dickens summarizes the first verse of a popular song for three voices by Thomas Moore (1779–1852) appropriate for a night walk:

> Oh, Lady fair! where art thou roaming?
> The sun has sunk, the night is coming.
> Stranger, I go o'er moor and mountain,
> To tell my beads at Agnes' fountain.
> And who is the man, with his white locks flowing?
> Oh, Lady fair! where is he going?
> A wand'ring Pilgrim, weak, I falter
> To tell my beads at Agnes' altar.
> Chill falls the rain, night winds are blowing,
> Dreary and dark's the way we're going. (1802)

Chapter 14   Ninth weekly number
                                                                                                    26 January 1861

IT is a most miserable thing to feel ashamed of home.

IT is a most miserable thing to feel ashamed of home. There may be black ingratitude in the thing, and the punishment may be retributive and well deserved; but that it is a miserable thing, I can testify.] These reflections appear to have an autobiographical element similar to the embarrassment Dickens felt when his father was imprisoned for debt. Recalling how Bob Fagin insisted on escorting him home from work after a bout of sickness at the blacking factory, Dickens explains: 'I was too proud to let him know about the prison', where his parents resided. So after several efforts to 'get rid of him' he bid his companion goodbye. Dickens then walked up boldly to a house near Southwark Bridge, knocked on the door and waited as if to be admitted (Forster 1.2.27).

Home had never been a very pleasant place to me

Home had never been a very pleasant place to me. . . . But, Joe had sanctified it. . . . I had believed in the front door . . . the kitchen as a chaste though not magnificent apartment . . . the forge as the glowing road to manhood] The representation of home as the source of virtue and emotion played a central role in the creation of a Victorian ideology about domestic life. This paragraph appears to conflate emphasis on home as a sacred place with a comic allusion to the Lares and Penates, the household gods who presided over the homes and domestic concerns of the ancient Romans.

Once, it had seemed to me

the dust of small-coal,] Blacksmiths used small or slack coal – coal broken into small pieces – because it was cheap.

For, though it includes what I proceed to add

I never ran away and went for a soldier or a sailor.] Young men enlisted for a variety of motives: destitution, restlessness, the desire to escape parental authority or a bad master. Others fled to escape responsibility for an illegitimate child or because they were lured by the prospect of an extended debauch on the recruiting money (Myerly 54). Later, Pip momentarily considers enlisting for India as a private (chapter 40), a statement which signifies absolute desperation: 'none but the worst description of men enter the regular service', noted the Duke of Wellington. Outcasts, tramps, petty thieves, bumpkins, fools and others desperate from poverty joined the ranks; enlisting for service in India, where assignments were longer and the climate was unhealthy, offered an especially bad bargain (Myerly 3).

the virtue of industry,] For possible allusions to Hogarth's series of engravings, *Industry and Idleness* (1747), see chapter 19, note on pp. 172–3.

What I wanted, who can say?

What I dreaded was, that in some unlucky hour I, being at my grimiest and commonest, should lift up my eyes and see Estella looking in at one of the wooden windows of the forge. I was haunted by the fear that she would, sooner or later, find me out, with a black face and hands, during the coarsest part of my work, and would exult over me and despise me.] The fear of being watched in humiliating circumstances can be traced directly to personal experience. After the blacking warehouse moved from Hungerford Stairs to a building on the corner of Chandos and Bedford streets, Dickens describes how he and Bob Fagin worked, 'for the light's sake', near the window. As the two tied and labelled pots of blacking, passers-by often stopped to watch the boys at work. On one occasion, when 'quite a little crowd' had gathered, Dickens noticed his father approach. 'I saw my father coming in at the door . . . when we were very busy, and I wondered how he could bear it,' he wrote of the painful experience of being involuntarily observed (Forster 1.2.32).

Chapter 15

AS I was getting too big for Mr. Wopsle's great-aunt's room

AS I was getting too big for Mr. Wopsle's great-aunt's room,] Dame schools were really infant schools. They received children as soon as they could speak and walk and continued up until the pupils were 7. Such schools, in effect, functioned as public nurseries. Evening schools from 1839 onwards took children between the ages of 12 and 16.

a comic song . . . bought for a halfpenny.] Songs, bought cheaply in bulk from presses such as Catnach and Pitts, were sold in the streets by ballad-sellers for a penny (Cotsell 51).

the only coherent part . . . were the opening lines,] The words may represent a composite version of different songs: 'The Astonished Countryman' ('When first I came to London Town'), 'When I arrived in London Town' and 'When I to London first came in'. The last appeared in *The Universal Songster* (1825, 1.245). 'Too rul loo rul' is a familiar refrain. Ballads, comic songs and folk-songs often told of young men going to London. Some, like Dick Whittington (d.1423), made their fortune; others, like the subject of this one, met with trouble. To be 'done very brown', or 'to do thoroughly', is slang meaning to be taken in or deceived. The expression occurs in *PP*: ' "He goes in rayther raw, Sammy," said Mr Weller . . . "and he'll come out done so ex-ceedin' brown, that his most formilar friends won't know him" '(43). Compare also the words of 'The Yorkshire man in London'. Another variant, used for advertising purposes by Robert Warren and sung to the tune of 'Auld Lang Syne', goes as follows:

> When to Lunnun town I came,
> On a visit, on a visit,
> When first to Lunnun town I came,
> Good lauk! how folks amazed me:
> For some I seed with Boots so bright,
> That they reflected back the light,
> I at them gaz'd with sike delight,
> By gum they almost crazed me
> Fol di rol, etc. (John Johnson, 'Oils and Candles', box 1)

a dramatic lay-figure,] A lay figure was a jointed wooden figure of the human body used by artists as a model to display shawls, draperies, etc. Pip means that he was not given any lines to learn and was used as a mute foil for Wopsle's own acting.

CHAPTER FIFTEEN   137

It was pleasant and quiet

when the tide was low, looking as if they belonged to sunken ships that were still sailing on at the bottom of the water.] The ebb tide in this reach of the river could lower ships or barges from a vantage-point behind the battery walls by about four feet. The sails most likely belonged to Thames sailing barges, capacious, sea-worthy craft, despite their shallow draught and low freeboard (Tomlinson and Tomlinson, 1934).

whenever the light struck aslant afar off, upon a cloud or sail or green hillside] Low hills on the Essex shore about a mile away are easily visible from Cliffe marshes.

Miss Havisham and Estella and the strange house and the strange life appeared to have something to do with everything that was picturesque.] By the early nineteenth century, 'picturesque' had become a general term of approval for scenes perceived to be not only pleasing but also interesting on account of their irregularity, disorder and even decay. 'Picturesque' was coined in the eighteenth century to express admiration for the idealized landscapes and gardens depicted in the work of seventeenth-century painters like Nicholas Poussin, Claude Lorraine and Salvator Rosa. In Britain the concept was then applied to the principles of landscape gardening developed by William Kent and Humphry Repton before being extended to include the fashionable preference among travellers for the wild scenery of Wales, the Lake District and Scotland.

"That's true, Pip

a set of shoes all four round] On average, saddle horses required shoeing once every four weeks except during the winter season. Blacksmiths charged about five shillings for a set of four, bringing the annual cost of nine sets of shoes to about £2 5s (Kitchiner, 1827, 2.12).

But Joe had got the idea of a present in his head

shark-headed screws] A trade term for 'round-headed' screws, which were introduced about 1800. Their predecessors were all flat-headed and had no point (Bridgeman 315).

"Well," said Joe, still harping on it

And if it was a toasting-fork, you'd go into brass and do yourself no credit. And the oncommonest workman can't show himself oncommon in a gridiron – for a gridiron IS a gridiron,"] Most brass items were produced by braziers, who worked with a hammer, or by specialists in brass foundries, who cast 'every variety of ornamental and useful article from brass' (*Complete Book of Trades* 67). A wrought-iron gridiron for broiling meat or fish would be a more appropriate item for a young apprentice. Toasters, long-handled forks with brass stems and tines or prongs, were common from the sixteenth century and were used for toasting bread or muffins on an open fire. Bronze, copper and brass long-handled forks became popular later once brass production emerged as a major activity in the eighteenth century, with Bristol and Birmingham as the principal centres. Simple, functional designs gradually gave way to ornate work as the market for twisted tines and shafts and ornamental handles developed (Strong 226).

"Yes, Joe; but what I wanted to say

if you could give me a half-holiday to-morrow, I think I would go up-town] A work week was six full days. Half-days, for an apprentice, would be at his master's discretion.

Now, Joe kept a journeyman at weekly wages

Now, Joe kept a journeyman at weekly wages] Originally the paragraph began without the introductory adverb; but since this is the first mention of Orlick it appears that Dickens added the 'Now,' to alert the reader. Rosenberg cites this revision as an instance of Dickens's vigilance with transitions and the kind of constant reworking evident at this stage of composition. A former, more awkward introduction of the journeyman – heavily deleted but deciphered by Rosenberg – reads: 'whom I have purposefully withheld from mentioning until now' (*Norton* 428). A similar instance recurs in chapter 19 with the introduction of Trabb's boy as 'the most audacious boy in all that countryside'. The initial 'Now,' present in the MS, was lost from subsequent versions but is adopted by Rosenberg (118, 428).

a journeyman at weekly wages] Originally, a journeyman was someone who was employed to work by the day (*journée*) and was paid daily for his labour. Unlike an apprentice, a journeyman received no systematic instruction and was therefore unable to advance his career or establish his own business. For this reason, journeymen were often equated with servants and looked down on as men lacking 'rational employments' and given to drinking, card-playing and singing indecent songs. By the middle of the century, the term was used to describe any mechanic who was hired to work for another, whether by the month, the year or any other period. A skilled journeyman in the iron trade in the 1830s could earn between thirty and forty shillings a week, if he were good at wrought-iron work; second-rate hands earned much less (Porter, 1836, 3.241–3; Adolphus 3.390; Buchanan 408; *Complete Book of Trades* 408).

whose name was Orlick.] 'Horlick' appears among the names listed in the *Book of Memoranda* to be ticked off after use (14). John Cayford (see chapter 2) states in his

'Recollections' that he supplied the name 'Orlick' (a grocer's boy he knew) and the idea for the fight between Joe and his journeyman, which Dickens reportedly based on Cayford's account of his having picked up and thrown down a journeyman 'of exceedingly bad quality and treacherous temper' who attempted to provoke Cayford into a fight (Richards 465–6).

He pretended that his christian name was Dolge – a clear impossibility] 'Dolge' originally appeared as 'Doolge' in the Book of Memoranda (14). The first version suggests ooziness and marshes, associations Dickens retains in Orlick's chosen lodging, the sluice-keeper's, and in his habit of lying around on Sundays 'on sluice gates'. The name is clearly 'impossible' since no such Christian name exists.

Cain or the Wandering Jew,] Cain, the biblical archetype of an outcast, slew his brother Abel, was driven from Eden for his crime and was destined to wander in distant lands 'as a fugitive and a vagabond' cut off from the presence of the Lord (Genesis 4.8–16). The Wandering Jew is a mythical figure based on a man who is said to have taunted Jesus on his way to crucifixion: when Jesus paused, he denied him any rest and urged him to move more quickly. The scoffer was subsequently condemned to wander the earth until the second coming of Christ. The Wandering Jew reappears in folk-legends under various guises, sometimes as a wise man who urges repentance and righteousness on others. Interest in the legend continued into the nineteenth century, providing a subject for German, French and British writers.

He lodged at a sluice-keeper's out on the marshes,] Sluice-keepers monitored the flow of water from drainage channels and dikes, and adjusted the sluice by opening or closing the upper portion of a wooden gate erected across a stream or brook. This system of drains and floodgates served to protect the rich alluvial topsoil from being swept away by flooding. A small house or cottage allowed keepers to attend to their work at all hours. For a possible 'original' of the house 'out on the marshes', see chapter 52, note on p. 378. Self-acting sluices introduced later in the century made sluice-keepers redundant. There were sluice gates on the canal that ran across the marsh to Cliffe Creek about a mile west of Cliffe village (Gadd, 1926, 184). See Appendix 4, map p. 449.

This morose journeyman had no liking for me.

When I was very small and timid, he gave me to understand that the Devil lived in a black corner of the forge, and that he knew the fiend very well: also that it was necessary to make up the fire, once in every seven years, with a live boy, and that I might consider myself fuel.] Bogey tales and stories of dangerous predatory figures filled Dickens's childhood reading. See 'Nurse's Stories' (AYR 3.517–21).

he always beat his sparks in my direction,] Fragments of hot metal fly off when iron or steel is hammered on an anvil. William Mavor describes work in the forge in one of his lessons for children:

Come, let us go to the smith's shop. What is he doing: He has a forge: he blows the fire with a great pair of bellows to make the iron hot. Now it is hot. Now he takes it out with the tongs, and puts it upon the anvil. Now he beats it with a hammer. How hard he works! The sparks fly about: pretty bright sparks! What is the blacksmith making: He is making nails, and horse-shoes, and a great many things. (*The English Spelling-Book*, 1819)

"I'd be a match for all noodles and all rogues," returned my sister

noodles]   A simpleton, a stupid or silly person (*OED*).

"You're a foul shrew, Mother Gargery," growled the journeyman

Mother Gargery,"]   'Mother' could be used as a prefix instead of 'Mrs', particularly to address a lower-class elderly woman.

"What did you say?" cried my sister

I must remark of my sister, what is equally true of all the violent women I have ever seen, that passion was no excuse for her, because it is undeniable that instead of lapsing into passion, she consciously and deliberately took extraordinary pains to force herself into it, and became blindly furious by regular stages;]   Subsequent observers have corroborated the apparently self-induced nature of some hysterical fits and the 'quality of volition and deliberateness' evident in convulsions (Shorter, 1992, 97). Compare also the description of Mrs Snagsby's behaviour in *BH*, a woman who responds to stress by 'delivering herself a prey to spasms' (25).

"Ah-h-h!" growled the journeyman

I'd hold you under the pump,]   Perhaps a variant of one of the punishments given to scolds, who were tied to ducking-stools and immersed in water as an inducement to curb their tongue. Both ducking-stools and stocks were in use in various parts of England during the early part of the century (Southey, 1807, 204 n.). Hand-cranked pumps to raise water were common, especially in country districts, where several houses might share a single facility. Plumbing and piped water became standard in many parts of England by the 1840s.

"O! To hear him!" cried my sister

threw her cap off,]   Many women in the eighteenth and early nineteenth century wore a light muslin cap over their hair when indoors, secured by a broad ribbon

CHAPTER FIFTEEN   141

which passed under the chin. Compare also Miss Pocket, who wears 'a very hideous one, in the nature of a muslin mop' (chapter 29). Some also wore a cap under a bonnet.

a perfect Fury]   The Furies (Erinyes in Greek mythology) were avenging goddesses whose role was to punish crimes, especially those committed against one's kin. 'Furies' derives from the Latin, *Furiae*.

What could the wretched Joe do now

whether he was man enough to come on?]   A slang expression meaning to start a fight.

"Abroad," said Miss Havisham; "educating for a lady

"Abroad . . . educating for a lady;]   Estella's destination was France (chapter 33), an anachronistic detail in view of the proposed early date of the action (see Appendix 1) since England and France were still at war in 1812. Most likely she would have gone to Paris, which offered 'numerous establishments for the education of young ladies' (Planta 341). Schools of this kind, collectively known as 'finishing' schools, flourished from the beginning of the century onwards both in France and in England. They catered primarily to a homogenous group of 'young ladies', offering dancing, music and other forms of refinement in preparation for the marriage market rather than intellectual training (Burstyn 24). The year Maria Beadnell spent in Paris (1829–30) created a painful separation for Dickens, traces of which perhaps inform this scene (Slater 51). In 'Sentiment' (*SB*), a haughty, self-important MP expresses hostility to such establishments, exclaiming, after his daughter elopes from Minerva House, Hammersmith: 'I'll bring in a bill for the abolition of finishing schools'.

As I was loitering along the High-street

the bookshop]   Wright's 1838 *Topography* lists three bookshops in Rochester High Street.

the affecting tragedy of George Barnwell,]   Forms of this 'old London story' about a ruined apprentice include 'The Ballad of George Barnwell' and George Lillo's *The London Merchant; or, The History of George Barnwell* (1731), to which Dickens refers. Lillo's, a domestic tragedy in prose, relates the fall of an innocent London apprentice who, seduced by Sarah Millwood, a prostitute, robs his employer and murders his uncle. In Lillo's hands, Barnwell becomes a complex figure, full of doubt and remorse, and profoundly penitent after his arrest for murder. Lillo adds Maria Thorowgood, the daughter of Barnwell's master, as a foil to Millwood and confines the action to London. The play was immediately popular; productions continued for many decades as 'proper entertainment for apprentices at Christmas and Easter', until growing contempt for the play's melodrama and pathos led to its eclipse. Revivals ceased in 1819, the first year with no production in London during the Christmas season. High-spirited youths of the middle class led astray by women were later accused of 'Barnwellizing', that is mixing with 'the ladies of the saloon, and escorting them through all the luxury of brawls, brandy, and brothells – cards, dice, d–n–t–n . . .' (Wight, 1833, 8). Minor references to *The London Merchant* appear in *PP* (10), *BR* (4) and *MC* (9).

No sooner did he see me, than he appeared to consider that a special Providence had put a 'prentice in his way to be read at;]   Compare *Hamlet* (5.2.208–9): 'There's a special providence in the fall of a sparrow'. For Wopsle's début on stage as Hamlet, which this reference may anticipate (Gager 274, 294), see chapter 31.

just as the street and the shops were lighting up.]   Oil-lamps supplied most public lighting until the introduction of gas to illuminate streets in the 1820s. See chapter 33, note on pp. 280–1.

As I never assisted at any other representation of George Barnwell

As I never assisted at any other representation of George Barnwell, I don't know how long it may usually take; but I know very well that it took until half-past nine o'clock that night, and that when Mr. Wopsle got into Newgate, I thought he never would go to the scaffold, he became so much slower than at any former period of his disgraceful career.]   The play is in five acts; a dramatic reading within about three hours is feasible. Beginning after tea late in the afternoon, the reading could have taken up to 9.30 before Barnwell was arrested. Several short scenes follow, however, before Barnwell greets his executioners by saying 'Tell 'em I'm ready' and is marched off to be hanged. Dickens added the detail about Newgate prison (see chapter 20, note on p. 182); in Lillo's play, Barnwell is held in an unspecified dungeon.

I thought it a little too much that he should complain of being cut short in his flower after all, as if he had not been running to seed, leaf after leaf, ever since his course began.]   A paraphrase of Barnwell's closing lines:

> Early my race of wickedness began and soon has reached the summit. Ere nature has finished her work and stamped me man, just at the time that others begin to stray, my course is finished. Though short my span of life and few my days, yet count my crimes for years and I have lived whole ages. (5.10.11–15)

When Barnwell began to go wrong,]   Barnwell's fall begins shortly after Millwood invites him to call on her. Young, innocent and bashful, he is easy prey for a skilled woman like Millwood, who incites in Barnwell 'desires I never knew before' (1.5.58). As his pulse 'beats high', his senses hurry and he finds himself 'on the rack of wild desire' (1.8.17). Millwood quickly gains the upper hand, despite the youth's honesty and loyalty to his master, whose money the prostitute covets.

Wopsle, too, took pains to present me in the worst light. At once ferocious and maudlin, I was made to murder my uncle with no extenuating circumstances whatever;] Wopsle's interpretation of the murder overlooks the conflicting emotions Barnwell expresses when he attacks his unsuspecting uncle. He also seems to ignore the fact that Millwood is executed as an accomplice; even her servant, Blunt, calls her 'the shameless author' of Barnwell's ruin. The ballad portrays Millwood as an accessory hanged for her part in the uncle's murder; Barnwell, by contrast, escapes abroad, but is later 'hang'd in chains' for a murder committed in Poland (Part 2.175–6).

Millwood put me down in argument, on every occasion;] Barnwell has no defence against Millwood. He fails to stick to his resolve to avoid her after they first meet; he gives in to her demands to steal, and later robs and murders his uncle at her instigation.

it became sheer monomania in my master's daughter to care a button for me;] Maria Thorowgood, the daughter of the London merchant to whom Barnwell is apprenticed, loves Barnwell and remains true to him, in spite of his descent into crime.

all I can say for my gasping and procrastinating conduct on the fatal morning, is, that it was worthy of the general feebleness of my character. Even after I was happily hanged] Lillo's Barnwell goes to his death exalting the goodness of his employer's daughter and asking her to pray for his dying soul. Full of self-blame, he affirms that justice and mercy 'are in Heaven the same' and that justice, 'in compassion to mankind, cuts off a wretch like me, by one such example to secure thousands from future ruin' (5.10.20–1).

It was a very dark night when it was all over

Beyond town, we found a heavy mist out, and it fell wet and thick. The turnpike lamp] Entrances to turnpike roads were frequently lit by a lamp with three separate reflectors attached to the turnpike house (see below): two were positioned to throw light along the road in opposite directions; the third directed light across the road and down on to the gate or turnpike, a horizontal wooden bar that could be swung on a vertical pivot (Loudon, 1857, 604).

The road Pip takes was sealed off with a crossbar in 1712 as part of England's turnpike system (Jessup 48) introduced in 1706 to raise revenues from users for the repair of main roads. Travellers were required to pay a graduated price ranging from one penny to a shilling or more. On passing through, they received a small ticket, approximately 1° inches square, printed with the name of the turnpike road and the tollkeeper who issued it (Johnson Collection, 'Toll-gates and tickets').

A turnpike gate stood at the bottom of Strood hill, half a mile from Rochester bridge at the junction of Strood High Street and Frindsbury Road (Hasted, 1798, 1.555; see Appendix 4, map p. 449). The gate was removed on 30 November 1876 (Gadd, 'The Turnpike Gate', 1926, 238–9) when a series of acts starting in 1872 (35 & 36 Vict., c. 85) abolished tolls on turnpikes. On 1 November 1895 the last tollgate on a public road in Britain was shut down (J. W. Gregory 194).

the turnpike house.]   Small cottages or houses, some of which were elegantly designed with a cupola and a lamp, accommodated turnpike-keepers, collectors of tolls who supervised the entrance to each turnpike. A turnpike gatehouse, erected in 1786, stood in Strood High Street near the old Angel Inn (Gadd, 'The Turnpike Gate', 1926, 238–9). One had to pass through this gate *en route* to Lower Higham from Rochester.

"You are late," I remarked.

late,"]   When Pip and Wopsle meet up with Orlick it must be about ten o'clock. Pip later specifies that they reached the Jolly Bargemen – about an hour's walk away – at eleven.

"Ay! There's some of the birds flown from the cages.

The guns have been going since dark, about. You'll hear one presently."]   This comment and Orlick's remark in the previous paragraph about coming in 'close behind' Pip contribute to the alibi Dickens establishes for him. Nevertheless, Orlick's admission about hearing shots fired after dark to warn of escaped convicts raises questions about the consistency of Dickens's account of Orlick's movements in the next chapter. If the guns had been going for so long, why did Pip not hear them as he loitered 'along the High-street' at the time when 'the shops were lighting up'? The fact that Orlick knows so much about the firings remains at odds with the attempt to place him in Rochester, where, it seems, the guns could not be heard. By his own account he arrived in town shortly after Pip and remained there, as we are told, 'all the evening'. Further discrepancies in his alibi are discussed in chapter 16, note on pp. 147–8.

The subject was a suggestive one to me

Mr. Wopsle, as the ill-requited uncle of the evening's tragedy, fell to meditating aloud in his garden]   On the evening of the fatal attack, Barnwell's uncle walks alone in a wood, shadowed by his nephew (armed with a pistol and a sword), and speaks of his fear of 'some danger' lurking unseen:

A heavy melancholy clouds my spirits. My imagination is filled with gashly forms of dreary graves and bodies changed by death, when the pale lengthened visage attracts each weeping eye and fills the musing soul at once with grief and horror, pity and aversion. . . . The mind scarce moves; the blood, curdling and chilled, creeps slowly through the veins; fixed, still, and motionless, like the solemn object of our thoughts, we are almost, at present, what we must be hereafter, till curiosity awakes the soul and sets it on inquiry. . . . O Death, thou strange mysterious power, seen every day yet never understood but by the incommunicative dead, what art thou?
(3.6. 1–15; 3.7. 1–3)

at Camberwell.]   In the ballad, the murder occurs in a wood outside Ludlow, an old market-town approximately twenty-four miles south of Shrewsbury in Shropshire. Lillo places the uncle's residence in a village near London. According to tradition, it occurred 'in the grounds formerly belonging to Dr. Lettsom, and now those of the Grammar-school at Camberwell, in Surrey' (Timbs, 1865, 1.316). In the eighteenth century, Camberwell was a village on the southern edge of London and a renowned local beauty spot.

It was very dark, very wet, very muddy, and so we splashed along.]   Early in the century, local and main routes were unlit and poorly maintained. Many roads in this portion of Kent were built on clay or chalk, which held water and became sodden after rain, making them vulnerable to the heavy traffic of wheeled vehicles and horses, pack animals, sheep, cattle and pigs.

Innovations introduced by Thomas Telford (1757–1834), and later by John Loudon Macadam (1756–1836), did much to improve these conditions, especially after Macadam's system won full support in the 1820s. Roads built from small, broken stones reduced attrition from carriage wheels by providing an elastic foundation which absorbed much of the shock and diffused damage from weight. Convex surfaces facilitated drainage and made roads less likely to turn to mud when it rained or to dust in hot, dry weather. The result was a steady improvement in both the safety and the comfort of coach travel. By 1840, Britain's road system was widely regarded as the best in the world.

Mr. Wopsle died amiably at Camberwell, and exceedingly game on Bosworth Field, and in the greatest agonies at Glastonbury.]   Two of the three scenes in the play feature protracted deaths. Barnwell's uncle dies 'amiably' after he is fatally stabbed while walking near his residence in Camberwell (see note above) and calls on 'All-gracious Heaven' to 'Bless with thy choicest blessings my dearest nephew, forgive my murderer, and take my fleeting soul to endless mercy!', not realizing who has done the deed (*London Merchant* 3.7.12–16). In the conclusion of *Richard III*, Richard dies fighting valiantly on foot after losing his horse and killing no fewer than five Richmonds at Bosworth Field in Leicestershire (*Richard III* 5.4.9–12). No great Shakespearian death scene occurs at Glastonbury, a town in central Somerset, whose location Dickens apparently mistook for Swinstead Abbey, Lincolnshire, the scene of King John's death. In 1842, Dickens saw Macready play King John and went behind the scenes after the performance to congratulate him on his role, which concludes shortly after the king is brought in, dying of poison (King John 5.7.28–34).

Thus we came to the village.

The way ... took us past the Three Jolly Bargemen, which we were surprised to find – it being eleven o'clock – in a state of commotion,] Public houses kept no uniform closing hours, although most shut down before midnight. Country pubs kept shorter hours because most of their customers rose early.

We were running too fast to admit of more being said

a surgeon,] Surgeons were not highly esteemed early in the century. The term signified someone trained through an indentured apprenticeship to set bones, bleed, cup, and make incisions into the body. Surgery, wrote Cornelius Celsus, is 'that branch of the art which teaches how to remove or to prevent disorders by the application of external remedies by the use of the hands and employment of instruments' (*Re Medicina*, quoted in *Complete Book of Trades* 420). Physicians, by contrast, held a university degree and enjoyed greater prestige by virtue of their theoretical knowledge.

Advances in the study of anatomy occurred when surgeons built a hall at the Old Bailey and enlarged it in 1746 after obtaining permission from Parliament to receive for dissection the bodies of executed malefactors. Further improvements followed as the apprenticeship system was strengthened and pupils prepared for various licensing examinations in the 1840s and 1850s. Until the introduction of anaesthesia in the 1840s and antiseptic practices in 1867, however, the surgeon's work was restricted mainly to dangerous emergency measures.

Chapter 16   Tenth weekly number
                                                  2 February 1861

With my head full of George Barnwell

George Barnwell,]   The hero of Lillo's play. See chapter 15, note on pp. 141–2.

Joe had been at the Three Jolly Bargemen

Joe had been at the Three Jolly Bargemen . . . from a quarter after eight o'clock to a quarter before ten. While he was there, my sister . . . had exchanged Good Night with a farm-labourer going home. The man could not be more particular as to the time at which he saw her . . . than that it must have been before nine. When Joe went home at five minutes before ten, he found her struck down on the floor, and promptly called in assistance. The fire had not then burnt unusually low, nor was the snuff of the candle very long; the candle, however, had been blown out.]   The details narrow the approximate time of the attack on Mrs Joe. The condition of the fire and the candle suggests that both had been carefully attended to, not the case had the assault occurred within minutes of Joe's departure to the pub at quarter past eight. Testimony from the labourer reduces the interval even further, to a ten- or fifteen-minute period around nine o'clock.

This would allow Orlick fifty or more minutes to walk four miles to Rochester and watch out for Pip, who, as we know, passes by the turnpike house about ten in the evening on his way home with Wopsle. Most puzzling, therefore, in view of these clues and Dickens's realistic presentation of the attack, is Pip's subsequent statement (see below), which provides Orlick with a firm alibi. If Orlick had been seen 'about town all evening' and 'in divers companies in several public-houses' in Rochester, how could he have been in Pip's village, lurking outside the forge intent on murder?

Now Joe, examining this iron with a smith's eye

The hue and cry going off to the Hulks,]   The hue and cry was originally a legal phrase summoning help from bystanders to pursue a felon. It is used here to indicate that an alarm was raised with the local authorities on the assumption that an escaped prisoner from one of the hulks was responsible for the attack.

Now, as to Orlick

he had gone to town exactly as he told us when we picked him up at the turnpike, he had been seen about town all the evening, he had been in divers companies in several public-houses, and he had come back with myself and Mr. Wopsle.]   A literal reading of this account conflicts with the information used to determine the approximate time of the assault on Mrs Joe. If she was attacked around nine in the evening, the assailant could hardly be someone whose observed movements appear to rule out his presence in the village at a time when the attempted murder occurred.

It was horrible to think that I had provided the weapon

The contention came, after all, to this; – the secret was such an old one now, had so grown into me and become a part of myself, that I could not tear it away.] Dickens may have used a similar rationalization to keep secret the misery he endured in 1824 at the blacking factory:

> From that hour until this at which I write, no word of that part of my childhood which I have now gladly brought to a close, has passed my lips to any human being. . . . From that hour, until this, my father and my mother have been stricken dumb upon it. I have never heard the least allusion to it, however far off and remote, from either of them. I have never, until I now impart it to this paper, in any burst of confidence with anyone, my own wife not excepted, raised the curtain I then dropped, thank God. (Forster 1.2.32–3)

Only a chance remark years later prompted a partial confession about his own 'servitude' and his family's struggle with poverty on their return to London in 1822. Although Dickens chose not to complete the autobiographical narrative he began in the 1840s, he continued to reconstruct fictional variations of his 'fall'. Pip's description of the experiences he underwent at Satis House are perhaps the most sustained and searching of any Dickens wrote.

The Constables, and the Bow-street men from London

The Constables, and the Bow-street men from London] For constables, see chapter 4, note on p. 53. The Bow Street men were semi-professional police attached to Bow Street, London's oldest and most prestigious police-court. The Bow Street men, or 'runners', originated from a patrol of four plain-clothes 'thief-takers', part-time investigators first used by Henry Fielding to solve crimes and recover stolen property during the novelist's service at Bow Street as magistrate (1749–54). Fielding's success and that of his half-brother, John Fielding (magistrate from 1755 to 1760), led to the gradual pre-eminence of the court in Bow Street and the establishment of seven other police-courts on the same model in 1792 under the provisions of the Middlesex Justices Act (10 Geo. IV, c. 45).

Successive magistrates at Bow Street continued to employ amateur police as the power and prestige of this office grew. In the course of time, the Runners extended their jurisdiction over the whole of Middlesex and those parts of Essex, Surrey and Kent closest to the metropolis, including the Hoo peninsula. 'We endeavour to make ourselves useful every where we are invited,' commented Sir Richard Birnie, the court's chief magistrate (*BPP, Crime and Punishment: Police* 4.30).

CHAPTER SIXTEEN   149

The establishment of the Metropolitan Police in 1829 (2 & 3 Vict., c. 47), however, adversely affected Bow Street, after which date the responsibility of this office for detecting and pursuing criminals was significantly reduced. The Bow Street Runners were disbanded in 1839.

in the days of the extinct red waistcoated police] The novel's syntax indicates confusion about the Runners' dress, for the costume described here was worn by members of a Horse Patrol established in 1805 and not by the original Runners, who wore no uniform. Members of the later group were well armed and wore a black leather hat, a double-breasted blue overcoat with yellow buttons, blue trousers and a scarlet waistcoat. Similarly attired foot patrolmen were introduced by Sir Robert Peel in 1822, the last addition to London's law enforcers until the establishment of an unarmed, professional police in 1829 (Babington 194, 212). Dickens makes a similar mistake when he describes 'the Bow Street runners' as having 'no other uniform than a blue dress-coat, brass buttons . . . and a bright red cloth waistcoat' in answer to George Thornbury's request for information about the old 'red-breasts' on 18 April 1862 (*Letters* 10.71–2).

were about the house for a week or two. . . . They took up several obviously wrong people . . . and persisted in trying to fit the circumstances to the ideas, instead of trying to extract ideas from the circumstances.] By statute, the Runners received a guinea a week; outside London, they received extra pay plus travelling expenses together with a share of parliamentary rewards that were given for the seizure and conviction of criminals. Their small salaries, and the fact that they could be hired by private citizens or institutions, led to their downfall and replacement by a better-paid, professional force. Ten years earlier, Dickens had expressed his view that the old Bow Street Runners were 'utterly ineffective' as a 'Preventive Police' and 'as a Detective Police . . . very loose and uncertain in their operations':

> To say the truth, we think there was a vast amount of humbug about those worthies. Apart from many of them being men of very indifferent character, and far too much in the habit of consorting with thieves and the like, they never lost a public occasion of jobbing and trading in mystery and making the most of themselves. ('A Detective Police Party', *HW* 1.409)

See also Dickens's satire against the Bow Street Runners in *OT* (30–1), and Paroissien (1992, 201–3).

Long after these constitutional powers had dispersed

constitutional powers] The Bow Street Runners, whose claim to legitimacy lay in the authority of the Bow Street magistrate, to whom they reported.

Her sight was disturbed, so that she saw objects multiplied, and grasped at visionary teacups and wine-glasses instead of the realities; her hearing was greatly

impaired; her memory also; and her speech was unintelligible.] The symptoms described here, including Pip's later reference to 'A tremulous uncertainty of the action of all of her limbs', are consistent with a severe head trauma of the kind Mrs Joe had suffered. Local haemorrhaging in the brain and axonal sheer injury (the result of severe blows to the head), when axons are sheered off from nerve fibres conducting impulses away from nerve cells, could easily lead to severe visual, auditory and cognitive damage.

Doctors have praised the accuracy of Dickens's account of Mrs Joe's aphasic efforts to make herself understood, her loss of speech, and the 'tremulous uncertainty' of her limbs, likening the symptoms to those of patients suffering from a 'focal contusion of the brain' caused by a severe blow to the head (Brain 125–6).

However, her temper was greatly improved

a confirmed habit of living] Sir Thomas Browne, *Hydriotaphia; or, Urn Burial* (1658), ch. 5: 'The long habit of living indisposeth us for dying.'

Again and again and again, my sister had traced upon the slate

traced upon the slate a character that looked like a curious T,] An ability to communicate in writing rather than through speech is consistent with Mrs Joe's injury. Lesions in the area of the temporal lobe will affect one's comprehension of speech or verbal communication. Expression through writing or drawing, however, might remain possible even after a heavy blow to the head. In the opinion of one doctor writing in 1924, Dickens 'would not realize the significance of his observations from a scientific medical standpoint, but the fact remains that he has described nothing that is not in keeping with present neurological knowledge' (Strachan 782).

Chapter 17

I NOW fell into a regular routine of apprenticeship-life

I NOW fell into a regular routine of apprenticeship-life, which was varied . . . by no more remarkable circumstance than the arrival of my birthday and my paying another visit to Miss Havisham]   See Appendix 1.

So unchanging was the dull old house

I felt as if the stopping of the clocks had stopped Time in that mysterious place, and, while I and everything else outside it grew older, it stood still. Daylight never entered the house. . . . It bewildered me . . .]   This passage and similar descriptions of Satis House in chapters 11 and 29 convey some of the personal fascination Restoration House held for Dickens. For the allusion to the stopped clocks, see chapter 29, note on p. 253.

Imperceptibly I became conscious of a change in Biddy

Her shoes came up at the heel, her hair grew bright and neat, her hands were always clean. She was not beautiful – she was common, and could not be like Estella – but she was pleasant and wholesome and sweet-tempered.]   Compare Dickens's description of Jane Pitt in 'The Schoolboy's Story', Christmas 1853, as 'a sort of wardrobe-woman' who looked after the boys' clothing at the school where Old Cheeseman teaches:

> She had come at first, I believe, as a kind of apprentice – some of our fellows say from a Charity . . . and after her time was out, had stopped at so much a year. . . . However, she had put some pounds in the Savings' Bank, and she was a very nice young woman. She was not quite pretty; but she had a very frank, honest, bright face . . . [and] was uncommonly neat and cheerful, and uncommonly comfortable and kind. (*Christmas Stories*, 1956, 52)

She had not been with us more than a year (I remember her being newly out of mourning at the time it struck me),]   For a deceased spouse or child, women wore mourning dress for a year and a half. For deceased aunts, uncles, nieces and cousins, women usually wore some form of mourning apparel for six to nine months.

My sister was never left alone now

It was summer-time, and lovely weather.]   See Appendix 1.

"Biddy," said I, after binding her to secrecy

"I want to be a gentleman."] Literally, labouring boys born in the country had almost no opportunity to improve their status. Historical developments over several centuries, however, provide a realistic context for the story of Pip's social transformation. Admittedly, the events of the novel accelerate the speed of his rise from a lowly blacksmith's apprentice to a wealthy gentleman. Yet, for all the rapidity of this imagined sequence, such changes in fortune were not uncommon. Nor was it impossible to raise oneself, as Dickens had done, through determination and hard work above one's original station.

The term 'gentleman' to some still carried a feudal connotation (literally one who is entitled to bear arms) whose import had become fused with later layers of meaning. These centred around concepts that placed gentlemen above yeomen but below the nobility and connected the rank with ownership of land and the wealth property conferred (OED). The term also referred to the moral and elusive qualities of 'gentlemanliness' one acquired through birth. A gentleman is 'a man in whom gentle birth is accompanied by appropriate qualities and behaviour'. 'The original meaning of the word gentleman, which it has never entirely lost, was nearly, if not quite, the same as that of its French equivalent *gentilhomme*. It denoted the fact that the person to whom it was applied was a member of one of a certain set of families, or the holder of a certain definite official or professional rank' (Stephen, 1862, 330).

Eliding the requirement of birth, a gentleman might also be 'in general a man of chivalrous instincts and fine feelings' (OED), as increasing emphasis on moral qualities rather than on birth and wealth shaped the new, democratic definition of gentlemanly behaviour. Proponents of this revised code emphasized honour, decency, self-esteem and honesty as goals to which any man might aspire, irrespective of his birth. The word 'gentleman', as Mr Twemlow comments, may be used 'in the sense in which the degree may be attained by any man' OMF (4.17).

Important social developments helped bring about this expansion in meaning and loosen England's hierarchical class divisions. These changes include: the role primogeniture played among the aristocracy; new opportunities for social advancement for those who succeeded in trade and manufacturing; and openings for social mobility made possible by education and by the expansion of the franchise in the nineteenth century.

Movement among classes at the top occurred because England's aristocracy relied on primogeniture for its continuance. Under this system estates and titles passed only to the eldest son or daughter, instead of being divided each generation among all family members. By excluding all but the firstborn from inheriting family estates, parents compelled their younger children to make their own way, forcing them to move 'down' among the gentry or affluent merchant class, whose wealth had obvious attractions, especially for young men brought up for no profession or occupation. Alternatively, increasing concentrations of wealth among merchants and later among manufacturers offered members of the middle class an opportunity to move 'up'. In the course of their rise, businessmen and factory-owners acquired land and titles, contributing further to the social mobility characteristic of English life early in the nineteenth century. Education also allowed some middle-class men to pass beyond class barriers by entering the Church of England, the law, and the Army – professions which all carried sufficient respectability for admission into 'society'.

Such changes prompted mixed responses. Opponents deplored instances of social levelling; others, with liberal views, welcomed those whose moral attributes and behaviour earned them the prized designation of 'gentlemen'. Uncertainty about qualifications fuelled an earnest debate – a point the novel makes by examining the conflicting significations of 'gentleman' in the mid-century. A broadened definition of the term also prompted warnings about the need for vigilance. Impostors like Compeyson could prey all too easily on the unsuspecting – a cautionary note Dickens sounds in chapters 22 and 42.

Where should we be going, but home?

jiggered] A mild oath, one that originated in the Navy: 'I'm jiggered if he don't tell a lie' (Frederick Marryat, *Dog Fiend*, 1837, 36).

Chapter 18   Eleventh weekly number
                                                9 February 1861

It was the fourth year of my apprenticeship to Joe

the fourth year of my apprenticeship]   Another detailed sequence follows. See Appendix 1.

There was a group assembled . . . at the Three Jolly Bargemen, attentive to Mr. Wopsle as he read the newspaper aloud. . . . A highly popular murder had been committed, and Mr. Wopsle was imbrued in blood to the eyebrows.]   Early in the century De Quincey remarked in 'On Murder as One of the Fine Arts' (1827) on the appeal murder cases exerted and how newspaper accounts fostered a class of 'Murder Fanciers' and 'amateurs and dilettanti in various modes of carnage' (1). De Quincey theorized that the spectacle of murder attracted readers and that almost everyone revealed 'a critical or aesthetic valuation of fires and murders'. Although Coleridge, for example, ignored the sensational Ratcliff murders of 1811, he told De Quincey how he was thrown 'into a profound reverie upon the tremendous power which is laid open in a moment to any man who can reconcile himself to the abjuration of all conscientious restraints, if, at the same time, [he is] thoroughly without fear' (62). Increased coverage given to the trial of murderers both in newspapers and in staid publications like the *Annual Register* documents this phenomenon (Boyle, 1969). In particular, the trial and execution on 9 January 1824 of John Thurtell (*DNB*) for the murder of William Weare near St Albans attracted extraordinary attention and seems to provide a watershed in the degree to which newspapers made murder 'their staple of interest' (Fonblanque 2.195). Thurtell's stirring self-defence at his trial also impressed several literary men including Scott, Bulwer Lytton, Hazlitt, Theodore Hook and Charles Lamb. Modern historians question the assertion that the deeds of Thurtell and others reflected a dramatic increase in crime. But they agree that the perception of an explosion of murder and violence reflects heightened anxiety about public order apparent in the press and among readers of a range of newspapers. A later wave of sensational crimes (and equally sensational newspaper reports) in the mid-fifties evidently had a similar impact on readers of *AYR* familiar with the deeds of William Palmer (1824–56), 'the Rugeley poisoner', and other notorious villains of the period.

A highly popular murder had been committed

The coroner, in Mr. Wopsle's hands, became Timon of Athens; the beadle, Coriolanus.]   The history of the English coroner's office dates from the twelfth century when coroners (derived from *corona*, 'a crown') were established to provide 'a mechanism both for administering justice and for insuring that the royal interest in certain sources of revenue was recorded, protected, and exploited'. In the course of time, however, the duties of officeholders narrowed to investigating cases of sudden, unexpected, unexplained, unnatural or violent death. Inquests were held in, or as close as possible to, the parish where death occurred. Also in attendance were a clerk, witnesses, jurymen and parish officials, one of whom might be the beadle. Defects in the system were inevitable since coroners were unpaid and were men without legal or medical training. Regulations for the disposal of the dead introduced in 1836 by the Births and Deaths Registration Act (6 & 7 Will. IV, c. 86) brought a greater degree of professionalism into post-mortem proceedings; further improvements occurred after the County Coroners Act of 1860 (23 & 24 Vict., c. 116), which introduced a salary system for the payment of coroners and established their right to hold proper inquiries into non-homicidal deaths (based on Forbes, 1978).

Timon and Coriolanus were historical figures on whom Shakespeare based *Timon of Athens* (1607) and *Coriolanus* (1607–8). Both roles provide opportunities for forceful, flamboyant acting. Imitating the mannerisms of a coroner at work also provides amusement to the company assembled at the Sol's Arms *BH* (11).

"I know you do," said the stranger

the law of England supposes every man to be innocent, until he is proved – proved – to be guilty?"]   Trial by jury was one of the boasted privileges of Englishmen. In the words of William Blackstone, it was the 'grand bulwark' of English liberties which 'cannot but subsist so long as this palladium remains sacred and inviolate' (*Commentaries*, 4.342–3).

English criminal procedure rests on two assumptions: the presumption of innocence; and the principle that there is no crime without criminal intent. The first derived from English Common Law (i.e. common to the whole country regardless of local customs) as the reciprocal right of trial by jury. The second is the Judaeo-Christian notion, transmitted to criminal procedure by Canon Law, that sin or crime is essentially a mental act, an act of will, before it becomes overt and physical (Williman 100). Jaggers's willingness to act on these two postulates and apply them evenhandedly accounts for his standing in the criminal community and the way people fawn on him, knowing also something of his success at winning acquittals. See also below.

"Certainly you know it.

"Do you know that none of these witnesses have yet been cross-examined?"]   The rule-bound nature of the judicial process, application of strict rules of evidence, and emphasis on the obligation of the prosecution to prove its case, all constituted part of the 'grand bulwark' of English liberty. The cross-examination of witnesses, which did not become common until the second half of the eighteenth century (Beattie 374–5), was particularly important since it served as the principal means by which barristers or attorneys (the latter in magistrates' courts) defended clients. For the conduct of trials, see also chapter 42, note on page 333.

"Undoubtedly. Now, turn to that paper.

to reserve his defence?"] A standard legal move by which a client is advised to say nothing pending the preparation of his defence and initiation of the trial.

"Never mind what you read just now, sir

You may read the Lord's Prayer backwards,] 'Our Father', the Lord's Prayer, was the prayer Jesus taught his disciples in answer to their request, 'Lord, teach us to pray' (Matthew 6.9–13; Luke 11.2–4). Participants in Satanic rituals sometimes recited the verses backwards in an attempt to summon the Devil.

"And that same man, remember," pursued the gentleman

after deliberately swearing that he would well and truly try the issue joined between Our Sovereign Lord the King and the prisoner at the bar, and would a true verdict give according to the evidence, so help him God!"] The words are from the oath taken by jurors when they were empanelled. The procedure called for jurors to step forward after their names were called and read for a second time. The crier then reported, 'Vous avez John Doe' (or whatever the name), after which each swore to the following:

> You shall well and truly try and true deliverance make between our sovereign lord the king and the prisoners at the bar whom you shall have in charge, and a true verdict give according to your evidence. So help you God.

The clerk marked each juror sworn; when there were twelve, they were counted, their names read for the third time and a proclamation for evidence against the accused was also read. 'Look upon the prisoner you that be sworn . . . ,' said the crier. 'Hear the evidence.' Then the trial commenced (Baker, 1986, 285). There was no age limit, but jurors had to be freeholders to the value of 40s or (in a city or town) owners of 40s worth of goods. They were twelve in number; by custom, women were excluded.

The stranger did not recognise me

my second visit to Miss Havisham.] After 'Havisham' AYR reads 'His appearance was too remarkable for me to have forgotten'.

Amidst a wondering silence

Our conference was held in the state parlour, which was feebly lighted by one candle.] After 'candle' MS reads 'which was very cold.'

CHAPTER EIGHTEEN

"My name," he said, "is Jaggers

Jaggers,] 'Jag', to pierce or stab, and 'yaeger', an anglicized version of *jaegar*, a German or Swiss hunter, have been proposed as possible etymologies for the lawyer's name; 'Jaggers' also appears to combine a pun on the lawyer's sharpness (like a dagger) and on his ability to 'stagger' others with questions and a 'jagged' style of dealing with people (Peacock 400). Compare also two slang terms: 'Jock gaggers', nineteenth-century 'Flash' for men who lived on wives or whores, and Hotten's 'JAGGER, a gentleman' (Hotten 160). The landlord of a coffee-house in St Martin's Lane, London (the Army and Navy), was also called Mr Jaggers (Wight, 1827, 197).

I am a lawyer in London. I am pretty well known.] Jaggers is an attorney, not a barrister – an important distinction. The cost of attending one of the Inns of Court, the difficulty in obtaining legal briefs, and the attitudes towards attorneys prevailing early in the nineteenth century created a gulf between these two groups of professionals. Barristers, whose training qualified them to plead cases in the higher courts, were said to live behind 'an almost impenetrable barrier' across which attorneys and men of middling means could not pass. Lord Campbell, writing in 1810, commented that, once a barrister, you lived 'on a footing of perfect equality with men of high birth, of the best education, and the most elegant manners'. On the circuit, barristers were not even permitted to use public transport or lodge at public inns. Such practices ensured their professional distance from any unseemly association with attorneys (based on Gatrell 506).

Changes occurring around 1800 account for the emerging status of attorneys and their consequent public recognition. Perhaps most significant were the opportunities attorneys had to work in London's recently opened police or magistrates' courts (see chapter 16, note on p. 148). Cases typically required the defence or prosecution of those charged with a variety of felonious charges, the majority of which were capital offences. Thus industrious, conscientious and intelligent attorneys had scope for practice. This situation, combined with increasing press coverage of crime and the widespread reporting of cases that made the news, meant that capable attorneys could indeed become 'pretty well known'. For Jaggers to have earned fame enough to have come to the attention of both Magwitch and Miss Havisham is entirely plausible in realistic terms (chapters 50 and 49).

One such individual who worked chiefly in the criminal courts and rose to public prominence was James Harmer (1777–1853), a possible model for Dickens's formidable lawyer (Gatrell 435). Harmer, the son of a Spitalfields weaver and orphaned at 10, was articled to an attorney in 1792, married early and then set himself up in practice in 1799. Harmer worked almost exclusively in the criminal courts, gaining experience which made him a strong advocate of reform in criminal procedure. He was later elected alderman of the ward of Farringdon Without in 1833. The following year he was made sheriff of London and Middlesex, having given up in 1833 a legal practice said to have been worth £4,000 a year (*DNB*).

It was in the courts, however, that Harmer's career and fame were made. He took great trouble to investigate cases of prisoners whom he believed had been wrongly committed, thereby winning a considerable reputation among those in need of his

"Now, Joseph Gargery, I am the bearer of an offer

an offer to relieve you of this young fellow, your apprentice.] As of November, some three full years remained. Statutes governing the conditions under which apprentices served made release from their contracts difficult. Apprentices were freed if their master became insolvent or died; for their part, masters could chastise apprentices but could not, of their own accord, discharge them. But cancellations of indentures were possible if both parties consented.

"Yes, I do keep a dog."

"Yes, I do keep a dog."] See chapter 3. The 'pet dog' referred to there never makes an appearance in the novel.

"Bear in mind then, that Brag is a good dog

Brag is a good dog, but Holdfast is a better.] Jaggers cites exactly the English proverbial saying, the point of which is to remind people that discretion is preferable to boasting. Compare also: 'Trust none, for oaths are straws, men's faiths are wafer-cakes,/And Holdfast is the only dog, my duck' (*Henry V* 2.3.47–8).

great expectations."] See pp. 21–2 for a note on the novel's title.

"I am instructed to communicate to him," said Mr. Jaggers

a handsome property.] See chapter 39, note on p. 314.

"Now, Mr. Pip," pursued the lawyer

it is the request . . . that you always bear the name of Pip.] Perhaps an ironic allusion to Charles Lever's hero, Potts, a dreaming snob with absurd pretensions. Potts concedes that his given names, Algernon Sydney, 'do a deal'. But he laments the bathos of 'Potts', the son of Peter Potts, a Dublin apothecary. 'Can a man hope to make such a name illustrious?' he asks, as he considers such fanciful alternatives as Pozzo di Borgo and Pottinger (*A Day's Ride*, 6).

Similarities beyond the alliterative monosyllabic names of the two narrators prompt speculation about the extent of Dickens's borrowings from Lever and his supposed determination to show a fellow serialist How to Do It, having failed to deliver the commercial appeal Dickens initially believed a book by Lever would hold for readers of AYR. Possible resemblances include: the dreaming nature of Potts and Pip, the former who confesses to building imaginary castles to live in for his own pleasure rather than to astonish his friends (20), and the latter who casts himself as 'the young Knight of romance', destined 'to marry the Princess' (29); a sustained focus on rank and class in the form of narratives illustrating the progress of two snobs who aspire beyond their station; and two love-struck young men unhappily infatuated with unsuitable women. See also Lever's use of the phrase 'great expectations' on 29 September 1860 within days of Dickens alighting on what he considered 'a good name' for the novel he planned to take the place of Lever's failing enterprise (p. 3). This much said, artistry and major differences in the treatment of snobbery set the two books so far apart as to make comparisons between the two 'interesting' yet 'all but meaningless' (*Norton* 419). For an extended discussion of Lever's achievements and the differences between GE and *A Day's Ride*, see Rosenberg's 'Lever's Long Day's Journey into Night' (*Norton* 410–22), but compare Meckier (1998) for a different assessment of Dickens's debt to Lever. See also notes to chapters 48 and 58 on the endings of both novels.

"Never mind what you have always longed for, Mr. Pip," he retorted

under some proper tutor?] Tutors commonly prepared young boys or youths for entry into university, providing an alternative, for those who could afford it, to boarding schools and academies. Anglican clergymen frequently resorted to tutoring in order to supplement their income.

"First," said Mr. Jaggers, "you should have some new clothes

twenty guineas?"] The equivalent in contemporary terms of about £880.

He produced a long purse

a long purse,] A knitted or crocheted purse with two pouches secured by rings.

Joe laid his hand upon my shoulder

like the steam-hammer,] Steam-hammers were capable of a wide range of adjustments from pounding iron to producing a light tap; they were also used for driving piles into the ground, an application widely employed by bridge-builders. James Watt may have been the first to envision the use of steam for driving and pounding, but a drawing made in 1839 by James Nasmyth is usually cited as the first practical model, which was later patented in 1842 (Bunch and Hellemans, 1993, 183).

O dear good Joe

O dear good Joe. . . . O dear good faithful tender Joe,] The apostrophe and its repetition and expansion have been cited as a mannerism Dickens learned from Carlyle. The stylistic trait, however, is by no means connected with a Carlylean idea (Oddie 34).

Mr. Jaggers had looked on at this

as one who recognised in Joe the village idiot and in me his keeper.] Keepers were commonly employed, engaged for a modest sum, to provide basic care for harmless lunatics as an alternative to incarceration. John Conolly (1794–1866) was a leading advocate of the non-restraint policies that challenged in the 1830s the earlier practice of removal and confinement to which almost all deranged persons were subject (Sutherland, 1995, 74). Jibes about rural half-wits and degenerates were common. Data gathered later in the century indicate that the intelligence quotient of the rural population 'has consistently fallen below that of the urban population as measured for schoolchildren' (Laslett 135). See also chapter 49, note on pp. 369–70.

"Which I meantersay," cried Joe

bull-baiting and badgering me,] Bull-baiting had once flourished in Elizabethan times when bulls were tethered from behind in specially built arenas 'and worried by great English bull-dogs'. Later regarded as a barbarous pastime, 'persons of rank' abandoned the sport and left it in the early nineteenth century only to 'the lowest and most despicable part of the people' (Strutt 257). The practice was officially suppressed in 1835 by the Cruelty to Animals Act (5 & 6 Will., c. 59). The use of dogs to attack badgers, which were released either from a cage or from a hole dug for the purpose, also drew criticism. Legislation introduced by Richard Martin in 1822 provided some measure of protection for cattle and horses. Efforts by the Society for the Prevention of Cruelty to Animals (founded in 1824) and subsequent legislation in 1835 (see above) suppressed most popular country sports but failed to eradicate either cockfighting or dog fighting. Upper-class bloodsports such as fox hunting, deer stalking and shooting remained immune to legislation.

"Well, Mr. Pip, I think the sooner you leave here

You can take a hackney-coach at the stage-coach office] Hackney-coaches – four-wheeled vehicles drawn by two horses – plied for hire in large cities. They could also be engaged at a stage-coach office, or a posting inn, or hired at designated stands where they waited in ranks. The date of their introduction to London is disputed: some claim they came first from Paris in 1662, others maintain that hackney-coaches

14 Rochester Castle, Cathedral and bridge over the Medway, c.1800

operated as early as 1625. Hackney-coaches for hire soon challenged the use of sedan chairs and prompted attempts by the government to limit their number, but by 1833 all restriction had been abolished (based on Timbs, 1865, 2.256, and Timbs, 1867, 392–3). Two other kinds of public transport early in the century were also available: stagecoaches, which ran daily carrying passengers between two recognized stages; and mail-coaches, which carried mail and some passengers.

In 'Hackney Coach Stands' Dickens identifies a class of hackney-coaches particular to London: ponderous, rickety old vehicles – 'great, lumbering, square concern[s] of a dingy yellow colour', with red axletrees and green wheels (SB). Coaches of this variety continued to operate during the 1830s until 'dapper green' cabs like hansoms (patented in 1834) and omnibuses (introduced in 1829) gradually drove the older hackney-coaches out of business.

Something came into my head

a hired carriage.]   Carriages hired to carry one or two passengers from one point to another along the road were more genteel, faster and more expensive than public stagecoaches. Carriages were generally lighter vehicles, pulled by either two or three horses, one of which the post-boy rode.

"Pip's a gentleman of fortun' then," said Joe

gentleman of fortun']   This was a usual expression for a man with money. Examples from *The Times* reveal several variants: 'a young gentleman of fortune', 'a young gentleman of good fortune' and 'a gentleman of independent fortune' (19 Oct. 1810, p. 3, col. d; 15 July 1840, p. 7, col. c; 4 July 1842, p. 5, col. f). This information was supplied by Susan Shatto.

Infinite pains were then taken by Biddy

I doubt if they had more meaning in them than an election cry,]   The OED cites this as the first recorded instance of the phrase, 'election cry', presumably a campaign slogan used by candidates running for national office. Canvassing for representatives often involved rowdy, drunken displays and the use of tactics for which Dickens expressed contempt. See his account of the North Northamptonshire by-election he covered as a young reporter for the *Morning Chronicle* in 1835 (*Letters* 1.105–10).

The sun had been shining brightly all day

I saw Biddy come and bring him a pipe and light it for him.]   Labourers, countrymen and others lower down the social scale generally preferred pipes (see Magwitch, chapter 40, and Wemmick at home, chapter 25). Middle- and upper-class men often used snuff, which was common until the introduction of cigars about 1804. Cigarettes, commonly smoked by women, did not appear until the early 1850s.

Chapter 19 Twelfth weekly number
16 February 1861

Joe and Biddy were very sympathetic and pleasant

the rich man and the kingdom of Heaven,]

> Then said Jesus unto his disciples, Verily I say unto you, that a rich man shall hardly enter into the kingdom of heaven. And again I say unto you, It is easier for a camel to go through the eye of a needle, than for a rich man to enter into the kingdom of God. (Matthew 19.23–4; also Luke 18.20–5, Mark 10.23–5)

Under the provisions of the Act of Uniformity of 1662 (14 Car. II, c. 4), this reading was assigned for 24 April in accordance with the practice of designating passages from the Bible for reading aloud at specific times of the year (see Table of Lessons, *BCP*). Although chosen for its obvious irony, the lesson reinforces other seasonal markers suggestive of spring: references to warm, sunny weather (chapters 18 and 19), and to Pip's arrival in London just as fresh strawberries become available at Covent Garden Market (chapter 20).

After our early dinner I strolled out alone

I felt . . . a sublime compassion for the poor creatures who were destined to go there . . . to lie obscurely at last among the low green mounds.] Compare Gray's 'Elegy Written in a Country Churchyard' (1751):

> Beneath those rugged Elms, that Yew-Tree's Shade,
> Where heaves the Turf in many a mould'ring Heap,
> Each in his narrow Cell for ever laid,
> The rude Forefathers of the Hamlet sleep. . . .
>
> The Boast of Heraldry, the Pomp of Pow'r,
> And all that Beauty, all that Wealth e'er gave,
> Awaits alike th'inevitable Hour.
> The Paths of Glory lead but to the Grave.

The description of the speaker's arrival in the gloomy churchyard, left alone in 'darkness' to contemplate the graves around him after the departure of others from the landscape, is perhaps also echoed in the novel's opening chapter. References to the 'Elegy' occur in both Dickens's *Speeches* (9, 37, 185) and in his *Letters* (4.552, 5.708–9). Emphasis on 'death, burial, and monuments' also occurs in Dickens's 1860 essay in the *UT* series, 'City of London Churches' (*AYR* 3.85–9),

Now more low wet grounds

henceforth I was for London and greatness:] Dickens absorbed from childhood reading a sense of London's legendary importance as a place where adventures begin:

> What an amazing place London was to me when I saw it in the distance, and how I believed all the adventures of all my favorite heroes to be constantly enacting and re-enacting there, and how I vaguely made it out in my own mind to be fuller of wonders and wickedness than all the cities of the earth, I need not stop here to relate. (*DC* 5)

So, when we had walked home and had had tea

I took Biddy into our little garden by the side of the lane,] The forge adjoining the smith's in Chalk had a small garden at the side of the house (Gadd, 'The Forge', 1926, 234–6). See also chapter 2, note on p. 40. A second reference to the garden occurs in chapter 35.

"Whether you scold me or approve of me," returned poor Biddy

Yet a gentleman should not be unjust, neither,"] 'What is it', Thackeray asked, 'to be a gentleman?':

> Is it to have lofty aims, to lead a pure life, to keep your honour virgin; to have the esteem of your fellow-citizens, and the love of your fireside; to bear good fortune meekly; to suffer evil with constancy; and through evil or good to maintain the truth always? Show me the happy man whose life exhibits these qualities, and him we will salute as a gentleman, whatever his rank may be; show me the prince who possesses them, and he may be sure of our love and loyalty. (*The Four Georges*, 1862, 225–6)

> What is it to be a gentleman? It is to be honest, to be gentle, to be generous, to be brave, to be wise, and, possessing all these qualities, to exercise them in the most graceful outward manner. Ought a gentleman to be a loyal son, a true husband, and honest father? Ought his life to be decent – his bills to be paid – his tastes to be high and elegant – his aims in life lofty and noble?
> ('The Snob Royal', *The Book of Snobs*, 1846–7, *Works* 9.12)

Compare also the observation of Fitzjames Stephen, who noted in 1862 'a constantly increasing disposition to insist more upon the moral and less upon the social element' of the word 'gentleman', so that in the course of time 'its use may come to be altogether dissociated from any merely conventional distinction'. Accordingly, he concluded, 'A man whose personal qualities fit him to take his place in such a society may properly, or at least intelligibly be described as a gentleman, whatever else he may either have or want'(330–1).

But morning once more brightened my view

Mr. Trabb, the tailor:]   Before the widespread use of sewing machines in the second half of the nineteenth century and the development of wholesale clothing factories, tailoring was almost exclusively a home industry variously organized according to the volume of work undertaken. Large houses employed several 'cutters', or foremen, who cut to measures taken from 'the persons of the customers'. Cutters also served as 'finishers', who waited 'upon the higher orders of the gentry when the suits are commanded to be fitted on, as well as when the orders are first received'. Other tasks fell to journeymen employed merely to sew together the seams of the clothes prepared for them by the cutters. Specialists in specific departments were also common with some excelling in 'the cut and make of the breeches', others in waistcoats and still a few who 'never descend below *the coats*' (*Complete Book of Trades* 431). Trabb appears to have only a small volume of business since Pip makes no reference to any employees at work cutting, trimming and sewing. *Wright's Topography* for 1838 lists four tailors, all of whom had premises in the High Street.

Mr. Trabb had sliced his hot roll

sliced his hot roll]   The meal suggests a degree of financial comfort. Hot rolls – small loaves rolled or doubled before baking – first appeared among the affluent in the mid-eighteenth century and gained popularity in the course of time.

"My dear sir," said Mr. Trabb

"My dear sir,"]   A formal but also rather patronizing style of address.

"Hold that noise," said Mr. Trabb

taking down a roll of cloth, and tiding it out in a flowing manner]   Relying on the tailor to supply the cloth for suits was a comparatively recent development:

> Less than a century ago, it was a usual custom for gentlemen to purchase their cloths and velvets [from a draper], and to employ a tailor to make them into clothes. . . .This required a practical knowledge of the material. It also meant that the customer assumed that the tailor would employ only good

materials. Putting the whole into the tailor's hands has . . . the bad effect that it has become extremely difficult to judge the correctness of his charges, or the extent of his profits. (Webster, 1844, 1014)

Mr. Trabb then bent over number four

the nobility and gentry,]   Five titles define the nobility or peerage, hereditary landed proprietors with estates of 10,000 or more acres (about 18 square miles) and incomes of over £10,000 a year. In descending order, the five divisions are duke, marquess, earl, viscount and baron. Beneath this group of from 300 to 400 families were the gentry, smaller landed proprietors with estates ranging from 1,000 to 10,000 acres and with annual incomes ranging from £1,000 to £10,000 (Brown 7). Members of this class had no titles, unless they were knights or baronets. To serve the gentry, fashionable tailors required 'very large capitals' owing to 'the great extent of credit taken' by members of this class. By laying on 'an adequate profit for such indulgence', however, most fashionable tailors 'threaded their way to eminence through many a toilsome maze'. London tailors, by contrast, generally received payments more promptly (*Complete Book of Trades* 433).

I selected the materials for a suit

to send the articles to Mr. Pumblechook's on the Thursday evening,]   A suit could be produced in four days if the tailor put aside work on other orders. Suits required intricate hand-sewing, especially for the buttonholes and cuffs.

"I know, sir, that London gentlemen cannot be expected to patronise local work, as a rule:]   London tailors offered formidable competition on account of their eminence (they were incorporated in 1480), their numbers and the renown for excellent work earned by tailors in Cork Street, Burlington Gardens and Sackville Street. A census taken in 1834 counted 14,552 tailors in the whole metropolitan district (*Complete Book of Trades* 428–32). London tailors enjoyed the further advantage of a near-monopoly of catering to officers in the Army. Thackeray satirized the extravagance of regimental uniforms in his description of a tailor's bill as an 'absurd catalogue of insane gimcracks and madman's tomfoolery' ('A Visit to Some Country Snobs', *Works* 9.141).

After this memorable event

the hatter's, and the bootmaker's, and the hosier's,]   Representatives of all three had premises in Rochester High Street in the 1830s. Hat-making was an old-fashioned trade, and England was considered 'the country of hats'. The industry owes its eminence to an Elizabethan statute requiring the wearing of hats on Sundays by every male over 7 (*Complete Book of Trades* 291). Hats required three separate operations: blocking, shaping and finishing. Shapes were made on blocks by means of a hot iron and were then covered with silk, which was sewn up the side in a transverse seam. Finishing referred to the process by which the crown and the lining were sewn on – a difficult task often performed by women. Boots were still custom-made from a last kept by a local cobbler. Ready-made uppers might be used, but typically the rest of the boot was finished by hand. One man might make up to four or five pairs of boots a week. Hosiers made and sold stockings, socks, underclothes, and woollen and cotton garments.

Mother Hubbard's dog whose outfit required the services of so many trades.]

> She went to the tailor's
> To buy him a coat . . .
>
> She went to the hatter's
> To buy him a hat . . .
>
> She went to the barber's
> To buy him a wig . . .
>
> She went to the cobbler's
> To buy him some shoes . . .
>
> She went to the seamstress
> To buy him some linen . . .
>
> She went to the hosier's
> To buy him some hose;
> But when she came back
> He was dressed in his clothes.
> (*The Comic Adventures of Old Mother Hubbard and Her Dog* (1805), cited in Opie)

I also went to the coach-office and took my place for seven o'clock on Saturday morning.] Early in the nineteenth century, seven coaches a day set out to London from Rochester. In addition, 'carriages of every description [are] almost continually passing between London, Dover, Deal, Margate, etc. which greatly facilitate the communication with the capital' (Denne 315). The limited number of seats made booking a place advisable. Mail-coaches augmented the old stagecoach system, which began in 1658, with an improved service in the 1780s, whose efficiency and speed increased with modernized roads (see chapter 15, note on p. 145) and advances in coach design and construction. Coach travel reached its peak in the 1830s when some 3,000 vehicles operated and either began or ended their journey in London. Coaching establishments in England employed about 150,000 horses and 30,000 coachmen, guards, horse-keepers and hostlers. By about 1836 the supremacy of mail-coaches and stagecoaches was defeated by railway trains, which travelled much faster and carried more passengers (Pratt 51–5, 325). For a note on the system of 'posting', see chapter 53, p. 382.

"But my dear young friend," said Mr. Pumblechook

Here is a chicken had round from the Boar, here is a tongue] Most hotels and taverns served food on and off the premises. Cutlery and complete place-settings, including table linen, could be provided, delivered by a waiter. A boiled beef tongue was often served with poultry, instead of ham. Alternatively, cold tongue pickled in spices and salt was equally popular. Customers preferred beef or ox tongue, but unscrupulous dealers often substituted horse tongue.

Mr. Pumblechook helped me to the liver wing

the liver wing,]

> [W]hen the liver and gizzard have been trussed and cooked with the fowl, the wing to which the liver is attached may be regarded as the choice portion of the bird, and should be offered to the person entitled to the most consideration in this respect. (Beeton 1270)

The custom of designating the liver wing as a particular favour appears to derive from the Romans' preference for the livers of geese and other fowl, and from the later practice of force-feeding fowls in order to enlarge their livers and bring the birds to an artificial state of obesity.

We drank all the wine

the turnpike] The turnpike entrance was on the north bank of the Medway in the adjoining town of Strood (see chapter 15, note on pp. 143–4).

We shook hands for the hundredth time at least

carter] A carter, one who conveyed goods. Compare also waggoner, chapter 42, note on p. 328.

So, Tuesday, Wednesday, and Thursday, passed

It being market morning at a neighbouring town some ten miles off,] Maidstone,

Gravesend, Aylesford, Newington and Sittingbourne are all within a ten-mile radius of Rochester.

I went circuitously to Miss Havisham's by all the back ways

rang at the bell constrainedly, on account of the stiff long fingers of my gloves.] Unsoiled gloves signalled respectability and freedom from dirty physical toil. Worn by someone who, unaccustomed to them and who also, according to prevailing rules of etiquette, would not ordinarily wear them indicates pretentiousness. Compare also Miss Skiffins's punctilious retention of her gloves in company (chapter 37), a sign of her anxiety to conform to propriety. To the poor and those who worked with their hands, gloves were both impractical and expensive.

"Ay, ay!" said she

"I have seen Mr. Jaggers. I have heard about it, Pip.] Miss Havisham's subsequent comments to Pip reveal familiarity with the main points Jaggers covered when he made known his 'unusual business' to Pip and Joe in the previous chapter. Her knowing these details represents a serious breach of client confidentiality on Jaggers's part. It would appear that Dickens made this concession to the plot, which requires Pip to draw the wrong inference from Miss Havisham's pointed remarks.

She stretched out her hand

She stretched out her hand, and I went down on my knee and put it to my lips.] Both gestures date from the ceremonial etiquette of court service to royalty: monarchs offered their hands to be kissed; inferiors knelt before their masters. Hand-kissing, however, also prevailed outside court as a token of respect or esteem when incorporated into a salutation, either on entering a room or on greeting one's hostess on formal occasions.

And now those six days which were to have run out so slowly

some flip] Flip, a hot mixed drink made with either ale or wine. Traditionally, it was heated by plunging a hot poker reddened in the fire into the drink, imparting to the mixture a pleasant burned taste. Other ingredients included the 'yolk of a new-laid egg, beaten up . . . with a glass of sound sherry, nutmeg and powdered sugar' (Hewett and Axton 51–2).

Chapter Nineteen 171

It was a hurried breakfast with no taste in it.

throwing an old shoe after me] Throwing an old shoe after a friend was a time-honoured custom supposed to impart luck and prosperity (Opie and Tatem, 1989). When David and Emily leave with Barkis on the day of his wedding to Peggotty, David sees Mr Peggotty 'prepared with an old shoe, which was to be thrown after us for luck' (*DC* 10).

I walked away at a good pace

and the light mists were solemnly rising as if to show me the world,] Compare the exit of the narrator from Rochester on Christmas Day after entertaining the travellers the night before with the uplifting story of Richard Doubledick: 'And now, the mists began to rise in the most beautiful manner, and the sun to shine; and as I went on . . . I felt as if all Nature shared in the joy of the great Birthday' ('The Road', *Seven Poor Travellers*, *HW*, Christmas 1854, 36). See also below.

and I had been so innocent and little there, and all beyond was so unknown and great,] Thoughts about innocence associated with childhood occupied Dickens earlier in the summer of 1860 as he found himself 'rambling about the scenes amongst which my earliest days were passed'. Speaking as the Uncommercial Traveller, Dickens describes how he reacted as 'a man' to scenes from which he had departed as a child:

> Ah! who was I that I should quarrel with the town for being changed to me, when I myself had come back, so changed, to it! All my early readings and early imaginations dated from this place, and I took them away so full of innocent construction and guileless belief, and I brought them back so worn and torn, so much the wiser and so much the worse! ('Dullborough Town', *AYR* 3.278)

Heaven knows we need never be ashamed of our tears

Heaven knows we need never be ashamed of our tears. . . . I was better after I had cried,] A shift in affective behaviour with an emphasis on sensibility occurred in the 1750s following several developments. The growth of the culture of sensibility was partly rooted in a new scientific understanding of the body and the mind, as evidenced in David Hartley's materialistic psychology (see his *Observations on Man*, 1749), which drew on the associationist nerve theory of Locke and others. Similar ideas spread in France and in England, popularized both by Joseph Priestley (1773–1804) and by French and English novelists, who emphasized the heart as the site of feeling. A willingness to endorse public displays of emotion, including tears, also proved compatible with Evangelicalism, aiding further the acceptance of unrestrained emotional behaviour indicative of a new obligation of compassion and consolation. Hence the propensity to weep for friends, for strangers or for humanitarian principles was viewed as the affirmation of a new sensitivity (Gatrell 230).

Those who subscribed to these theories recognized the existence of flaws in human nature and in the social order. At the same time, they affirmed a belief either in innate goodness or in the view that sensibility could be taught by example. For Dickens, emphasis on feelings served partly to counter Benthamite calculation and those political economists who advocated selfishness as the best guide to civic virtue. Magwitch's penchant for tears (see chapters 3, 5 and 39) unites him with the new sensitivity, a characteristic he shares with Joe, who combines physical strength with mildness and who sheds tears without embarrassment when deeply moved (see chapters 18 and 57).

So subdued I was by those tears

clear of the town,] That is, across the Medway and heading south-west on the London road.

when we changed horses,] Drivers changed horses when they stopped at posting inns to drop off and pick up passengers. Distances between stages varied from seven to twelve miles. For further details of Pip's journey from Rochester to London, see chapter 20, note on p. 172.

We changed again, and yet again

And the mists had all solemnly risen now, and the world lay spread before me.] After 'spread' MS reads 'was'. Compare Milton's *Paradise Lost* (1667): 'Some natural tears they dropped, but wiped them soon,/The world was all before them, where to choose/Their place of rest, and providence their guide' (12.645–7); and Wordsworth's *Prelude* (1850): 'The earth is all before me' (1.14–15).

THIS IS THE END OF THE FIRST STAGE OF PIP'S EXPECTATIONS] The novel's division into three stages suggests an affinity with the fictional convention of portraying life as a journey: John Bunyan in *Pilgrim's Progress* (1678) and William Hogarth in *Industry and Idleness* (1747) both employed this widely imitated device. The term 'stages' was used by Hogarth to indicate 'progress', an idea Dickens incorporates here. Pip's linear journey takes him from his village to London and introduces him to a series of worldly attractions. Each serves as an obstacle the traveller must confront on a journey whose course carries metaphorical implications for his own mortality.

In this respect, Pip's apprenticeship and the subsequent cancellation of his indentures owing to his new status as a gentleman of fortune reconstruct old warnings traditionally given to young men as they began the world. Dickens's 'Vade Mecum', however, analyses the dilemma of a young man facing a greater challenge than Hogarth's two apprentices. In *Industry and Idleness* Frances Goodchild and Thomas Idle follow separate trajectories, respectively exhortations to the rewards of hard work or warnings about ruin brought on by sloth. Pip, by contrast, faces a future complicated beyond the need to make a choice between two stark alternatives: for him, good and bad commingle in deceptive and disturbing ways. One consequence is that the 'apprentice' must acquire greater sophistication if he is to master the challenges of mid-Victorian urban life. To succeed, he must accept his own improved circumstances without renouncing those he leaves behind in his former, humble sphere of life. See also chapter 58, note on pp. 315–16. For Dickens's use of Hogarth, see Harvey; Steig; and Paul B. Davis.

Volume I of the 1861 three-volume edition ended here.

Chapter 20   Thirteenth weekly number
                                                                                                         23 February 1861

THE journey from our town to the metropolis

THE journey from our town to the metropolis, was a journey of about five hours.] Averaging about six miles an hour to cover the thirty miles from Rochester to London by stagecoach was typical of the period. Stops to change horses and pick up and discharge passengers were frequent; unpaved and badly maintained roads added more time. Travel between Rochester and London and other parts of Kent did not improve substantially until the introduction of trains. In 1858, the London, Chatham and Dover Railway opened, reducing the journey between the metropolis and Dickens's 'Kentish house' just outside Rochester to 'little more than an hour's Railway ride' (*Letters* 9.196).

    The highway to London followed Watling Street, a Roman military road which ran from Canterbury to London via Rochester and then north-west to Wales. After crossing the Medway and ascending Strood Hill and then Gad's Hill, coaches passed through Chalk, Milton, Gravesend and Northfleet as the road ran parallel to the Thames. Beyond Dartford lay Crayford, Bexley Heath, Welling, Shooter's Hill, Greenwich and the Old Kent Road. Southwark, three miles west of Greenwich, was the last town before coaches crossed London Bridge and arrived at one of London's posting inns (*The Kentish Traveller's Companion*, 1779, pl. 1). See Appendix 4, map p. 443. This way into London was one of seven 'great openings' through which the majority of visitors passed entering from different parts of the country (Grant, 1839, 1.2).

    Dickens describes a journey by coach from London to Dover via 'the old high road' as it ran alongside the river 'between Gravesend and Rochester' in 'Travelling Abroad' (7 April 1860, *AYR* 2.557–62). Nostalgic comments about 'old road-side public house[s]' and the eclipse of stagecoaches by the advent of rail travel appear in his farewell address to the public as the editor of *Bentley's Miscellany* ('Familiar Epistle from a Parent to a Child', 5 [March 1839], 219–20). See also 'Dullborough Town' and 'An Old Stage-Coaching House' (*AYR* 3.274–8, 9.540–3).

the metropolis,] Metropolitan London in the early 1800s stretched from Poplar in the east to Hyde Park Corner in the west. The northern and southern boundaries included those parts of Middlesex and Essex and Surrey and Kent (the home counties) closest to the Thames. Three separate cities made up the metropolitan area: the City of London proper and the cities of Westminster and Southwark. See also below.

the four-horse stage-coach] Stagecoaches held twelve or more passengers. Four were accommodated inside; the remainder and the driver rode outside. A four-horse team was standard for a coach with this capacity.

the ravel of traffic] The prosperity that followed England's victory over France in 1815 accounts for the growth of London's horse-drawn traffic in the ensuing decades.

By 1839 some 1,200 cabriolets operated, in addition to which over 600 hackney-coaches plied for hire and competed with 400 or more horse-drawn omnibuses (Grant, 1837, 1.9). Large goods-waggons pulled by teams of horses, and sheep, cattle and pigs driven into town for auction at Smithfield market (see below), added to the chaotic conditions prevailing in the heart of the city (Reader 16). The city's first parking regulations date from 1820 in an attempt to clear streets blocked by unlawfully parked carriages and other vehicles. See also below.

Cross-Keys, Wood-street, The Cross Keys in Wood Street, Cheapside, one of London's former coaching inns, served as a terminus for coaches travelling between London and towns in the south-east. Its sign and name derived from the nearby church of St Peter's, whose emblem is two keys crossed. Coaching inns had dining-rooms on the ground floor and projecting balustraded galleries above leading to individual rooms. Large coaching inns, which employed a blacksmith, a vet, a coach-maker and a wheelwright, kept several hundred horses on hand, reserving some for use on regular coach routes and others for posting and private hire.

The rapid decline of coaching inns in London dates from about 1830, following the introduction of horse-drawn omnibuses in 1829 and the development of railway travel a decade later. In 'Dullborough Town' (*AYR* 3.274 [30 June 1860]), Dickens recalls arriving by coach in Wood Street when he left Chatham alone in September 1822 to join his family in London (Allen, 1988, 73). The inn was demolished in 1865 (Timbs, 1867, 453).

Cheapside, London.] Londoners regarded Cheapside, a principal thoroughfare, as the 'epitome of the wealth and splendour of the metropolis' (Shepherd, 1829, 71). Originally Cheap, or West Cheap, the street extends from the Poultry and Bucklersbury to St Paul's and Newgate Street. One observer commented: Cheapside was so crowded on both sides with pedestrians and the middle so packed with vehicles that one had to walk 'a considerable distance' before crossing to the opposite side (Grant, 1839, 1.7–9). Another described the accumulation of 'the world's material wealth' in Cheapside as without parallel anywhere on the earth:

> Dazzling stores of costly gems and the precious metals, displayed in glittering profusion, look out upon us from the shop-windows; and all that industry, ingenuity, and the rarest talent can furnish to the demands of luxury, is here offered to its acceptance. All the ends of the earth have sent in their choicest contributions, and whatever the treasures of the natural world, controlled and combined by the skill of man, can supply for the satisfaction of his most urgent wants or his slightest caprice, is here gathered together and submitted for his approval. (Charles Manby Smith, 1857, 362–3)

We Britons had at that time

We Britons had at that time particularly settled that it was treasonable to doubt our having and our being the best of everything:] Self-congratulation and complacency were common well into the middle of the century among some authors. Wrote Macaulay in 1830: 'when we compare our own condition with that of our ancestors, we think it clear that the advantages arising from the progress of civilization have far more than counterbalanced the disadvantages arising from the progress of population'. While Britain's numbers had increased tenfold, he added, 'our wealth has increased a hundredfold' ('Southey's Colloquies', 1.263). Addressing Parliament two decades later, Queen Victoria thanked God that 'tranquillity, good order, and willing obedience to the laws continue to prevail generally throughout the country' (*Annual Register*, 3 February 1852).

I was scared by the immensity of London,]

> The first thing which strikes a person on his visiting London for the first time is its amazing extent. In walking through its streets he fancies himself in a vast world of houses, out of which there is no escaping. (Grant, 1837, 1.1)

From east to west London stretched about eight miles; its circumference was thirty miles. The metropolitan area in 1830 was divided into 153 parishes, and eighty squares and over 10,000 streets, lanes, rows and alleys contained a population of roughly 2 million (Grant, 1837, 1.2). By contrast, the combined population of the cathedral city of Rochester and the adjacent dockyard town of Chatham a decade later just exceeded 17,000 (*Miniature Road-Book of Kent*, 1842).

rather ugly, crooked, narrow, and dirty.] Early nineteenth-century London presented dramatic contrasts. Visiting Little Britain (see below) early in the century, Washington Irving described the locality as 'a cluster of narrow streets and courts, of very venerable and debilitated houses', several ready to tumble down, 'the fronts of which are magnificently enriched with old oaken carvings' ('Little Britain', 2.83–4). Elsewhere, wrote another observer:

> The principal streets are open and airy . . . they are paved in the middle for carriages, with large stones in a very compact manner, forming a small convexity to pass the water off by channels; and on each side is a broad level path, formed of flag-stones, raised a little above the centre, for the convenience of foot passengers. (Adolphus 3.434)

Overall, the predominant impression appears to have been one of confusion, density and hurrying crowds. Commenting on the London he saw in 1832, James Hogg, the Ettrick Shepherd, noted that all the people in the principal streets 'seemed to be in as great a hurry as if Death himself had been following hard at their heels' (Grant, 1837, 1.7).

Mr. Jaggers had duly sent me his address

Little Britain . . . "just out of Smithfield, and close by the coach-office."] A former parish which derives its name (old Britain Street) from the Dukes of Brittany who lodged there centuries ago. The street called Little Britain still exists and runs west from Aldersgate Street, across present-day King Edward Street, to Smithfield Market (see below). The distance from the coach-office in Wood Street to Jaggers's is just under a mile. See Appendix 4, map pp. 442–3. This was an appropriate location for a law office on account of its proximity to the heart of London's 'law district'. The Justice Hall of the Old Bailey, Newgate Prison, the principal Inns of Court, and chambers occupied by solicitors and lawyers were all within a short walk, forming an area that was reputed to conduct 'nine-tenths of the whole court business of the country' in the nineteenth century (Charles Knight, 1851, 675). Nearby in Pasternoster Row booksellers, printers, publishers and stationers provided additional amenities to members of the legal profession. For Smithfield, see below.

a hackney-coachman,]   All hackney-coaches were licensed and regulated by a body of commissioners. Coach proprietors paid a weekly sum of ten shillings for their licences and were required to display their licence number on both sides of the coach. The commissioners set standards for the height of horses, and for rates and distances under specific conditions. For journeys under a mile the fee was one shilling; the fare for longer distances rose according to the time or to the miles travelled (George Gregory, 1806, 2.377). By 1800 over 800 hackney-coaches operated in London and Westminster. See also chapter 18, note on pp. 160–2.

as many capes to his greasy great-coat as he was years old,]   Coachmen wore overcoats with removable capes extending almost to the waist with as many as four separate layers.

a folding and jingling barrier of steps,]   Passengers used folding steps to enter and exit from the coach, as described in *PP*: 'The fat boy . . . let down the steps, and held the carriage door invitingly open' (4).

getting on his box . . . decorated with an old weather-stained pea-green hammercloth,]   The term appears to derive from an earlier period of travel when coach-owners brought along a hamper of food for the journey which was placed outside the coach facing the horse and used as a seat for the driver. Subsequent refinements in coach design included a box which the coachman used to store tools and equipment for the coach and horses (Kitchiner, 1827, pt 2, pp. 170, 204).

Hammercloth was a coloured drapery with a fringe frequently used to cover the driver's seat and box. By the nineteenth century, the hammercloth had become 'one of the principal ornaments to a carriage: according to the fullness of the plaiting of the cloth, its depth, and the quantity of trimming thereon, is the cost thereof, which varies from £10 to £40'. Possibly the term derived from *hammockcloth*, an ornamented and decorated cloth put over the back of a horse. Alternatively, it may be a corruption of 'Hamper cloth', the cloth people used to cover the food-hampers (Kitchiner, 1827, pt 2, p. 204).

with six great coronets outside,]   Coronets painted on the door of the coach signify a former aristocratic owner. Peers often sold back unfashionable carriages to coach-makers who, in turn, passed them on to hackney-coach proprietors at a low price. Many of the hackney-coaches and chariots for hire in London and in other large towns originated this way (*Complete Book of Trades* 150). In SB, Dickens wrote that panels ornamented with a faded coat of arms, 'in shape something like a dissected bat', indicated that the coach was one of London's 'time-honoured institutions' ('Hackney Coach Stands').

ragged things behind for I don't know how many footmen to hold on by, and a harrow below them, to prevent amateur footmen from yielding to the temptation.] Coaches designed originally for private use had a hind footboard and handles for servants, who travelled at the back, accompanying the family on short distances. This frame – the 'Hind Standard' – could be removed and a rumble or boot attached to convert into two seats suitable for a longer journey.

A wooden frame attached to the coach with iron teeth or tines prevented boys or youths from jumping on and hitching a free ride. The device resembled an inverted harrow and was considered essential when the coach had no footman behind, 'otherwise you will be perpetually loaded with idle people'. Unauthorized riders at the back were also deterred when voices from a crowded street cried out to the coachman to use his whip and 'Cut! Cut behind!' (Kitchiner pt 2, pp. 82–3).

I had scarcely had time to enjoy the coach

how like a straw-yard it was,] 'Why should hackney coaches be clean? Our ancestors found them dirty and left them so,' Dickens noted in 'Hackney Coach Stands' (SB). Straw in carriages helped insulate passengers against the cold. Meeting Dickens one day in November 1835, an American journalist describes how he hailed a cab carrying John Macrone, the publisher of SB. First, Macrone's head appeared, 'From out of the smoke of the wet straw', after which he saw Dickens (cited in Carlton, 1957, 403). Straw-yards – literally yards covered with straw – offered 'economical equestrians' a way to reduce the expense of maintaining a saddle horse from November through February. By sending horses there, owners avoided costs like shoeing and the expense of maintaining a private groom.

a rag-shop,] A shop where rags and old clothes were sold. Irish immigrants and Jews dominated London's extensive trade in second-hand clothing and displayed heaps of odorous, worn-out clothes and rags 'far from pleasant' to one's nostrils in musty-smelling shops (Mayhew and Binny 39).

the horses' nose-bags were kept inside,] Generally, horses' 'vitals' were provided by the cab driver and were served up to the animals 'in small bags, fastened to their own heads' (Grant, 1846, 1.263). Most coachmen allowed a hard-working horse 'four good feeds a day'. These included a sack of oats, some straw, chaff and a little bran (Kitchiner, pt 2, p. 13).

The coachman glanced at Mr. Jaggers's name

"A shilling – unless you wish to make it more."]   Legislation introduced by Parliament in 1808 (48 Geo. III, c. 87) and in 1831 fixed coach fares. A shilling would have been the correct fare, according to rates recently set. The London Hackney Carriage Act of 1831 (1 & 2 Will. IV, c. 22) gave drivers the option of charging either by distance or by time. Fares were fixed at one shilling for up to a mile and then sixpence for every half-mile beyond that. Alternatively, passengers paid one shilling for up to thirty minutes and sixpence for every additional fifteen minutes (Kitchiner, pt 2, p. 317).

London's hackney-coachmen were quick to overcharge strangers. One defence the visitor had against 'their practiced eye' was to request transport over a certain distance rather than to a specific destination. That way drivers would not dispute the distance, 'which they do when you specify a location'. Visitors were also encouraged to inquire from passers-by about the distance before engaging a coach; and, if you had luggage, you were advised to bargain with the coachman for the amount since 'he will probably ask you a half more than the regular fare' (Grant, 1846, 1.256, 258). Waiters and coachmen who take advantage of youthful travellers appear in *DC* (9, 19).

"He is not," returned the clerk.

"He is in Court]   Presumably at one of the courts in the Old Bailey, which served as crown courts and tried criminal cases.

With those words, the clerk opened a door

a velveteen suit and knee-breeches,]   In the first half of the nineteenth century, such a costume was worn only by elderly or old-fashioned gentlemen.

I began to say that I hoped

fur cap]   Most likely a cap made from cat fur, popular among lower-class men and boys. Tom Chittling in *OT* (18), Mr Krook in *BH* (5) and Rogue Riderhood in *OMF* (3.3) are typical examples.

Mr. Jaggers's room was lighted by a skylight only

two dreadful casts on a shelf of faces peculiarly swollen, and twitchy about the nose.] Swollen features and distorted noses characterize victims of hanging or throttling. The

> face, chest, shoulders, arms and hands, are swelled and livid, and often a bloody mucus issues from the mouth and nose . . . [the mark of the cord or rope] is evident around the neck, forming a livid, depressed circle.
> (T. R. Beck, 1825, 106)

Instructions for making a death mask call for the following procedure. First, one applies a coat of oil or a strong lather of soap and water to the face and hair to prevent the adhesion of plaster when it is spread carefully over the face and head. After the plaster has set, the head is then pressed into a flat dish containing more plaster, where the head reclines, as on a pillow. Uncovered parts of the head may then receive the same treatment. When the mould is hard enough it may be removed in three pieces. The same steps can be used with live models either by inserting quills into the nostrils or by leaving small openings for the same purpose (Hutton, 1892, 620).

Plaster casts made from death masks of executed criminals and notorious murderers often went on sale not long after the hangman had removed the bodies from the scaffold. Thomas De Quincey, writing in 1827 about the voyeuristic interest in murderers in the early nineteenth century, speaks of purchasing a plaster cast of John Williams (executed for the Ratcliff Highway murders of 1811), displayed in a shop in a dirty London side-street (1862, 4.64). De Quincey also notes that it was not uncommon for surgeons who assisted at the dissection of murderers to maintain their own private collection of casts, especially when the body of a celebrated murderer had provided the corpse for their anatomical inquiries (29).

Death masks apparently originated in ancient Rome, where their popularity owed more to a respectful interest in the deceased than to the macabre curiosity typical in Dickens's time. The display of masks in England received a boost after the introduction of phrenology early in the nineteenth century, from which period dates the vogue for collecting plaster heads of criminals for ostensibly scientific purposes. Several collections of life and death masks of the infamous and the famous still exist in the Black Museum of Scotland Yard, London, Castle Museum, Norwich, Dundee Art Gallery and Museum, and the Anatomy Department of the University of Edinburgh. Madame Tussaud's and Newgate Prison itself encouraged public interest by preserving casts of criminals' heads for viewing: a sketch in the *Illustrated London News* as late as 1873 depicts a warder showing visitors (a well-dressed family of four) standing in a place off the entrance hall a collection of casts taken from the heads of criminals who had been hanged in front of the prison ('Sketches of Newgate', 161). Gatrell links the interest in casts with the earlier vogue for commissioning portraits of condemned prisoners shortly before their execution. Sir James Thornhill, Nathaniel Dance, William Mulready, and George and Robert Cruikshank all drew, sketched or painted murderers before they expired on the scaffold (1996, 254–5).

high-backed chair . . . of deadly black horsehair, with rows of brass nails round it like a coffin;] Chairs like this were often made of oak and upholstered leather held down by a row of brass studs or nails. See also the description in *DS* of the twenty-four chairs standing around Mr Dombey's dining-table (30).

I sat down in the cliental chair

knowing something to everybody else's disadvantage,] The phrase appears to be a variation of one used by lawyers attempting to contact heirs or beneficiaries and commonly inserted as an announcement into newspapers. For the correct form, often repeated, see R. L. Stevenson, *The Wrong Box*: if this should meet the eye of [blank], 'he will hear SOMETHING TO HIS ADVANTAGE' (1889, ch. 14). This information was supplied by Susan Shatto.

oppressed by the hot exhausted air, and by the dust and grit that lay thick on everything.] Private coal-fires and smoke from factories, breweries, bakehouses, gasworks and numerous industrial sources polluted London's air and that of all major cities and towns in England. The Towns Improvement Clauses Act of 1847 (10 & 11 Vict., c. 34) represents an early attempt to address the problem of air filled with smuts and gritty from coal smoke.

When I told the clerk that I would take a turn in the air

go round the corner and I should come into Smithfield. So I came into Smithfield, and the shameful place, being all asmear with filth and fat and blood and foam, seemed to stick to me.] Smithfield, London's only 'live' cattle market, adjoined Little Britain. Originally an area of nearly five acres devoted to the sale of cattle and horses, and to horse racing, in 1685 it was paved, drained and railed in to form the world's largest market for the sale of cattle, sheep and pigs. Henceforth, markets were held here twice a week, every Monday and Friday. To many, Smithfield was synonymous with a 'shocking' barbarity to animals:

> The scenes of cruelty . . . practised by the drovers towards the cattle, sheep, and pigs, are of the most shocking kind. No person of humane mind can pass through Smithfield . . . without the greatest violence being done to his feelings, at the manner in which the poor animals are treated. (Grant, 1846, 2.182)

Reformers also objected to the presence of slaughter-houses in a crowded part of the city and to the unsanitary conditions under which they operated – butchers slaughtered sheep and cattle in 'the most horrible [underground] dens which can be conceived'; other nuisances were created by the presence of 'knackers' yards, tainted sausage-makers . . . tripe-dressers, cat's-meat boilers, catgut-spinners, bone-houses, and other noxious trades' all in the immediate vicinity (Charles Knight, 1851, 798; Timbs, 1867, 561).

HW participated in the campaign to close the market and published many articles about it (see Select Bibliography). The sale of live cattle continued until 1855, when the market was abolished by Parliament (Smithfield Market Removal Act, 14 & 15 Vict., c. 61).

I saw the great black dome of Saint Paul's bulging at me] The apex of the dome of St Paul's, black from the soot of coal fires, and approximately 365 feet high, is easily visible from the vicinity of Smithfield. Dickens makes a similar observation about the 'bulging' appearance of 'large edifices' in 'One Man in a Dockyard' (*HW* 3.553). The cathedral and its famous dome (completed 1709) were the work of Sir Christopher Wren (1632–1723), who submitted a new design in response to a request for something 'handsome and noble' to replace the old medieval cathedral partially destroyed by the Great Fire of London in 1666.

a grim stone building which a bystander said was Newgate Prison.] The reference is to the prison built in 1769 and rebuilt in 1782 by George Dance II (1741–1825); it stood on the east side of Old Bailey Street close to the site of the ancient city wall and took its name from the city's fifth principal gate. Dance deliberately emphasized massive solidarity and security: great blind outer walls of Portland stone three feet thick; bold rustication and Doric corners; and two wings extending to right and left added to the prison's dominating effect. The keeper's house, with close-set windows, stood in the centre; two entrance-lodges on either side, 'stamped with gloomy grandeur and severity', created a visceral sense of power.

In the early nineteenth century, Newgate housed about 800 prisoners, mixing debtors and capital felons and serving as a detention centre for the secure custody of prisoners about to be tried or executed (Wakefield, 1831, *Works* 228). Subsequent legislation attempted to separate inmates into categories and address abuses that gave Newgate a reputation that persisted well into the nineteenth century. Changes in penological practice (see chapter 32, note on pp. 271–3) further mitigated the evil conditions so long associated with Newgate, whose origin as a prison dates from the twelfth century.

the roadway covered with straw to deaden the noise of passing vehicles;] This practice continued in many parts of London until the introduction of wooden pavements later in the century (Charles Knight, 1851, 679). Visitors to London generally found the noise level overwhelming:

> The first rather startling phenomenon that greets the ear of a stranger who drops thus suddenly into the arms of the metropolis, is the uninterrupted and crashing roar of deafening sounds, which tell of the rush of the current of London's life-blood through its thousand channels. (Charles Manby Smith, 1857, 395)

The crack of drivers' whips, shouts, and the sound of horses' bells, the confused trampling of hoofs, and 'the hoarse brawling of link-boys, watermen and cads' added to the din that prevailed throughout the day and well into the night (Wight, 1833, 3).

from the quantity of people standing about, smelling strongly of spirits and beer, I inferred that the trials were on.]   The 'trials' refers to the former quarterly 'Sessions' at the Justice Hall (commonly called the Sessions-house and rebuilt in 1834 as the Central Criminal Court) in Old Bailey street adjacent to Newgate prison. To accommodate the volume of cases, the quarterly Sessions in London were later doubled to accommodate the number handled by superior or assize judges when they met for *oyer and terminer* ('to hear and bring to an end') and to 'deliver the gaol'. Trials drew spectators on account of the 400 or so prisoners to be tried during each session and provided public excitement in anticipation of the hangings that would follow outside the prison. In *TTC*, Dickens expressed contempt for 'the tainted crowd' trials attracted, who paid 'to see the play' in which interest mounted in proportion to the seriousness of the crime and the severity of the punishment (2.2).

While I looked about me here

minister of justice]   The phrase appears to be Dickens's invention, used ironically to describe one of the Newgate gatekeepers. 'Minister' in this context refers to a subordinate or underling.

asked me if I would like to step in and hear a trial or so: informing me that he could give me a front place for half-a-crown, whence I should command a full view of the Lord Chief Justice in his wig and robes – mentioning that awful personage like waxwork, and presently offering him at the reduced prices of eighteenpence.]   The commercialization of the scaffold existed at many levels. Newgate officials were notorious for making money (up to almost £300 a year) by taking fees from spectators who could afford to indulge their curiosity. Some paid to view prisoners in the condemned cell, others to secure good seats at important trials. Newgate turnkeys took similar advantage of opportunities their employment offered by accepting bribes to admit prostitutes or wives and children (Gatrell 385).

A high gallery inside offered spectators a commanding view of the court proceedings below. To the right, a bench extended the length of one wall with desks at intervals for the use of the judges. In the body of the court were a dock underneath the gallery for prisoners, to the left the witness-box and then the jury-box. In the centre around a green-baize table sat defence and prosecution counsel facing 'a formidable row of law-books' in the middle of the table. The Lord Chancellor, England's chief justice, sat in the centre of the bench in the chief seat, dressed in fur-trimmed blue robes and a gold chain. From the bench, the Lord Chancellor and the other judges in their wigs and robes were positioned so they could keep jury, witnesses and prisoners within the same line of view (Charles Knight, 1851, 681).

where the gallows was kept,]   The gallows were stored within the prison walls and assembled outside Newgate in preparation for executions. The apparatus included the scaffold with its small, collapsible platform, and barriers and guards to keep spectators at a distance. The device caused the prisoner to fall on the removal of a supporting pin. Although hanging was supposed to be a quick and certain form of execution, it usually caused a slow, painful death. The 'new drop', introduced in 1783 as a replacement for the three-cornered gallows that had stood at Tyburn (the junction of Oxford Street, Bayswater and Edgware Roads) failed to live up to its expectations of efficiency. Few died cleanly: some were decapitated when the ratio between body weight and the length of the drop was badly miscalculated; most choked to death over several minutes, kicking their bound legs and losing control of their bowels; and some required assistance from the hangman to finish them off. This ritual remained embedded in metropolitan and provincial urban life until the collapse of the capital code in the 1830s. Hangings occurred once or twice a year in many assize towns and after each of the eight Sessions held annually in London at the old Sessions House. After 1830 hangings declined, restricted solely to murderers, until the last public execution outside on 27 May 1868 (Gatrell 30, 45–6).

where people were publicly whipped,] Prisoners were whipped both in 'private', within the gaol or house of correction, and in public, either by the common hangman or by someone hired for the occasion. Victims suffered intensely: sentences sometimes directed that the prisoner should be whipped 'severely' or 'until his back be bloody'. Vagrants, 'incorrigible rogues', prostitutes and individuals convicted of petty larceny (the theft of goods worth less than a shilling) were among those most commonly whipped. The frequency of public whippings began to decrease from 1700 onwards as corporal punishment fell increasingly into disfavour, although public whippings continued to be ordered, especially at the quarter sessions, until the end of the eighteenth century (Beattie 461–2, 614).

Efforts to abolish flogging entirely began in 1823 but were defeated, although the public whipping of women had been abolished in 1817 (53 Geo. III, c. 75), followed by the elimination of whipping women in private in 1820 (1 Geo. IV, c. 57) and whipping for minor offences under the Vagrancy Act of 1824 (5 Geo. IV, c. 83). However, the Juvenile Offenders Act of 1847 (10 & 11 Vict., c. 82) allowed courts of summary jurisdiction to order offenders under 14 to be whipped, and the flogging of adults was re-introduced in 1863 by the Security from Violence Act (26 & 27 Vict., c. 44) for garrotting and robbery with violence during the outbreak of garrotting in 1862–3 (Tobias 138). Prison authorities continued to use the birch and the cat-o'-nine-tails and retained the option to inflict corporal punishment until a Royal Commission in 1938 recommended its abolition.

the Debtors' Door, out of which culprits came to be hanged:] This was a side-door, originally designed to admit and discharge debtors from the prison. The same door was later reserved for a second purpose when, at the suggestion of John Howard, prison authorities began to use it to escort condemned prisoners to the scaffold after public executions were moved from Tyburn to Newgate in 1783 (see above). Condemned prisoners passed through the debtors' hall, temporarily screened from their fellow-inmates by black curtains, and exited via Debtors' Door to the street, where they were hanged (Timbs, 1867, 704, 698). The practice of confining debtors in Newgate ended in 1815 when Whitecross Prison in Whitecross Street, Cripplegate, opened solely to hold debtors. The euphemistic name persisted, however, and reference to 'the debtors' door' continued until the abolition of public executions outside Newgate in 1868.

"four on 'em" would come out at that door the day after tomorrow at eight in the morning, to be killed in a row.] Newgate's 'new drop' (see above) was constructed with three cross-beams. Ropes attached to each could accommodate as many as eighteen victims. Multiple executions continued to occur into the second decade of the nineteenth century, providing a horrible public spectacle in which rows of offenders were exhibited. These included, on some occasions, 'ten or twenty children' in a line (Bennett, 1818, 27, 303). Executions outside Newgate prison were usually conducted at eight in the morning.

Support for this 'ancient practice', justified in the name of deterrence, continued despite criticism from reformers. Henry Grey Bennett, MP, a supporter of prison reform, advocated multiple executions on the grounds that they conveyed an unequivocal message to those whom the law had found 'hopeless', individuals incapable of reform:

> Nine-tenths of [those executed] commit offences from misery, from the seduction of others, from the neglect or want of parents. If, then, reformation of these miserable beings is not to be looked to, but their punishment alone is to be considered, experience has shown, that the milder punishment does not deter. The choice is then narrowed, and we must recur again to the disgraceful severities of our ancestors. (1818, 303–4)

The majority of crimes for which people were executed between 1822 and 1827 were offences against property, including forgery, sheep-stealing, horse-stealing and highway robbery. Less common were executions for rape, other violent crimes and 'unnatural offences' (*The Hangman's Record*, 1909). The Old Bailey has been judged the bloodiest court in the kingdom: 'At the peak of the crime wave of the 1780s its judges presided over what has aptly been termed a judicial carnage' (Gatrell 544).

which, I took it into my head, he had bought cheap of the executioner.] The clothes of executed prisoners were traditionally the perquisites of the hangman, who made a little extra money by selling them. Equally popular was the halter in which the victim suffered: the rope was cut into the smallest pieces possible and sold to spectators at a shilling each (Southey 63).

The public regarded London's hangmen as minor celebrities ever since records of the public executioner began in 1601. Individuals were initiated with a theatrical ceremony conducted by the Recorder of London and other legal officials. Kneeling before a table on which were displayed a well-sharpened axe, a pair of leg irons, handcuffs, other fetters and a small coil of rope, the candidate swore 'to hang or behead and to draw and quarter, or otherwise destroy all felons and enemies of the peace of our loyal King, and of his subjects duly sentenced according to law, and that I will do the like unto father, mother, sister, or brother, and all other kindred whatsoever, without favour or hindrance – so help me God'. After the oath-taking, the hangman rose, a black veil was thrown over him and all assembled groaned in unison. Then death bells tolled as the presiding judge cried out: 'Get thee hence,

Wretch' (*The Groans of the Gallows!* 5–6). From 1828 to 1871, John Calcraft served as London's executioner (*The Hangman's Record*, 1909).

I dropped into the office

Bartholomew Close;] A square or court formerly part of the enclosed grounds of the ancient Priory of St Bartholomew in the vicinity of Little Britain. Dickens later refers to 'the iron gate of Bartholomew Close', which was locked every night, restricting passageway between Little Britain and Aldersgate Street.

a red-eyed little Jew . . . with a second little Jew] London's Jewish population numbered around 20,000 in 1849. Charles Dickens, Jr, notes that 'Within the memory of living men' the Jews of the metropolis rarely settled outside their own quarter, a ghetto east of the City embracing Bevis Marks, Aldgate, Houndsditch, the Minories, Whitechapel and Petticoat Lane (1879, 125). Most of these Jews were poor Ashkenazi, political refugees from Poland and Germany let into England after Cromwell in 1656 rescinded the order given in 1290 to expel them. Poor Jews, like those depicted here, necessarily settled for marginal occupations at the edge of or outside the law. Dealing in second-hand clothing remained one of their characteristic occupations throughout the century. See also below.

a lamp-post,] For the introduction of gas-lighting into London, see chapter 33, note on pp. 280–1.

"Oh Jaggerth, Jaggerth, Jaggerth! all otherth ith Cag-Maggerth, give me Jaggerth!"] The speaker's inability to produce sibilants and his use of an inorganic initial 'h' (see also 'hown' and 'Habraham') are traits typically associated with the speech of poor Jews, most of whom were recent immigrants from Germany and Poland. Other mispronunciations noticed by Dickens include those of a Jew in *LD* (2.26) who speaks only five words ('a tyfling madder ob bithznethz'), and the similar nasal consonants that characterize the speech of Barney in *OT* (42), an associate of Fagin's ('I'b dot certaid you cad'). Riah, the good Jew in *OMF* Dickens offered as amends for Fagin, has a distinctive speech indicated by syntax and word-choice rather than by pronunciation. Some observers maintained that well-to-do Jews generally spoke without a lisp in speech 'quite free from that accent that mostly distinguishes the less wealthy descendants of Abraham' (Thomas Cross 1.149).

The phrase 'Cag-Maggerth' comes from *Cag-mag*, a slang term for rotten meat or offal 'dressed up' and sold to the public by butchers 'at the price of good and wholesome food' ('Cag-mag Butchers!', 1838, 4). According to this source, many 'filthy rascals' had amassed immense fortunes this way. Much of the business centred around London's meat markets – Newgate, Leadenhall and Clare Market – but Whitechapel Market in London's principal Jewish quarter was thought to be the most notorious stronghold of this 'abominable, stinking, disgusting' trade. See also below.

"Oh yes, sir! Every farden."

farden."] A London dialectical pronunciation of farthing, one quarter of a penny.

This terrible threat caused the two women

raised the skirts of Mr. Jaggers's coat to his lips several times.] Most coats worn by men during this period had coat-tails at the back. Riah uses an identical gesture in OMF (2.5). According to Mrs Eliza Davis, the Jewish woman who reproached Dickens for his portrait of Fagin, kissing the hem of a garment 'is strictly Polish'. She admitted that Turkish Jews might use it, though she had never seen it practised in England except once by a Polish Jewess ('Fagin and Riah', *Dickensian* 149).

The suitor, kissing the hem of the garment again

on thuthpithion of plate."] The charge was for either stealing or receiving stolen silver plate. Plate-receivers were reputed to have fixed crucibles 'always in readiness, to melt any quantity of plate brought in'. After the plate was melted, weighed and cast off, they purchased the silver at about one shilling and three pence per ounce under the current market price; alternatively, they received a liberal payment for the melting and then the thief disposed of the goods at his own discretion (*Old Bailey Experience* 410). Both felonies were punishable by either gaol or transportation.

"You're too late," said Mr. Jaggers.

"I am over the way."] A colloquialism meaning on the other side, that is, prosecuting rather than defending.

My guardian threw his supplicant off

My guardian threw his supplicant off with supreme indifference, and left him dancing on the pavement as if it were red-hot.] Possibly the petitioner is refused because his brother 'fences' silver, an illicit trade in which Jews, by tradition, were implicated. Or perhaps his wealth (money is no object, he asserts) implicates him as one of the 'cag-mag' butchers, reportedly many of whom were ' "accursed Jews" ' engaged in selling offal as they vied with each other 'in their nasty ways' and dishonest practices ('Cag-mag Butchers!' 4).

"Oh!" said Mr. Jaggers, turning to the man

like the Bull in Cock Robin pulling at the bell-rope;] The bullfinch in the nursery rhyme 'Who Killed Cock-Robin?'

Who'll toll the bell:
I said the Bull,
Because I can pull,
I'll toll the bell.

And the birds of the air
Fell a-sighing and a-sobbing,
When they heard the bell toll
For poor Cock-Robin

"Spooney!" said the clerk

"Spooney!"]   An eighteenth-century term for a simpleton or fool, now obsolete.

"He is dressed like a 'spectable pieman.

a 'spectable pieman. A sort of a pastrycook."]   Piemen might wear an ordinary hat or a white hat, an apron and perhaps a white jacket. Many wore breeches and carried a handbell to advertise their goods (Cunnington and Lucas 127).

London's streets were crowded with 'peripatetic pastry-cooks' who wound in and out of the crowds shouting: 'Hot kidney pudd'ns!' – 'Hot mutton pies, and no <u>vet</u> 'uns – all hot!' – 'Brandy balls!' – 'Cock-tail!' – 'Hot <u>sassenges</u> – all hot!' (Wight, 1833, 58). The decline in home baking from the early nineteenth century onwards accounts for the increase in the number of street-sellers of cooked food and baked goods. A 'respectable' pieman may have been an ironic allusion on account of the frequency with which itinerant piemen and owners of cheap cook-shops were exposed in the press for selling contaminated baked goods ('Meat and Murrain', 1865, 202–4).

The window indicated was the office window.

the wire blind,]   Wire blinds were affixed to windows to reduce heat and light during the summer months (Loudon, 1833, 560).

My guardian then took me into his own room

a pocket flask of sherry]   Sherry was the most popular of the fortified wines carried in pocket flasks (Hewett and Axton 141).

"Barnard's Inn,"]   Barnard's was one of ten Inns of Chancery, houses or sets of collegiate buildings in London which began as places of residence for students and apprentices of the law. Many resembled Oxford colleges with a hall, chapel, library and residential rooms. Barnard's Inn (see Plate 15) at 23 Lower Holborn, opposite

Furnival's Inn, derived its name from Lionel Bernard (pronounced Barnard), a former tenant, who rented the original building from its owner, Dr John Mackworth. Barnard's Inn had a hall 'of very small dimensions . . . totally devoid of all architectural ornaments' (Ireland, 1800, 191). Until the eighteenth century, the ten Inns of Chancery were subordinate to the Inns of Court, four principal Inns in London which had the exclusive right of admitting men to practise at the Bar and of instructing and examining for that purpose. The distinction between the Inns of Chancery and the Inns of Court had been lost by the nineteenth century, and in Dickens's time all fourteen Inns existed as legal societies with corporate property whose chambers were let to solicitors and individuals unconnected with the law. For the Inns of Court, see Apendix 3.

outrunning the constable.]   A colloquial phrase which meant to spend more than one could afford. In a literal sense, one might have to evade a constable sent by a creditor to recover money that was owed.

I then found that Wemmick

shaking hands with my guardian.]   For Pip's tendency to shake hands, see chapter 21, note on p. 192.

Chapter 21

CASTING my eyes on Mr. Wemmick as we went along

he appeared to have sustained a good many bereavements; for, he wore at least four mourning rings, besides a brooch representing a lady and a weeping willow at a tomb with an urn on it. I noticed, too, that several rings and seals hung at his watch-chain, as if he were quite laden with remembrances of departed friends.] This display suggests pretension and manifests a degree of 'vulgarity' characteristic of someone unschooled in the ways of polite society: 'So completely is modesty the true spirit of good breeding, that any kind of display in poor or rich, high or low, savors of vulgarity' (*The Habits of Good Society*, 1860, 47).

Individuals frequently left bequests to relatives and friends for the purchase of mourning jewellery and other kinds of *memento mori* to be worn as tokens of respect and sorrow. Varieties of mourning rings existed. Some were gold, others were enamelled or set with miniatures, locks of hair from the deceased, or precious and semi-precious stones. Many also employed iconographic devices traditionally associated with death: willow trees, wreaths, wheat ears (the full ear reaped in maturity) or a snake swallowing its own tail (eternity). The motif on the brooch was one of the more popular and enduring icons.

Rings and a bunch of seals (either engraved stones for sealing letters or pieces of coloured glass) were worn as ornamental appendages attached to a watch-chain. The watch, in this case, would have been a pocket-watch worn in the fob pocket, a small opening in the waistband of breeches used for carrying valuables.

"You may get cheated, robbed, and murdered, in London.

"You may get cheated, robbed, and murdered, in London.] MS reads 'That depends upon what you call very wicked. You'.

Versions of London as the 'dissolute city', revived in Romantic poetry, connect with an old literary tradition that portrayed towns in moral terms. More recently, visitors to the metropolis were warned of the dangers to be found there: cheats and wretches 'who are always keeping a sharp look out to entrap' the property of visitors, cheat them and 'rob and perhaps murder the unprotected, and . . . make a prey of the unsuspecting'; 'smashers' and 'jobbers' who passed on forged banknotes; thieves who walked off brazenly with luggage taken from a hackney-coach; dexterous pickpockets; 'flimpers', who tripped and hustled their victims as they stole from their pockets; beggars; violent housebreakers; and 'women of the town', many of whom lured customers to places where their victims were beaten and robbed (*The London Guide, and Stranger's Safeguard* . . . ,1818, vi, passim).

He wore his hat on the back of his head

His mouth was such a post-office of a mouth] The comparison draws on two recent developments: the introduction of slots in the front doors of houses in the 1840s through which letter carriers could insert mail and the erection of Britain's roadside letter boxes, the most distinctive of which were the re-designed fluted-column pillar boxes introduced in 1857. These boxes with a slightly protruding horizontal aperture replaced earlier models whose vertical slits had not offered great security or protection from rain. Both innovations resulted from the inauguration of the Uniform Penny Postage on 10 January 1840 and had two unforeseen consequences: the greatly increased use of envelopes and the elimination of fees to be collected each time letters were delivered. With prepaid mail, all the carrier had to do was to drop letters through slits in people's front doors, as Rowland Hill had suggested in his pamphlet, *Post Office Reform*, 1837 (Muir 117).

Harriet Martineau, writing in a letter to an American friend about the introduction of the penny postage, commented:

> We are all putting up our letter-boxes on our hall doors with great glee . . . The slips in the doors are to save the postmen's time, – the great point being how many letters may be delivered within a given time, the postage being paid in the price of the envelopes, or the paper. So all who wish well to the plan are having slips in their doors. (Martineau 3.250)

Prior to 1840, letters were handed in at London's General Post Office or at receiving houses located in shops throughout the metropolitan area. After 8 p.m. when the shops closed, letters could be put through a slot which had been cut in the shutter of the receiving house (Muir 23–4).

the top of Holborn Hill] Holborn Hill was at the east end of Holborn, a main thoroughfare running east to west from New Oxford Street to Newgate Street. The hill, one side of which was formed by the Fleet Valley, remained an obstacle to horse-drawn traffic until Holborn Viaduct, which carried the road across the valley on a series of arches, opened in 1869. See Appendix 4, map pp. 442–3.

"Yes," said he, nodding in the direction.

"At Hammersmith, west of London."] MS reads 'At Hornsey, north of London.' Presumably Dickens changed the location when he recognized Hammersmith, on the north bank of the Thames about five miles west of Barnard's Inn, would serve as a place for Pip and his companions to develop their skill as oarsmen. In 1801 Hammersmith was an attractive village of about 6,000 crossed by two great roads from London: one which ran through Kensington to Brentford and one which ran through Bayswater, Notting Hill and Shepherd's Bush to Uxbridge.

We entered this haven through a wicket-gate

a melancholy little square . . . and the most dismal houses . . . I had ever seen . . . while To Let To Let To Let, glared at me from empty rooms,] Compare the earlier, extended description of Gray's Inn published as 'Chambers' in *AYR* on 18 August 1860. In it, the Uncommercial Traveller evokes a similar melancholy atmosphere, likening the Inn's dirty windows and door-posts to gravestones and pronouncing the entire building 'one of the most depressing institutions in brick and mortar' known to the children of men (*AYR* 3.453). See also below. Elsewhere, Dickens comments on the tendency to cover properties to let in 'a perfect suit of bills' and encrust buildings in more fragments of notices than the number of barnacles a ship's keel gathered after a long voyage in *DC* (41) and in 'Bill-Sticking' (*HW* 2.601).

Another writer, however, called Barnard's Inn 'a most picturesque little enclosure'. Reportedly, former inhabitants at the beginning of the century 'had the most beautiful view' from the windows, one that stretched as far as Hampstead and Islington. 'The inhabitants grew, and were proud of, their grapes, nectarines, and peaches' (Fitzgerald 164).

"Try Barnard's Mixture."] Evidently an analogy to the kind of slogan used for advertising tobacco.

He led me into a corner

He led me into a corner and conducted me up a flight of stairs – which appeared to me to be slowly collapsing into sawdust, so that one of these days the upper lodgers would . . . find themselves without the means of coming down] Speaking as the Uncommercial Traveller in 'Chambers', Dickens made a similar point about crumbling staircases:

> Imagination gloats over the fulness of time, when the staircases shall have quite tumbled down – they are daily wearing into an ill-savoured powder, but have not quite tumbled down yet – when the last old prolix bencher all of the olden time, shall have been got out of an upper window by means of a Fire-Ladder, and carried off to the Holborn Union . . . (*AYR* 3.453)

I put out my hand

I put out my hand, and Mr. Wemmick at first looked at it as if he thought I wanted something.] Pip appears to compound two social errors. In shaking hands, the rule is that the person in the superior position (i.e. class or age) holds out his hand first. A gesture of friendship and equality on the basis of such a short acquaintance indicates a second breach in decorum: 'Familiarity, on first introduction, is always of bad style, often even vulgar,' warned the arbiters of 'society' (*The Habits of Good Society*, 1860, 38).

"I have got so out of it!" said Mr. Wemmick

"except at last."] The customary farewell handshake to a criminal, shortly before he was executed.

When we had shaken hands and he was gone

saying to myself that London was decidedly overrated.] The narrator of 'Dullborough Town' registers a similar sense of disappointment when he describes his first coach journey as a youth from Rochester to London: 'There was no other inside passenger, and I consumed my sandwiches in solitude and dreariness, and it rained hard all the way, and I thought life sloppier than I had expected to find it' (AYR 3.274).

Mr. Pocket, Junior's, idea of Shortly

a pottle of strawberries] Pottles were cone-shaped wicker or 'chip' baskets, which held about twelve ounces and were used as a dry measure for the sale of fruit. Victorians regarded strawberries, together with raspberries and gooseberries, as 'the most wholesome fruit which this country affords'. Strawberries had a short season and were sold only in June (Keith Imray, 1842, 818).

"Dear me!" he exclaimed.

I went to Covent Garden Market to get it good."] Covent Garden was widely regarded as the best source for fruit, vegetables and flowers in London:

> There is more certainty of being able to purchase a pine-apple here, every day in the year, than in Jamaica and Calcutta, where pines are indigenous. Forced asparagus, potatoes, sea-kale, rhubarb-stalks, mushrooms, French beans, and early cucumbers, are to be had in January and February; in March, forced cherries, strawberries, and spring spinach; in April, grapes, peaches, and melons, with early peas; in May, all forced articles in abundance. The supply of forced flowers, of greenhouse plants, and in summer of hardy flowers and shrubs, is equally varied and abundant; and of curious herbs for domestic medicines, shrubs, distilleries, &etc., upwards of 500 species may be procured at the shop of one herbalist. (Timbs, 1867, 559)

Founded in 1670, the market occupied a three-acre site and was open three days a week (Tuesday, Thursday and Saturday). The name refers to the former garden of the Convent of Westminster, which lay between the north side of the Strand and Long Acre. For over a century, the market was 'a strange assemblage of shed and penthouse, rude stall, and crazy tenement, coffee-house and gin-shop, intersected by narrow and ill-lit footways, until the area was cleared for a new market in 1829'

(Timbs 1867, 559). The quadrangle with two exterior colonnades on the north and south sides in front of shops and a central building with an open roof and shops on each side designed by Charles Fowler still stand, but the market closed for business in November 1973, when the market moved to a new site at Nine Elms, Battersea.

"Pray come in," said Mr. Pocket, Junior.

our table . . . will be supplied from our coffee-house] London's original coffee-houses (the first dates from 1652) limited their business to beverages. Coffee-drinking later spread to taverns where food was sold and meals were catered outside the premises. Eventually, taverns like these adopted the preferred name of coffee-houses.

15 Barnard's Inn, c.1800

Chapter 22 Fourteenth weekly number
2 March 1861

As he was so communicative

I further mentioned that as I had been brought up a blacksmith in a country place, and knew very little of the ways of politeness, I would take it as a great kindness in him if he would give me a hint whenever he saw me at a loss or going wrong.]   Conduct manuals like Day's *Hints on Etiquette and The Usages of Society* (1834) and 'how to' books written for 'those who do not know what is proper' also called attention to the importance of manners. 'GOOD Manners, have often made the Fortune of many, who have had nothing else to recommend them; ILL Manners, have as often marred the hopes of those who have had everything else to advance them' (Kitchiner, 1825, 26). See also below.

"I don't take to Philip," said he

"I don't take to Philip," said he, smiling, "for it sounds like a moral boy out of the spelling-book, who was so lazy that he fell into a pond, or so fat that he couldn't see out of his eyes, or so avaricious that he locked up his cake till the mice ate it, or so determined to go birds'-nesting that he got himself eaten by bears who lived handy in the neighbourhood.]   The target seems to be one of the many didactic reading primers and spelling books popular during the early part of the century. Sir Richard Philips (1767–1840), author of *Reading Exercises for the Use of Schools, on a New and Improved Plan* (1820), to whom Dickens may allude specifically, populated his book, described in the title as a sequel to William Mavor's widely used *English-Spelling Book*, with several 'moral boys'. Harry Thoughtless, for example, earned a reputation for mean and nasty behaviour by pulling off the wings of flies, Robin, 'the spoiled boy', indulged and pampered by his parents, grew increasingly quarrelsome and obstinate until his mother fell ill and he suddenly imagined what would happen if both his parents died, while Mendaculus, a youth of good parts and an amiable temper, began to live up to his name when he started to keep bad company and developed 'the odious practice of lying' (47–9, 63, 11–12).

"Would you mind Handel for a familiar name?

There's a charming piece of music by Handel, called the Harmonious Blacksmith."]   That is, the air and variations from Handel's Harpsichord Suite No. 5 in E Major (1720). The nickname, which has no connection with the circumstances of the work's composition, was first used after the composer died. The centenary of Handel's death (London, 14 April 1759) had recently been celebrated at the Handel Festival, held at the Crystal Palace on 20 June 1859 (Joseph Irving, *Annals*, 1875).

This I would not hear of

It was a nice little dinner – seemed to me then, a very Lord Mayor's Feast] Banquets given by each new Lord Mayor of London on his installation were known for their splendour. They were generally considered the equal of Royal Banquets, Ministerial Dinners and 'well-mounted aristocratic entertainments' (*London at Dinner*, 1858, 20). The custom originated in the fifteenth century as a way to honour outgoing Lord Mayors and welcome new office-holders on 9 November every year. 'Even in these moderate times the Lord Mayor's feast is a Gargantuan institution, involving the services of twenty cooks, the slaughter of forty turtles, and the consumption of somewhere about fourteen tons of coal' (*Dickens's London Guide*, 1878, 111).

lap of luxury] A common figurative variant of this phrase; see Maria Edgeworth, 'Brought up in the lap of luxury' (*Moral Tales*, 1816, 1.6, 36).

the boiled fowl] Boiled fowl was typically prepared by trussing the bird, rubbing the breast with lemon, wrapping it in buttered paper and boiling it with sliced vegetables and bouquet garni (Beeton 702–3). Common domestic fowl was reputedly 'rather slow of digestion', but the mild quality of its meat was prized.

"True," he replied. "I'll redeem it at once.

in London it is not the custom to put the knife in the mouth. . . . and that while the fork is reserved for that use, it is not put further in than necessary. . . . Also, the spoon is not generally used over-hand, but under.] Conduct manuals frequently made a similar point:

> <u>In all cases</u>, the observances of the Metropolis (as the seat of refinement) should be received as the standard of good breeding. . . . Never <u>use your knife to convey</u> your food to your mouth, <u>under any circumstances</u>; it is unnecessary, and glaringly vulgar. Feed yourself with a <u>fork</u> or <u>spoon, nothing else</u> – a knife is only used for cutting. (Day 4, 20)

Dickens's passage may owe something to one of Lord Chesterfield's letters to his son (Letter 59, 25 July 1741), in which Chesterfield explains the importance of 'a genteel, easy manner' and the disadvantages of not knowing how to act. 'Awkwardness can proceed but from two causes; either from not having kept good company, or from not having attended to it'. Dinner in particular proves a trial to 'the awkward fellow' because he has so much to do:

> there he holds his knife, fork, and spoon, differently from other people; eats with his knife to the great danger of his mouth, picks his teeth with his fork, and puts his spoon, which has been in his throat twenty times, into the dishes again. . . . When he drinks, he infallibly coughs in his glass, and besprinkles the company. Besides all this, he has strange tricks and gestures;

such as snuffing up his nose, making faces, putting his fingers in his nose, or blowing it and looking afterwards in his handkerchief, so as to make the company sick.

As Lord Chesterfield concedes, none of this is in any degree criminal; 'but it is highly disagreeable and ridiculous in company, and ought most carefully to be avoided, by whoever desires to please' (Stanhope, *Letters* 1.145–7). In the words of Day, 'Nothing indicates a well-bred man more than a proper mode of eating his dinner. A man may pass muster by <u>dressing well</u>; and may sustain himself tolerably in conversation; but if he is not perfectly "au fait," <u>dinner</u> will betray him' (25). I am grateful to Nancy Metz for supplying this and a second reference to Chesterfield (see chapter 27, note on p. 238).

"Now," he pursued, "concerning Miss Havisham.

Her father was a country gentleman down in your part of the world,] Miss Havisham's father belonged to a class 'found in and about every country town': professional and mercantile people who enjoyed some local prestige but who did not belong to 'the <u>old</u>, solid, "Country People" ', the descendants of patrician families, 'the Squirearchy, with incomes of from seven to ten thousand a year' (Day 14).

Many held newcomers to prosperity in contempt: 'I respect the aristocracy of birth and of intellect. I do not respect the aristocracy of wealth,' Sir Robert Peel is said to have complained (Escott 13). Herbert's apparent ignorance of the gap between 'county people' and the 'merely great little' separates him from his mother, a woman obsessed with the significance of such social nuances.

and was a brewer.] Several categories of brewer existed in the nineteenth century. Top-ranked were the large commercial or 'common' brewers who supplied numerous public houses and taverns with beer and ale. Many of these brewers lived and worked in London, the owners of companies whose names remain familiar today (see below). A second group were country brewers, a class to which Mr Havisham evidently belonged, suppliers on a smaller scale who brewed and sold beer locally to independent publicans in market-towns and villages. Brewing victuallers also existed, individual publicans or owners of taverns who brewed beer for consumption by their regular customers. In addition, amateur or private brewing continued to flourish among farmers and people living in the country, although William Cobbett, a strenuous advocate of this practice, noted signs of its decline early in the nineteenth century.

I don't know why it should be a crack thing to be a brewer; but it is indisputable that while you cannot possibly be genteel and bake, you may be as genteel as never was and brew.] England's changing social mobility (see chapter 17, note on pp. 152–4) accounts for some of Herbert's puzzlement; additional developments appear to have shaped attitudes towards brewers, making them relatively favoured entrants into society set apart from bakers and others in trade. Time had conferred some degree of respectability on them (brewers were incorporated by Henry VI in 1438, making them fourteenth among the city companies), allowing generations of brewers the opportunity to acquire wealth and social prominence. This was particularly true in London, whose large market for the sale of beer accounts for the ascendancy of brewing families like Calvert, Whitbread, Truman, Parson, Hope, Thrale, Meux and Murray, Charrington and Moss and Courage, representatives of whom also made their way into Parliament. From 1700 to 1740 no fewer than twelve brewers sat as MPs, a figure that fell and later rose and almost doubled in the forty years between 1780 and 1820.

The connection of brewing with Quakers, begun in 1781 when Robert Barclay purchased the Thrale brewery in Southwark, further strengthened the respectability of this industry. Advances in brewing techniques also played a role by introducing reliability and consistency into the product, thereby helping representatives from the major houses secure their hold on customers. Two publications proved particularly useful: Michael Combrune's *Essay on Brewing* (1761) and John Richards's *Philosophical Principles of the Science of Brewing* (1784). Each advocated the need for precision in the preparation of beer and a scientific approach to production, both of which were possible with the introduction of reliable thermometers and the invention of the sacchrometer, a type of hydrometer used to measure the specific gravity of liquids. Shortly after, brewers received royal approval. In May 1787, George III and Queen Charlotte visited Samuel Whitbread's brewery in Chiswell Street, London, thus helping to advance the image of brewing as a prosperous and highly respectable trade. Just over sixty years later, a special article in the *Illustrated London News* described a visit in 1847 to the brewery of Barclay & Perkins in Southwark, Thrale's old business, as 'one of the "Privileged Sights" of the metropolis' ('A Visit', February 1847, 92). Among the recent entries in the visitors-book at the time the article appeared were Ibrahim Pasha and Prince Louis Napoleon.

"Yet a gentleman may not keep a public-house; may he?"

"Yet a gentleman may not keep a public-house; may he?" said I.
"Not on any account," returned Herbert; "but a public-house may keep a gentleman.]   The distinction is between owning something and enjoying income derived from it as opposed to earning the money by one's own labour.

Well! Mr. Havisham was very rich]   Rochester's local history offers a success-story connected with brewing possibly known to Dickens. Alderman Thomas Stevens, the original owner of the house on Gad's Hill which Dickens bought in 1856, started life as an ostler, married the widow of the innkeeper who first employed him, and later turned to brewing. Stevens flourished, became wealthy, built Gad's Hill Place in 1780 and gained civic prominence, serving as the mayor of Rochester in 1787 and in 1801 (Forster 8.3.209; Thomas Frost, 1890, 22; Harris, 1916).

A further local link between wealth and brewing may have been suggested to Dickens when he sought a model for the imaginary residence of a prosperous Rochester brewer. Restoration House stood out as the former home of several leading citizens and mayors. It was also close enough to Woodham's brewery to suggest an actual connection which, were records available, one might be able to prove (see chapter 8, note on p. 90).

"Stop a moment, I am coming to that.

Her father privately married again – his cook, I rather think."]   A private marriage, that is a union solemnized without the posting of banns in the parish church of one of the parties, was illegal according to Hardwick's Act of 1753 'for the Better Prevention of Clandestine Marriages' (26 Geo. II, c. 33). Exempt from these statutory regulations were members of the royal family, Jews and Quakers. The Act was repealed in 1823 when the Marriage Act of that year (4 Geo. IV, c. 76) declared clandestine marriages valid, but the officiating minister a felon (Cross and Livingstone, 1974, 887, 619). An entry in Dickens's *Book of Memoranda* for 1855 reads: 'The Man who marrys his Cook at last, after being so desperately knowing about the sex' (30). From the mid-eighteenth century onwards, cross-class unions were not uncommon. Not only did peers occasionally marry their mistresses, or working-class women, but wealthy and prominent women also chose men from lower social grades with comparable frequency, although these cases tended to generate more attention through publicized accounts in the press of runaway marriages and elopements. Dickens alludes to this phenomenon in *PP* when Rachel Wardle attempts to elope with Alfred Jingle (9–10).

"My good Handel, so he was.

Take another glass of wine,]

> Wine is the most agreeable and best of all liquors; taken in moderation and at proper times, it imparts vigour both to the body and mind, and gives to life an additional charm; in a medical point of view it is one of the most valuable gifts which Providence has bestowed upon man. (Keith Imray, 1842, 826)

Why I was trying to pack mine into my tumbler

worthy of a much better cause,]   A common saying now almost proverbial. See *Cymbeline*: 'Thou mayst be valiant in a better cause,/But now thou seem'st a coward' (3.4.70–1).

"There appeared upon the scene – say at the races

I never saw him, for this happened five-and-twenty years ago (before you and I were, Handel)]. See Appendix 1.

he got great sums of money from her . . . on the plea that when he was her husband he must hold and manage it all.]   The legal status of married women as mere possessions of their husbands extended also to their property, thus providing unscrupulous men with opportunities like this to swindle their fiancée or wife. The process of enabling women to retain their money and property when they married did not begin until the Married Women's Property Act of 1870 (33 & 34 Vict., c. 93), which allowed women to retain £200 of their own earnings.

"It's not that," said he

the wedding dresses were bought, the wedding tour was planned out]   The wedding dresses, including those for the bridesmaids, would have been chosen by the bride but in consultation with her attendants as to the colour, material and style (*Etiquette of Marriage*, [1902], 49). By the mid-nineteenth century, members of 'fashionable society' and those in 'the middle ranks of life' customarily left for a tour immediately after the wedding ceremony:

> It is a practice which is highly consistent with female modesty, and we may add gives a relish to connubial bliss. . . . A few weeks recreation is highly necessary as a relaxation of the mind after the tedious anxieties and appliances of courtship. . . . The place you visit, and the length of time you devote on this happy occasion, must be dictated according to your own pleasure. If a tour on the Continent, four or six months is generally occupied, but if only to the lakes [of northern England], or some fashionable resort, four, six, or eight weeks. (T. E. G., 1847, 80–1)

"At the hour and minute," said Herbert

"at which she afterwards stopped all the clocks . . . and she has never since looked upon the light of day."]   The situation Dickens outlined to Collins to serve as the framework for the 1858 Christmas number of *HW* has been suggested as a possible germ of Miss Havisham's reclusive behaviour (Clarendon xiii–xiv). Writing on 6 September 1858, Dickens proposed this 'hint' for *A House to Let*:

> Some disappointed person, man or woman, prematurely disgusted with the world for some reason or no reason, (the person should be young, I think) retires to an old lonely house . . . with one attendant: resolved to shut out the world and hold no communication with it. The one attendant sees the absurdity of the idea – pretends to humour it – but really tries to slaughter it. Everything that happens – everybody that comes near . . . shews beyond mistake that you can't shut out the world – that you are in it to be of it – that you get into a false position the moment you try to sever yourself from it – and that you must mingle with it, and make the best of it, and make the best of yourself into the bargain. (*Letters* 8.650)

If Collins and he could plot out a way of doing this together, Dickens concluded, 'I would not be afraid to take my part'. Dickens's specific assignment, 'Going in Society', went so well that two months later he wrote to warn W. H. Wills, his subeditor of *HW*, of a possible complication: his 'introduced paper for the Xmas. No.' involved 'such an odd idea', one 'so humorous, and so available at greater length', that he entertained the possibility of cancelling it and making it 'the Pivot round which my next book shall revolve' (*Letters* 8.709–10). See also chapter 40, note on p. 317.

It had not occurred to me before

"A capitalist – an Insurer of Ships."]   A capitalist in this context refers to anyone who could raise money to buy a portion of common stock in a partnership when a company was first formed. An insurer or underwriter subscribed his name to a contract 'whereby one party, in consideration of a stipulated sum, undertakes to indemnify the other against certain perils or risks to which he is exposed, or against the happening of some event' (Adolphus 3.206).

The prominence of the marine insurance business in London dates from the early decades of the nineteenth century. After the destruction of French and Spanish naval power at Trafalgar in 1805, the Royal Navy controlled the seas, allowing Britain to dominate the major trade routes, free from any European rival. The adaptation of steam to sea transport (see chapter 54, note on p. 385) and the continued expansion of the mercantile fleet brought further trade to the industry that monitored this growth by registering ships, underwriting their cargoes, and offering owners and merchants insurance premiums. Several corporations specializing in marine insurance developed, helped by legislation passed in 1719–20 allowing companies to offer merchants protection or indemnity against the dangers goods faced during a sea voyage. The largest of these was Lloyd's, which soon became the authoritative source of marine intelligence in London (see also chapter 34, note on p. 286). Lloyd's and other marine insurers based their premiums on several variables: the length of the voyage, the time of the year and the seaworthiness of the vessel. Insurers sold policies to ship-owners from any country, but they provided no coverage to someone whose government declared war on Britain (based on George Gregory, 1806, 2.162).

Social opportunities for those connected with ships, trade and related maritime activities flourished under these circumstances. In 'a mercantile country like England, people are continually rising in the world. Shopkeepers become merchants, and mechanics manufacturers; with the possession of wealth they acquire a taste for the luxuries of life, expensive furniture, and gorgeous plate' (Day 3). Dickens's own early exposure to the maritime world through his father, who worked for the Navy, and through contact with shipping and ships during the years he spent in Chatham, may have informed Pip's perceptions about the 'grand ideas' he had 'of the wealth and importance of Insurers of Ships'. In the MS, Herbert's occupation appears throughout instead as 'merchant'. Possibly Dickens altered his calling at a later stage to avoid any possible reference to Charley, his eldest son, who, after working in the business-house of Barings for three or four years, had gone out to Hong Kong in May 1860, 'strongly backed up' by the company 'to buy Tea on his own account, as a means of forming a connexion and seeing more of the practical part of a merchant's calling, before starting in London for himself' (*Letters* 9.246–7; Rosenberg, 1972, 319). Dickens also revised Herbert's intention to go to China. See below.

"In the City."] London's principal insurers were all located around the Royal Exchange. In a strict sense, 'the City' denotes a geographical area of approximately one square mile administered by the Lord Mayor and Corporation of London. This body assumed responsibility for policing the City, attending to roads, lighting, watching, cleaning and the removal of 'nuisances'. Temple Bar and Holborn Bar marked the western limits; the boundary stretched east to Aldgate and Tower Hill. Smithfield and Moorfields marked the extent to the north and the Thames to the south. The City originally had eight gates, but these were all demolished by the end of the eighteenth century, with the exception of Temple Bar, which was removed in 1870 to ease traffic congestion.

"I shall not rest satisfied

"I shall not rest satisfied with merely employing my capital in insuring ships.] Free trade policies introduced in the 1820s by William Huskisson (1770–1830) as president of the Board of Trade made it possible for individuals to underwrite cargoes and import goods following a renewal of European trade after the restoration of peace in 1815. Increased trading opportunities also prompted changes in Britain's customs regulations during the same period. Prior to 1803 importers were required to pay duties on 'almost every description of foreign and colonial goods at the time of their importation'. This system limited trade and restricted the activities of many merchants. Higher costs were also passed on to consumers, who, 'in addition to the ordinary profits of trading, had to pay an additional profit to reimburse the merchant for the advancement of the duty' (Porter, 1836, 3.269–71).

Life Assurance shares,] Shares in assurance or joint-stock companies were available to those with funds. Such companies typically also handled insurance premiums against casualties from fire or wrecks at sea. By the 1840s some seventy companies operated in London, forty of which specialized in life assurance and the rest in fire protection. Many of the former possessed immense capital (*Dictionary of Trade*, 1844).

and cut into the Direction.] A colloquialism meaning to strike a path and advance as through obstacles.

do a little in the mining way.] The destruction of Spanish sea power at Trafalgar in 1805 and the collapse of the Spanish empire early in the nineteenth century attracted British commercial interests to South America. Large amounts of gold, silver, lead, copper, tin, sulphur and salt tempted investors willing to back mining companies operating in the Andes and elsewhere (*Dictionary of Trade*, 1844). Dickens alludes to the dangers associated with this market in both *DS* and *DC*. Mrs Pipchin's husband died pumping water out of Peruvian mines, while Aunt Betsey's financial misfortunes stem, in part, from her having done badly in the same mines.

chartering a few thousand tons on my own account.]   This was a popular option for small investors working through chartered companies which hired ships to deliver cargoes abroad: 'Many of the most important and extensive classes of British commerce have been, and some still are, carried on by means of chartered companies' (Adolphus 3.219).

Overseas trade by charter-party – the charter or deed between a merchant and a ship-owner – had flourished in England for several centuries since the establishment of the Russia Company (1553), the Eastland Company (1579) and the Turkey Company (1581). More recently, the monopolistic practices established by Cromwell in 1651 had prevented free trade between other nations and Britain's colonial possessions. 'England, it must be observed, was a great trading country, her mercantile capital was very great, and likely to become still greater and greater every day' (Adolphus 2.170).

"to the East Indies, for silks, shawls, spices, dyes, drugs, and precious woods.]   The Royal Navy's presence in South-East Asia enabled merchants to challenge Dutch colonial interests in the region and promote British commercial expansion. The term 'East Indies' originated as a name for both the continent and the islands to the east and the south of the river Indus as far as the borders of China. New Guinea, New Holland, the Philippine Islands and Van Diemen's Land were excluded. Shawls, made from either a blend of silk and wool or cashmere, were among the prized imports from the East Indies. Among the imported spices were cinnamon, cloves, ginger, mace, nutmeg, pepper and pimento. Dyeing stuffs – a broad term for various dyes – included cochineal, fustic, indigo, lac dye, logwood, madder roots, safflower, shumac and yellow berries. Salt, opium, amber and musk came from Assam, which the Burmese ceded to Britain in 1826. Many valuable woods came from Ceylon, including teak, calamander wood, ebony, rose-wood, satin-wood and sapan-wood (based on *Dictionary of Trade*, 1844, and Porter, 1836, 3.274).

"I think I shall trade, also," said he

"I think I shall trade, also,"]   Nineteenth-century usage distinguished between a merchant who dealt wholesale in a single commodity and the 'only real Merchant' who brought his goods for sale into the country by sea. Merchants in this category were regarded as 'seated at the very head of the trading genus' placed 'on the actual pulsation of the nation's commercial prosperity, carrying abroad and selling its productions' (*Complete Book of Trades* 329).

Herbert's desire to become a merchant differs sharply from the assumptions about commerce that the novel attacks as false. Proponents of gentility found it demeaning to work for one's money, regarding inherited wealth as the sole means of social worth. Belief in the contaminating effects of all forms of business or trade was so strong that some asserted that even financial misfortune presented only a temporary setback.

Extremists argued that one could still return to one's former status 'by the desistance from the exercise' of trade, 'even without the aid of letters of rehabilitation' (Adolphus 1.472). For Pip's revised views and recognition of the need to work for one's living, see chapter 58, note on pp. 415–16.

"to the West Indies, for sugar, tobacco, and rum. Also to Ceylon, specially for elephants' tusks."] After 'rum.' MS reads 'Also to China, for teas'. Barbados in 1627 was the first of several islands in the Caribbean to become a British possession; Jamaica, seized from Spain in 1655, was the largest and most important. The introduction of sugar cane as a plantation crop in the seventeenth century led to Britain's near-monopoly and to the establishment of a refining business at home which supplied sugar to North America and much of Europe. 'Sugar is more extensively used in this country [England] than in any other on the globe, and until of late years the refining business has been almost entirely confined to us' (*Dictionary of Trade*, 1844).

Originally brought to England from Mexico in 1586, tobacco was later transplanted to Tobago, where it was successfully cultivated and introduced to other British possessions. Tobacco followed sugar in importance in the economy of the West Indies. Rum, made from the distilled liquor obtained from the fermented juice of the sugar cane, or molasses, was another major export until high duty, temperance activity and unsettled conditions in the West Indies cut rum consumption in Britain by about a third. Additional commodities imported from the West Indies include cotton, coffee, chocolate nuts, ginger, pimento, indigo and various hard and soft woods. In return, British merchants exported wrought iron, copper, brass, pewter, silver, watches, cotton and woollen goods, and 'every article of food and clothing, furniture, ship chandlery, military stores, coals for firing, and every article of accommodation and luxury' (Adolphus 2.152–3).

Trade in ivory also flourished, the main suppliers of the British being Africa, India and Ceylon. Importers sold the ivory to manufacturers of knife handles, piano keys and billiard balls, of mathematical instruments, to toymakers, and to artists for miniatures (*Dictionary of Trade*, 1844).

"Yes. I am in a counting-house, and looking about me.

counting-house,] A place for the transaction of a merchant's business and repository of his commercial books and accounts.

"Then the time comes," said Herbert

"Then the time comes," . . . **"when you see your opening. And you go in and you swoop upon it and you make your capital, and then there you are!"]** In the context of the 1820s, this may have been an attainable dream; read in the context of the crash of 1857 and the depression that followed, readers of the serial version of the novel perhaps paid greater attention to the novel's emphasis on the need to face diminished expectations and reduced prospects. A succession of American firms going bankrupt in 1857, followed by a glut of manufacturing goods on the international market and a drop in prices, earnings, and employment rates in Britain created a temporary crisis the novel possibly reflects (Lohman, Jr, 53–66).

Yet, having already made his fortune in his own mind

half-price to the Theatre;]   Most London theatres offered the main piece (a five-act play), followed by a two-act farce; other variants included four or five short pieces and occasionally the 'afterpiece' performed first. One paid full price for both plays, but the custom had prevailed since early in the eighteenth century of admitting playgoers to the house for a reduced charge at the end of the third act of the main piece. Patrons referred to this as the 'second price' or 'half-price', the cost of which ranged from three shillings in the boxes to sixpence in the top galleries. The Opera and Haymarket theatres held out against this practice (Hogan xxxvi–xxxviii).

Westminster Abbey,]   Westminster Abbey, on the north bank of the Thames near the Houses of Parliament and Westminster Hall, has served as the setting for the coronation of English monarchs since 1066 and principal burial-place of royalty and distinguished persons. The present Abbey was begun in 1245 under Henry III and lavishly rebuilt in the French style with a huge nave (103 feet high), flying buttresses and rose windows in the transepts. The Abbey's close connection with the monarchy saved it from the fate of most English abbeys during the Reformation, when many were turned into parish churches or plundered for their stone. Dickens's body lies in the south transept, which is also known as Poets' Corner.

we walked in the Parks;]   Centuries ago, London's several parks catered primarily to the aristocracy and provided opportunities to hunt deer and wildfowl, to skate in the winter and to play the French game of Paille-mail (striking a ball with a wooden mallet through an iron ring), which was introduced in the reign of Charles I. By the nineteenth century, London's fourteen royal parks and pleasure grounds – 'the lungs of London', in the words of William Pitt, 1st Earl of Chatham – had adapted to the needs of the general public and were used primarily as somewhere to walk (Timbs, 1867, 642).

Hyde Park, Green Park and St James's Park all lie relatively close to Westminster Abbey. To the north and on the western boundary of Mayfair is Hyde Park, London's largest park, with open space for walking and riding (see below). St James's, an elegant and beautiful park, extends towards Pall Mall; Green Park, the smallest of these three, adjoins St James's Park and extends north to Piccadilly and west to Hyde Park Corner.

and I wondered who shod all the horses there,]   Rotten Row on the south side of Hyde Park offered a mile-and-a-half gallop for saddle-horses and was popular with fashionable riders late in the afternoon, especially during the London 'season', a period of concentrated social activities from the first of May until the end of July tied to the sitting of Parliament, which began in November and ended formally on

12 August. Each afternoon people assembled in their carriages and drove around at little more than a walking pace. Among them were 'great ladies, virtuous British Matrons and their conventionally innocent daughters' and women of 'the demi-monde' (Sir William Hardman, 1923, 212). Admiring men on horseback added to the congestion, making Hyde Park during the afternoon perhaps the most densely crowded part of London. Hackney-coaches and -cabs, however, were excluded from Hyde Park. The scene described here takes place on a Sunday.

On a moderate computation

the London streets . . . so brilliantly lighted] The streets appear brilliant because several of London's main thoroughfares were illuminated by gas, which had been selectively introduced from 1806 onwards. See chapter 33, note on pp. 280–1.

a porter mooning about Barnard's Inn, under the pretence of watching it,] The Inns of Court and Chancery employed porters as gatekeepers or attendants to watch over the property and monitor visitors. For the Inns and security, see chapter 40, note on p. 316.

On the Monday morning at a quarter before nine

On the Monday morning] See Appendix 1.

It appeared to me that the eggs from which young Insurers were hatched, were incubated in dust and heat, like the eggs of ostriches,] Ostriches make partial use of the heat of the sun to hatch their eggs, a practice responsible for their proverbial reputation as birds which desert their nests and show little regard for their young (OED).

a back second floor up a yard,] After 'yard' MS reads 'with a look into another second floor rather than any look out, and of a grimy presence in all particulars'. A 'back second floor' simply meant a back room on a floor two storeys above the ground floor.

I waited about until it was noon

'Change,] Literally an exchange, a place where merchants meet to transact their business with ship-owners and underwriters. Since 1600, London's 'Bourse', or Exchange, on Cornhill and Threadneedle Street (originally built by Sir Thomas Gresham in 1566) has been known as the Royal Exchange. This building, with its courtyard, loggia and upper storey, was destroyed by the Great Fire in 1666 and replaced by the New Exchange (the work of James Peacock) to which Pip refers. Fire also destroyed this building on 18 January 1838, shutting down the Exchange until a third opened on the same site on 1 January 1845 designed by William Tite and remained in use until 1939.

I saw] MS reads 'saw at once, quite as plainly as I ever saw afterwards,'

fluey men sitting there under the bills about shipping, whom I took to be great merchants, though I couldn't understand why they should all be out of spirits.] 'Fluey' literally means dusty. The merchants who look glum appear to be 'defaulters'. This class of men, John Capper explained, were 'individuals of previous high character' who, through unforeseen losses, entered rashly into speculation 'in the hope of extricating themselves from their difficulties, by an anticipated rise in some particular stock'. Of the respectability of the Stock Exchange, 'there can be no question'. But fraud and improper dealings were not unknown (Capper, 'Bulls and Bears', *HW* 8.520–1).

a celebrated house which I then quite venerated, but now believe to have been the most abject superstition in Europe,] Several coffee-houses and taverns in the vicinity of the Royal Exchange had become renowned in the eighteenth century as meeting places for merchants, sea captains and marine underwriters to eat and transact business. Writing as an older man, Pip finds their 'celebrated' reputation overstated and incompatible with the indifferent food and service they now provide.

a little garden overlooking the river,] Many of the larger houses in Hammersmith (see chapter 21) had gardens which ran down to the Thames and looked over to the Surrey shore.

Mrs. Pocket was sitting on a garden chair

Mrs. Pocket's two nursemaids] MS reads 'two nurse maids who had a general air of being Mrs. Pocket's proprietors'.

an appearance of amiable dignity.] MS reads 'enthusiasm, and I thought she was the sweetest woman I had ever seen'.

I found, now that I had leisure to count them

when a seventh was heard, as in the region of air, wailing dolefully.] Compare William Blake, 'To the Muses' (1783): 'Whether in Heaven ye wander fair,/. . . Or the blue regions of the air,/Where the melodious winds have birth'.

Millers, who was the other nurse

and I was curious . . . what the book could be.] After 'be' MS reads 'Mrs. Pocket reads all the time. At last she looked at me again and asked me if I was "fond of travelling?" I was so very much surprised by the abstract character of the question that I answered "No" – which, without any intention or meaning whatever on my part, seemed agreeable to Mrs. Pocket. "No," she said; "so much hurry and trouble, isn't there?" and Flopson then struck in with the observation, "It ain't the thing for you, Mum;" upon which Mrs. Pocket said, "No Flopson," and laughed and went on reading'.

Mrs. Pocket acted on the advice

Thus I made the second discovery on that first occasion, that the nurture of the little Pockets consisted of alternately tumbling up and lying down.] The portrait of Mrs Pocket contrasts sharply with the emphasis on domestic competence and housekeeping proclaimed in Mrs Ellis's *Daughters of England* and in similar publications. 'To understand the Economy of House-hold Affairs is not only essential to a Woman's proper and pleasant performance of the duties of a wife and a mother, but is indispensable to the comfort, respectability, and general welfare of all Families, – whatever their circumstances' (Kitchiner, 1825, 2). Compare also John Timbs: 'Domestic Economy, which consists in the Management of a Family and the Government of a Household, is nowhere better understood than in England.... The practical knowledge of the domestic duties is the principal glory of a woman' (1847, 9).

Chapter 23 Fifteenth weekly number
9 March 1861

Chapters 23 and 24 are the most extensively revised of any in the novel, save the two last chapters. For details of the deleted and added passages, see below. All of the alterations, amounting in total to almost 400 words, in which Mrs Coiler becomes a neighbour rather than an insinuating mother-in-law, suggest that Dickens attempted to reduce her resemblance to Mrs Hogarth, his own 'wicked' mother-in-law, whom he charged with spreading malicious rumours about the reasons for the tension between him and Catherine Dickens. The personal implications are further decreased by giving Mrs Pocket aristocratic pretensions and a family background in no way similar to his wife's (Rosenberg, 1973, 90–101; *Norton* 455–61; Cardwell xxviii–xxix).

Mr. Pocket said he was glad to see me

He was a young-looking man . . . and his manner seemed quite natural.] MS reads 'He was quite a young-looking man, in spite of his perplexities, and his manner seemed unstudied and natural'.

"Belinda,] The use of 'Belinda' by earlier writers links the name with nymphs, romantic figures and court belles. Compare Belinda, courted by the cynical Heartfree in Sir John Vanbrugh's *The Provok'd Wife* (1697), Pope's heroine in *The Rape of the Lock* (1712), and Maria Edgeworth's *Belinda* (1810), a novel about contemporary English society commended by the heroine of *Northanger Abbey*.

in an absent state of mind,] MS reads 'with great sweetness'.

orange-flower water?] The aqueous solution known as orange-flower water, made from the white flowers of the orange tree, has various uses, including a flavouring agent in pastries, puddings, cordials and perfumes.

I found out within a few hours

I found out within a few hours . . . because he had never got one.] This paragraph was added at the proof stage. One consequence is to sharpen the satire against Mrs Pocket, whose tendency to boast of her connections reveals a major breach in etiquette: 'Nothing therefore will more irretrievably stamp you as vulgar in really good society than the repeated introduction of the names of nobility, or even distinguished personages in reference to yourself' (*The Habits of Good Society*, 1860, 49). The changes also serve to decrease the similarities between Mrs Pocket and Catherine Dickens, from whom Dickens had been separated for just over two years. See below.

a certain quite accidental deceased Knight. . . . I believe he had been knighted himself for storming the English grammar . . . and for handing some Royal Personage either the trowel or the mortar.] The satire is aimed at those who protested that rewarding individuals for increasingly trivial accomplishments devalued the aristocracy. In Disraeli's *Sybil; or, The Two Nations* (1845), one character objects that 'A baronetcy has become the distinction of the middle class; a physician, our physician for example, is a baronet; and I dare say some of our tradesmen; brewers, or people of that class. An attempt to elevate them into an order of nobility, however inferior, would partake, in some degree, of the ridiculous' (2.11.107). Taken to an extreme, some knighthoods apparently occurred unexpectedly, on chance occasions, perhaps in the manner of the late Sir Thomas Tippins, who was said to have been knighted 'in mistake for somebody else' (OMF 1.10).

Traditionally, the monarch controlled entrance into the aristocracy, making land ownership, birth, education and marriage the principal means by which some gained social prominence and advanced over others. This practice began to change within a decade after the accession of Charles II in 1660, as the power to confer honours passed from the monarch into the hands of his ministers and baronetcies were increasingly used to reward politicians for state service. Men thus elevated to the peerage nevertheless generally had solid claims to a landed background; for those who lacked connections with the old élite, the tendency prevailed to confer a knighthood rather than a hereditary title for specific achievements. Individuals receiving such honours included soldiers, statesmen, scholars, lawyers, antiquaries, mathematicians, physicians, merchants and learned writers.

'Knight' and 'Baronet' both carry the title 'Sir'; baronets occupy a higher rank, belonging to the lowest order of the peerage, below a baron and above a knight, and require the abbreviation 'Bt' after the surname to differentiate them from knights. The title of baronet is 'an hereditary dignity' which owes its origin to James I, the founder of the order, who, in his anxiety to settle and civilize Ireland, tried to maintain peace 'by selecting an élite from the most wealthy and distinguished families of the landed-gentry' (Debrett, 1824, vii). In the event of the monarch's heeding advice from someone to oppose the bestowal of a knighthood or a baronetcy, the Prime Minister, the Lord Chancellor and the Archbishop of Canterbury could prevail in the case of disagreements.

watch and ward] That is, to remain on watch or active duty.

she had grown up highly ornamental, but perfectly helpless and useless.] This is an example of the 'barren blooming' Mary Wollstonecraft had attacked in 1792: as a result of 'a false system of education', middle-class and upper-class women were often treated as 'the frivolous sex' and discouraged from cherishing nobler ambitions (*Vindication of the Rights of Women* 79).

to mount to the Woolsack, or to roof himself in with a mitre.] The Woolsack, a large square bag of wool without back or arms and covered with cloth, is the seat of the Lord Chancellor in the House of Lords; mitres are the tall caps worn by bishops, who are also entitled to sit in the Lords.

taken Time by the forelock] A proverbial phrase encouraging one to act immediately and grasp any available opportunity. The expression derives from the conventional depiction of the Greek god Occasio as bald except for a forelock.

Mr. Pocket took me into the house and showed me my room

Drummle and Startop.] Initially, 'Drummle' appeared as 'Jumble' before Dickens settled on the change. Drummle's 'heavy' and 'sluggish complexion' and his 'idle' behaviour and habit of lolling around (GE 25) have much in common with 'drumly' or 'drubly'. As an adjective applied to water, 'drumly' means turbid, or discoloured with matter in suspension; referring to the sky or to the day, 'drumly' signifies troubled, gloomy, cloudy or the opposite of clear. By contrast, Startop is cordial, clear and friendly. For Drummle's Christian name, see below.

Both Mr. and Mrs. Pocket had such a noticeable air

Both Mr. and Mrs. Pocket had such a noticeable air of being in somebody else's hands, that I wondered who really was in possession of the house ... until I found this unknown power to be the servants.] The Pockets reverse the arrangements with servants that prevailed in well-ordered families. 'In every household there must be the hands to do the work, the head to guide and to control the workers. The proper tasks must be assigned to each, the work must be done in an efficient way' (Christine G. T. Reeve, 1893, 497). Others emphatically agreed: the correct attitude to display was firm, unhesitating leadership from the master and mistress, matched by obedience and subservience from servants. Only in this situation could harmony prevail with both parties working together in strict adherence to their respective stations. The servant's subordinate status was more than a social fact; it was even reinforced by the law (Horn, 1996, 130).

to keep a deal of company down stairs.] To entertain friends and fellow-servants below the stairs, where the kitchen and other utility rooms were typically located. Employers usually prohibited this practice or established strict rules for visitors.

They allowed a very liberal table to Mr. and Mrs. Pocket, yet it always appeared to me that by far the best part of the house to have boarded in, would have been the kitchen] Augustus and Henry Mayhew joked about emboldened servants in a novel illustrated by Cruikshank and first published in 1847. One sketch shows the cook, the housemaid and two male servants sitting around in comfort by the fire and ignoring an agitated bell summoning one of them to the drawing-room. The caption reads: 'Oh ah! Let 'em ring again!' (*The Greatest Plague of Life; or, The Adventures of a Lady in Search of a Good Servant*, n.d., 263).

CHAPTER TWENTY-THREE 213

By degrees I learnt

educated at Harrow and at Cambridge,]   Harrow, at Harrow-on-the-Hill, Middlesex, was founded in 1572. It is one of England's most famous boys' public schools, which traditionally provide access to the universities of Oxford and Cambridge. Boys attending Harrow and other fee-paying boarding schools (compare Compeyson, chapter 42) generally received a classical education (Greek and Latin) in preparation for university entrance or a career in the Church or one of the liberal professions.

a Grinder.]   A slang term for someone who coached pupils for entrance examinations to the public schools. Most probably the instruction would have entailed helping the boys to 'cram' for Latin and Greek. For 'blade', see chapter 24, note on p. 223.

the house I saw.]   MS reads 'Whether he [Matthew] was ever sensible in my day of anything like a waste of his life or of anything in it, will be deducible perhaps from my occasional record of him'. Dropped from the proofs.

Mr. and Mrs. Pocket had a toady neighbour

Mr. and Mrs. Pocket ... neighbour;]   MS reads 'Mrs. Pocket had a mother'. The revision to 'neighbour' distances Mrs Coiler and thereby softens the satire against mothers-in-law, the long-standing object of humour and complaint. Dickens himself had reason to express hostility about the dependent behaviour of his own in-laws and Mrs Hogarth's role in the public quarrel that preceded his separation from Catherine Dickens in 1858. Perhaps prompted by second thoughts and now some two years later, Dickens altered this passage in the proofs by decreasing any resemblance between the Pockets' domestic circumstances and those that had prevailed in his own family circle (Rosenberg, 1973, 100; *Norton* 460). See below for similar changes.

she agreed with everybody,]   MS reads 'everybody (except Mr. Pocket)'.

blessed everybody,]   MS reads 'everybody (with the same exception). When visiting at the house, she usually maintained one gentle, uniform continual watery assertion of Mrs. Pocket. If her feelings towards Mr. Pocket ever had assumed that hydraulic form of demonstration, I might have been better able to account for it now and then'.

I had the honour of taking her down to dinner]   Etiquette requires men to escort their dinner partners to the table. One goes down to dinner, descending from a drawing-room, or other reception room on the first floor to the dining-room on the ground floor.

"But dear Mrs. Pocket," said Mrs. Coiler

"But ... so much luxury and elegance"]   MS reads ' "But my dear Belinda has so large a family," said Mrs. Coiler, "and requires so much affection –" '.

"And she is of so aristocratic a disposition

"And she is of so aristocratic a disposition –"] MS reads 'And she is of so sweet a disposition, and ever was as a child; for if she had plenty to eat and drink, and was never interfered with, she was always so amiable'.

"that it is hard," said Mrs. Coiler,

Coiler,] MS reads 'Coiler, with red eyelids'.

It came to my knowledge

It came to my knowledge ... the cook had mislaid the beef.] Dickens substituted this whole passage in proof for the one below in the MS:

> "How do you think her looking, Mr. Pip?" asked Mrs. Coiler with an air of extreme solicitude.
> "Mrs. Pocket Ma'am?" I said: considering it an odd question to put to me, who had never seen its fair subject before.
> "Yes. My dear dear Belinda."
> Bluff was the only word I could have used with honesty; but not being honest under the moistened eye of Mrs. Coiler, I said "delicate". She highly approved of the reply, and was resuming "With Belinda's large family—" when Mr. Pocket, whom I had observed to be out of sorts at the bottom of the table, struck into our conversation.
> "Pray Mrs. Coiler," said Mr. Pocket, "is anything the matter?"
> "Matter? No," said Mrs. Coiler, with a kind of jocund resignation.
> "You seemed to be low, Ma'am, I thought," said Mr. Pocket.
> "Why should I be low," answered Mrs. Coiler, with a sprightly tear, "at dear Belinda's table?" /To

Drummle, whose christian name was Bentley,] The surly ill humour, violence and emphasis on his native stock, together with Jaggers's reference to him as the 'Spider' (chapter 26), link Drummle with Swift's description of the Spider in *The Battle of the Books* (1704). When a wandering Bee alights near the Spider's web, the latter boasts: 'I am a domestic animal, furnished with a native stock within myself. This large castle ... is all built with my own hands, and the materials extracted altogether out of my own person.' In reply, the Bee asks:

> Whether is the nobler being of the two, that which, by a lazy contemplation of four inches round, by an overweening pride, feeding and engendering on itself, turns all into excrement and venom, producing nothing at all, but flybane and a cobweb; or that which, by an universal range, with long search, much study, true judgement, and distinction of things, brings home honey and wax. (552)

The connection between Drummle and 'Spider' may have been reinforced by Dickens's knowledge of Swift's target. The recognized object of his satire was none other than the despotic and irascible scholar Richard Bentley (1662–1742). His quarrelsome behaviour may have recalled that of his Victorian namesake and publisher Richard Bentley (1794–1871) with whom Dickens struggled over money and copyright issues from 1837 to 1841.

the book I had seen Mrs. Pocket reading in the garden, was all about titles,] Pip later refers to this as 'the red book', apparently an allusion to *Webster's Royal Red Book*, which listed Members of the House of Peers in alphabetical order and gave their town address. Other well-known guides include several compiled by John Debrett (d.1822), who published his *New Peerage* in 1784 and the first edition of *Debrett's Peerage of England, Scotland, and Ireland* in 1802. This and other titles continued to flourish under Debrett's name, together with *Burke's Peerage*, properly entitled *A Genealogical and Heraldic History of the Peerage and Baronetage of the United Kingdom*, compiled by John Burke and first published in 1826. The volumes provided information about the descent of peers, the collateral branches of their families, and a listing of marriages, births and issue.

recognised Mrs. Pocket as a woman and a sister.] A joking allusion to the seal of the Anti-Slavery Society, which shows a black slave kneeling in chains and saying, 'Am I not a man and a brother?' The seal derived from a Wedgwood cameo modelled in 1786.

the page] Young boys were commonly employed either in addition to or as an alternative to one or more maids. Typically, they performed a range of menial duties such as attending fires, carrying coal, cleaning shoes, etc. The larger the household, the more specialized the work. A later reference in this chapter to 'a dissipated page' makes it sound as if the Pockets have more than one.

Mrs. Coiler then changed the subject

the opposite side of the table.] After 'table.' MS reads 'We had all sorts of things for dinner and Mrs. Pocket sweetly consumed them at the head of the board. Startop afterwards disrespectfully informed me when I said how sweet she was, that I had better say how sticky. I was rather disposed to say it, too, before I had done with the family'.

After dinner the children were introduced

After dinner the children were introduced. . . . There were four little girls, and two little boys, besides the baby who might have been either, and the baby's next successor who was as yet neither.] With Herbert and his sister Charlotte, who died before she was fourteen (chapter 30), the Pocket children total ten, the number to which Catherine Dickens also gave birth. Introducing children after dinner was not the best form:

> If you should happen to be blessed with those lovely nuisances, children, and should be entertaining company, never allow them to be brought in after dinner, unless they are particularly asked for, and even then it is better to find some excuse. (*Etiquette for Gentlemen*, 1838, 34)

Flopson, by dint of doubling the baby at the joints

like a Dutch Doll,] A jointed wooden doll well known for the flexibility of its limbs. The dolls were exported from Nuremberg, Germany, a primary source since the sixteenth century for the production of toys on a large scale. Other varieties of 'Dutch' or 'peg' dolls had delicately and elaborately painted coiffures, grey kiss-curls, or were carved with a projecting comb on the top of their head.

who had clearly lost half his buttons at the gaming-table.] Metal buttons plated with silver or gold were of modest value and were sometimes used by compulsive gamblers to bet.

I was made very uneasy in my mind

a sliced orange steeped in sugar and wine,] A fruit punch combining wine with orange syrup made from squeezed orange juice boiled with powdered sugar (Timbs, 1847, 92).

We all looked awkwardly at the tablecloth

while this was going on] After 'on' MS reads 'and nothing extraneous was heard save an inarticulate moaning from Mrs. Coiler'.

The baby was the soul of honour

by little Jane.] After 'Jane', MS reads 'while Mrs. Pocket read her book placidly oblivious of everything else'.

It happened that the other five children

in a distant, Missionary way he asked them certain questions] After 'Missionary' MS reads 'solemn parental'. Compare Mrs Jellyby in *BH* who, preoccupied with her 'African duties', had 'a curious habit of seeming to look a long way off' when she was engaged with her 'telescopic philanthropy' (4).

Whitlow:] An inflammatory sore or swelling in a finger or thumb, often found in the terminal joint. Victorian medical practitioners identified three kinds of whitlow, each varying according to severity. The first was an inflammation, confined to the surface of the skin, the second a subcutaneous inflammation, and the third one in which the membrane covering the bone at the end of the finger is attacked. Bruises, scratches and pricks from a needle or other sharp instrument were listed among the most common causes of the injury. Remedies included the application of lunar caustic (nitrate of silver) or a warm poultice of linseed or bread (Keith Imray, 1842).

to poultice it] For poultice remedies, see chapter 2, note on p. 42.

In the evening there was rowing on the river.

In the evening there was rowing on the river. As Drummle and Startop each had a boat, I resolved to set up mine, and to cut them both out.] Promoters of rowing recommended regular practice and long trips on the Thames. Young gentlemen benefited from both because they

> are good for body and soul, and promote sound and practical philosophy, in improving the health and the bodily vigour. (Wood, 1857, vi.).

A skiff or gig was the preferred boat: under 30 feet long and with room for four oarsmen, the craft was suited to long trips of up to thirty miles a day upstream on dead water, about six hours' rowing, altogether (De Colquhoun, 1857, 5).

I at once engaged to place myself under the tuition of the winner of a prize-wherry who plied at our stairs,] Competitive rowing on the Thames dates from the late seventeenth century; by 1800, races had become a popular form of entertainment drawing crowds of spectators to watch contests among professional watermen, several thousands of whom worked on the Thames, ferrying people to and from the numerous stairs along the river, or earning their living as lightermen rowing barges. Scullers typically competed for high stakes: winners might receive a brand-new wherry – a stoutly built boat designed to carry about eight passengers and managed either by one sculler or two oarsmen – or a purse of sovereigns. Mogg's map of the Thames in 1827 shows sixty-six river stairs between Battersea and the Isle of Dogs. In the second half of the century, as penny steamers began to capture the passenger market and as piers began to replace stairs, watermen disappeared from the river (based on Halladay 7–10). In 'Down With the Tide', Dickens refers with pride to his having 'graduated . . . under a fireman-waterman, and winner of Kean's Prize Wherry' (*HW* 6.484).

There was a supper-tray

Mr. Pocket was in good spirits,] MS reads 'Mr. Pocket was in quite good spirits (Mrs. Coiler having gone away)'.

"Speak to your master?" said Mrs. Pocket

"Speak to your master?" said Mrs. Pocket, whose dignity was roused again. "How can you think of such a thing? Go and speak to Flopson. Or speak to me – at some other time."] A serious breach of protocol: a well-trained servant would have known to have taken up the question of the cook's misconduct below stairs. Likewise, on no account should the host initiate and exchange with a servant:

> Never at any time, whether at a formal or a familiar dinner party, commit the impropriety of talking to a servant: nor address any remark about one of them to one of the party. Nothing can be more ill-bred. You merely ask for what you want in a grave and civil tone, and wait with patience till your order is obeyed. (*Etiquette for Gentleman*, 1838, 34)

"This is a pretty thing, Belinda!" said Mr. Pocket

"Here's the cook lying insensibly drunk . . . with a large bundle of fresh butter made up in the cupboard ready to sell for grease!"] Misuse of alcohol and the pilfering of foodstuffs and small items by servants were concerns even in well-regulated households. In this instance, the cook has set the butter aside as 'grease' with the intention of using it for her own ends. Grease, dripping and other kitchen-stuff would customarily be sold to rag-and-bottle and marine-store dealers and the proceeds duly recorded in the household accounts. The best antidote to such abuses was vigilance and careful supervision by the mistress of the house.

"Sophia has told you," said Mrs. Pocket.

"Sophia] MS reads 'That detestable Mary Anne'.

"Am I, grandpapa's granddaughter

grandpapa's granddaughter,] This phrase was inserted in the proofs.

"Besides,] MS reads 'Is it Mary Anne's position, or mine, to find out misconduct in the cook? Besides'

There was a sofa where Mr. Pocket stood

There was a sofa where Mr. Pocket stood, and he dropped upon it in the attitude of the Dying Gladiator.] This statue, dating from the third century BC in the Capitoline Museum in Rome was well known in the nineteenth century from Byron's description in *Childe Harold's Pilgrimage*, 1812–18 ('I see before me the Gladiator lie:/He leans upon his hand – his manly brow/Consents to death, but conquers agony,/ And his droop'd head sinks gradually low': Canto 4, stanza 140) and from frequent graphic reproductions. The statue has been correctly renamed 'The Dying Gaul'.

Chapter 24

AFTER two or three days

ordered all I wanted of my tradesmen,]   Young gentlemen who belonged to 'the fast set' received credit on easy terms and showed little restraint using it. Bulwer Lytton's Guy Bolding lived in much the same way as a 'fast man' at Oxford: 'so "fast" had he lived that there was scarcely a tradesman at Oxford into whose books he had not contrived to run' (*The Caxtons*, 1849, pt 13, ch. 4).

Tradesmen readily extended credit to gentlemen for two reasons: they welcomed their business and they knew that the threat of arrest and imprisonment for non-payment, which was theirs by law, left them in a strong position to recover money owed. In fact, the existing system (see chapter 57, note on pp. 408–9) so favoured tradesmen that opposition from the business community delayed efforts by reformers to abolish imprisonment for debt until the second half of the nineteenth century (Lester, ch. 3).

I was not designed for any profession, and that I should be well enough educated for my destiny if I could "hold my own" with the average of young men in prosperous circumstances.]   Education, widely regarded as an 'indispensable requisite for good society', required the development of one's mental powers, 'especially the <u>comprehension</u>'. 'A man should be able, in order to enter into conversation, to catch rapidly the meaning of anything that is advanced' (*The Habits of Good Society*, 1860, 61).

The agenda set for Pip resembles Dickens's own 'higher personal cravings'. According to Forster, strong motivation accounts for Dickens's assiduous attendance 'in the British Museum reading-room' when he was about Pip's age. Forster explains how Dickens himself referred to those days as 'decidedly the usefullest to himself he had ever passed', a judgement his biographer endorsed: 'No man who knew him in later years, and talked to him familiarly of books and things, would have suspected his education in boyhood, almost entirely self-acquired as it was, to have been so rambling or haphazard as I have here described it' (Forster 1.3.45).

When these points were settled

When these points were settled, and so far carried out as that I had begun to work in earnest, it occurred to me that if I could retain my bedroom in Barnard's Inn, my life would be agreeably varied,]   See Appendix 1.

Wemmick was at his desk, lunching – and crunching

a dry hard biscuit;]   This was unleavened bread made from a mixture of flour, milk and water, kneaded into a tough paste and made thin in order that it could be completely cooked in the oven. The paste was usually divided into round pieces and sprinkled with flour before it was baked (Keith Imray 806). Biscuits like this were prepared for the Royal Navy in bakehouses established by the government; hence the term 'sea biscuit'. Twelve ovens at Deptford were capable of supplying each day biscuits for 2,040 men (*Complete Book of Trades* 19).

"Always seems to me," said Wemmick

a man-trap]   Landowners used spring-loaded iron traps hidden in the grass to deter poachers and trespassers. Some were strong enough to crush the bone; others had sharp serrated edges; while some resembled 'the jaws of an old woman to whom time had left nothing but gums'. According to Hardy, men living in the 1880s recalled the use of these devices up to the 1840s (*The Woodlanders*, 1887, 47).

I accepted the offer.

a clerk who looked something between a publican and a rat-catcher]   The comparison appears to suggest a paradoxical blend of the publican's professional affability and a rat-catcher's reputation for dishonesty and criminality. Rat-catchers belonged to a class of individuals in London who merited caution, 'vagabonds' and the 'veriest scoundrels' who practised illegal activities under the guise of rat-catching. Some, 'properly speaking', were dog-stealers; others, 'prowling at will through your establishment under the pretence of ascertaining the holes and runs of rats', operated in conjunction with 'many of the thieves and house-breakers of London', to whom they passed information of any valuables they noticed (Rodwell, 1858, 86). A set of rat-catchers also operated on the Thames, moving from ship to ship, ostensibly to set traps but often, in fact, working in league with 'Lumpers', dishonest cargo-handlers who received stolen goods when they were dropped overboard (Colquhoun, 1800, 69). Other categories of rat-catcher included reliable and trustworthy men who contracted to visit premises on a regular basis in order to keep the rat population under control, while a third group caught rats in the sewers 'for those gentlemen who keep sporting dogs'. Members of this body, on receiving an order for rats, went forth into London's sewers armed with 'a bull's eye lantern, a strong wire cage, and a short rake'. For several hours they waded waist-deep in 'the muck and filth of the description which the closets and sinks of London furnished', disturbing creatures in their hiding-places and catching and caging rats, an easy prey, dazzled with the light (Rodwell 183).

the Bailey."]   See chapter 56, note on p. 400.

a smelter who kept his pot always boiling, and who would melt me anything I pleased]   See chapter 20, note on p. 187.

a face-ache tied up in dirty flannel,]   Flannels soaked in warm water or me poultices served as common remedies for facial inflammation caused by a toothache or an abscess.

These?" said Wemmick, getting upon a chair

"These are two celebrated ones. Famous clients of ours that got us a world of credit.] Since much of Jaggers's reputation rests on his success in defending clients, how might he have benefited from cases he lost? The career of James Harmer (see chapter 18, note on pp. 157–8), the attorney who worked strenuously on behalf of clients the crown ultimately executed, provides a useful perspective. The result of Harmer's efforts, in the words of one of his contemporaries, was the 'immense reputation' he won for himself 'amongst the classes whose natural destination was the Old Bailey' (Ballantine, 1882, 83). Compare also Edward Gibbon Wakefield, who, asked for advice by someone wishing to help a witness accused of forgery, replied: entrust the prisoner's defence to Mr Harmer, 'whose experience and skill as an attorney in criminal matters are well known' (1831, 222).

Two cases in particular illustrate zeal and determination: his defence of Henry Fauntleroy (1785–1824), a wealthy banker hanged for forgery, and of a more obscure individual, Edward Harris, executed for robbing a woman. In both instances, Harmer conducted energetic and exhaustive investigations, working assiduously to unravel a motive and counter-motive. He collected affidavits, publicized the cases in the *Weekly Despatch* and rounded up help from benevolent activists opposed to the use of the death penalty in crimes other than murder. Harmer also wrote – and encouraged others to to write – petition the Home Secretary for clemency (see chapter 56, note on pp. 405–6), and in the case of Harris sent his assistant to Robert Peel and approached Peel himself as well (Gatrell 436–8). All to no avail. But these and other public campaigns on behalf of his clients did much to enhance his professional reputation. The fact that the second of Jaggers's two clients (whose deaths represent milestones in the early stage of his career) was a forger provides a further tentative link with Harmer. See also below.

This chap . . . murdered his master,] The most publicized murder of this kind was probably that of 73-year-old Lord William Russell, whose throat was slit in the early morning of 6 May 1840 as he lay in bed. Russell's Swiss valet, F. B. Courvoisier (1817–40), was tried and convicted of the murder, the object of which was robbery. Dickens attended Courvoisier's execution on 6 July 1840 (*Letters* 2.87 n.).

"Like him? It's himself, you know.

The cast was made in Newgate, directly after he was taken down.] See chapter 20, note on p. 180.

"No," returned Wemmick.

"Only his game. (You liked your bit of game, didn't you?)] 'Game', a slang term for a prostitute. Fauntleroy, who over nine years embezzled half a million pounds from his partners and his bank's creditors, was also a notorious womanizer. His gains from forgery served to finance a dissolute life squandered on mistresses in town and country and on gambling (*DNB*).

"You're right," said Wemmick

"it's the genuine look. Much as if one nostril was caught up with a horsehair and a little fish-hook.] A similar detail characterizes the strange old man questioned by the two apprentices visiting Lancaster in 'The Lazy Tour of Two Idle Apprentices' (1857). Asked if criminals are hanged facing the castle, he replies:

> His cravat appeared to trouble him. He put his hand to his throat, and moved his neck from side to side. He was an old man of a swollen character of face, and his nose was immovably hitched up on one side, as if by a little hook inserted in that nostril. (ch. 4, *HW* 16.387)

See also chapter 20, note on p.180.

He forged wills, this blade did. . . . You were a gentlemanly Cove, though . . . and you said you could write Greek. Yah. . . . What a liar you were!] Executions for forgery between 1770 and 1830 attracted public attention, owing to a sustained campaign to remove the crime from the capital statutes. Several cases stood out, like that of the swindler Fauntleroy, 'the most celebrated metropolitan criminal of the 1820s' (Gatrell 387). His composure on the eve of his execution, and the fact that he and other forgers were well-educated gentlemen (Joseph Hunton, for example, was a wealthy Quaker), added to his notoriety and to the public's interest. Forgery statistics also mocked the supposed deterrent value of the capital statutes for the offence. In 1817 only fourteen people were hanged for forgery, yet 31,280 forged notes were presented to the Bank of England in that year alone (Radzinowicz 1.537–8). Despite these and other anomalies, including Peel's consolidation of forgery statutes in 1830, the crime remained a capital one until 1832. In his second letter to the editor of the *Daily News* on 26 February 1846, Dickens comments how the death penalty invested forgers with a notoriety not given to them when they were transported for life (Paroissien, 1985, 219). A 'blade' was a gallant or a free-and-easy fellow, 'cove' slang for man or companion and 'Bounceable' a colloquial adjective meaning full of bounce or swagger.

"Sent out to buy it for me, only the day before."] Theatrical gestures of this kind were not uncommon among notorious criminals living in the condemned cells. Mourning rings could be easily obtained from any one of several shops in London that specialized in the sale of mourning paraphernalia.

"Oh yes," he returned

"Get hold of portable property."] 'Personal' rather than 'portable' is the correct legal adjective used to distinguish property recoverable by personal action as opposed to 'real property', that is an estate or interests in land, which are recoverable only by a real action (*OED*). 'Portable' in this context serves as a synonym for chattels or movables. The same phrase appears in *DC* when David, at the bidding of Mrs Micawber, takes 'portable articles of property' to the pawnbroker (11). Perhaps someone in Dickens's family invented the term. If so, it would have had a special resonance for the author who, like David Copperfield, frequently ran similar errands when the Dickens family lived on the edge of financial collapse not long before John Dickens's arrest for debt on 20 February 1824.

"If at any odd time when you have nothing better to do

Walworth,] At this time, a small village about three miles from central London, on the south bank of the Thames between Kennington Park Road and the Old Kent Road with Camberwell to the south.

"Well," said Wemmick, "you'll see a wild beast tamed.

a wild beast tamed.] Possibly an echo of James 3.8. 'For every kind of beasts, and of birds, and of serpents, and of things in the sea, is tamed, and hath been tamed of mankind'.

For several reasons, and not least because I didn't clearly know

We dived into the City, and came up in a crowded police-court,] Police-courts were known as magistrates' courts, 'public offices' and 'police-offices', depending on the period in question (Paroissien, 1993, 114). The inferior courts dealt primarily with misdemeanours (offences less than a felony) and dispensed summary justice, where offenders were tried by magistrates rather than by juries. Summary offences included offences against property, vagrancy, drunkenness, prostitution and minor larceny. Magistrates or stipendiary police-magistrates presided, sitting on the bench, while attorneys on either side conducted their cases.

my guardian had a woman under examination or cross-examination – I don't know which – and was striking her, and the bench, and everybody present, with awe.] Dickens attacked the use of bullying tactics by lawyers in *PP* (34) and again in the preface to the Cheap Edition of the novel in 1847.

thief-takers] The Bow Street Runners (see chapter 16, note on pp. 148–9).

he seemed to me to be grinding the whole place in a mill;] The 'mills of justice' is an old figure of speech.

he was not on the side of the bench,] Jaggers therefore defends his client against a charge brought by the Crown or the state.

Chapter 25 Sixteenth weekly number
16 March 1861

BENTLEY DRUMMLE, who was so sulky a fellow

who was so sulky a fellow]   The recurring use of 'sulky' by Jaggers and Pip (see chapters 26 and 38) possibly connects Drummle with entry 90 in the *Book of Memoranda:* 'A thoroughly sulky character – perverting everything – making the good, bad – and the bad, good'. Compare Kaplan, who suggests that the notation may refer to Rogue Riderhood in *OMF*.

in Somersetshire,]   Somerset, a predominantly rural county in the south-west of England. See also chapter 43, note on p. 336.

"Very much," was Wemmick's reply

a stewed steak – which is of home preparation – and a cold roast fowl – which is from the cook's-shop.]   Stewed steak was fried first in butter or fat, lightly browned and then cut into serving-sized pieces. After water and seasonings were added the meat was covered and cooked gently for two to three hours (Beeton 1578). Chopped mushrooms, port or madeira were often included to enrich the flavours. Cooked food from a cook's shop could either be purchased and taken out or eaten on the premises.

"That's it!" returned Wemmick.

regular cracksmen]   A slang term for housebreakers or burglars.

"Dread him," said Wemmick.

No silver, sir. Britannia metal, every spoon."]   Britannia metal (a compound of tin, antimony, copper and brass metal) was an inexpensive substitute for silver widely used in the manufacture of cutlery, tea-pots, salvers, candlesticks, snuffers, bread-baskets, etc.

"Ah! But <u>he</u> would have much," said Wemmick

He'd have their lives, and the lives of scores of 'em.]   This statement is compatible with the continued existence of over 200 capital statutes as late as the 1820s, but in practice executions for housebreaking with larceny were rare (Radzinowicz 1.154). The penalty for this offence was abolished in 1835 (3 & 4 Will. IV, c. 44).

"Massive?" repeated Wemmick.

a gold repeater,]   Repeater watches, introduced early in the eighteenth century, enabled owners to learn the hour and the last quarter by pressing a pendant or lever. This action wound up the mainspring of the repeating train, and the hours were then struck on a bell shaped to the inside of the watch-case. The addition of the repeating mechanism to the movement increased the size of casings, making the early repeaters larger and deeper than any watches manufactured since the sixteenth century, hence the need for a strong chain to secure them to one's waistcoat pocket. Gold cases were often elaborately chiselled or engraved (Hayward 7–8). The introduction of friction matches in 1827 hastened the decline of repeaters since matches made obtaining a light easy, thereby undercutting the need to tell time in the dark by pressing the striking mechanism.

Reference to the 'massive' quality of Jaggers's watch-chain and to his gold repeater may have carried personal significance. On 4 December 1858 the watch-makers of Coventry presented Dickens with a gold repeater specially built by them in recognition of his efforts to raise money for the city's new Institute. In gratitude, Dickens pledged the givers that the watch thenceforth would be his companion and never absent from his side until 'I have done with time and its measurement' (*Speeches* 286; 'Coventry's Watch', 1951, 17).

At first with such discourse

we had arrived in the district of Walworth.]   The route required crossing London Bridge and heading south along the Borough High Street and into the Old Kent Road. Walworth lay to the west. Dickens's reference to it as presenting the aspect of 'a rather dull retirement' resembles comments he made in 1836 about Walworth as 'a straggling miserable place' sprinkled with houses at irregular intervals 'of the rudest and most miserable description' ('The Black Veil', SB).

It appeared to be a collection of back lanes

a little wooden cottage in the midst of plots of garden, and the top of it was cut out and painted like a battery mounted with guns.]   The cottage resembles one kept by Smollett's Commodore Trunnion, who is described as keeping 'garrison in his house'

> as if he were in the midst of his enemies, and makes his servants turn out in the night, watch and ward (as he calls it) all the year round. His habitation is defended by a ditch, over which he has laid a drawbridge, and planted his court-yard with patereroes continually loaded with shot, under the direction of one Mr. Hatchway who ... lives with [the commodore] as his companion.
> (*The Adventures of Peregrine Pickle*, 1751, ch. 2)

I highly commended it.

I think it was the smallest house I ever saw; with the queerest gothic windows (by far the greater part of them sham), and a gothic door almost too small to get in at.] The architectural features incorporate two late-eighteenth-century fashions in domestic architecture: 'cottage ornée' and the Gothic. The first called for artfully rustic buildings, usually of asymmetrical plan. This vogue was the product of the picturesque cult and was popular with small property holders. The Gothic style, a taste for sham castles and false medievalism, began with Arbury Hall in Warwickshire (c.1760–70) and is most famously exemplified by Horace Walpole's Strawberry Hill (c.1750–70). As the Gothic Revival spread, parapets, pointed arches, turrets, crested roofs and an intentional irregularity and verticality made their way even into ordinary houses built throughout much of the nineteenth century (based on Fergusson, 1862).

The bridge was a plank

The bridge was a plank, and it crossed a chasm about four feet wide and two deep.] Bridges and moats derive from other Gothic features associated with castles built on estates in the country. Wemmick's concern for privacy and comfort reflects a trait observers characterized as a typically national one:

> What we call in England a comfortable house is a thing so intimately identified with English customs as to make us apt to say that in no other country but our own is this element fully understood; or at all other events that the comfort of any other nation is not the comfort of this. The peculiarities of our climate, the domesticated habits of almost all classes, our family reserve, and our large share of the means and appliances of easy living, all combine to make what is called a comfortable home perhaps the most cherished possession of an Englishman. (Kerr, 1864, 77)

"At nine o'clock every night, Greenwich time," said Wemmick

Greenwich time,"] The old observatory built by Wren at Greenwich (1675) on the south bank of the Thames housed a succession of important clocks by which time in Britain was measured. When the time ball installed in 1833 was dropped at precisely one o'clock each day, it served as a signal to ships on the Thames and to chronometer-makers in Clerkenwell. In 1884 an international agreement established that the meridian passing through the Royal Observatory should be the zero or prime meridian from which meridians east and west up to 180 degrees were to be measured.

"At the back, there's a pig, and there are fowls and rabbits

a pig . . . fowls and rabbits;] Keeping livestock in a semi-urban setting recalls a version of 'cottage economy' practised by those working men who subscribed to the notion of domestic self-sufficiency; by raising a supply of vegetables, eggs and meat, one created a pleasant feeling of independence. Such 'sober, industrious and domestic habits' in the common man were widely regarded as 'the best security against pauperism' (Loudon, 1857, 1074–5, 1043). See also below.

I knock together my own little frame, you see, and grow cucumbers;] Interest in producing cucumbers early in the season was an enthusiasm shared by even 'the humblest tradesmen'. Cucumbers were forced by growing them under a glazed wooden frame in a bed of hot dung in a minimum temperature of 58°. Efforts to produce the first crop began early in February (Loudon, 1827, 569, 299).

Then he conducted me to a bower

Then he conducted me to a bower about a dozen yards off . . . approached by . . . ingenious twists of path . . . and in this retreat our glasses were already set forth. Our punch was cooling in an ornamental lake. . . . This piece of water (with an island in the middle . . .) was of a circular form, and he had constructed a fountain in it, which, when you set a little mill going . . . played to that powerful extent that it made the back of your hand quite wet.] The layout reflects (perhaps in parody form) the emphasis Victorian landscape gardeners placed on creating landscapes that were both useful and ornamental. The stratagems employed here – flowing water, a stream, a pond and cascade, together with twists in the path and a bower – resemble those used by eighteenth-century landscape gardeners. Decorative buildings 'introduced more for their picturesque effect as parts of external scenery, than as absolutely necessary', writes Loudon, belong equally in the large country estate and in the garden of the labourer's cottage:

> This may be reckoned too humble a country residence for the consideration of the country gardener; but we conceive it to be of very great importance to the general good, that these should be improved, and their inhabitants ameliorated. What we shall advance is founded on the general principle, that whatever renders the cottager more comfortable and happy at home, will render him a better servant and subject, and in every respect a more valuable member of society. (1827, 1027)

Not mentioned in the novel, but understood by Victorian readers and subject to the same aesthetic considerations, is the water-closet or privy. Loudon recommended placing it in a hidden part of the garden behind the house, approached not by a direct cul de sac path but by one so contrived that the visitor could not be seen, coming or going, from either the windows of the house or the public road (1027).

punch was cooling]   Spirits, water, lemons and sugar were among the basic ingredients. See also chapter 4, note on p. 63.

"This is a fine place of my son's, sir," cried the old man

This spot and these beautiful works upon it ought to be kept together by the Nation, after my son's time, for the people's enjoyment."]   As early as 1810, Wordsworth had spoken of the Lake District as 'a sort of national property' for the 'persons of pure taste' who admire and visit it (1977, 92), but the idea of giving a building to the state was an advanced one. The National Trust, the recipient of most buildings and areas of the countryside 'left to the nation', was not founded until 1895. The Society for Protecting Ancient Buildings was founded by William Morris earlier, in 1877, but did not own any buildings until the twentieth century. In 1852, Apsley House, the home of the Duke of Wellington, was opened to the public on the Duke's death, but the house remained in the Spencer family.

"You're as proud of it as Punch

as proud of it as Punch;]   Comparisons with 'Punch' as the embodiment of pride replaced earlier ones (with peacocks, pigs or dogs with two tails, Lucifer) around the middle of the nineteenth century. The *OED* cites Mrs Gaskell's *Mary Barton* (ch. 5, 1848) as the first recorded use of the phrase. From the 1820s, Punch became increasingly associated with entertainment for children rather than with the adult comic figure derived from the seventeenth-century Italian *Pulcinella*.

Proceeding into the Castle again

heating the poker,]   A red-hot poker inserted into the cannon's touchhole would ignite the powder charge.

The interval between that time and supper

several manuscript confessions written under condemnation – upon which Mr. Wemmick set particular value as being, to use his own words, "every one of 'em Lies, sir."]   The Old Bailey authorities, often led by the prison chaplain, made a strenuous effort to encourage felons to profess their guilt and penitence. Genuine and self-serving motives characterized these endeavours: confessions helped legitimize the punishment and ease the minds of those who sent hundreds to the scaffold, while the chaplain took seriously repentance as a preparation for the afterlife since he believed felons faced a merciful creator. But many condemned prisoners refused to comply, stoutly insisting on their innocence to the discomfort of all members of the execution party. Wemmick's scepticism expresses a view others shared that confessions extracted from hardened criminals in the face of certain death and delivered in formulaic phrases were far from heartfelt, since the species 'all have the same stamp'. As one authority noted:

> ... the whole of the last dying speeches and confessions, trials and sentences, from whatever part of the country they come, run in the same form of quaint and circumstantial detail: appeals to Heaven, to young men, to young women, to Christians in general, and moral reflection. We have seldom met with one of different character. ('Street Ballads', 1861, 405)

Wemmick's other 'felonious' curios appear to be variants of what Fonblanque termed the public's 'Diseased Appetite for Horrors' evident in the sale of relics associated with sensational crimes: the hangman often disposed of his rope in inch-length pieces; the barn in which William Corder murdered Maria Martin in 1828 was 'sold in tooth picks'; and 'the hedge through which the body of Mr. Weare was dragged, was purchased by the inch' (Fonblanque 2.194).

tobacco-stoppers] Pipe-smokers used tobacco-stoppers to press the tobacco down into the bowl of a pipe while smoking.

a brazen bijou over the fireplace designed for the suspension of a roasting-jack.] This was an ornamental brass bracket supporting the roasting-jack, a clockwork device for cooking a roast attached to a rotating spit.

Chapter 26

IT fell out, as Wemmick had told me it would

dinner dress,]

> At a formal dinner-party the evening suit is imperative, with dress-coat, white or black waistcoat, black trousers, and white tie. When dining with friends with whom one is on terms of familiarity, the dinner-jacket may be substituted for the coat. Black ties often take the place of white. Patent-leather shoes or boots must be worn . . . His varnished shoes must show no trace of mud or dust.
>
> The pocket-handkerchief used with evening dress must be of white cambric . . . . It ought to be of fine quality. (Humphry, 1897, 81)

he washed his clients off, as if he were a surgeon or a dentist.] Compare Pontius Pilate, who 'washed his hands' of Christ's blood (Matthew 27.24), and Lady Macbeth, whose 'accustomed action' of washing her hands as she walks in her sleep conveys guilt for spurring on her husband to murder Duncan and Banquo (*Macbeth* 5.1). Clearly, surgeons and dentists washed their hands for Dickens to make the comparison, although the full implications of washing as a protection against infection were not fully understood until Joseph Lister introduced carbolic acid as a disinfectant in 1867.

like a perfumer's shop.] The comparison provides further evidence of Pip's social transformation: 'The patrons of perfumery have always been considered the most civilised and refined people of the earth' (Piesse, 1855, vi). In the 1850s, perfumers typically sold a wide variety of perfumed soaps (almond, camphor, honey, white Windsor, brown Windsor, sand, fuller's earth), milks or emulsions, hair dyes, depilatories, absorbent powders, cold cream, oils and pomades, hair washes, tooth powders and tooth washes (Piesse).

There were some people slinking about as usual

As we walked along westward,] Soho, their destination (see below), lies west of Jaggers's office in Little Britain.

He conducted us to Gerrard-street, Soho

to Gerrard-street, Soho, to a house on the south side. . . . Rather a stately house of its kind,] Gerrard Street in the district of Soho, north-east of Piccadilly, had several handsome houses formerly tenanted by the nobility and gentry in the eighteenth century. By the early 1800s the region had declined, mingling faded grandeur with the colourful activity and bustle associated with more recent foreign immigrants who had settled there. Today, Soho is bounded by Regent's Street, Oxford Street, Tottenham Court Road and Piccadilly.

He took out his key and opened the door,] Reference to the key seems to contradict Wemmick's earlier comment about Jaggers's apparent immunity from thieves (chapter 25).

Dinner was laid in the best of these rooms

The table was comfortably laid – no silver in the service, of course] The use of Britannia metal (chapter 25) flouts the middle-class practice of using silver cutlery: 'At every respectable table you will find *silver* forks; being broader, they are in all respects more convenient than steel for fish or vegetables' ('Agogos' 27).

dumb-waiter,] Dumb-waiters were invented in England about 1740. After adaptation elsewhere later in the century, they became common pieces of dining-room furniture. They typically consisted of a central pedestal supporting one or more revolving trays or shelves for dishes, glasses, decanters, bottles and other table requisites. Having them close to hand allowed one to dispense with the services of a table waiter.

There was a bookcase in the room

books . . . about evidence, criminal law, criminal biography, trials, acts of parliament,] A prolific literature about crime catered to a variety of preferences and pockets. Professional books included volumes about evidence (a growing field in the 1820s), medical jurisprudence, forensic medicine, and numerous collections of state trials, case-histories and criminal biographies. The latter, often of the confessional variety and one of the staples of the 'lower-class publishers', were complemented by numerous 'Newgate Calendars' based on an earlier series of lives of notorious criminals (see also chapter 40, note on p. 323). Typical titles included Paul Lorraine's *The Ordinary of Newgate*, Captain Alexander Smith's *Lives of the Most Noted Highwaymen* (five editions between 1713 and 1719), *A General and True History of the Most Famous Highwaymen, Murderers, Street-robbers, etc.* (1742), *Adventures of Famous Highwaymen and Other Public Robbers* (c.1834) and the five volumes of the *Malefactors' Register* (1779). Among government publications were Select Committee Reports, Reports of Royal Commissions and the Old Bailey Sessions Papers. Broadsides, chapbooks and later penny dreadfuls and the penny newspapers satisfied a similar taste for crime among humbler readers (James, 1974, *passim*). Dickens's own library contained volumes of state trials, celebrated crimes and Parliamentary reports (*Letters* 4.719, 722, 724).

"The Spider?" said I.

"The Spider?"] For Jaggers's choice of nickname for Drummle, see chapter 23, note on pp. 214–15.

She was a woman of about forty, I supposed

She was a woman of about forty, I supposed – but I may have thought her younger than she was.] After 'her' MS and AYR read 'older than she was, as it is the manner of youth to do'. Molly's supposed age fits in well with the projected overall chronology of the novel. See Appendix 1.

her face looked to me as if it were all disturbed by fiery air, like the faces I had seen rise out of the Witches' caldron.] The comparison is with one of the Weird Sisters, apparitions which hover in the air, vulture-like, as they stir their cauldron of exotic ingredients popularly supposed poisonous (*Macbeth* 1.1, 4.1).

She set the dish on,

a noble dish of fish . . . a joint of equally choice mutton . . . and then an equally choice bird.] The dinner follows a conventional pattern in which the host serves fish followed by two entrées, one brown and one white. A choice of fruit and port wine concludes the meal. Some observers considered dinner 'at a bachelor's snuggery' with six to ten guests 'the perfection of all' forms of social dining (*London at Dinner*, 1858, 27).

Years afterwards, I made a dreadful likeness of that woman, by causing a face that had no other natural resemblance to it than it derived from flowing hair, to pass behind a bowl of flaming spirits in a dark room.] Evidently an allusion to a Victorian parlour game of viewing faces in a darkened room by the light of a bowl of flaming spirits. Dickens recounts one such instance related to him by a guest at a dinner given by Harvard's notorious Professor J. W. Webster (1793–1850), a year before Webster disposed of the man he murdered by cutting him up and incinerating him:

> Webster suddenly told the servants to turn the gas off and bring in that bowl of burning materials which he had prepared, in order that the company might see how ghastly they looked by its weird light. All this was done, and every man was looking, horror-stricken, at his neighbour; when Webster was seen bending over the bowl with a rope round his neck, holding up the end of the rope, with his head on one side and his tongue lolled out, to represent a hanged man! (*Nonesuch* 3.591)

In 'Christmas at Noningsby', *Orley Farm* (1862), Trollope describes the illumination of a 'ghost' with light from a large dish aflame with burning brandy at a children's party (22).

"I'll tell you, however," said I

We said that as you put it into your pocket very glad to get it, you seemed to be immensely amused at his being so weak as to lend it."] Drummle bears partial resemblance to a borrower Dickens sketched in 1857 who later scoffs privately at the generosity of the lender:

> The knowing man in distress, who borrows a round sum of a generous <and> friend. Comes, in depression and tears, dines, gets the money – and gradually cheers up over his wine, as he obviously entertains himself with the reflection that his friend is a damned fool to have lent it to him, and that *he* would have known better. (*Memoranda* 69)

In about a month after that

he went home to the family hole.] After 'hole.' MS reads 'He called me Blacksmith, when he went away, qualified to be an indifferent hostler or a bad gamekeeper.'

Chapter 27 Seventeenth weekly number
23 March 1861

"I write this by request of Mr. Gargery

Barnard's Hotel] The use of 'hotel' as a synonym for 'inn' illustrates ignorance of Barnard's original function as a residence for law students. Initially, Pip made the same mistake (chapter 21).

'Your ever obliged, and affectionate Servant,] Biddy ends her letter correctly; letter writers were instructed:

> Always remember that the terms of compliment at the close of a letter – 'I have the honour to be your very obedient servant,' etc. are merely forms – 'signifying nothing'. Do not therefore avoid them on account of pride, or dislike of the person addressed. (*Etiquette for Gentlemen*, 1838, 20)

I received this letter by the post

Monday morning,] See Appendix 1.

I had begun to be always decorating the chambers

I enjoyed the honour of occupying a few prominent pages in the books of a neighbouring upholsterer.] Pip's later ironic view of his extravagant use of credit contrasts with his earlier tendency to boast of having all he wanted of his tradesmen (chapter 24). By the 1830s the trade of upholstery had become 'one of multifarious occupations', employing a wide range of skilled workers capable not only of stuffing chairs, sofas and beds but also of making beds, cabinets and looking-glasses. The business also included openings for carvers and gilders, mercers, and woollen and linen drapers. Other work performed by upholsterers included arranging draperies for window curtains, cutting carpets and turning their attention 'even to the decorative part' of rooms (*Complete Book of Trades* 87, 458–9, 92). By the end of the century, the term meant decorator in the sense we speak of an interior decorator (Panton 1).

a boy in . . . top boots . . . a blue coat, canary waistcoat, white cravat, creamy breeches] The Mayhew brothers satirized the fashion for fancifully dressed pages in *The Greatest Plague of Life* whose heroine decks out a former workhouse boy in a claret jacket with 'three rows of sugar-loaf buttons . . . and . . . a pair of nice quiet dark-coloured pantaloons' (222). The livery Pip selects suggests an outfit adopted by post-boys, youths who carried letters on horseback. Leather top-boots, which rose to just below the knee, were worn with the tops – often a lighter colour – turned down and had a low square heel and rounded toe. Loops on either side made it easier for the wearer to pull on the boot. Originally worn by yeomen farmers and gentlemen, top-boots later spread to jockeys, coachmen, post-boys and, finally, to boys employed in service. The habit of dressing pages in livery persisted until the end of the century.

Affluent young men in furnished apartments often employed a uniformed male servant as a sign of respectability. 'Do you keep livery-servants?' was one of the most prominent of the great public questions of the day, according to Charles Manby Smith. Smith himself had a boy, 'Bung', the 'ever-active Mercury of the house'. On suitable occasions, Bung was brought up from the basement, where he did much of his menial work, and would dress up to receive guests, who would see 'Bung brilliant in a clean face, a milkwhite collar, and "dicky", neat slippers, and a showy suit of rather faded livery, a little tarnished in the lace and buttons, only a few sizes too big for him' (Charles Manby Smith, 1857, 286). Wages, livery and maintenance for a single male servant could cost as much as £60 a year in the 1820s (Porter, 1836, 2.14).

For, after I had made this monster . . . and had clothed him . . . I had to find him a little to do and a great deal to eat; and with both of those horrible requirements he haunted my existence.] The allusion is to Mary Shelley's 'ghost-story', *Frankenstein; or, The Modern Prometheus* (1818). Dr Frankenstein's experiment goes awry when the monster he creates turns on him and haunts him for refusing to provide the monster with a female counterpart. Pip later reverses the comparison, seeing himself as 'the misshapen creature' made by Magwitch. See chapter 40, note on p. 324.

This avenging phantom was ordered to be on duty

avenging phantom] An allusion to *Frankenstein*. See above.

at eight on Tuesday morning] This early arrival (impossible had Joe come directly) is later explained when Joe tells Herbert that he came to town 'yesterday afternoon'.

With his good honest face glowing and shining

the last-patented Pump.] Pump technology continued to evolve throughout the century. By the 1850s, hand-cranked pumps in public thoroughfares either lifted water, forced it or worked by combining the two operations (Gwilt, 1842).

"I am glad to see you, Joe. Give me your hat

But Joe, taking it up carefully with both hands, like a bird's-nest with eggs in it, wouldn't hear of parting with that piece of property, and persisted in standing talking over it in a most uncomfortable way.] To well-bred men, mastery of hat etiquette was almost as important as knowing how to use a knife properly. 'It is a piece of superlative folly for men who dine at a house to take their round hats into the drawing-room: it answers no purpose at all; and the necessity of giving them to a servant on entering the dining-room, creates confusion' (Day 25).

Joe's comic antics may owe something to Lord Chesterfield's sketch of 'an awkward fellow':

> When an awkward fellow first comes into a room, it is highly probable, that his sword gets between his legs, and throws him down, or makes him stumble, at least; when he has recovered this accident, he goes and places himself in the very place of the whole room where he should not; there he soon lets his hat fall down, and, in taking it up again, throws down his cane; in recovering his cane, his hat falls a second time, so that he is a quarter of an hour before he is in order again. If he drinks tea or coffee, he certainly scalds his mouth, and lets either the cup or the saucer fall, and spills either the tea or coffee in his breeches. (Letter, 25 July 1741, 1.146)

A century later, Thomas Tegg endorsed Chesterfield's witty picture of 'the ill-bred man'. In a 'Manual' written to direct the steps of a practical man 'upon his first going into life', Tegg commented that clumsy behaviour, 'we own, has nothing in it criminal; but it is such an offence to good manners and good breeding, that it is universally despised; it makes a man ridiculous in every company, and, of course, ought to be avoided by every one who would wish to please' (242–3).

"Which you have that growed," said Joe

your king and country."] George III.

"Thank God," said Joe, "I'm ekerval to most.

he's had a drop."] Joe's description of Wopsle's fortunes accurately suggests the realities of life in the theatre, all too frequently distorted by the spell or enchantment performers created. 'Delusive appearances!', commented Pierce Egan:

> The life of an Actor, viewed in the most advantageous situation, is far from proving a bed of roses; it is true he is cherished by hope; but more frequently depressed by fears; subject to the keen shafts of envy; and tortured by caprice. . . . It cannot be denied he is hero for the time being; but then *his* THRONE is never secure. (Egan, 1825, 3–5)

Only the foremost actors enjoyed professional standing and earned, like tragedian W. C. Macready and comic actor William Farren (1725–95), £30 a week. Others received much less; the pay for 'third-rate performers' varied from seven to ten guineas, while 'shoals of other actors and actresses' were engaged at rates ranging from two to five guineas (Grant, 1837, 1.60–1). For Wopsle, it is plausible that he purchased his leading part rather than received money to perform. See chapter 47, note on p. 361.

All this time (still with both hands taking great care of the bird's-nest)

Joe was rolling his eyes round and round the room,]   Pip's expensive decorating habits and dandy clothing manifest a form of vulgarity, for ostentatious display 'is an assumption of delicacy superior to the majority' (*The Habits of Good Society*, 1860, 55).

the flowered pattern of my dressing-gown.]   Gentlemen at home often wore long, loosely tied dressing-gowns in the morning over a shirt, waistcoat and trousers; patterned and brightly coloured silk or rich brocades were the fabrics of choice in the 1830s (Sichel 19–20). Some criticized the practice: 'Avoid dressing-gowns; which argue dawdling, an unshorn chin, a lax toilet, and a general lazy and indolent habit at home. Begin your day with a clean conscience in every way' (Thackeray, 'On Tailoring – and Toilette in General', *Sketches and Travels in London*, 1847–50, 238).

I took what Joe gave me

the crumpled playbill]   Playbills affixed to walls or posts, or distributed by hand to pedestrians in the streets, advertised coming attractions.

a small metropolitan theatre,]   Prior to the Theatres Act of 1843 (6 & 7 Vict., c. 68), the Letters Patent issued by Charles II in 1662 had effectively limited the production of serious or 'legitimate' drama to London's Drury Lane and Covent Garden theatres. Their monopoly of acted drama, however, failed to carry a similar monopoly over forms of dramatic entertainment that fell outside a strict definition of 'drama'. These forms included: melodrama, burlettas, extravaganzas, farces, operettas and other forms of performance that were within the law. Non-patent theatres, whose numbers increased steadily during the early decades of the nineteenth century, catered primarily to the popular taste for spectacle and entertainment until the 1843 Theatres Act finally broke the monopoly on 'serious' drama held by the two Patent theatres. The assumption that Wopsle could have played Hamlet at 'a small metropolitan theatre' before 1843 has prompted an attempt to question the early dating of the novel's action (Clinton-Baddeley). Dickens appears to refer to no particular theatre or performance, presenting instead a composite version based on his extensive knowledge of London theatres dating from the 1830s.

announcing the first appearance, in that very week, of "the celebrated Provincial Amateur of Roscian renown, whose unique performance in the highest tragic walk of our National Bard has lately occasioned so great a sensation in local dramatic circles."]   The description parodies the florid and hyperbolic style of contemporary playbills. Quintus Roscius Gallus (d.62 BC) was a famous Roman actor; actors commonly regarded Shakespeare's Hamlet as the ultimate test of their skill.

"Why," said Joe, "yes, there certainly were a peck of orange-peel.

a peck of orange-peel.] A peck is a dry measure equal to eight quarts. Throwing orange peel at members of the cast was a gesture of mockery, frequent even in the more respectable theatres. Visiting Drury Lane theatre on Boxing Night 1862, William Hardman recorded:

> The first piece was acted in dumb show, not a word we could hear. The fights in the pit and gallery were frequent. The shower of orange peel from the gods into the pit was quite astounding. The occupants of the latter place made feeble efforts to throw it back again, but, of course, never got it any further than the first tier of boxes. (229)

On the night Pip and Herbert visit, the actors are pelted with nuts (chapter 31).

Partickler, when he see the ghost. Though I put it to yourself, sir, whether it were calc'lated to keep a man up to his work with a good hart, to be continiwally cutting in betwixt him and the Ghost with 'Amen!'] The Ghost appears on the battlements in the opening scene. Despite the absence of any stage directions, the practice developed for the actor playing Hamlet to walk across the Ghost's path when he entered saying, 'I'll cross it though it blast me' (*Hamlet* 1.1.127). The derisive cries of 'Amen' may have been provoked by Wopsle's solemn tone, a legacy of his performances as parish clerk.

if the ghost of a man's own father cannot be allowed to claim his attention, what can, Sir? Still more, when his mourning 'at is unfortunately made so small as that the weight of the black feathers brings it off, try to keep it on how you may."] A hat with black feathers was an accepted item of any Hamlet's costume. Traditionally, Hamlet knocked off his hat, as a token of terror and amazement, when he saw the ghost. The undersized hat Wopsle wears thus spoils one of his great moments by continually and prematurely falling off (Clinton-Baddeley 157).

"Do you take tea, or coffee, Mr. Gargery?

tea, or coffee,] For tea, see chapter 2, note on p. 42. By the nineteenth century, coffee, together with tea, was popular among all classes and one of the nation's principal beverages. Carefully prepared and used in moderation, coffee was described as 'an exhilarating, grateful beverage' (Keith Imray, 1842, 826).

"Why, yes, Sir," said Joe

"me and Wopsle went off straight to look at the Blacking War'us. But we didn't find that it come up to its likeness in the red bills at the shop doors;] The warehouse in question belonged to Day & Martin, London's leading manufacturer of liquid shoe blacking. This company maintained an imposing headquarters on the north side of High Holborn between Red Lion Street and Kingsgate Street: 'From the arched entrance, the premises extend to a distance of upwards of two hundred feet northward, to a street running parallel with Holborn; and the working parts of the factory are nearly a hundred feet in width'. The whole manufactory was 'built on a scale of great magnificence', making the warehouse a popular tourist attraction in the years following its erection in 1832 ('A Day at Day and Martin's', 1843, 511).

The distinctive labels attached to Day & Martin's pots of liquid blacking were well known from their use as display bills, which the firm produced by taking advantage of developments in printing technology:

> If we examine one of "Day and Martin's" labels, we see that nearly the whole of the ground consists of a kind of lace-work, printed in red on white paper, the meshes or interstices being probably about one-twentieth of an inch in diameter. The ground-work, occupying about sixteen square inches, is diversified by several compartments printed in black ink; one, for instance, containing a view of the front façade of the factory; another, the name of the firm; a third, the retail price of the commodity contained in the bottle; a fourth, the number of the house, curiously bedecked with a double enunciation of the name of the firm; and two others containing remarks and directions to the purchaser. All these are printed with black ink on the white paper, no red lace-work being seen here. Above these are letters printed in black and white on a wavy or undulating ground of black, red, and white; while at the top are black letters, and at the bottom letters in white, red, and black, printed on, or at least interspersed among, the lace-work ground itself. (514)

Advertising campaigns by rival manufacturers of blacking added further to public interest in the commodity. Competition was so intense that owners were said to have retained 'poets of high reputation to sing the praises of their paste and product'.

The relative newness of blacking accounts for consumer interest in a product that enabled men to polish their shoes at home instead of having to go to the shoe-black boy at the street-corner. The gradual introduction of paving and improvements in street conditions also hastened the adoption of this 'agent of cleanliness' in homes, conveniently available in brown glazed pots. The vogue for blacking persisted for much of the century until the introduction of creams and polishes suitable for fine leather, rather than the 'strong' leather used for boots, pushed the 'old-fashioned' blacking out of the market (Humphry, 1914, 2.141). The personal implications this product had for Dickens are well known (Forster 1.2.19–33) and perhaps account for the anachronistic reference to the 'red bills', whose appearance and circulation postdate the novel's early setting and presumed date of Joe's visit to London in 1816. See Appendix 1.

"as it is there drawd too architectooralooral."] The reference is to the design on the Day & Martin label (see above). Joe's difficulty with the word 'architectural' may owe something to mispronunciations ascribed to Londoners. *Black's Picturesque*

Tourist of Scotland (1851) cites 'tural lural' as one cockney's attempt to say 'truly rural' (Scott, 1975, 172). Compare also Jerry Cruncher's description of his former occupation as that of an 'Agricultooral character' in *TTC* (3.9).

I really believe Joe would have prolonged this word

wicket-keeping.] The wicket-keeper in cricket stands behind one set of three sticks (stumps) fixed upright in the ground and topped by two small pieces of wood called bails. His job is to catch balls tipped or missed by the batsman, who defends the wicket against the ball, delivered by the bowler on the opposing team. Nine other players are positioned elsewhere to field the ball, if it is hit.

the slop-basin,] Slop-basins or slop-bowls date from the early nineteenth century and were used to hold the rinsings of tea, coffee or other beverages: 'He threw the slops . . . into the sugar-dish instead of the slop-basin' (Scott, *Guy Mannering*, 1815, 53).

As to his shirt-collar, and his coat-collar

As to his shirt-collar, and his coat-collar, they were perplexing to reflect upon – insoluble mysteries both. Why should a man scrape himself to that extent, before he could consider himself full dressed?] Shirt-collars and coat-collars of the period were often turned up high with two sets of points extending to the cheeks. The points were stiff and lined with buckram to obtain a stand-up effect, an obvious sacrifice of comfort to fashion on the part of the wearer (Sichel 16).

I had neither the good sense nor the good feeling

he heaped coals of fire on my head.] Proverbs 25.22: 'For thou shalt heap coals of fire upon his head and the LORD shall reward thee'.

"Which I fully believed it were, Pip," said Joe

(wot a pipe and a pint of beer do give refreshment to the working-man, Sir, and do not over stimilate),] Dickens differed sharply with those who advocated abstinence from all forms of alcohol. Instead, he supported the working man's right to enjoy a drink and argued for moderation. Reformers concerned about the consumption of cheap gin persuaded the government in 1836 to promote beer as an alternative by decreasing the tax on beer.

"Which I say, Sir," replied Joe

"Miss A., or otherways Havisham.]   Not knowing whether or not to aspirate 'is simply a habit of ill-bred people everywhere throughout the three kingdoms. Nor is the plea of dialect any real excuse' (*The Habits of Good Society*, 1860, 69).

"Pip, dear old chap, life is made of ever so many partings

one man's a blacksmith, and one's a whitesmith, and one's a goldsmith, and one's a coppersmith.]   Whitesmiths and coppersmiths work respectively in tin and copper, making various objects and utensils. Both proceed by filing and polishing as distinguished from hammering out articles on an anvil. Tinsmiths were called whitesmiths because they worked with 'whited iron', a fusion of two plates of tin and a piece of malleable iron in the centre to give the tin strength and durability. 'Whitesmith' was also a popular term for 'Brightsmiths', which was used to apply generally to any smith who filed rather than hammered his work (*Complete Book of Trades* 407).

Chapter 28

IT was clear that I must repair to our town next day

I had secured my box-place] Youthful travellers often believed that the box-seat next to the driver conferred a 'distinguished eminence' on the passenger (*DC* 19). Veterans, however, complained that the box-place was uncomfortable: 'If it was cold, you were frozen, if it rained, you were soaked, and if it was dusty, you were smothered' (Albert Smith 15). In addition, one had to hold the reins when the driver got down and listen to his boring, commonplace stories. Coachmen, for their part, thought that sitting next to the driver induced talkativeness in passengers (Thomas Cross 1.223).

half-crown] A former silver coin of the value of two shillings and six pence.

An obliging stranger, under pretence of compactly folding up my bank-notes for security's sake, abstracts the notes and gives me nutshells;] Trickery of one kind or another prevailed in London's streets in the early part of the century, especially ploys on 'decent-looking' persons from the country, whose innocence 'duffers and ring-droppers' ruthlessly exploited. One common scheme was to pose as a blunt and honest seaman with expensive foreign articles to sell which, in reality, had no value at all, a trap into which many a countryman, anxious to take a present to his wife or daughter, fell with ease (*Old Bailey Experience* 421–2). I have been unable to document this particular ruse, but the size of bank notes (7° inches by 4° inches) made them suitable for folding. See also chapter 21, note on p. 190.

Having settled that I must go to the Blue Boar

the archway of the Blue Boar's posting-yard;] See chapter 13, note on p. 132.

It was the afternoon coach by which I had taken my place

as winter had now come round,] See Appendix 1.

until two or three hours after dark.] See below.

Our time of starting from the Cross Keys was two o'clock.] Afternoon coaches for Rochester, approximately five hours away, left the Cross Keys, Wood Street, at 1.45 p.m., 4.45 p.m., 6.46 p.m. and 7.30 p.m. (*The Post Office London Directory for 1839* 148). Starting at two during the winter months, a traveller would arrive about seven in the evening, some two or three hours after dark.

I arrived on the ground with a quarter of an hour to spare,] Confusion and bustle inevitably attended the departure of coaches at one of London's coaching establishments. Numerous packages in transit arrived at the booking office, and a motley crowd of people of both sexes and of all ranks from peers to labourers milled around. The coaches themselves were generally neat, elegant and polished. Names were painted on the 'hinder part', bodies highly varnished and the company's symbol or name painted on the door panels. Well-groomed horses with their attendant keeper and harnesses 'all in the nicest order' completed the picture (Thomas Cross 1.2).

At that time it was customary to carry Convicts

At that time it was customary to carry Convicts down to the dockyards by stage-coach. As I had often heard of them in the capacity of outside-passengers, and had more than once seen them on the high road dangling their ironed legs over the coach roof, I had no cause to be surprised when Herbert . . . told me there were two convicts going down with me.] Convicts sentenced to hard labour at one of five royal dockyards in the south-east (Deptford, Woolwich, Chatham, Sheerness and Portsmouth) travelled on public coaches in the company of armed guards. This practice began shortly after the government passed the Hulks Act (1776) and continued well into the nineteenth century. Those sent to Chatham would have taken the Rochester coach, *en route* for the dockyards on the south bank of the Medway just beyond the boundary of the old cathedral city. In the nineteenth century, the dockyards were surrounded by a high wall almost a mile in length; the main entrance was (and is) through a spacious gateway, flanked by embattled towers. Hard work and a rigorous regimen awaited them there (see below).

The method of delivering prisoners by public coach prompted vigorous criticism in 1819 from Henry Grey Bennett (1777–1836), the radical MP for Shrewsbury (1806; 1811–26), prison reformer and advocate of social justice for convicted offenders:

> some are chained on the tops of coaches; others, as from London, travel in an open caravan, exposed to the inclemency of the weather, to the gaze of the idle and the taunts and mockeries of the cruel. . . . Men and boys, children just emerging from infancy, as young in vice as in years, are fettered together . . . and paraded through the kingdom . . . [women, too, were brought up in the same manner] ironed together on the top of coaches.
> (Bennett, 1819, 23–4)

The graphic quality of the incident Pip describes may have been based on direct observation made when Chatham (a royal dockyard since 1567) was still a centre for the construction of wooden warships during the age of sail and a destination for prisoners sentenced to hard labour. Dickens frequently visited the dockyard during the years his father was stationed there from 1817 to 1822; living in the town as a child and later making journeys to and from London himself, he might well have witnessed such a scene. Inspecting Chatham dockyard shortly after completing GE, however, the Uncommercial Traveller describes a changed place, one dominated by the noisy activity that accompanied the building of *Achilles*, the British navy's first iron-built warship:

> Ding, Clash, Dong, BANG, Boom, Rattle, Clash, BANG, Clink, BANG, DONG, BANG, Clatter, BANG BANG BANG! What on earth is this! This is, or soon will be, the Achilles, iron armour-plated ship. Twelve hundred men are working on her now. . . . Twelve hundred hammerers, measurers, caulkers, armourers, forgers, smiths, shipwrights; twelve hundred dingers, clashers, dongers, rattlers, clinkers, bangers bangers bangers! (29 August 1863, AYR 10.13)

Convict labourers could still be seen, but those present in the dockyards from 1856 onwards belonged to Chatham's recently opened public works prison and not to hulks stationed on the Medway, as had been the case in former days. This new group of prisoners were employed in draining and reclaiming St Mary's Island, a tidal marsh, in preparation for expanding the government's naval facilities at Chatham dockyard. By the mid-century, however, the practice of employing convict labour had lost its appeal. 'Visit St. Mary's Island, Chatham or Portsmouth Dockyard, where the convicts are at work, and a score of able-bodied men are drawing along an empty handcart, doing the work of one of their number only, because where one goes the whole gang must follow' (Barry, 1863, 145). See also below on working conditions.

"See! There they are," said Herbert

the Tap.] A colloquial term for the tap-room, a room in a public house or tavern where liquors are sold on tap.

They had been treating their guard, I suppose

They had been treating their guard, I suppose, for they had a gaoler with them, and all three came out wiping their mouths on their hands.] Scenes like this were not uncommon. John Ward, convicted of burglary in the Midlands in 1841, describes how he was ironed with six other prisoners and marched to a coach when they were all 'called . . . away to the Hulks'. In the bustle of getting ready prior to departure, each man 'drank a pint of beer', before the coach set off carrying the guard and his prisoners. A similar ritual occurred 'every time we changed horses', since the guard 'allowed us to take more refreshment'. Gin and ale on the road, Ward observed, 'seemed to shorten the night's fatigue' ('Diary', 1841, 41–2).

It was easy to make sure

The great numbers on their backs,] See chapter 1, note on p. 30.

as if they were lower animals;] Darwinian terminology appears to inform this ironical description, whose import, on re-reading, illustrates a premise crucial to the evolutionary hypothesis proposed in the *Origin of Species*: that no organism has been independently created and that each is the lineal descendant of the other. One consequence of this insight (presumably available to the retrospective narrator) is that we can now see interconnections our earlier constructions of reality denied. As the author of the second of the three essays on Darwin's work explained to readers in AYR on 7 July 1860:

> We are no longer to look at an organic being as a savage looks at a ship – as at something wholly beyond his comprehension; we are to regard every production of nature as one which has had a history. ('Natural Selection', AYR 2.299)

This position implies that the history of each species is not discrete or individualistic but rather connected with all other living beings. In Darwin's terms, there is an 'infinite complexity of the relations of all organic beings to each other and to their conditions of life, causing an infinite diversity in structure, constitution, and habits' (chapter 4, 'Summary of chapter').

their ironed legs, apologetically garlanded with pocket-handkerchiefs;] See below.

But this was not the worst of it.

the whole of the back of the coach had been taken by a family removing from London, and that there were no places for the two prisoners but on the seat in front, behind the coachman.] Seating plans for coaches varied according to the size of the vehicle and offered passengers a choice between 'inside' seats at 4d or 5d a mile and 'outside' seats at 2d or 3d. Coaches generally accommodated at least four passengers inside, up to eight outside at the back and seven passengers, in two rows, in front, in addition to the driver ('Coaches', 1, Johnson Collection). Wherever one sat, however, the coaches provided little comfort. Robert Surtees, who travelled extensively, making horses and sporting matters his fictional speciality, commented that even the very 'latest and best of the old stage-coaches were dreadful, slow and uncomfortable. . . . Who hasn't a lively recollection of those musty old horrors?' (*Plain or Ringlets?* 1860, 184 ff.).

Hereupon, a choleric gentleman, who had taken the fourth place on that seat, flew into a most violent passion, and said that it was a breach of contract to mix him up with such villainous company] Angry travellers typically ascribed such incidents to 'the levelling spirit of the age', occurrences of which became increasingly familiar as new means of transport developed. Compare the anecdote told in Disraeli's *Sybil, or; The Two Nations* (1845) about two ladies travelling by train from Birmingham who sat opposite two men chained together: "A countess and a felon! So much for public conveyances", said Lord Mowbray (2.11.104).

that curious flavour of bread-poultice, baize, rope-yarn, and hearthstone, which attends the convict presence.]   Convicts wore uniforms made from baize, a coarse woollen material with a long nap, and undertook many menial forms of labour, including untwisting old ropes for re-use and making (or mining) hearthstone, a composition of powdered stone and pipeclay, which was widely sold as a soft stone to whiten hearths and doorsteps. Bread-poultices were made by mixing bread and boiling water and spreading the soft substance on muslin or linen; their most frequent intention was 'to soothe a part [of the body] which is irritated, and to allay inflammation' (Henry H. Gregory 56). Possibly convicts used bread-poultices, secured by 'pocket-handkerchiefs', to ease the chafing and protect scabs and sore areas aggravated by their leg irons.

At length, it was voted that

sat behind me with his breath on the hair of my head.]   The description is in fact quite literal: seated next to the driver on the box-seat, Pip occupies a place below the two convicts, who, accommodated behind him, sit on the front part of the roof and rest their feet on the driver's box. Later, when they bend over, cowering forward to use Pip as a screen against the wind, they are inches from his head.

The weather was miserably raw

we had left the Half-way House behind,]   Coaches bound for Gravesend, Rochester, Chatham, Canterbury and Dover stopped at the Guy, Earl of Warwick, in Welling, Kent, approximately eleven miles east of London. By this time, passengers would have been on the road for nearly two hours and about halfway to Gravesend. See Appendix 4, map pp. 444–7.

a couple of pounds sterling . . . before losing sight of him,]   Each reference to pounds or notes in this section appeared in the MS as 'guineas'.

"How should I know?" returned the other.

"How should I know?" returned the other. "He had 'em stowed away somehows. Giv him by friends, I expect."]   Money continued to circulate among prisoners, despite the confiscation of all currency when prisoners arrived at the hulks. Some received money from friends; others foiled the authorities, using their comparative wealth to buy tea, tobacco, rum or anything they wished, despite the prospect of severe punishment for those caught with money in their possession (Ward 43, 45, 49–50). Convicts were also paid for their labour, earning from 2*d* to 9*d* a day as labourers and up to a shilling or more for those who worked as artificers (*BPP, Crime and Punishment, Transportation*, 1, 28th S. C. Report 26 June 1798; Third Report, 27 June 1812). Some also supplemented their allowance by working at night after they had been locked down, 'or on wet and foggy days, in which they do not go ashore', to produce models and other artifacts they sold in the dockyards.

"So he says," resumed the convict I had recognised

a pile of timber in the Dockyard]   That is, Chatham dockyard (see above). In the days of wooden ships, huge piles of seasoned timber stood everywhere. These 'beams are handled and dandled, and raised and lowered, and moved hither and thither, and fashioned and fitted by men like myself, as an ordinary occurrence' (Dickens and Horne, 'One Man in a Dockyard', *HW* 3.553). Moving timber often fell to convicts; for additional forms of convict labour, see below.

"Not a ha'porth.

ha'porth.]   That is, a half-penny, an inconsequential amount.

a Lifer."]   After 'Lifer.' MS reads 'That's what he took by *his* motion, and that's all I know of him.' 'Lifer' is slang for a convict sentenced to transportation for life. The practice of sending convicted felons overseas originated with an Elizabethan statute in 1597–8 (39 Eliz. I, c. 17) and continued for nearly two centuries until the War of Independence (1775–83) forced the British to discontinue sending prisoners to America. Subsequent statutes in 1778–9 and 1784 (19 Geo. III, c. 74, and 24 Geo. III, s. 2 c. 56) upheld the power of courts to impose the sentence of transportation; in 1787, a further Act (27 Geo. III, c. 2) specified New South Wales as a new destination for unwanted criminals.

"A most beastly place.

Mudbank, mist, swamp, and work; work, swamp, mist, and mudbank."]   Convict labour in and around the dockyards followed a simple rule. The tasks given to prisoners were generally 'the most irksome and disagreeable' forms of work available: raising sand or gravel, cleaning the river and 'any other service for the benefit of the Navigation' of the rivers specified under the first hulks legislation (16 Geo. III, c. 43). At Chatham prisoners were 'also employed in mud-work, cleaning the river Medway and other places of mud' (*BPP, Crime and Punishment, Transportation*, 1, 'Report from the Select Committee on Punishments', 27 September 1831, 48).

Convicts also assisted in the construction of military forts or installations, or worked ashore in the dockyards. Those with skills were often employed as masons, bricklayers, blacksmiths, sawyers, carpenters, shipwrights or brickmakers; others worked in gangs as 'common labourers' under close supervision by overseers and guards. Their tasks included stowing timber, loading and unloading ships, clearing mud and soil to build a foundation for a new wharf, landing and loading ballast, breaking up unserviceable gun-carriages, and other heavy tasks. Convicts worked from sunrise to sunset with an interval for dinner. Their productivity was restricted, one observer noted, because 'they labour under some disadvantage on account of their irons' (BPP, *Crime and Punishment, Transportation,* 1, 'Second Report from the Committee on the Laws Relating to Penitentiary Houses', 10 June 1811, 183).

Rain, mist and fog, and the long hours of winter darkness, further reduced their performance ashore because such conditions prompted attempts to escape. As a counter-measure, authorities kept prisoners aboard, where security was greater. Confined to one of the hulks, naval-style discipline prevailed. Convicts spent the day washing the decks above and below and carrying out other shipboard chores (BPP, *Crime and Punishment. Transportation* 1, 'Report From the Select Committee on Finance', 26 June 1798, 16–17; 'Appendix B', Third Report, 27 June 1812).

After overhearing this dialogue

the boot]   A receptacle for luggage and parcels near the external steps of the coach.

at the first lamp on the first stones of the town pavement.]   Literally, 'the first stones' of Rochester begin on the south bank of the Medway, whose shoreline forms the city's north-western boundary. The bridge leads directly into Rochester High Street, where the coach would stop at each of the city's two posting inns. The Blue Boar, whose apparent original was the Bull, was only a short distance from the bridge. See Appendix 4, map p. 450.

As to the convicts, they went their way with the coach, and I knew at what point they would be spirited off to the river. In my fancy, I saw the boat with its convict crew waiting for them at the slime-washed stairs, – again heard the gruff "Give way, you!" like an order to dogs – again saw the wicked Noah's Ark lying out on the black water.]   Coaches continuing south proceeded along Rochester High Street towards Chatham. Several actual landing-places along the Medway existed, including Admiralty wharf about a mile further south. Stairs at this wharf would have served to embark prisoners and convey them by boat to one of the hulks moored in Upnor reach opposite Chatham dockyard. Possibly Dickens refers to these same stairs when he describes crossing the river and landing near the dockyard in 'Chatham Dockyard' (*AYR* 10.12).

Earlier, Dickens had specified a different landing-place, perhaps conflating the 'stairs' referred to here with a 'landing-place made of rough stakes and stones' described in chapter 5, from which the escapees were transferred to a rowing boat. After the order 'Give way, you!' had been given to the convict crew, Pip and Joe watched the boat set off for the black hulk, 'lying out a little way from the mud of the shore', a location that seems to point to Egypt Bay as Dickens's model. For Egypt Bay, see chapter 5, note on p. 45.

The coffee-room at the Blue Boar was empty

Boots] A servant employed at the hotel to clean the boots of guests.

The waiter (it was he who had brought up

the Great Remonstrance from the Commercials] Literally, the 'Great Remonstrance' was a petition objecting to the acts of Charles I, passed by the Puritan Parliament in 1641. Elsewhere, Dickens refers to this incident as 'a great opposition in the Parliament to a celebrated paper put forth by [John] Pym and [John] Hampden and the rest, called "THE REMONSTRANCE," which set forth all the illegal acts that the King had ever done, but politely laid the blame of them on his bad advisers' (*CHE*, ch. 33). Dickens's enthusiastic reading of Forster's recently published *Arrest of the Five Members*, recorded in a letter to Forster dated 2 May 1860, may have prompted Dickens to mention 'the Great Remonstrance' again (*Letters* 9.244–6). For 'Commercials', see chapter 13, note on p. 133.

a dirty old copy of a local newspaper] An anachronism: newspapers published in Rochester during the nineteenth century all postdate the novel's early setting. Wright describes the *Rochester Gazette* (established 1821) as a weekly 'of some standing in the county' (1838, 43). It was published every Tuesday by Messrs Caddell & Son in the High Street (Bagshaw 101). Other papers included the *Rochester and Chatham Journal* (1854) and the *Chatham and Rochester News* (1859).

"Our readers will learn, not altogether without interest

the Mentor of our young Telemachus,] Mentor was the comrade and old man whom Odysseus left in authority over his house and slaves during his absence 'to guard them well'. The goddess Athene assumes Mentor's shape when Telemachus, Odysseus' son, prays to her for help on leaving to search for his father (*Odyssey*, bks 3–4). The laboured style of the paragraph, overweight with allusions and learning, parodies journalistic practices of the day. A case for the sustained significance of the literary reference has been made on the grounds that Pip, like Telemachus, searches for his father, travels, matures and has various mentors (Warner 52–4).

Quentin Matsys was the BLACKSMITH of Antwerp.] Quentin Matsys (or Quintin Massys), a Flemish painter (*c*.1466–1530), reputedly began life as a blacksmith.

VERB. SAP."] This is an abbreviation of the Latin tag, *verbum sapienti satis est*: 'a word to the wise is sufficient'.

I entertain a conviction, based upon large experience

if . . . I had gone to the North Pole, I should have met somebody there, wandering Esquimaux or civilised man,] The long search for naval explorer Sir John Franklin (1786–1847) and members of his ill-fated voyage in 1847 kept the Arctic regions much in the news during the second half of the nineteenth century. The expedition tragically failed when Franklin and 129 officers and men abandoned their ice-bound ships and struggled in vain to walk 1,000 miles out of the Arctic circle.

Chapter 29 Eighteenth weekly number
30 March 1861

BETIMES in the morning I was up and out.

I loitered into the country on Miss Havisham's side of town – which was not Joe's side;] That is, country to the south-west of Rochester as opposed to the area where Dickens located the forge, some four miles to the north-east of the city on the Hoo peninsula.

She had adopted Estella

She reserved it for me to restore the desolate house, admit the sunshine into the dark rooms, set the clocks a going, and the cold hearths a blazing, tear down the cobwebs, destroy the vermin – in short, do all the shining deeds of the young Knight of romance, and marry the Princess.] The fantasy appears to echo Charles Perrault's description of the arrival of the prince in 'Sleeping Beauty' when he makes his way through interlacing brambles and thorns to enter the castle, awaken the princess and rouse the sleeping members of the palace. For Dickens, journeys into the past were often journeys into romance and a picturesque version of the Rochester and Chatham of his boyhood home. Evocations of scenes from this region, still fresh in his imagination, occur in 'The Doom of English Wills' (*HW* 2.1) and in 'One Man in a Dockyard' (*HW* 3.553).

I had stopped to look at the house as I passed; and its seared red brick walls, blocked windows, and strong green ivy clasping even the stacks of chimneys with its twigs and tendons . . . had made up a rich attractive mystery, of which I was the hero.] The thick ivy and twigs continue the fairy-tale motif, suggesting the thick hedge through which the prince makes his way when he seeks entrance to Sleeping Beauty's Castle. Ivy also grew (and continues to grow) on the walls of Restoration House. One former owner noted that its proliferation was so rapid 'that it is necessary to cut a very large quantity away every year, sometimes nearly half a ton' (Aveling 459). For the red brick walls and blocked windows, see chapter 8, note on p. 90.

Forster describes one of Dickens's favourite walks during the 1860s. Leaving Gad's Hill, he passed through Strood, crossed the bridge into Rochester and walked along the High Street before turning west through the Vines, 'where some old buildings . . . had a curious attraction for him'. One of these was Restoration House in Crow Lane, which he would pass *en route* to Fort Pitt, one of two fortified points built between 1805 and 1819 to protect the dockyards at Chatham from possible attack by land during the Napoleonic wars. He would then recross the Medway and head east for Frindsbury, a small village on the north bank of the river. From there, Dickens made his way back to Gad's Hill by striking through some fields and returning to the main London road (Forster 8.3.215). See Appendix 4, map p. 449.

Dickens's fascination with the house continued long after he finished the novel.

On 6 June 1870, while at work on MED and three days before he died, he is reported to have walked over from Gad's hill, accompanied by his dogs. 'On this occasion he was seen by several persons leaning on a fence in front of Restoration House [dividing the Vines from Crow Lane], and apparently examining the old mansion with great care' (Langton, 1883, 238).

I knew to my sorrow . . . that I loved her against reason, against promise, against peace, against hope, against happiness, against all discouragement that could be.] Compare the responses of Astrophil, in Sidney's *Astrophil and Stella*, recognizing how passion enslaves and degrades as much as it elevates:

> What, have I thus betrayed my libertie?
> Can those blacke beames such burning markes engrave
> In my free side? or am I borne a slave,
> Whose necke becomes such yoke of tyranny? (sonnet 47)

A sense of torture and misery originating from Maria Beadnell's coolness later in the relationship characterizes letters Dickens wrote when he spoke of the 'utter desolation and wretchedness' he felt receiving 'so many displays of heartless indifference' during their meetings of late (*Letters* 1.17).

By this time we had come to the house

I found his room to be one just within the side door, with a little window in it looking on the court-yard.] The description of Orlick's quarters as a sentry-box may have been based on a room with several small windows, each about a foot square, added to the south wing of Restoration House.

In its small proportions, it was not unlike the kind of place usually assigned to a gate-porter in Paris.] A gatekeeper, or concierge, occupies a single room or small quarters at the entrance to a block of flats.

"No," said he; "not till it got about

with convicts and Tag and Rag and Bobtail] Tag, rag, and bob-tail, or tag-rag and bob-tail, are contemptuous expressions for 'that lowest class of the community', ruffians or 'scuffle-hunters', who, under the guise of offering their services as porters or in some other manual capacity, pilfer and steal (Colquhoun, 1800, 75).

My eye had been caught by a gun with a brass-bound stock

a brass-bound stock] Brass was fastened to the butt of stocks on long guns and used to bind the barrel to the stock; it was also added as an inlay to the stock for decoration. Most likely the reference is to a muzzle-loading sporting gun (based on Peterson, 1964, and *Complete Book of Trades* 288). Orlick threatens Pip with a gun with 'a brass-bound stock' in chapter 53.

She gave me her hand.

She gave me her hand.] 'The etiquette of hand-shaking [with ladies] is simple. A man has no right to take a lady's hand till it is offered' (*The Habits of Good Society*, 1860, 326).

We sat in the dreamy room

she had but just come home from France,] Compare Dora Spenlow in *DC*, who has just returned from 'finishing her education at Paris' when David first meets her at Mr Spenlow's house and '[falls] into captivity' (26).

Truly it was impossible to dissociate her presence from all those wretched hankerings after money and gentility that had disturbed my boyhood . . . that had first made me ashamed of home] Pip's fear that his humble background and secret connection with convicts would jeopardize his relationship with Estella resembles concerns that troubled Dickens arising from the social disparity between Maria Beadnell, the daughter of a banker, and himself, the son of a father who had been imprisoned for debt (Edgar Johnson 1.68–72; Slater 51).

"Then you don't? Very well.

you shall be my Page, and give me your shoulder."] Estella uses 'Page' playfully in its former, medieval sense, addressing Pip as if he were a young boy from a good family who had been placed in a great household for a limited period of time to learn the ways of polite society. When walking outdoors, a lady might put her hand on the shoulder of a manservant (who walks slightly in front of her) for support.

There was no discrepancy of years between us

we were of nearly the same age,] See Appendix 1.

The time so melted away

our early dinner-hour drew close at hand,] In some families 'dinner is taken early in the afternoon, and in others, although later, still not towards evening' (Kerr, 1864, 111).

He always carried (I have not yet mentioned it, I think)

a pocket-handkerchief of rich silk and of imposing proportions,] Silk handkerchiefs for men rarely measured less than thirty-one square inches (Braun-Ronsdorf 29).

He complied, and we groped our way down

we groped our way down the dark stairs together. While we were still on our way to those detached apartments across the paved yard at the back,] This description suggests that dinner is served in the detached dwelling house (see chapter 11, note on p. 115).

This brought us to the dinner-table

Mr. Jaggers presided,] Typically the lady of the house would call on the person of highest rank to assist her, especially if it were necessary to carve meat (*London at Dinner*, 1851, 47):

> To perform faultlessly the honours of the table, is one of the most difficult things in society . . . [the host's] great business is to put every one entirely at his ease, to gratify all his desires, and make him, in a word, absolutely contented with men and things. . . . He behaves [to all guests] without agitation, without affectation; he pays attention without an air of protection; he encourages the timid, draws out the silent, and directs conversation without sustaining it himself. (*Etiquette for Gentlemen*, 1838, 29)

and were waited on by a maid-servant whom I had never seen in all my comings and goings, but who, for anything I know, had been in that mysterious house the whole time.] Domestic servants were expected to efface themselves as much as possible: 'The idea which underlies all is simply this: The family constitutes one community, the servants another. Whatever may be their mutual regard and confidence as dwellers under the same roof, each class is entitled to shut its door upon the other, and be alone' (Kerr, 1864, 76).

After dinner, a bottle of choice old port was placed before my guardian . . . and the two ladies left us.] By custom, ladies withdrew to the drawing-room after dinner, allowing the gentlemen to remain for conversation and a bottle of port (circulated clockwise around the table) before joining the ladies (*London at Dinner* 23).

I think Miss Pocket was conscious

played at whist.] Whist became popular in England from about the mid-seventeenth century. The game is ordinarily played with four persons, of whom two sit opposite each other as partners. All fifty-two cards are used. Card-playing remained in vogue during the early Victorian period when it was considered ill-bred to read in company. As older ladies were used to saying, 'Books were not fit articles for drawing-rooms' (Thackeray, *Four Georges*, 90).

My guardian lay at the Boar

My guardian lay at the Boar in the next room to mine.] After 'to' MS reads 'me, and before he went to bed I could hear him dipping Miss Havisham's into the washing basin and blowing it out of himself like a whale. It would have been better for me if I could have done the same'.

Chapter 30   Nineteenth weekly number
                                                                             6 April 1862

As we were going back together to London

I would go on along the London-road while Mr. Jaggers was occupied, if he would let the coachman know that I would get into my place when overtaken.] The projected walk would take Pip down Rochester High Street, across the Medway and north-west through Strood. From there, the road continued in the same direction and ran parallel to the south bank of the river Thames. The present A2 takes much the same course. See Appendix 4, map pp. 446–7.

I was thus enabled to fly from the Blue Boar immediately after breakfast. By then making a loop of about a couple of miles into the open country at the back of Pumblechook's premises, I got round into the High-street again,] This 'loop' had to be to the west in the opposite direction from the river Medway. See Appendix 4, map p. 450 and Appendix 2.

It was interesting to be in the quiet old town once more

the quiet old town] The cathedral, its precincts and the clerical atmosphere surrounding stately houses in the vicinity impart an air of repose, a mood to which Pip occasionally responds. See Plate 14 and also Appendix 2.

it was not disagreeable to be here and there suddenly recognised and stared after.] In 'Dullborough Town' the Uncommercial Traveller records a different experience as he walks along the High Street looking 'in vain for a familiar face'. Nettled by the phlegmatic response of the inhabitants, none of whom recognizes the famous author, the Traveller accosts the town greengrocer and tries to prompt the man's memory by telling him that he had left the town as a child. The greengrocer 'slowly returned, quite unsoftened and not without a sarcastic kind of complacency, Had I? Ah! And did I find it had got on tolerably well without me?' (*AYR* 3.275–6).

Casting my eyes along the street

an empty blue bag.] Blue bags were commonly used for several purposes. An entry in Julia Mills's journal about an 'incident' one Friday morning reads: 'Man appears in kitchen, with blue bag, "for lady's boots left out to heel". Cook replies, "No such orders" ' (*DC* 38). Compare also the blue bags solicitors, lawyers and their assistants used for briefs and legal papers: see *BH* (2), *DC* (17, 25), and Edward Sk–n–st–n, the lawyer and husband of the heroine of the Mayhew brothers' *Greatest Plague of Life* (63).

I had not got as much further down the street

the post-office,]   In the 1830s the post office was located on the north side of Rochester High Street (*Wright's Topography*, 1838).

shooting round by a back way.]   Alleys, courts and roads in the vicinity of the cathedral lend plausibility to the tactics employed by Trabb's boy.

This time he was entirely changed. He ... was strutting along the pavement ... "Don't know yah!"]   The satire is not lost on Pip, who had complacently admired an appropriate 'cheerful briskness' in the gait of Trabb's boy and the light of 'honest industry' beaming in his eyes as he walked determinedly to his place of employment. Gentlemen, by contrast, were exhorted not to be seen in a 'hurry': a man of sense, Thomas Tegg noted in his comments on manners, 'may be in haste, but he is never in a hurry ... To be in a hurry, is proof that the business we embark in is too much for us, it is the mark of little minds, that are puzzled and perplexed when they should be cool and deliberate' (266). Similarly, walking fast in the streets was regarded as a mark of vulgarity, something that may appear well in a mechanic or a tradesman, but was not suited to the character of a gentleman or a man or fashion.

He wore the blue bag in the manner of my great-coat,]   Tied loosely around his neck and draped over his shoulders.

across the bridge]   An 'elegant stone bridge' over the Medway linked Rochester and Strood (*Kentish Traveller's Companion*, 1779, 107). Each time Pip visits or leaves Rochester, he must cross it – a local detail Dickens downplays (see Plate 14). This bridge, which had been built in 1388 on the site of two earlier bridges, was replaced by a new cast-iron bridge in 1856. Several months after the new bridge (designed by Sir William Cubitt) was opened on 13 August 1856, the old stone bridge was demolished. In June 1859 the contractor for the works sent Dickens one of the stone balustrades as a remembrance. Dickens ordered a sundial, had the balustrade 'duly stonemasoned' and set up the gift on the lawn behind Gad's Hill Place (*Letters* 9.76–7). References to the stone bridge occur in *PP* (5) and *DC* (13).

into the open country.]   Once beyond Strood, Pip would have been clear of houses and signs of habitation. Today, the town extends out towards Gad's Hill and beyond as suburbs encroach on former open spaces and countryside.

The coach, with Mr. Jaggers inside

As soon as I arrived, I sent a penitential codfish and barrel of oysters]   Cod was caught in abundance off the coast of Norfolk and Lincolnshire and in the mouth of the Thames; the city of Rochester sent oysters, cultivated in the creeks and inlets of the Medway, 'in great quantities' to London, Holland and Germany (*Dictionary of Trade*, 1844; Dugdale, 1819, 4.1344). Oysters were considered very nutritive, easily digested and agreeable to the stomachs 'of most people' (Keith Imray 793). Compare the 'peace-offering' brought 'from town' by Thackeray's narrator and given to Mrs Ponto, his hostess: 'a cod and oysters from Grove's, in a hamper about the size of a coffin' ('On Some Country Snobs', *Works* 9.114).

I found Herbert dining on cold meat

I sometimes sent him to Hyde Park-corner to see what o'clock it was.] Hyde Park lay about two miles west of Barnard's Inn. There used to be a clock mounted on the gate at the south-east corner.

"Now, Handel," Herbert replied

we are looking into our gift-horse's mouth with a magnifying-glass.] The proverb, dating from the fourteenth century, is 'to look a gift-horse in the mouth'.

"I should think it was a strong point," said Herbert

You'll be one-and-twenty before you know where you are,] See Appendix 1.

"I ought to have," said Herbert

I want to make myself seriously disagreeable to you for a moment – positively repulsive."] Herbert's attempt to discourage Pip's pursuit of Estella (without any success) has been likened to Astrophil's friend, whose 'right healful caustiks' attempt to counter his lovesickness (Endicott 159).

"Oh yes! and so the dustman says

the dustman] A street-cleaner contracted to remove household filth, dirt and accumulated refuse of any kind. Dustmen toured the streets with a horse and cart calling out 'Dust, ho! Dust, ho!' Everything they gathered was taken to dust-heaps, where the contents of carts were dumped and then thoroughly sifted and classified for sale to various specialists. The collection of dust and the dust business receive extended treatment in OMF (Cotsell 30–4).

marine-store-shop] Marine stores began as shops in maritime districts that bought and sold ironwork, cordage, sails, provisions and other supplies for sea-going vessels.

> Brassy's shop is a museum of everything that is worth little or nothing – of old iron, old copper, old brass, old tools, old panels of oak and mahogany,

old cranks and cogwheels and fragments of incomprehensible machines, to which you may add the rusty keys of forty thousand perished locks, and coils of rope and shreds of broadcloth strung together in huge mops up on wires.
(Charles Manby Smith, 1857, 220)

In time, marine stores expanded into junk shops that bought and sold any old and used goods. For Dickens's description of the latter kind of dealer, see Krook's Rag and Bottle Warehouse in *BH* (5) and Shatto (1988, 59, 63). Mayhew draws a distinction between marine stores and 'rag-and-bottle' shops based principally on the latter's concentration on dripping and 'every kind of refuse in the way of fat or grease', but concedes that differences between the two in practice were often hard to maintain (Mayhew, 1967, 2.108).

May I ask you if you have ever had an opportunity of remarking . . . that the children of not exactly suitable marriages, are always most particularly anxious to be married?"] The question relates closely to troubles in Dickens's life at the time. Less than a year before the publication of this chapter, his daughter Kate married Charles Alston Collins on 17 July 1860, to Dickens's great distress. He felt, not without reason, that she married to escape a household made unhappy by his own marital problems and painful separation from Catherine Dickens in May 1858. Sixteen months after Kate's wedding, in November 1861, Charley, Dickens's oldest son, married Bessie Evans, the daughter of Frederick Evans, Dickens's former publisher, with whom he had quarrelled. 'I wish I could hope that Charley's marriage may not be a disastrous one. There is no help for it . . .' (*Letters* 9.494). The probable date of the composition of this chapter (March 1861) may have followed discussions between father and son about Charley's intended marriage (19 November 1861) not long after Charley returned from Hong Kong in January 1861.

"I don't know," said Herbert.

Kew.] A riverside district near Richmond, Surrey, and site of Kew Palace, whose extensive pleasure grounds the widow of Frederick Lewis, Prince of Wales, helped convert on her husband's death in 1751 into the Kew Royal Botanic Gardens. The project, developed with assistance from the Earl of Bute, was further augmented by Sir Joseph Banks, whose gift of an immense collection of plants and seeds he had obtained during his voyages helped make Kew England's richest botanical garden.

"Yes. Perhaps I ought to mention," said Herbert

Her father had to do with the victualling of passenger-ships. I think he was a species of purser."] Herbert recognizes that his mother would reject Clara because she was the daughter of a purser, a man associated with provisioning ships and with trade.

Chapter 31

On our arrival in Denmark,

On our arrival in Denmark, we found the king and queen of that country elevated in two arm-chairs on a kitchen-table, holding a Court.]   Fielding makes comic use of *Hamlet* in *Tom Jones* (16.5) on the occasion of Tom's visit to the theatre with Partridge and Mrs Miller, although the humour of this scene arises from the credulous responses of the schoolmaster while Dickens's satire is aimed at the inept performance of the actors. *Hamlet* opens on the battlements of Elsinore Castle in Denmark. In Act 1, scene 2, Claudius, the new king, now married to Hamlet's mother, addresses the court – the scene referred to here. The lack of realistic stage props, common among small metropolitan theatres with few resources, frequently produced unintentionally comic effects noticed also by other observers. According to à Beckett, the 'Stage Monarch' was often found perching on 'a very uncomfortable throne, raised on a rickety platform, with scarcely room for his feet', while the 'Stage Prince', even at the height of his power, had to march about in processions 'with a pasteboard crown on his head'. Similarly, the 'royal ermine' was rarely anything better than 'flannel with tufts of worsted fastened on to it' (18–19).

The whole of the Danish nobility were in attendance; consisting of a noble boy in the wash-leather boots of a gigantic ancestor, a venerable Peer . . . and the Danish chivalry with a comb in its hair and a pair of white silk legs, and presenting on the whole a feminine appearance.]   Among the 'Danish nobility' are Laertes, his father Polonius, the King's trusted minister, and one other member of the Danish court, perhaps played by a woman.

My gifted townsman stood gloomily apart, with folded arms,]   Wopsle, as Hamlet, stands in the classic pose of isolation. He is inconsolable over the loss of his father and communes bitterly with himself as Claudius dedicates the remainder of the day to celebration and carousing.

Several curious little circumstances transpired

The late king of the country]   Hamlet's father, whom Claudius murdered to take the kingdom of Denmark and marry his brother's wife.

The royal phantom also carried a ghostly manuscript round its truncheon,]   Horatio reports to Hamlet how his father's ghost carried a truncheon or baton, formerly a symbol of office or of military command and authority:

> Thrice he walk'd
> By their oppress'd and fear-surprised eyes,
> Within his truncheon's length; whilst they, distill'd

>   Almost to jelly with the act of fear,
>   Stand dumb and speak not to him. (*Hamlet* 1.2.202–6)

In this instance, the actor carries his prompt wrapped around the short staff, the cause of derisive comments from members of the audience.

It was this, I conceive, which led to the Shade's being advised by the gallery to "turn over!" – a recommendation which it took extremely ill.] People seated in the cheapest seats traditionally behaved in a noisy, ill-mannered way. Audiences were particularly hard on performers who displeased them. In such cases they 'rise from their seats, and express their indignation not only in loud hisses, groans, etc. but by the most violent gestures'. Audiences would cry out, 'Off, off!' and make an uproar so great 'that not one word of what was said on stage, with one or two occasional exceptions, was heard'. 'This is an insult to us! Give us back our money!' (Grant, 1837, 1.92–4).

"the kettle-drum."] A cylindrical side drum used for martial music and not the timpani of the classical orchestra.

The noble boy in the ancestral boots, was inconsistent representing himself, as it were in one breath, as an able seaman, a strolling actor, a gravedigger, a clergyman, and a person of the utmost importance at a Court fencing-match. . . . This gradually led to a want of toleration for him, and even – on his being detected in holy orders, and declining to perform the funeral service – to the general indignation taking the form of nuts.] Dickens learned about the practice of doubling up on roles as a boy on the occasion of outings to the Theatre Royal in Rochester. Remembering a performance of *Macbeth* he had seen, he records in 'Dullborough Town' how he was impressed by the fact that the witches 'bore an awful resemblance to the Thanes and other proper inhabitants of Scotland', and the 'good King Duncan' kept coming out of his grave and calling himself somebody else' (*AYR* 3.276). See also his comments on 'exclusiveness' in a speech to the General Theatrical Fund, 14 April 1851 (*Speeches* 121).

In this imaginary instance, one actor begins as the 'noble boy' (a Lord in 1.2) and goes on to play a succession of parts. There are no lines for an able seaman, but seamen are listed in the cast together with soldiers and attendants. Strolling players visit Elsinore Castle (2.2, 3.2), and Act 5 opens in a churchyard, where gravediggers prepare for Ophelia's burial at which a priest later assists when the funeral party arrives. In Act 5, scene 2, Osric, the court fop, enters with a message from the king that he is ready to back Hamlet in a fencing match with Laertes.

Upon my unfortunate townsman all these incidents accumulated

whether 'twas nobler in the mind to suffer, some roared yes, and some no,] See *Hamlet* 3.1.56–60:

> To be, or not to be – that is the question;
> Whether 'tis nobler in the mind to suffer
> The slings and arrows of outrageous fortune,
> Or to take arms against a sea of troubles,
> And by opposing end them?

When he asked what should such fellows as he do crawling between earth and heaven,]   See *Hamlet* 3.1.129–32: 'What should such fellows as I do crawling between earth and heaven? We are arrant knaves, all; believe none of us'.

When he appeared with his stocking disordered (its disorder expressed, according to usage, by one very neat fold in the top,]   In Act 2, scene 1, Ophelia tells Polonius how Hamlet had visited her 'with his doublet all unbrac'd;/No hat upon his head, his stockings fouled,/Ungarter'd, and down-gyved to his ankle' (78). A disordered stocking (falling down on one leg) was a conventional signal of mental distress widely employed by actors playing Hamlet in the eighteenth and nineteenth centuries.

a flat iron]   Heated irons replaced equipment designed to press and smooth out creases late in the sixteenth century, by which time fabrics had become smooth enough to respond to heat when dampened. Introduced by the Dutch, who lead the way with decorative brass irons, two kinds of iron became common: (1) the box iron, which was hollow and designed to contain a heated cast-iron slug or burning charcoal; (2) the flat iron or sad (i.e. solid or heavy) iron, made from solid cast iron and heated on the fire. Many varieties of flat irons existed, designed to smooth different parts of a garment. Flat irons continued in use until self-heating irons (gas or electric) replaced them towards the end of the nineteenth century (McNeil 931–4).

On his taking the recorders . . . he was called upon unanimously for Rule Britannia.]   When the strolling players enter again with recorders, Hamlet calls for one and asks Guildenstern to play for him (3.2.336 ff.). 'Rule Britannia' is the song originally composed for the masque *Alfred* (1740) by James Thomson:

> When *Britain* first, at heaven's command,
> Arose from out the azure main;
> *This* was the charter of the land,
> And guardian angels sung *this* strain:
>   "Rule, *Britannia*, rule the waves,
>   *Britons* never will be slaves."

Theatre audiences were familiar with the song from nautical melodramas which customarily closed with 'the theatrical tar, or British seaman', waving the Union Jack over his head to the air of 'Rule Britannia' (à Beckett 9).

When he recommended the player not to saw the air thus,]

> Speak the speech, I pray you, as I pronounc'd it to you, trippingly on the tongue; but if you mouth it, as many of our players do, I had as lief the town-crier spoke my lines. Nor do not saw the air too much with your hand, thus, but use all gently; for in the very torrent, tempest, and, as I may say, whirlwind of your passion, you must acquire and beget a temperance that may give it smoothness. (3.2.1–10)

But his greatest trials were in the churchyard

But his greatest trials were in the churchyard:]   In Act 5, scene 1, Hamlet returns to Denmark in time to witness the burial of Ophelia who, driven mad with grief, drowned after she fell into a stream.

I believe it is well known in a constitutional country that Mr. Wopsle could not possibly have returned the skull . . . without dusting his fingers on a white napkin . . . but even that innocent and indispensable action did not pass without the comment, "Wai-ter!"]   In this famous passage Hamlet first muses on the skull of Yorick, his former playfellow, and then (according to the stage direction) throws it down having taken the skull from the gravedigger (5.1). The use of a handkerchief to dust his fingers was introduced by William Macready, the great tragedian. George Henry Lewes reacted negatively to Macready's reliance on this costume accessory: Macready was 'too fond of a cambric pocket-handkerchief to be really affecting' (Lewes 35). The handkerchief, however, became 'an essential part of the Hamlet myth' (Quillian 25). Dickens first makes reference to the stage business of Hamlet holding the skull on a handkerchief in MC, where Mr Norris 'dusted his fingers as Hamlet might after getting rid of Yoric's skull' (17).

The joy attended Mr. Wopsle through his struggle with Laertes on the brink of the orchestra and the grave, and slackened no more until he had tumbled the king off the kitchen-table, and had died by inches from the ankles upward.]   Hamlet grapples with Laertes, Ophelia's brother, in the grave; later, they meet to duel. In the spectacular conclusion, Laertes wounds Hamlet with a poisoned foil, only to suffer the same fate when foils are exchanged in the ensuing scuffle. Gertrude inadvertently drinks from a poisoned cup prepared by the king for Hamlet, whereupon Laertes admits his treachery and implicates Claudius. Hamlet kills Claudius and then dies, with Horatio, his friend, bidding him good night and wishing him heavenly rest.

We had made some pale efforts in the beginning

there was something decidedly fine in Mr. Wopsle's elocution . . . because it was very slow, very dreary, very up-hill and down-hill, and very unlike any way in

which any man in any natural circumstances of life or death ever expressed himself about anything.]   Actors generally received some elocutionary instruction, although aspiring players were frequently left to their own devices, aided solely by recitation books compiled with speeches 'well calculated to display the talents of the speaker' (Egan, 1825, 21). Consequently, nineteenth-century actors were notorious for their 'unnatural' diction: 'By turns they bellow'd like the wind,/And then to whisper had a mind,/Till each resolved to act a part/And give a spec'men of his art' (à Beckett 1).

We made all the haste we could down stairs

a Jewish man with an unnaturally heavy smear of eyebrow,]   Dickens added 'Jewish' in the proofs. Compare Fagin, who has 'thick red eyebrows' (OT 12). The representation of Jews in Dickens's fiction created much discomfort. One of the first to object, Mrs Eliza Davis, wrote on 22 June 1863 that 'Charles Dickens, the large hearted, whose works plead so eloquently and so nobly for the oppressed of his country', has encouraged 'a vile prejudice against the despised Hebrew' ('Fagin and Riah', *Dickensian*, 1921, 145–6). Fagin, she added, admitted only a single interpretation, and she invited Dickens to 'atone for a great wrong'.

The presence of a good Jew, Riah, in OMF and the textual revisions to OT in 1867 indicate Dickens's growing awareness that he had not treated Jews fairly (Paroissien, 1992, 208). Elsewhere in OMF, however, Jews appear as 'asthmatic and thick-lipped' with 'big rings on their forefingers', figures consistent with conventional representations of Jews as 'bloated and bejewelled' in *Punch* cartoons (see Cotsell 151 and ff.).

"Mr. Waldengarver," said the man

"Waldengarver?" I repeated]   Conventional theatrical wisdom maintained that adopting a foreign pseudonym was essential for a career on stage. ' "Your own!" exclaims Isaac, offering advice to Pippo, "you must be mad!/Your own, and not a foreigner's! – absurd!/You'll make a wretched failure, take my word;/The thing's impossible . . ." ' (*The Maid and the Magpie*, 1858). Dickens speaks caustically of the fashion in 'Private Theatres' (SB):

> With the double view of guarding against the discovery of friends or employers, and enhancing the interest of an assumed character, by attaching a high-sounding name to its representative, these geniuses assume fictitious names, which are not the least part of the play-bill of a private theatre. Belville, Melville, Treville, Berkeley, Randolph, Byron, St. Clair, and so forth, are among the humblest; and the less imposing titles of Jenkins, Walker, Thomson, Barker, Solomons, etc., are completely laid aside.

The suggestion (Hudson) that 'Waldengarver' may be a composite of the names of four London theatrical stars of the early nineteenth century (Wallack, Vandenhoff, Woolgar and Verbruggen) has been challenged by Rosenberg (1977), who proposes a more likely connection with the Waldegrave family. Two possible candidates are Samuel Waldegrave (consecrated Bishop of Carlisle on 11 November 1860) and Lady Frances Waldegrave, the Bishop's cousin-by-marriage and oldest daughter of the tenor John Braham, Dickens's friend.

"A few steps, please.

"How do you think he looked? – I dressed him."] Jews worked in theatres as dressers and suppliers of costumes, a consequence, presumably, of their long-standing connection with the secondhand clothing business (Paroissien, 1992, 136). For Dickens's use of one such Jewish supplier, see *Letters* 6.186.

I don't know what he had looked like

a large Danish sun or star hanging round his neck . . . that had given him the appearance of being insured in some extraordinary Fire Office.] The symbol of the Sun Fire Office, a London insurance business founded in 1786, was a circular design of the sun with flames radiating from its circumference. Offices and houses protected by the company displayed a large metal badge bearing this symbol. The badge served to advertise Sun Fire and to identify buildings to the company's private fire brigade, which answered calls when a fire broke out.

I modestly assented

we all fell through a little dirty swing-door, into a sort of hot packing-case immediately behind it.] Wopsle at least has the semblance of a private dressing-room, a luxury denied many. Actors frequently made do with shared space, such as the 'miserable room, lighted by candles' common to the gentlemen performers Dickens describes in 'Private Theatres' (*SB*).

"But I'll tell you one thing, Mr. Waldengarver," said the man

a large red wafer] Wafers, small discs of flour mixed with gum and colouring, were first moistened and then used to seal letters or to attach to papers to create the impression of a seal.

Without distinctly knowing whether I should have been more sorry

he sat until two o'clock in the morning, reviewing his success and developing his plans. . . . I have a general recollection that he was to begin with reviving the Drama, and to end with crushing it; inasmuch as his decease . . . without a chance or hope.]. This appears to be an allusion to the efforts of the Syncretic Society (established in 1839), whose members wished to break the monopoly of the patent theatres and who wrote plays theatrical managers refused to produce (see *Letters* 4.78 n.; Jacobson 161–2). Just over twenty years later, Dickens wrote of the decline of the theatre from another perspective, worrying in 'Dullborough Town' about the consequences of Mechanics Institutes replacing theatres, as one had done in Rochester.

Chapter 32   Twentieth weekly number
13 April 1861

ONE *day when I was busy with my books*

"I am to come to London the day after to-morrow]   Sending Estella to London brings Pip into her orbit again and serves Miss Havisham's plans for her adopted daughter. A succession of gaieties in London provided opportunities for marriageable daughters to meet eligible young men; and anyone with aspirations to 'society' moved there during the Season, whose opening in February coincided approximately with the parliamentary sittings. The pace quickened at the end of March, when fox-hunting concluded, and gathered momentum throughout April, May and June. The Season always ended with an extra whirl of activities before Parliament adjourned in July. '*In all cases*, the observances of the Metropolis (as the seat of refinement) should be received as the standard of good breeding' ('Agogos'12).

"Next thing to it," returned Wemmick

We are in a banker's-parcel case]   That is, defending a client accused of either forgery or robbery. A banker's parcel might contain business papers, reissuable county bank-notes, money orders, specie, rings and jewellery (*The Post Office London Directory*, 1839, 1086–7). Jaggers appears to have specialized in such cases ever since one of his early clients, a forger, 'got [him] a world of credit' (GE 24).

"Yah!" said Wemmick, touching me on the breast with his forefinger

Would you like to have a look at Newgate? Have you time to spare?"]   On two occasions (November 1835 and June 1837) Dickens arranged to visit Newgate, perhaps drawn there to satisfy his curiosity whetted by Fielding, Gay and Smollett, in whose work the prison looms so large, and also for compelling reasons of his own (*Letters* 1.88, 278 n.). Expressing interest a year before his first appointment, Dickens wrote in a sketch originally published in the *Morning Chronicle* on 23 October 1834:

> What London pedestrian is there who has not, at some time or other, cast a hurried glance through the wicket at which prisoners are admitted into this gloomy mansion [Newgate], and surveyed the few objects he could discern, with an indescribable feeling of curiosity? The thick door, plated with iron and mounted with spikes, just low enough to enable you to see, leaning over them, an ill-looking fellow . . . with . . . an immense key in his left hand. Perhaps you are lucky enough to pass, just as the gate is being opened; then, you see on the other side of the lodge, another gate, the image of its predecessor, and two or three more turnkeys, who look like multiplications of the first one . . . ('Criminal Courts', *SB*)

Two years later, in 'A Visit to Newgate', Dickens offered readers a guided tour of the interior. 'We saw the prison, and saw the prisoners; and what we did see, and what we thought, we will tell at once in our own way' (SB). Brief references to Newgate appear in chapters 16 and 25 of *OT*; material from his first visit also provided the basis for the description of Fagin's last night alive (52) and, evidently, for some of the details about the condemned men in this chapter. See below.

Custom permitted the curious to tour the prison almost at will well into the first third of the nineteenth century. Visits to the condemned cells were common, sanctioning a voyeuristic interest consistent with a legal system that staged public whippings and executions before large crowds. Evangelicals were also among those who began to visit the condemned. Their motives were primarily to do good and offer comfort and spiritual support to felons facing imminent death.

We were at Newgate in a few minutes

We were at Newgate in a few minutes,] The prison in Old Bailey Street and Newgate Street was only a few minutes from the coach-office in Wood Street, Cheapside, where Pip awaited Estella's arrival from Rochester.

we passed through the lodge where some fetters were hanging up on the bare walls among the prison rules, into the interior of the jail.]

> How one shudders at the mere mention of the name – NEWGATE! A sense of horror possesses the mind when looking at the massive blocks of granite composing its walls, the iron-barred windows, and the terrible manacles suspended over the doors to deter men from breaking the laws of the country. Truly Newgate has a grim and sombre aspect! (*Newgate*, Johnson Collection, Box 4)

The main entrance was through one of two lodges on either side of the centrally located keeper's house. In 'Criminal Courts', Dickens writes that as a schoolboy he used to think the fetters over Newgate's Debtors' Door 'were a *bonâ fide* set of irons, just hung up there, for convenience sake, ready to be taken down . . . and riveted on the limbs of some refractory felon!' (SB). Fetters attached to bare walls inside the lodge, however, served a useful purpose. As late as the first two decades of the nineteenth century, prisoners 'committed for felony' and even those awaiting trial in Newgate and in other London prisons continued to be ironed. Bennett (see chapter 28) questioned the legality of this practice, suspecting it might be contrary to the law, but he justified it 'for the purposes of safe custody'. Ironing prisoners arose, he explains, in response to the 'indiscriminate admission of strangers' into prisons, a practice which increased the chances of escapes when the number of visitors almost equalled that of prisoners 'within the walls'. 'The wearing of irons was then a mark of distinction, and thus rendered their chances [of escape] less favorable' (Bennett, 1818, 39).

In addition to the display of fetters, there was also a collection of ropes used by the hangman and casts taken from the heads of notorious criminals after their execution outside Newgate (Timbs, 1867, 698; see also chapter 20). Prison Rules, pertaining to general conduct or to rules governing the use of a particular room, were often attached to the walls.

At that time, jails were much neglected, and the period of exaggerated reaction consequent on all public wrong-doing – and which is always its heaviest and longest punishment – was still far off.] Dickens refers to the conditions and policies of the Hanoverian period when Newgate prison typified the abuses that prevailed under the old system. Overcrowding was often chronic: the prison was designed for 427 prisoners but held 822 in 1818 (Bennett, 1818, 5). Inadequate sanitation and the promiscuous mixing of prisoners regardless of their age or sex complicated the problem. Citing a Report submitted to the House of Commons four years earlier, Bennett wrote in 1818:

> There was no separation of the young from the old, the children of either sex from the hardened criminal. Boys of the tenderest years, and girls of the ages of ten, twelve, and thirteen were exposed to the vicious contagion that predominated in all parts of the prison; and drunkenness prevailed to such an extent . . . that unaccompanied with riot, it attracted no notice. (Bennett 6)

Deficient provision for the sick often meant that the prison chaplain received no notice of illness among the prisoners until 'he got a warning to perform a funeral'. The failure of prison authorities to provide bedding and supply uniforms added to the discomfort of prisoners. Some, like the man 'in a well-worn olive-coloured frock coat' Wemmick visits, wore their own clothes, others dressed in rags. Prison dietaries were another issue: most were so deficient that inmates could hardly survive without assistance from friends. 'I am no friend to luxury in prison,' wrote Bennett, commenting on food allowances in Newgate in 1818, but 'the torture of famine and disease is not in the sentence of the law, which inflicts imprisonment: least of all is it warrantable previous to conviction, when safe detention is all that is contemplated'. Bennett recommended one and a half pounds of 'best wheaten bread' a day and two pounds of meat weekly. That 'is the least that a prisoner requires, of the ages of fifteen to thirty; and I have no doubt, that the allowance of food in Newgate is not equal to the sustentation of the human frame' (35).

Starting in the 1770s, voices crying out about the evil conditions common in English gaols were heard with increasing frequency. Efforts by John Howard (1726–90), Jeremy Bentham (1748–1832), Samuel Romilly (1757–1818), Elizabeth Fry (1780–1845) and Patrick Colquhoun (1745–1820) awakened the public conscience and publicized conditions which had existed in prisons throughout the country for many years. Howard's influential *State of the Prisons in England and Wales* (1777), for example, cited data he gathered over three years of intense research and told a horrifying story of mismanagement and cruelty. In many extreme cases, he reported, prisoners expired on the floors 'in loathsome cells' from neglect and lack of food.

Conditions like these arose because county and city gaols were private institutions.

They were run by unpaid officials who were under no obligation to report to local or national authorities. Prisoners generally had to pay for services – food, drinking water, bedding – an arrangement that led to profiteering and abuse. They were also incarcerated in conditions severely detrimental to their health. '[S]corbutic distempers' and toes mortified 'or quite rotted from their feet' were among the results Howard frequently encountered during his visits. Starvation, the lack of medical supplies, filth, vermin, contagion and 'the stench from the sewers' often proved fatal. 'It is a shocking thing to destroy in prisons the morals, health, and (as is often done) the lives of those whom the laws consign only to hard labour and correction' (Howard 37).

Howard's report prompted improvements among some local authorities. Support grew for the need to classify prisoners and separate men from women and debtors from hardened criminals by housing them in different wards. In 1815 prison fees allowing gaolers to charge for their services were abolished by law (55 Geo.II, c. 50). But, without inspectors to enforce the provisions of the Act, efforts to redress abuses often remained ineffective. Legislation to introduce compliance occurred in 1835 (5 & 6 Will. IV, c. 38), when all English prisons were brought under the authority of the Secretary of State and justices were required to furnish quarterly reports on the condition of their gaols. Standards of hygiene, organization and the safety of those held in custody also continued to improve. Acts in 1865 (28 & 29 Vict., c. 18) and 1877 (40 & 41 Vict., c. 53) finally brought all the gaols in Britain under the powers of the Secretary of State. Thus by 1861 the horrors people associated with Newgate and the excesses of England's 'bloody code' had long been tamed by a period of government legislation.

Centralization, however, drew criticism from some who feared that reforms had gone too far. Sydney Smith, for example, worried that gaols had become 'soft', thus depriving the criminal justice system of its former deterrent effect. Improving gaols, others argued, raised conditions in them above those in which many of the poor and aged worked and lived. Dickens shared the view that the correction of earlier public wrong-doing had prompted a period of 'exaggerated reaction' and voiced objections both here and in *DC* when David questions why large expenditures on prisons went unchallenged while an uproar would occur 'if any deluded man had proposed to spend half the money – on the erection of an industrial school for the young, or a house of refuge for the deserving old' (61). And, watching meals delivered to inmates in their cells, Copperfield observes 'a striking contrast between these plentiful repasts of choice quality, and the dinners, not to say of paupers, but of soldiers, sailors, laborers, the great bulk of the honest working community; of whom not one man in five hundred ever dined half so well' (61). *DC* also criticized the expensive 'separate' system for its inability to keep prisoners in complete isolation and prison authorities for their eagerness to see penitence in men whose 'love of deception' made officials easy victims of guile they never suspected. Elsewhere, Dickens argued against coddling lazy prisoners, maintaining that pickpockets, 'sturdy vagrants', drunkards and begging-letter writers should be given 'a kind of work' they least liked to do ('Pet Prisoners', *HW* 1.103). Complaints about high costs associated with turning 'penal places' into 'penal palaces' and providing criminals with conveniences and comforts beyond the means of many working men received a further airing on 11

May 1861 in Beard's 'Dialogue Concerning Convicts' (AYR 5.156).

So, felons were not lodged and fed better than soldiers (to say nothing of paupers), and seldom set fire to their prisons with the excusable object of improving the flavour of their soup.] Compare Carlyle, who also denounced authorities for coddling prisoners in 'Model Prisons' (*Latter-Day Pamphlets*, 1850): in August 1850, convicts in London's Parkhouse Model Prison set fire to their quarters. The riots which occurred in Chatham at St Mary's Convict Prison, however, appear to be a more immediate source of these comments. Two months before the publication of the novel's twentieth instalment on 13 April, serious trouble began on Tuesday, 12 February 1861 at the new facility (1856) designed to hold convicts who earlier in the century would have been sent to Australia (Presnail 216). Tensions between prisoners and guards had surfaced earlier in the year when several men complained, not for the first time, 'of the badness of the food'. Following more incidents of insubordination and hostile exchanges, a full-scale revolt erupted as dinner was served on the 12th. Guards were captured and some were seriously injured; the Chief Warden's office was sacked, and prison records and papers burned, as a wild uproar spread unchecked until 400 Royal Marines and 500 troops 'of the line' were called in. Armed soldiers quickly weeded out the ringleaders, and severe reprisals soon followed (*The Times*, 13 and 19 February 1861).

Newspaper coverage of the 'Revolt of the Convicts at Chatham' showed little sympathy with the prisoners' objections to their diet: their rations, wrote a reporter from *The Times*, '[are] greatly superior to [those] given in any union workhouse' (13 February 1861). Testimony from C. P. Measor, the Deputy Governor of the prison, went further, asserting that 'Men in the position of criminals, who get 27 oz. of excellent white bread, 5 or 6 oz. of good beef, three quarters of a pint of by no means indifferent soup, and cocoa and gruel in addition, as their ordinary diet, cannot be said either to have much grievance on the ground of quantity' (15 February 1861). Returning to this issue four days later, *The Times* pointedly compared the weekly rations served to prisoners at Chatham with those given to inmates of the neighbouring union workhouse in the town:

Chatham Convict Prison	*Chatham Union Workhouse*
189 oz bread	112 oz bread
42 oz cooked meat, 'free from bone, etc.'	16 oz meat pudding and vegetables
7 pints of tea	1 oz tea
5˘ pints of 'good soup'	4 oz cheese
7 pints of cocoa or gruel	7 oz butter
7 lb. of vegetables	
cheese and porter on Sundays	
	(19 February 1861)

It was visiting time] 'Visiting time' belongs to the era before Newgate and other gaols in England came under the authority of the government. In those pre-centralized days, visitors enjoyed almost free and unsupervised access to prisons. According to the 'Report from the Committee on Laws Relating to Penitentiary Houses' filed on 31 May 1811, prison authorities extended 'to [male] offenders of every description' the privilege of allowing friends and family members access to their yards, where prisoners could communicate freely with outsiders. Women prisoners, however, were more closely supervised and could only communicate with friends through a railing at one end of their quarters (*BPP, Crime and Punishment, Transportation*, 1, 6).

Expediency accounts for this practice, since most inmates could not survive without food, clothing and other essentials supplied by friends and family members. The presence of outsiders, however, created rather than solved problems – a point Bennett emphasized in his letter attacking management policies current in Newgate early in the century. 'The indiscriminate visiting of the prison of Newgate by all persons, whether male or female, who claim any relationship with the prisoners, is altogether opposed to the moral improvement of those who are confined'. Specifically, he warned that free intercourse between prisoners and their criminal associates outside abetted rather than diminished crime. Some of the worst 'and most extensive burglaries have been plotted' in Newgate. 'Forged notes have been both fabricated and passed there, and coining itself has been carried on within its walls'.

Equally disturbing was the sexual immorality encouraged by the present system of visiting, which permitted London's 'most profligate and abandoned females' free access to the prison:

> A woman has only to state herself to be the wife of a prisoner, and although she may be well known as a common street-walker by every turnkey she must pass, she is admitted without farther inquiry. (Bennett, 1818, 8)

Bennett declined to elaborate further on 'the gross scenes' observable each day 'in open daylight'. Instead, he invited readers to use their imagination and contemplate what happened when women spent the night:

> It is easier to conceive than to describe the horrid profligacy and indecency attending such a system as this, in wards, each containing several beds, most of which are not separated from each other even by a single curtain.
> (Bennett, 1818, 7–8, 283–4)

a potman was going his rounds with beer;] The sale of beer to prisoners was a long-established practice based on the fact that inmates, including debtors, had to support themselves during their confinement. Prisoners drank beer and other liquors as a matter of course, since prison authorities failed to supply fresh water or other non-alcoholic beverages.

Bennett regarded 'The introduction of spirituous liquors' as another flaw of the open system, which allowed visitors to flout 'public acts of parliament' and the 'regulations of the court of aldermen'. Cursory searches by the turnkeys failed to have the desired effect; when spirits were discovered, a trifling bribe usually stalled any opposition. To the consternation of Bennett and others, unhappy prisoners often resorted to drink, opting to 'stupefy themselves' and get rid of 'all reflection' rather than contemplate their misdeeds in a sober frame of mind (1818, 6–7).

It struck me that Wemmick walked among the prisoners

It struck me that Wemmick walked among the prisoners, much as a gardener might walk among his plants.]   This metaphor, and the reference to 'Wemmick's greenhouse' two paragraphs later, perhaps owes something to the appearance of Newgate's interior before extensive alterations later in the century. Asked in 1811 to describe how the wards were lighted, the Keeper of Newgate at that time responded with a description that evokes some features of a typical greenhouse: 'The windows are iron-barred, and there are wooden frames, which are papered with greased paper, so as to admit light and exclude air'. Windows were generally kept open during the day and closed at night by shutting the paper casement (*BPP, Crime and Punishment, Transportation*, 1, 'Appendix, No. 1, Committee on Laws Relating to Penitentiary Houses', 1811, 49).

Almost as soon as he had spoken

(whom I can see now, as I write)]   This is one of several occasions when Pip makes explicit the retrospective nature of his story. Similar references occur in chapters 18, 56, and 58. The significance of this gap between the events of his life and his subsequent narration is discussed in the Introduction.

in a well-worn olive-coloured frock-coat,]   Frock-coats were men's double-breasted coats with skirts that extended to the knees. The coat-tails extended equally at the back and the front.

"Yes, it was too strong, sir – but I don't care."'

but I don't care."]   Prisoners awaiting execution were known to exhibit indifference and even an 'unbecoming merriment'. They also sought relief 'in the constant application of intoxicating stimulants'. 'I saw Cashman [executed 1817], a few hours before his execution, smoking and drinking with the utmost lack of concern and indifference,' Bennett added (1818, 14). Thirty years later, Dickens made a similar comment when he argued against public executions on the grounds that they could provoke bravado rather than fear among some criminals. 'Well! We must all die at one time or other; and to die game . . . is just the thing for the man of spirit' (*Daily News*, 9 March 1846; Paroissien, 1985, 227). Fauntleroy's display of composure on the eve of his execution in 1824 was another case in point and added to the public controversy aroused by hanging forgers.

"No, no," said Wemmick, coolly

"Served His Majesty this man. Was a soldier in the line and bought his discharge."] These details may contain an allusion to Robert Swan, a 32-year-old private in the Scotch Fusilier Guards, whom Dickens observed in the condemned cells when he visited Newgate in 1835 (see above). Swan, convicted of robbery with menace, was subsequently reprieved. His two companions, John Smith and John Pratt, both convicted of homosexual acts, were hanged outside Newgate on 27 November 1835 (Carlton 406). Buying one's discharge was a recognizable way to leave the Army.

"If what I had upon me when taken

"I should have asked the favour of your wearing another ring] See chapter 21, note on p. 190, for Wemmick's collection of mourning rings, given to him by clients attempting to curry favour.

"I'll accept the will for the deed," said Wemmick.

tumblers.] Commenting on the variety of tumblers, Darwin, who joined two London pigeon clubs to pursue his fascination with the birds, noted the 'short-faced tumbler' and the 'common tumbler'. Both were so-called on account of their flying at a great height and then 'tumbling in the air head over heels'. Other breeds of pigeon included the pouter, the turbit, the Jacobin, the trumpeter and the fan-tail (20).

"All right," said Wemmick

"A Coiner,] In the decade before Parliament passed the Coinage Offences Act of 1832 (2 & 3 Will. 4, c. 34), seventy-three offenders were sentenced to death under the provisions of the old law (Radzinowicz 1.600–1). On 22 November 1827, Edward Lowe was drawn to the scaffold on a sledge and executed at Newgate for coining (*The Hangman's Record*, 1909). The last forger to be hanged outside Newgate was Thomas Maynard, a friendless and obscure customs clerk in financial difficulties, who died on 30 December 1829 (Gatrell 581).

The Recorder's report is made to-day, and he is sure to be executed on Monday.] The Recorder of London served as the chief law officer of the Corporation of London and presided over trials at the Old Bailey, 'with relays of judges or serjeants assisting him as the court dealt with several hundred prisoners per session' (Gatrell 509). After prisoners had been sentenced, it fell to the Recorder to review the cases of all criminals capitally convicted at the City of London and County of Middlesex Sessions held at the Old Bailey and submit a report to the Home Secretary of State (see also chapter 56, note on p. 404). This review provided an opportunity to try over 'all the cases that have been determined by the Judges and Juries, seeking out reasons in good character, and in the complexion of the crime, in order to be enabled to recommend the remission of the punishment' to the monarch (Bennett, 1818, 30–1).

Solicitors were appointed to the office of Recorder by the Lord Mayor and aldermen. Lawyers viewed this procedure with scepticism because it guaranteed neither legal competence nor learning. The two Recorders who served in the early years of the nineteenth century (Sir John Silvester, 1803–22, and Newman Knowlys, 1822–33) were both perceived as 'dismal specimens, more or less corrupt' (Gatrell 509). Additional duties included arranging a date for the Quarter Sessions. See also chapter 56.

"Is this young gentleman one of the 'prentices or articled ones

'prentices or articled ones]   For apprentices, see chapter 7, note on p. 73; 'articled ones' refers to a clerk articled to a lawyer for a specific period of training in return for which his parents had paid a substantial premium to the law firm. Lawyers also employed salaried clerks, like Wemmick, who worked without the prospect of advancement, and copying clerks, whose principal work constituted making copies of legal documents by hand.

Chapter 33

IN her furred travelling-dress

furred travelling-dress,]   Styles for women travellers emphasized the practical and the durable: tweed, serge, Irish frieze, homespun and other all-wool materials were preferred; satin, brocade or rich heavy silks were judged 'quite out of place' (C. E. Humphry, 1900, 67).

> As to travelling dress, it cannot be too quiet, nor too unobtrusive, more especially if ladies are travelling without the escort of any male relative. Light but warm in cold weather, light and cool in summer, no gaudy colours or fly-away trimmings should be allowed. (*Etiquette of Modern Society*, [1881], 61)

Ladies' travelling coats and other outdoor wear, however, were often trimmed with fur around the collar and cuffs and down the front.

"I am going to Richmond," she told me.

there are two Richmonds, one in Surrey and one in Yorkshire,]

> [Richmond] is esteemed the finest village in England, whether considered with respect to the great variety of beautiful and finely variegated prospects it affords, or the great number of superb and elegant buildings, and magnificent gardens, with which the whole neighbourhood abounds. Richmond is situated in the county of Surrey, and at a distance of twelve miles from the metropolis.
> (*The London Guide*, 1818, 59)

The environs were partly cultivated and partly wooded, 'diversified by rising spires, villages, mansions, and inferior habitations' (*Picturesque Tour of the River Thames*, 1828, 131). Richmond in Yorkshire about 140 miles north of London is 'one of the most picturesquely placed towns in England' situated on the river Swale above which, on a precipice, 'rises the great castle of the Breton earls, magnificent even in decay' (*Handbook for Travellers*, 1867, 309).

She drew her arm through mine

She drew her arm through mine, as if it must be done,]   Etiquette required a gentleman to offer his right arm when escorting a lady from one room to another (Day 16).

a waiter who had been staring at the coach like a man who had never seen such a thing in his life,] Travellers often remarked on the idiosyncratic or peculiar behaviour of waiters. Albert Smith contended that waiters usually came in no more than two denominations: 'the Haughty and the Mouldy'. Or, if they belonged to neither, they were generally 'familiar' (1855, 27).

a diminishing mirror] These are usually round or oval in shape with convex glass surrounded by a carved and gilded frame. They are so-called because convex glass allows one to see at a glance a reduced image of almost the whole room.

an anchovy sauce-cruet, and somebody's pattens.] Anchovy sauce was often served as a savoury appetizer on toast to be eaten before drinking wine. Cruets of the sauce, together with other condiments, were among the relishes and spices typically available in stagecoach houses where passengers stopped for refreshments while the horses were changed ('An Old Stage-Coaching House', AYR 9.540). For 'pattens', see chapter 13, note on p. 126.

a copy-book] Copy-books were widely used in classrooms to teach children penmanship. They were generally issued in quarto size, complete with proverbs and moral tags such as 'Indolence is the inlet to all misfortunes' and 'Banish every inordinate loose desire'. In the blank space below pupils copied what was written, thus improving simultaneously their penmanship and their mind (Heal ix).

I was, and I am, sensible that the air of this chamber

the air of this chamber . . . might have led one to infer that . . . enterprising proprietor was boiling down the horses for the refreshment department.] Worn-out, diseased and old horses were taken to a knacker's yard, slaughtered, and the carcasses put to various uses after the hides had been stripped for sale. Hoofs and bones boiled down provided the basic ingredients for glue; dogs' meat was prepared from the flesh.

"Very superior indeed.

He is nobody's enemy"] See chapter 11, note on p. 116.

"Two things I can tell you," said Estella.

the proverb that constant dropping will wear away a stone,] Several versions of the expression exist. Compare 'All the waters wear the stones' (Job 14.19).

I rang for the tea, and the waiter

Moses in the bullrushes typified by a soft bit of butter in a quantity of parsley,] As a baby, Moses was placed in a basket of rushes by his mother beside the river when Pharaoh ordered the execution of all male Jewish children (Exodus 1–2).

a powdered head,] See chapter 40, note on p. 320.

a casket of precious appearance containing twigs.] The best teas come from the young, soft leaves picked from the top of the bush; twig tea, from stems, produces an inferior, weaker drink when steeped in hot water.

The bill paid, and the waiter remembered

Turning into Cheapside and rattling up Newgate-street,] See Appendix 4, map p. 443.

I should have been chary of discussing my guardian

a sudden glare of gas. It seemed, while it lasted, to be all alight and alive . . . and when we were out of it, I was as much dazed for a few moments as if I had been in Lightning.] Experiments to illuminate houses and factories by burning gas from heated coal date from the late eighteenth century; but it was Friedrich Albrecht Winzer (anglicized to Winsor) who stimulated national interest in gas lighting when he lit one side of Pall Mall in London in 1807 from an apparatus in his house there. Five years later, Parliament approved a scheme for a larger central installation and the London Gas, Light and Coke Company came into being, initiating a widespread and immediate demand for gas-lighting:

> Among the recent improvements of the metropolis, none perhaps merit greater celebration than the present brilliant mode of lighting public streets, shops, etc. with gas. This beautiful substitute for the former imperfect plan of securing a public light, is rapidly extending its benefits, in consequence of the incorporation of the "Gas Light and Coke Company" on the 30th of April, 1812. (*Leigh's New Picture of London*, 1818, 320)

By 1820, fifteen of the principal cities of England and Scotland had been equipped with gas-lighting and at the mid-century hardly a town or village of any consequence lacked a gas supply (McNeil 208–9).

Startled reactions on encountering gas-lit streets for the first time were not uncommon. John Quincy Adams, a visitor to London in December 1816, found the new gas-lights in the City, near the Mansion House, 'remarkably brilliant', shedding a light 'almost too dazzling for my eyes' (Nevins 169). Profound economic and social consequences followed. In industry and commerce, gas-lighting extended the working day, especially in winter; streets became safer to frequent after dark, it made possible evening classes, thus enabling adults to gain an education after a day's work, and it made it easier for dinner, until now taken around three in the afternoon, to slip into the evening. Prior to the introduction of gas, blinking oil-lamps in the streets, dim tallow candles in shop windows and rush lights and candles were the only forms of illumination.

So, we fell into other talk

what parts of London lay on this side of it, and what on that.] The journey to Richmond from the City would take Pip and Estella through distinct areas defined by sociological and geographical boundaries. Making their way west from the City, the centre of business and commerce, they would cross Holborn and the region of the Inns of Court and the Temple before passing through Soho and then along Shaftesbury Avenue and Piccadilly in the direction of Hyde Park. Government offices, Parliament and the river lay to the south; to the north, Mayfair and aristocratic London.

she had never left Miss Havisham's neighbourhood until she had gone to France, and she had merely passed through London then in going and returning.] The description suggests a route to the Continent taken before 1820 when travellers left the port of London by sail or steam packet: 'From London vessels proceed to the French coast almost every day; to Holland three times a-week; to Belgium frequently; to Hamburg twice a-week and to Lisbon and Cadiz every week'. This practice prevailed for some years after 1815 (Porter, 1836, 2.49).

Travel to France changed in 1821 when David Napier introduced cross-Channel steamers that ran between Dover and Calais (Spratt 9). The popularity of this service gradually increased, especially after the mid-century when railways began to provide fast and direct access to the Continent by taking passengers to Dover and Folkestone for embarkation. Passenger traffic on this route expanded in 1862 when rail companies obtained permission from Parliament to own or work steam-boats.

The same year, the London, Chatham and Dover and South Eastern Company and the London, Brighton and South Coast Company exploited this new privilege by introducing an improved link between London and the Channel ports. Under this arrangement, train timetables were co-ordinated with the arrival and departure of steamers from Dover and Folkestone, a move which reduced further travelling time between London and the Continent (Burtt 3). Dickens travelled frequently to France later in his career and was a passenger on the 'tidal train' travelling to London when it crashed at full speed on 9 June 1865 near Staplehurst in Kent.

We came to Richmond all too soon

our destination there, was a house by the Green:] Richmond Green lies to the south-west of the former village. In 1818 the Green was 'a very pleasant spot, being surrounded with lofty elms, and by the fine houses of many persons of distinction' (*The London Guide, Describing the Public and Private Buildings* 62). Twenty years later, another writer noted that this 'large open space . . . does not belie its name' and was still surrounded 'with many comfortable-looking houses, and rows of venerable trees' (Mackay, 1840, 1.134).

where hoops and powder and patches,] Hooped petticoats remained in vogue throughout the eighteenth century. Women also applied perfumed powder to their hair and wore patches – small pieces of black silk or sticking plaster – on their face to conceal a blemish or more commonly to show off their pale complexion. See also below for farthingales.

embroidered coats, rolled stockings, ruffles, and swords, had had their court days many a time.] The list evokes the aristocratic court fashions of the eighteenth century when men wore swords, bucklers, garters, gold-laced coats, embroidered vests and cocked hats. By the 1850s, these were seen as a 'miserable relic of bygone times' (*London at Dinner*, 1858, 35–6).

Some ancient trees . . . cut into fashions] See chapter 11, note on p. 115.

A bell with an old voice

Here is the green farthingale, Here is the diamond-hilted sword, Here are the shoes with red heels and the blue solitaire,] Farthingales, introduced into England from the Continent in the sixteenth century, held the voluminous folds of a lady's gown away from her feet, allowing the skirts to skim the ground. Different versions of the farthingale existed, including the later hooped skirt, all cage-like garments which, if worn with care, added an air of elegance to the wearer, provided she walked smoothly with rather slow steps, appearing to glide along, her feet unseen. Gentlemen carried swords or rapiers with beautifully fashioned hilts whenever they appeared in public, thus adding a decorative touch to their apparel further augmented with brightly coloured shoes and a solitaire, a loose necktie of silk or broad ribbon (based on Wildeblood 1973, 73, 75).

Mr. Pocket was out lecturing

he was a most delightful lecturer on domestic economy, and his treatises on the management of children and servants were considered the very best text-books on those themes.] The choice of topic is obviously ironic. One author of a treatise for use in schools defined 'domestic economy' as 'the arrangement, regulation, and management of all the persons who compose a household. . . . It is, in fact, the art of rendering domestic life respectable and comfortable' (Gleig 1).

(with a relative in the Foot Guards)] To go out with 'a relative' was often a euphemistic excuse maids used when they asked permission to walk with an admirer or male caller. Soldiers were most commonly the object of maids' affections and notorious for accosting maids and nurse-maids as they walked in parks, taking their employers' children on excursions. In defence of Ninette (*The Maid and the Magpie*), it was said that she 'Never had cousins in the Grenadiers' (3). The Foot-Guards, formerly a body of carefully selected foot-soldiers for special guard duty, is the proper name of three infantry regiments: the Coldstream, Grenadier and Scots Fusilier Guards.

Chapter 34 Twenty-first weekly number
20 April 1861

Yet Estella was so inseparable from all my restlessness

the canary-breasted Avenger] Pip's servant dressed in ostentatious yellow livery: the most fashionable colour.

So now, as an infallible way of making a little ease great ease

making a little ease great ease,] A popular but non-proverbial expression.

I began to contract a quantity of debt.] See chapter 24, note on p. 220.

we put ourselves down for election into a club called The Finches of the Grove: the object of which institution I have never divined, if it were not that the members should dine expensively once a fortnight, to quarrel among themselves as much as possible after dinner, and to cause six waiters to get drunk on the stairs.] Dickens takes the club's name from a phrase spoken by Tilburina, a character in Puff's 'The Spanish Armada', a farcical play-within-the-play in Sheridan's *The Critic; or, A Tragedy Rehearsed* (1779): finding herself unable to rejoice as the sun rises and all 'the feather'd warblers tuned their notes', she laments, 'But O to me, no joy can they afford!/ . . . nor lark,/linnet, nor all the finches of the grove!' (2.2). The choice of name is no more improbable than many of the odd and humorous names clubs adopted throughout the nineteenth century. Among the 'queerly-named' clubs of the times are: Mum, Ugly, Lying, Odd Fellows, Humbugs and the Great Bottle club (Neville 39).

Victorian men's clubs evolved from eighteenth-century coffee-houses, where men first gathered to drink coffee, read the newspapers and discuss business. Over time, identifiable groups emerged, leading eventually to the proliferation of clubs separated one from the other by distinctive interests. All, however, were private and exclusive and worked to maintain a sense of privilege. Each was self-governing with its own set of rules (the Finches, as Pip notes, refused admission to anyone under 21) and elected nominees only on the unanimous approval of all members. Successful nominees paid an initial entrance fee (from £20 to £30) and thereafter annual dues (£5 to £10), thus perpetuating a system of limited access. Wealth, social status and professional interests dictated club membership.

Young men considered obtaining entry 'into a respectable club' essential to their status. Without it, no one would consider them accomplished men about town (Thackeray, 'Mr. Brown the Elder Takes Mr. Brown the Younger to a Club', 1849, *Sketches and Travels* 261). Clubs, however, differed widely in their facilities, ranging from the grand in Pall Mall with servants and well-stocked libraries to small clubs limited solely to dining, like the one described here. Small clubs restricted their membership to fewer than fifty. Their atmosphere tended to be intimate and not unlike the society founded by Douglas Jerrold called 'Our Club', whose forty members met on Saturday evenings for dinner in Clunn's in Covent Garden (Sir William Hardman, 1923, 200). They rarely admitted guests and indulged in little speechmaking. The sole rationale for meeting regularly was the pleasure members took in seeing each other, eating well and enjoying amusing talk.

The Finches spent their money foolishly

(the Hotel we dined at was in Covent-garden),] The club's location in Covent Garden (see chapters 21 and 45), an area west of the City and north of the Strand, hints at its lesser status. Fashionable and famous establishments like Almack's, Crockford's, Brooke's, the Carlton, the Reform, the Turf and the Athenaeum in Pall Mall and St James's Street were some distance away.

in a cab of his own,] Cabriolets, or cabs, introduced in 1820 from Paris, were open, two-wheeled, horse-drawn vehicles with a reputation for being 'very liable to accidents' (Timbs, 1867, 393).

the posts at the street corners.] Many of London's main streets were encumbered with posts, which were used to display placards, advertisements and the times of theatre performances, hence the term 'bill-posting' (Timbs, 1867, 349).

head-foremost over the apron, and I saw him on one occasion deliver himself . . . like coals.] A leather apron covered the legs of a passenger in a cabriolet, affording some protection against rain and cold. Drummle's arrival is likened to the delivery of a sack of coals, dumped from the back of a coalman as he tips the sack over his shoulders and upside down into the householder's coal-bin.

until I came of age.] See Appendix 1.

In my confidence in my own resources

buying a rifle and going to America, with a general purpose of compelling buffaloes to make his fortune.] Thinking of America as the land of opportunity had become a commonplace, though not an entirely accurate one, by 1800. Published letters by emigrants, handbills and misleading posters suggested that even the penniless could thrive there. The novel's early chronology, however, makes the route to fortune named here an anachronistic reference. Until the Erie Canal opened to connect the Hudson River with Lake Erie in 1825, access to the Great Plains and the west, where buffalo roamed in vast herds, was severely restricted. Thereafter, the American buffalo, or bison, was hunted ruthlessly and to near-extinction by the mid-century. Their wholesale slaughter by Europeans occurred because buffalo tongues were prized as a delicacy; they were also shot for sport from trains on the completion of the transcontinental railroad at Promontory Point, Utah, on 10 May 1869.

I was usually at Hammersmith about half the week

taught the young idea how to shoot,]   That is, to develop. From 'Spring' in James Thomson's *The Seasons* (1728): 'Delightful task! to rear the tender thought,/To teach the young idea how to shoot,/To pour fresh instruction o'er the mind,/To breathe the enlivening spirit, and to fix/The generous purpose in the glowing breast' (l.1152–5).

Every morning, with an air ever new

If we all did what we undertake to do . . . we might live in a Republic of the Virtues.]   An ironic allusion to Rousseau's use of the phrase a Republic of Virtue in his *Social Contract* (1762) when he discusses the community's right to force men to be free in the name of a unitary, single truth. Some have found in Rousseau's advocacy of a direct democracy a dangerous strain of thought consistent with a popular dictatorship or a totalitarian democracy. (I am grateful to Edgar Rosenberg for identifying Rousseau's phrase.)

go to Lloyd's"]   London's most prominent marine insurance company, so-called because it originated in Edward Lloyd's Coffee House in Lombard Street, a resort from 1692 for merchants and ship-owners and, eventually, emporium of mercantile news and the city's recognized centre for underwriters and those who did business with them. In 1770, Lloyd's Society was established; retaining the old name, the 'New Lloyd's' moved to the Royal Exchange and opened for business in 1774.

If we had been less attached to one another

"not unwholly unconnected," as my local paper might put it, "with jewellery,"]   The euphemistic language suggests the cautious reporting of criminal cases or perhaps the incompetence of subeditors of small newspapers.

like a booted Cupid]   Cupid, the son of Mercury and Venus, was the Roman god of love. Typical representations of him portrayed a young boy with bare feet.

We ordered something rather special for dinner

a bundle of pens,]   Quill pens, which were sold in bundles.

Each of us would then refer

Each of us would then refer to a confused heap of papers at his side, which had been thrown into drawers, worn into holes in pockets, half-burnt in lighting candles, stuck for weeks into the looking-glass, and otherwise damaged.]   This mode of keeping accounts ran counter to practices recommended in Victorian manuals. Maintain your financial records with the utmost exactness, books counselled. Devote an hour a week to the task, ask the tradesmen who supplied food and other essentials to send their bills every Monday, and check and cast up each one before making a payment. Obtain receipts, even for the smallest amount, and keep a clear record of all other expenses. 'Aim at the happy mean – be Liberal without being lavish, be Prudent without being Penurious' (Kitchiner, 1825, 2, 44). Pip's and Herbert's domestic mismanagement may have reflected concerns Dickens expressed about his own older sons (Rosenberg, 1972, 319).

We shut our outer door on these solemn occasions

its heavy black seal and border.] Etiquette dictated that letters to gentlemen should always be sealed with wax (*Etiquette for Gentlemen*, 1838, 21), while mourning practices dictated the use of black wax and paper with black borders along the edges on appropriate occasions.

The letter was signed TRABB *&* CO.

TRABB & CO.,] Trabb combines the two trades of tailor and undertaker – a plausible arrangement because Victorian funeral practices required men skilled in the use of large quantities of cloth. Nineteenth-century undertakers often described themselves as Furnishing Undertakers to convey the range of services they provided, for example: supplying mourning dress for the bereaved family and the family servants, and for mutes and other attendants; decorating the house where the funeral reception was held; and providing additional trappings, including capes, yards of silk, crape, or cloth for hat-bands and grave clothes for the deceased.

Mrs. J. Gargery had departed this life on Monday last,] The language of the formal announcement borrows a locution from the prayer for the Church militant, asking the Lord for comfort and saying: 'And we also bless thy holy name for all thy servants departed this life in thy faith and fear' (*BCP*). See also Appendix 1.

Chapter 35

IT was fine summer weather again

IT was fine summer weather again,] See Appendix 1.

At last I came within sight of the house

put in a funereal execution and taken possession.] The legal phraseology adapted from a bailiff's right to seize the goods of a debtor conveys the extent to which undertakers took over the house when they made their funeral arrangements.

Writing in 'Trading in Death', Dickens referred to mid-century funeral practices as 'A system of barbarous show and expense'. Such ostentation, he thought, could do no honour to the memory of the dead and did 'great dishonor to the living'. As a consequence the most solemn of human occasions had now become associated with 'unmeaning mummeries, dishonest debt, profuse waste, and bad example in an utter oblivion of responsibility' from which no class escaped. Competition among the middle class for 'superior gentility' in funerals – 'the gentility being estimated by the amount of ghastly folly in which the undertaker was permitted to run riot' – descended even to the poor (*HW* 6.241).

Two dismally absurd persons, each ostentatiously exhibiting a crutch done up in a black bandage . . . were posted at the front door;] Two mutes from the undertaker's hold staves draped in black cloth and stand guard outside the house, performing a task previously undertaken by family servants. By the 1830s this practice had become common among ordinary people in imitation of the 'conductor' and his staff from the College of Heralds, the body which orchestrated the funeral rites of nobles and important figures during the sixteenth and seventeenth centuries. Dickens ridiculed the practice of employing mutes to hold staves draped in black in a *HW* essay in 1850: 'There they stood, for hours, with a couple of crutches covered over with drapery: cutting their jokes on the company as they went in' and breathing strong fumes of rum and water ('From the Raven in the Happy Family', *HW* 1.241).

These and similar practices added needlessly to funeral expenses, all in an attempt to honour the dead. In answer to his own question about why people spend more money upon a death than upon a birth, Mr Mould, the undertaker in *MC*, observes:

> It's because the laying out of money with a well-conducted establishment, where the thing is performed upon the very best scale, binds the broken heart, and sheds balm upon the wounded spirit. Hearts want binding, and spirits want balming when people die; not when people are born. (19)

Another sable warder (a carpenter, who had

sable warder] 'Sable', formerly a heraldic term, was widely used as a general (poetic or rhetorical) synonym for black.

a kind of black Bazaar, with the aid of a quantity of black pins.] Draped black cloth has transformed the 'best parlour'. Specially manufactured black pins were used by undertakers to secure the hangings and keep the fabric in place (Penny, 1981, 29).

putting somebody's hat into black long-clothes,] Long black bands of cloth (or silk or crape) were attached to men's hats as a sign of mourning – a custom dating from Elizabethan funeral processions. By the end of the nineteenth century hat-bands, or 'weepers', had almost totally disappeared.

Poor dear Joe, entangled in a little black cloak

entangled in a little black cloak tied in a large bow under his chin . . . seated apart at the upper end of the room; where, as chief mourner, he had evidently been stationed by Trabb.] The custom of wearing cloaks (supplied by the undertaker) dates from Elizabethan times; arranging mourners in hierarchical groups was an essential part of Victorian and earlier funeral practice, the point of which was to emphasize differences rather than minimize them.

Biddy, looking very neat and modest in her black dress

Biddy . . . in her black dress,] Family servants wore mourning when a family member died; typical attire for females included black dresses, black shawls and black bonnets. Later reformers denounced this practice as an instance of 'innate vulgarity' (*Sylvia's Home Journal*, 1879, quoted in Morley 72).

I . . . began to wonder in what part of the house it – she – my sister – was.] By custom bodies were laid out at home and kept there until they were buried. Women assisted at both home births and laying out the dead.

So, we all put our pocket-handkerchiefs to our faces

it being a point of Undertaking ceremony that the six bearers must be stifled and blinded under a horrible black velvet housing with a white border, the whole

looked like a blind monster with twelve human legs,]   Standard practice called for six bearers to carry the coffin on their shoulders; obscured by the low-hanging pall, only their knees and feet remained visible. Compare the image in *TTC* of a walking coffin that haunts young Jerry Cruncher: after spying on his father's 'fishing' expedition, Jerry gets the idea that he is pursued by a coffin, 'hopping on behind him, bolt upright upon its narrow end', and following him upstairs as he scrambles into bed (2.14).

And now, the range of marshes lay clear before us

And there,]   MS reads 'there, Joe and I standing side by side against the very grave stone on which the <convict> fugitive had put me that dismal evening long ago'.

Of the conduct of the worldly-minded Pumblechook

even when those noble passages were read which remind humanity how it brought nothing into the world and can take nothing out, and how it fleeth like a shadow and never continueth long in one stay,]   From 'The Order for Burial of the Dead' in *BCP*: 'We brought nothing into this world, and it is certain we can carry nothing out' (1 Timothy 6.7; Job 1.21). 'While the corpse is made ready to be laid into the earth, the priest shall say . . . Man that is born of a woman hath but a short time to live, and is full of misery. He cometh up, and is cut down, like a flower; he fleeth as it were a shadow, and never continueth in one stay'.

"How am I going to live?" repeated Biddy

the new school nearly finished here . . . the new schools are not like the old,]   On nineteenth-century maps a cottage marked 'school-house' stood between Stonehouse Inn and Mockbeggar House (Gadd, 1929, 40). In 1864 the government erected a National School in Cooling for thirty-five children under the supervision of a single mistress (*Kelly's Directory: Kent*, 1882, 133). Anglican day schools, built under the auspices of the National Society for Promoting the Education of the Poor in the Principles of the Established Church, were introduced in 1809; by 1831 the Society had opened 1,300 new establishments.

The professionalization of school teaching and the introduction of a modest government initiative in 1839 to set aside money to train teachers and staff schools with competent personnel distinguish the new schools from the old. The government also began a pupil-teacher system, inspired by European examples, in an attempt to improve instructional standards. The British and Foreign School Society administered schools for Nonconformists.

"I should think from the colour of his clothes

"I should think . . . he is working in the quarries."]   Chalk and limestone were mined locally.

Early in the morning, I was to go.

Early in the morning,]   See Appendix 1.

Chapter 36   Twenty-second weekly number
27 April 1861

HERBERT and I went on from bad to worse

and Time went on, whether or no, as he has a way of doing; and I came of age] See Appendix 1.

Herbert himself had come of age

eight months before me.]   This statement puts Herbert's birthday around March, making him Pip's senior by about eight months.

In the outer office Wemmick offered me his congratulations

tissue-paper]   A term formerly used for the kind of paper on which bank-notes were printed.

It was November,]   See Appendix 1.

"This is a bank-note," said I

for five hundred pounds."]   The Bank of England issued notes in denominations ranging from £1 to £1,000 (*Leigh's New Picture of London*, 1818, 452). Five hundred pounds, paid in quarterly instalments, puts Pip securely among those at the high end of the middle class, a group estimated at about 90,000, whose earnings ranged from £150 to £500 a year. Compare the incomes of the privileged upper classes, whose annual incomes ranged from £3,000 to £50,000 and with those at the other end of the middle class. Teachers, for example, earned on average £88 a year in the mid-century, while the stipend for Church of England ministers averaged £213 a year in 1866 (Levi, 1885, quoted by Lewis). Information from the Bank of England shows that prices have increased approximately forty-fold since the mid-nineteenth century, which would make Pip's income, in equivalent terms today, about £200,000. Such conversions, however, need to be treated with caution since the relationship between prices and wages during the two eras varies greatly and renders comparisons of income alone somewhat misleading.

"When that person discloses," said Mr. Jaggers

discloses,"]   Dickens originally wrote 'appears' but substituted 'discloses' in all three instances in this paragraph.

"Mr. Pip," said Wemmick

"I should like just to run over . . . the names of the various bridges up as high as Chelsea Reach. Let's see: there's London, one; Southwark, two; Blackfriars, three; Waterloo, four; Westminster, five; Vauxhall, six."]   Chelsea Reach refers to a stretch of the river that runs through Chelsea, formerly a village on the north bank of the Thames and western limit of the metropolis. Moving west from Old London Bridge, an ancient stone structure dating from the twelfth century which was finally replaced in 1831, the bridges are Southwark (1819), Blackfriars (1769), Waterloo (1817), Westminster (1750) and Vauxhall (1816). Bridges constructed after Vauxhall Bridge include Hammersmith Suspension Bridge (1827), Hungerford Suspension Bridge (1845) and Chelsea Suspension Bridge (1858). For Old London Bridge, see chapter 46, note on p. 356.

The names of the bridges help date the novel's internal action. References to horse travel, old London Bridge, the predominance of watermen and the relative absence of steamers on the Thames provide further topographical evidence of the novel's setting early in the nineteenth century. The introduction of rail services to London in December 1836 had a major impact on London's environment: gradually, inhabitants began to move out into the surrounding countryside as additional bridges were erected across the Thames. By 1861 nine bridges rather than six spanned the river between Chelsea Reach and the Upper Pool, a distance of approximately six miles. For other changes to London occurring during the period covered by Pip's narration, see chapter 39, note on pp. 306–7.

Chapter 37

DEEMING Sunday the best day

the Union Jack] The Union flag, national flag of the United Kingdom. The British Union Flag was designed in 1606 to symbolize the union between England and Scotland under James I. This Union was formalized in 1707 through the Act of Union; with the addition of Ireland in 1801 the country became the United Kingdom. At this time, the Union flag was designed to incorporate the three crosses of St George, St Patrick and St Andrew, the patron saints of England, Ireland and Scotland respectively.

"You made acquaintance with my son, sir," said the old man

Wine-Coopering."] Wine coopers belonged to the 'wet' division of the trade, distinct from 'dry' coopers, who made barrels for a variety of dry goods. Wet coopering called for skilled work in order to make casks holding liquids absolutely watertight. Staves had to be hand-sawed and jointed at the edges, and then placed round the inner edge of an iron hoop. Next a stout wooden hoop was knocked down the barrel as far as it would go before the staves were warmed and bent. Flat top and bottom pieces were inserted, after which the wooden hoops were replaced by iron ones (*Trades for London Boys*, 1908). The introduction of machinery later in the century simplified the production of wooden barrels and eventually displaced wine coopers who worked by hand.

"No," said the old gentleman

Liverpool;] Liverpool, 'a great and important commercial town' in Lancashire on the eastern bank of the estuary of the Mersey, 178 miles north-west of London (Dugdale 3.1075). The city's prominence as a port dates from the seventeenth century; subsequent economic growth arising from shipping soon made Liverpool the foremost Atlantic port for trade in sugar, cotton, tobacco and slaves shipped from Africa to America and the West Indies. 'Fortunes are made here', wrote Southey, 'with a rapidity unexampled in any other part of England'. Certainly adventurers failed; 'yet with all the ups and downs of commercial speculation Liverpool prospers beyond all other ports' (*Letters* 107, 223). The city may have been on Dickens's mind since the visit he made to 'the dock-quays of Liverpool' in search of material he included in 'Poor Mercantile Jack', published in *AYR* on 10 March 1860 (2.462).

It was worth any money to see Wemmick

Miss Skiffins:] Dickens included the name 'Skiffins' in his *Book of Memoranda*

(14). Possibly he had seen it on a shop in the Kent Road, some ten minutes away from Wemmick's house in the district of Walworth (F[itch] 307).

Miss Skiffins was of a wooden appearance

She might have been some two or three years younger than Wemmick,]   After 'some' MS reads 'few'. Dickens gives Wemmick's age as 'near 50' (see p. 345), which makes Miss Skiffins a woman in her late forties.

The cut of her dress from the waist upward, both before and behind, made her figure very like a boy's kite;]   An effect achieved by tight-lacing; see chapter 11, note on p. 120.

While Miss Skiffins was taking off her bonnet

(she retained her green gloves during the evening as an outward and visible sign that there was company),]   See The Catechism: 'An outward and visible sign of an inward and spiritual grace' (*BCP*). The gesture suggests overcompensation: ladies wore gloves indoors only on ceremonial occasions and always removed them for meals. Compare Mrs Micawber, who, discomposed by the sudden appearance of Steerforth's 'respectable serving-man' at David and Dora's, hastily put on her brown gloves 'and assumed a genteel languor' (*DC* 28). 'Ladies should never dine with their gloves on – unless their hands are not fit to be seen' (Day 23).

Having thought of the matter with care

to help Herbert with some present income – say of a hundred a year, to keep him in good hope and heart – and gradually to buy him on to some small partnership.]   An income of about £100 a year would permit a frugal young man to live in relative comfort. Allowing for inflation and multiplied about forty-fold, in present terms Herbert would enjoy about £40,000 a year.

"You are right," he returned.

"You hit the nail on the head.]   A proverb dating from the sixteenth century.

After a little further conversation to the same effect

a jorum of tea]   A large drinking-bowl.

We ate the whole of the toast

some clean old chief of a savage tribe, just oiled.] Possibly the comparison comes from a description Dickens encountered while reading accounts of tribes in remote regions of the world. Forster mentions, speaking of Dickens's seaside reading in 1851, that he had 'a surprising number of books of African and other travel' and showed for this genre 'an insatiable relish' (Forster 6.3.57).

The Aged's reading reminded me

he required as much watching as a powder-mill.] Powder mills, which manufactured gunpowder, required all employees to take extreme care against accidentally producing a spark or a light. Precautions included removing iron-shod boots and surrendering matches, tinder-boxes or any other means of striking a spark or igniting a flame. Dickens uses the analogy elsewhere: Aunt Betsey objects to taking a tour of Doctors' Commons because she regarded 'all Courts of Law as a sort of powder-mills that might blow up at any time' (DC 23). Reports of fatal explosions occurred in the papers with some regularity (Joseph Irving, Annals, 27 May 1861 and 24 October 1861).

By-and-by I noticed Wemmick's arm

Miss Skiffins stopped it with the neatness of a placid boxer, took off that girdle or cestus] The magic girdle of Aphrodite, which makes men fall ardently in love with her. Hence, irresistibly attractive women are said to be wearers of Aphrodite's cestus. 'Cestus' also applies to the boxing glove Romans bound to their wrist with tight leather bands often weighted with iron or lead. Dickens would have known of cestus and boxing from his studies at Wellington House Academy.

At last, the Aged read himself into a light slumber.

a black bottle with a porcelain-topped cork, representing some clerical dignitary] Coloured and fancifully shaped glass bottles most likely contained either cordials or imported liqueurs. Cork bottle-stoppers designed for reuse were often topped with porcelain.

Before a week was out, I received a note from Wemmick

we found a worthy young merchant or shipping-broker . . . who wanted intelligent help, and who wanted capital, and who in due course of time and receipt would want a partner.] A ship-broker was a mercantile agent who transacted the business for a ship when it came into port. Ship-brokers often combined this work with the business of marine insurance (Simmonds 1858).

half of my five hundred pounds down,] Pip later asks Miss Havisham for £900, bringing the cost of Herbert's partnership to £1,150 (chapter 49). The high price commonly paid for apprenticeship fees (£200 to £300, according to the *Complete Book of Trades* 333) and partnerships, especially with the great overseas trading companies, restricted those who entered to the sons of the wealthiest of the merchant élite, rich farmers, the squirearchy and the nobility (L. Stone and J. C. F. Stone 233–5).

The whole business was so cleverly managed

Clarriker] The name appears in the list Dickens kept in his *Book of Memoranda* (14).

I had the greatest difficulty in restraining my tears of triumph when I saw him so happy . . . At length, the thing being done, and he having that day entered Clarriker's House . . . I did really cry in good earnest . . . to think that my expectations had done some good to somebody.] Revisions to the MS suggest that Dickens sought to intensify Pip's response to his own good actions. Originally, Dickens wrote: 'I cried in good earnest'; and later added: 'I did really cry in good earnest,' ending the sentence and the paragraph with 'when I went to bed'. The phrase 'to think that my expectations had done some good to somebody' represents a further revision made to the proofs.

The importance Dickens attached to this reflection can be inferred from its repetition (in similar phrasing) at the beginning of chapter 52 and from the last sentence he jotted down in the 'General Mems.' 2: 'The one good thing he did in his prosperity, the only thing that endures and bears good fruit' (Harry Stone, 1987, 323).

'The very emphasis that Dickens gives this note, placing it as his last comment on the whole plan, gives it almost the status of a leading "moral". . . . It is entirely consistent with Dickens's mainly sentimental and individualistic ethic that Pip's one good deed should have its reward, even for himself' (House, 1948, 184).

Chapter 38

Twenty-third weekly number
4 May 1861

IF that staid old house near the Green at Richmond

O the many, many nights and days through which the unquiet spirit within me haunted that house when Estella lived there! Let my body be where it would, my spirit was always wandering, wandering, wandering, about that house.] The lover who stands before the house of his mistress frequently appears in classical poetry; for example, Horace, *Odes* 3.10; Catullus 67; Tibullus 1.29. Compare also David Copperfield haunting Dora's house on Norwood Road (*DC* 26, 33).

The lady with whom Estella was placed

They were in what is called a good position, and visited, and were visited by, numbers of people.] Members of society in the nineteenth century observed an elaborate 'calling' etiquette, the responsibility for which fell mainly to wives since husbands were generally considered too busy to spare time for visiting. Callers left cards (more than one if other family members were included in addition to wives), each inscribed in copper-plate with the visitor's name, title and address. Calls were returned after a suitable interval, thereby initiating the process of reciprocal entertaining. Callers generally tried to avoid mornings when most people were busy, preferring instead afternoons or a specific day appointed for visiting (Wildeblood, 1973, 170–1).

In Mrs. Brandley's house and out of Mrs. Brandley's house

I suffered every kind and degree of torture that Estella could cause me. . . . She made use of me to tease other admirers,] Maria Beadnell's flirtatious behaviour caused the youthful Dickens great pain. Slater argues that the 'torture' described here and elsewhere in the novel more likely originates from an examination of old wounds and slights rather than from Ellen Ternan's actions following their meeting and subsequent relationship (73).

I saw her often at Richmond

there were pic-nics, fête days, plays, operas, concerts, parties, all sorts of pleasures,] The social meetings of the fashionable world consisted of balls, musical parties and routs:

> No metropolis boasts of more amusements than London, when the veil which ordinarily hides them from the casual observer is drawn aside. During the

season scarcely a day passes without two or three morning concerts, and balls are to be found in great profusion. (*Leigh's New Picture of London*, 1818, 340)

Throughout this part of our intercourse

and it lasted, as will presently be seen, for what I then thought a long time]   See Appendix 1.

I should have replied

that Love was commonly reputed blind,]   *The Merchant of Venice* 2.6.36: 'But love is blind, and lovers cannot see/The pretty follies that themselves commit'.

From Estella she looked at me

with her witch-like eagerness . . . she was most weird;]   An extended allusion to *Macbeth*. Compare the earlier reference to Molly (chapter 26) and one of the Weird Sisters, whom Miss Havisham also resembles in this scene.

It was with a depressed heart

the faded tatters of old banners that I have seen hanging up in cathedrals.]   Banners displayed in cathedrals were faded and tattered primarily because they were old. Some, as Thackeray notes, had been wrenched from former enemies and were hung as reminders of England's military conquests (*Four Georges*, 1862, 186). Others, symbols of investiture and power, were carried in processions on various occasions and served as decoration when not in use. The practice of embellishing churches and cathedrals with furnishings of this kind dates from medieval times (*New Catholic Encyclopedia* 2.51–2).

only we were skilful now, and played French games]   French cards, like English, have the same number (fifty-two), use the same names for the four suits but differ in the figured cards, which are whole-length. Games suitable for two players include quinze, vingt-et-un and piquet.

I lay in that separate building across the court-yard.

I therefore got up and put on my clothes, and went out across the yard into the long stone passage, designing to gain the outer court-yard and walk there]   Evidently Pip leaves the detached cottage and traces his way back to the main part of the house in an attempt to get into the main courtyard. Miss Havisham's wanderings make it difficult to gain the outer yard undetected.

On a certain occasion when the Finches were assembled in force

Mr. Drummle had not yet toasted a lady; which, according to the solemn constitution of the society, it was the brute's turn to do that day.] Ritual toasting was a common practice in men's clubs and usually took place after dinner when members circulated decanters of port and other wines. Ladies named on these occasions were frequently the reigning beauty of the season. Often a special glass was used for the purpose, inscribed with the name of a woman or with verses in her honour.

This was the only retort

barbed with wit,] From the prologue to Sheridan's *School for Scandal*, 1777: 'And half mistrustful of her Beauty's store,/She barbs with Wit those Darts too keen before' ('A Portrait' Addressed to Francis Anne Crewe').

we always talked about coming down to that Grove, as a neat Parliamentary turn of expression] The phrase appears to be a variant of 'to come down to the House', used by MPs when they plan to attend or make an appearance in the House of Commons.

I made him the extreme reply that I believed he knew where I was to be found.] Pip issues a challenge to a duel with deadly weapons, a practice confined principally to aristocrats and army officers. For duels to proceed, both sides then appointed seconds to negotiate the conditions of the combat and make sure that agreements were observed. Opponents who declined to fight lost their honour.

The object was not necessarily to kill but to fire a prescribed number of shots or to draw first blood, after which the duel would be stopped. Killing one's opponent was a felony; anyone tried and found guilty was sentenced to be hanged. Opposition to duelling mounted over time; by the 1840s it had come to be regarded as an 'execrable relic of barbarism' (Millingen 1.6). Efforts by the Anti-Duelling Association (founded 1842), the amendment of the Articles of War in 1844 to punish officers involved in attempting to promote a duel, and the final abolition of the practice incorporated in the Army Discipline and Regulation Act of 1879 (42 & 43 Vict. c. 33) led to its demise. 'In a democratic age and under a settled government [duelling] is doomed to extinction' (*Encyclopaedia Britannica*, 11th edn, 8.642).

Whether it was possible in a Christian country to get on without blood

Whether it was possible in a Christian country to get on without blood, after this, was a question on which the Finches were divided.] Clubs undertook to mediate in disputes between members. Outbursts of temper and bad feeling were punished according to the rules governing the club, and actions taken were moved, seconded and voted, with the ballot recorded for the occasion (Ralph Neville 39).

At a certain Assembly Ball

At a certain Assembly Ball at Richmond (there used to be Assembly Balls at most places then),] 'Every country town had its assembly-room – mouldy old tenements, which we may still see in deserted inn-yards, in decayed provincial cities, out of which the great wen of London has sucked all the life' (Thackeray, *Four Georges*, 1862, 87). These former centres of social life dominated by local gentry flourished from the mid-eighteenth century onwards. The rooms, public facilities, were used for various purposes, including ballroom dancing following the introduction of the quadrille from France and later the waltz from Germany. Rooms built for dancing were usually large and often decorated with gilt columns, pilasters and mirrors. Other functions held in assembly rooms included dinners, concerts, lectures and dramatic readings.

In the Eastern story

In the Eastern story, the heavy slab . . . was slowly wrought out of the quarry, the tunnel for the rope . . . was slowly carried through the leagues of rock, the slab was slowly raised . . . the rope was rove to it and slowly taken . . . to the great iron ring. All being made ready . . . and the hour come, the sultan was aroused . . . and the sharpened axe that was to sever the rope . . . was put into his hand, and he struck with it, and the rope parted . . . and the ceiling fell.] The reference is to the story of Misnar's pavilion, originally published as 'The Continuation of the Tale of the Inchanters; or Misnar, the Sultan of the East' in *Tales of the Genii* (1764), whose carefully prepared catastrophe Dickens compares to the blow about to land on Pip. Ostensibly a translation from the Persian by Sir Charles Morell, but in fact the invention of the Reverend James Ridley, the tale relates how the Sultan's vizier builds an opulent palace which is actually a trap designed to cave in on command and crush a pair of evil enchanters who have defeated the Sultan's armies and seized his throne:

> Studious that no one might interrupt or betray my Designs, I inclosed a Place near the Mountains surrounded with Trees, where I began to build a Pavilion, which I gave out was erected in Honor of my Lord the Sultan. Within this Pavilion I concealed a massy Stone, which was sawn out of the solid Rock, and which, by the Help of several Engines, was hung upon four pillars of gold and covered the whole Pavilion.
>
> The rope which upheld this massy Stone passed through one of the golden Pillars into the earth beneath, and by a secret Channel cut in the Rock was carried onward through the Side of the Mountain, and was fastened to a Ring of Iron in a Cave hollowed out of the Rock on the opposite side.

Dickens knew this book well. Forster recounts how, as a young boy, Dickens became famous 'in his childish circle' for having written a tragedy called *Misnar, the Sultan of*

India; Ridley's *Tales of the Genii* is also mentioned by David Copperfield in an explicitly autobiographical passage as one of the books belonging to a small collection 'in a little room upstairs' left to him by his father (Forster 1.1.8; *DC* 4).

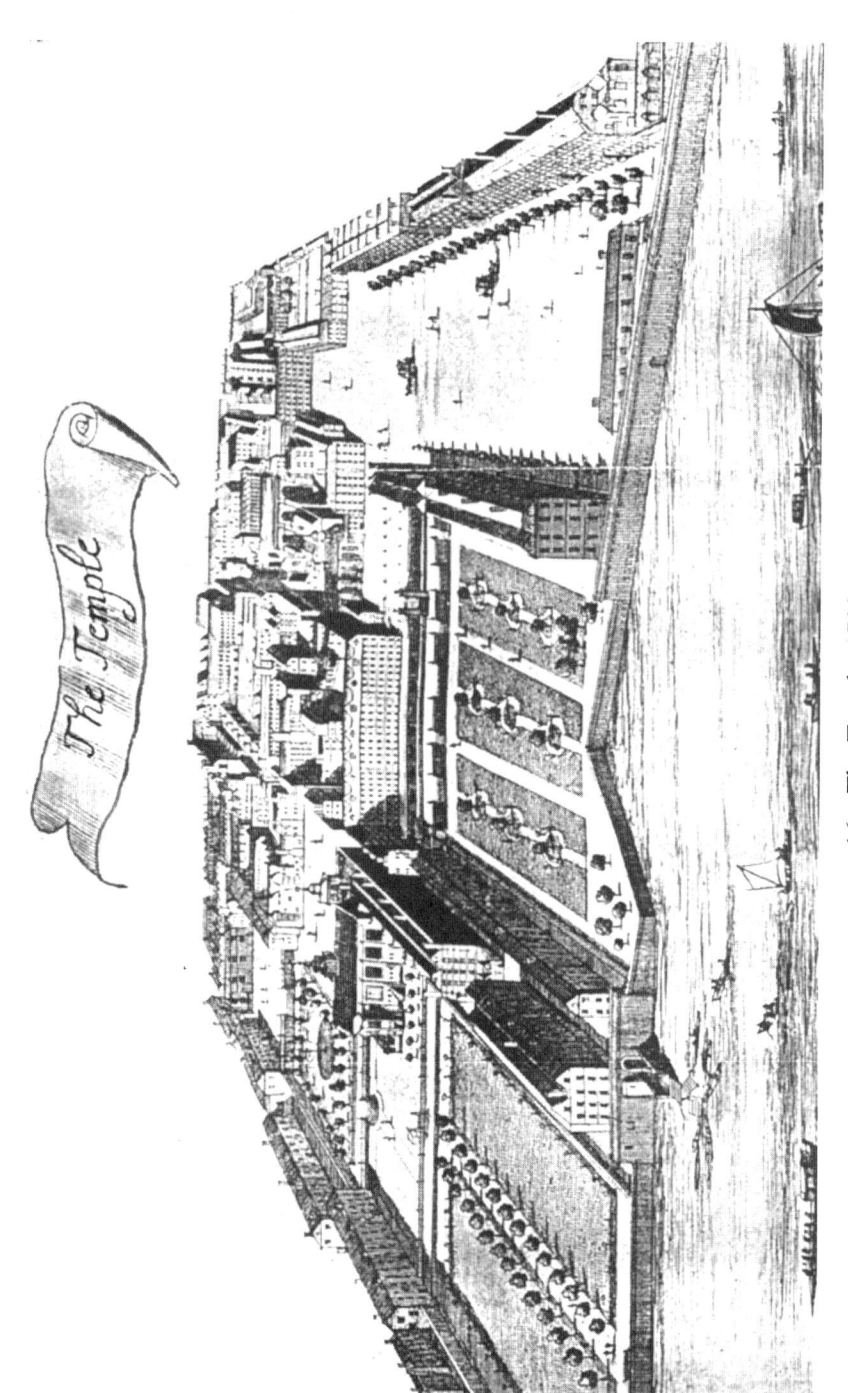

16 The Temple, 1720

17 Staircase leading to a set of chambers

Chapter 39 Twenty-fourth weekly number
11 May 1861

I WAS three-and-twenty years of age.

my twenty-third birthday was a week gone.]   See Appendix 1.

We had left Barnard's Inn . . . and lived in the Temple. Our chambers were in Garden-court, down by the river.]   See Plate 16 and Appendix 3.

Business had taken Herbert on a journey

Business had taken Herbert on a journey to Marseilles.]   Contemporary readers may have read into Herbert's 'business' in Marseilles a reference to the recently signed 'Commercial Treaty' between Britain and France, an issue which had dominated several newspapers since January 1860. Signed on 20 January and hailed as a great triumph by the advocates of free trade, the provisions of the treaty called for the total abolition of British duties on French manufactured goods (silks, gloves, artificial flowers, watches, leather, china and glassware) in return for the removal of restrictions by the French government on all the staples of British manufacture such as iron, steel and coal. A deliberate allusion, of course, remains incompatible with the dating of the action and would represent one of the novel's few anachronisms.

The port of Marseilles, a 'busy and flourishing city' with 'few fine public buildings or sights for strangers' (*Hand-Book for Travellers in France* 484), was the focus of French and Mediterranean commerce in the nineteenth century. Descriptions of the port appear in *PI* and in *LD* 1.1. Herbert's destination may also owe something to Dickens's tendency to connect him with his own oldest son, Charley, and the fact that Charley had recently landed at Marseilles on his return from China (*Letters* 9.382).

It was wretched weather; stormy and wet, stormy and wet

and mud, mud, mud, deep in all the streets.]   The language is euphemistic; medical authorities tended to speak more directly:

> In many great towns the streets are little better than dunghills, being frequently covered with ashes, dung, and nastiness of every kind. Even slaughter-houses, or killing shambles, are often to be seen in the very centre of great towns. The putrid blood, excrements, etc. with which these places are generally covered, cannot fail to taint the air, and render it unwholesome. (Buchan, 1784, 113)

According to calculations undertaken by Mayhew, four-fifths of London street-dirt consisted of horse manure and cattle dung. Ground dust from stone-paved roads mixed with rain during wet weather added a further layer of detritus 'known by the name of "mac mud," or simply "mud" ' (1967, 2.181–202). For Dickens's extended description of the mud, mist and darkness typical of London in November, see the opening paragraphs of *BH* and Shatto (1988, 22–3). Improvement in the state of metropolitan streets came later in the century.

driving over London from the East,] The winds that prevail in London during the late autumn come from the east and bring wet, stormy weather in November. Traditionally, the east wind is associated with unpleasantness and portents of trouble: 'The dreaded *East* is all the wind that blows,' writes Pope in *The Rape of the Lock*, as Umbriel repairs to 'the gloomy Cave of *Spleen*' (4.20). Folk-lore and biblical tradition appear to account for the east wind's adversarial qualities. See, for example, Genesis 41.5–6, Exodus 10.13, Psalms 48.7, and Ezekiel 17.10 and 27.26.

gloomy accounts had come in from the coast, of shipwreck and death.] Newspapers kept a tally on the loss of life and the destruction of coastal shipping following severe storms in the autumn and winter of 1860–1 (Joseph Irving, 1875).

Alterations have been made in that part of the Temple

Alterations have been made in that part of the Temple since that time, and it has not now so lonely a character as it had then, nor is it so exposed to the river.] The gradual embankment of the Thames, the start of which dates back to 1767, systematically altered the appearance of the river. Quays and a sweeping promenade replaced extensive tidal mud flats; new buildings and wharves encroached on the former natural shoreline; reducing the width of the river also deepened the water and made the waterway better suited for shipping ('The Thames Embankment', April 1844, 159, 164).

The most dramatic alteration, to which Pip refers, began in 1860, when the Metropolitan Board of Works undertook the systematic embankment of the north shore of the Thames in three sections (25 & 26 Vict., c. 93). The project began at Waterloo Bridge and proceeded east towards the Temple and Blackfriars:

> The foundations [of the Embankment] are laid upon a connected line of iron caissons and concrete, upon which is built the brick granite-faced embankment-wall; behind which, and underneath the roadway, it is proposed to construct the subways and sewers, an arrangement which will add much to the stability of the embankment-wall. . . . The section between Temple Gardens and Blackfriars bridge will be constructed on arches, so as to admit of the passage under it to docks between the roadway and the shore of barges and lighters; besides a subway for gas and water pipes and electric telegraphs. The embankment will pass by an easy curve to the level of Bridge-street, Blackfriars, where the line of roadway will be continued by the new street to Mansion House. (Quoted in Timbs, 1867, 773–4)

Other features included the addition of landing-stairs for small craft and piers for steam-boats. The Embankment wall itself was to be enriched with 'mouldings of a simple character' and massive blocks of granite to carry ornamental lights and recesses with seats.

One contemporary observer described the turmoil attending the project as 'The invasion of the metropolis by an army of excavators and bricklayers' and expressed doubts if the ensuing chaos would ever cease (Dodd 359). In fact, work on the north bank was completed in 1870 when the new Victoria Embankment was opened by the Prince of Wales. In 1865 a similar land-reclamation project commenced on the south shore and progressed upstream from Westminster to Vauxhall. The principal features of these huge undertakings remain in place today.

a storm-beaten lighthouse.]   Advances in civil engineering and the development of reflector lamps helped meet the demand for the construction of lighthouses around Britain's shores owing to increased shipping from the end of the eighteenth century onwards. An article in HW published in 1851 notes that foreigners were struck with admiration at a coastline so well provisioned ('Lighthouses and Light-Boats', 2.373). The modern pharos, 'shapely yet substantial, with [their] powerful illuminating apparatus of lamp and lenses', were capable of shining ten, twelve or twenty miles across the waves (W. H. Davenport Adams 6).

the staircase lamps were blown out . . . the lamps in the court were blown out . . . the lamps on the bridges and the shore were shuddering,]   Lamps stationed above each staircase entrance may still be seen today; these would have been oil-lamps (see Plate 17). Lamps on bridges to the east visible from Pip's quarters (Blackfriars, Southwark and Old London Bridge) may have burned gas, the source of most public lighting from the 1820s onwards.

the coal fires in barges]   That is, coal fires in galleys aboard barges on the Thames.

I read with my watch upon the table

Saint Paul's, and all the many church-clocks in the City – some leading, some accompanying, some following – struck that hour.]   John Hollingshead remarks on the density of churches standing within the one-mile radius of the City in a HW essay, 'All Night on the Monument' (17.147). For St Paul's Cathedral, see chapter 20, note on p. 182. Dickens jokes elsewhere in PP (40) and NN (11) about the irregularity with which church clocks in London struck the hour.

What nervous folly made me start

reading-lamp]   Oil-burning lamps were an alternative to candles before the widespread use of gas for indoor illumination. Kerosene (or paraffin) replaced oil at the end of the 1860s, to give way, in turn, to electricity at the end of the century.

Moving the lamp as the man moved

his age was about sixty.] This description agrees with the calculations Dickens made before completing the last third of the novel (see pp. 344–5). Approximately seventeen years have passed since the opening, at which time Pip was 6 and Magwitch in his early forties. This interval allows sufficient time for Magwitch to have gone back and forth to Australia and made his fortune (see below). See also Appendix 1.

I relinquished the intention he had detected

for I knew him!] Magwitch's reappearance fuses two conventions: the outcast's return and the inheritance convention (see below). In this instance, however, Dickens extends the device far beyond his first use of it in 'The Story of the Convict's Return' (*PP* 6; Reed 223–5).

"I've been a sheep-farmer, stock-breeder

"I've been a sheep-farmer, stock-breeder, other trades besides, away in the new world," said he; "many a thousand miles of stormy water off from this."] Grazing sheep and cattle were the first activities in New South Wales to bring wealth to the early settlers and attract others with capital. In 1810 there were 26,000 sheep and 12,500 cattle in New South Wales and Van Diemen's Land; within eleven years, these figures had increased to 290,000 sheep and 103,000 cattle (A. G. L. Shaw 93). John Macarthur, one of the pioneers of the Australian sheep and cattle industry, argued that 'no occupation, except agriculture, is to be found at this period in New South Wales for any considerable number of convicts which would make a return to defray the cost' of shipping them nearly sixteen thousand miles overseas and providing for them until they were established. Labours connected with 'the tillage of the earth and the rearing and care of sheep and cattle', he also contended, were best-calculated to help felons reform. 'When men are engaged in rural occupations their days are chiefly spent in solitude – they have much time for reflection and self-examination and they are less tempted to the perpetuation of crimes than when they are herded together in towns' (quoted in Shaw 93–4). A second and much later route to success occurred after the discovery of gold in Ballarat, Victoria, in 1851.

"I've done wonderful well.

"I've done wonderful well. There's others went out alonger me as has done well, too, but no man has done nigh as well as me.] By the 1850s, Australia had earned a reputation for opportunity to anyone willing to work hard and apply himself. Openings existed for both convicts and free settlers alike:

It is remarkable that the most successful settlers have been those who, transported for fourteen or twenty-one years, or life, on obtaining their liberty, as was usual at the end of six or eight years, abandoned all idea of returning to England – a country synonymous to them with hard work and low pay – and settled on farms, intent on making everything round them as like "home" as possible. (*Sidney's Australian Hand-book,* 1849, 45)

Samuel Sidney, also author of the weekly publication, *Sidney's Emigrant Journal,* made a similar point to the hard-working poor in England, provided they showed the tough, resilient spirit Dickens gives Magwitch: 'Action is the first great requisite of a colonist; to be able to do anything, to need the least possible assistance, to have a talent for making shift'. Prior knowledge of agriculture, he continued, is inessential and 'quite unnecessary on an Australian stock or sheep farm'. Men from cities who had never noticed a sheep before, except in a butcher's shop, made good shepherds or hut-keepers (*Sidney's Australian Hand-book* 40, 44). Others extolled the openings the colony offered in terms similar to Samuel Smiles's best-selling manual, *Self-Help* (1859). An anonymous publication, *Australia: Who Should Go; How to Go; What to Do When There* (1852), vigorously promoted the concept of self-improvement and the need to seize opportunities that the new continent offered: to get on in Australia, 'a man must be steady, industrious, and wide awake'. Knowing the value of saving money and working hard, even 'a very dull fellow' could get work and prosper. Among the trades wanted were shepherds, farm servants, agricultural labourers and female servants (2, 4).

He watched me as I laid my purse upon the table

I separated two one-pound notes. . . . They were clean and new,] The 'small-note era' began in 1797 and lasted for twenty years. In December 1817 the Bank of England resumed cash payments but did not suspend the issue of one-pound notes, despite mounting concern with incidents of forgery associated with their circulation. In 1819 the government appointed a Commission to inquire into measures to check forgers. Numerous proposals were submitted, most of which urged the adoption of intricate and expensive designs. None of the 180 recommendations was taken up, and the true expedient for opposing forgeries was ignored until 1821 when 'the issue of small notes was wholly discontinued and sovereigns were brought into circulation' (Wills and Dickens, *HW* 1.618). The newness and clean state of the notes indicate their recent issue, which could be as late as 1821, a date compatible with the suggested historical setting of the novel outlined in Appendix 1.

"Put it," he resumed, "as the employer of that lawyer

Portsmouth,] Britain's main naval port in the nineteenth century, seventy-two miles south-west of London. John Dickens was sent here to work in the Pay Office at the end of 1807 and remained until he was transferred back to London on 1 January 1815

(Allen, 1988, 27). Charles was born in a suburb of Portsmouth on 7 February 1812. Unlike Chatham, Portsmouth features infrequently in Dickens's works.

"Yes, Pip, dear boy, I've made a gentleman on you!

I swore that time, sure as ever I earned a guinea, that guinea should go to you. I swore arterwards, sure as ever I spec'lated and got rich, you should get rich.] Magwitch's route to wealth – hired hand, shepherd, and overseer of a farm – resembles steps taken by a convict mentioned by Sidney to illustrate opportunities for advancement abroad. The accomplishments of this exemplary felon lend plausibility to Magwitch's achievements, as do accounts of the rise of other convicts familiar to Dickens from government reports (see below). Magwitch's will and self-determination, a code Dickens admired and lived by himself, lend further credibility to his rise.

I lived rough, that you should live smooth;]. Life in the bush, the remote outback where sheep were raised, *was* 'rough' and far from the 'sober, orderly, conventional arrangements of an English rural parish'. There were no roads or villages, and 'little law and less gospel' (*Sidney's Australian Hand-book* 26, 14).

Accommodation for those tending sheep or cattle was spartan: a wooden hut thatched with bark and a crude bedstead made from a bullock's hide stretched over four posts driven into the ground was about as much as one could expect (Sidney, 1854, 31). Utensils included only a frying pan, iron pot, bucket and tin dish. Occasionally huts had a brick chimney; more generally smoke from the fire escaped through a hole in the roof. A cupboard, a camp-bed and a simple table with a stool were the only furnishings (Wilkes 2.261). Convict-servants received two full suits of clothes each year, in addition to food (wheat, beef or pork, tea, tobacco and sugar), while wages were 'only allowed at the option of the master' (Cunningham 2.189).

These conditions had been noted earlier, although Sidney's observations on bush life lacked the edge of critics like Henry Grey Bennett, MP. Bennett expressed shock at the primitive arrangements that prevailed in the colony of New South Wales under Lachlan Macquarie (Governor, 1810–21), whose subjects lived 'in the state of nature' unchanged since the coastal region was first settled in 1788. Surely it was not Britain's intention, Bennett chided, citing Macquarie's own description, to turn settlers and convicts 'adrift into the woods, without churches, schools, courts, barracks, hospitals, and all the other accommodations of civilised nations' (Macquarie, *Letter*, 1821, 22).

"Look 'ee here, Pip. I'm your second father.

When I was a hired-out shepherd in a solitary hut, not seeing no faces but faces of sheep till I half forgot wot men's and women's faces wos like,] Shepherds typically earned between £17 and £35 a year (*Sidney's Australian Hand-book* 66).

The lack of female companionship, to which Magwitch obliquely refers, shocked some observers. Vice 'of the most frightful and demoralising character is created and fostered by the want of female population'. To counter the harmful consequences of a 'one-sexed state', help from England was necessary: 'It is into these districts that the humanising influences of woman must be brought, by the aid of Government'. Otherwise, the consequences of the 'fearful disproportion of the sexes' (estimated at six men to one woman) 'become too horrible to be recorded' (*Sidney's Australian Hand-book* 26–7; Samuel Sidney, 1852, 32). 'Where the female does not amount to an eighth of the male population, no wonder crimes of the deepest dye should prevail amongst individuals naturally so depraved' (Cunningham 2.288).

Government investigators made a similar point: 'The general tendency of the evidence indicates that unnatural crimes are far more common in the penal colonies than would be supposed from the number of convictions for those offences' (*BPP, Crime and Punishment, Transportation*, 3, 'Select Committee Report', August 1838, xxvii). '[U]nnatural crimes' in this context refers both to acts of male homosexuality and to 'connexions with animals', a practice that existed 'particularly in the remote districts' of the Australian colonies. Shepherds rather than the stock-men, Reverend William Ullathorne, the witness, added, were less frequently offenders, unlike the latter, who were 'a much more dissolute set'. Ullathorne lacked evidence to support these allegations but offered his view that 'when a bad man is under the dominion of a passion of that kind, he will gratify that passion in any manner that suggests itself to his imagination' ('Evidence' 26). For Dickens's familiarity with the Molesworth Report, see chapter 1, note on p. 34.

'but wot, if I gets liberty and money,] A conditional pardon allowed former felons to buy and hold land, enter into trade and support themselves. Conditional pardons served two important objectives: they helped convicts to reform by giving them opportunities they would never have if they returned to England, and they decreased the government's costs by encouraging self-sufficiency in men who would otherwise remain a financial burden. Pardoned convict settlers played an important role in the colony's economy; in 1821, for example, they had over 92,618 acres of land in cultivation and owned 40,643 'head of horned cattle' and 221,079 sheep: 'By far the greater part of the trade of the Colony is in their hands. . . . In fact, to them we owe our existence as a Colony' (Macquarie 69).

I'll make that boy a gentleman!'] See below.

"Look 'ee here!" he went on, taking my watch out of my pocket

taking my watch out of my pocket, and turning towards him a ring on my finger,] Magwitch's proprietary survey of Pip's possessions and the room resembles the actions of Mr Testator's mysterious visitor, who comes up the stairs one night and enters his chambers furnished with items Mr Testator had found stored in the cellar of Lyon's Inn. Having lulled himself over time into believing that the furniture was his own, Mr Testator froze 'to the marrow' when the visitor stepped past him and examined 'first the writing-table, and said, "Mine;" then, the easy-chair, and said, "Mine;" then, the bookcase, and said, "Mine;" then, turned up the corner of the carpet, and said, "Mine!" – in a word, inspected every item of furniture from the cellar, in succession, and said, "Mine!" ' ('Chambers', *AYR*, 3.456; Spence 114–15; Foll 112–13)

And your books too. . . . You shall read 'em to me, dear boy!] Reverence for books among illiterates was not uncommon, especially in Australia. According to Samuel Sidney, 'the greatest favour' he could bestow on a neighbour was to lend him a book. Illiterate servants also valued books:

> Night after night, especially in wet seasons, I have seen them [bush servants] sitting in a circle round a fire, baking their dampers in the wood ashes, each man with a pipe and a pot of tea before him, listening with the intentness of children while the "best scholar" read the story. (*Sidney's Australian Hand-book* 30–1)

"They shall be yourn, dear boy

Let me finish wot I was a telling you, dear boy. From that there hut and that there hiring-out, I got money left me by my master (which died, and had been the same as me), and got my liberty and went for myself.] Real convicts in the early days of the colonies had taken a similar path by earning their freedom, buying land and turning to agriculture or raising sheep and cattle (*BPP, Crime and Punishment, Transportation*, 3, Molesworth Committee, 'Report', 1838, xx). Exaggerating these accounts, however, could obscure the purpose of transportation, a point Dickens made to Lord Normanby in 1840 (*Letters* 7.818). Perhaps hoping to counter stories people read in the newspapers about the fortunes left by men who had been transported many years ago, Dickens makes sure he conveys no false encouragement to felons, a warning issued earlier in 1803 by the Reverend Sydney Smith, who argued that by converting capital punishment into transportation and then founding a colony peopled by criminals the government held forth 'a very dangerous, though certainly a very unintentional encouragement to offences':

> And when the history of [New South Wales] has been attentively perused in the parish of St. Giles, the ancient avocation of picking pockets will certainly not become more discreditable from the knowledge, that it may eventually lead to the possession of a farm of a thousand acres on the river Hawkesbury. ('Australia', *Works*, 2.42).

"It warn't easy, Pip, for me to leave them parts

"It warn't easy, Pip, for me to leave them parts, nor yet it warn't safe.] Magwitch says later, 'By G—, it's Death!' Attempting to return home without a full pardon was a capital offence. The death penalty for doing so pre-dates transportation to Australia and derives from the earlier period when England shipped its unwanted criminals to plantations in America. Returning to England or being at large before the expiration of one's term was first made a capital felony in 1717 (4 Geo. I, s. 2 c. 11). Several later statutes reinforced the penalty, although in practice it was rarely acted on. Of the fourteen transports convicted in 1810 for unlawfully returning home, only one was executed. Parliament passed an Act for abolishing capital punishment in case of returning from transportation (4 & 5 Will. IV, c. 67) in 1834 (Radzinowicz 1.154–5, 4.307). See also below.

"Yes. And to sleep long and sound," he answered

I've been sea-tossed and sea-washed, months and months."]

> To survive such a voyage is quite enough for a young and stout man, and, as to women and children, how are they to survive it, crowded together in the hold of a ship, that ship knocked about by storms and tempests, the ears dinned with the rattling of the thunder, and the soul terrified by the dreadful flashes of lightning? (Cobbett 209)

Ships transporting convicts were seaworthy, and no convict ship was wrecked before 1833. But all of them pitched and rolled in the heavy swells, often making the passage 'wet' (Shaw 117). The voyage from New South Wales – some 15,900 miles – took from four to six months. The passage was slow under sail because ships stopped at least twice for water and supplies. Cape Town and Rio de Janeiro were typical ports of call on the home journey. Faster times out were recorded later in the century when the ships were required to take fewer goods to the colony: more space for supplies meant fewer stops to replenish (Cunningham 1.1). The return voyage on the same route, however, was usually slower on account of the prevailing westerlies.

"I was sent for life. It's death to come back.

There's been over-much coming back of late years, and I should of a certainty be hanged if took."] The 'over-much coming back' probably alludes to the 'ticket-of-leave' men. Prisoners in this category were given a conditional pardon which released them from forced government labour and enabled them to work on their own. But it did not grant them the right to return to England, a freedom reserved only for those who received an absolute pardon from the colonial governor and full restoration of their rights. Much earlier, reports circulated of an increase in the number of unlawful returns, but John Henry Clapper, the Superintendent of the Convict Establishment, which included all of England's hulks, stated before a Select Committee on 21 July 1831 that he knew of no executions as a result. Usually, returned transports 'are capitally convicted, sentence of death recorded, and then they are transported for life'. Men originally sent to Australia for life were treated the same way, receiving the same sentence a second time (BPP, *Crime and Punishment, Transportation*, 1.53). In 1857 the sentence of transportation was abolished, although the government continued to send some long-term prisoners to Western Australia.

Miss Havisham's intentions towards me, all a mere dream

Miss Havisham's intentions towards me, all a mere dream;] The story Dickens contributed in 1858 to 'A House to Let' (see chapter 22, note on pp. 201–2) contains 'interesting little resemblances to details' in *GE* (Clarendon xiv). Foremost among them is the rise and fall of a fairground dwarf, Mr Chops, a man preoccupied with the idea that he is 'entitled to property'. Drawing the winning lottery ticket at Egham races (compare Epsom races, where Magwitch meets Compeyson) allows him to fulfil his hopes. He leaves Mr Magsman, the travelling showman who employs him, and goes into society, only to discover false companions, lose his money and fall. He eventually returns to Magsman's travelling show and dies. Other incidentals include an echo of Compeyson in Mr Chops's false companion, Normandy, a man of 'wery genteel appearance' who sets up 'a chay and four greys' at lodgings in Pall Mall (compare Magwitch's notion that Pip must have horses and live near Hyde Park) and the way Mr Chops learns to write, taught by a young man without arms, who also works for Toby Magsman. Magwitch later relates how he was instructed by a travelling giant, an alteration in the manuscript from a dwarf (xiv). Much of the story is related by Magsman, whose vernacular expressions occasionally resemble Magwitch's.

The ironic manipulation of the inheritance convention (a device inherited from Smollett and Fielding) represents one of the achievements of *GE*. Legacies and wills confer wealth and respectability on Oliver, Dick Swiveller (*OCS*) and Martin Chuzzlewit; in *BH*, *GE* and *OMF*, the experience of wealth is shown to test and corrupt those who wait in attendance on it. The convention was also widely used by Scott, Thackeray, Collins, the Brontës and others (Lansbury 79; Reed 268–88).

He had rolled a handkerchief round his head

He] Dickens had originally written: 'There was still much of the old marsh character upon him, for he'.

I softly removed the key to the outside of his door,] Dickens overlooks this detail in the following chapter when Pip comments the next morning that 'By-and-by' Magwitch's door opened 'and he came out'.

the clocks of the Eastward churches] That is clocks belonging to churches in the City east of the Temple. See also above.

THIS IS THE END OF THE SECOND STAGE OF PIP'S EXPECTATIONS] Stage Two consists of twelve instalments published weekly between 23 February and 11 May 1861. Four instalments consisted of single chapters (chapters 22, 29, 38 and 39); the remaining eight each has two chapters. The second volume of the three-volume edition of the novel ended here.

Chapter 40   Twenty-fifth weekly number
                                                                         18 May 1861

The impossibility of keeping him concealed

I was looked after by an inflammatory old female, assisted by . . . her niece . . . they were always at hand when not wanted; indeed that was their only reliable quality besides larceny.] Women similar to college scouts were employed as cleaners and laundresses; in 'Chambers', Dickens expresses a similarly low opinion of these attendants, linking them with inefficiency and petty larceny (*AYR* 3.456). Joe later pays off the laundress, having found her drawing off feathers from the spare bed and stealing coal, wine and spirits (chapter 57).

This course I decided on

to the adjacent Lodge]   At one of the gates. See Temple ground plan, p. 441.

the watchman]   Printed 'Rules and Orders' issued in June 1822 detailed the duties of porters, watchmen and warders responsible for protecting the Temple. Following a Report on Security undertaken in 1821, Parliament specified that all public gates to the Temple should close at night, and that evening and night watchmen should institute patrols and proclaim the time of night every half-hour (Inner Temple archives). Porters also remained on duty throughout the day, under strict orders to keep out beggars and examine any suspicious basket or bundle brought in after dark 'as a precaution against the dropping of children' ('Rules and Orders', June 1822).

a man crouching in a corner.]   Watchmen were also required to inspect staircases in each building twice during the night 'in order to drive out of the Temple all such loose and disorderly persons as shall be found lurking in the staircases, or strolling about' (Archives).

It troubled me that there should have been a lurker

Fountain-court . . . the Lane,]   See Temple ground plan, p. 441.

his door with his seal on it]   Wax seals were commonly placed on doors or chests for security (*OED*). The practice does not appear to have been peculiar to the Temple or the Inns of Court either before or after they lost their predominantly legal character.

By-and-by, his door opened

By-and-by, his door opened and he came out.]   See chapter 39, note on p. 314.

"Yes, dear boy. I took the name of Provis."

Provis."] This alias appears in the *Book of Memoranda* among the list of names Dickens kept (14). Possibly he came across the name in the *Times* of 17 September 1853: a criminal named Tom Provis was found guilty of imposture in a case in the Gloucester Assizes (see also *Letters* 7.149 and n.). Also, a 'Mr Provice' appears in Dudley Costello's 'The Incomplete Letter Writer' (*HW* 9.475 and Gerson 302); the name contains the hint of 'Providence', which may have appealed to Dickens.

"Magwitch," he answered, in the same tone

"Magwitch,"] 'Magwitch' and a variant 'Mag' appear in one of the lists from which Dickens drew the names of future characters for *GE* in his *Book of Memoranda* (14). 'Mag' perhaps anticipates 'Magwitch' or exists as a recollection of Mr Magg ('Our Vestry', *HW* 5.549) or of David Mag and Thomas Mag, both names Dickens entertained for David Copperfield before he settled on 'Copperfield'. Kaplan (14 n.) suggests that 'Mag' might also point to an early version of Toby Magsman from 'Going into Society', Dickens's contribution to *A House to Let* (1858). Compare also 'Mugswitch', one of several names invented by W. E. Aytoun when he cautioned Dickens and other novelists against putting 'rubbish' into their pages, including choosing 'euphonious appellations' for their characters ('Advice to an Intending Serialist', *Blackwood's Magazine*, 1846; rpt in Collins, 1971, 211).

The name also appears to conflate *magus* (magician) with *witch*; alternatively, the first syllable may connect the name with 'magpie', a bird associated with pilfering and hoarding, or with 'magsman', a confidence man (Friedman, 1986).

A claim made in 1986 (Hoefnagel) that Magwitch's name and other jottings on the fly-leaf of a copy of Johnson's *Dictionary* Dickens owned antedate all other notes Dickens made about the novel was challenged on calligraphic grounds in 1987 (Tillotson). Subsequent investigations have proved conclusively the inauthenticity of these notes as memoranda in Dickens's hand referring to the novel (Meckier, 1992).

"chrisen'd Abel."] Dickens evidently hesitated before he chose Abel, striking out George and another name before introducing Abe, to which he added the 'l' (*Norton* 462). The biblical Abel, a shepherd, was murdered by his older brother, Cain, a farmer, when Yahweh rejected Cain's sacrifice for no obvious reason (Genesis 4.1–8). Magwitch's given name perhaps hints at his success as a sheep farmer in Australia and later persecution by a sworn enemy (Compeyson) aided by the Cain-like outcast Orlick. In the New Testament, Abel is the prototypical martyr, whose 'righteous blood' is shed when he dies for his faith (Matthew 23.35, Hebrews 11.4, 12.24). In *OMF*, Dickens uses the phrase 'Better to be Abel than Cain' as a chapter title (4.7). The name Abel had a brief vogue among Puritans but has not been used widely since the seventeenth century.

He ate in a ravenous way that was very disagreeable

He ate in a ravenous way that was very disagreeable, and all his actions were uncouth, noisy, and greedy.] 'Making a noise in chewing or breathing hard in eating, are both unseemly habits, and ought to be eschewed'. Readers of *Hints on Etiquette* were also charged not to make 'a disgusting noise with their lips, by inhaling their breath strongly whilst taking soup – a habit which should be carefully avoided' (Day 21–2).

"I'm a heavy grubber, dear boy," he said

heavy grubber,] A slang expression for someone with a hearty appetite. The phrase is used by a London chimney sweep in Paul Pry, *Oddities of London Life* (1838): 'She chucks ony von tater at me, and a bit of meat vot aint of no use to sich a heavy grubber as I am' (1.235).

Sim'larly, I must have my smoke . . . it's my belief I should ha' turned into a molloncolly-mad sheep myself, if I hadn't a had my smoke."] Tobacco was included by many masters as part of the supplies allowed shepherds in the bush (*Sidney's Australian Hand-book* 22, 66). 'Indeed, without the aid of that magic care-killer, the pipe,' one observer believed that the greater part of the convict population would have taken to the bush in a week after their arrival, before exposure to solitude had 'attuned their minds to rural prospects and industrious pursuits' (Cunningham 2.190–1). Early in the century, smoking was almost uniformly regarded as a 'low' habit and unfit for civilized society (Day 27). For other signs of coarseness, see below.

As he said so, he got up from table

Negro-head.] A strong, black plug tobacco which had been softened with molasses or syrup and pressed into cakes, which were generally called Cavendish. The product was not unlike 'shag tobacco', which was treated with molasses when picked, then boiled in a decoction made from the stalks and finally formed into rolls. Shag tobacco, widely regarded as an inferior kind, was variously called Oroonoko, Pigtail, or Roll tobacco (*Dictionary of Trade*, 1844).

"I mustn't see my gentleman a footing it in the mire of the streets

Horses to ride, and horses to drive, and horses for his servant to ride and drive as well.] To provide for such symbols of wealth and gentility, Pip would need a groom, a coachman and perhaps a coach-house as well.

Shall colonists have their horses (and blood 'uns, if you please, good Lord!) and not my London gentleman?] 'Colonists' in this context refers to the free settlers, or the 'Exclusives', the élite of New South Wales, including military officers, civilian administrators and a small group of well-heeled settlers with assets of £1,000 or more (*Sidney's Australian Hand-book* 2). Members of this class generally opposed the idea of penal rehabilitation and resisted attempts by former felons to enter polite society. 'Emancipists', in their view, remained inherently tainted, despite their having won their freedom and acquired, like Magwitch, considerable wealth. Lines drawn between the two classes, in fact, remained so distinct in New South Wales that 'Any connexion with convicts would at once preclude admission' to the circle of residents with claims to gentility. Should 'an officer or other person, contract marriage ties with any of the lower classes, he would forthwith be shut out' (Wilkes 2.220).

"We'll show 'em another pair of shoes]   A colloquial expression meaning 'a different matter'. Compare Wegg's comment: 'That, sir, is quite another pair of shoes' (OMF 1.15).

"Well," he returned, "there ain't many.

Botany Bay;]   Explorers led by Captain James Cook landed at Botany Bay, a coastal inlet just south of Sydney, New South Wales, in April 1770. The variety of unclassified plants and animals enabled Joseph Banks (1743–1820) and his fellow-botanists to accumulate so many specimens and drawings that Cook named the low, flat shores 'Botany Bay' to commemorate their triumph.

Almost eighteen years later eleven ships from England's First Fleet under the command of Captain Arthur Phillip anchored there in January 1788 with a different mission: the establishment of Britain's first penal settlement in Australia. Following the advice of Banks, and anxious to solve the crisis of England's hulks created by the rebellion of the American colonies (see chapter 2, note on p. 46), the government looked for a solution. The argument for colonizing Australia appeared to make sense because it offered a cheaper alternative to building new gaols. It also gave politicians a chance to remove large numbers of the country's 'criminal classes' to a remote place 'beyond the seas' far from civilized life. Convict labour, furthermore, could help a new settlement find its feet and expand further Britain's territorial possessions. Economic and strategic arguments thus added to the appeal of Australia and won support for the main motive, which was to empty England's gaols as quickly and cheaply as possible.

Within one week of arrival, finding the soils too sandy, the water supply inadequate and the bay too shallow for his ships, Phillip moved the settlement about five miles north to Sydney harbour, where he discovered better conditions. A period of hardship followed for convicts and soldiers alike, as short rations and work in extreme conditions with inadequate supplies took their toll. Brutal discipline, believed necessary to maintain order under precarious conditions, made life worse. But the penal settlers maintained their hold on the land as they struggled to produce food and fight off the demoralized torpor associated with the early years of the colony.

A Second and Third Fleet brought supplies and more convict labourers in 1790 and 1791. A new and more promising settlement inland developed at Parramatta, where a convict succeeded in growing wheat and maize. And as the acres under cultivation increased (some private and the rest public) signs appeared by 1792 that the colony of New South Wales would become self-supporting. The discovery in 1813 of a way through the Blue Mountains revealed the 'outback' so crucial to the establishment of the sheep-farming industry. Further development followed with the arrival of the first free settlers in 1815 and the establishment of additional communities.

The name Botany Bay, however, quickly entered the language as a synonym for Australia, a distant place to which convicts were delivered with finality. Giving evidence before a Select Committee on 3 April 1811, James Ives, Keeper of Horsemonger Lane gaol, Southwark, stated: 'I know that every one that ever I have heard of or known would do anything in the world rather than go to Botany Bay, or return there again; they have a general dislike to transportation, to going out of this country'. Convicts, he added, do not like Botany Bay because it cut off all communication with their homeland. It also rendered useless any money they might carry with them because it could buy no comforts there (BPP, *Crime and Punishment. Transportation*, 1, 'Appendix . . . . 31 May 1811', 84–5). Compare also the author of *Old Bailey Experience*: 'The only punishment [convicts] dread is transportation; they hold all others in contempt' (42).

"Dear boy," he returned

"there's disguising wigs can be bought for money, and there's hair powder, and spectacles, and black clothes – shorts and what not.] Wigs and hair powder belong to the eighteenth century when men used powder (pulverized and scented starch) to whiten wigs (*Dictionary of Trade*, 1844). Powder, which was introduced towards the end of the sixteenth century, also served to keep hair 'clean' before regular washing became common. Its application called for an elaborate ritual. One began by spreading out a white powdering cloth on the carpet and then setting to work with a powder puff and powder knife in an effort to apply powder evenly to the forehead and temples (Bourchier, 1873, 1.343). An annual tax on powder, introduced in 1795 (35 Geo. III, c. 112), discouraged its use, particularly by barbers, who required it to dress hair and wigs (*Complete Book of Trades* 26). By the mid-nineteenth century, hair powder was almost extinct, except for use by 'eccentric belles and aristocratic footmen' (Rimmel, 1865, 208).

'Shorts', or knee-breeches worn with silk or worsted stockings, belong to the same period; trousers superseded knee-breeches in the early decades of the nineteenth century. Beginning in the latter half of the eighteenth century, black became the predominant colour for English gentlemen and professional men (e.g. doctors and lawyers).

"And so I swear it is Death," said he

Death by the rope, in the open street not fur from this,] Newgate Prison was nearby. See Appendix 4, map pp. 442–3. The practice of executing felons on a scaf-

CHAPTER FORTY 321

fold erected outside in the street continued until 1868. Under the provisions of the Capital Punishment Amendment Act (31 & 32 Vict., c. 24), authorities were required henceforth to conduct hangings within the privacy of the prison walls.

As he was at present dressed

in a seafaring slop suit, in which he looked as if he had some parrots and cigars to dispose of,] The comparison conveys a sense of disapproval. Slops, the dress of sailors, typically consisted of loose trousers and a short, coarse woollen jacket called a pea-coat. Returning from abroad, seamen often came back with exotic birds from the tropics; together with soldiers, they were among the first to smoke cigars, a habit which, in social terms, signalled a rough-and-ready individual disdainful of the prejudice against smoking in general, an attitude which prevailed among the respectable middle class well into the century (Altick 240–9). Innumerable parrots 'brought from foreign parts', Dickens noted in 'Bound for the Great Salt Lake' (AYR 9.444), frequently ended up in public houses in London's dockside area.

something between a dean and a dentist.] Possibly alliteration influenced the comparison. Deans in their ecclesiastical dress wore long black coats while the attire of prosperous London dentists often matched the well-appointed rooms from which they worked. One retrospective account by a patient describing a visit in 1830 spoke of the dentist's coat, 'fancy waistcoat and slippers, all of the brightest colours' and commented that he thought 'this peculiar costume seemed to indicate its suitability for either day or night wear'. By the 1880s, frock coats had become common and prevailed until the introduction of white drill jackets in the later 1930s. The professional status of dentists emerged in the second half of the nineteenth century, following the foundation of the College of Dental Surgery in 1856 and the Medical Act of 1858, which granted members of the Royal College of Surgeons the right to institute examinations and award certificates of fitness to successful candidates. Prior to that time, dentistry had been a trade in the hands of the uneducated and unqualified, a sideline practised by blacksmiths, hairdressers, corn-doctors and cuppers (J. Menzies Campbell 82–5, 18).

There being to my knowledge

in Essex-street, the back of which looked into the Temple,] Essex Street off the Strand lies about 200 feet west of Garden Court and forms the western boundary of the Middle Temple (see Temple ground plan, p. 441). The Strand and the river are respectively to the north and the south.

Mr. Jaggers nodded.

New South Wales,] The territorial definition of New South Wales changed significantly during the course of the century. In 1788 the phrase was applied to the eastern half of the Australian continent, although usage restricted it to the penal and agricultural colonies established on the eastern seaboard between 1788 and 1835. During that period it was a narrow strip about 860 miles in length on which the government, churches, gaols, gallows 'and all other appendages and excrescences of civilisation' existed. Beyond and to the west lay 'a vast, and, in great part, undiscovered tract of land in a state of nature, the property of the Crown, rented by the settlers and the squatters, who raise the flocks and herds, in which the true wealth of Australia lies' (*Sidney's Australian Hand-book* 14). In 1842 opposition from residents led to a ban on any further importation of convicts into the colony.

"I communicated to Magwitch – in New South Wales

he was not at all likely to obtain a pardon;] A pardon was the king's prerogative. See chapter 56, note on pp. 405–6.

Wemmick was out

I went straight back to the Temple,] See Appendix 4, map pp. 442–3.

Next day the clothes I had ordered

from head to foot there was Convict in the very grain of the man.] Specifically, 'convict' here refers to someone undergoing a sentence of penal servitude (that is, a sentence of not less than three years), but more important is the metaphorical implication of indelibility. In every aspect of Magwitch's demeanour, Pip sees a residual coarseness that sets him apart from respectable circles of English life.

This attitude appears to be consistent with Dickens's belief that the hardened criminal, whatever the circumstances responsible for that conditioning, remains an outsider incapable of joining society despite his financial success in Australia.

The influences of his solitary hut-life

his solitary hut-life ... gave him a savage air that no dress could tame;] Prolonged exposure to hardship in the outback coarsened men, but beneath their rude appearance, their lack of manners and their 'strange oaths' lay sterling characteristics: frugality, industry and courage. These virtues of Sidney's 'Australian Stockman', whom Magwitch loosely resembles, need 'only cultivation to ripen into all that we most admire in our old Saxon yeomanry' (*Sidney's Australian Hand-book* 32). Born into a low sphere of life and living a solitary existence, or 'with companions as rude as himself', the outdoors man rarely loses the 'barrack way[s]' Pip and Herbert instinctively reject in Magwitch, until growing familiarity with him alters their perception.

Concludes Sidney: 'truly among these men there is a richer and riper harvest to be gathered than among the party-coloured pagans on whom year after year hundreds of thousands of pounds are expended, with infinitely small returns'.

his great horn-handled jack-knife]   A large folding pocket-knife with a handle inlaid with an animal's horn.

pannikins]   Metal drinking-cups made from tinned iron.

Words cannot tell what a sense I had

all the crimes in the Calendar,]   'Calendar' refers to *The Newgate Calendar*, subtitled 'the Malefactors' Bloody Register', a generic title for the various compilations of criminal biographies popular during the eighteenth and nineteenth centuries. Most *Calendars* ran to several hundred pages per volume. Some included fine engravings of criminals' portraits or trial and execution scenes, expensive productions beyond the reach of common readers. The accounts contained much that was sensational and salacious, although publishers professed moral didacticism as their goal in making these records of England's most notorious criminals available to the public. The first five-volume edition of *The Newgate Calendar*, beginning with crime stories from 1700, appeared in 1774; subsequent editions and reissues remained popular throughout the nineteenth century.

enlist for India as a private soldier.]   See chapter 14, note on pp. 134–5.

I doubt if a ghost could have been more terrible to me

I doubt if a ghost could have been more terrible to me,]   Joe's comment about the difficulties Wemmick faced in the opening scene of *Hamlet* when he met the ghost (chapter 27) and Wemmick's later description of Compeyson sitting behind Pip in another theatre on a later occasion 'like a ghost' (chapter 47) are two of three allusions to Shakespeare's play. Taken together, all three reinforce the existence of former ties and obligations to others. Further emphasis on the need to swear by one's commitment, as the ghost commands Hamlet, occurs when Magwitch orders Herbert to promise – 'Lord strike you dead on the spot, if ever you split' – total secrecy about his visit to Pip. See also below.

a complicated kind of Patience]   Patience, the English term for solitaire, a card game played by dealing out the cards and then assembling them in special groups according to established rules. Because the game is played by one person it is easy for players to introduce minor rules of their own, which accounts for the many variants that exist.

surveying me with the air of an Exhibitor,] Magwitch's behaviour is compared with Frankenstein's. See below.

The imaginary student pursued by the misshapen creature he had impiously made, was not more wretched than I, pursued by the creature who had made me,] Victor Frankenstein, Mary Shelley's student of natural philosophy, pursues and is pursued by the monster he created. The novel's close relates how Frankenstein dies aboard his ship, exhausted and ill after tracking his 'demonical enemy' to the Arctic wastes.

This comparison has been described as 'curiously double-edged' (Sadrin 235–6). In the first half of the sentence, Pip is equated with Frankenstein, Mary Shelley's 'imaginary student'; in the second, he is the monster, the creation of Magwitch, who now pursues him. The word 'creature' similarly refers both to Pip and to Magwitch. Dickens's reworking of Mary Shelley's ideas are discussed by Crawford and by Stubblefield. See also chapter 27, note on p. 237.

"Quiet! It's Herbert!" I said

with the airy freshness of six hundred miles of France upon him.] Herbert had just come from Marseilles (see chapter 39, note on p. 305). Dickens appears to have associated travel in France with beneficial effects. Summer visits in the 1850s and then later trips across the Channel, either alone or with a companion, perhaps account for this.

"It's all right, dear boy!" said Provis

split] A slang expression meaning to inform or betray.

Chapter 41

Twenty-sixth weekly number
25 May 1861

Never quite free from an uneasy remembrance

the street was empty when I turned back into the Temple. . . . As I crossed by the fountain, I saw his lighted back windows]   For a possible route, see Appendix 4, p. 441. The proximity of Essex Street would have made Magwitch's lodgings visible from the staircase entrance to Pip's chambers in Garden Court.

"What am I fit for?

to go for a soldier.]   See chapter 14 note on p. 134.

"My good Handel, is it not obvious

with Newgate in the next street,]   See Appendix 4, map pp. 442–3.

He came round at the appointed time

a "fashionable crib" near Hyde Park, in which he could have "a shake-down."]   Underworld slang for a house and a bed respectively. In the nineteenth century the 'higher orders' and *'people of condition'* congregated in Hyde Park every Sunday afternoon, 'as thick as idle moths' on a sunny day, exhibiting their taste in clothes and discussing the state of Europe, 'a *mêlée* of equestrians, pedestrians, and charioteers; Dukes and Duchesses, horses and carriages, Lords, ladies, grooms, pimps, panders, and black-legs' (Wight, 1833, 42). For Hyde Park, see also chapter 22, note on p. 206.

Chapter 42

"DEAR boy and Pip's comrade.

I am not a going fur to tell you my life, like a song or a story-book.] Printed on a single sheet or broadside, and sold by street hawkers and itinerant salesmen, the lives of notorious criminals were among the most popular subjects for ballads, many of which were doggerel accounts of criminals' careers composed in the form of confessions and prepared for sale at the time of the prisoner's trial and execution. 'Story-books', or novels about criminals, enjoyed an equal vogue, especially in the 1830s. See also chapter 43, note on p. 337.

In jail and out of jail, in jail and out of jail, in jail and out of jail. There, you've got it. That's *my* life pretty much,] This account of Magwitch's 'life' begun 'in jail' and spent 'in jail and out of jail' illustrates one of the failures in the system of criminal justice: 'Deep-seated and serious as the mischief in . . . [the case of the young] evidently is, either nothing would be done . . . or something very useless' (Dickens and Morley, 'In and Out of Jail', HW 7.241).

Over two hundred prisons in England and Wales served to confine felons, petty offenders, debtors, and people arrested pending trial. London offered a wide variety of penal establishments, ranging from: the Tower (see chapter 54, pp. 386–7) for 'State delinquents of rank'; to several debtors' prisons; Bridewells (see below); a military prison (the Savoy); and Newgate.

"I've been done everything to, pretty well

I've been locked up, as much as a silver tea-kettle.] Household silver was commonly kept under lock and key to protect it from burglars and dishonest servants.

I've been carted here and carted there, and put out of this town and put out of that town,] Legislation dating from the sixteenth century permitted the removal of the indigent and other 'undesirables' by parish authorities. The practice was designed to save money and reduce expenses incurred by providing relief. Extra-legal devices such as oral warnings of arrest and notices posted outside villages and towns also threatened vagrants and beggars with immediate arrest, unless they left the district immediately. See Paroissien, 1992, 88–9.

stuck in the stocks,] That is, placed in a sitting posture between two planks, the upper of which was movable, secured at either end to posts in the ground. Each plank had holes cut to receive the offender's ankles. This form of discipline (inflicted chiefly on idlers, drunkards and vagrants) dates from medieval times and belonged to the old belief that punishments carried out in public served to deter others. By the early nineteenth century, the stocks had fallen into disuse and were abolished in 1837, together with the pillory, a more serious form of corporal punishment and the cause of loss of life when vindictive crowds stoned unpopular victims to death (McLynn 282–3; Walker 1192).

and whipped]   See chapter 20, note on p. 184.

and worried and drove.]   That is, driven from place to place like cattle, the fate of many vagrants whose wandering habits under existing statutes rendered them 'Rogues and Vagabonds', subject to imprisonment for six months. Hanoverian statutes were sufficiently vague as to allow authorities to prosecute persons who wandered abroad and failed to give 'a good account of themselves'. Many fell into this category, including gypsies, fortune-tellers 'pretending skill in Physiognomy', petty chapmen, unlicensed pedlars and persons who pretended to go to work 'in Harvest, without a proper Certificate from the Parish' (17 Geo. II, c. 5, and subsequent Acts).

down in Essex, a thieving turnips for my living.]   Essex, one of the four Home Counties, lies to the north-east of the Thames. Turnips, together with clover, were regarded as 'the two main pillars of the best course of British husbandry' (Loudon, 1857, 854). Turnips served as food for sheep and cattle in winter, they contributed to the fertility of the soil, and they were widely used in soups and stews.

– a tinker – and he'd took the fire with him,]   Tinkers were itinerant workmen who performed makeshift repairs to metal utensils and household articles. They relied principally on soldering and hammering out metal, hence their need for a fire, which they built in a brazier. Carrying a brazier evidently set tinkers apart from other trampers, vagrants and roving travellers in search of work. In *DC*, one of the 'ferocious-looking ruffians' who threatens David during his flight to Dover stands out in his memory: 'a tinker, I suppose, from his wallet and brazier' (13).

'This is the way it was

measured my head,]   An allusion to phrenology, a quasi-respectable theory of human behaviour based on the assumption that 'the agitation of a man's brain by different passions, produces corresponding developments in the form of his skull' ('Our Next-Door Neighbour', *SB*). Dickens admitted to Charles Lever in February 1860 to believing in phrenology 'as an essential part of the truth of physiognomy' (*Letters* 9.216). Phrenologists assigned behaviours to specific contours of the head and arranged character traits hierarchically, starting with the animal propensity of Amativeness (number 1) at the lowest part of the back of the head, and progressing to the perceptive and reflective faculties (numbers 22–35) located in the forehead. Phrenology was founded by Johann Kaspar Spurzheim (1776–1832) and spread by Franz Joseph Gall (1758–1828) and George Combe (1788–1858).

Although by 1826 'craniological mania' was said to have spread like the plague and possessed 'every gradation of society from the kitchen to the garret', its advances in the fields of penal reform, psychiatry and education were far less explicit. Later in the century, scrutiny of the criminal's head picked up momentum in an attempt to identify the 'criminal type', but the greatest application developed in the field of racial anthropology (Cooter 135, 259).

Collections of skulls and plaster casts of heads were a further manifestation of the vogue for phrenology. Some were open to the public, such as the Museum of Comparative Anatomy of Paris, under the care of Baron Cuvier and Spurzheim, while others belonged to individuals. Mr Deville, a London lamp-manufacturer, began his collection in 1817 and amassed over 5,000 skulls and casts. Among them were examples illustrating painters, sculptors, architects, navigators, poets, musicians, pugilists, criminals and the insane (Timbs, 1865, 3.262–3).

giv me tracts what I couldn't read,] The idea for giving prisoners moral and religious tracts dates from the 1770s. Jonas Hanway, John Howard and other reformers advocated combining solitary confinement and hard labour with religion in an attempt to correct behaviour and accustom prisoners to good habits of hard work and self-discipline. Emphasis on religion assumed the possibility of achieving an inner change as an alternative to bodily torment and punishment. By the late 1830s, religious and moral instruction served as the guiding objective at London's Millbank prison (1816); likewise, Pentonville (completed in 1842), which was widely regarded as the most comprehensive expression of Victorian penal philosophy, relied heavily on attempts to turn its inmates into Christian citizens (Christopher Harding *et al.* 119, 149–53).

"Tramping, begging, thieving, working sometimes when I could

"Tramping,] 'Tramps' (AYR 3.230–4) provides a series of 'notes' on the kinds of tramp Dickens encountered during his own walks in Kent on bright summer days. Unlike the solitary and reflective figures Wordsworth encountered on public roads earlier in the century, the tramps whom Dickens met often tended to be gruff bullies or artful beggars adept at wheedling money for drink. Most vicious, by far, 'of all the idle tramps' was 'the tramp who pretends to have been a gentleman'. This shameful creature lolled about 'hedge tap-rooms' in his ragged clothes, ready to sponge on the poorest boy 'for a farthing' or interpose '(if he could get anything by it) between the baby and the mother's breast' (232).

a bit of a labourer, a bit of a waggoner, a bit of a haymaker, a bit of a hawker,] All were marginal occupations undertaken by unskilled workers for little pay. A waggoner drove a waggon, a strongly built, four-wheeled vehicle for the conveyance of sacks of coal, wheat, flour or other heavy goods. Waggons were pulled by a team of draught horses from either end, making waggons suitable for use in narrow streets and wharves where it was impossible to turn around. The load was discharged at either side, not at the ends (William Bridges Adams 280). Migrants and others helped with hay-making; a hawker earned his living as an itinerant salesman offering miscellaneous wares. Regulations passed in 1810 (50 Geo. III, c. 41) required hawkers to take out a licence.

A deserting soldier in a Travellers' Rest, what lay hid up to the chin under a lot of taturs,] Efforts to catch deserters from His Majesty's service extended to keeping a watch for soldiers and sailors, together with felons and thieves, and circulating a list of names and descriptions among civil authorities. Desertion ranked as a major crime; those who were caught were lashed with a knotted 'cat' and tattooed with the 'deserter's escutcheon', the letter 'D', on the left shoulder, to prevent men from enlisting, deserting and then repeating the process for bounty money (Chandler 173; Myerly 84). Travellers' Rests were charitable houses providing cheap shelter for tramps and other homeless people on the move. In slang parlance, 'travellers' included ruffians, beggars and thieves.

a travelling Giant what signed his name at a penny a time] Dickens originally wrote 'travelling dwarf'. Unusually tall people often exploited their stature and made a career by exhibiting themselves. Robert Hale, 'the Imperial Norfolk Giant' (died 1851), was widely regarded as one of London's curiosities, standing at 7 feet 6 inches and weighing 33 stone. Hale visited the United States in 1848, where he remained for two years attached to Barnum's Circus. On 11 April 1851 he was presented to Queen Victoria, who gave him a gold watch and chain (Timbs, 1865, 2.295). Other well-known giants included 'The French Giant' (7 feet 4 inches), the 'Yorkshire Youth' (7 feet 8 inches) and the 'The Cambridge Giant', all of whom travelled about the country as central attractions of theatrical shows ('Human Freaks', Box 1, Johnson Collection).

"At Epsom races, a matter of over twenty year ago

Epsom races,] Epsom, formerly a village and spa eighteen miles south-west of London, declined when the wells were closed in 1702, only to be revived with the introduction of horse racing, which began on the Surrey Downs in 1779 when the 12th Earl of Derby put up the first stakes. Annual races held there over four days in June soon made Epsom 'the metropolis of English racing' (Wills and Dickens, *HW* 3.241). The two principal races, held on consecutive days, are the Oaks (named after the earl's country seat) and the Derby.

The selection of Epsom as the site for the first meeting of the two criminals adds to the novel's verisimilitude, for the races attracted not only fashionable people but also conjurers, dramatic troupes and performers, thimble-riggers, rogues, cheats, trampers and criminals of all kinds. The population of Epsom on Derby Day surged into 'millions', and large tents were erected for the sale of food and drink; gambling and dice went on at 'a fearful rate' (*HW* 3.241; Grant, 1839, 1.88–93).

a matter of over twenty year ago,] Dickens added 'over' to the original reading. The MS shows his deliberations over the time period. The earlier readings are: '<say five and twenty years ago>'; '<more nor five and> twenty years ago'; and 'a matter of twenty years ago'. See also note below.

His right name was Compeyson;] The manuscript also suggests hesitancy over Compeyson's name, which appears here and in chapter 45 as 'Compey'. In chapter 47, Dickens uses 'Compeyson' and retains this version throughout. Literally, 'Compeyson' means 'co-countryman'. Both names appear in the *Book of Memoranda* (14).

"He set up fur a gentleman, this Compeyson

he'd been to a public boarding-school and had learning.] Compeyson's moral failings were hardly representative of the advantages Dickens associated with the 'sound, liberal, comprehensive education' good public boarding-schools imparted. 'A boy there is always what his abilities or his personal qualities make him' (*Speeches* 333–6). See also chapter 23, note on p. 213.

" 'Yes, master, and I've never been in it much.'

Kingston Jail . . . on a vagrancy committal.] The county gaol at Kingston-upon-Thames, Surrey, was small and dirty, typical of prisons and lock-ups all over the country in the later part of the eighteenth century. When John Howard toured it in 1782 he noted that prisoners were not given any employment (197). In *OT*, Blathers and Duff visit this same cage or lock-up to investigate a rumour about two men and a boy held there possibly connected with the attempted robbery in Chertsey (31).

Vagrancy (from the Latin *vagari*, 'to wander') legislation proliferated under the Elizabethan Poor Law in an attempt to restrict the movement of suspicious persons with no visible means of support. A subsequent Act passed in 1743–4 referring to 'Idle and Disorderly Persons' recognized several classes of vagrant, including 'Persons, who not having the wherewithal to maintain themselves, live idly without employment, and refuse to work for the usual Wages' (17 Geo. II, c. 5). Convictions under this and subsequent Acts carried one month's imprisonment (Colquhoun, 1806, 442–3). Kingston, so-called from the sixth century because kings resided here, is now a large town ten miles south-west of London.

"I went to Compeyson next night

Compeyson's business was the swindling, handwriting forging, stolen bank-note passing, and such-like.] Forging bills of small denomination and uttering or passing stolen bank notes belong specifically to 'the small note era' of 1797 to 1817 (Wills and Dickens, *HW* 1.618). Both were capital crimes, but before the Bank of England's introduction of one-pound notes in 1797 forging bank-notes was rare. After the one-pound note was introduced, the total number of prosecutions for forgery in the next twenty years rose to 870. 'In the days of uttering forged one-pound notes by people tempted up from the country, how many hundreds of wretched creatures . . . swung out of a pitiless and inconsistent world' ('Night Walks', *AYR* 3.350).

To pass stolen notes, thieves altered serial numbers and issue dates stamped on each bank-note by cutting out some numerals and inserting others. Efforts by banks to circulate information and supply lists of notes reported stolen failed to deter swindlers. But nine years after the resumption of gold currency in 1817 convictions by the Bank of England had dropped to under a hundred, and only eight people were executed during that period. In 1830 the death sentence for all minor offences, including forgery, was repealed (HW 1.618).

Embezzlement, another of Compeyson's activities, increased from the 1850s onwards, with women often the victims of schemes to defraud them of money or property much in the way Miss Havisham suffers. The case of Miss Frederica Johnstone offers a representative example widely reported at the time when one Vincent Collucci attempted to swindle her out of £1,900. First, the two became engaged to be married. Collucci then obtained £250 from his fiancée on the pretence of having to go to Italy to see his mother. Collucci returned to find that Miss Johnstone had changed her mind about marrying him, but by that time she had given him £2,000. When she asked for the return of her letters to him, the ungallant Italian demanded a further £2,000. Pretending to comply, Miss Johnstone employed someone to hand over a packet supposedly containing the letters. Collucci was arrested, tried at the Old Bailey in October 1861 and sentenced to three years' penal servitude, much to his surprise (Irving, *Annals*, 1875; Sir William Hardman 63).

"There was another in with Compeyson

as was called Arthur – not as being so chrisen'd, but as a surname.] The comment seems to suggest Magwitch's ignorance about names since the 'Arthur' referred to is Arthur Havisham and not a Mr Arthur. See the note Herbert writes to Pip at the end of the chapter: 'Young Havisham's name was Arthur. Compeyson is the man who professed to be Miss Havisham's lover'.

some years afore,] See Appendix 1.

the king's taxes.] The phrase refers to revenues derived from the Crown's urban estate, commercial and residential property mainly in central London, the surplus of which is paid to the Exchequer in return for the civil list approved by Parliament to help meet the expenses of the royal family. This arrangement dates from 1760 and the reign of George III. The current value of the properties managed by the Crown estate is a record £2.61 billion (*Financial Times*, 10 July 1997, 9).

with the horrors on him,] The popular term for *delirium tremens*, a disorder which 'arises from excess in drinking spiritous liquors, or from the abuse of opium' (Keith Imray 204). The symptoms Magwitch observes in Arthur Havisham – screaming, sweating, the inability to sleep soundly, and peevishness – are among those typically associated with the affliction. Individuals also suffered, like Arthur, from hallucinations of a desperate and despondent character. In the words of one physician: the patient 'fancies he is attacked by robbers, and struggles as if he were defending himself, or he supposes that a swarm of bees are hovering around him, and he moves his arms as if he were driving them away' (Keith Imray 205). Compare also the extended description in *PP* of the delusions tormenting the dying clown in 'The Stroller's Tale', the 'low pantomime actor' who dies 'emaciated by disease' brought on by habitual drinking (3).

Victorian medical opinion differed about the treatment. Some doctors recommended granting requests for spirits (Havisham is 'quieted' after being given 'some liquor') or other stimulants when patients became very insistent, but the consensus was that sleep was the best course. Small and repeated doses of opium were prescribed every six hours in more serious cases 'until sleep be procured' (Keith Imray 205).

"I might a took warning by Arthur

(over nigh Brentford] Originally 'a long irregularly built town without any public building or structure which merits description' eight miles west of London. The town, however, was a place of considerable trade, 'owing to its position as a thoroughfare on the Great Western Road, and situation on the Thames, which affords so much facility to the market boats and other sources of active employment' (Dugdale, c.1830, 1.268). Brentford is now part of the metropolitan borough of Hounslow.

"Compeyson's wife, being used to him

Has her keeper been for her? . . . Did you tell him to lock her and bar her in?'] Arthur Havisham assumes that his sister, dressed all in white, must be mad and under the care of a personal keeper employed by the family. Arrangements like this were common among those who could afford to pay for a private companion.

"Not to go into the things that Compeyson planned

black slave.] For slavery in Britain, see chapter 12, note on p. 125.

"There ain't no need to go into it," he said

for misdemeanour,] In criminal law, a misdemeanour represents the lowest technical degree of public wrong, an offence that can be tried summarily by justices of the peace sitting without a jury. Compare a felony, a far more serious indictable offence requiring a judge and jury. Until the reform of England's 'Bloody Code' in the 1830s, every felony conviction tacitly carried both a forfeiture of land, goods or both and the prospect of capital punishment. For forfeiture, see also chapter 54, note on pp. 394–5.

"Well!" he said, "I <u>was</u>, and got convicted.

afore I could get Jaggers.]   See Appendix 1.

"When we was put in the dock

"When we was put in the dock, I noticed first of all what a gentleman Compeyson looked . . . and what a common sort of a wretch I looked. When the prosecution opened and the evidence was put short . . . I noticed how heavy it all bore on me, and how light on him. . . . But, when the defence come on, then I see the plan plainer;]   This 'plan' of 'separate defences, no communication', and the deliberate putting 'short' or withholding of evidence makes sense given the novel's historical context when justice at the Old Bailey was often rough and ready, and trials notoriously slapdash, on account of the speed with which judges conducted proceedings. The court met eight times a year, and during each session relays of judges tried between three and five hundred cases in the course of several days. In 1833 trials at the Old Bailey lasted for an average of 8° minutes each, although capital trials took longer (Gatrell 536).

Other procedural flaws built into the legal system almost inevitably ensured discrimination and unfairness. At the time, a general bias against 'prisoners' prevailed, reducing all cases to a single denominator. The role of the defence counsel was severely limited, and the laws of evidence showed few signs of sophistication (Gatrell 359). Summing up the features that made for the rapidity of criminal trials in the early eighteenth century, one historian offers these reasons:

> the scheduling of trials close to the happening of the crimes, sometimes within a few days; prompt pretrial evidence-gathering and sifting by the JPs; the virtual absence of lawyers for the prosecution or defence; the conversational informality of the trial; the constant resort to the accused as a testimonial resource; the recurrent use of jurors who were long experienced in jury work, men who needed comparatively little formal instruction on the essentials of criminal law and procedure; and the guidance that the jury received from the judge, who exercised an unrestricted power to comment on the merits.
> (Langbein 115)

Class bias among judges and jurors also played a role in sentencing – a point Dickens makes in the favourable treatment of Compeyson. 'Character remained as central to judges' decisions in the 1820s as ever in the previous century. It was the key variable in sentencing. It is referred to in nearly every appeal mentioned in this chapter [19] and in this book' (Gatrell 540).

'My lord and gentlemen,]   The correct way to address the presiding judge and members of the jury.

up hill and down dale]   A *Midsummer Night's Dream* 2.1.2: 'Over hill, over dale'.

in Bridewells and Lock-Ups?]   Bridewells were Houses of Correction established for the confinement and deterrence of idle persons. The name derives from Henry VIII's Bridewell Palace in Blackfriars, London, erected near St Bridget's (St Bride's) holy well. In 1553, Edward VI gave the palace to the City of London as a workhouse for unruly apprentices and vagrants. Subsequently the name was applied generally to Houses of Correction, where the idle were sent to labour in order to learn 'the habits of industry'. Work performed in the latter was menial and generally unpleasant: picking oakum, breaking stones – something tedious and repetitive.

Lock-ups were places for the safe custody of those awaiting trial. Magwitch's use of 'lock-up' to signify a house or room for the temporary detention of offenders is anachronistic. The first recorded use is 1859 (*OED*).

And when it come to speech-making, warn't it Compeyson as could speak to 'em . . . wi' verses in his speech, too. . . . And when the verdict come, warn't it Compeyson as was recommended to mercy . . . and warn't it me as got never a word but Guilty?]   Trial protocol in cases of felony permitted an appeal to the jury on the delivery of a verdict but before a judgement had been given. The legal purpose of the *allocutus*, or 'speaking to', was to allow convicts after a guilty verdict to allege anything which could prevent the court from giving judgement. Prisoners were brought to the bar, usually in irons, and then asked: 'Is there any reason why sentence of ———— should not be pronounced on you?'

One frequently used answer was 'I pray [the benefit of] the clergy', a remarkable privilege of importance in English criminal law dating from the eleventh century. During the reign of William the Conqueror, successful pleas from the clergy led to the separation of the ecclesiastical courts from secular courts, one consequence of which was that clerics who committed any of the serious crimes termed felonies could be tried only in an ecclesiastical court and were thereby amenable only to such punishments as that court could inflict. Subsequent developments extended this privilege to 'clerks' of all kinds, to all persons eligible for ordination although not actually ordained, and eventually during the reign of Henry III to all males who could read. Inevitably this broadened provision of the original statute invited abuse, including exploitation by illiterate criminals, who took to learning a few words by heart, typically the first verse of Psalm 51, the so-called 'neck-verse', which began 'Miserere mei, Deus'. In response to abuse, this 'benefit' was gradually whittled away and finally abolished when Parliament passed the Criminal Law Act (7 & 8 Geo. IV, c. 28) of 1827 (Baker, 1986, 293; Turner 97). Reference to 'verses' possibly alludes to this practice. After 'too' Dickens originally wrote 'and, to the best of my belief, Latin too'.

And when we're sentenced, ain't it him as gets seven year, and me fourteen,]   Between 1805 and 1817, prisoners sentenced to transportation received either seven or fourteen years. A third sentence – for life – was reserved for those whom the law regarded as incapable of reform and best removed permanently from the country (Bennett, 1819, 57). A period of work in one of the government's dockyards usually preceded the journey to Australia. See also below.

and ain't it him as the Judge is sorry for . . . done so well,] Dickens originally wrote after 'him' 'as the Judge's voice trembles over'.

"I had said to Compeyson that I'd smash that face of his

We was in the same prison-ship, but I couldn't get at him for long, though I tried.] Critics of the hulks like John Howard, Sir William Blackstone, and Hepworth Dixon often pointed to the poor security and the failure of authorities to keep apart prisoners who, ashore, would have been separated.

The black-hole of that ship warn't a strong one,] Each of the prison ships reserved several 'dark cells' into which refractory prisoners were confined, 'where light is totally excluded, and bread and water is the diet'. Howard, visiting three 'miserable objects' in 1788 punished 'for attempting to break out', describes how they were let down 'into a dreadful, dark and deep hole at the bottom of the ship, where they lay, almost naked, upon a little straw' (Howard 255; *BPP, Crime and Punishment: Transportation*: 1, 5, 'Report from the Select Committee on Secondary Punishments', 27 September 1831).

"Of course he'd much the best of it to the last

I was put in irons,] That is, shackled with a bracelet around the ankle and returned to the ship's 'black-hole', the usual punishment for prisoners who attempted to escape.

brought to trial again, and sent for life.] Prisoners sentenced to transportation for life were read the following verdict: 'It is therefore ordered and adjudged by this Court, that you be transported upon the seas, beyond the seas, to such a place as His Majesty, by the advice of His Privy Council, shall think fit to direct and appoint, for the term of your natural life' (quoted in Robert Hughes 129). Critics of the hulks system argued that it had many faults. For many of the prisoners the preliminary confinement and labour proved 'too severe for the far greater number of those who are confined' in the prison ships. The practice also failed to distinguish between degrees of guilt because it recognized 'no proportion of punishment to several offences', treating first-time offenders and hardened criminals the same way. And, Howard asked, 'Is it not contrary to justice and humanity' to send those who are not sentenced for life 'to a settlement so remote that there is no probability of their return?' (257).

Chapter 43 Twenty-seventh weekly number
1 June 1861

A new fear had been engendered in my mind

the consequence.]   After 'consequence' MS reads 'that he would put the rope round his neck'.

becoming an informer,]   Since the eighteenth century, civil authorities had relied on individuals to come forward with information that might lead to the prosecution and conviction of offenders. Reforms in criminal law introduced by Peel in 1826 curtailed the granting of so-called parliamentary rewards to those volunteering information, but police-courts retained their power to 'remunerate' anyone who had been active in the apprehension of certain offenders. The establishment of the Metropolitan Police in 1829 further undermined reliance on informers, although 'the information trade' did not diminish significantly until after 1839 (Radzinowicz 2.153). Such individuals were popularly detested. See Noah Claypole (*OT*), Mr Gashford (*BR*), Barsad and Cly (*TTC*).

Next day, I had the meanness to feign

across the water,]   A colloquial expression referring to the sea, as in the Jacobite toast, 'the king over the water', meaning the Pretender in France.

"Is this a cut?" said Mr. Drummle.

a cut?"]   Victorians recognized 'cutting' as a way to convey one's unwillingness to be approached by a person deemed unworthy or embarrassing (Day 7). Some regarded the practice as a 'silly gesture' far too 'promptly resorted to': 'In the first place, it is vulgar, and a custom which the vulgar affect. It is pretentious, and seems to say, "You are not good enough for me to know" ' (*The Habits of Good Society* 314). However, cutting was justifiable among young ladies when it became the only means of ridding themselves of annoying attention.

"Yes," I assented. "I am told it's very like your Shropshire."

Shropshire."]   An oversight; in chapter 25, Dickens names 'Somersetshire' in south-west England as Drummle's county. Shropshire, on the border of Wales and north of Somerset, is hilly and bears no resemblance to the marshy peninsula east of Chatham, where Pip grew up.

I felt here, through a tingling in my blood

the nearest box.]   Coaching inns and coffee-houses had their tables petitioned off from each other on three sides, allowing customers a degree of privacy.

Then, Drummle glanced at me

I felt inclined to take him in my arms as the robber in the story-book is said to have taken the old lady and seat him on the fire.]   A deed traditionally attributed to Dick Turpin (1706–39) and members of the 'Essex Gang' when they broke into the house of an old woman in Loughton, Essex. In response to repeated denials that she had any money, Turpin finally seized his victim and said: 'If you won't tell us I will sit you on the grate'. The threat was carried out, forcing the widow to relinquish upwards of four hundred pounds, with which the robbers escaped (*The Complete Newgate Calendar* 3.90).

Chapter 44

"And what wind," said Miss Havisham

"And what wind . . . blows you here, Pip?"]   *2 Henry IV* (5.3.84–5):

> *Falstaff*: What wind blew you hither, Pistol?
> *Pistol*: Not the ill wind which blows no man to good.

Though she looked steadily at me

I read in the action of her fingers, as plainly as if she had told me in the dumb alphabet,]   More commonly, the finger-alphabet, which is used to translate the letters in every word into a visual equivalent. Efforts to communicate manually with the deaf date from the sixteenth century. Pioneers of finger-spelling and manual systems include Peter of Ponce (died 1584), Giovanni Bonifacio, John Bulwer and George Dalgarno (Bender ch. 5). Dickens's introduction in 1842 to Laura Bridgeman, the famous blind deaf mute at Boston's Massachusetts School for the Blind, memorably impressed him with the potential of the manual alphabet, especially under the supervision of Samuel Gridley Howe (1801–76), Laura's teacher, whom Dickens befriended (*AN* ch. 3).

"Because," said I, "I began the service myself

more than two years ago,]   See Appendix 1.

"Don't be afraid of my being a blessing to him," said Estella

you visionary boy – or man?"]   In MS, Dickens wrote 'you silly boy'. The juxtaposition of 'boy' and 'man', and reference to a vision that has faded, suggests Wordsworth's 'Immortality' ode. Pip and Wordsworth's speaker both review their childhood and reflect on the vicissitudes and joys of growth and development.

All done, all gone! So much was done and gone

I went out at the gate,]   See chapter 8, note on p. 90.

then struck off to walk all the way to London.]   Dickens was himself a regular and avid walker: 'I performed an insane match against time of eighteen miles by the milestones in four hours and a half, under a burning sun the whole way,' he noted in August 1843 (*Letters* 3.547), referring to one of his more concerted efforts. In

October 1857 he undertook the reverse of Pip's journey by walking thirty miles from Tavistock House in London to Gad's Hill in Kent ('Shy Neighbourhoods', *AYR* 3.155). For dating, see Forster 8.5.232, and Edgar Johnson 2.lxxv). Pedestrian feats like this were by no means uncommon. The poor walked everywhere as a matter of course, and many others as a form of recreation: 'Walking is no doubt the best exercise for unblemished health and unimpaired strength' (Kitchiner, 1827, pt 1, p. 247).

It was past midnight when I crossed London Bridge.

London Bridge.]   MS reads 'old London Bridge.' For further details about the Bridge, see chapter 46, note on p. 356.

Whitefriars.]   The name derives from the monastery founded in 1241 by the white-robed Carmelites and later dissolved in the sixteenth century by Henry VIII. The precinct was also a former sanctuary, an ecclesiastical place where fugitives from justice enjoyed immunity from arrest. Henry VIII abolished most sanctuaries (32 Hen. VIII, c. 12), though these places, which became in the course of time de facto dens of thieves, were not finally eradicated until 1623 (Baker, 1971, 281). Timbs notes that by 1865 scarcely any trace of old Whitefriars remained, with the exception of 'some buildings named "Hanging Sword Alley" ', a reminder of the number of fencing schools formerly located there (1865, 1.101).

As it seldom happened

I came in at that Whitefriars gate after the Temple was closed,]   The Temple was closed to the public every evening at dusk, although several wicket gates supervised by porters remained open for residents until 11 p.m. For Pip's route, see Appendix 4, p. 441.

I did not take it ill that the night-porter examined me with much attention]   See above and chapter 40, note on p. 315.

Chapter 45   Twenty-eighth weekly number
8 June 1861

T URNING *from the Temple gate*

Fleet-street,] Named after the river Fleet, Fleet Street extends eastwards from the Temple Bar, the western limit of the City, to the junction of Faringdon Street and Bridge Street. Covent Garden, London's principal fruit, flower and vegetable market, lay to the west. See Appendix 4, map p. 441.

and drove to the Hummums in Covent Garden.] The building stood nearby at the corner of Russell Street in Covent Garden (see chapter 21) and served as a hotel after its conversion in the eighteenth century from a Turkish-style sweating-bath with tiled walls, marble steps, hot and cold baths and a cupola roof. The name derives from the Arabic *Hammam*, 'a Bagnio, or Place for Sweating', and was retained until the hotel was demolished later in the century (*Leigh's New Picture of London* 340; and Timbs, 1867, 38–9).

a Divinely Righteous manner.] Monarchs (both ancient and modern) claimed a sacred status. A specifically Christian dimension to the monarchy originated with the medieval Carolingian kings, who initiated a religious coronation ceremony in the eighth century. The anointing of the king during his coronation signified a God-given mandate to rule. The idea persisted through the centuries before losing credibility in England during the eighteenth century. In 1689 the Bill of Rights redefined the role of the monarch as someone who governed at the consent of the people and not of God.

As I had asked for a night-light

the good old constitutional rushlight of those virtuous days – an object like the ghost of a walking-cane, which instantly broke its back if it were touched . . . was placed in solitary confinement at the bottom of a high tin tower, perforated with round holes] Rushes dipped in fat were first used as tapers during the seventeenth century. Although they gave a feeble light, they proved popular with the poor after the introduction of a tax on candles in 1709 and continued in use beyond the repeal of the tax in 1831. Meadow rushes were picked green, cut to a length of twelve to eighteen inches, peeled, then soaked in grease and dried. Prepared rushes were then placed in holders or iron clips and mounted on a wooden base. The 'ghost of a walking-cane' was the thin strip of rush supporting the grease-soaked pith. In this case, a perforated iron tin protects the strip of rush which, if touched, would instantly crumble (based on Hartley 647). William Cobbett, a staunch believer in traditional ways, wrote: 'I was bred and brought up mostly by rushlight and do not find that I see less clearly than other people. My grandmother, who lived till 90. . . never I believe burnt a candle in her life' (quoted in Hartley 647). In 'Lying

Awake' (*HW* 6.145–6) Dickens refers twice to the night-light in his room when he lies abed, unable to sleep.

the eyes of this foolish Argus.]   Argus, the Greek monster with a hundred eyes who was appointed to watch Io, the mistress of Zeus, lulled to sleep and then slain by Hermes. At the command of Zeus' wife, Hera, the eyes were transplanted into the tail of the peacock.

Whatever night-fancies and night-noises crowded on me

Not long before, I had read in the newspapers, how a gentleman unknown had come to the Hummums in the night, and had gone to bed, and had destroyed himself, and had been found in the morning weltering in blood.]   Details like this made their way into many newspapers, including *The Times*. Compare the paragraph 'Sudden Death' reporting the demise of William Lambert, 'a gentleman of property from Yeovil, Somersetshire', who was found dead at the New Hummums Hotel, Covent Garden, shortly after his arriving in London 'in search of medical advice' (19 April 1845, p. 7, col. f).

"That's all right," said he, rubbing his hands.

"I left a note for you at each of the Temple gates,]   Ten gates served the Temple. There were two principal gates in Fleet Street (the gate to Middle Temple Lane and one to Inner Temple Lane), two in the Strand (Palsgrave Place and Devereux Court), New Court and West Lodge to the west, Mitre Court and Ram Alley Gates to the north-east, and the eastern Whitefriars Gate at which Pip arrived. Until the embankment of the Thames in 1865, there was also the Water Gate leading to the pier known as the Temple Stairs on the Middle Temple's southern boundary (see Appendix 4, map on p. 441).

"– had made some little stir in a certain part of the world

the government expense—"]   Transported convicts bound for Australia were commonly said to travel 'at His Majesty's expense'.

"And him I found.

Tom, Jack, or Richard,]   To preserve Wemmick's variation of the more commonplace Tom, Dick or Harry, Dickens frequently had to correct 'Harry' to 'Richard' in the MS.

"He <u>was</u> puzzled what to do

Under existing circumstances there is no place like a great city when you are once in it. Don't break cover too soon. Lie close. Wait till things slacken, before you try the open, even for foreign air."] Compare Caleb Williams's description of London as 'an inexhaustible reservoir of concealment' for someone, like himself, on the run. Changing one's clothing, lodging in an obscure part of the town and assuming a disguise are other preliminaries Williams adopts. He even resolves to walk only at night and use caution when approaching 'the window of [his] apartment, though upon the attic story' in accordance with the principle of not wantonly or unnecessarily exposing himself to risk, 'however slight that risk might be' (William Godwin, *Caleb Williams*, 1794, 3.8). In the next chapter, Wemmick makes the case for hiding Magwitch in a tenement 'well away from the usual heap of streets great and small' and suggests a system for communicating with blinds designed not to reveal the sender.

"Mr. Herbert," said Wemmick

the Purser line of life,] See chapter 30, note on p. 261.

"The house with the bow-window," said Wemmick

down the Pool there between Limehouse and Greenwich,] The Pool, a four-mile stretch of the Thames, begins at London Bridge and continues downstream towards Greenwich, the site of a famous military hospital. Limehouse, a commercial and maritime region on the northern shore, is about 2° miles east of London Bridge (see Appendix 4, map p. 444). For the subdivisions of the Pool, see chapter 46, note on p. 349.

kept, it seems, by a very respectable widow who has a furnished upper floor to let,] A case has been made on the grounds of locality and the presence of bow windows for a specific house known locally as 'a lodging house used by masters and the like of the cargo boats coming up the Thames' (Major 32). The house was demolished in the 1930s. See also chapter 46, note on p. 349.

It's altogether out of all your beats, and is well away from the usual heap of streets great and small.] Maritime and seafaring activities predominated along the shore; inland, the country was still remote and not heavily populated early in the century.

a foreign packet-boat,] Packet-boats were passenger-boats so-called because they carried letters, dispatches and bankers' parcels in sealed bags to and from foreign countries.

"Well, sir! Mr. Herbert threw himself into the business with a will

he was summoned to Dover, and in fact he was taken down the Dover road and cornered out of it.]   The Channel port of Dover in Kent lies sixty miles south-east of London. Wemmick's feint was evidently executed by crossing London Bridge into Southwark and setting off along the Dover Road or Watling Street, which ran parallel to the Thames as far as Gravesend (see Appendix 4, map pp. 444–6). Turning left or north off the main road, known also as the Old Kent Road, one could head back towards the river and make one's way to the waterside region described in the next chapter.

Dates

Herbert Pocket speaks of Miss Havisham's matter having happened "five and twenty years ago." at that time, Pip is – say 18 or 19. Consequently it happened 6 or 7 years before Pip ~~/~~ and Estella — who is about his age — were born.

But say that the matter was a year or so in hand – which it would be – that would reduce it to ~~4 or 5 years~~ 5 or 6 years before they were born.

Magwitch tells his story in the Temple, when Pip is 23. Magwitch is then about 60. Say Pip was about 7 at the opening of the story. Magwitch's escape would then be ^about^ 16 years ago. If Magwitch says he first knew Compey about 20 years ago, that would leave about 4 years for his knowledge of Compey and whole association with him up to the time of the escape. That would also make him about 40 when he knew Compey, and Compey was younger than he.

When Magwitch ~~knew Comp~~ became known to Compey the end of Miss Havisham's matter would thus have taken place about 7 or 8 years before.

Estella, as Magwitch's child, must have been born

(Dates) 2

about 3 years before he knew Compey.

The Ages in the last stage of Pip's Expectations - stand thus:

Pip   about   23

Estella   "   23

Herbert   "   23

Magwitch   "   60

Compey   "   52 or 53

Miss Havisham " 56 (I judge her to have been the elder in the love time.)

Biddy " 24 or 25

Joe " 45

Jaggers 55, Wemmick near 50, and so forth.

General Mems: 1

Miss Havisham and Pip, and the Money for Herbert. So

Herbert made a partner in clarriker's

    Compeyson. How brought in?

    Estella, Magwitch's daughter

    Orlick – and Pip's entrapment - and escape

      – To the flight

        Start

        Pursuit

                    /Both overboard
        Struggle- xxxx the untuned
        together -Compeyson drowned -
        Magwitch rescued by Pip. And
Then: taken. –

Magwitch tried, found guilty, & left for

                            Death

        Dies presently in Newgate

        Property confiscated to the Crown.
Herbert goes abroad:
      Pip perhaps to follow.

Pip arrested when ii too ill to be moved - lies in the

chambers in Fever. Ministering Angel Joe.

   Recovered again, Pip goes humbly down to the

old marsh Village, to propose to Biddy.

      Finds Biddy married to Joe

General Mems: 2.

So goes abroad to Herbert (happily married to Clara Barley), and becomes his clerk.

The one good thing he did in his prosperity, the only thing that endures and bears good fruit

Ti_de_

Down at   up

  9 AM   3 PM

   till   till

   3 PM   9 P. M

Down 9 PM

till 3 morning

    Down at 9 ♠ A.M. till 3 P. M Wednesday

    Up at 3 PM – till 9. P.M. Wednesday

    Down at 9 PM. till 3 A. M Thursday morning

    Up at 3 AM. till 9. AM Thursday morning

        when the boat starts

Chapter 46

Eight o'clock had struck before I got into the air

air . . . scented . . . by the chips and shavings of the long-shore boat-builders, and mast oar and block makers.]   The waterside communities of Rotherhithe, Wapping, Deptford, Ratcliff and Poplar were important centres for boat-building and allied trades in the early nineteenth century (Hartwell). See also below. Blocks – oval-shaped pulleys housed in wood or metal frames – are used for all running ropes aboard a sailing vessel. Their manufacture, by hand, until Mark Isambard Brunel designed machinery for their mass production, was essential to Britain's maritime industry.

All that water-side region of the upper and lower Pool below Bridge, was unknown ground to me, and when I struck down by the river, I found that the spot I wanted was not where I had supposed it to be, and was anything but easy to find.]   That is, the south bank of the Thames east of Southwark in the vicinity of Bermondsey, formerly a thickly populated region, full of crowded recesses and known for its impenetrability to outsiders (see Appendix 4, map p. 444). A visitor noted: one is 'astonished at the number of canals and drawbridges, and basins . . . at the odour of tar and pitch . . . at the clink of hammers, [and] the creaking of cranes and pulleys' (Mackay, 1840, 2.65, 68).

Public houses and 'slop sellers' – small businesses offering everything designed to catch 'a sailor's eye' – also abounded. 'Ship joiners – ship carpenters – mathematical instrument makers, with their sign-posts of gilded captains peering through telescopes, – provision shops – rope makers – vendors of ship biscuits, even ship booksellers, – ironmongers – dealers in marine stores, are strangely mixed together' (Beames 97). Along the shore, ships rode at anchor in snug basins, attended by 'a swarming hive of amphibious labourers'. The fruits of Dickens's 'waterside wanderings' in search of local colour also found their way into OMF (Forster 9.5.291).

'The Pool' refers to a four-mile stretch of the Thames between London Bridge and Deptford divided into the upper and lower Pool. Further divisions include the upper pool from London Bridge to Union Hole; the middle pool from Union Hole to Wapping New Stairs; the lower pool from the stairs to Horse Ferry pier, near Limehouse; and a fourth stretch of the river from Limehouse to Deptford (James Dugdale 3.528). Beyond lies Bugsby's Hole, the lower limit of the Port of London, some 6° miles down-river from London Bridge (see Appendix 4, map pp. 444–5). The river's width through this section averages between 400 and 500 yards. Water traffic in the Pool increased substantially towards the end of the eighteenth century, forming a congested mass of sailing vessels, lighters, barges, punts and watermen's wherries.

It was called Mill Pond Bank, Chinks's Basin; and I had no other guide than . . . the Old Green Copper Rope-Walk.]   Dickens may have taken the name 'Mill Pond Bank' from an elongated sheet of water called Mill Pond in the Rotherhithe region on the Surrey bank of the river. Such ponds were constructed to retain tidal waters, which, released, drove windmills, watermills and tidemills operating various kinds of revolving machinery. 'Chinks's Basin' (another artificially enclosed area designed to maintain a water level unaffected by fluctuations in the tide) appears to be wholly fictitious and possibly derives from '<?Chinkle/?Chinkb> Chinkible', three variants Dickens listed in his *Book of Memoranda* (14). For rope-walk, see below.

It matters not what stranded ships

It matters not what stranded ships repairing in dry docks I lost myself among, what old hulls of ships . . . what ooze and slime and other dregs of tide, what yards of ship-builders and ship-breakers, what rusty anchors . . . what mountainous country of accumulated casks and timber,] Nineteenth-century commentators remarked that the Thames, although not Britain's longest river, was certainly its busiest and without question the commercial centre of the world. The shoreline from London Bridge east towards Blackwall was

> almost one continued great magazine of naval stores, containing three large wet docks, thirty-two dry docks, and thirty-three yards for the building of ships for the use of merchants, besides the places allotted for the building of boats and lighters; and the King's yards lower down the river for the building of men of war. (*The London Guide*, 1818, vi–vii)

the stump of a ruined windmill,] Formerly there were three windmills in the area (Gadd, 1937, 120), one of which was an old one 'that stood in the north-west corner' of a swampy field called Windmill Field, not far from the rope-walk (E. J. Beck, quoted in Major 33).

Old Green Copper Rope-Walk – whose long and narrow vista I could trace in the moonlight, along a series of wooden frames set in the ground, that looked like superannuated haymaking-rakes which had grown old and lost most of their teeth.] The manufacture of ropes, shrouds, cables and hawsers remained an indispensable maritime industry in the days of sail. Rope-making involved several distinct operations. The process began by combing and straightening fibres of hemp in the hatchelling house and then pulling the fibres over a board of closely spaced iron spikes known as a hatchel board (Dickens's 'superannuated haymaking-rakes'). The fibres were then taken and spun into yarn by a spinner who walked backwards from a turning frame, adding fibres from a bundle around his waist. Completed yarns were taken to the tarring house and dipped in hot tar to preserve them.

Tarred yarn was then removed to the laying-floor of a rope-walk, where the strands in turn were laid into rope. Usually a timber roof protected the machinery and covered the length of the rope walk, although the sides remained open, revealing the minimal equipment the operation required as rope-makers twisted strands of hemp into a continuous length with the help of a turning machine.

The spinner, who carries a portion of dressed hemp round his middle, attaches one end of two threads to two spindles of the wheel, which is then set a going at an equal turn: he retires backward from the wheel, spinning out both his threads until he reaches the farther end of the walk. He makes fast and commences anew. When a quantity of yarns are done, a few are brought back together and made into a strand by turning any number in a jack-wheel, the workman as before going down the walk and keeping the yarns separate. Several of these strands make a rope, and many such ropes constitute a cable, for holding safely the largest ships at anchor. (*Complete Book of Trades* 394)

Selecting from the few queer houses upon Mill Pond Bank

a house with a wooden front and three-stories of bow-window (not bay-window, which is another thing),] The distinction between a 'bow window' and a 'bay window' refers to the window's shape: all windows that project from a wall are bay windows but only those with curved projections are bow windows. Number 670 Trinity Street (now Rotherhithe Street) has been suggested as a possible original for Mrs Whimple's house, one of seven demolished in the summer of 1934. The house in question, known locally as Balcomb Mill, was an old one with four slender pillars supporting a large, old-fashioned bow-window, with many small panes, on the first floor. It stood at the end of the terrace where the road turned sharply, close to the river. The bow window and windows in the attic all commanded a clear view of the Thames (based on Gadd, 1937, and Major).

the death of Captain Cook . . . Majesty King George the Third in a state-coachman's wig, leather breeches, and top-boots, on the terrace at Windsor.] Several versions of the violent death of Captain James Cook in 1779 at the hands of Hawaiian natives existed; paintings by James Webber (1784) and George Carter (1785) were widely reproduced as engravings. A framed picture of the same subject hung on the walls of the sitting-room occupied by Mr Jarndyce's three wards (*BH* 6).

An 1812 portrait of George III outside Windsor Castle, Berkshire, by Charles, or Carl, or Christian Rosenberg (1745–1844) was equally popular and often reproduced. The painting shows the king in profile wearing a black hat with a cockade, buff-coloured breeches and top-boots. It was in an outfit like this he became known to many of his subjects (Hill, 1959, 58). 'Rain or shine, the King rode every day for hours; poked his red face into hundreds of cottages round about, and showed that shovel hat and Windsor uniform to . . . all sorts of people, gentle and simple' (Thackeray, *Four Georges*, 150).

"Yes," returned Herbert, "and you may suppose

gout.]

It is a matter of notoriety that Gout is a disease of the rich, and not of the poor and working class of society; that it attacks more especially those who lead a luxurious and sedentary life, who pamper their appetite with rich dishes and sauces, who overload the stomach with a variety of articles of food at each meal, and indulge in the free use of wine, thus inducing a state of plethora, or, in other words, charging the system with a greater quantity of nutritive and excrementitious matter, than can be thrown off by the natural outlets of the body (Keith Imray 320).

Fever and pain in the joints, especially in those of the feet and hands, were among the most common symptoms. Patients in the nineteenth century could expect little relief beyond that conferred by the dubious practices of bloodletting and purgation. Dietary recommendations were equally bleak: a regimen of farinaceous substances (sago, arrow-root and panada) supplemented with chicken broth and toast, and the restriction of fluids to barley water, tepid whey and weak black tea.

He persists, too, in keeping all the provisions . . . and serving them out. . . . His room must be like a chandler's shop."] Chandlers – so called because they made and sold candles – later became more general retailers. In the nineteenth century they sold a wide range of goods, including staples like bread, butter, cheese, and pickled and cured meats.

"What else can be the consequence," said Herbert

a Double Gloucester] A hard English cheese made in Gloucestershire and produced in large rounds weighing between twenty-six and thirty pounds. Double Gloucester is so called because it is aged twice as long as a single Gloucester (four months as opposed to two).

"Mrs. Whimple," said Herbert

Gruffandgrim."] Other variants of the nickname appear in *CH* (Gruff and Tackleton) and in *OMF* 4.4 (Gruff and Glum).

Herbert had told me on former occasions

completing her education at an establishment at Hammersmith,] Three kinds of educational opportunity existed for girls and young ladies early in the nineteenth century: charity schools for the poor, private tuition at home with a governess, and boarding schools for children from middle-class families. Schools in this third category varied widely in proficiency and standards, especially since their number increased rapidly between 1800 and 1850. Most combined instruction in the first

18 Old London Bridge, c.1800

19 The Custom House

four rules of arithmetic, reading, writing, and perhaps a little French and Italian. The classical languages almost invariably were not offered to girls, nor were the sciences, astronomy and other subjects since condescending ideas about women's intellectual capabilities and emphasis on their need to acquire 'accomplishments' to prepare girls for marriage dominated attempts to determine a suitable curriculum (Kamm passim). See also 'finishing' schools (chapter 15, note on p. 141).

"That's it!" cried Herbert

his grog]   A naval drink (one quart of water to a half-pint of rum) credited to Admiral Edward Vernon (1684–1757), who issued an order on 21 August 1740 forbidding the serving of raw spirits on board ships under his command. The practice of cutting the daily ration (half a pint of neat rum or brandy before noon) in two and serving a mixture twice a day was quickly adopted by the admiralty in an attempt to combat drunkenness. The drink was named 'grog' after the grogram coat Vernon wore, although the custom of mixing water with spirits at sea to counteract unwholesome water may pre-date this derivation. The addition of sugar and lemon juice made grog an anti-scorbutic (Smyth).

Herbert, who had been looking at the fire

the Temple stairs,]   A wharf known as Temple Stairs or Temple Bridge lay just beyond Middle Temple gardens (see Temple ground plan, p. 441). The stairs had been used by lawyers since the fourteenth century to board barges when they travelled to and from Westminster Hall. A second wharf, also beyond the gardens, was constructed following the embankment of this portion of the Thames in 1767. These stairs were built for the use of the two Temple societies (Baker, 1991, 20).

I liked this scheme, and Provis was quite elated by it.

We agreed that . . . Provis should never recognise us if we came below Bridge and rowed past Mill Pond Bank.]   The distance from London Bridge to Limehouse Reach is about 2° miles.

When I had taken leave of the pretty gentle dark-eyed girl

as old as the hills, and might swear like a whole field of troopers,]   'Old as the hills' is a proverb dating from the sixteenth century. The expression 'to swear like a trooper' seems to have been made famous by John Galt's popular *Annals of the Parish* (1821): 'He swore like a trooper that he would get an act of parliament to put down the nuisance' (ch. 8).

All things were as quiet in the Temple

there was no lounger in Garden-court. I walked past the fountain twice or thrice before I descended the steps that were between me and my rooms,] See Appendix 3. Tom Pinch in MC takes a similar route, glancing down the steps to look for his sister (45).

Next day, I set myself to get the boat.

At first, I kept above Blackfriars Bridge; but as the hours of the tide changed, I took towards London Bridge.] That is, upstream and west in the direction of Waterloo Bridge and Westminster Bridge; adjusting to the length of flood from high water, he then rows east from the Temple stairs and downstream towards London Bridge. (See Plate 18).

It was Old London Bridge in those days,] The bridge Pip knew in his youth was replaced by a new bridge about 60 yards upstream, begun in 1825 and completed and opened in 1831. Old London Bridge dated back to 993, when a wooden bridge succeeded earlier structures built on the same site by the Romans. After fire destroyed this bridge in 1136, a new stone bridge was constructed in 1209 and, despite a long history of repairs, the stone bridge proved adequate until 1823, when Parliament agreed to build a new one.

The addition of houses to Old London Bridge and subsequent rebuilding and alterations over the centuries helped add to the bridge's reputation as one of London's sights. 'It does not appear ill to the foot passenger', wrote one observer in 1818, 'yet it is still a clumsy piece of patch-work, when viewed from the water. The arches are nineteen in number, and all unequal; and, upon the whole, this Gothic pile is a disgrace to the metropolis of Great Britain' (*The London Guide*, 1818, 21). See also below.

at certain states of the tide there was a race and a fall of water there which gave it a bad reputation. But I knew well enough how to "shoot" the bridge] To 'shoot the bridge' is to negotiate the rapid flow of water through 'the eddy-chafed arches and starlings of the old bridge' (chapter 46). Starlings were made by driving pilings into the bed of the river in the outline of a boat pointed up- and down-stream. The enclosure formed by timbers bolted together was then filled with large stones to form a platform which provided a base for one of the bridge's twenty piers and starlings supporting the 926-foot-long structure (Forbes 15). As a means of support, the starlings proved extremely effective since the bridge lasted for 653 years; but their effect on the water-borne traffic was less successful because they

> contracted the spaces between the piers to such a degree as to occasion, at the retreat of every tide, the fall of five feet, or a number of temporary cataracts, which, since the foundation of the bridge, have occasioned the loss of many thousands of lives. The number of arches was nineteen, of unequal

dimensions, and greatly deformed by the starlings and the houses on each side, which overhung and leaned in a terrific manner. In most places they hid the arches, and nothing appeared but rude piers. (James Dugdale 3.534)

in the Pool, and down to Erith.] For the Pool, see above. Nineteenth-century Erith, Kent, was a small town and river port about fifteen miles downstream from the Temple stairs. In the 1840s it enjoyed a brief vogue as a watering-place and resort with pleasure gardens; when the North Kent Railway connected Erith with London, the town gradually developed and became a residential and industrial centre. From the Temple Stairs to Erith and back Pip covers about 30 miles.

Chapter 47 Twenty-ninth weekly number
 15 June 1861

Some weeks passed without bringing any change.

SOME weeks passed]   This reference and a second (see below), together with others in chapters 48 and 49, carefully delineate the passing of time in this section of the novel. See Appendix 1.

We waited for a hint from Wemmick.]   Thus in MS only; all printed versions read: 'We waited for Wemmick' (*Norton* 339).

There were states of the tide

There were states of the tide when, having been down the river, I could not get back]   See chapter 46, note on pp. 356–7.

the Custom House,]   London's Custom House on Lower Thames Street between London Bridge and the Tower stood on the site of three earlier buildings. The first (1385) was built originally to collect the 'Great Custom' on wool. The building referred to here (designed by David Laing, 1817; Plate 19) has Greek Ionic porticoes flanking a round-arched centre and an imposing 500-foot frontage looking on to the river. The building accommodated merchant brokers and 300 officers and clerks employed in the collection of government duties.
  A spacious quay, mooring-places and wharves to the right and left made the Custom House a centre of activity on the Thames (James Dugdale 3.532; Charles Knight 123).

I was not averse to doing this, as it served to make me and my boat a commoner incident among the water-side people there.]   Rowing on this part of the river became much less frequent after the completion of the Thames Embankment project in 1864 (see chapter 39, note on pp. 306–7; Plate 19). By narrowing the river, engineers increased the ebb and flow of tidal water, which, combined with the rise in steam traffic, effectively halted rowing between Westminster and London Bridge.

One afternoon, late in the month of February

late in the month of February,]   See Appendix 1.

as far as Greenwich]   Greenwich, a former royal residence, lies almost six miles down river from the Temple Stairs on a sheltered bend of the Thames. Its popularity increased in the late 1830s when steamers and trains made local attractions accessible. Crowds were drawn to the waterside taverns and pubs for whitebait dinners, to the

20 Steamers at London Bridge wharf

21 Gravesend

Easter fair, the royal parks and the Royal Hospital. By the mid-century, a further transformation was evident. Docks and ancillary trades spread along the river, and rapid urbanization changed a former waterside retreat into a densely populated town. The Royal Hospital operated until 1869 when the declining number of pensioners prompted the government to close it and move the Royal Naval College here in 1873.

As it was a raw evening and I was cold

The theatre where Mr. Wopsle had achieved his questionable triumph, was in that water-side neighbourhood (it is nowhere now),] Wopsle's 'small metropolitan theatre' (chapter 31) appears to be based on a composite derived from Dickens's memories of several non-patent or unlicensed 'minor' theatres familiar to him from his youth (Clinton-Baddeley 157). An even lower category of small theatres included those that sold main parts to 'donkeys . . . prevailed upon to pay for permission to exhibit their lamentable ignorance and boobyism on the stage of a private theatre' 'Private Theatres' (SB). Performing trifling parts in them was a recognized way in which to advance one's career as an actor in London (Egan, 1825, 52).

reviving the Drama,] See chapter 31, note on p. 268.

He had been ominously heard of . . . as a faithful Black, in connexion with a little girl of noble birth, and a monkey . . . as a predatory Tartar of comic propensities, with a face like a red brick, and an outrageous hat all over bells.] Details from playbills chart Wopsle's 'decline' through roles common in popular melodramas. From Hamlet, he 'falls' to playing the 'Stage Negro', an 'old constitution-loving and sentiment-spluttering' figure deeply imbued with a love for Britain. By the 1840s, this version of the Negro had almost disappeared, to be replaced by the Stage Negro as 'a vulgar dancing brute, with a banjo in his hand'. 'Lowly born' lovers tragically addicted to 'the very inconvenient practice' of loving above their station were other stock figures. Stage makeup tended to be overdone with liberal use of chalk, cork and paint (à Beckett 14–15, 22, 1); carmine, a red pigment found in cochineal, was also used to redden cheeks (*HT* 1.6). Performing dogs, horses, monkeys and other animals also featured prominently in early nineteenth-century melodramas; the 'predatory Tartar' refers to *Timour the Tartar* (1811), a famous equestrian drama by M. G. M. Lewis. See also below.

I dined at what Herbert and I

what Herbert and I used to call a Geographical chop-house – where there were maps of the world in porter-pot rims on every half-yard of the tablecloths, and charts of gravy on every one of the knives – to this day . . . within the Lord Mayor's dominions] Stained tablecloths and streaky cutlery resembling marine charts evidently characterize similar eating establishments within the City of London, the administrative district directly under the Lord Mayor. Chop-houses generally specialized in 'substantial English' fare at modest prices and catered to the needs of a man who 'has been taking strong exercise all day' and who had 'the appetite of a Saxon' (*London at Dinner*, 1858, 8–10). Some diners complained about the limited menu and the predictable response of waiters to inquiries about the fare: 'Chops, sir; steaks; welsh-rabbit, kidneys, poach'd eggs, eggs on ham', washed down with porter or beer (Albert Smith, 1855, 10).

There, I found a virtuous boatswain

a virtuous boatswain in his Majesty's service . . . who wouldn't hear of anybody's paying taxes . . . though he was very patriotic.] The entire paragraph burlesques the nautical melodramas popularized by Charles Dibdin (1745–1814), Edward Fitzball (1792–1873) and Douglas William Jerrold (1803–57), whose plays exploited the 'Jolly Jack Tar'. This figure of the sailor-hero, a lineal descendant of the sailors in Smollett's novels (*Roderick Random*, *Peregrine Pickle*), flourished well into the 1850s, especially in the minor theatres. The boatswain (pronounced 'bos'n') was a seaman with multiple responsibilities including: inspecting the sails and rigging each day; supervising all deck activities, such as weighing and dropping anchor and handling the sails. He issued orders using a silver boatswain's pipe.

like a pudding in the cloth,] Suet puddings, sweet or savoury, were tightly wrapped in a cotton cloth before they were cooked by immersing them in boiling water.

a young person in bed-furniture,] An actress wearing a costume made from ornamental bed-hangings or drapery. Improvising outfits from draperies used for four-poster beds was not uncommon. See the lady in the May Day procession who is 'attired in pink crape over bed-furniture' ('The First of May', *SB*).

Portsmouth] For Portsmouth, see chapter 39, pp. 309–10.

"Fill, fill!"] From Thomas Moore's popular drinking song: 'Fill the bumper fair!/ Every drop we sprinkle/O'er the brow of care/Smoothes away a wrinkle' (*Irish Melodies*, 1807–34).

Swab,] Nautical slang for a naval officer wearing epaulettes. The term derives from a mop made of old rope used for cleaning and drying the deck of a ship.

a star and garter] The insignia of the Order of the Bath, the oldest order of chivalry, instituted by Edward III in 1348 and limited to the sovereign and twenty-four Knights Companion. The most distinctive features are the Star, the Garter and the blue diagonal ribbon.

the Admiralty,] The administrative department in Whitehall in Parliament Street near Charing Cross responsible for the management of Britain's armed fleet. The department also supervises the ordering, building, fitting and repairing of ships for sea, and oversees all commissions, pensions and promotions. Originally, the Admiralty was directed by either the Lord Admiral or the Board of Admiralty.

the Union Jack,]   See chapter 37, note on p. 294.

by the fin.]   Theatrical tars customarily spoke distinctively, combining nautical jargon – 'Belay, there!' – with jocular terms such as 'timber' for legs and 'fin' for a hand or an arm.

everybody danced a hornpipe;]   Lively dancing was indispensable to nautical melodrama.

The second piece was the last new grand comic Christmas pantomime

The second piece was the last new grand comic Christmas pantomime; in the first scene of which . . . I detected Mr. Wopsle with red worsted legs. . . . But he presently presented himself under worthier circumstances. . . . The business of this enchanter . . . being principally to be talked at, sung at, butted at, danced at, and flashed at with fires of various colours, he had a good deal of time on his hands.]   The origins of English pantomime as an exclusively Christmas-time entertainment date from the early eighteenth century when French fairground performers put on 'night scenes' using *commedia dell'arte* characters. Subsequent developments introduced openings drawn from classical mythology, whose figures evolved into such types as Harlequin, Pantaloon and Columbine. By the end of the eighteenth century fairy-tale openings had replaced mythical materials as these farces or afterpieces gradually expanded to fill a major portion of the bill. Further changes included the introduction of 'dame roles' played by men, 'principal boys' played by women in tights, elaborate trick-work utilizing traps, hinged properties and instantaneous transformations. Dickens attended pantomimes as a child in Chatham and even saw Grimaldi act 'in the remote times of 1823' (*Letters* 1.382). Later, he wrote: 'We revel in pantomimes . . . because . . . a pantomime is to us, a mirror of life; nay more, we maintain that it is so to audiences generally' ('The Pantomime of Life', *Bentley's Miscellany* 1[March 1837], 291).

Shortly before composing this episode, Dickens attended a pantomime and melodrama at one of London's cheap theatres on 28 December 1860 (Johnson and Johnson 337); he appears to have drawn on this visit for the essay he contributed to *AYR* on 25 February 1860 ('Two Views of a Cheap Theatre') and for the account of Wopsle's performance, first as the subterranean manufacturer of thunderbolts dressed in 'red worsted' stockings, and then as 'a sententious Enchanter', who helps two young lovers overcome opposition from the young woman's father:

> The Spirit of Liberty was the principal personage in the Introduction, and the Four Quarters of the World came out of the globe, glittering, and discoursed with the Spirit, who sang charmingly. . . . In an allegorical way . . . we and the Spirit of Liberty got into a kingdom of Needles and Pins, and found them at

war with a potentate who called in to his aid their old arch-enemy Rust, and who would have got the better of them if the Spirit of Liberty had not in the nick of time transformed the leaders into Clown, Pantaloon, Harlequin, Columbine, Harlequina, and a whole family of Sprites, consisting of a remarkably stout father and three spineless sons. . . . After this era in our existence, we went through all the incidents of a pantomime; it was not by any means a savage pantomime in the way of burning or boiling people, or throwing them out of window. (AYR 2.418)

Actors wore different-coloured stockings to signify their occupation: ordinarily, grey worsted was reserved for rustics and dark-blue for 'the Stage Countryman' (à Beckett 12).

Coming up from the antipodes] That is, through a trapdoor.

There was something so remarkable in the increasing glare

ascended to the clouds in a large watch-case,] A comic reference to a stage lift.

"I had a ridiculous fancy that he must be with you, Mr. Pip

like a ghost."] An allusion to *Hamlet*. See chapter 40, note on p. 323.

Chapter 48

The second of the two meetings referred to

about a week after the first.]   See Appendix 1.

I had strolled up into Cheapside,]   For Cheapside, see chapter 20, note on p. 175.

I was going to excuse myself

the lights were springing up brilliantly in the shop windows,]   For gas-lighting indoors, see chapter 33, note on pp. 280–1.

and the street lamp-lighters, scarcely finding ground enough to plant their ladders on]   Lamplighters carried a ladder to reach street gas-lamps, which had to be lit and extinguished by hand until the advent of electric street-lighting later in the century.

my rushlight tower at the Hummums]   See chapter 45, note on pp. 340–1.

At the office in Little Britain

the pair of coarse fat office candles . . . were decorated with dirty winding-sheets,]   The winding sheet is the solidified dripping of grease clinging to a candle and resembling a folded sheet, like a shroud. In popular superstition, a winding-sheet on a candle is considered an omen of death or calamity (OED).

"So, Pip! Our friend the Spider," said Mr. Jaggers

"has played his cards. He has won the pool."]   That is, he has beaten the other players in a card game and won the total amount of the stakes and fines.

"Hah! He is a promising fellow – in his way

If he should turn to, and beat her—"]   The husband's right of correction dates from the early sixteenth century, although the right was not an absolute one. It could not be exercised at will but only as a punishment for misbehaviour and that punishment, moreover, was not to be excessive. No definitive legal precedents, however, existed by which one might measure reasonable chastisement beyond the popular belief in the ancient doctrine that it was lawful for a husband to beat his wife provided that the stick he used was no thicker than his thumb. The survival of this claim, for which there was little legal authority, may have testified, comments one recent observer, 'to the strength of the conviction that not only should wife-beating be legal, but that the question of reasonable severity should be one for the individual husband' (Doggett 6–8). See also chapter 59, note on pp. 419–20.

"That's his secret.

many a long year."]   Dickens originally wrote 'a score of years' but substituted a less specific phrase when he reconsidered the novel's internal dating in the latter stages of the composition. Similarly, Dickens altered Wemmick's "A score of years ago " in MS to read "A score or so of years ago".

"A score or so of years ago

the Old Bailey]   The Justice Hall adjoining Newgate Prison. See also chapter 56, note on p. 400.

some gipsy blood in her]   Romany gypsies (of Hindu origin), resident in England since the sixteenth century, attracted suspicion: many viewed them as wild and lawless, and judged them indifferent to the Christian view of marriage as a sacrament. They were also linked with horse-stealing, confidence tricks and other forms of theft. Novelists tended to portray gypsy women as dark, wild and sexually attractive: Molly's good looks and her 'great quantity of streaming hair' (chapter 26) align her with Alice Marwood in *DS*, a 'supremely handsome' woman whose dark skin, hair and 'reckless and regardless beauty' suggest a similar ethnic origin and erotic appeal (33).

The presence of 'gipsy' blood in Estella, too, creates what Rosenberg calls 'an interestingly crooked' parallel between her and Lever's Catinka, a gypsy fortune-teller loved by Potts. On the day we gain our first glimpse of Estella in chapter 8, by coincidence, the adoptive father of Catinka (a clown) comments to Potts in chapter 30: 'Would that some rich person – it should be a lady – kind and gentle, and compassionate, could see her and take her away, from such associates, and this life of shame, ere it be too late' (*Norton* 420).

"Mr. Jaggers was for her," pursued Wemmick

He worked it himself at the police-office, day after day for many days, contending against even a committal; and at the trial where he couldn't work it himself, sat under Counsel, and – everyone knew – put in all the salt and pepper.]   The first round of Molly's defence occurred in one of London's lower courts before a stipendiary police-magistrate or a justice of the peace. Failing to prevent a committal, Jaggers saw his client indicted and imprisoned pending a trial by jury in a higher court. As a young attorney in a capital case, Jaggers had to yield to the lead counsel (in real life this would have been a King's Counsel), a barrister who advised on questions of law and conducted cases in court. The phrase, to 'put in all the salt and pepper', has not been traced but clearly refers to the role Jaggers takes in preparing final details relating to the case.

married . . . over the broomstick] A colloquial expression for a common-law marriage, that is one constituted by the consent of the parties and capable of proof by public knowledge. Such unions were routine between about 1750 and 1850, especially among miners, sailors, canal workers or 'navvies', costermongers, sweeps and dustmen (Paul Johnson 498–9). Related phrases from the time include 'living tally', 'besom weddings' and 'jumping over the besom', a bundle of rods or twigs used either as a birch or as a broom.

near Hounslow Heath.] An extensive open area near Hounslow in Middlesex approximately eleven miles west of London and former haunt of highwaymen. The Staines and Hanworth roads border the area to the north and south respectively.

Chapter 49 Thirtieth weekly number
22 June 1861

PUTTING Miss Havisham's note in my pocket,

I went down again by the coach next day.] See Appendix 1.

I alighted at the Halfway House, and breakfasted there, and walked the rest of the distance;] See chapter 28, note on p. 248. Walking from this point, Pip would have about nineteen miles to cover before arriving in Rochester between four and five in the afternoon. See Appendix 4, map pp. 445–7.

The best light of the day was gone

The nooks of ruin where the old monks had once had their refectories and gardens, and where the strong walls were now pressed into the service of humble sheds and stables,] Apparently a reference to some of the stones of a former bridge-chapel erected in 1396 which at a later date were used to build part of the stables attached to the Crown Inn in Rochester High Street (Gadd, 1929, 46).

The cathedral chimes] See Appendix 2.

the rooks, as they hovered about the grey tower and swung in the bare high trees of the priory-garden,] The 'grey tower', or central tower and spire, of Rochester Cathedral, is 156 feet high. The priory garden lies to the east and takes its name from the original priory founded in 1080.

An elderly woman whom I had seen before

the supplementary house across the back court-yard,] See the 'detached dwelling-house' in chapter 11, note on p. 115.

She asked this question

an unwonted tone of sympathy.] MS reads tone of sympathy 'that choked me'.

She presently rose from her seat

a yellow set of ivory tablets, mounted in tarnished gold, and wrote upon them with a pencil in a case of tarnished gold that hung from her neck.] A writing-tablet was a small, thin sheet or surface, or pair of surfaces hinged or fastened together, used for writing notes and often carried in the pocket. Tablets were made of wood, ivory or other materials and appear to have been used predominantly by women. David Copperfield, hoping to encourage domesticity in Dora, presents her one day with an old account-book of his aunt's and 'a set of tablets, and a pretty little pencil case and box of leads, to practice housekeeping with' (*DC* 41).

I knew not how to answer

That she had done a grievous thing in taking an impressionable child to mould into the form that her wild resentment, spurned affection, and wounded pride, found vengeance in, I knew full well. But that, in shutting out the light of day, she had shut out infinitely more; that, in seclusion, she had secluded herself from a thousand natural and healing influences; that, her mind, brooding solitary, had grown diseased, as all minds do and must and will that reverse the appointed order of their Maker; I knew equally well.] Dickens frequently remarks on the ill consequences for children of selfish adult behaviour. These observations resemble the charge brought against Mrs Clennam, whom the narrator accuses of reversing 'the order of Creation, and breath[ing] her own breath into a clay image of her Creator. Verily, verily, travellers have seen many monstrous idols in many countries; but no human eyes have ever seen more daring, gross, and shocking images of the Divine nature, than we creatures of the dust make in our own likeness, or our own bad passions' (*LD* 2.30). Compare also the narrator's reflections in *DS* on the 'enforced distortions' men work on Nature: 'Coop any son or daughter of our mighty mother within narrow range' and see what horrible consequences follow (47).

Reference to 'a thousand natural and healing influences' aligns this passage with an idea central to British Romanticism. Elsewhere, Dickens wrote that Nature has the power to engage our 'Natural affections and instincts', but like 'other beautiful works of [the Almighty], they must be reared and fostered' (*NN* 47).

I looked into the room where I had left her

I saw a great flaming light spring up. In the same moment I saw her running at me, shrieking, with a whirl of fire blazing all about her, and soaring at least as many feet above her head as she was high.] Fatal accidents arising from women's dresses catching fire prompted repeated warnings in the press. The flammability of the materials, open fireplaces and the popularity of bell-shaped crinoline dresses and skirts account for public concern, which, by 1860, 'had become almost a panic', prompted by as many as ten deaths in the first eight weeks of 1861 (Witt 153–4). 'Take what precautions we may against fire, so long as the hoop is worn, life is never safe. All are living under a sentence of death which may occur unexpectedly in the most appalling form' (*Illustrated News of the World*, 1863, quoted in Gernsheim, 1963, 47).

Pip's haunting final image of Miss Havisham has also been suggestively read in the context of Dickens's revision of earlier views he held about the non-restraint of the insane. Possibly public scandals and disclosures associated with John Conolly, a friend of Dickens and a leading opponent of incarceration in the 1830s, prompted a change in his thinking evident in the portrayal of mental illness in GE (Sutherland, 1995, 75). Harmless madness, such as the delusions that plagued Mr Dick (*DC*), Dickens came to realize, needed to be distinguished from those forms of madness that were dangerous: 'Like the pyromaniac Bertha Mason [in *Jane Eyre*], in her uncontrolled violence, Miss Havisham arsonizes her house, and destroys herself'. Better, one might conclude, that the poor woman had been confined and manacled rather than given the freedom with which Betsey Trotwood ministered to Mr Dick (Sutherland, 1995, 83).

I had a double-caped great-coat on

I had a double-caped great-coat on,] Voluminous greatcoats with a removable shoulder-cape date from the early nineteenth century. The coats often reached to the knees or ankles, and were popular with coachmen and travellers since the heavy outer capes provided warmth and protection against rain. A similar coat with a removable cape known as an Inverness overcoat or cloak was also popular. According to the *Gentleman's Herald* of 1859, this garment, named after the town in the Scottish Highlands, was so common that 'gentlemen of rank will not wear it' (quoted in Witt 156). Waterproof outer garments introduced about 1823 by Charles Mackintosh began to replace greatcoats with shoulder-capes later in the century.

That I got them off, closed with her, threw her down, and got them over her; that I dragged the great cloth from the table for the same purpose . . . that we were on the ground . . . and that the closer I covered her, the more wildly she shrieked and tried to free herself;] Victorian doctors recommended these steps when a dress caught fire, instructing victims to lie down (or be forced to the ground) and roll over and over since a horizontal position tended to keep flames from spreading rapidly towards the neck and head. Covering someone with a hearthrug, table-cover or shawl was also suggested as an effective way to extinguish flames. Burns from the dresses 'of females catching fire' were listed among the worst kind of accidents with fires (Keith Imray 101).

Though every vestige of her dress was burnt

they had covered her to the throat with white cotton-wool,] This was the recommended procedure for dressing burns after they had been washed carefully.

> The cotton employed should be finely carded, and then applied over the burned surface in thin layers one over another, until there is a covering sufficiently thick to exclude the air, and protect the parts from undue pressure; bandages are then to be applied over the whole of this envelope, so as to keep up a moderate and equal degree of pressure.

In the case of mild burns, doctors recommended removing the bandages within ten to fourteen days; for severe burns, which produced abundant discharge, the bandages were to be removed frequently and replaced with fresh dressings (Keith Imray 105).

I found, on questioning the servants

in Paris,]   Paris was a frequent destination for affluent travellers. The city offered a range of good hotels, many with English-speaking waiters, splendid and elegant coffee-houses, restaurants, gardens, walks, museums, theatres, operas, exhibitions, concerts, balls and other forms of amusement (Planta 82, 93). The voyage from London to Calais by steam-packet took up to fourteen hours; from Calais, passengers covered the remaining 162 miles to Paris by diligence in about thirty-two hours (Planta 10–11). Passports, issued on application to the French ambassador in Portland Place, London, were required for all travellers.

As I could do no service there

'I forgive her.' "]   After 'her' a final paragraph in the serial instalment published in *AYR* on 22 June 1861 reads: 'It was the first and the last time that I ever touched her in that way. And I never saw her more' (5.292).

Chapter 50

When Herbert had been down to Hammersmith

in the cooling liquid] Nineteenth-century medical practice emphasized the importance of excluding air from severely blistered skin. Burns were generally dressed with carron oil and other liniments made from a combination of olive oil or linseed oil and lime water spread on a cloth and applied directly to the burned skin two or three times a day. At a later stage, Turner's Cerate replaced the fluids. This emollient was advertised as a gentle 'drying ointment' made from palm oil, olive oil, yellow wax and Venetian turpentine (Buchan 639–40, 737).

Alternative methods of excluding air quickly included covering burns with flour or enveloping them completely in cotton wool. Before the application of cotton wool, immersing the burned parts in cold water, if practical, was also advised. Physicians recommended changing dressings once a week or more frequently in the case of a heavy discharge from the damaged skin (Keith Imray 101).

"So you did. And so he is.

You remember his breaking off here about some woman that he had had great trouble with] In chapter 42, Magwitch referred in passing to his 'Missis as [he] had the hard time wi' '.

"Now, whether," pursued Herbert

she had shared some four or five years of the wretched life he described to us at this fireside,] See Appendix 1.

fearing he should be called upon to depose about this destroyed child, and so be the cause of her death, he hid himself . . . kept himself dark . . . and out of the way of the trial,] This was a realistic decision on Magwitch's part as well as a necessary contrivance by Dickens in order for Magwitch to take Molly's oath at her word. Infanticide was regarded as murder and remained a capital felony until the Infanticide Act of 1922 (12 & 13 Geo. V, c. 18), when the killing of a new-born became the equivalent of manslaughter (*Encyclopaedia Britannica*, 1937, 15, 179).

"Particularly? Let me remember, then

'a round score o' year ago, and a'most directly after I took up wi' Compeyson.'] See Appendix 1.

"I think in my seventh year."

"I think in my seventh year."]   Magwitch appeared in 'the churchyard' on Christmas Eve, approximately a month after Pip's sixth birthday in November. This statement conflicts slightly with Dickens's earlier calculation in which he had written: 'Say Pip was about 7 at the opening of the story' (see 'Dates', p. 344).

"Ay. It had happened some three or four years then

"Ay. It had happened some three or four years then, he said, and you brought into his mind the little girl so tragically lost, who would have been about your age."]   In the MS, Dickens wrote 'about four years' and described Magwitch's daughter as Pip's age without further qualification, making her about 6 or 7 when the novel opens. For the dating of Molly's trial, see Appendix 1.

Chapter 51   Thirty-first weekly number
29 June 1861

Any way, I could scarcely be withheld

at the corner of Giltspur-street by Smithfield, I left Herbert to go his way into the City, and took my way to Little Britain.]   See Appendix 4, map pp. 442–3.

"Put the case that he lived in an atmosphere of evil

"Put the case . . . that all he saw of children, was, their being generated in great numbers for certain destruction. Put the case that he often saw children solemnly tried at a criminal bar, where they were held up to be seen; put the case that he habitually knew of their being imprisoned, whipped, transported, neglected, cast out, qualified in all ways for the hangman, and growing up to be hanged.]   Early in the nineteenth century no separate legal or court system existed for juveniles, and children as young as 7 were tried, imprisoned and transported on the same grounds as adults. Growing concern over the youthfulness of criminal offenders expressed in the periodical press prompted efforts by reformers to campaign for changes in the legal system in order to separate children from hardened criminals and prevent their descent into a life of crime. Early legislation designed to treat children as children when brought before the law includes the 1840 Infant Felon Act (3 & 4 Vict., c. 90) and the Juvenile Offenders Act (10 & 11 Vict., c. 82) of 1847. The first provided for the care and education of infants convicted of stealing; under the provisions of the second, magistrates were allowed to exercise summary disposition in cases of petty larceny committed by those under 14 and to discharge the offender without punishment, if they thought best. The arrest, trial and punishment of children represents one of the many 'shameful instances of neglect of children' Dickens continued to record ('The Short-timers', *AYR* 9.397). See, for example, *OT*, chs 11 and 43, and Paroissien (1992, 250).

"Put the case, Pip, that here was one pretty little child

here was one pretty little child out of the heap, who could be saved;]   Most likely from prostitution: young and unprotected girls in London were often ' "hocussed" and then ravished . . . scarcely a night elapses, but the most brutal violations take place, in houses, considered generally, most respectable of their kind' ('Decoying a Young Girl into a Brothel', 1838, 1).

At the first meeting of the Associate Institute for Improving and Enforcing the Laws for the Protection of Women in 1846, members attending spoke of the need to combat the existence of 'a widely organised and systematic traffic in Seduction and Prostitution, carried on by the agency of the Brothel-Keeper and Procurer . . . directed to ensnare and effect the ruin of young and unprotected females'. To supply brothels with young victims, agents were sent out into the country, where they inserted coded advertisements in newspapers, visited houses for the registration of servants, and watched coach offices and railway stations for young victims alone and unattended (*The First Report*, 21 July 1846, 7–8).

Efforts by reformers did little to deter procurers, who operated with near-immunity in their attempts to seduce girls as young as 12 and draw them into service. The government was slow to intervene and refused to take action, critics contended, because some of its own members were deeply implicated 'in this career of sensuality'. 'Dukes, lords, magistrates, bankers, and men prominent in the army and navy, and even ministers of the church, have been active ringleaders, patrons, and abettors of the cruel and destructive vice' (*The Female's Friend*, April 1846, 78).

Continued activity by reformers to stimulate legislation to protect 'young persons' from prostitution met with little success. Eventually Select Committees in the 1870s reporting on infant mortality, 'baby-farming', conditions in lying-in houses and the seduction of young women stirred the government to action.

"You did,'" said Wemmick.

spluttering like a bad pen.]   That is, scattering ink like a badly pointed and split quill pen. Compare 'A hard-nibbed pen which could be warranted not to splutter' (*PP* 33).

Chapter 52

From Little Britain

It was the only good thing I had done, and the only completed thing I had done, since I was first apprised of my great expectations.] Compare the wording in the 'General Mems: 2'. See chapter 37, note on p. 347.

Clarriker informing me on that occasion

a small branch-house in the East] Herbert later names Cairo (chapter 55), the capital of Egypt, as his destination. Britain's presence in the eastern Mediterranean dated from about 1800 and arose from attempts to counter Russian and French designs on the disintegrating Ottoman Empire and the overland route through Suez to the East. Trading patterns, in the first half of the century, fell into two principal divisions: the inland, Red Sea trade with its centre in Cairo, and the Mediterranean trade based primarily on the ports of Suez and Alexandria (*Dictionary of Trade*, 1844). The closing off of England's cotton supply owing to the American Civil War (1861–5) and the need of manufacturers to find an alternative source increased British commercial interests in Egypt, to which Dickens may indirectly allude here.

But there was recompense in the joy

airy pictures of ... the land of the Arabian Nights,] To many nineteenth-century Englishmen, Cairo summoned up 'the grand Cairo of the Arabian Nights'. John Capper, recalling his arrival there on a night of 'surprising loveliness', falls into a similar train of thought as he describes the 'lotus land' he encountered on a moonlit walk through the city. 'The whole scene, with its nocturnal stillness, its mosques, fountains, latticed windows, and fantastic gateways, conjures up vividly before me the legends of the Thousand and One Nights. It seems, indeed, like a picture, cut out of that wonderful volume' ('Cairo', *HW* 16.66). Dickens knew this collection of oriental tales (translated into French in twelve volumes 1704–8, and from French into several English versions) as a child and retained his fondness for the stories throughout his life.

Of our going up the Nile and seeing wonders] Public interest in attempts by Sir Richard Burton (1821–90) and other explorers to find the source of the Nile remained high throughout the 1850s, especially following the discovery of Lake Victoria Nyanza by John Hanning Speke (1827–64). On 3 August 1858 Speke expressed his belief that the lake he had discovered was the 'source reservoir' of the Nile. The verification of his claim at the meeting of the Royal Geographical Society on 11 May 1863 created a sensation, and Speke and his companion, Captain James Augustus Grant (1827–92), were credited with solving 'the problem of all ages'. The Nile, which flows from central Africa to its delta on the Mediterranean Sea, is the world's longest river.

We had now got into the month of March.

We had now got into the month of March.]   See Appendix 1.

On a Monday morning

On a Monday morning,]   See Appendix 1.

"Walworth. Burn this as soon as read.

"Walworth. . . . Early in the week, or say Wednesday]   MS reads 'or say Wednesday, if the tide should suit'.

When I had shown this to Herbert

we considered what to do.]   MS reads after 'do': 'Down to that time we had never interchanged a word on the subject of my being disabled, but of course it could be kept out of view no longer'.

It had seemed to me

Hamburg, Rotterdam, Antwerp. . . . Any foreign steamer . . . would do.]   All three cities were accessible by steamer from London in the 1820s, when services to Continental ports expanded rapidly. Steam-packets to Dunkirk, Hamburg, Ostend and Calais began in 1825, operated by General Steam Navigation, the company which introduced steamship travel on the Thames and the first to offer passenger services to foreign ports (R. J. B. Knight 38). The company advertised widely in London newspapers, including *The Times*, *The Morning Chronicle*, *The Herald* and *The Post*. One of their posters issued in 1826 referred to 'First Class and Powerful Steam Packets' starting from the Custom House or Tower pier, with weekly boats to Rotterdam taking twenty-six hours and services to Hamburg with a passage of fifty-four hours (see Plate 20; Cornford, 1924, 1, 4, 7, 27). Eight years later, the travelling time remained almost the same. Packets run by General Steam Navigation Company left for Hamburg and Rotterdam every Wednesday and Saturday morning, making the crossing in fifty-four and twenty-six hours respectively. Other destinations included Ostend, Antwerp (three boats every ten days), Boulogne, Calais and Dieppe ('Shipping', Box 6, Johnson Collection).

I had always proposed to myself to get him well down the river in the boat: certainly well beyond Gravesend, which was a critical place for search or inquiry if suspicion were afoot.] For one or more oarsmen in training, this thirty-five-mile trip down the Thames was a realistic plan. Gravesend (see Plate 21), a popular market-town and resort near the mouth of the river, was an obvious checkpoint for the Thames river police to search for a fugitive from justice. The town marked the limit of the jurisdiction of the London Custom House (chapter 47, note on p. 358), whose officers used the port to monitor ships leaving and entering the Thames. It was here that Customs officials also boarded in-bound vessels to collect duty on foreign goods. Below Gravesend, and adjacent to the Hoo peninsula, the river broadened considerably. Early in the century, wide expanses of water merged with desolate tracts of marshland undisturbed by signs of habitation or activity. See also chapter 54, note on pp. 383–4.

As foreign steamers would leave London at about the time of high-water, our plan would be to get down the river by a previous ebb-tide. . . . The time when one would be due . . . could be calculated pretty nearly,] See chapter 54, note on p. 384.

Herbert assented to all this

to get at once such passports as were necessary;] Travellers to the Continent generally had to apply to the London offices of individual ambassadors of the country they wished to visit. Applications for Hamburg were received at the Hanseatic Consul, 76 Cornhill; passports for Rotterdam were obtained from the ambassador at 11 Prince's Street, Cavendish Square. One alternative was to apply to the Agent for Aliens in Ball Court, Cornhill. The document issued in the 1830s was a sheet of paper about eleven inches square specifying the bearer's name with the date and a list of places to be visited. The application procedure was considerably less formal than is the case today ('Shipping' Box 6; 'Passports' folder, Johnson Collection).

"If you are not afraid to come to the old marshes

the little sluice-house by the limekiln,] A sluice gate with a house attached to it on the canal which ran across the marsh to Cliffe Creek has been proposed as a possible model (see Appendix 4, map p. 447). Near the sluice-gate end of the canal stood a flint-walled building which originally had a tiled roof; next to it was an old, dilapidated wooden hut erected on a brick foundation. This was never a habitable place but merely a shanty used by the man who attended the sluice gates (Gadd, 'The Lime-Kiln and the Sluice-House', 184). For lime-kilns and the lime industry on the Hoo peninsula, see chapter 53, note on p. 380.

It is so difficult to become clearly possessed of the contents

inside passenger,]   See chapter 28, note on p. 247.

jolting away knee-deep in straw,]   In 'Dullborough Town', Dickens evokes a similar journey but in reverse, when he writes autobiographically of his journey from Rochester to London as a child in 1822:

> Through all the years that have since passed, have I ever lost the smell of the damp straw in which I was packed – like game – and forwarded, carriage paid, to the Cross Keys, Wood-street, Cheapside, London? There was no other inside passenger, and I consumed my sandwiches in the solitude and dreariness, and it rained hard all the way, and I thought life sloppier than I had expected to find it. (*AYR* 3.274)

For straw on carriage floors, see chapter 20, note on p. 178.

My inn had once been a part

a part of an ancient ecclesiastical house, and I dined in a little octagonal common-room, like a font.]   This inn 'of minor reputation down the town' with its 'little octagonal common-room' perhaps owes something to the Mitre Hotel in Chatham. Adjoining the bar of the Mitre in Dickens's time was 'a small common room, furnished with dark and heavy furniture of somewhat ecclesiastical design and appearance and with a serving hatch communicating with the bar' (Gadd, 1929, 51–2). Rochester High Street ran straight through the town and into adjoining Chatham, whose own main street was 'down the town' in relation to Rochester.

My heart was deeply and most deservedly humbled

Towards the marshes I now went straight, having no time to spare.]   The distance between the inn and the sluice house is about five miles. See Appendix 4, map p. 449.

Chapter 53 Thirty-second weekly number
6 July 1861

The direction that I took

The direction that I took, was not that in which my old home lay, nor that in which we had pursued the convicts. My back was turned towards the distant Hulks as I walked on, and, though I could see the old lights away on the spits of sand, I saw them over my shoulder.]   Lower Higham, Pip's former 'village', is about three miles south-west of Cliffe. See Appendix 2 and Appendix 4, map on p. 449.

limekiln]   This area and the district further west towards Gravesend were well known for their lime-kilns, the leading feature of the landscape, according to accounts by contemporary visitors (*Summer Excursions in the County of Kent*, 1847, 193). Large deposits of limestone found in north-east Kent made possible the production of lime, one of the earliest industries on the Hoo peninsula.

Stone or brick lime-kilns in one of two external shapes (cylindrical or square) were shaped inside like an egg and were filled with alternating layers of burning coal and limestone broken into fist-sized pieces (Loudon, 1857, 625). A ramp or inclined plane of earth enabled workers to load coal and lime from the top of the kiln. Sods or turf provided insulation to keep the heat as intense as possible. Apertures at the bottom admitted air. The product, burned limestone or calcined lime, is a powerful caustic; combined with water, it generates great heat and forms hydrate of lime or slaked lime. Lime was used extensively in the building trade and was regarded at the time as 'the most essential ingredient in all cements' (Buchanan). Large quantities of lime were also exported to farming communities in Essex and Sussex (Willmott 2). Kilns were located close to quarries (see below).

It was another half-hour before I drew near to the kiln.

The lime was burning with a sluggish stifling smell, but the fires were made up and left, and no workmen were visible.]   Draw kilns, or perpetual kilns, loaded with alternating layers of lime and coal and covered with turf, could be left to burn slowly for at least twenty-four hours. Often they burned for as long as four or five days. As the limestone was thoroughly burned and the coal depleted, workmen added more fuel and limestone from the top and raked out the calcined lime below. The 'stifling' smell comes from the fuel in the kiln. Lime, when burned, gives off odourless carbon dioxide. Among the likely emissions are soot, which occurs when coal is burned in closed spaces with little ventilation, and sulphur dioxide, a malodorous gas whose smell resembles the heavy, choking smell of rotten eggs.

Hard by, was a small stone-quarry.]   Carbonate of lime was mined from limestone quarries. A composite Ordnance Survey map of the region printed late in the nineteenth century shows a chalk quarry about a mile inland at the foot of the escarpment on which Cliffe stands. Chalk mined from this quarry was taken by a canal which ran across the marsh about a mile west of Cliffe village. At Cliffe Creek chalk and lime were loaded on to sailing barges and shipped up the Thames.

The sudden exclusion of the night

he found the flint and steel he wanted, and began to strike a light. I strained my sight . . . but I could only see . . . the blue point of the match;] Orlick lights the match by first igniting dry materials in the tinder-box with a spark struck from the flint and steel. Friction or Lucifer matches, as they were first known, were not invented until 1827, making this an anachronistic detail.

The man was in no hurry

a flare of light . . . showed me Orlick.] In allegorical terms, the encounter resembles Pilgrim's meeting with Apollyon, or the Devil, in Bunyan's *Pilgrim's Progress* (Q. D. Leavis 321).

"You're a liar. And you'll take any pains

to the last brass farden!"] That is, to the lowest possible coin, a copper farthing, one quarter of a penny.

"More than that," said he

"I won't have a rag of you, I won't have a bone of you, left on earth. I'll put your body in the kiln] The combined action of caustic lime and fire, in due course, would obliterate all trace of a body. The setting and Orlick's incantatory language suggest an affinity with a giant from nursery rhymes and fairy-tales: 'Fee, fi, fo, fum – /I smell the blood of an Englishman/Be he alive or be he dead/I'll grind his bones to make my bread'.

"You with a uncle too!

weazen] A slang term for the throat.

he dropped your sister with it, like a bullock,] In the slaughter-house, bullocks and other cattle were felled or 'dropped' by a heavy blow to the head.

"Ah!" he cried, laughing, after doing it again

"the burnt child dreads the fire!] A proverbial expression (*Oxford Dictionary of English Proverbs*).

The resolution I had made did not desert me

fly out into the night.] Marginal instructions in the manuscript read: 'Printer, two white lines here'. The intervening double spacing between this paragraph and the next presumably was designed to suggest a lapse of time between Pip's fainting and his regaining consciousness after the rescue. Modern editions ignore the injunction (Rosenberg, 1972, 304–5).

Entreating Herbert to tell me

Finding that the afternoon coach was gone . . . he resolved to follow in a post-chaise.] The decision to hire a small light vehicle carrying only one or two passengers appears to be a realistic detail consistent with the need for speed and Pip's earlier departure. Post-chaises for private hire were always available at large coaching establishments, which kept horses and post-boys ready to leave at short notice. Posting, however, was expensive: in addition to tolls, turnpike fees and tips, the carriage and a pair of horses cost 1s 6d a mile, plus 3d a mile for the post-boy, who rode one of the horses as a postilion.

they went out to the sluice-house: though by the town way to the marshes, which I had avoided.] Evidently Herbert's party takes a parallel route about half a mile to the west. See Appendix 4, map p. 449.

Wednesday morning was dawning

The winking lights upon the bridges] Blackfriars Bridge, Southwark Bridge and London Bridge would have been visible to the east and Waterloo Bridge to the west.

Chapter 54

Thirty-third weekly number
13 July 1861

We loitered down to the Temple stairs

It was then about high-water – half-past eight.] An extant sheet of notes made by Dickens before he wrote this chapter reveals that he consulted a table of tides for the Thames (see p. 348). The action opens on a Wednesday morning in March; high tides for that day occurred at 9 a.m. and 9 p.m. The early departure, therefore, takes advantage of these conditions. See also below.

Our plan was this.

Our plan was this.] Dickens made further careful preparations prior to describing the aborted flight down the Thames. On 22 May 1861 he hired a steamer to sail from a large wharf at the terminal of the railway at Blackwall to Mucking Flats (see below) and beyond to Southend almost fifty miles away on the north shore of the Thames estuary. He undertook this excursion, Forster explains, 'To make himself sure of the actual course of a boat in such circumstances, and what possible incidents the adventure might have':

> Eight or nine friends and three or four members of his family were on board, and he seemed to have no care, the whole of that summer day . . . except to enjoy their enjoyment and entertain them with his own in shape of a thousand whims and fancies; but his sleepless observation was at work all the time, and nothing had escaped his keen vision on either side of the river. The fifteenth chapter of the third volume is a masterpiece. (Forster 9.3.287)

The tide, beginning to run down at nine, and being with us until three, we intended still to creep on after it had turned, and row against it until dark.] Their objective is to cover approximately twenty-seven miles before the tide turned and use the remaining three hours of daylight in which to make slower progress through Lower Hope Reach to a point about ten miles beyond Gravesend (see map on pp. 447–8). Thirty miles in about six hours on dead water, i.e. without resistance from the tide, was considered good progress, a fair day's work for practised oarsmen (De Colquhoun 9).

We should then be well in those long reaches below Gravesend, between Kent and Essex, where the river is broad and solitary, where the water-side inhabitants are very few, and where lone public-houses are scattered here and there,] To get to this point, the oarsmen must travel through seventeen 'reaches', sections of the river that can be seen in one view (see map on pp. 444–8). Beyond Gravesend, twenty-seven miles below London Bridge, are Hope Reach, a 3°-mile stretch of water, and Sea Reach. This reach, the largest, most important and last reach of the Thames, extends for nearly thirteen miles, from Mucking Flats to the Nore, as the river runs through the counties of Essex on the north shore and Kent on the south. On both banks the shores are flat and marshy; on the Essex side, rise the low Laindon Hills opposite the deserted terrain Pip describes in the novel's first chapter.

Oarsmen viewed the journey from London Bridge to Gravesend Reach and beyond as a challenge. Distances between stopping-places increased lower down the river. The tide also became an important factor:

> [it] runs so strong that rowing against it for many miles is out of the question; but, for the same reason, the rate of travelling with the tide is very great (about seven or more miles an hour, fair rowing). The distance *down* from London to the Nore or Southend cannot be accomplished in one tide; but up from Southend to London Bridge, it may be done by starting one hour after the flood from Southend. (Wood 53)

This same authority suggested that it was not advisable to go beyond Gravesend in one tide, 'as the tide would barely serve as far as Hole Haven, which is ten miles further down'. Hole Haven on Canvey Island is the place where they rest for the night. See below.

Gravesend in the nineteenth century was 'a place of little picturesque beauty, but of considerable commercial importance, being the first port on the river, and consequently connected in a particular manner with its navigation' (*Picturesque Tour of the River Thames*, 1828, 161).

The steamer for Hamburg, and the steamer for Rotterdam would start from London at about nine on Thursday morning.] After 'morning' MS reads 'and would be in our part of the river at about noon'. Steamers for Continental ports typically left from piers adjacent to London Bridge and the Customs House on the full tide.

We should know at what time to expect them, according to where we were, and would hail the first;] Since Pip knows that each boat leaves at nine o'clock and has approximately thirty-seven miles to cover at speeds up to 6 m.p.h., he can estimate with some accuracy the time of their arrival in Hope Reach. Dickens appears to have worked out the rates of travel quite carefully. Smoke from the first steamer is spotted at 1.30 p.m., indicating that the ships covered the distance at about 6 m.p.h. This speed fits with limits steamers observed on the Thames and remains consistent with the performance of vessels operating in the 1820s. I have been unable to document the practice of hailing steamboats in order to stop them.

We knew the distinguishing marks of each vessel.] Sea-going steamers of the period had side-mounted paddles (boxed in) some fifteen feet in diameter. Wooden hulls, up to eighty feet long with a beam between twelve and fifteen feet, a single square sail and a twenty-five-foot smokestack would have given each common features, perhaps distinguished only by company markings and the name on the bow. The majority of passengers sat in the saloon; up to twelve private cabins were available.

At that time, the steam-traffic on the Thames

At that time, the steam-traffic on the Thames was far below its present extent, and watermen's boats were far more numerous.] Pip writes from the perspective of almost forty years, during which period water traffic on the Thames changed considerably. At the time of Magwitch's attempted escape, watermen maintained their supremacy; and their boats, plying from numerous stairs between Westminster Bridge and London Bridge, accounted for much of the waterborne traffic on the river in central London. Below London Bridge, however, sail predominated: most of the coastal traffic relied on sail; and sail retained its monopoly for services to North America, Britain's colonies and other distant ports since steamers in the early decades of the nineteenth century proved far less suited to ocean routes on account of their need to carry coal as fuel.

Steamers, however, came into their own on shorter routes – a development which began as early as 1815. Their challenge was evident in two traditional spheres: from about 1815 steam vessels offered increasing competition on short routes above London Bridge and on the longer routes (formerly the preserve of sail) to Greenwich, Margate, Ramsgate and Continental ports in France, Belgium, Holland and Germany (David Smith 95). Thus, by about 1860, the presumed time when Pip composes his memoirs, it was accurate to comment that few watermen survived. If they did, wrote one observer, 'it must be beyond the [western] limits of the bridges and the range of the half-penny, penny, and two-penny steamers, which would peril the safety of his wherry and the lives of his fare'. The 'jolly young waterman' of the days of George III 'has been effectively banished from the London river' (Charles Manby Smith, 1853, 103). Others noted a comparable change in steam traffic as speed, dependability and improved safety soon overwhelmed the inconveniences of sail. 'Countless thousands' annually pass up and down the Thames 'in steam-packets', Porter recorded in 1836, so that 'within the last five years [steam vessels] have, in a great degree, superseded the use of sailing vessels' (2.46–8). Steamers retained their supremacy until about mid-century when they, in turn, were surpassed in popularity by trains operating between London and points on the north Kent shore (Thornton 2).

barges, sailing colliers, and coasting-traders,] 'Barge' is a general term for a large flat-bottomed vessel used for the transport of coastal freight. Barges lack keels, so they can operate effectively in shallow water and remain upright when they are grounded.

Increased use of sea coal shipped from Newcastle, Sunderland, Blyth, Scotland, and Wales later expanded the coastal trade from nearly five hundred colliers in 1788 to 4,500 by the middle of the nineteenth century, as the demand for fuel increased. The practice was for the ships to dock and wait for lightermen to unload the coal, which was then transported to the principal London dealers for sale to smaller retailers (Anderson 4.701; *Dictionary of Trade*, 1844).

Sailing colliers (two-masted, and square-rigged on both the fore and main mast) were strong, bluff-bowed, broad-sterned boats used to transport coal. Coastal traders, by definition, restricted their trips to coastal waters and generally sailed back and forth between specific ports. Many paintings by J. M. W. Turner portray the density of inshore boat traffic during the early decades of the century.

skiffs and wherries,]   The term 'skiff' has two applications: generally, to light boats designed for rowing or sailing; and in a more limited sense to a long, narrow racing boat for one sculler. Wherries are light rowing boats used on rivers to transport goods or passengers; a sleek version for a single sculler also exists.

Old London Bridge was soon passed

old Billingsgate market with its oyster-boats and Dutchmen,]   Billingsgate market on Lower Thames Street between London Bridge and the site of the former Custom House (see chapter 47, note on p. 358) specialized from the end of the seventeenth century in the sale of fish. 'Old' Billingsgate, 'a collection of wooden pent-houses, rude sheds and benches', disappeared when the market was extended and rebuilt in the 1840s. Fishing vessels tied up to a floating quay at night, and the fish was brought ashore in baskets (Timbs, 1867, 54–5) and sold in lots by 'Dutch auction' – the practice of starting with an excessive sum and then working backwards (*Complete Book of Trades* 236).

Billingsgate was also the centre of London's oyster trade, which employed several hundred men and boys. The annual shipments in the 1840s totalled around fifty tons and came from several sources: from artificially formed and cultivated oyster beds in the estuary of the Thames, from Purfleet and Colchester in Essex, and from nurseries in Hampshire, Dorset and Scotland (*Dictionary of Trade*, 1844). Strict regulations helped oysters flourish by banning their sale between May and August during the breeding season.

The presence of Dutch boats off Billingsgate was a common sight on account of Holland's monopoly of the eel trade. Popular lore claims that the Dutch were granted this privilege because they were willing to continue shipments of eels to London during the height of the bubonic plague in 1665 (Thompson 30). In the 1840s two main Dutch companies operated, each with five boats designed with large wells in which large quantities of live eels were kept until they were sold.

the White Tower and Traitors' Gate,]   The White Tower, or Keep, a massive fort originally built to defend or command the City of London and added to by successive monarchs, dates from the eleventh century. Commonly known as 'the Tower of London', the stronghold stands on the north bank of the Thames just under a mile from the site of old London Bridge. The White Tower, so named from its having been originally whitewashed, also served as the principal detention centre for state prisoners (Timbs, 1867, 791–806).

Traitors' Gate was the popular name for the water-gate entrance to the Tower from the Thames. The name derives from the practice, 'in former and more arbitrary times', of using this gate 'to convey state prisoners by water, to and from the Tower' (Anderson 4.48). Prisoners arriving by boat under heavy guard were then taken to dungeons in the Tower to await trial for treason and, if convicted, beheading. The gate itself was a stone arch, before which was a flight of stone steps washed by the tide.

In 1865, Timbs called Traitors' Gate 'a modernized sham' which had lost 'its ancient dignity'. 'The whole of the upper part is [now] crammed with offices, and disfigured in every possible manner; and the gloom of Traitors' Gate is now broken up by the blatant noise of steam-machinery for hoisting and packing war-weapons' (1865, 1.50). Timbs also noted that the moat had been drained in 1843, after the water level had fallen in previous years, and then filled up and turfed to provide exercise for troops garrisoned there. Sheep occasionally grazed on the grass. The moat was last in commission in 1830 when the Duke of Wellington ordered it to be cleaned and filled with water should riots accompany agitation for the Reform Bill of 1832 (1867, 794).

the Leith, Aberdeen, and Glasgow steamers,] During the winter months in cooler weather large quantities of slaughtered meat were shipped to the metropolis by steam vessels from Aberdeen, Leith (the port of Edinburgh) and Glasgow (Porter, 1836, 3.93–4), three of Scotland's principal ports. The number of steamers used to transport other goods and passengers also increased in the course of the century once steamers had demonstrated their reliability on short sea routes around the coast of Britain.

here, were colliers by the score and score, with the coal-whippers plunging off stages on deck, as counterweights to measures of coal swinging up,] For sailing colliers, see above. Early in the nineteenth century, colliers outnumbered all other vessels on the Thames (*Summer Excursions in the County of Kent*, 1847, 172–4) until steamers and then trains provided the principal means of transporting coal from the north of England to the metropolis.

Men called 'coal-whippers' removed almost all coal from colliers by hand, transferring it to lighters or barges capable of holding almost sixty tons of coal (Horne, *HW* 1.92). They usually operated in gangs of nine or so and set to work having first agreed upon a price per ton for the removal of the coal:

> Some of them descend into the hold, and fill baskets or boxes with coals, and others draw up the laden baskets by means of ropes, pulleys, and a stage of steps, and empty the contents into the barges. The work is the coarsest and rudest kind of manual labour.

Nine men working in this mode would 'whip' about eighty tons of coal a day (Charles Knight 495). When the lighter alongside the collier was full, it was allowed to float with the tide to the wharf of one of the numerous coal-merchants engaged in the London coal trade (*Complete Book of Trades* 154–5). Coal-handling machines for unloading ships were invented and one was tried on the Thames in 1805, but efforts by coal-whippers blocked the use of such devices until the second half of the century (Forbes 15; Sheppard 195).

Mill Pond stairs.] Several sets of stairs existed on the Surrey shore of Limehouse and Deptford reaches, but none with this name.

We touched the stairs lightly

He had a boat-cloak with him, and a black canvas bag,] A boat-cloak was 'A mantle for the officer going on duty; when left in the boat it is in the coxswain's charge' (Smyth).

he looked as like a river-pilot as my heart could have wished.] Trinity House Company, the prestigious fraternity founded in 1515 to train and license pilots, recognized two classes of men: River Pilots, who guided ships between London Bridge and Gravesend, and Channel Pilots, who took ships out to sea through the channels between sandbanks at the mouth of the estuary, and on to Dover or even further. In fact, river pilots wore no specific uniform until 1899, when they adopted the dress of navy blue and jackets with brass buttons. Presumably, Magwitch's outfit would have looked something like this (Grosvenor 83; *Tables of the Rates of Pilotage*, 1862).

Again among the tiers of shipping

under the figure-head of the John of Sunderland making a speech to the winds (as is done by many Johns), and the Betsy of Yarmouth with a firm formality of bosom and her knobby eyes starting two inches out of her head,] Figureheads – ornamental and painted carvings placed over the cutwater of a ship – included designs, birds (usually eagles) and male and female figures, either full-length or half-length. The 'John' from the north-eastern port of Sunderland may have been a serious-looking gentleman, formally dressed in a neck-cloth and jacket, hence Pip's reference to his making a speech. The 'many Johns' speaking 'to the winds' appears to contain a double allusion: to St John the Baptist, patron saint of missionaries, perhaps gesturing as he cries 'in the wilderness' (Matthew 3.3; Mark 1.3; Luke 3.4), and to Lord John Russell (1792–1878), Foreign Secretary under Aberdeen and Palmerston, and Prime Minister (1846–52), who on 24 July 1861 delivered his farewell address to the electors of the City of London when he vacated his seat preparatory to elevation to the House of Lords (McMaster 431; Joseph Irving, *Annals*, 1875).

The second figurehead of the bare-breasted Betsy from Great Yarmouth, Norfolk, a coastal fishing port about 120 miles north-east of London, reflects a nautical superstition that a naked woman was believed to have the power to calm a storm at sea. The 'staring' eyes evidently represent another superstition: they are the '*occuli*' traditionally painted on the bow of ships to ward off evil spirits.

pumps going in leaky ships,] Wooden ships required almost continuous pumping because as the timbers and planks moved slightly sea-water inevitably seeped through into the bilges. Caulking with hemp slowed the rate at which water trickled through.

Lightermen,] Lightermen worked aboard lighters, flat-bottomed barges used for unloading coal from colliers (Horne). They operated within a limited range, working in the Pool and on the river not much below or above the bridges. Lightermen led a rough life. They were exposed to all kinds of weather and put in long hours of heavy labour, often at night, to accommodate tides and the movement of ships (*Trades for London Boys*, 1908). See also below.

The air felt cold upon the river

By imperceptible degrees, as the tide ran out, we lost more and more of the nearer woods and hills, and dropped lower and lower between the muddy banks, but the tide was yet with us when we were off Gravesend.] At this point in the journey, the vertical rise and fall of the water is about eighteen feet. Beyond Gravesend, the estuary begins to broaden considerably as shallows and mud banks appear on either side, exposed by the ebbing tide.

As our charge was wrapped in his cloak, I purposely passed within a boat or two's length of the floating Custom House,] The 'floating Custom House' most probably refers to a galley, an open boat with six to eight oars, used on the Thames by customs officers. For the work of customs officers, see below.

two emigrant ships,] Emigrant ships in the days of sail were large wooden vessels with flat bottoms (to enable them to sit upright at low tide), square sterns and full, rounded hulls (Greenhill and Gifford 79). Living conditions aboard made the four-month passage to Australia something of an ordeal: one emigrant described the interior as 'A long, dark gallery, on each side of which were ranged the berths – narrow shelves open to every prying eye – where . . . the inmates were to be packed, like herrings in a barrel, without room to move, almost without air to breathe' (Sidney, 1854, 141).

Historians offer different explanations for the 20 million people who left Britain between 1815 and 1914. Some argue that emigration served as a safety valve by providing opportunities abroad – the United States and British colonies were the principal destinations – for unemployed rural labourers and other victims of distress. Work by recent historians questions the view that economic hardship prompted people to leave and that emigration protected England from serious social upheaval during the nineteenth century. They emphasize instead that many emigrants were self-motivated urban people who were drawn abroad by reports from friends who had gone before and done well. Dickens shared a view held by Caroline Chisholm, Angela Burdett Coutts and others that life in one of Britain's colonies offered opportunities that were often denied at home. Dickens provides a brief portrait of a group of emigrants crowded aboard a ship off Gravesend in *DC* (57); Australia, for the Micawbers and Mr Peggotty's family, is a land where blessings fall on them and they all do 'nowt but prosper' (63).

a large transport with troops] This was either a government ship or a private merchant vessel sailing under contract for the government. In both cases the ship would serve as a supply vessel, carrying troops, both cavalry and infantry, horses, artillery, baggage, field equipage and all other requisites for service abroad (Adolphus

2.264). Ships were also commissioned by the government to transport prisoners to New South Wales and other penal colonies.

And soon the tide began to slacken, and the craft lying at anchor to swing, and presently they had all swung round, and the ships that were taking advantage of the new tide to get up to the Pool, began to crowd upon us in a fleet,]   Gravesend was where inbound ships anchored, awaiting a favourable wind and tide to complete their passage up the river to the Pool. Outbound vessels stopped at Gravesend to take on water, provisions, livestock and passengers. Gravesend also offered travellers a final opportunity to say goodbye to friends and family members. When David Copperfield and his old nurse go down to Gravesend to take their leave of Mr Peggotty and his party, they find the ship in the river 'surrounded by a crowd of boats' and immediately hire their own so they can put off and go on board for an emotional parting (*DC* 57).

Our oarsmen were so fresh

like my own marsh country,]   The south shore of Essex bordering the Thames is also fronted by extensive mud-flats, which run out from the mainland for as much as a mile, covered by water ranging from two to twelve feet at high tide.

the winding river turned and turned,]   Beyond Gravesend, the river turns north into Lower Hope Reach before straightening out into Sea Reach and Hole Haven, their destination. See Appendix 4, map on pp. 446–8.

the great floating buoys]   Three kinds predominated: conical, spherical and cans. Can and spherical buoys varied from between five and twelve feet in height. Trinity House, the guild established in the reign of Henry VIII, was responsible for the maintenance of all aids to navigation around the coasts of England and Wales.

the last green barge, straw-laden, with a brown sail,]   The manufacture of straw goods in London and in other towns required the importation of foreign straw on a large scale. The raw product, after it had been cleaned and bleached, was braided and then plaited into hats, baskets, artificial flowers, mats and other items. Treating straw with the fumes of burning sulphur gave English straw goods 'an enviable whiteness' unobtained by manufacturers elsewhere (*Complete Book of Trades* 419–20; Simmonds, *Dictionary of Trade*, 1858).

Imported straw was moved up and down the river in sailing barges. The brown, tanned sail belonged to a Thames sailing barge: a vessel with a distinctive square bow, shallow-draughted, capacious and yet seaworthy, despite its low freeboard (Tomlinson and Tomlinson). Some were rigged with stepped masts, so they could pass under bridges or through canals. Others, which worked only on the Thames and the Medway and around the south-east coast, had a fixed mast amidships and no top mast or a sail over the stern (Dear and Kemp 10; *Dictionary of Trade*, 1844).

ballast-lighters,] Ballast lighters, low, flat-bottomed vessels propelled by oars, supplied extra weight for the holds of sailing ships when they were unloaded to counterbalance the effect of wind and give wooden ships stability so they could carry sail without danger of upsetting. Gravel, sand and stones dug from the Thames (often by convict labour) or iron or lead were the materials most frequently used as ballast for empty ships (*Dictionary of Trade*, 1844).

a little squat shoal-lighthouse on open piles, stood crippled in the mud on stilts and crutches, and slimy stakes stuck out of the mud . . . and red landmarks and tidemarks stuck out of the mud,] This was Mucking Flats Lighthouse off Mucking Creek on the north bank of the river some thirty-two miles from London Bridge. It was painted black and white in alternate horizontal bands and connected to the shore by a long footbridge, built on piles and painted white (*Dickens's Dictionary of the Thames*, 1880, 125). A temporary light was first installed here in October 1849; reference in the novel to the permanent structure (erected two years later and tended by two keepers) makes this an anachronistic detail. The light served to warn vessels of Blythe Sand, a shoal which extends to Hole Haven (see below). England's first lighthouse, the timber-built Eddystone Lighthouse off the south-eastern coast of Cornwall, was erected in 1700.

We pushed off again

It was much harder work now,] By late afternoon, the oarsmen had lost the advantage of the tide as it ebbed and by about three they faced the returning flood, which set at a maximum average of 2.8 knots, hence the need for effort. The direction and strength of the wind are additional factors affecting the tides of the Thames (John Irving 1–2).

As the night was fast falling

the first lonely tavern] The inn on Canvey Island, six miles further downstream. See Appendix 4, map p. 452 and below.

At this dismal time

thowels.] A variant spelling of 'thole', a rowlock.

At length we descried a light and a roof

**ran alongside a little causeway made of stones that had been picked up hard-by. Leaving the rest in the boat, I stepped ashore, and found the light to be in a window of a public-house. It was a dirty place enough, and I dare say not

unknown to smuggling adventurers;] The description suggests the landing at Hole Haven Creek, which forms the western boundary of Canvey Island. Steps within the entrance of the creek offered an accessible landing place at all states of the tide, making the creek 'of great utility to fishermen in all weathers' (Nicholls 143–4). The steps were also handy for the Lobster Smack Inn, a remote public house which, in the nineteenth century, offered beds and food. The inn and landing place would have been visible from the steamer Dickens hired. Canvey Island, a small, low-lying island approximately 4° miles long west-south-west of Leigh, is formed by a channel which runs from Leigh up to South Benfleet; its 2,600 acres of marshland were used primarily as pasture for cattle (James Dugdale 2.363). Hole Haven Creek is now a popular yacht anchorage.

Many resorted to smuggling in the 1820s, the result of high tariffs, a labour market depressed by high unemployment and the discharge of 120,000 highly trained seamen from the Navy after 1815 (Shanes 34).

the "Jack"] A common labourer, one who performs odd jobs.

With this assistant, I went down to the boat again

bandboxes] Bandboxes – light wooden or cardboard boxes covered with paper – were originally constructed to store 'bands' or ruffs worn in the seventeenth century. Later, they were adapted for storing caps, hats and millinery.

While we were comforting ourselves by the fire

who had a bloated pair of shoes on . . . that he had taken a few days ago from the feet of a drowned seaman washed ashore] A variant of this image occurs in the description of 'the swollen saturated clothes' Dickens saw in the Paris Morgue on one of his visits ('Lying Awake', *HW* 6.147). For persons drowned in the Thames, see below.

a four-oared galley] The Thames River Police (founded in 1798) used similar vessels, rowed by three men, two pulling a 'rowing' oar each, and one a pair of sculls, shorter lighter oars, both operated by a person seated midway between the sides of the boat ('Down with the Tide', *HW* 6.484). The jurisdiction of the River Police extended along the course of the Thames as it ran through the counties of Middlesex and Surrey and Essex and Kent, but their most common and busiest area of supervision lay between Westminster Bridge and Greenwich (Grant, 1838, 193–224). The 'sitters' subsequently referred to are passengers as distinct from either the rowers or the steersman.

"They put in with a stone two-gallon jar

rattling physic] That is, a cathartic or purge of great severity.

"You thinks Custum 'Us, Jack!" said the landlord.

Custum 'Us] Custom House officers were appointed by the Crown. In their earliest role, they collected duties on wool, the Crown's most productive source of revenue in the fourteenth century. Gravesend was their original base until the centre of operations moved to the Port of London in the seventeenth century (Cruden 102). Customs officials working on the river had numerous responsibilities. They collected duties on a wide range of imports, examined bills of entry for all incoming ships, cleared outward-bound vessels, checked passenger-lists and tallied the number and tonnage of ships entering the Port of London. In addition, Customs men enforced quarantine regulations and watched for smugglers. Ships engaged in coastal trading were the only vessels they did not have to check (Jukes Pritchard Jones).

"Done with their buttons?" returned the Jack.

small salad.] A slang expression for mustard and cress.

This dialogue made us all uneasy

On the whole we deemed it the better course to lie where we were . . . then to get out in her track, and drift easily with the tide.] The deep-water channel for steamers lay close to Canvey Island, making it relatively easy to put off from Hole Haven and get into the steamer's track. Leaving from the south side of the river would have been difficult on account of the exposure of Blythe Sands. A boat would have had to push off more than an hour before the steamer left London in order to catch the tide and then hang about in the channel, fighting the strong ebb tide for four or five hours until the steamer arrived (Gadd, 1929, 144–5).

I lay down with the greater part of my clothes on

in the direction of the Nore.] The Nore anchorage lay to the east opposite Sheerness, where the Medway joins the Thames estuary and the sea. The Nore lightship was a floating beacon 'always to be illuminated at sun set, or sooner, if the gloominess of the weather should require it'. The light began in 1730 with two large lanterns suspended at each end of a sloop; replaced by a single more powerful light in 1825, the signal finally evolved into a single revolving light in 1850 (*Dickens's Dictionary of the Thames*, 1880).

When he looked out from his shelter in the distance

By that time it wanted but ten minutes of one o'clock, and we began to look out for her smoke.] These appear to be realistic calculations, based on actual timetables (see note above). The relatively flat shores on both sides of the river and a smokestack over twenty feet high would have made the steamer visible from a distance, despite bends in the river.

But, it was half-past one before we saw her smoke

I saw a four-oared galley shoot out from under the bank but a little way ahead of us,] Dead Man's Point, a low point of land a mile or so east of Hole Haven, may have provided cover for the officers' boat (Gadd, 1929, 148).

Startop could make out, after a few minutes

the beating of her paddles] Early steam ships were powered by paddles, large wheels housed on each side of the boat in boxes. 'The paddle steamer was, *par excellence*, a comfortable steamer and was conspicuously steady in a rough sea' (Burtt 5). Paddles rather than screw propellers prevailed until about 1875, by which time screws came to the fore when railway and shipping companies abandoned the construction of paddle vessels.

It was but for an instant that I seemed to struggle

that instant past, I was taken on board the galley. Herbert was there, and Startop was there; but our boat was gone, and the two convicts were gone.] This description differs from the one Dickens originally projected in his working plans for the novel. See p. 346.

The Jack at the Ship was instructed

Probably, it took about a dozen drowned men to fit him out completely;] Casualties on the Thames in the nineteenth century were high: Timbs reports that some 500 persons were drowned each year. The collision of vessels accounts for a number of these deaths, one third of which occurred in the Pool of London, a section of the river below Old London Bridge (1867, 687).

Apart from any inclinations of my own

I foresaw that, being convicted, his possessions would be forfeited to the Crown.] Until the Forfeiture Act of 1870 (33 & 34 Vict., c. 32), which abolished forfeitures for treason and felony, the Crown automatically claimed the goods of felons, suicides and persons convicted of treason. What Pip does not foresee, and what the demands of the plot evidently compel Dickens to overlook, is that Pip,

Herbert and Startop were accomplices or accessories to Magwitch's attempted escape. In cases of felony, the law classified four parties to a crime: (1) the principal in the first degree, i.e. the man who actually commits the felony; (2) the accessory at the fact, or the principal in the second degree, i.e. the man present at the commission of the felony aiding and abetting; (3) the accessory before the fact, i.e. he who counsels, procures, or commands the felony; (4) the accessory after the fact, i.e. he who 'receives and comforts' the felon, thus aiding him to escape justice (Holdsworth 3.308). In the language of the Accessories and Abettors Act of 1861 (24 & 25 Vict., c. 90), any one who 'shall aid, abet, counsel, or procure the commission of any indictable offence . . . shall be liable to be tried, indicted and punished as a principal offender' (quoted in Ashworth 411).

Chapter 55 Thirty-fourth weekly number
20 July 1861

He was taken to the Police Court next day

He was taken to the Police Court next day, and would have been immediately committed for trial, but that it was necessary to send down for an old officer of the prison-ship . . . to speak to his identity. Nobody doubted it; but, Compeyson, who had meant to depose to it, was tumbling on the tides, dead, and it happened that there was not at that time any prison officer in London who could give the required evidence.] Prisoners could be charged at any one of the nine 'public offices' in London established under the provisions of the Middlesex Justices Act of 1792 (10 Geo. IV, c. 45), each with three stipendiary magistrates and a number of constables, but prisoners had to be identified before they were tried. Dickens attempts to make the delay credible. It would take time to send inquiries to Chatham, locate a prison officer from one of the hulks (perhaps difficult because fifteen or sixteen years had elapsed since Magwitch had been confined), and bring him to London to testify. Missing the current Sessions, in turn, means waiting until the next, during which interval Magwitch's health worsens, allowing him to die peacefully rather than violently at the end of the hangman's rope.

I imparted to Mr. Jaggers my design

Jaggers] After 'Jaggers' MS reads 'on the first day of the proceedings'.

we must memorialise by-and-by, and try at all events for some of it. But, he did not conceal from me that although there might be many cases in which the forfeiture would not be exacted, there were no circumstances in this case to make it one of them.] A memorial is a document prepared on request by a solicitor and sent to counsel, narrating the facts and circumstances and setting out the questions on which the counsel's opinion is sought. In Magwitch's case, no grounds for exemption to forfeiture existed: he was a convicted felon and an illegally returned transport.

There appeared to be reason for supposing

the drowned informer had hoped for a reward out of this forfeiture,] For rewards to informers, see chapter 43, note on p. 336.

When his body was found . . . so horribly disfigured that he was only recognisable by the contents of his pockets,] The absence of any investigation into the precise cause of Compeyson's death is consistent with customs that prevailed early in the century. Although the presentation of medical testimony at inquests had become common by the 1820s, it was customary not to conduct a post-mortem examination when the cause of death – for example drowning or falling from a great height – was obvious and unquestionable (Forbes 44). Moreover, this corpse had been in the water long enough to preclude any sophisticated attempt (even if one had been possible) to ascertain details that might indicate Magwitch's culpability for his enemy's death. Furthermore, drowning constituted the single greatest cause of non-occupational accidental death in London during the early part of the century, and police officers in the galley had seen Compeyson fall into the Thames (Forbes, 23). See also chapter 56, note on p. 403.

in a case he carried.]   MS reads 'in the case of the watch he wore'.

"We shall lose a fine opportunity

Cairo,]   For international trade in the Mediterranean and the Near East, see chapter 52, note on p. 376.

"I am afraid that must be admitted," said Herbert

the red book]   See chapter 23, note on p. 215.

On the Saturday in that same week

one of the seaport mail coaches.]   John Palmer (1742–1818) introduced mail-coaches in August 1784 as an alternative to the older, slower system of delivering mail by post-boys, men or boys, who rode alone with the mail carried in a canvas bag. Within six years of the first run from Bristol to Bath to London, Palmer successfully challenged the government's long-standing monopoly on delivering letters with his innovative method of sending mail by fast coaches travelling with an armed guard. Fares paid by four inside passengers helped defray the costs and added to the popularity of the new system, whereby fast, reliable vehicles left London and travelled to all parts of the country. By 1790, the changes Palmer introduced had revolutionized the whole pattern of travel and mail delivery in Britain (Margetson 90). 'These vehicles perform their duties with undeviating constancy, are furnished, at stated places, with relays of horses, and meals are provided for the passengers, at a limited price, at the inns where they stop in the course of the day' (Adolphus 3.284).

I thought this odd; however, I said nothing

Camberwell Green,]   Camberwell, Surrey, formerly a village with a green about a mile south of Walworth within the London borough of Southwark. St George's Church, Camberwell, has been proposed as the original (Fitch, 1908).

As the gloves were white kid gloves

white kid gloves,]   Wemmick's dress, in this respect, conforms with the rule for grooms: 'The gloves must be white as the linen' (*The Habits of Good Society* 425).

That discreet damsel was attired as usual

the altar of Hymen.]   The god of marriage.

I acted in the capacity of backer, or best-man

pew opener]   Pews in the form of enclosed compartments were originally reserved for certain worshippers. Initially this arrangement was for women and then for persons of rank; subsequently, an increasing number of middle-class families adopted the practice of taking a 'sitting' or hiring a pew to signify their standing in the parish. Admitting worshippers to these locked compartments fell to pew openers, often elderly women, described by Dickens in 'The City of the Absent' as generally not 'too bright' (*AYR* 9.494). The practice of exclusive seating gradually declined during the nineteenth century following the Church Building Act of 1818 (58 Geo. III, c. 45) which authorized the building of 214 churches to accommodate expanded urban populations and made the majority of pews free.

"Who giveth this woman to be married to this man?"]   From the 'Solemnization of Matrimony' (*BCP*).

beaming at the ten commandments.]   Exodus 29.3–17.

Breakfast had been ordered at a pleasant little tavern

Breakfast had been ordered . . . a mile or so away upon the rising ground beyond the Green;]   'Breakfast', after the marriage ceremony, was a meal eaten in the middle of the day at which soup, entrées and game were commonly served. The meal was so-called because English canonical law dating from the seventeenth century stipulated that marriages celebrated in a parish church had to be performed between the hours of 8 a.m. and 12 noon, otherwise they were uncanonical (but not invalid). The Marriage Act of 1886 (49 & 50 Vict., c. 14) extended the appointed hours for solemnizing marriages in parish churches to 3 in the afternoon (Rodes 116–18; Eversley and Craies 119). Denmark Hill is the only rising ground in the vicinity.

a bagatelle board]   Bagatelle was a game played on a board slightly rounded and elevated at one end and with a rim around the edges to contain balls struck with a small cue. Players score when balls run downwards, falling into compartments formed by standing nails and holes deep enough to hold balls as they roll towards the bottom. The origin of the game is obscure; bagatelle boards in England, frequently found in inns, appear to date from the first half of the nineteenth century.

We had an excellent breakfast

"Provided by contract,]   Wemmick paid a fixed sum for the meal, having arranged the particulars by agreement beforehand.

Chapter 56

Being far too ill to remain in the common prison

he was removed . . . into the Infirmary.] Recognition of the need to provide prisoners with both spiritual and physical care dates from the late eighteenth century when magistrates were first permitted to appoint chaplains (1773) and surgeons to gaols (1774). Facilities for the medical treatment of convicts, nevertheless, remained limited because prison officials often worried that relaxed discipline in the infirmary might tempt prisoners to feign illness or even deliberately injure themselves in order to take advantage of 'this chink in the penal order' (Morris and Rothman 85, 107).

It happened on two or three occasions

he was humble and contrite,] The description of Magwitch's penitent state echoes the words of the Collect for the first day of Lent, which asks: 'Create and make in us new and contrite hearts, that we worthily lamenting our sins, and acknowledging our wretchedness, may obtain of thee, God of mercy, perfect remission and forgiveness' (*BCP*).

When the Sessions came round

the Sessions] For 'Sessions', see chapter 20, note on p. 183. A square court separated Newgate prison from the old brick sessions-house, where all prisoners from London and Middlesex were sent for trial. On the north side or front of the building

> are two flights of steps leading to the court room, which has a gallery on each side for the accommodation of spectators. The prisoners are brought to this court from the prison by a passage that closely connects the two buildings; and there is a convenient place under the session-house in the front, for detaining the prisoners till they are called upon their trials. There are also many rooms for the grand and petit jury. (Anderson 4.117)

The court itself was spacious. The judges presided from a bench at the upper end; below them at a table were the counsel and solicitors, and in front of them the clerk of the arraigns with his attendant officers (Adolphus 3.505).

At that time, it was the custom

At that time, it was the custom . . . to devote a concluding day to the passing of Sentences, and to make a finishing effect with the Sentence of Death. . . . I could scarcely believe, even as I write these words, that I saw two-and-thirty men and women put before the Judge to receive that sentence together.] Hurried trials for felons and collective sentencing remained a feature of the administration of justice in London and throughout England until the first decades of the nineteenth century. Court proceedings began with accused offenders being brought together and arraigned in batches as their names were called; individual trials then followed, many lasting only a few minutes, after which jurors gave their verdicts, often huddling together in close proximity to the accused and spectators. The same jury would then hear another batch of cases and continue in the same manner through the duration of the session or assizes. According to one observer, trials at the sessions averaged about eight and a half minutes each as men 'were taken up to be knocked down like bullocks, unheard' (*Old Bailey Experience* 59–60; Beattie, chapter 7).

Several factors account for this rapid pace. Trials moved quickly because disputes about evidence were few, defence counsels played a relatively minor role, and judges rarely found the need to sum up beyond giving simple directions to the jury. Jurors, too, lost little time arriving at decisions, partly because many had gained previous experience with the variety of verdicts possible and partly because the range of punishments was narrow. Passing the sentences brought the whole process to an emotional climax. See below.

The whole scene starts out again

The whole scene starts out again in the vivid colours of the moment, down to the drops of April rain on the windows of the court, glittering in the rays of April sun. . . .
The sun was striking in at the great windows of the court, through the glittering drops of rain upon the glass, and it made a broad shaft of light between the two-and-thirty and the Judge, linking both together . . . to the greater Judgment that knoweth all things and cannot err.] The description in both paragraphs appears to conflate two literary allusions. First, the implied connection between 'the glittering drops of rain' and the light which links the judged with those who judge carries echoes of Portia's speech during the trial scene in *The Merchant of Venice*:

> The quality of mercy is not strain'd;
> It droppeth as the gentle rain from heaven
> Upon the place beneath. It is twice blest:
> It blesseth him that gives and him that takes.
> 'Tis mightiest in the mightiest; it becomes
> The throned monarch better than his crown. . . .
> It is enthroned in the heart of kings,
> It is an attribute to God himself;
> And earthly power doth then show likest God's
> When mercy seasons justice. (4.1.179–92)

Second, the passage as a whole reflects the assize sermon. This was one of the Church's set pieces, a ritual sermon delivered by the sheriff's chaplain at the opening of all court sessions. Typically, this address turned on themes of obvious relevance to the occasion, the Great Assizes before which in time each man and woman would be called, the equality of all before God and each person's accountability for his deeds. See, for example, John Wesley's sermon, 'The Great Assize', preached on 10 March 1758 at St Paul's Church, Bedford, the day before the commencement of the quarterly Assizes in the city. Taking Romans 14.10 as his subject – 'We shall all stand before the judgment seat of Christ' – Wesley, the influential Methodist leader, sermonized:

> A few will stand at the judgment seat this day, to be judged touching what shall be laid to their charge. And they are now reserved in prison, perhaps in chains, till they are brought forth to be tried and sentenced. But we shall all, I that speak and you that hear, 'stand at the judgment seat of Christ'.
> (Sermon 15, Outler 1.372)

Earlier, Dickens made a similar point in his fifth letter to the editors of the *Daily News* in 1846:

> and, when the judge's faltering voice delivers sentence, how awfully the prisoner and he confront each other; two mere men, destined one day, however far removed from one another at this time, to stand alike as suppliants at the bar of God. (Paroissien, 1985, 240)

Charles Knight describes the old Sessions House as 'a square hall of sufficient length, and breadth, and height, lighted up by three large square windows on the opposite wall, showing the top of the gloomy walls of Newgate' (681).

in the dock,]   The dock for prisoners was located underneath the visitors' gallery of the old Justice Hall.

The sheriffs with their great chains and nosegays,]   The responsibilities of sheriffs in the nineteenth century had narrowed to summoning potential jurors for selection and service, and to ensuring the safe custody of prisoners. Two sheriffs, ceremoniously dressed in robes and chains, attended trials as representatives of London and the county of Middlesex, a practice which originated in the thirteenth century under King John.

The custom of carrying nosegays at the Old Bailey began in the mid-eighteenth century after two judges and several jurymen died from 'jail-fever', a form of typhus endemic in crowded cells and prisons. To counter the virus – mistakenly thought to be airborne – officials carried posies of sweet-smelling flowers and herbs. In fact, nosegays offered no protection beyond providing some relief from the smell of unwashed prisoners. Howard described the effect of his prison visits on his own clothes as so offensive that

> in a post-chaise I could not bear the windows drawn up; and was therefore obliged to travel commonly on horseback. The leaves of my memorandum-book were often so tainted, that I could not use it till after spreading it an hour or two before the fire: and even my antidote, a vial of vinegar, has, after using it in a few prisons, become intolerably disagreeable. (Howard 4)

Unhygienic conditions among prisoners at the Old Bailey persisted. Even after the provision of underground channels and filtered air in the Sessions House in 1841 (Timbs, 1867, 506), outbreaks of 'jail-fever' spread from prisoners to court officials. In May 1870 the fever raged 'so violently' as to enter the court and cause the death of the Lord Mayor, another judge and several other members of the Bar and the jury (*Newgate . . . Curious Facts* 23). At the start of the new law term each May and September, judges carry bouquets of flowers and scatter sweet herbs around the court as a reminder of this former custom.

other civic gewgaws and monsters, criers, ushers, a great gallery full of people – a large theatrical audience] Many factors contributed to the drama occasioned by trials at the Old Bailey. The spectacle was heightened by the traditional arrangement of the trial space and furniture. On one side the jury sat in its box, while the prisoner stood in the dock before the judge, who presided from his elevated bench, removed from the verbal battle below. Members of the public, seated outside the bar, looked on, mute observers distanced from the actual trial. Clothes and court rituals added to the display. The Lord Mayor wore a sword and a scarlet robe, furred, and bordered with black velvet. Numerous attendants carrying maces and wands and the wigs worn by the justices, who were also dressed in splendid robes, heightened the pageantry in an attempt to invest the legal proceedings with an atmosphere of solemnity and dignity.

Being here presently denounced, he had for a time succeeded in evading the officers of Justice, but being at length seized while in the act of flight, he had resisted them, and had – he best knew whether by express design, or in the blindness of his hardihood – caused the death of his denouncer, to whom his whole career was known. The appointed punishment for his return to the land that had cast him out, being Death, and his case being this aggravated case, he must prepare himself to Die.] The capital sentence passed on Magwitch cites the specific offence: his unlawful return. Earlier, Pip had expressed his fear that, in view of Magwitch's prior record and return from transportation 'under a life sentence', lenient treatment at the trial was impossible, especially since Magwitch had 'occasioned the death of the man who was the cause of his arrest' (chapter 54). 'Occasioned', however, implies a subsidiary or incidental role free from intention, a 'truth' Pip notes that he never had any reason to doubt. Rather, it was Compeyson's sudden action that capsized Pip's boat, as the two convicts went down, locked together in a fierce struggle, until Magwitch disengaged himself, 'struck out, and swam away'.

More problematic in realistic terms is the fact that Dickens conveniently overlooks the legal precedent for prosecuting Pip, Herbert and Startop as accessories after the fact who had knowingly assisted a felon in an attempt to evade the law (see chapter 54, note on pp. 394–5). Fiction, however, requires only the willing suspension of the reader's belief, a compact the events of Magwitch's trial fail to disturb.

The sun was striking in

There was some hushing, and the Judge went on with what he had to say to the rest. Then, they were all formally doomed, and some of them were supported out, and some of them sauntered out with a haggard look of bravery, and a few nodded to the gallery, and two or three shook hands, and others went out chewing the fragments of herb they had taken from the sweet herbs lying about.] Hanging verdicts and the practice of collective sentencing produced extremes of emotion. Judges delivered their final words and sermonized; condemned prisoners received the sentence of death variously. An account by a local reporter covering the trial and sentencing to death of two agricultural protesters at Salisbury assizes in 1831, together with other offenders, conveys this culminating moment of the courtroom drama:

> there were . . . no dry eyes in the crowded court. The tears of pity, of compassion, or regret, at the necessity of such severity were to be seen flowing and chasing one another down the cheeks not merely of the spectators, but of those who had long been accustomed to hear the last dreadful sentence which a human being has the power of passing on a fellow-creature in this world. [The judges] were frequently obliged to rest their faces on their extended hands, and even then the large drops were to be seen falling in quick succession. . . . Every one [of the prisoners] was in a state of dreadful agitation – some sobbing aloud and others with a pallid cheek. . . . [After the death sentence] their mothers, their sisters, and their children clasped them in their arms with an agonizing grasp – the convicts . . . gave way, they wept like children. . . . Nature had begun to play with every force, and the heart was broken. (*Dorset County Chronicle*, 1831, quoted in Robert Hughes 30)

I earnestly hoped and prayed

I earnestly hoped and prayed that he might die before the Recorder's Report was made,] After each sessions, the Recorder of London (see chapter 32, note on pp. 276–7) drew up a table of condemned names and indicated which petitions (if any) deserved consideration. He completed this task quickly and sent his report to the Home Secretary, who, in turn, reviewed all appeals to mitigate sentences and prepared further notes and recommendations to present to the king for his consideration. See below. In effect, the Recorder's report carried a finality whose summary prisoners in the condemned cells awaited with dread.

I began that night to write out a petition] Petitions were variously addressed (see below) and followed a model. The petitioner had to refer to the convicted person's 'good conduct', achievements and general circumstances, and go on to implore the king to spare the life of the person in question. The document closed with signatures of a number of witnesses and supporters ('Crime' Box 3, Johnson Collection). Most appeals were to commute capital sentences, but they did not address the hanging code exclusively. Prominent among petitioners were grandees and members of the gentry, but the procedure was open to all and widely used. Although some petitioned out of obligation to dependants, and a few out of expedience,

> most acted disinterestedly against the injustice perceived in particular verdicts or sentences, moved by commonsensical ideas of fair trial and proportioned punishment which were remote from the discretionary principles of the judges' law. (Gatrell 417)

The petitioning system entered its 'golden age' during the first thirty years of the nineteenth century. Between 1812 and 1822, the Home Office was flooded with appeals at the rate of about 1,300 a year, a frequency which nearly doubled by the later 1830s (Gatrell 197).

Home Secretary of State,] 'Home Secretary' is an abbreviated title for the Secretary of State for Home Affairs, the senior cabinet member who was responsible for domestic law and order, and who received all appeals. As Home Secretary from 1822 to 1830 (with a five-month break from 1827to 1828), Sir Robert Peel was subjected almost daily 'to impassioned pleas for mercy in the correspondence and affidavits which flooded his desk after each assize circuit and Old Bailey Sessions' (Gatrell 572).

I wrote out other petitions to such men in authority as I hoped were the most merciful, and drew up one to the Crown itself.] Appeals could be addressed to any office-holder or government member. The officials implied here might have included all members of the 'nominal' or 'Great' or 'Grand' or 'Honorary' cabinet, whose existence continued during the first three decades of the nineteenth century. This cabinet consisted of the king's confidential servants (fifteen ministers with portfolios who reported to the Prime Minister), the principal officials of the royal household, the Archbishop of Canterbury, the Speaker of the House of Commons and the Lord Chief Justice. One of the functions of the Cabinet Council was to review the capital sentences of the Old Bailey and advise the sovereign on the exercise of the prerogative of mercy; hence the origin of the phrase the 'hanging cabinet' (Aspinall and Smith 11.86).

In London the king exercised his prerogative directly; hence Pip's address to the Crown. Under the provisions of the constitution, the king retained a relic of direct rule claimed by medieval monarchs. This ancient emblem of his majesty as God's representative on earth gave the sovereign power to mitigate the sentences of judges through his prerogative of mercy and pardon all offences against either the crown or the public (Gatrell 200). Pardons, issued under the Great Seal, in effect, made the offender 'a new man' acquitted of all corporeal penalties and forfeitures annexed to the offence for which he obtained his pardon (Adolphus 2.713).

Decisions to mitigate sentences were distressingly uneven (see Gatrell, ch. 20). Appeals that failed usually bore a pencilled notation, 'The law to take its course'. Fortunately, the archaic proceedings of the Grand Council decreased in the 1830s to the extent that the Whigs were able to abolish the Council in 1837. By that date the Recorder's report had become redundant because the number of prisoners sentenced to execution had fallen dramatically: by 1837 only eight persons, all murderers, were executed in England (Gatrell 565).

I could not keep away from the places where they were, but felt as if they were more hopeful and less desperate when I was near them. . . . I would roam the streets of an evening, wandering by those offices and houses where I had left the petitions.] After 'petitions' MS reads 'and thence to the prison where he was confined, and thence back again'.

The reference is to the streets in the vicinity of Whitehall just south of Charing Cross. This part of London has been called 'The heart of the Executive of England' on account of the numerous government offices located between Whitehall and St James's Park (Charles Knight 99). In order of appearance as one walks southwards along Whitehall are the Admiralty, the Treasury and the Horse Guards. This last building, designed by William Kent in 1753, stands on the site of the guardhouse to the old Palace of Whitehall (hence the name of the street) and houses numerous government officials, including the Secretary of State for War and the Secretary of State for the Colonial and the Home Department. A little further along is Downing Street, the official residence of the Prime Minister, which runs off Whitehall; to the west is St James's Palace, a former royal residence and court in frequent use until the accession of Queen Victoria. Government offices are also located in the adjacent Carlton House Terrace and Pall Mall, the scene of pioneering street-lighting by gas in 1807.

The daily visits I could make him

Seeing, or fancying, that I was suspected of an intention of carrying poison to him, I asked to be searched] Once under a capital sentence with no hope of a commutation, a strict mode of confinement was observed to prevent escapes or suicides (Wakefield). Suicide attempts were common 'by persons of a better station', Wakefield thought, because forgers and others, unlike common thieves, tried hard to escape the disgrace of a public execution (231).

some other prisoners who attended on them as sick nurses] Prisoners awaiting trial, and some few who were detained in Newgate on non-capital charges, were pressed into service. Some acted as servants, others helped out in the infirmary (Wakefield 249).

Mindful, then, of what we had read together

say] After 'say' MS reads 'through my rush of tears'. 'Surely Dickens blotted the tears not because they obscured any intended irony but because he saw them as blemishes on Pip's dignity: the weeping fit is all out of place' (*Norton* 452). See also below.

"O Lord, be merciful to him, a sinner!"] Pip misrepresents the concluding words to the parable. See Luke 18.10–13:

> Two men went up into the temple to pray; the one a Pharisee, and the other a publican.
> The Pharisee stood and prayed thus with himself, God, I thank thee that I am not as other men are, extortioners, unjust, adulterers, or even as this publican. I fast twice in the week, I give tithes of all that I possess.
> And the publican, standing afar off, would not lift up so much as his eyes unto heaven, but smote upon his breast, saying, God be merciful to me a sinner.

The substitution of 'him' for 'me' has occasioned speculation that the misquotation directs authorial irony back at a self-satisfied Pip; counter-arguments stress the improbability of such a reading, especially in view of Dickens's adaptation of the novel for public reading. This (unperformed) version ends with the final prayer over Magwitch and emphasizes in its exclusive focus on the relationship between the hero and the convict how Pip's reaction to Magwitch, begun in fear and pity, ends in sympathy and love unqualified by social uneasiness (Collins, 1975, 306; Cardwell xlix; *Norton* 452–3).

Chapter 57 Thirty-fifth weekly number
27 July 1861

Now that I was left wholly to myself

I put bills up in the windows;] For the posting of bills, see chapter 21, note on p. 192.

The late stress upon me had enabled me to put off illness, but not to put it away; I knew that it was coming on me now, and I knew very little else, and was even careless as to that.] Pip's breakdown occurs in a moment of prolonged strain; variants of this convention, 'the *sine qua non* . . . of restored or reconstructed identity' (Bailin 79) appear in *OCS* (Dick Swiveller), *MC* (Martin Chuzzlewit), *BH* (Esther Summerson), *LD* (Arthur Clennam) and *OMF* (Eugene Wrayburn), and in works by other Victorian novelists. Collapses due to stress were familiar to medical observers:

> The passions have great influence both in the cause and cure of diseases. How the mind affects the body, will, in all probability, ever remain a secret. It is sufficient for us to know, that there is established a reciprocal influence betwixt the mental and corporeal parts, and that whatever injures the one disorders the other. (Buchan 124–5)

"Hundred and twenty-three pound, fifteen, six.

"Hundred and twenty-three pound, fifteen, six. Jeweller's account, I think."] The 'two men' Pip sees looking at him are special bailiffs sent by the sheriff, who has issued a writ for Pip's arrest on *mesne* process. In this case, insolvency proceedings had been initiated by a jeweller on his signing an affidavit attesting that he had sold and delivered goods to Pip amounting to the value of £123 15s 6d.

Once in the bailiff's custody, the debtor could immediately obtain his release by paying the sum he owed, plus the penal sum of £10 for costs, or he could post bail. Failing to comply, early nineteenth-century debtors went to a debtors' prison and remained there until they could seek assistance to petition for release. Under the provisions of Lord Redesdale's Act of 1813 (53 Geo. III, c. 102), which established the Court for the Relief of the Insolvent Debtor, the debtor initiated the relief process by petitioning the court to release him on the condition that he gave up all his present property and agreed to subject any further assets to the court. This petition had to be accompanied by a schedule of assets, a gaoler's certificate of the causes of detainer, and the retainer of an attorney. (In Pip's case, the debt and costs are paid by Joe).

Imprisonment for debt dates back to a series of thirteenth-century statutes granting the creditor the right to imprison a debtor, even if he lacked the means to pay his debts. Occasionally, the monarch would release debtor-prisoners, and various charitable bequests existed to assist debtors in getting out of prison. Mounting opposition over the centuries introduced minor provisions for relief such as requiring creditors to pay 'a reasonable maintenance' for prisoners whom they insisted stay in gaol (22 & 23 Car. II, c. 20) and increasing the minimal amount of delinquent indebtedness required before a creditor could start proceedings from £2 in 1725 (11 Geo. I, c. 21) to £20 in 1827 (7 & 8 Geo. IV, c. 71). The Relief Act of 1813 (noted above), and subsequent statutes in 1820, 1826 and 1861 carried the reform impetus further. The Act of 1861 (24 & 25 Vict., c. 134) abolished the Court for the Relief of Insolvent Debtors and eliminated the former distinction between merchants or traders, who, by law, could plead bankruptcy, and ordinary insolvents, for whom imprisonment was the only alternative to paying their creditors (based on Lester, ch. 3). Imprisonment for debt was not formally repealed until the Debtors Act of 1869 (32 & 33 Vict., c. 62). Compare John Dickens. After repeated attempts to elude creditors, Dickens's father was arrested on 20 February 1824 at the suit of James Karr, a baker of Camden Town, for a debt of £40 (Allen, 1988, 94).

"You had better come to my house," said the man.

"You had better come to my house . . . I keep a very nice house."] In the eighteenth and early part of the nineteenth century it was common practice for a bailiff or sheriff's officer to keep a house – popularly known as a sponging-house – for regular use as a place of preliminary confinement for debtors.

That I had a fever and was avoided

That I had a fever and was avoided, that I suffered greatly, that I often lost my reason, that the time seemed interminable, that I confounded impossible existences with my own identity . . .] The symptoms correspond closely with textbook descriptions of patients suffering from a severe fever: an increased pulse rate, loss of appetite, general debility, pain in the head, severe anxiety and weariness. The psychic nature of Pip's illness has also been stressed (Kaplan, 1975, 156–8). The role of the nurse is to observe 'which way Nature points, and to endeavour to assist her operations'. 'Our bodies are so framed, as to have a constant tendency to expel or throw off whatever is injurious to health. This is generally done by urine, sweat, stool, expectoration, vomit, or some other evacuation' (Buchan 136).

I was a brick in the house-wall, and yet entreating to be released from the giddy place where the builders had set me;] Compare the description of a similar wish to be free expressed by Esther Summerson in *BH*. During her illness, she dreams about being one of the beads 'in a flaming necklace' strung together somewhere 'in great black space' and wants more than anything 'to be taken off from the rest' and escape that 'dreadful thing' (35).

I was a steel beam of a vast engine, clashing and whirling over a gulf,] Experimental beam engines (steam engines whose action of raising and lowering a long lever, or beam, allowed mechanical effort to be obtained from the engine) were pioneered by John Roebuck (1718–94) and James Watt (1736–1809). The whirling and clashing probably refers to Watt's 'sun and planet' gear to obtain a rotary motion by connecting the piston rod to the beam via a system of rods forming a parallelogram. This arrangement, known as the 'parallel motion', provided a prototype of the beam engine which persisted for many years (Bunch and Hellemans 164; Singer et al. 4.186). The most notable application of the beam engine during the first half of the nineteenth century was in American river and coastal steamships, where it was known as the walking beam engine (McNeil 281).

After I had turned the worst point of my illness

in the shaded open window,]   A good supply of fresh air was thought essential to all invalids: 'Nothing is more desired by a patient in a fever than fresh air. It not only removes his anxiety, but cools the blood, revives the spirits, and proves every way beneficial' (Buchan 161). See also below on the importance of ventilating a sick-room.

cooling drink,]   Water, thin gruel, decoctions of tamarinds, apple-tea and orange-whey were among the beverages recommended. Patients were given 'cooling liquors' in order 'to abate the heat, attenuate the humours, remove spasms and obstructions, promote perspiration, increase the quantity of urine, and, in short, produce every salutary effect in an ardent or inflammatory fever' (Buchan 159).

After which, Joe withdrew to the window

O God bless this gentle Christian man!"]   As the apotheosis of the Christian gentle man, Joe represents the final democratization of the concept of the gentleman. In this respect, rank, birth and wealth defer to a code of conduct accessible to all. Compare Mr Twemlow's redefinition of gentleman in *OMF*: 'I use the word, gentleman . . . in the sense in which the degree may be attained by any man' (4.16).

"Pretty nigh, old chap.

the news of your being ill were brought by letter, which it were brought by the post and being formerly single he is now married though underpaid for a deal of walking and shoe-leather,]   Two weeks earlier, an article published in *AYR* on 13 July 1861 offered support for the postman's long-standing claim for higher wages, referred to the difficulty of supporting a wife and children on his meagre earnings, and characterized the job as an arduous one which required the postman to walk himself 'off his legs' ('Hear the Postman!' 5.366).

Evidently, Biddy had taught Joe to write.

My bedstead, divested of its curtains, had been removed . . . and the carpet had

been taken away, and the room kept always fresh and wholesome] Medical authorities regarded the ventilation of bedrooms as crucially important, especially for the sick:

> If fresh air be necessary for those in health, it is still more so for the sick, who often lose their lives for want of it. . . . No medicine is so beneficial to the sick as fresh air. It is the most reviving of cordials, if it be administered with prudence. (Buchan 84)

Carpets and thick curtain hangings around beds were considered obstacles to the circulation of fresh air and were removed. To breathe the 'vitiated air' of a badly ventilated room was judged 'not good for one's system' and as dangerous to the sick as living on unwholesome or innutritious food (Sir James Clark, *The Sanative Influence of Climate,* quoted in Timbs, 1847, 27). Similar steps to create a 'fresh' atmosphere free from dust and dirt were taken when women were confined at home for the delivery of a baby. 'The valences of the bed, and carpets had better be removed' (Chavasse, 1843, 55).

"Well, old chap," said Joe

coddleshell] i.e. 'codicil'.

a cool four thousand . . . I never discovered from whom Joe derived the conventional temperature of the four thousand pounds] Dickens had originally written 'three thousand'. The colloquial use of the adjective applied to a large sum of money, possibly signifying 'deliberately or calmly counted, reckoned, or told' (*OED*), dates from the eighteenth century. Compare 'He had lost a cool hundred, and would play no more' (Fielding, *Tom Jones* 8.12), and 'My Table alone stands me in a cool thousand a quarter' (Smollett, *Humphry Clinker*, 201, 1771).

Joe nodded. "Mrs. Camels," by which

five pound fur to buy rushlights] Rushlights were a cheap form of lighting used mainly by people living in the country. See also chapter 45, note on pp. 340–1.

"That's it, Pip," said Joe

the county jail."] Maidstone county gaol, erected in 1747, provided wards for debtors and felons and dungeons for the condemned (Howard 191). Prisoners were sent here after they stood trial in Rochester, whose old city gaol behind the Town Hall provided only temporary accommodation (Bagshaw 99).

For, the tenderness of Joe was so beautifully proportioned

Wellington boots."]   There were two styles: a high boot which covered the knee but was cut away behind, and a shorter boot, worn under trousers. Both were named in honour of Sir Arthur Wellesley, 1st Duke of Wellington (1769–1852).

It was on the third or fourth occasion

the Temple Gardens]   The gardens were a prominent feature of the Temple in the nineteenth century, a plot of fresh green grass and 'an oasis of trees and verdure amid the wilderness of brick and mortar' on every side.

> The houses that form this pleasant square are high and regular, and have a solemn and sedate look, befitting the antiquity and historical sanctity of their site, and the grave character of the people that inhabit them. Here are the Temple Gardens, sacred to the Goddess of Strife . . . flowers blossom, trees cast a refreshing shade, and a fountain maketh a pleasant murmur all the year; but each room in that precinct is a den inhabited by a black spider, who sucks the blood of foolish flies. (Mackay, 1840, 1.29–30)

Enclosed in the letter

a receipt for the debt and costs on which I had been arrested.]   See note on p. 408 above.

Chapter 58 Thirty-sixth weekly number
3 August 1861

It was evening when I arrived

a very indifferent chamber among the pigeons and post-chaises up the yard.] The Bull in Rochester had three rooms in an annexe located over the stables and coach-houses, and reached by a separate staircase from the yard (Gadd, 1929, 50). David Copperfield suffered a similar fate at the Golden Cross in London until Steerforth demanded his removal from 'a little loft over a stable' (*DC* 19).

"William," said Mr. Pumblechook, mournfully

**William, bring a watercress."
"Thank you," said I shortly, "but I don't eat watercresses."
"You don't eat 'em," returned Mr. Pumblechook, sighing and nodding . . . and as if abstinence from watercresses were consistent with my downfall.]** Victorians, like their immediate ancestors and the Greeks and Romans, attributed numerous healing properties to watercress, this 'simple fruit of the earth'. English herbalists from the sixteenth century onwards claimed that it could cure toothache, hangovers and unfashionable freckles, and some authorities even credited it with the ability to increase sexual appetite. Harvested locally in Gravesend, Kent, by market gardeners, watercress was also gathered from the banks of the Thames and its tributaries, sold throughout London by costers for a few pence a bunch and, on account of its cheapness, consumed in great quantities. From the mid-century, demand in London exceeded local supply, but the railway enabled watercress from Hampshire and Dorset to be delivered to the capital within a day or so of harvesting. Among the working people of London, watercress was known as 'the poor man's breakfast': they would gather it from the river banks and eat it on its own for breakfast or, if bread was available, as a sandwich (Kelly, 1882, 2; Watercress Information Service, Southampton).

"Little more than skin and bone!"

like the Bee,] The bee, as a model of industry and self-improvement, is most typically represented in Isaac Watts's 'Against Idleness and Mischief' (Song 20 of his *Divine Songs*, 1715): 'How doth the little busy bee/improve each shining hour,/ And gather honey all the day/From every opening flower!'

The schoolhouse where Biddy was mistress, I had never seen

The schoolhouse] See chapter 35, note on p. 290.

but, the little roundabout lane by which I entered the village for quietness' sake, took me past it.]   On this occasion Pip follows Cliffe Road to Stonehouse Inn. But instead of turning left, over Dusty Hill to the village, he continues as far as Lilly Church farm. This route also takes him into Gore Green along a road bordered on one side by an orchard and on the other by a row of lime trees (Gadd, 1929, 40).

But, the forge was a very short distance off

under the sweet green limes,]   Lime or linden trees ran along the lane from Lilly Church farm to Gore Green (Gadd, 1929, 41).

'It's my wedding day," cried Biddy

"and I am married to Joe!"]   Five asterisks and two blank lines follow Biddy's exclamation, evidently a typographical attempt to draw attention to the impact of this statement on Pip. No significant temporal break occurs since Joe, Biddy and Pip all return to the forge shortly after the church ceremony. See also below.

"And Joe and Biddy both, as you have been to church to-day

are in charity and love with all mankind,]   Compare the words of the priest to the communicants:

> Ye that do truly and earnestly repent you of your sins, and are in love and charity with your neighbours, and intend to lead a new life, following the commandments of God, and walking from henceforth in his holy ways; Draw near with faith, and take this Holy Sacrament to your comfort; and make your humble confession to Almighty God, meekly kneeling on your knees. (BCP)

"Now let me go up and look at my old little room

good-by!"]   In the MS, Dickens instructed the printer to provide 'two white lines' between the close of this paragraph and the beginning of the next. In this instance, the break appears to signal the lapse of time during which Pip returns to London, settles his affairs and then sets out to join Herbert in Cairo.

I sold all I had, and put aside as much as I could

I sold all I had, and put aside as much as I could, for a composition with my creditors – who gave me ample time to pay them in full]   Compare the advice given to the rich man wishing to enter heaven in Luke 18.22: 'sell all that thou hast, and distribute unto the poor, and thou shalt have treasure in heaven: and come, follow me' (also alluded to in chapter 19).

Bankruptcy law, before 1825, had not recognized any formal system whereby creditors could agree among themselves as to how a debtor's assets might be distributed. The Act of 1825 (6 Geo. IV, c. 16, ss. 6–7) introduced an important change, the concept of a composition:

> On the issuance of a bankruptcy commission and the debtor having passed his last examination, nine-tenths of the creditors in number and value could agree to accept an offer of the debtor to pay a certain amount in the pound. If accepted, a new contract came into effect . . . The debtor was then free to carry out his business, subject only to the payment agreed upon in the composition. Under a composition or a deed of arrangement, bankruptcy law now recognized that the debtor and his creditors could settle their affairs and avoid the filing of a formal bankruptcy. (Lester 36)

Clarriker and Co.,] 'The word Company signifies persons associated for the purpose of carrying on a particular branch of trade . . . and implies, in a general sense, that [the partners] do so with a joint stock'. Compare traders in a regulated company: 'They do not form a company at all. It is only a subscription' (Adolphus 3.139).

Many a year went round

a partner in the House;]

> Partners are joint-tenants in all the stock and partnership effects; and they are so not only of the particular stock in being at the time of entering into the partnership, but they continue joint-tenants throughout whatever changes may take place in the course of trade. . . . The whole of this doctrine seems to arise out of the very principle upon which partnership is founded, namely, probable profit, and the risk of loss; the advantages or disadvantages of which cannot, in common justice, be confined to one side only, but must be reciprocal throughout. (Adolphus 3.138–9)

We were not in a grand way of business, but we had a good name, and worked for our profits, and did very well.] Trading companies made demands on those who ran them. The young merchant had to acquire particular information about the interests, productions, government, tariff and maritime laws of the countries to which he sent his goods. The work also required knowledge of the money, weights, language and 'course of exchange, and wants of those countries in which he has found favour' (*Complete Book of Trades* 332).

In a modest, less assertive manner, Pip restates the 'golden rules' to which David Copperfield attributed his success: 'the habits of punctuality, order, and diligence' and determination to concentrate on one object at a time, 'no matter how quickly its successor should come upon its heels' (*DC* 42). Success in business earned through steady application and self-help also sets Pip apart from George Barnwell by making him more like the 'good' apprentice, albeit on a reduced scale. Lillo envisaged for Thorowgood, his hero, all 'the blessings Heaven bestows', including monetary rewards from 'The populous East', with its 'glittering gems, bright pearls, aromatic spices, and health-restoring drugs' (3.1.20–6). On Pip's modest success, see also chapter 59, note on p. 420.

I often wondered how I had conceived that old idea of his inaptitude,] The criticism of Herbert that Pip expressed earlier (see chapter 34) may have owed something to Dickens's assessment of his son Charley, about whom he had written to Miss Coutts on 14 January 1854:

> He is very gentle and affectionate. . . . His inclinations are all good; but I think he has less fixed purpose and energy than I could have supposed possible in my son. . . . With all the tenderer and better qualities which he inherits from his mother, he inherits an indescribable lassitude of character – a very serious thing in a man – which seems to me to express the want of a strong, compelling hand always beside him. (*Letters* 7.245)

but had been in me.] In the original version of the novel, the MS continues after these words and incorporates the initial paragraphs of what is now chapter 59 through to the paragraph beginning, ' "My dear Biddy, I have forgotten nothing in my life . . . " and ending with the phrase, "Biddy, all gone by!" ' Following four deleted lines, the MS closes with a meeting between Pip and Estella (now remarried after Drummle's death) in Piccadilly, after which he never saw Estella again. This ending (printed below) was first published by Forster in the third volume of his *Life* (1874), where he included it as a footnote to his commentary on the novel.

A proof of the ending, unearthed at the Morgan Library by Rosenberg, provides what he calls the 'most nearly impeccable text' of the novel's original ending in existence (see below). This version reveals how Dickens altered his original 'It was four years more, before I saw her myself' to 'two' and how he removed the adverbial 'Then I had heard of her', writing instead 'I had heard of her . . . '. In addition, a comparison with the proof also shows how Forster prints the ending as a single paragraph, thus obscuring the optical effect and sense of tempo Dickens achieved by laying out the conclusion in four separate paragraphs (*Norton* 507–8):

> It was two years more, before I saw herself. I had heard of her as leading a most unhappy life, and as being separated from her husband who had used her with great cruelty, and who had become quite renowned as a compound of pride, brutality, and meanness. I had heard of the death of her husband (from an accident consequent on ill-treating a horse), and of her being married again to a Shropshire doctor, who, against his interest, had once very manfully interposed, on an occasion when he was in professional attendance on Mr. Drummle, and had witnessed some outrageous treatment of her. I had

heard that the Shropshire doctor was not rich, and that they lived on her own personal fortune.

I was in England again – in London, and walking along Piccadilly with little Pip – when a servant came running after me to ask would I step back to a lady in a carriage who wished to speak to me. It was a little pony carriage, which the lady was driving; and the lady and I looked sadly enough on one another.

"I am greatly changed, I know; but I thought you would like to shake hands with Estella too, Pip. Lift up that pretty child and let me kiss it!" (She supposed the child, I think, to be my child.)

I was very glad afterwards to have had the interview; for, in her face and in her voice, and in her touch, she gave me the assurance, that suffering had been stronger than Miss Havisham's teaching, and had given her a heart to understand what my heart used to be. [MS ends here.] (*Norton* 359)

The existence of two endings (see Introduction, pp. 11–14) has fuelled an extensive critical debate, with proponents opting for one or the other. Forster, Charles Dickens, Jr, George Gissing, G. K. Chesterton, and William Dean Howells were among the earliest to vote in favour of the ending Dickens discarded, but it was the decision of George Bernard Shaw to restore the original to the edition of *GE* he edited in 1937 that intensified the controversy (*Norton* 511–12). In his introduction, Shaw was also the first to point to a resemblance between Dickens's original ending and the incident Lever uses to signal the close of Potts's narrative, published in *AYR* on 23 March 1861, some twelve weeks before Dickens composed the final number of *GE* in mid-June. This similarity – an unconscious borrowing, Shaw speculated – perhaps accounted for Dickens's sense that 'there was something wrong' with Pip's chance encounter with Estella in London. With his doubts confirmed by Bulwer's objections, Shaw contended that, 'Accordingly, [Dickens] wrote a new ending, in which he got rid of Piccadilly' (xvi).

Potts's final meeting with Catinka occurs shortly after he has returned from the Crimea:

> It was about two years after this – my father had died in the interval, leaving me a small but sufficient fortune to live on, and I had just arrived in Paris . . . I was standing one morning early in one of the small alleys of the Champs Élysées, watching with half-listless curiosity the various grooms as they passed to exercise their horses in the Bois de Boulogne. . . .
>
> I crossed the road, and had but reached the opposite pathway, when a carriage stopped, and the old horse drew up beside it. After a word or two, the groom took off the hood, and there was Blondel! [the horse Potts had bartered away thirty chapters earlier]. But my amazement was lost in greater shock, that the Princess, whose jewelled hand held out the sugar to him, was no other than Catinka!
>
> I cannot say with what motive I was impelled – perhaps the action was too quick for either – but I drew nigh to the carriage, and, raising my hat respectfully, asked if her highness would deign to remember an old acquaintance. "I

am unfortunate enough, sir, not to be able to recall you," said she, in most perfect Parisian French.

"My name you may have forgotten, madame, but scarcely so either our first meeting at Schaffhausen, or our last at Bregenz."

"These are all riddles to me, sir; and I am sure you are too well bred to persist in an error after you have recognised it to be such."

With a cold smile and a haughty bow, she motioned the coachman to drive on, and I saw her no more. (AYR 4.572; *A Day's Ride*, chapter 48)

Opinions differ as to why Dickens agreed to Bulwer's suggestion to revise the ending. Sadrin (171–5) lends support to Shaw's suggestion that the affinity between the endings of the two serials might have been embarrassingly close and that Bulwer, whose novel was to follow GE, would have been specially sensitive to the resemblance, and thus strong in urging his friend to abandon it (see p. 5n). Cardwell dismisses the notion of borrowing as without 'similarity in character or in situation' (482). Rosenberg notes, appropriately, that Lever 'could afford to get rid of Catinka' because, one paragraph later, he had a second ending up his sleeve (*Norton* 421): Potts finds a year-old letter from his other love, Kate Whalley, the young lady in mourning, whose family, attempting to track him down, had invited him to Wales; Potts accepts and sets off that night to live happily ever after in Wales (*A Day's Ride*, chapter 48).

Chapter 59

For eleven years, I had not seen Joe nor Biddy

eleven years] MS reads 'eight'.

an evening in December,] The novel now comes full circle, having opened on Christmas Eve almost sixty years ago.

I had heard of her, as leading a most unhappy life

as being separated from her husband, who had used her with great cruelty,] By mid-century wife-beating had emerged as a matter of public concern in England and one treated with regularity by journalists and novelists. In the words of Frances Power Cobbe, members of the English public 'read of the beatings, burnings, kickings, and "cloggings" of poor women well-nigh every morning in their newspapers' (56). The same writer also estimated that about 1,500 women were brutally assaulted in England and Wales each year, an average of more than four attacks on women every day, most of whom, Cobbe believed, were wives (71–2).

The lack of reliable data makes it difficult to determine if the incidence of wife-beating had in fact increased during the century; what is clear is that tolerance for this behaviour diminished in proportion to the successful prosecution of abusive husbands in the courts. Two reasons account for this: first, from 1828 onwards the extension of summary jurisdiction made it easier for wives to pursue prosecutions for assault without the expense and delay of a jury trial; second, the establishment of a police force in 1829 allowed constables to make arrests and prosecute offenders (Doggett 114).

Within the novel's hypothetical time-scheme, a legal separation from Drummle would have been difficult to obtain since women did not win the right to remain separated from abusive husbands until the Matrimonial Causes Act of 1884 (47 & 48 Vict., c. 68). This statute, the result of a parliamentary campaign dating from the 1850s to increase the penalties for aggressive assaults on women and children, removed a husband's right to have his wife imprisoned if she refused to consent to cohabitation and the restitution of conjugal rights.

Drummle's ill-treatment of Estella possibly reflects a combination of these mid-century developments. It may also owe something to the abusive behaviour of Sir George Chapple Norton, MP, whose unsuccessful case against Lord Melbourne in 1836 for alienating his wife's affections Dickens alluded to in the case of Bardell versus Pickwick (Sutherland, 1989, 469). Caroline Norton subsequently provided a fictionalized account of her marriage in *Stuart of Dunleath* (1853). This autobiographical novel, subtitled 'A Story of Modern Times', recounts the suffering of Eleanor at the hands of her 'brute of quality' husband, Sir Stephen Penrhyn. However, no truly significant change in the law came before 1891. In the case of *R. v. Jackson* the Court of Appeal swept away centuries of judicial authority by finally making it illegal for a husband to beat or imprison his wife (Doggett 142).

"I work pretty hard

"I work pretty hard for a sufficient living, and therefore – Yes, I do well."] Pip's affirmative reply to Estella's question further emphasizes the self-help ideal underpinning his eventual success. One is happiest, Carlyle argued, producing something important to oneself and to society: 'Blessed is he who has found his work; let him ask no other blessedness' (*Past and Present*, bk 3, ch. 11). Smiles, in his best-selling *Self-Help* (1859), restates a similar doctrine recast in what has been termed 'the progressive democratization of the gentlemanly ideal' (Gilmour, 1986, 108). See especially Smiles's last chapter, 'Character: The True Gentleman', in which he states:

> Riches and rank have no necessary connection with genuine gentlemanly qualities. The poor man may be a true gentleman – in spirit and in daily life. He may be honest, truthful, upright, polite, temperate, courageous, self-respecting and self-helping – that is, be a true gentleman. (*Self-Help* 240)

"I have often thought of you," said Estella.

> "I have often thought of you," said Estella.
> "Have you?"
> "Of late, very often. There was a long hard time when I kept far from me, the remembrance of what I had thrown away when I was quite ignorant of its worth. But, since my duty has not been incompatible with the admission of that remembrance, I have given it a place in my heart."
> **"You have always held your place in my heart," I answered. And we were silent again until she spoke.]** Dickens introduced this brief passage of dialogue at a very late stage in correcting the proofs (the addition can only be traced to the *Harper's* text of the novel, which was published from advance copies sent specially to America). Almost certainly 'the very last touches Dickens added' to *GE* before he revised the final sentence, the interpolation serves to remind readers of 'the genuine efficacy of Estella's reformation' (*Norton* 503–4).

I took her hand in mine

I took her hand in mine, and we went out of the ruined place; and, as the morning mists had risen long ago . . . so the evening mists were rising now,] Compare the scene in *Paradise Lost* after Eve's last words to Adam:

> The Cherubim descended; on the ground
> Gliding meteorous, as Ev'ning Mist

> Ris'n from a River o're the marish glides . . .
> In either hand the hastning Angel caught
> Our ling'ring Parents, and to th' Eastern Gate
> Led them direct . . .
>   then disappeer'd.
> They, looking back, all th' Eastern side beheld
> Of Paradise, so late thir happie seat . . .
> Som natural tears they drop'd, but wip'd them soon;
> The World was all before them, where to choose
> Thir place of rest, and Providence thir guide:
> They hand in hand with wandring steps and slow,
> Through Eden took thir solitarie way. (12.628–30; 637–49)

I saw the shadow of no parting from her.] This sentence concludes the serial text of the novel, the early American editions based on the text of *AYR* and the first edition printed in 1861 (see Introduction p. 11). A year later, preparing the Library Edition of 1862, Dickens introduced a further revision (see below), which he allowed to stand in the Charles Dickens Edition of *GE* in 1868 and which has been adopted by all subsequent editors:

> I saw no shadow of another parting from her

In the MS, this sentence originally appeared as:

> I saw the shadow of no parting from her, but one.

Dickens cancelled 'but one' in proof. One plausible guess at Dickens's intentions is offered by Rosenberg:

> He may simply have disliked the phrase on artistic grounds: in playing these shapely sentences by ear, he may well have discovered that last chord to be a needless, needlessly distracting obtrusion on an already long and moving sentence, which reaches its appropriate climax in the parting words to which the cadences lead up. Possibly, too, he objected to the mawkishness of the phrase or, more emphatically, refused to end the novel on a quasi-religious note as being out of harmony with the scene – the note, precisely, that the phrase "but one" conveys. (*Norton* 502)

Interestingly, Bulwer Lytton, generally characterized as the proponent of the 'happy' ending, had concluded one of his own earlier novels in a way that bears some resemblance to the revised ending Dickens furnished in response to his friend's reservations. (I am grateful to Nancy Metz for drawing this possible link to my attention.) In *Eugene Aram* (1832), the final scene closes with the two lovers meeting on a memory-laden occasion after a passage of many years and former trials. Returning from abroad, Walter seeks out Miss Lester's house in 'a small country town', pauses at the gate, and on being admitted to the parlour, is left alone for a few moments as the past 'rushed sweepingly over him'. Regaining his self-possession, he sees Ellinor standing before him:

> Changed she was, indeed; the slight girl had budded into a woman; changed she was indeed; the bound had for ever left that step, once so elastic with hope; the vivacity of the quick, dark eye was soft and quiet; the rich colour had given place to a hue fainter, though not less lovely. . . .
> "Ellinor!" said Walter, mournfully, thank God! We meet at last!" . . .
> "We are alone in the world – let us unite our lots. Never, through all I have seen and felt . . . never have I forgotten you, my sweet and dear cousin. Your image has linked itself indissolubly with all I conceived of home and happiness, and a tranquil and peaceful future; and now I return, and see you, and find you changed, but oh, lovely! . . ."

For an entertaining and thorough discussion of the vexed issue of Bulwer's meddling, see Rosenberg's essay, 'Putting an End to *Great Expectations*' (*Norton* 491–527). See also the Introduction, pp. 11–14.

APPENDIX ONE

The Sequence of Events in Pip's Narrative

[Note: All page references are to the *Norton* edition of the novel]

The 'events' include all those that occur in the main narrative and those that belong to the embedded histories of Compeyson's two victims, Miss Havisham and Magwitch. The hypothetical dating of their narratives is based on historical information given in the text, on the sequence Dickens constructed and maintained as he planned his weekly instalments, and on the extant notes he made before he wrote the last third of the novel (see below). Allusions that establish the storytelling time of the narrator, as Pip looks back on his life many years after the incidents he relates, are noted in specific chapters when they take place. The significance of the gap between episodes which happened in the past and Pip's recounting of them as he looks back on his youth later in life is addressed in the Introduction.

All calculations are based on two assumptions: (1) that Magwitch returns to England in November 1820, shortly after Pip's 23rd birthday; and (2) that Dickens carefully planned the main action and inner chronology, whose duration of sixteen or seventeen years he successfully integrated within the novel's historical framework. Evidence for dating the action rests on numerous historical references, perhaps the most important of which for my purposes are the two one-pound notes mentioned in chapters 10, 28 and 39. Anxious to make restitution for the gift Magwitch sent Pip when he was a 'poor boy', Pip returns the money many years later (this time 'clean and new', instead of the soiled notes covertly passed to him in the Three Jolly Bargemen), saying to Magwitch: 'You can put them to some other poor boy's use' (239; chapter 39).

For the bank notes to be of service, they would have to be legal tender, a requirement whose historical implications Dickens fully understood. Ten years earlier, he and W. H. Wills had explained to readers of *Household Words* how the Bank of England had first issued one-pound notes in 1797 and later instructed a Select Committee in 1819 to find a way to reduce the number of forgeries prompted by the issue of notes in small denominations. No 'true expedient' for decreasing the capital crime of forgery, they wrote, was adopted until 1821. That year, the issue of small notes 'was wholly discontinued' and the Bank reintroduced the circulation of gold sovereigns, making one-pound notes illegal tender.

External documents corroborate the care Dickens took with the novel's historical dating and chronology. To make sure of the interconnections which bind the main characters, Dickens paused before writing chapters 47 and 48 and set down two half-sheets of notes headed '<u>Dates</u>' and '(Dates) 2' (see pp. 344–5). These extant memoranda, themselves undated but evidently composed not long after Dickens concluded the 'Second Stage' of Pip's story, served as a guide before he wrote the weekly numbers revealing the interlocking histories of Miss Havisham, Compeyson, Magwitch, Molly and Jaggers. The first sheet reviews the central chronologies of the novel, while the second lists the ages of the chief characters, a crucial matter in view of their intimately linked histories. Integrating the information about ages from both the notes and the novel, and working from the year 1820 (chosen for the reason given above), we can see a remarkable consistency in the chronology showing the novel's imagined events in relation to each other and in relation to selected historical markers embedded in Pip's narrative. All dates of birth derive either from the list of ages supplied in the memoranda marked 'Dates' or from facts given in the novel and interpreted in relation to its historical setting. Italicized entries provide selected historical facts relevant to the system of transportation.

HYPOTHETICAL CHRONOLOGY

1. *Events before the novel opens*

1760: Birth of Magwitch

1764: January: birth of Miss Havisham. ('This is my birthday, Pip' 72; chapter 11). Dickens noted that 'I judge her to have been the elder in the love time'. Compeyson appears to arrive on the scene c.1790, making her about 26 and Compeyson 22 when they meet.

Miss Havisham's mother 'died when she was a baby'. She was 'a spoilt child' whose father 'denied her nothing' (141; chapter 22).

Mr Havisham later privately marries his cook; they have a child (Arthur Havisham); his second wife dies, and the boy, Miss Havisham's half-brother, becomes 'a part of the family', residing at Satis House (142; chapter 22).

Arthur Havisham grows up – 'riotous, extravagant, un-dutiful – altogether bad' (142; chapter 22). His father disinherits him, but softens before he dies, leaving Arthur well off, 'though not nearly so well off as' his elder stepsister (142; chapter 22).

1765: Birth of Jaggers

Magwitch's early childhood: 'I first become aware of myself, down in Essex, a thieving turnips for my living'. 'I was a ragged little creetur' (259; chapter 42).

1768: Birth of Compeyson, who subsequently attends a public boarding school, acquires 'learning' and the smooth ways 'of gentlefolks' (260; chapter 42).

1770: Birth of Wemmick

1771: Birth of Mrs Gargery, who is 'more than twenty years older' than Pip (12; chapter 2).

1775: Birth of Joe Gargery

1775: Birth of Molly. 'She was a woman of about forty, I supposed – but I may have thought her younger than she was' (165; chapter 26).

1787: *13 May: First Fleet leaves Spithead for Australia to found penal settlements in New South Wales at Botany Bay, Sydney, Parramatta and Norfolk Island (1788).*

1790: A 'certain . . . showy-man' appears on the scene, pursues Miss Havisham, professing devotion and practising on her affection in a 'systematic way'. He extorts money and induces her to buy out her brother's share of the brewery; they make plans for an elaborate wedding. Date based on the account of Miss Havisham's history provided by Herbert (142; chapter 22). Compare, however, Dickens's initial calculation in 'Dates' that 'the end of Miss Havisham's matter' occurred 'about 7 or 8 years' before Magwitch met Compeyson, an estimate he subsequently abandoned in favour of the less specific 'some years before'. See chapter 42.

Reports of Jaggers's successes at the Bar catch Miss Havisham's eye: she reads of his exploits in the newspapers 'before I and the world parted' (298; chapter 49). She stores away this knowledge to draw on it later.

Matthew Pocket, Herbert's father, warns Miss Havisham, his cousin, that Compeyson is not 'a true gentleman'; Miss Havisham, blinded by love, refuses all advice. Herbert adds: 'Your guardian was not at that time in Miss Havisham's councils' (143; chapter 22).

1792/3?: January: projected date for Miss Havisham's wedding to coincide with her birthday (72; chapter 11). But Compeyson jilts Miss Havisham, having successfully bilked her of substantial sums. She falls seriously ill; recovering, she 'laid the whole place waste' (143; chapter 22). Later, she contacts Jaggers, placing her financial affairs in his hands. She also asks him to look for 'a little girl to rear and love,' and save from her fate (298; chapter 49).

When Herbert recounts these events in 1815, he speculates that Compeyson may already have been married (he is when Magwitch meets him in 1800). He also adds that relatives suspected that Compeyson acted 'in concert' with her half-brother, Arthur, and that both 'shared the profits' (143; chapter 22).

1794: *The Transport Commissioners of the Transport Board (founded 1689) are revived and given responsibility for provisioning ships to transport convicts to Australia. In 1817 control of the business of transports reverted to the Navy Board.*

1795: Magwitch and Molly marry 'over the broomstick' (293; chapter 48). Magwitch tells Herbert in 1820 that they had been together 'some four or five years'. Their little girl, Estella, was about 2 or 3 at the time of Molly's trial.

1796–7: Birth of Biddy

1797: March: Herbert Pocket born. Herbert reaches his majority 'eight months before me' (217; chapter 36).

November: Pip born. Cf. 303; chapter 50, where Pip tells Herbert that he met Magwitch in the churchyard 'in my seventh year', which makes the opening date Christmas Eve 1803. In 'Dates' Dickens notes: 'Say Pip was about 7 at the opening of the story'. This comment makes for a small discrepancy since, according to the text, Pip would have turned 6 just before the novel opens. Reference to November as the month of Pip's birthday occurs twice. See chapters 36:217 and 39:236.

Estella born. Dickens gives 23 for Estella's age in '(Dates) 2'; cf. chapter 8: 49: 'she was of about my own age'. Other references reinforce the closeness of their ages.

1800: June: Epsom Races, Surrey. Magwitch meets Compeyson for the first time – 'a matter of over twenty years ago' – on the night after the Derby (260; chapter 42). The following night, Compeyson takes on Magwitch as his 'pardner', and Magwitch becomes 'a poor tool' in Compeyson's hands, a victim of the other's craft and learning. Magwitch appears to hint that Molly understood how 'overmatched' her husband was (262; chapter 42).

Magwitch meets Arthur Havisham at Compeyson's house in Brentford, Middlesex. Magwitch describes Arthur as another accomplice of Compeyson's: 'Him and Compeyson had been in a bad thing with a rich lady some years afore' (261; chapter 42). Arthur Havisham is now reduced by guilt and drink and is haunted by the figure of his half-sister – 'all in white' – whose ruin he engineered with Compeyson. A suitable amount of time has elapsed to make Arthur's decline seem credible. The second or third time Magwitch visits Compeyson's, Arthur Havisham dies prematurely, aged c.32 (262; chapter 42).

Molly is tried and acquitted of murder at the Old Bailey. Wemmick tells Pip this occurred 'A score or so of years' ago, and her acquittal constituted one of Jaggers's early successes (293; chapter 48). The scene of the struggle was a barn near Hounslow Heath, a deserted area approximately eleven miles west of London and not far from Compeyson's house in Brentford. After the trial, Jaggers takes Molly into service. Her child, 'some three years old', is believed to have been destroyed. Magwitch, her common-law husband, whom she had married when she was young, feeling pity and forbearance (and grief for the child he believes lost) lies low, assuming his presence would jeopardize her life. Magwitch first learns of Jaggers when Jaggers defends Molly (302; chapter 50).

Jaggers, fulfilling Miss Havisham's request, brings Estella to Satis House. Miss Havisham says Estella was 'two or three' at the time (299; chapter 49).

Compeyson uses Magwitch's anxiety about the trial to exploit him further, keeping him poor and making him work all the harder (300; chapter 50). Magwitch continues in Compeyson's services for about three or four years. Looking back on this dark period from a later perspective (1820), Magwitch comments that the trial and the loss of his baby daughter 'had happened some three or four years' before the churchyard meeting with Pip on Christmas Eve, 1803. Pip, aged 6, reminded him of the little girl he had so tragically lost (303; chapter 50).

1803: Late in their partnership, Magwitch and Compeyson are arrested for 'putting stolen notes in circulation' (262; chapter 42). They are tried and sentenced to transportation (fourteen and seven years respectively) and held for a period on one of the hulks. Both prisoners escape, unknown to each other, and swim ashore, landing on the marshes near Pip's village.

2. The novel opens: Pip narrates the 'First Stage' of his 'Expectations':

1803: Christmas Eve. Pip's story begins (chapters 1–2). 25 December, Christmas Day (chapters 3–5).

1804: Magwitch retried and transported to Australia for life, where he would have arrived later that year after a voyage of fifteen to sixteen weeks. This would give him about fifteen years in which to do 'wonderful well' before returning to England around November 1820 (237; chapter 39).

One evening late in December or early in January when the ground was hard with frost – 'a full year after our hunt upon the marshes' – Pumblechook takes Pip 'into town' in order to meet Miss Havisham (39; 45; chapter 7). Pip's first visit to Satis House in Rochester occurs the following morning (chapter 8). 'That was a memorable day to me, for it made great changes in me' (60; chapter 9).

A 'morning or two later' Pip resolves to make himself 'uncommon' by taking his education in hand and improve on the lessons he receives as a pupil at the village 'evening school' (61; chapter 10). Later he recounts how one Saturday evening at the Three Jolly Bargemen a mysterious stranger delivered the two one-pound notes.

1805: January, a week later, Pip returns to Satis House. He meets the toady relatives, passes Jaggers on the stairs and fights with Herbert. Afterwards, Estella proffers her cheek to Pip (75; chapter 11).

At the next visit seven days later, Miss Havisham tells Pip to return 'every alternate day' at noon and enter into 'a regular occupation' of pushing her in her chair round her room and across the landing (76; chapter 12). His trips settle into a steady routine: 'I am now going to sum up a period of at least eight or ten months' (76; chapter 12).

1806–11: This portion of the novel contains the fewest chronological markers, largely because little occurs in Pip's life beyond his trips to Satis House three times a week. His sense of frustration and entrapment mounts, aided by the nonsensical speculations of his sister and Pumblechook about his 'prospects' (78; chapter 12) and the deep shame he feels about his own humble surroundings and projected future as a blacksmith. 'We went on in this way for a long time,' Pip remarks, referring to the weekly routine and the kitchen councils at home (79; 78; chapter 12). As time slips by, Miss Havisham comments that Pip is 'growing tall' (79; chapter 12). Pip also adds: 'I was fully old enough now, to be apprenticed to Joe' (78; chapter 12). Legally, this means he was almost 14, bringing us to about 1811.

1811: Perhaps on his birthday or shortly thereafter Pip is 'bound' at Rochester Guildhall (chapter 13).

1812: Pip is now 'too big' for the school-room run by Mr Wopsle's great-aunt; instead, he studies at the Old Battery (88; chapter 15).
Noticing that he was 'getting on in the first year' of his time, Pip asks Joe for a half-day in order to visit Miss Havisham (89; chapter 15). Receiving him, she tells Pip to come once a year on his birthday. Estella has gone abroad to pursue her schooling in France (93; chapter 15). Orlick attacks Mrs Joe, attempting to murder her. The Bow Street Runners hang about the house 'for a week or two' (97; chapter 16). 'I now fell into a regular routine of apprenticeship-life' (99; chapter 17).

1813: November. Another birthday passes. The guinea he receives from Miss Havisham becomes 'an annual custom' (100; chapter 17). Pip begins to notice Biddy (100; chapter 17); later, he lets her into his secret: 'I want to be a gentleman'.

1815 late spring?: One Saturday night – 'it was in the fourth year of my apprenticeship to Joe' – Jaggers arrives in the village and informs Pip that he has 'come into a handsome property' and that he is authorized to offer Joe compensation for the loss of Pip's services (109; 108; 111; chapter 18). Pip notes how the kitchen door, customarily open 'on summer evenings', airs the room (113) and that the sun makes the roof of his bedroom warm (114), one of several seasonal markers worked into the chronology. In church on Sunday, Pip hears the parable about the rich man and the kingdom of heaven (115; chapter 19).

Monday: Pip visits Mr Trabb; later he dines with Pumblechook. Tuesday, Wednesday, Thursday pass; on Friday, Pip returns to Rochester to fit his new suit and take leave of Miss Havisham (123; chapter 19). On Saturday, Pip leaves the forge, fancying 'henceforth I was for London and greatness' as he departs from Rochester by the 7 a.m. coach (115; 119; chapter 19).

3. *Pip narrates the 'Second Stage' of his 'Expectations'*

1815: continued: A detailed sequence describes Pip's arrival in London and his first impressions of the next three days as he explores Little Britain, meets Herbert, hears the story about Miss Havisham's unhappy past, goes to the theatre and walks in the parks. On Monday he visits the Pockets in Hammersmith, where he also meets his fellow-students. Within 'two or three days', Pip establishes himself in his room in Hammersmith and then begins to go back and forth between Hammersmith and London, where he retains his bedroom at Barnard's Inn in order to keep Herbert company (154; chapter 24).

Adverbial phrases indicate how time is passing and how that time differs from the present: 'We used to walk between' Hammersmith and Barnard's Inn 'at all hours. I have an affection for the road yet (though it is not so pleasant a road as it was then), formed in the impressibility of untried youth and hope' (158; chapter 25). Looking back, Pip selects important events – his first visit to Wemmick's house in Walworth, followed by dinner the next day at Jaggers's in Soho (chapters 25 and 26) – and Drummle's departure about a month later 'to the family hole' (168; chapter 26).

One Monday morning Pip learns of Joe's impending visit, which begins another sequence chronicled in detail: his first trip back to Rochester on a Wednesday; overnight stay at the Blue Boar; visit to Satis House; second night in Rochester and return to London on Friday; going that evening with Herbert to see Wopsle play Hamlet (chapter 31). Remarks by Orlick – together with Pip's observation that Estella, whom he now sees for the first time in three or more years, 'was much changed' – register a further passage of time, as does Pip's comment that 'winter had now come round' when he makes this trip (174; chapter 28). Shortly afterwards, Pip notes that his majority is still off in the future, to which Herbert replies: You will be 21 'before you know where you are' (191; chapter 30). See also chapter 34 (208) for a further reminder ('until I came of age') that this event still lies in the future.

1816? One day 'when I was busy', Pip relates how he received a note telling him to expect Estella's arrival the day after tomorrow (198; chapter 32). She arrives, and Pip escorts her to Richmond (206; chapter 33).

After a further unspecified passage of time, Pip grows accustomed to his expectations (207; chapter 34). In moments of conscience, he reflects how his lavish habits have become ingrained, causing him to fall into debt and incur foolish expenses (208; chapter 34). 'As I am now generalising a period of my life with the object of clearing the way before me, I can scarcely do so better than by at once completing the description of our usual manners and customs at Barnard's Inn' (209; chapter 34). Herbert goes daily into the City; Pip applies himself to his studies and then spends about half the week in Hammersmith haunting Richmond; Pip and Herbert fall deeper into debt (211; 217; chapter 36).

Pip receives news that his sister has died (at age 39, according to this version of the novel's internal chronology: 212; chapter 34). He returns to the forge for the funeral and notes 'fine summer weather again', as if to suggest the next summer following his arrival in London in early June (212; chapter 35). The seasonal marker also ties in with other references to the time of the year: the Christmas opening and the detailed sequence which begins when Magwitch returns in November not long after Pip's 23rd birthday. On this occasion, he spends the night at the forge before returning to London the following day, making this one of several sequences in which the action slows down and a particular event occupies one or more days (217; chapter 35).

1817–18: March: Herbert turns 21 ('eight months before me'; 217; chapter 36). 'Time went on . . . and I came of age – in fulfilment of Herbert's prediction, that I should do so before I knew where I was' (217; chapter 36): 'It was November'. Pip is now to receive £500 a year, paid in quarterly instalments, but he learns nothing of his benefactor. He resolves, however, to assist Herbert and asks Wemmick for advice. Wemmick co-operates the following Sunday when Pip goes to Walworth; before the next week is out, Wemmick finds a good shipping broker and Pip puts down £250 to pay for Herbert's partnership.

1819: Before getting to 'the turning-point' of his life (226; chapter 37), Pip selects further incidents: he writes about Estella at Richmond and how she uses him to torture other suitors (227); Estella's teasing behaviour lasts for what seems to Pip to be 'a long time' (227; chapter 38), the exact duration of which is difficult to determine. The period may well extend from Estella's arrival in Richmond (perhaps in 1816) through to Pip's 23rd birthday in November 1820.

Pip escorts Estella to and from Satis House (228; chapter 38): he spends the night there for the first time and then returns to London the next day. Drummle toasts Estella at the Finches; peace is made between Pip and Drummle the following day. Pip and Herbert leave Barnard's for the Temple.

Appendix One 431

1820: Two years pass and bring the action forward to November 1820, after which date a series of important events takes place recorded in a chronological framework indicated either by the day or by the month, making this the most specifically sequenced portion of the novel. Further reference to these 'two years' occurs in chapter 44 when Pip explains to Miss Havisham how he had taken steps to help Herbert to a partnership. Late one stormy evening, a week after Pip's 23rd birthday, Magwitch returns (this event is expressed below as '®').

4. Pip narrates the 'Third Stage' of his 'Expectations'

®+1: Pip confirms Magwitch's story with Jaggers; secures lodgings for his benefactor in Essex Street; Herbert returns from Marseilles (chapter 40).

®+2: Magwitch comes round 'at the appointed time' for his meal (258; chapter 41). As he relates the first part of his life, we see how the separate stories of Magwitch and Miss Havisham tie together (264; chapter 42). Later that night, Pip resolves to see Estella and Miss Havisham.

®+3: Not finding Estella in Richmond the next day (265; chapter 43), Pip consults further with Herbert.

®+4: The following day, Pip goes to Satis House, setting off by the 'early morning coach' (265; chapter 43) to find Drummle at the Blue Boar. He then walks to Satis House and confronts Miss Havisham: 'who am I, for God's sake, that I should be kind?' she replies, telling Pip that he made his own snares (269; chapter 44). Pip leaves and walks back to London, arriving just after midnight to find Wemmick's note warning him not to go home. That same day, in Pip's absence, Wemmick moves Magwitch to a riverside house on learning that Pip's chambers were under surveillance.

®+5: The next morning, after spending a restless night at the Hummums, Pip goes to Walworth to consult Wemmick; he passes the day there before leaving in the evening to search for Magwitch's new lodgings at Mill Pond Bank. In front of the fire that evening, Magwitch, Pip and Herbert evolve their plan to practise rowing and keep in touch with Magwitch, who would signal that all was right from his window overlooking the river (282–3; chapter 46).

®+6 'I set myself to get the boat' (284; chapter 46).

1821: January, February: 'I was often out [on the Thames] in cold, rain, and sleet, but nobody took much note of me after I had been out a few times' (284; chapter 46).

'Some weeks passed without bringing any change'. 'One afternoon, late in the month of February' (285; chapter 47), Pip has dinner at a chop-house and goes to the theatre to see Wopsle. In the course of the play, Wopsle, from the stage, notices Compeyson sitting behind Pip 'like a ghost' (288; chapter 47). '[A]bout a week' later, Pip dines with Jaggers at his house a second time (290; chapter 48). Pip identifies Molly as Estella's mother.

The next day, Pip goes to Satis House, responding to a note delivered to him via Mr Jaggers on the evening of the dinner. He breakfasts at the Halfway House and walks 'into the town' after 'the best light of the day' had gone. Asks Miss Havisham for £900 to pay for the rest of Herbert's partnership (296; chapter 49). Miss Havisham breaks down: 'My Dear . . . I meant to save [Estella] from misery like my own. At first I meant no more' (298). Tells Pip the few facts she knows about Estella's adoption. Pip walks in the deserted brewery. Recalling the illusion that terrified him as a boy (55; chapter 8), he decides to look in on Miss Havisham before leaving and rescues her from almost certain death when her clothes catch fire (299; chapter 49).

At 6 a.m. the following day, Pip kisses Miss Havisham and returns to town. Herbert attends Pip, who is in pain from his burns, and recounts what he learned the previous evening from Magwitch's unfinished history. Using these details, Pip deduces the identity of Estella's father (303; chapter 50).

The next morning, Pip confronts Jaggers with his discoveries (chapter 51) and then settles business matters relating to Herbert's partnership.

March: Pip's left arm remains painful; on Monday morning, he receives a note from Wemmick: 'Early in the week, or say, Wednesday if the tide should suit, you might do what you know of' (310; chapter 52). After breakfast, Pip and Herbert check on departure times for steamers bound for Hamburg, Pip obtains passports and Herbert enlists Startop's help with the rowing. Pip returns home to find a note summoning him to the little sluice house on the marshes at nine either tonight or tomorrow. Pip resolves to set out for Rochester at once. After dining at 'an inn of minor reputation down the town' shortly after his arrival (312; chapter 52), he sets off to keep his appointment at the sluice house, where Orlick awaits him, intent on murder. Saved by Herbert and co., Pip learns that it 'is still Monday night'. By daylight on Tuesday morning, the party returns to the Temple. Pip immediately goes to bed and rests all day (322; chapter 53).

Wednesday morning dawns: a day typical of early March when hot spells alternate with blasts of cold wind (322; chapter 54). The rowing party spend the night at the inn on Canvey Island (327).

Friday: the Thames river police intercept Magwitch at 12.50 p.m. as he prepares to board the steamer for his escape. Compeyson drowns after grappling with Magwitch, who is captured, handcuffed and taken to a police-court before being lodged in Newgate pending his trial in a month at the next sessions (chapter 55).

Saturday: 'in that same week', Herbert leaves for Cairo. Pip meets Wemmick at the Temple, and Wemmick invites him to Walworth next Monday (336; chapter 55).

Monday: Wemmick and Miss Skiffins marry.

March/early April: Magwitch lies ill in Newgate infirmary, visited daily by Pip (chapter 56).

April: The sessions commence, and Magwitch, together with thirty-one others, receives the death sentence (340; chapter 56).

Pip immediately petitions the Home Secretary and continues his daily visits to the prison hospital. 'As the days went on', it became clear that Magwitch would soon die. Pip tells Magwitch that his daughter survived, found rich friends, and that he loves her. Magwitch dies (342; chapter 56).

'For a day or two', Pip lies exhausted in his chambers. He is arrested for debt (he owes £123 15s 6d to a jeweller) but collapses and becomes delirious (343; chapter 57).

End of May, first of June: Pip recovers sufficiently to talk with Joe. Pip's convalescence continues; a Sunday excursion in the country, walks in the Temple Gardens. Later, Joe leaves, enclosing with a note saying goodbye a receipt 'for the debt and costs' on which Pip had been arrested (350; chapter 57).

Pip goes to the forge to thank Joe – 'The June weather was delicious' – and arrives to find Joe and Biddy celebrating their wedding (354; chapter 58). Pip rests in his old room and then says goodbye.

July: Pip sells his possessions, leaves England and goes to join Herbert in Cairo (355; chapter 58).

September: 'I was clerk to Clarriker and Co.' (355; chapter 58).

[time passes] – 'Many a year went round' – and Pip becomes a partner.

1832: One December evening, Pip returns to the forge and sees Joe and Biddy for the first time in eleven years. He walks over to the site of Satis House –

'There was no house now, no brewery, no building whatever left, but the wall of the old garden' – and meets Estella (356; chapter 59).

[time passes]

1840: *22 May: Orders-in-Council abolish transportation to New South Wales, although for the next decade Britain continues to send convicts to the colony in small numbers. Growing opposition from colonists prompts the New South Wales Legislative Council to refuse convicts, forcing the government to comply.*

1850: *The flow of prisoners to Australia is diverted to Tasmania and Western Australia.*

1853: *Abolition of transportation to Tasmania (officially known as Van Diemen's Land after 1 January 1856), followed by a ban effective for Western Australia.*

1860–1: Pip writes his memoirs.

1868: *9 January: The last convict ship arrives in Western Australia.*

APPENDIX TWO
The Hoo Peninsula and Rochester

The 'marsh country' Pip claims as 'ours' belongs to a distinctive portion of north-east Kent, a spur-shaped area of land lying east of Gravesend between the Thames and the Medway. Descriptive passages, together with many specific details, support this assertion and the contention that sections of *Great Expectations* remain so distinctly rooted in the countryside as to give several chapters the characteristics of a regional novel. Dickens, of course, did not set out to write a guide book about Rochester and its environs or to scrutinize the Medway region with the thoroughness Thomas Hardy applied to Dorset under the pretence of chronicling the lives of the inhabitants of his imaginary Wessex. But at least two considerations ensured the indebtedness of *Great Expectations* to the topography of this region: Dickens's evident resolution to draw on childhood memories intimately linked with Chatham and Rochester, and the renewed interest in north-east Kent signalled by the delight he took in his new country home at Gad's Hill.

Some of Dickens's contemporary readers and later overzealous topographers have tended to exaggerate the novel's roots in a particular locality by proposing a *literal* correspondence between real villages and places and their fictive counterparts. Dickens's use of actual place-names for all his London settings (save one) and the verisimilitude of the descriptive passages based on the Hoo peninsula and its churchyards, villages and the nearby city of Rochester lend plausibility to claims of this kind. But inflexibility and a refusal to admit descriptions based on composites altered for fictional purposes lead to foolishness when commentators insist on *this* forge as the prototype for Joe Gargery's workplace, or on *that* church as the sole model for the graveyard where Pip's parents and siblings lie.

The same criticism applies to an attempt to place the 'neglected' brewery at the side of Miss Havisham's house (chapter 8) and provide definitive identifications of other topographical details. The circuitous walk taken by Pip to avoid passing the corn-chandler's in chapter 30, for example, only makes sense imaginatively, since the loop conflicts with the respective positions of the supposed originals in Rochester High Street. The seedsman's gabled premises lie at the other end, in the opposite direction from the inn where Pip and Jaggers stay and from the bridge over the Medway. But suppose their positions reversed: one either unavoidably passes in front of the shop or makes the detour Pip describes before re-entering the High Street by way of the Cathedral precincts further along the High Street towards the river (see map on p. 451). The location of the hulks is another instance; for, while hulks and two of their prisoners play a key role in the novel, the fact remains that, however vividly we might picture the apparent proximity of the prison ships ' 'right 'cross th' meshes' from Pip's fictional village, topographical evidence for their anchorage is conjectural at best (see chapters 2, 5 and 28).

We are on safer ground (quite literally) when we point to Rochester as the prototype of 'the market town' four miles from Pip's village. It is to Rochester's Guildhall the family marches on the solemn occasion of Pip's apprenticeship to Joe and to the Royal Victoria and Bull Hotel just across the High Street that they repair to have dinner on the windfall of the premium paid by Miss Havisham to the blacksmith for taking on his pupil (chapter 13). Though never given even an imaginary name (compare 'Cloisterham' in MED), distinct features of 'the quiet old town' appear throughout the novel. Its narrow High Street and various merchants, weekly market, the 'bridge', 'cathedral chimes', and adjacent 'echoing courts' unquestionably fix the locale, as does the 'large, dismal house' inhabited by the Miss Havisham 'up town'. Pip's fifteen-minute walk there on the occasion of his first visit, however, more than triples the time it would take to cover the real distance to Restoration House from Pumblechook's presumed gabled premises in Rochester's High Street (chapter 8). Thus, some walks and the location of recognizable landmarks answer to the needs of the novel rather than to those of observed reality.

By contrast, Pip's three marsh journeys represent a skilful blend of the real and the imaginary (chapters 3, 5 and 53). With respect to distance, direction and duration, Dickens supplies details as he might have logged them in the course of an afternoon excursion from his house on Gad's Hill just outside the city of Rochester. Take the first occasion on Christmas morning when, 'in the confusion of the mist', Pip finds himself 'too far to the right' and forced to correct his course by following the edge of the river back towards the Battery (chapter 3). Eight or nine hours later (the hours of this eventful day are ticked off with convincing realism), Pip returns to the scene, this time in the company of Joe, Wopsle and a file of soldiers led by their gallant sergeant.

The temporal setting, the sergeant's question about the distance of the forge from the marshes – 'Just a mile', replies Mrs Joe – and the carefully plotted directions add to the sense of verisimilitude. Shortly before dusk, the party sets off through the village and past the finger-post to search among the graves in the churchyard of St James's, Cooling, whose 'weird strangeness' drew Dickens on many of his afternoon walks, according to Forster. Reference to striking out 'on the open marshes, through a gate at the side of the churchyard', however, more obviously resembles the outlying terrain around St Mary's in Lower Higham, where a wicket-gate led from the church-yard to the marshes and to a five-barred gate at the end of the road, which confined cattle to their grazing ground (Gadd, 'Topography of *Great Expectations*', 136).

As the soldiers appear to move towards the river-bank at Higham Creek, near Cliffe fort, they head north-west in the direction of the old battery, the beacon and the gibbet illuminated by the setting sun. Beyond, lie the Thames and the Essex shore, approximately one mile across the river at this point. Guided by shouts, and after further corrections, the soldiers capture the two convicts. Then follows a march along 'a reasonably good path' at the edge of the Thames, evidently a reference to the sea-wall built along the shoreline around much of the Hoo peninsula and maintained by the Commission of Sewers (Burnett 22). An hour of this travelling brings the party to a 'landing-place made of rough stakes and stones', a destination approximately five miles from Cliffe Creek, their original point of departure. The description of the landing-place and the subsequent reference to the hulk 'lying out a little way from the mud of the shore' suggest Egypt Creek as a model for the location, the only one of three possible deep-water sites on the banks of the Thames consistent with the topographical details supplied earlier in chapter 5. (For contradictory information about the embarkation point, see chapter 28).

Much later in the novel (chapter 53) Pip makes a similar journey, this time mysteriously summoned to a hut used by workers attending the many lime-kilns to the west of the old battery. On this occasion, he confidently navigates his way there through the darkness by plotting his course in relation to geographical features that correspond to actual landmarks. 'The direction that I took, was not that in which my old home lay, nor that in which we had pursued the convicts'. Instead, he turns his back to the distant hulks and keeps them to the east, 'over my shoulder', as he walks directly towards the river. The Old Battery – to the south-west and near Higham Creek – and the particular lime-kiln he heads for were 'miles apart'. The presence of several kilns renders futile the reader's attempts to identify a specific kiln or specific hut. But reference to an occupation long associated with the area and to the 'sluggish stifling smell' of burning lime adds a compelling authenticity to one of the novel's more sensational chapters.

'Everyone in writing', Dickens commented on one occasion, 'must speak from his own experience' (*Letters* 7.460), a truth to which his use of Rochester, the marsh settings, the various London locales and the chapter devoted to the failed flight down the Thames all attest. Yet fictitious narratives, as Dickens also knew, necessarily depart from reality since any details we cite as evidence of accuracy and authenticity come to us via an agency that alters, colours and distorts by omission. Nowhere is the operation of the latter more apparent than in the 'interesting' portrait of Rochester's High Street offered by Pip on first returning to his old haunts. Recalling some of the particulars of his visit, Pip notes how occasional 'tradespeople', including Trabb's boy, disturb a sense of composure he detects in the 'quiet old town' which, on another occasion, he attributes to its clerical air, ruined cloisters and the sad, remote sounds of the nearby cathedral chimes (chapters 30 and 49).

But there was a section of the city's population, portrayed by a contemporary of Dickens in 1860, to which Pip paid little attention:

> *The people on the river* formed a distinct feature of Medway life. Tiers of colliers, mostly sailing vessels, might be seen [nearby] lying between Chatham Pier and Strood, five or six abreast, with some five hundred seamen among them; and, as these vessels changed from week to week, the neglected collier sailors on the Medway were to be counted by thousands in the course of the year. Great numbers of barge people, too, might be found on the stream and in the several reaches and creeks of the river. . . . The dedication of a parish church at Rochester to St. Nicholas, the patron saint of sailors, seems to indicate a special spiritual provision for men employed on the neighbouring waters; but no such provision appears to have been made, and little thought given to the matter, by the good people of the city. (Hobbes 2.260)

This compromise between the inventive requirements of the novelist and those of the journalist committed to reportage finds sustained expression in *Great Expectations* and constitutes one of the sources of this novel's continuing appeal to generations of readers.

APPENDIX THREE
The Temple, Little Britain and the River Thames

The removal of Pip and Herbert to the Temple, more than a year before Pip turns 23 in November 1820, represents another instance of Dickens's respect for actual topography, especially in the care he exerted in the selection of the London scenes of the novel. The Temple, with its walks, well-kept gardens and fine view of the Surrey hills on the opposite side of the Thames, improved significantly on the dingy 'collection of shabby buildings' that belonged to Barnard's Inn, Pip's first London domicile off Lower Holborn and north of the river (see Plate 16). By contrast, this new location on a summer morning was 'a temple of repose' where one could hear the 'whispering of leaves from the tall trees, and a soothing murmur from the river' (Manby Smith, 1857, 33) rather than the passage of heavy traffic up and down nearby Holborn Hill. And, as two of England's four Inns of Court, the Middle and Inner Temple (known collectively as 'the Temple') suggest an improvement of another sort: all four institutions customarily received the sons of noblemen and 'the better sort of gentlemen', unlike those of Chancery, whose inns attracted the sons of merchants and tradesmen (Adolphus 2.503).

The Inns of Court, so called because each in the thirteenth century belonged to the king's court, were collegiate properties with halls, chambers and libraries where law was practised and taught. Buildings belonging to the Middle and Inner Temple occupied an area between Fleet Street to the north and the Thames to the south and extended west to Essex Street and east to Whitefriars (see map on p. 441). Inside, 'sundry lanes and courts' connected buildings with suites of rooms, access to which was by staircases. Residents included law students, lawyers and individuals with no ties to the legal profession. The name 'Temple' derives from the Knights Templars, a twelfth-century contingent of knights who 'acted as Guardians to the roads for the protection of Pilgrims going to the Holy Sepulchres' (*The London Guide*, 1818, 113). The occupation of the Temple by lawyers dates from the 1340s following the decline of the Templars and their cessation as an order in 1313. By 1388, Middle and Inner Temple had emerged as two separate Inns of Court, each with its own professional and academic facilities for training lawyers.

In the case of *Great Expectations*, Pip's new location offered additional advantages. It is not far from Jaggers's office in Little Britain and close enough to Newgate to remind Magwitch of the fate awaiting him if he were caught: 'Death by the rope in an open street not fur from' Pip's chambers. Essex Street was equally near at hand, the locale chosen by Dickens for Magwitch's temporary lodgings in a 'respectable' house 'almost in hail' of Pip's rooms from which he could look back on Magwitch's lighted rear windows as he returns to his own staircase after crossing by the fountain in Middle Temple. With access to the Thames via its own stairs, the Temple also plays a role in the preparations for aiding Magwitch's attempted river escape, since the waterside landing offers Pip a perfect place to tie up his boat and develop a new routine. Either alone or with Herbert, he began frequently to go out 'as for training and practice' until he became a familiar figure on the river. Varying his routine with the tides, he was thus able to build up stamina for the long trip down-river 'well beyond Gravesend' and also maintain contact with Magwitch (later relocated 'down the Pool') by prearranged signals.

Dickens makes further use of the actual configuration of the Temple in two opposing ways. Its spacious and attractive gardens provide an ideal site for Pip's recuperation, when, under Joe's care, he is nursed back to health, leaning on Joe's arm as they walk in the warm sunlight of early summer and look at the river (chapter 57). Second, the 'lonely' and exposed position of Pip's chambers early in the century close to the river (chapter 39) adds to their apparent vulnerability on the night of the fierce wind and stormy weather signalling Magwitch's return from Australia. Furthermore, arrangements for the security of the Temple deepen the sense of mystery and expectancy, of watching and being watched.

Even Pip as a permanent resident is subject to scrutiny by the night porter on duty at the Whitefriars gate when, arriving late one evening and spattered in mud after a long walk from Rochester, he is examined 'with much attention' (chapter 44). Dickens may well have come across a copy of the printed 'Rules and Orders' issued in June 1822 specifying the duties of porters, watchmen and warders responsible for protecting the Temple. Following a report on Security undertaken in 1821, Parliament stipulated that all public gates to the Temple (ten in all) should close at night and that evening and night watchmen should institute patrols and proclaim the time of night every half hour (Inner Temple archives). And at all times they were under strict orders to keep out beggars and 'all loose and disorderly persons' and instructed to examine any suspicious basket or bundle brought in after dark 'as a precaution against the dropping of children' ('Rules and Orders', June 1822). Yet, in spite of efforts by porters and watchmen to monitor the various gates to the Temple, suspicious persons continued to pass in and out, as Pip discovers when he falls over 'a man crouching in a corner' as he descends his staircase in the darkness of the early morning following the unexpected arrival of his 'uncle'. Reference to details like these also corroborates Wemmick's thoroughness. His need to leave duplicate notes of warning to Pip is duly registered when he comments how he must go round later in the day to each of the gates to destroy potentially incriminating 'documentary evidence' (chapter 45).

Attending to this as part of his day's work would have been no difficult task for a law clerk employed in Little Britain. Mr Jaggers's gloomy office, situated among 'the distorted adjoining houses' of the neighbourhood, was less than a mile from the Temple. Equally important, its location gave the lawyer and his clerk easy access to the Old Bailey and Newgate gaol. And what better district to serve as a warning to the youth fresh from the country that the reality of 'London and greatness' might run counter to his cherished dreams? Taking two 'turns' in quick succession after arriving at his guardian's office, Pip sets out to explore the vicinity while waiting for Mr Jaggers. Neither walk in the big city proves auspicious. On the first, Pip confronts nearby Smithfield market before heading in the opposite direction to be oppressed by 'the great black dome of St Paul's, by the 'grim stone building' of Newgate prison, by inebriated crowds attending the Sessions and by the horrors of the state's stark apparatus of punishment and death. Restricting himself on the second walk to Little Britain and Bartholomew Close proves hardly more encouraging, a pattern which continues as Wemmick cautions Pip what to expect of London while conducting him to his next destination. They head west, perhaps down King Edward Street into Newgate Street and then up Holborn Hill to Lower Holborn and Barnard's Inn, less than a mile away. Rather than 'an hotel kept by Mr. Barnard' grand enough to make Rochester's Blue Boar no more than 'a mere public-house', Pip sees instead 'the dingiest collection of shabby buildings ever squeezed together in a rank corner as a club for Tom-cats'. Such are his quarters, interspersed with breaks at the Pockets' riverside home in Hammersmith, five miles to the west, until Pip and Herbert remove to Garden Court in the Temple several years later.

The flight down the Thames in chapter 54, for which Dickens prepares early in the second stage of Pip's expectations, conveys the same concern with accuracy. In this instance, Dickens went to considerable length to get things right. To make sure about 'the actual course of a boat in such circumstances', Forster reported, Dickens hired a steamer for the day to travel the full distance of the projected journey undertaken by the oarsmen. The waterside environment of the south bank of the Thames is evoked in equally compelling detail, this time the result of pedestrian excursions by the author. Following the track of one of Dickens's own forays into the region, Pip first makes his way through the area just east of Southwark, which Dickens selects as a suitable locale for Magwitch's hideaway. The wooden house with its bow-fronted windows most likely seems to have had an actual prototype. Yet, once again, Dickens irresistibly blends fiction with reality by providing plausible but imaginary names beyond the reach of the most determined source hunter.

APPENDIX FOUR

Maps

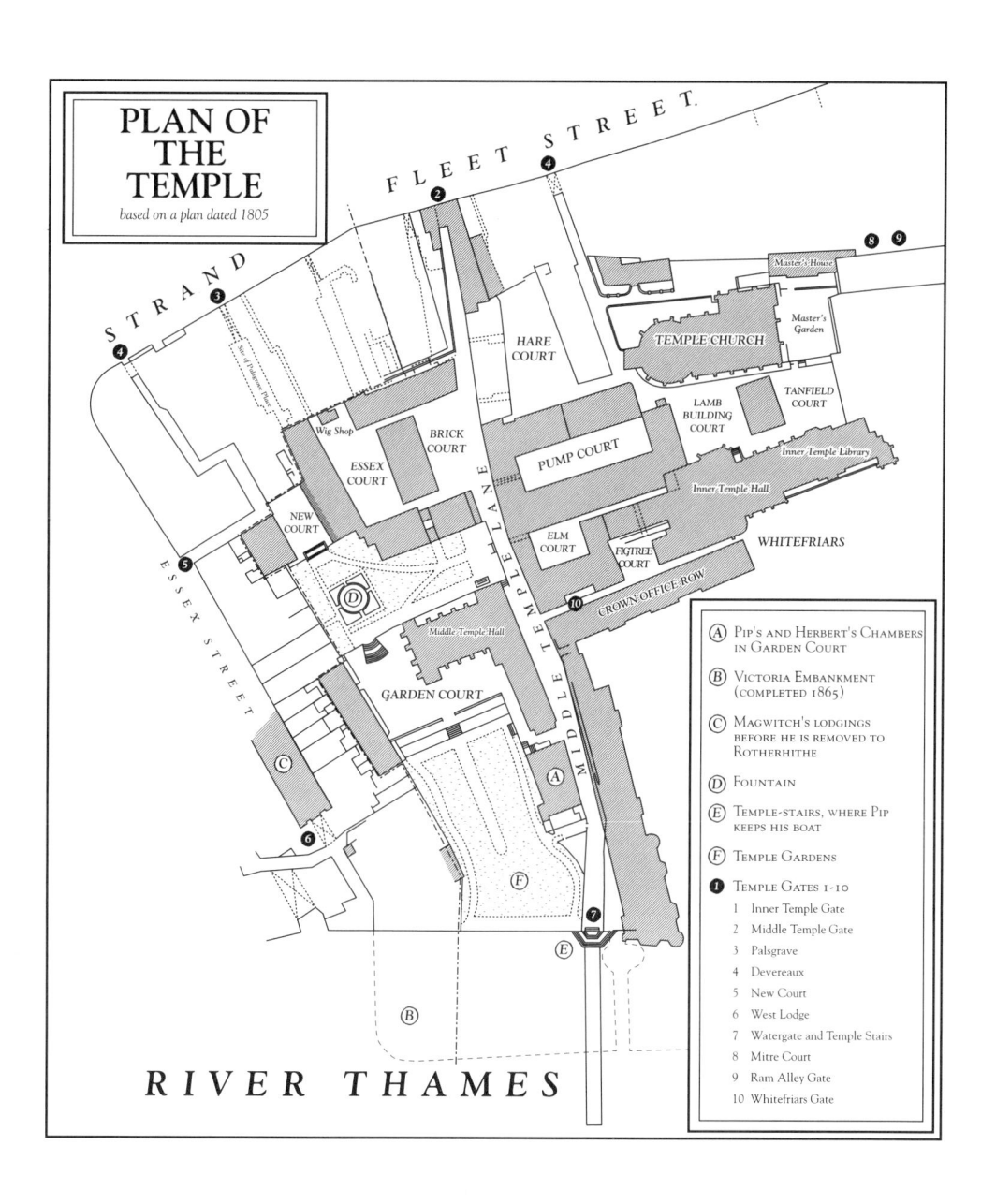

PLAN OF THE TEMPLE
based on a plan dated 1805

- Ⓐ Pip's and Herbert's Chambers in Garden Court
- Ⓑ Victoria Embankment (completed 1865)
- Ⓒ Magwitch's lodgings before he is removed to Rotherhithe
- Ⓓ Fountain
- Ⓔ Temple-stairs, where Pip keeps his boat
- Ⓕ Temple Gardens
- ❶ Temple Gates 1-10
  1. Inner Temple Gate
  2. Middle Temple Gate
  3. Palsgrave
  4. Devereaux
  5. New Court
  6. West Lodge
  7. Watergate and Temple Stairs
  8. Mitre Court
  9. Ram Alley Gate
  10. Whitefriars Gate

Mr JAGGERS' LITTLE BRITAIN

based on an 1855 map

KEY
- Gardens
- Buildings
- Buildings significant to Book

Appendix Four

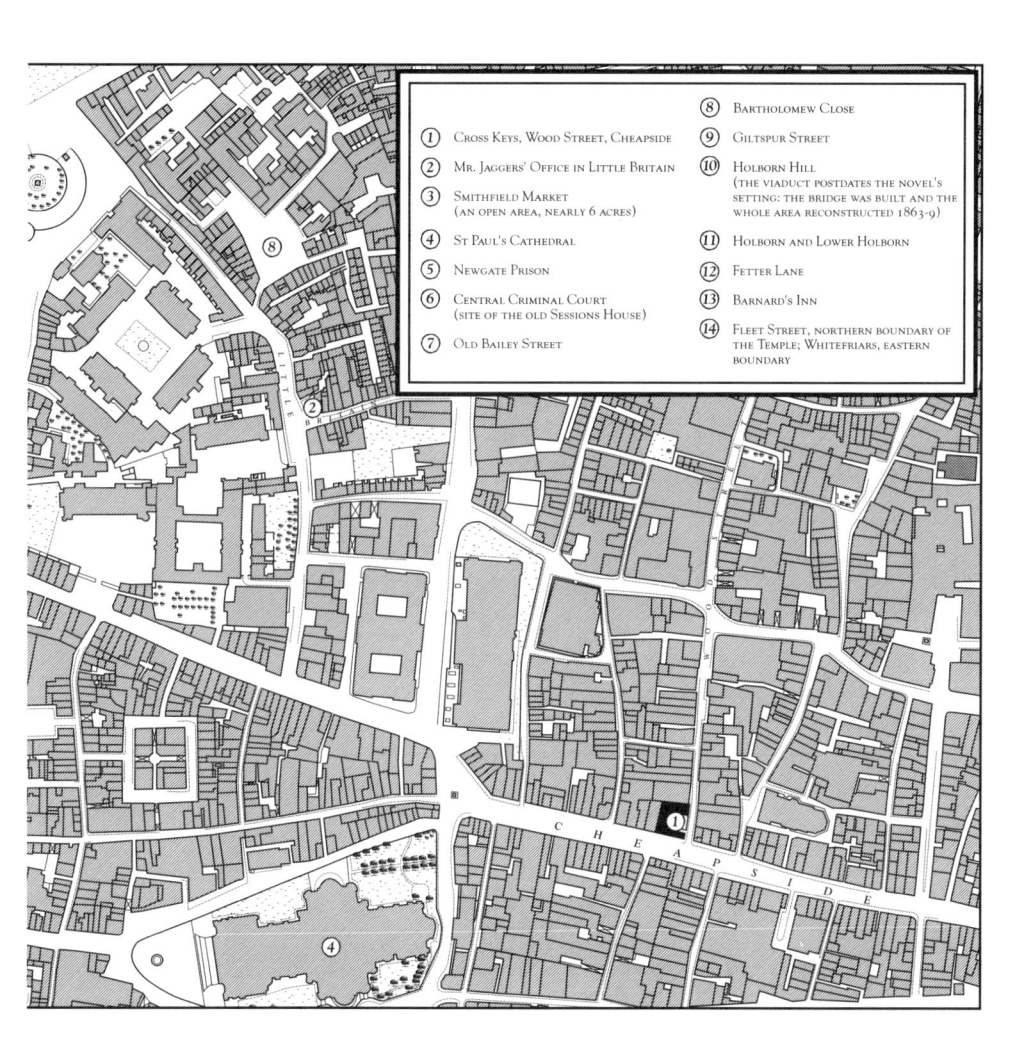

① Cross Keys, Wood Street, Cheapside
② Mr. Jaggers' Office in Little Britain
③ Smithfield Market (an open area, nearly 6 acres)
④ St Paul's Cathedral
⑤ Newgate Prison
⑥ Central Criminal Court (site of the old Sessions House)
⑦ Old Bailey Street
⑧ Bartholomew Close
⑨ Giltspur Street
⑩ Holborn Hill (the viaduct postdates the novel's setting: the bridge was built and the whole area reconstructed 1863-9)
⑪ Holborn and Lower Holborn
⑫ Fetter Lane
⑬ Barnard's Inn
⑭ Fleet Street, northern boundary of the Temple; Whitefriars, eastern boundary

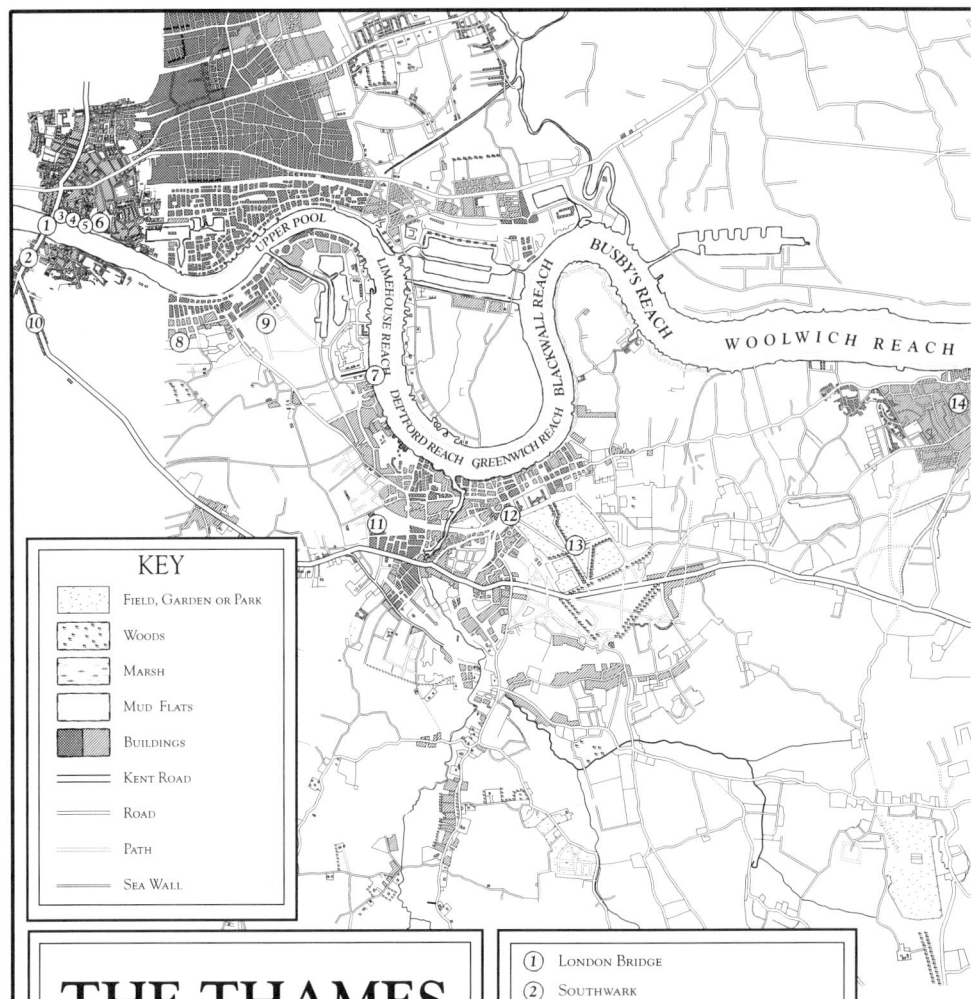

THE THAMES AND KENT ROAD FROM LONDON TO WOOLWICH

based on an 1844 map

KEY

- Field, Garden or Park
- Woods
- Marsh
- Mud Flats
- Buildings
- Kent Road
- Road
- Path
- Sea Wall

1. London Bridge
2. Southwark
3. Terminal for Steam Packets
4. Old Billingsgate Market
5. Custom House
6. Tower of London
7. Mill Pond Bank and Mill Pond Stairs
8. Bermondsey
9. Rotherhithe
10. Kent Street
11. Deptford
12. Greenwich
13. Greenwich Park
14. Woolwich
15. Shooters Hill
16. Welling
17. Erith
18. Bexley Heath
19. Dartford

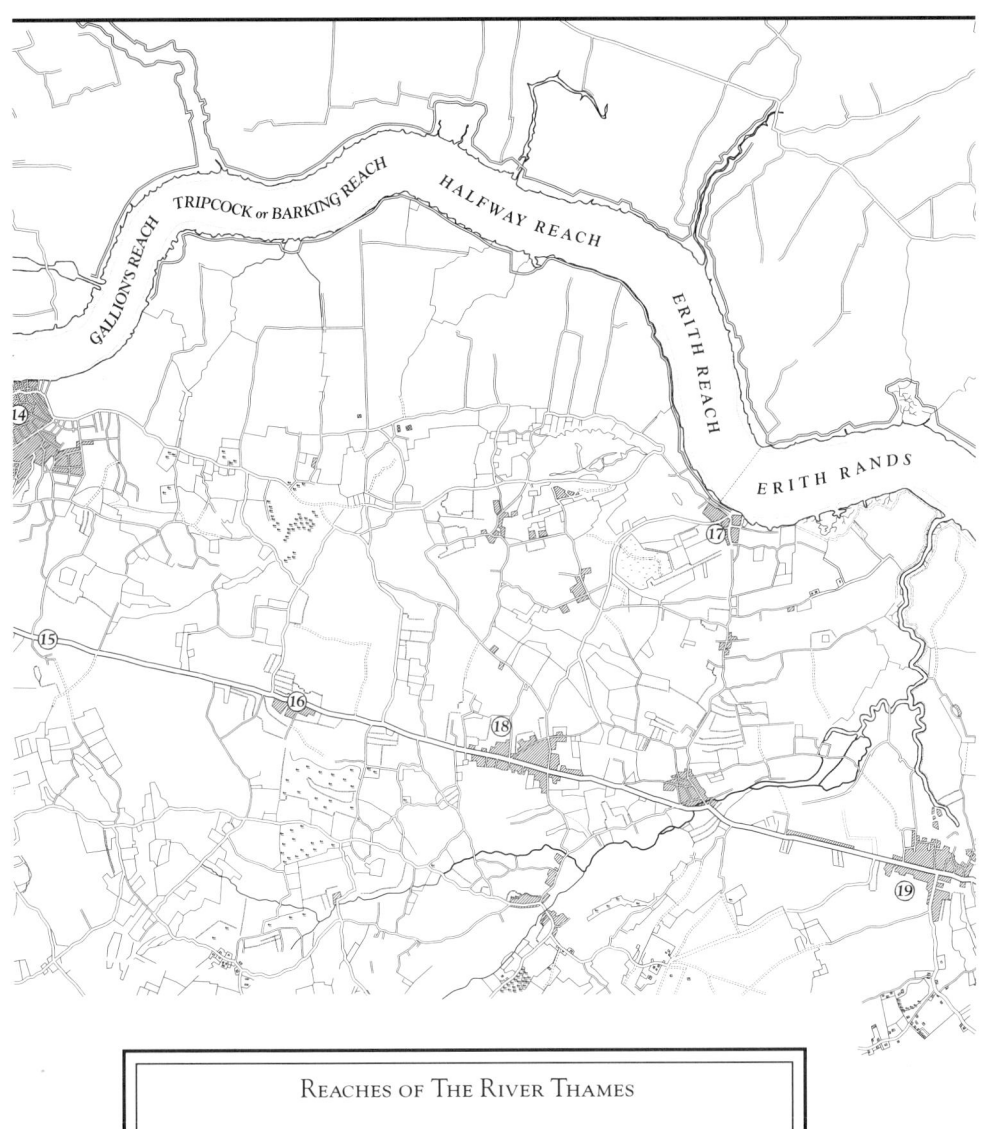

Reaches of The River Thames

Upper Pool	1 mile	Woolwich Reach	2 1/2 miles
Lower Pool	1 1/4 miles	Gallions Reach	1 1/2 miles
Limehouse Reach	1 1/2 miles	Barking Reach	2 miles
Deptford Reach	1 mile	Halfway Reach	2 miles
Greenwich Reach	1 mile	Erith Reach	2 miles
Blackwall Reach	1 1/4 miles	Erith Rands	1 1/2 miles
Busby's Hole (Reach)	1 1/4 miles		

20	Gravesend	31	Sea Wall
21	Higham Street	32	Hope Point
22	St Mary's, Higham	33	Cliffe
23	Chalk	34	Egypt Bay
24	Gad's Hill	35	St. James's, Cooling
25	Higham Creek	36	Hole Haven
26	Cliffe Creek	37	Canvey Point
27	Higham Creek Fort	38	Boundary of the River Thames
28	Cliffe Fort	39	London Stone
29	Sluice House	40	Frinsbury
30	Lime Kilns	41	Stroud
		42	Rochester

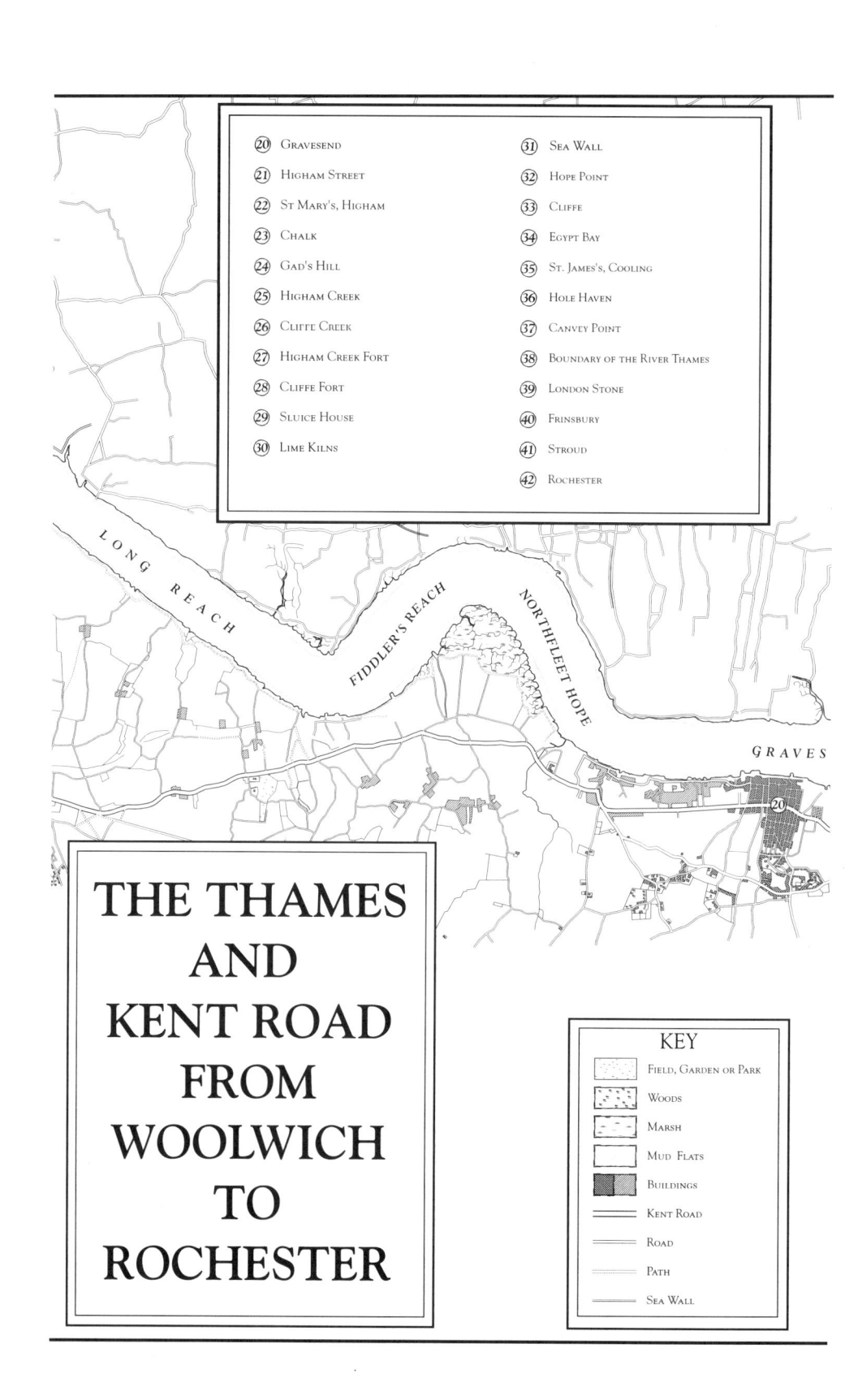

THE THAMES AND KENT ROAD FROM WOOLWICH TO ROCHESTER

KEY

- Field, Garden or Park
- Woods
- Marsh
- Mud Flats
- Buildings
- Kent Road
- Road
- Path
- Sea Wall

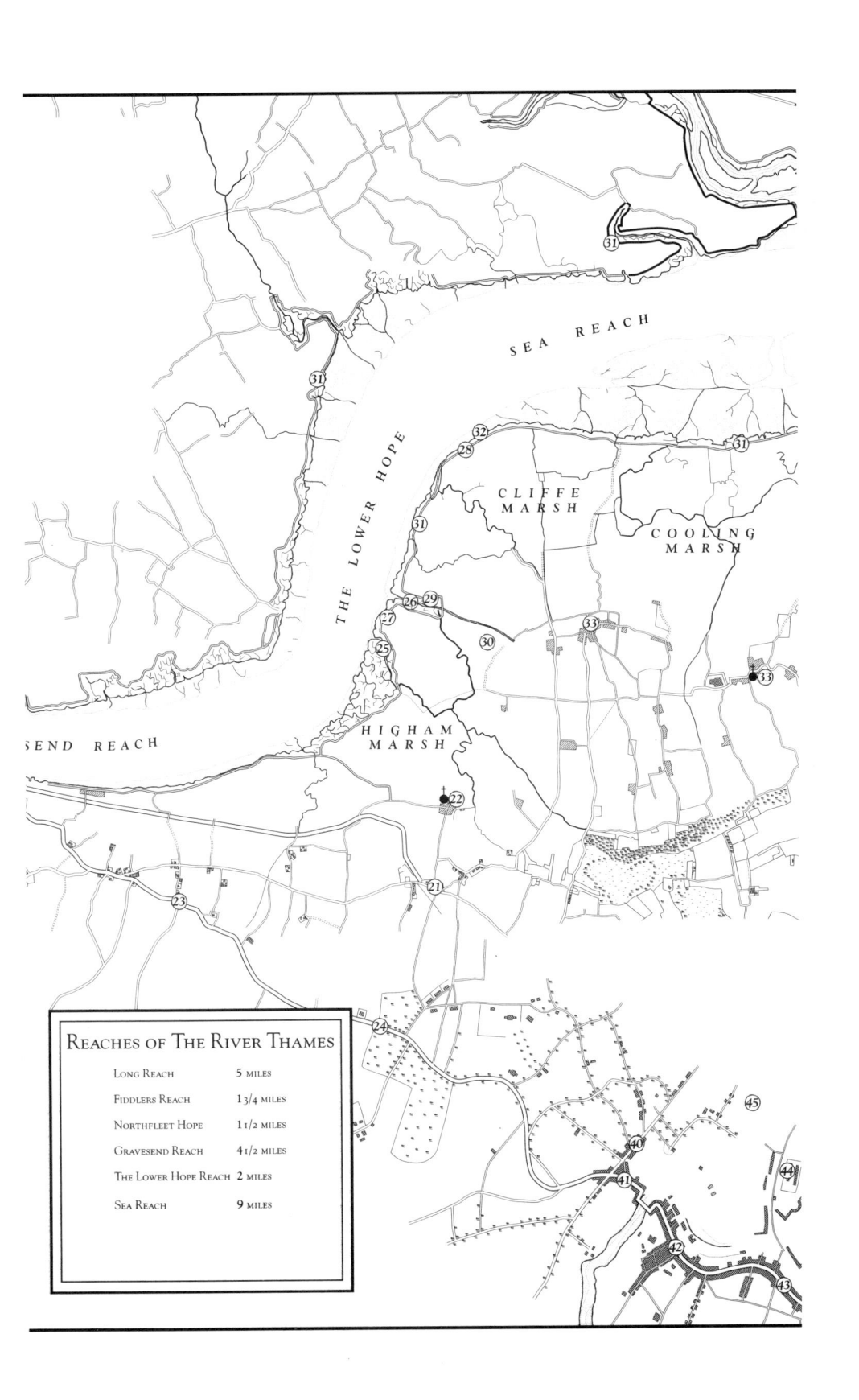

Reaches of The River Thames

Long Reach	5 miles
Fiddlers Reach	1 3/4 miles
Northfleet Hope	1 1/2 miles
Gravesend Reach	4 1/2 miles
The Lower Hope Reach	2 miles
Sea Reach	9 miles

- ㉞ Egypt Bay
- ㉟ St. James's, Cooling
- ㊱ Hole Haven
- ㊲ Canvey Point
- ㊳ Boundary of the River Thames
- ㊴ London Stone
- ㊵ Frinsbury
- ㊶ Stroud
- ㊷ Rochester
- ㊸ Chatham
- ㊹ Chatham Dockyard
- ㊺ Upnor Castle

THE THAMES AND MEDWAY ESTUARIES

based on an 1844 map

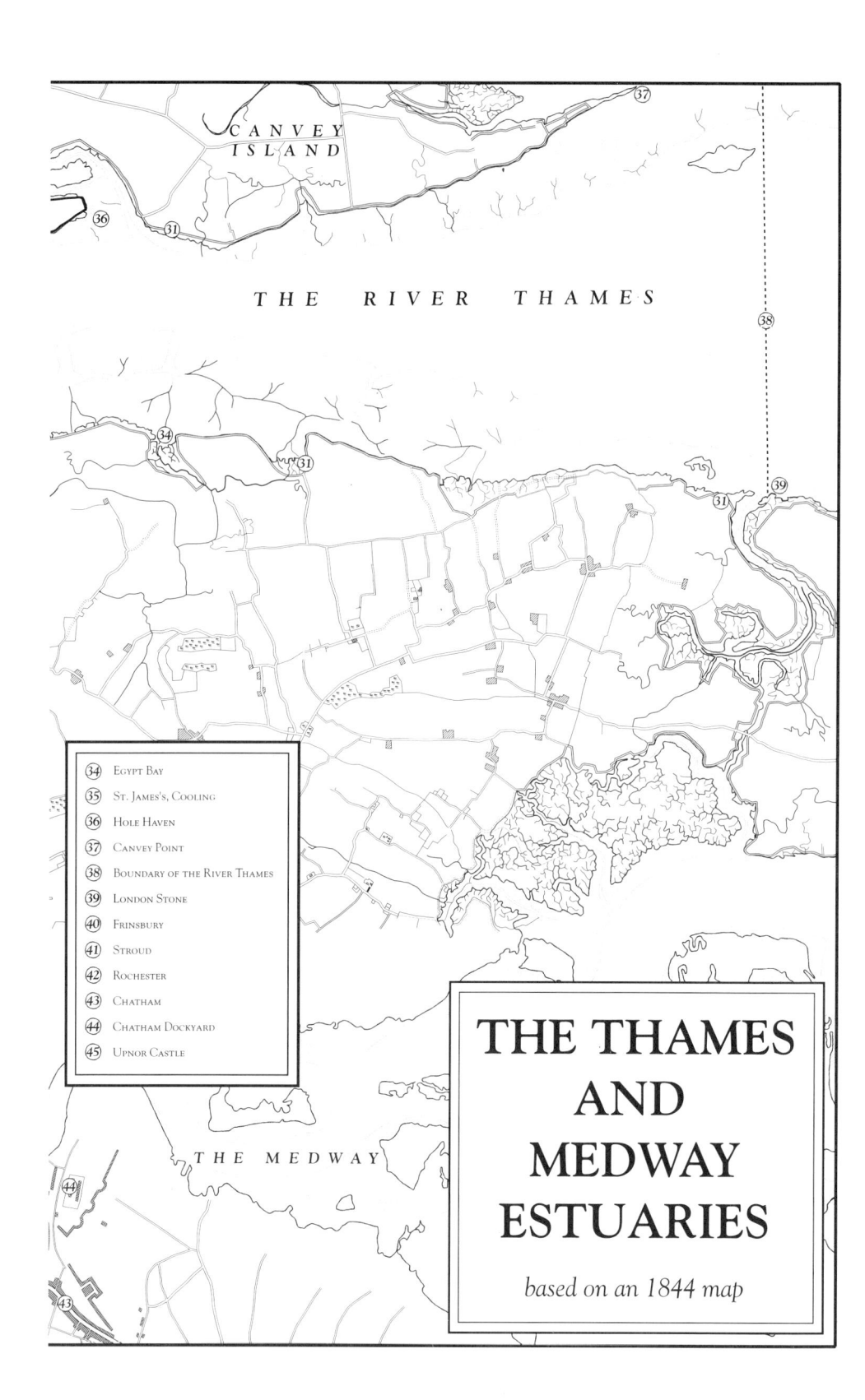

MAP OF THE HOO PENINSULA

KEY

- Main Roads
- Other Roads, Tracks
- Woods
- Mud Flats
- Marshes
- City, Town, Village

1. Chatham Dockyard
2. Upnor Castle
3. Gad's Hill
- A. St. Mary's, Lower Higham
- B. St. James's, Cooling

OUR TOWN: PIP'S ROCHESTER

based on an 1816 map

1. Miss Havisham's Satis (Restoration House)
2. The Vines
3. Woodham's Brewery
4. Satis House, Boley Hill
5. Blue Boar (Bull Inn)
6. Town Hall
7. The Mitre
8. Bridge across the Medway
9. Cathedral
10. Mr. Pumblechook's

STROOD

THE MARSHES

PART OF THE RIVER MEDWAY

KEY
- Woods
- Mud Flats
- Marshes
- Fields
- Gardens
- Buildings
- Important Buildings
- Buildings significant to Book

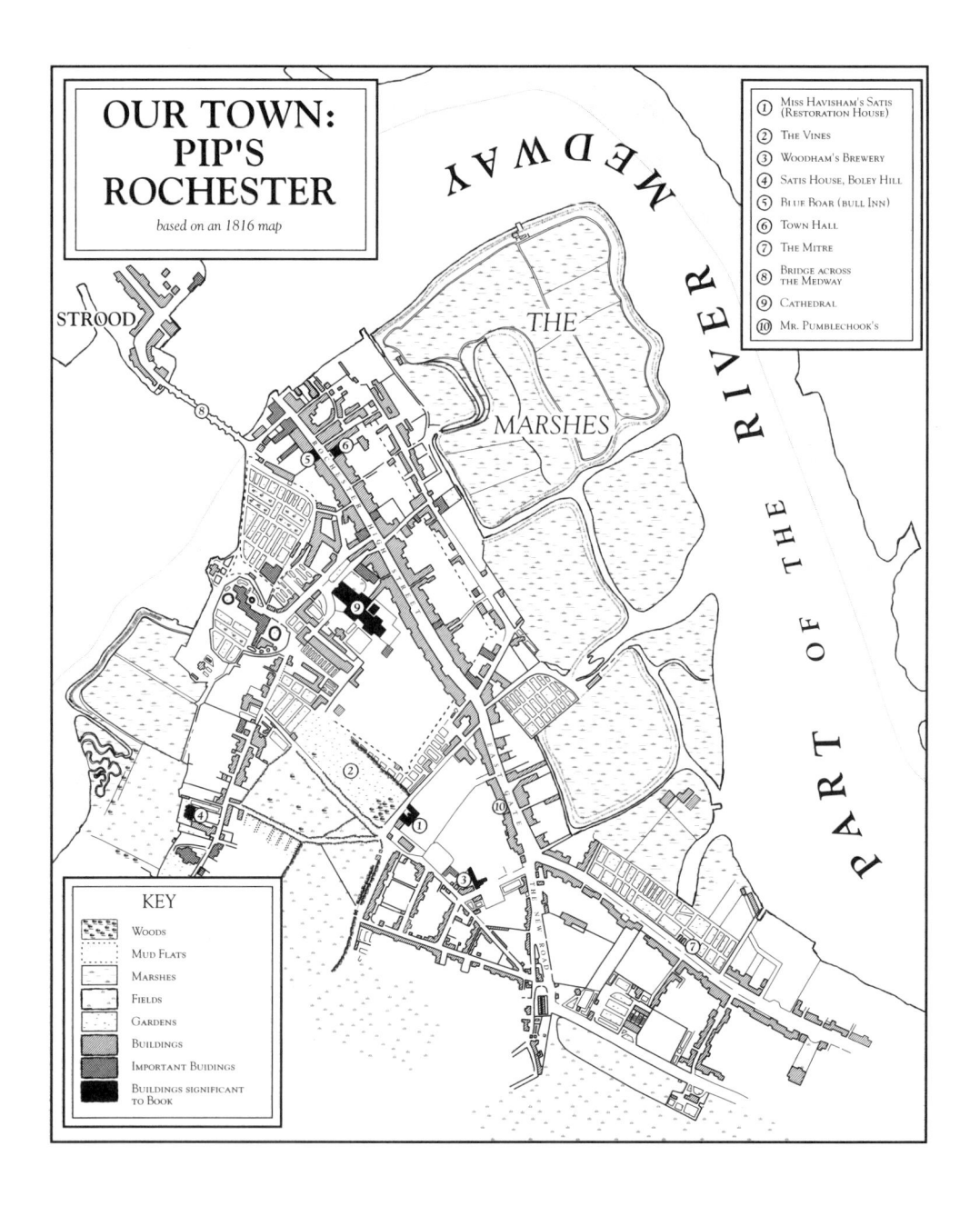

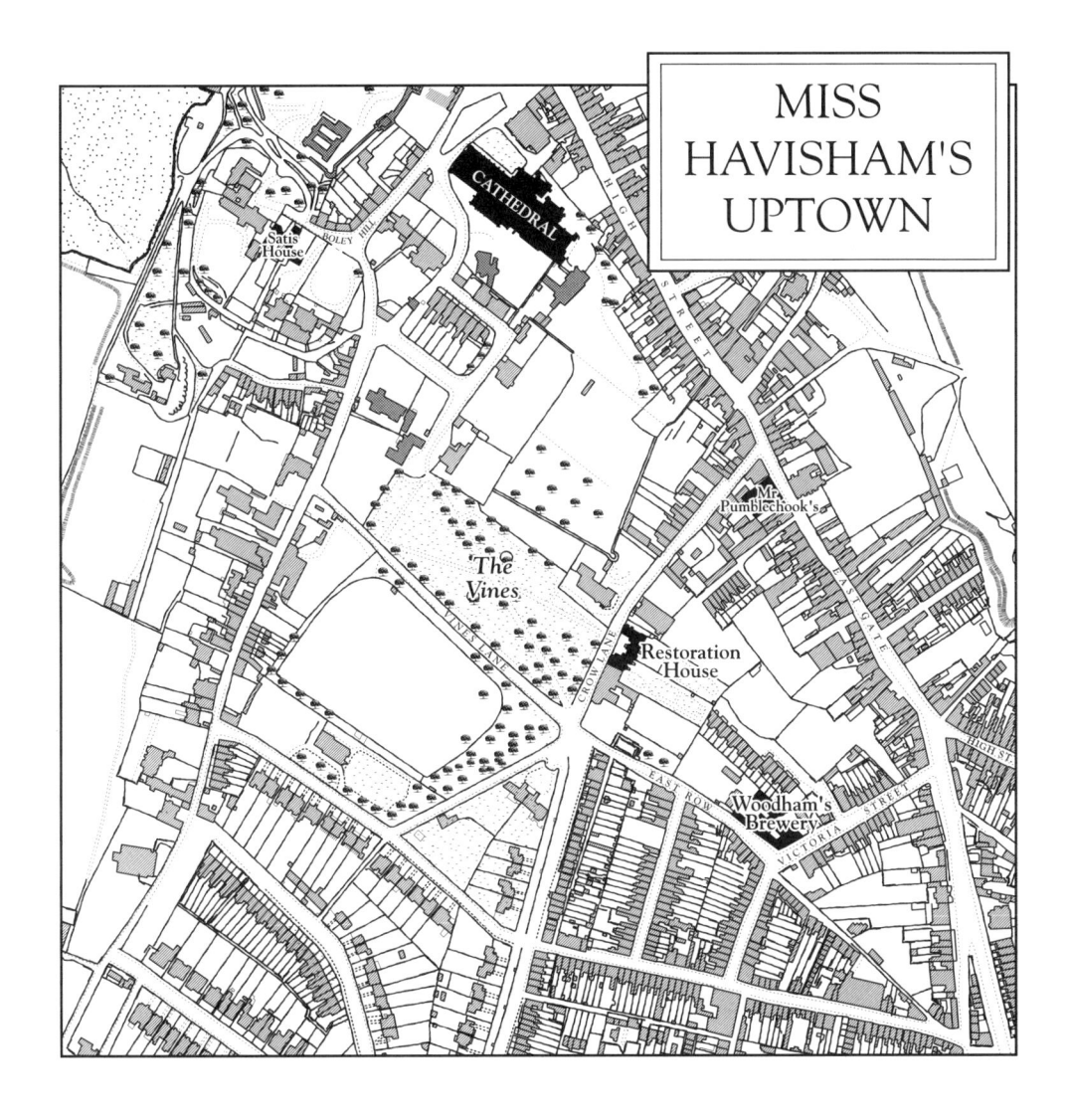

APPENDIX FOUR 451

MISS
HAVISHAM'S
UPTOWN

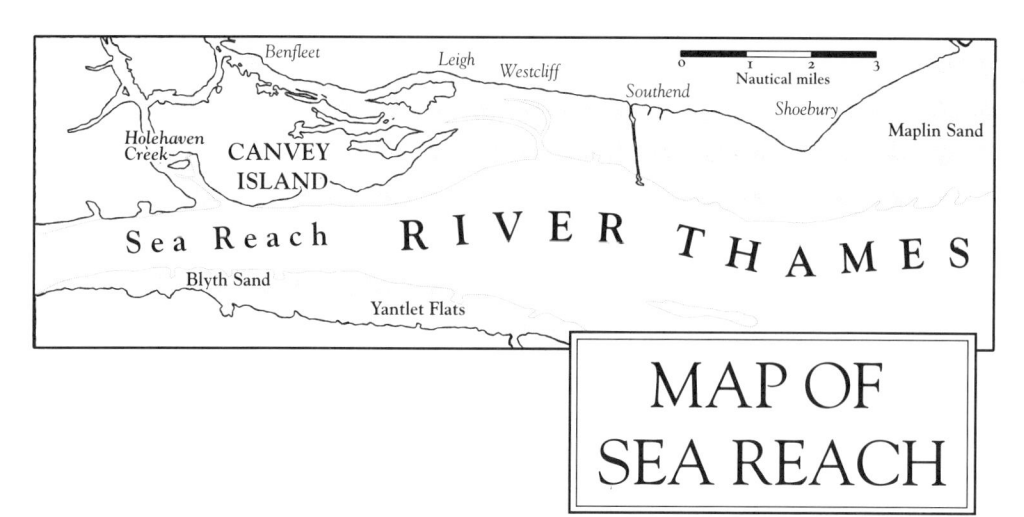

MAP OF SEA REACH

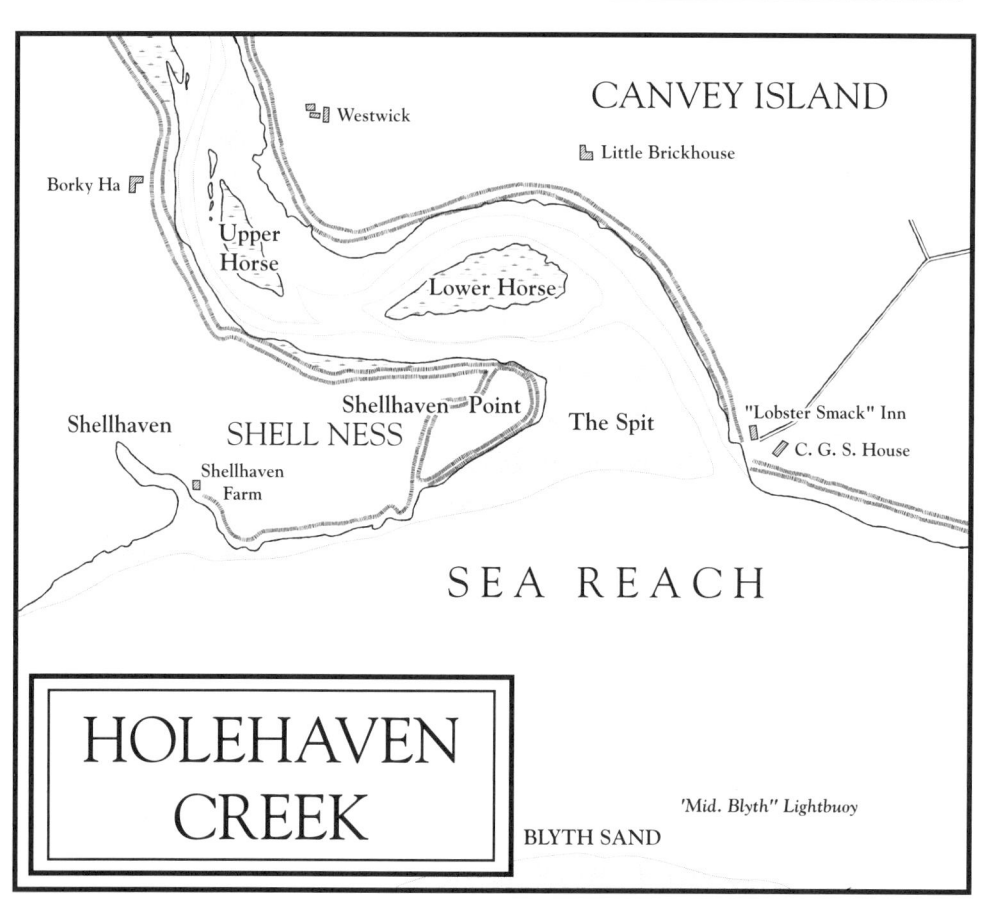

Benfleet, Leigh, Westcliff, Southend, Shoebury, Maplin Sand, Holehaven Creek, CANVEY ISLAND, Sea Reach, RIVER THAMES, Blyth Sand, Yantlet Flats

0 1 2 3
Nautical miles

HOLEHAVEN CREEK

CANVEY ISLAND

Westwick, Little Brickhouse, Borky Ha, Upper Horse, Lower Horse, Shellhaven, Shellhaven Point, SHELL NESS, The Spit, "Lobster Smack" Inn, C. G. S. House, Shellhaven Farm

SEA REACH

'Mid. Blyth' Lightbuoy

BLYTH SAND

APPENDIX FIVE
Serial Instalments in *All the Year Round*

The data below about the length of each instalment of GE illustrate the degree of control Dickens brought to his fifth weekly serial, a form he had clearly mastered late in his career, in spite of frequent and vociferous complaints about the 'thimblefuls' of space this format required. No rigid formula for the contents of each issue of AYR existed, but every weekly number consisted of 24 pages, 6 inches in width and 9˘ inches in length. The number of items varied from week to week, with most issues containing five or six, including a portion of an original work of fiction, which always occupied the lead.

The 'First Stage' of GE ran in twelve weekly portions between 1 December 1860 and 16 February 1861. Seven numbers consisted of two chapters; five were only a single chapter. The twelve instalments averaged 10.33 columns in AYR. Dickens contributed the shortest weekly number on 15 December, which was 2.08 columns below the average, and the longest on 19 January, the eighth. This number exceeded the average by 1.92 columns. The variations in chapters and in the length of the weekly portions indicate that Dickens had some flexibility within a format that emphasized uniformity.

The weekly instalments that constitute the Second and Third stage of Pip's expectations show a similar degree of control. Between 13 February and 24 May, four of the weekly instalments appeared as single chapters and the remaining eight as two chapters. Throughout, Dickens maintained an average of 10.56 columns in AYR, contributing his longest instalment (11.50 cols) on 16 March (chapters 25 and 26) and the shortest (9.05 cols), a single chapter (39), on 11 May. The longest overrun of the weekly average is .94 and the most significant underrun .89 short of the average weekly length.

The Third and final stage running from 18 May through 3 August tells much the same story. Eight of the instalments appeared with two chapters and four as single chapters. Weekly instalments averaged 10.25 columns; the longest overrun of 1.50 columns occurred on 8 June (chapters 45 and 46) and the shortest (chapters 58 and 59), the novel's two concluding chapters, on 3 August 1861.

Planning GE, Dickens also contemplated the simultaneous publication of the novel in monthly parts, an experiment he had tried with TTC. Although he decided against using this method again, MS and other evidence indicate that he continued to think of GE as a novel for publication in monthly parts. In this form, the novel's nine monthly numbers consisted of three stages, each of which in turn included three monthly numbers. The proposed monthly divisions are as follows: First Stage, first monthly number, chapters 1 to 7; second monthly number, chapters 8 to 13; third monthly number, chapters 14 to 19. Second Stage: fourth monthly number, chapters 20 to 26; fifth monthly number, chapters 27 to 33; sixth monthly number, chapters 34 to 39. Third Stage: seventh monthly number, chapters 40 to 36; eighth monthly number, chapters 47 to 53; ninth monthly number, chapters 54 to 59.

SERIAL INSTALMENTS IN AYR

Date	Instalment	Vol. and No.	Chapters	Columns in AYR
		FIRST STAGE		
01 Dec 1860	IV.84	1, 2	10.5	
08 Dec		85	3, 4	10.5
15 Dec		86	5	8.25
22 Dec		87	6, 7	9.5
29 Dec		88	8	9.5
05 Jan 1861		89	9, 10	10.5
12 Jan		90	11	10.75
19 Jan		91	12, 13	12.25
26 Jan		92	14, 15	10.25
02 Feb		93	16, 17	10.25
09 Feb		94	18	10.5
16 Feb		95	19	11.25
		SECOND STAGE		
23 Feb		96	20, 21	10.25
02 Mar		97	22	10.25
09 Mar		98	23, 24	11.25
16 Mar		99	25, 26	11.50
23 Mar		100	27, 28	11.25
30 Mar		V. 101	29	10.0
06 Apr		102	30, 31	11.0
13 Apr		103	32, 33	10.0
20 Apr		104	34, 35	10.75
27 Apr		105	36, 37	11.0
04 May		106	38	10.0
11 May		107	39	9.50
		THIRD STAGE		
18 May		108	40	10.5
25 May		109	41, 42	10.5
01 June		110	43, 44	9.75
08 June		111	45, 46	11.75
15 June		112	47, 48	10.5
22 June		113	49, 50	10.25
29 June		114	51, 52	10.5
06 July		115	53	10.0

13 July	116	54	11.0
20 July	117	55, 56	10.0
27 July	118	57	9.5
03 Aug	119	58, 59	9.25

The three 'Stages' of Pip's expectations also corresponded to a single volume of the three-volume edition of the novel published by Chapman Hall on 6 July 1861. The chapter numeration in this edition, however, began afresh with each volume instead of running continuously, as it did in the weekly format.

SELECT BIBLIOGRAPHY

(i) *Works by Dickens*

The Clarendon Dickens. Oxford: Clarendon Press, 1966–. Edition cited in quotations from
>   *The Pickwick Papers*. Ed. James Kinsey. 1986

The Penguin English Library. Harmondsworth: Penguin. Edition cited in quotatons from
>   *Dombey and Son*. Ed. Peter Fairclough. 1970
>   *Little Dorrit*. Ed. John Holloway. 1967
>   *Martin Chuzzlewit*. Ed. P. N. Furbank. 1978
>   *Nicholas Nickleby*. Ed. Michael Slater. 1978
>   *Our Mutual Friend*. Ed. Stephen Gill. 1971
>   *Sketches By Boz*. Ed. Dennis Walder. 1995
>   *A Tale of Two Cities*. Ed. George Woodcock. 1970

The Norton Critical Edition. New York/London is cited in quotations from
>   *David Copperfield*. Ed. Jerome H. Buckley. 1990

The Oxford Illustrated Dickens. 21 vols. London: Oxford UP, 1947–58. Edition cited in quotations from
>   *Christmas Stories*. Intro. Margaret Lane. London: Oxford UP, 1956. New Oxford Illustrated Dickens.
>   *A Child's History of England* (includes *Master Humphrey's Clock*)

Charles Dickens' Book of Memoranda. Ed. Fred Kaplan. New York: New York Public Library, 1981.
The Letters of Charles Dickens. Pilgrim Edition. 10 vols to date. Oxford: Clarendon, 1965–. Vols 1 and 2. Ed. Madeline House and Graham Storey. Vol. 3. Ed. Madeline House, Graham Storey and Kathleen Tillotson. Vol. 4. Ed. KathleenTillotson. Vol. 5. Ed. Graham Storey and K. J. Fielding. Vol. 6. Ed. Graham Storey, Kathleen Tillotson and Nina Burgis. Vol. 7. Ed. Graham Storey, KathleenTillotson and Angus Easson. Vol. 8. Ed. Graham Storey and Kathleen Tillotson.Vol. 9. Ed. Graham Storey. Vol. 10. Ed. Graham Storey.
The Letters of Charles Dickens. Ed. Walter Dexter. Nonesuch Edition. 3 vols. London: Nonesuch Press, 1938.
The Speeches of Charles Dickens. Ed. K. J. Fielding. Oxford: Clarendon Press, 1960.

(ii) *Articles in 'All the Year Round'*

Beard, Thomas. 'A Dialogue Concerning Convicts.' 5 (11 May 1861): 155–9.
Dickens, Charles. 'Bound for Salt Lake.' 9 (4 July 1863): 444–9.

Dickens, Charles. 'Chambers.' 3 (18 August 1860): 452–6.
Dickens, Charles. 'Chatham Dockyard.' 10 (29 August 1863): 12–16.
Dickens, Charles. 'The City of the Absent.' 9 (18 July 1863): 493–6.
Dickens, Charles. 'City of London Churches.' 3 (5 May 1860): 85–9.
Dickens, Charles. 'Dullborough Town.' 3 (30 June 1860): 274–8.
Dickens, Charles. 'The Martyr Medium.' 9 (4 April 1863): 133–6.
Dickens, Charles. 'Night Walks.' 3 (21 July 1860): 348–52.
Dickens, Charles. 'Nurse's Stories.' 3 (8 September 1860): 517–21.
Dickens, Charles. 'An Old Stage-Coaching House.' 9 (1 August 1863): 540–3.
Dickens, Charles. 'Poor Mercantile Jack.' 2 (10 March 1860): 462–6.
Dickens, Charles. 'The Short-timers.' 9 (20 June 1863): 397–401.
Dickens, Charles. 'Two Views of a Cheap Theatre.' 2 (25 February 1860): 416–21.
Dickens, Charles. 'Tramps.' 3 (16 June 1860): 230–4.
Dickens, Charles. 'Travelling Abroad.' 2 (7 April 1860): 557–62.
'Hear the Postman!' 5 (13 July 1861): 366–8.
'Infallible Physic.' 2 (3 March 1860): 448–52.
'Natural Selection.' 3 (7 July 1860): 293–9.
'Sacred to the Memory.' 15 (30 June 1866): 592–5.
'Species.' 3 (2 June 1860): 174–8.
'Transmutation of Species.' 4 (9 March 1861): 519–21.

(iii) *Articles in 'Household Words'*

Allingham, William. 'The Dirty Old Man. A Lay Leadenhall.' 6 (8 January 1853): 396–7.
Capper, John. 'Bulls and Bears.' 8 (28 January 1854): 517–23.
Capper, John. 'Cairo.' 16 (18 July 1857): 65–9.
Costello, Dudley. 'The Incomplete Letter-Writer.' 9 (1 July 1854): 474–6.
'Curious Epitaph'. 1 (11 May 1850): 168.
Dickens, Charles. 'Bill-Sticking.' 2 (22 March 1851): 601–6.
Dickens, Charles. 'A Child's Dream of a Star.' 1 (6 April 1850): 25–6.
Dickens, Charles. 'A Detective Police Party.' 1 (27 July 1850): 409–14.
Dickens, Charles. 'Down with the Tide.' 6 (5 February 1853): 481–5.
Dickens, Charles. 'From the Raven in the Happy Family [ii].' 1 (8 June 1850): 241–2.
Dickens, Charles. 'The Ghost of the Cock Lane Ghost Wrong Again.' 6 (15 January 1853): 420.
Dickens, Charles. 'It Is Not Generally Known.' 10 (2 September 1854): 49–52.
Dickens, Charles. 'Lying Awake.' 6 (30 October 1852): 145–8.
Dickens, Charles. 'A Monument of French Folly.' 2 (8 March 1851): 553–8.
Dickens, Charles. 'New Year's Day.' 19 (1 January 1859): 97–102.
Dickens, Charles. 'Our School.' 4 (11 October 1851): 49–52.
Dickens, Charles. 'Our Vestry.' 5 (28 August 1852): 549–52.
Dickens, Charles. 'Pet Prisoners.' 1 (27 April 1850): 97–103.
Dickens, Charles. 'The Spirit Business.' 7 (7 May 1853): 217–20.
Dickens, Charles. 'Trading in Death.' 6 (27 November 1852): 241–5.

Dickens, Charles. 'Well-Authenticated Rappings.' 17 (20 February 1858): 217–20.
Dickens, Charles. 'Where We Stopped Growing.' 6 (1 January 1853): 361–3.
Dickens, Charles, and Wilkie Collins. 'The Lazy Tour of Two Idle Apprentices, ch.4' 16 (24 October 1857): 385–93.
Dickens, Charles, and Richard H. Horne. 'One Man in a Dockyard.' 3 (6 September 1851): 553–7.
Dickens, Charles, Henry Morley, and W. H. Wills. 'In and Out of Jail.' 7 (14 May 1853): 241–5.
Dickens, Charles, and W. H. Wills. 'A Curious Dance Round A Curious Tree.' 4 (17 January 1852): 385–9.
Dickens, Charles, and W. H. Wills. 'The Doom of English Wills.' 2 (28 September 1850): 1–4.
Dickens, Charles, and W. H. Wills. 'The Heart of Mid-London' [Smithfield cattle-market]. 1 (4 May 1850): 121–5.
Hollingshead, John. 'All Night on the Monument.' 17 (30 January 1858): 145–8.
Horne, Richard H. 'The Cattle-Road to Ruin.' 1 (29 June 1850): 325–30.
Horne, Richard H. 'The True Story of a Coal Fire, ch. iii.' 1 (20 April 1850): 90–6.
Horne, Richard H., and Charles Dickens. 'Cain in the Fields.' 3 (10 May 1851): 147–51.
Macpherson, Ossian. 'Chip: The Smithfield Model of the Model Smithfield.' 2 (8 March 1851): 572–3.
Martineau, Harriet. 'Malvern Water.' 4 (11 October 1851): 67–71.
Morley, Henry. 'The Ghost of the Cock Lane Ghost.' 6 (20 November 1852): 217–23.
Morley, Henry. 'Infant Gardens.' 11 (21 July 1855): 577–82.
Morley, Henry and W. H. Wills.' Photography.' 7 (19 March 1853): 54–61.
Ollier, Edmund. 'Eternal Lamps.' 8 (22 October 1853): 185–8.
Payn, James. 'Spirits Over the Water.' 17 (5 June 1858): 580–3.
Sala, George A., and Charles Dickens. 'First Fruits.' 5 (15 May 1852): 189–92.
Thornbury, George Walter. 'Sherry.' 18 (13 November 1858): 508–14.
Wills, W. H., and Charles Dickens. 'Epsom.' 3 (7 June 1851): 241–6.
Wills, W. H., and Charles Dickens. 'Two Chapters on Bank Note Forgeries, ii.' 1 (21 September 1850): 615–20.
Wills, W. H., and John Docwra Parry. 'Chip: Nice White Veal.' 1 (10 August 1850): 467–8.

(iv) Unpublished Sources

Gadd, W. Laurence. 'The Topography of *Great Expectations*.' Typescript. 1925.
Johnson, John. *John Johnson Collection of Printed Ephemera*. Bodleian Library, Oxford.
Ward, John. 'Diary.' Transcript. National Library of Australia.

(v) Other Material

à Beckett, Gilbert Abbott. *The Quizzology of the British Drama*. London: Punch

Office, 1846.

Adams, William Bridges. *English Pleasure Carriages*. London: Charles Knight, 1837.

Adams, W. H. Davenport. *Lighthouses and Lightships: A Descriptive and Historical Account of their Modern Construction and Organization*. London: T. Nelson, 1870.

Adburgham, Allison. *Silver Fork Society: Fashionable Life and Literature from 1814 to 1840*. London: Constable, 1983.

Addison, William. *In the Steps of Charles Dickens*. London: Rich & Cowan, 1955.

Adolphus, John. *The Political State of the British Empire, Containing a General View of the Domestic and Foreign Possessions of the Crown; The Laws, Commerce, Revenues, Offices, and Other Establishments*. 4 vols. London: T. Cadell & W. Davies, 1818.

'Agogos' [Charles William Day]. *Hints on Etiquette and the Usages of Society*. London: Longman, Rees, Orme, Brown, Green & Longman, 1836.

Allen, Michael. *Charles Dickens' Childhood*. New York: St Martin's Press, 1988.

Allen, Michael. 'The Dickens/Crewe Connection.' *Dickens Quarterly* 5 (1988): 175–85.

Altick, Richard D. *The Presence of the Present: Topics of the Day in the Victorian Novel*. Columbus: Ohio UP, 1991.

Anderson, Adam. *An Historical and Chronological Deduction of the Origin of Commerce from the Earliest Accounts*. 4 vols. London: J. Walter, 1787–9.

Arlott, John, ed. *Oxford Companion to the World of Sports and Games*. London: Oxford UP, 1975.

Ashworth, Andrew. *Principles of Criminal Law*. Oxford: Clarendon Press, 1995.

Aspinall, A. and E. Anthony Smith, eds. *English Historical Documents, 1783–1832*. Vol. 11. New York: Oxford UP, 1969.

Australia: Who Should Go; How to Go; What to Do When There. Liverpool: Gabriel Thompson [1852].

Aveling, Stephen T. 'The Restoration House.' *Scribner's Magazine* 13 (April 1893): 453–62.

Babington, Michael. *A House in Bow Street: Crime and the Magistracy, London, 1740–1881*. London: Macdonald, 1969.

Bagshaw, Samuel. *History, Gazetteer, and Directory of the County of Kent*. Sheffield: G. Ridge, 1847.

Bailin, Miriam. *The Sickroom in Victorian Fiction*. New York: Cambridge UP, 1994.

Baillie, G. H., C. Clutton, and C. A. Ilbert, eds. *Britten's Old Clocks and Watches and their Makers*. 7th edn. New York: Bonanza Books, 1956.

Baker, J. H. *The Inner Temple: A Brief Historical Description*. London: The Honourable Society of the Inner Temple, 1991.

Baker, J. H. *An Introduction to English Legal History*. London: Butterworth, 1971.

Baker, J. H. *The Legal Profession and the Common Law*. London: The Hambledon Press, 1986.

Ballantine, William. *Some Experiences of a Barrister's Life*. 2 vols. London: R. Bentley, 1882.

Ballin, Ada A. *Health and Beauty in Dress from Infancy to Old Age*. London: A. C. Ballin, n.d.

Banbury, Philip. *Shipbuilders of the Thames and Medway*. Newton Abbot: David & Charles, 1971.

Banks, F. R. *The Penguin Guides. New Series: Kent.* Harmondsworth: Penguin Books, 1955.
Barrett, C. R. B. *The Trinity House of Deptford Strond.* London: Lawrence & Bullen, 1893.
Barry, P. *Dockyard Economy and Naval Power.* London: Sampson Low, 1863.
Bartlett, John. *Familiar Quotations.* 16th edn. Boston: Little, Brown, 1992.
Bartolomeo, Joseph F. 'Charlotte to Charles: The Old Manor House as a Source for *Great Expectations.*' *Dickens Quarterly* 8 (1991): 112–20.
Beames, Thomas. *The Rookeries of London: Past, Present and Prospective.* 2nd edn. London, 1852; rpt London: Frank Cass, 1970.
Beattie, J. M. *Crime and the Courts in England 1660–1800.* Princeton: Princeton UP, 1986.
Beaven, Edwin Sloper. *Barley: Fifty Years of Observation and Experiment.* London: Duckworth, 1947.
Beck, E. J. *Memorials to Serve for a History of the Parish of St Mary, Rotherhithe.* Cambridge: Cambridge UP, 1907.
Beck, Theodric Romeyn. *Elements of Medical Jurisprudence.* London: John Anderson, 1825.
Beckett, J. V. *The Aristocracy in England, 1660–1914.* Oxford: Basil Blackwell, 1986.
Beeton, Isabella. *Mrs Beeton's Book of Household Management.* [1861]. New edn. London: Ward, Lock & Co., 1915.
Belden, Daniel. 'Great Expectations, XXXI.' *Explicator* 35 (1977): 6–7.
Bender, Ruth E. *The Conquest of Deafness.* Danville, Ill.: Interstate Publishers, 1981.
Bennett, MP, Hon. H. G. *A Letter to the Common Council and Livery of The City of London, on the Existing Abuses in Newgate; Showing the Necessity of an Immediate Reform in the Management of That Prison.* 2nd edn. London, 1818. In *The Pamphleteer* 10 (1818): 277–324.
Bennett, Hon. Henry Grey. *Letter to Viscount Sidmouth, on the Transportation Laws, The State of the Hulks and of the Colonies in New South Wales.* London: J. Ridgway, 1819.
Bentley, Nicolas, Michael Slater, Nina Burgess. *The Dickens Index.* Oxford: Oxford UP, 1988.
Besant, Walter. *London in the Nineteenth Century.* London, 1909; rpt New York, 1985.
Bettelheim, Bruno. *The Uses of Enchantment: The Meaning and Importance of Fairy Tales.* New York: Alfred A. Knopf, 1976.
Bishop, Frederick. *The Illustrated London Cookery Book.* London: J. Haddon, 1852.
Blackstone, William. *Commentaries on the Laws of England.* 4 vols. 1769; rpt Chicago & London: U of Chicago P, 1979.
Boniface, Priscilla. *Hotels and Restaurants: 1830 to the Present Day.* London: HMSO, 1981.
Boswell for the Defence, 1769–1774. Yale Edition of the Private Papers of James Boswell. Ed. William K. Wimsatt, Jr, and Frederick A. Pottle. New York: McGraw-Hill, 1959.
Bourchier, Lady. *Memoir . . . of Sir Edward Codrington.* 2 vols. London: Longmans, 1873.
Bovil, E. W. *English Country Life, 1780–1830.* London, 1962.
Boyle, Thomas. *Black Swine in the Sewers of Hampstead: Beneath the Surface of Victorian Sensationalism.* New York: Viking, 1969.
Brain, Russell. *Some Reflections on Genius and Other Essays.* Philadelphia, Pa: J. B. Lippincott, 1960.

Braun-Ronsdorf, M. *The History of the Handkerchief*. Leigh-on-Sea: F. Lewis, 1967.
Brewing: A Book of Reference. In Six Parts. London: George Clark & Son, n.d.
Bridgeman, J. H. 'Shark-headed Screws'. *The Dickensian* 32 (1936): 315.
Brieger, Peter. *English Art, 1216–1309*. Vol. 14 of the *Oxford History of English Art*. Ed. S. R. Boase. Oxford: Clarendon Press, 1957.
Brook, G. L. *The Language of Dickens*. London: André Deutsch, 1970.
Brown, Julia Prewitt. *A Reader's Guide to the Nineteenth-Century English Novel*. New York: Macmillan, 1985.
Buchan, William. *Domestic Medicine; Or, A Treatise on the Prevention and Cure of Diseases by Regimen and Simple Medicines*. 8th edn. London: W. Strathan, 1784.
Buchanan, W. M. *A Technological Dictionary: Explaining The Terms of The Arts, Sciences, Literature, Professions, and Trades*. London: W. Tegg, 1846.
Bucknill, John Charles. *The Psychology of Shakespeare*. 1859. Rpt New York: AMS Press, 1970.
Bunch, Bryan H. and Alexander Hellemans. *The Timetables of Technology: A Chronology of the Most Important People and Events in the History of Technology*. New York: Simon & Schuster, 1993.
Burnett, C. B. *A History of the Isle of Grain, An Old Time Village in Kent*. Sheerness: Rigg, Allen, 1906.
Burstyn, Joan N. *Victorian Education and the Ideal of Womanhood*. New Brunswick, NJ: Rutgers UP, 1984.
Burtt, Frank. *Cross-Channel and Coastal Paddle Steamers*. London: Richard Tilling, 1934.
Byron, Henry T. *The Maid and the Magpie; or, The Fatal Spoon. A Burlesque Burletta*. London: Thomas Hailes, n.d.
'Cag-mag Butchers!' *London As It Is*. No. 1. 27 October 1838.
Calthorp, Dion Clayton. *English Dress from Victoria to George V*. London: Chapman & Hall, 1934.
Calthrop, Strachey, ed. *The Letters of the Earl of Chesterfield to his Son*. Vol. 1. London: Methuen, 1927.
Campbell, Elizabeth. '*Great Expectations*: Dickens and the Language of Fortune.' *Dickens Studies Annual* 24 (1996): 153–65.
Campbell, J. Menzies. *From a Trade to a Profession: Byways in Dental History*. Privately printed, 1958.
Carlton, William J. 'The Third Man at Newgate'. *RES* 8 (1957): 402–7.
Carlyle, Thomas. *Latter-day Pamphlets*. 1850. Centennial Memorial Edition, Vol. 20. Boston, Mass.: Dan Estes, n.d.
Carolan, Katherine. '*Great Expectations* and a *Household Words* Sketch'. *Dickens Studies Newsletter* 3(1972): 27–8.
Catalogue of the Library of Charles Dickens, Esq. Rpt from Sotheran's. Piccadilly Fountain Press, 1935.
Chance, Burton. 'Bishop Berkeley and His Use of Tar Water.' *Annals of Medical History*. 4 (1942): 454.
Chandler, David, gen. ed. *The Oxford Illustrated History of the British Army*. Oxford: Oxford UP, 1994.
Chapman, R. W, ed. 'On Travel and Carriages,' *Mansfield Park*. The Oxford Illustrated Jane Austen. Vol. 3. London: Oxford UP, 1970. Pp 561–5.

Chavasse, Pye Henry. *Advice to Mothers on the Management of Their Offspring*. London: Longman, Orme, Brown, Green & Longman, 1839.
Chavasse, Pye Henry. *Advice to Wives on the Management of Themselves, during the Period of Pregnancy, Labour, and Suckling*. 2nd edn. London: Longman, Brown, Green & Longman, 1843.
Chesterton, G. K. *Charles Dickens*. London: Methuen, 1906.
Clair, Colin. *Kitchen and Table: A Bedside History of Eating in the Western World*. London: Abelard-Schuman, 1964.
Clancy, Roger. *Ships, Ports and Pilots: A History of the Piloting Profession*. Jefferson, NC: McFarland, 1984.
Clarke, Ethne. *The Cup that Cheers*. London: Reader's Digest Association, 1983.
Clinton-Baddeley, V. C. 'Wopsle'. *The Dickensian* 57 (1961): 150–9.
Cobbe, Frances Power. 'Wife-Torture in England.' *The Contemporary Review* 32 (1878): 55–87.
Cobbett, William. *Cobbett's Twopenny Trash; or, Politics for the Poor*. No. 1. 1831.
Collins, Philip, ed. *Dickens: The Critical Heritage*. London: Routledge & Kegan Paul, 1971.
Collins, Philip, ed. *Charles Dickens The Public Readings*. Oxford: Clarendon, 1975.
Colquhoun, Patrick. *A Treatise on the Commerce and Police of the River Thames*. London: Joseph Mawmon, 1800.
Colquhoun, Patrick. *Treatise on Indigence*. London: J. Hatchard, 1806.
Combe, Andrew. *The Principles of Physiology Applied to the Preservation of Health and to the Improvement of Physical and Mental Education*. 15th edn. Edinburgh: Maclachan & Stewart, 1860.
Complete Book of Trades; or, The Parents' Guide and Youths' Instructor. London: John Bennett, 1837.
The Complete Newgate Calendar, ed. G. T. Cook. London: Navarre Society, 1926.
Coombe, Derek. *The Bawleymen: Fishermen and Dredgermen of the River Medway*. Rainham: Pennant Books, 1979.
Cooter, Roger. *The Cultural Meaning of Popular Science: Phrenology and the Organization of Consent in Nineteenth-Century Britain*. Cambridge: Cambridge UP, 1984.
Cornford, Leslie Cope. *A Century of Sea Trading, 1824–1924: The General Steam Navigation Company Limited*. London: A. & C. Black, 1924.
Cornford, Leslie Cope. *The Sea Carriers, 1825–1925: The Aberdeen Line*. Aberdeen: The Aberdeen Line, 1925.
Cornwallis, Sir William. *Essayes*. London: Edmund Mattes, 1600.
Cornish, W. R., et al. *Crime and Law in Nineteenth Century Britain*. Dublin: Irish Academic Press, 1978.
Cotsell, Michael. *The Companion to 'Our Mutual Friend'*. London: Allen & Unwin, 1986.
'Coventry's Watch.' *The Dickensian* 47 (1951): 117.
Cox, J. Charles. *Kent*. 6th edn, revised. London: Methuen, 1935.
Cox, J. Charles. *Pulpits, Lecterns, & Organs in English Churches*. London: Oxford UP, 1915.
Crawford, Iain. 'Pip and the Monster: The Joys of Bondage.' *Studies in English Literature* 28 (1988): 625–48.

Critchley, Macdonald. 'Miss Havisham Syndrome'. *History of Medicine* 1 (1969): 2–6.
Cross, F. L. and E. A. Livingstone, eds. *Oxford Dictionary of the Christian Church*. 2nd edn. London: Oxford UP, 1974.
Cross, Thomas. *The Autobiography of a Stage Coachman*. 2 vols. London: Kegan Paul, Trench, Trübner, 1904.
Cruden, Robert Pierce. *The History of The Town of Gravesend in the County of Kent and the Port of London*. London: William Pickering, 1843.
Cuddon, J. A. *The International Dictionary of Sports and Games*. New York: Schocken Books, 1979.
Cunningham, P. *Two Years in New South Wales: A Series of Letters*. 2 vols. London: Henry Colburn, 1827.
Cunnington, Phillis and Catherine Lucas. *Occupational Costume in England from the Eleventh Century to 1914*. London: Adam & Charles Black, 1967.
Currie, Richard A. 'All the Year Round and the State of Victorian Psychiatry.' *Dickens Quarterly* 12 (1985): 18–24.
Darwin, Charles. *The Origin of Species by Means of Natural Selection; or, The Preservation of Favoured Races in the Struggle for Life*. London: John Murray, 1859.
Davey, E. 'The Parents of Charles Dickens,' Our Monthly Gossip, *Lippincott's Magazine* 13 (June 1874): 772–4.
Davidson's. *The Only Correct Steam Traveller's Guide From London Bridge to the French Coast, and to Hull and the Humber*. London: [c.1839].
Davis, Paul B. 'Dickens, Hogarth, and the Illustrated *Great Expectations*.' *The Dickensian* 80 (1984): 130–43.
Day, C. W. *Hints on Etiquette and The Usages of Society*. 1834; rpt London: Turnstile Press, 1946.
'A Day at Day and Martin's.' *The Penny Magazine* 11 (31 December 1842): 509–16.
De Colquhoun [Sir Patrick Mac Chombaich]. *A Companion to the Oarsman's Guide*. Lambeth: Searle, Stangate, 1857.
De Quincey, Thomas. 'On Murder Considered as One of the Fine Arts.' In *The English Mail Coach and Other Writings*. Vol. 4. Edinburgh: Adam & Charles Black, 1862.
Dear, Ian and Peter Kemp, eds. *An A–Z of Sailing Terms*. Oxford: Oxford UP, 1992.
Debrett, John. *The Baronetege of England*. 5th edn. London: G. Woodfall, 1824.
'Decoying a Young Girl into a Brothel.' *London As It Is*. No. 6. 1 December 1838.
Delaney, John J. and James Edward Tobin. *Dictionary of Catholic Biography*. Garden City, NY: Doubleday, 1961.
Deneau, Daniel P. 'Pip's Age and Other Notes on *Great Expectations*.' *The Dickensian* 60 (1964): 27–9.
Denne, Samuel. *The History and Antiquities of Rochester and its Environs*. 2nd edn. Rochester: W. Wildash, 1817.
Dexter, Walter. 'Cooling versus Higham.' *The Dickensian* 20 (1924): 213–14.
Dickens, Charles, Jr. *A Dictionary of London, 1879*. Rpt as *Dickens's Dictionary of London, 1879: An Unconventional Handbook*. London: Howard Baker, 1972.
Dickens, Charles, the Younger. 'Introduction.' *Great Expectations*. London: Macmillan, 1904. Pp ix–xii.
Dickens, Charles, the Younger. 'Notes on Some Dickens Places and People.' *Pall Mall*

Magazine 9 (1896): 342–55.

Dickens, Sir Henry Fielding, W. Laurence Gadd, and Henry Smethan. 'Cooling v. Higham 1.' *The Dickensian* 21 (1925): 13–15.

Dickens's Dictionary of the Thames: From Oxford to the Nore. London: Charles Dickens, 1880.

A Dickens Pilgrimage. The Times Series. London: John Murray, 1914.

The Dictionary of Trade, Commerce, and Navigation. London: Brittain, 1844.

Dilnot, A. F. 'The Australian Miss Havisham: Some Reservations.' *Australian Literary Studies* 7 (1975): 206–8.

Dodd, George. 'The Metropolis and the Railways.' *Fortnightly Review*. 31 (15 March, 1866): 359–68.

Doggett, Maeve E. *Marriage, Wife-Beating and the Law in Victorian England*. Columbia, SC: University of South Carolina Press, 1993.

Dolby, George. *Charles Dickens as I Knew Him: The Story of the Reading Tours in Great Britain and America (1866–1870)*. 1885. Rpt New York: Haskell House, 1970.

The Duelist; or, A Cursory Review of the Rise, Progress, and Practice of Dueling. London: Longman, Hurt, Rees, Orme & Brown, 1822.

Dugdale, James. *The New British Traveller; or, Modern Panorama*. 4 vols. London: J. Robins, 1819.

Dugdale, Thomas. *England and Wales Delineated. Historical, Entertaining and Commercial*. 4 vols. London: L. Tallis, [c.1830].

Dumbould, Edward, ed. *The Political Writings of Thomas Jefferson: Representative Selections*. New York: Liberal Arts Press, 1955.

Edminson, Mary. 'The Date of the Action in *Great Expectations*.' *Nineteenth Century Fiction*. 13 (1958): 22–35.

Edmonstone, Sir Archibald. *The Christian Gentleman's Daily Walk*. London: Joseph Masters, 1850.

[Egan, Pierce]. *Boxiana; or, Sketches of Ancient and Modern Pugilism*. 2 vols numbered as 1 to 3. London: G. Smeeton, 1812.

Egan, Pierce. *The Life of An Actor*. London: C. S. Arnold, 1825.

Egan, Pierce. *New Series of Boxiana: Being the Only Original and Complete Lives of the Boxers*. 2 vols numbered as 4 and 5. London: George Virtue, 1828.

Ellacott, S. E. *The Story of Ships*. London: Methuen: 1958.

Encyclopaedia Britannica. 11th edn. 29 vols. New York, 1910–11.

Endicott, Annabel. 'Pip, Philip and Astrophil: Dickens's debt to Sidney?' *The Dickensian*, 63 (1967): 158–63.

Enfield, William. *The Speaker; or, Miscellaneous Pieces, Selected from the Best English Writers*. Derby: Henry Mozley, 1820.

Escott, T. H. S. *Social Transformations of the Victorian Age: A Survey of Court and County*. 1897; rpt Folcroft, Pa: Folcroft Library Editions, 1973.

Etiquette for Gentlemen: With Hints on the Art of Conversation. 2nd edn. London: Charles Tilt, 1838.

The Etiquette of Marriage. London: John Macqueen [1902].

The Etiquette of Modern Society: A Guide to Good Manners in Every Possible Situation. London: Ward, Lock [1881].

Evans, John. *An Excursion to Windsor in July 1810*. London: Sherwood, Neely &

Jones, 1817.
Eversley, William Pender, and William Feilden Craies. *The Marriage Laws of the British Empire*. 1910; rpt Littleton, Colo: Fred B. Rothman, 1989.
'Fagin and Riah.' *The Dickensian* 17 (1921): 144–52.
The Female's Friend. Journal of the Associate Institute for Improving and Enforcing the Laws for the Protection of Women. April 1846.
Fergusson, James. *History of the Modern Styles of Architecture*. London: John Murray, 1862.
Fielding, K. J. 'Dickens and Science.' *Dickens Quarterly* 13 (1996): 200–16.
Fildes, Valerie. *Breasts, Bottle and Babies: A History of Infant Feeding*. Edinburgh, 1986.
The First Report. 21 July 1846. Associate Institute for Improving and Enforcing the Laws for the Protection of Women. London: Brewster & West, 1846.
Fitch, Francis. 'Dickens and Walworth.' *The Dickensian* 4 (1908): 124–6.
F[itch], F. 'Letter to the Editor.' *The Dickensian* 3 (1907): 307.
Fitzgerald, Percy. *Bozland: Dickens' Places and People*. 1895; rpt Ann Arbor, Mich.; 1971.
Flemming, John and Hugh Honour. *The Penguin Dictionary of Architecture*. 4th edn. Harmondsworth: Penguin Books, 1991.
Flemming, John and Hugh Honour. *The Penguin Dictionary of Decorative Arts*. New edn. London: Viking, 1989.
Flinn, D. Edgar. *Our Dress and Our Food in Relation to Health*. Dublin: M. H. Gill, 1886.
Foll, Scott. '*Great Expectations* and the "Uncommercial" Sketch Book.' *The Dickensian*: 81 (1985): 109–16.
Fonblanque, Albany. *England Under Seven Administrations*. 3 vols. London: Richard Bentley, 1837.
Forbes, Thomas Rogers. *Crowner's Quest*. Transactions of the American Philosophical Society 68 (January 1978): 3–52.
Fraser, Russell. 'A Charles Dickens Original.' *Nineteenth-Century Fiction* 9 (1955): 301–7.
French, A. L. 'Old Pip: The Ending of *Great Expectations*.' *Essays in Criticism* 29 (1979): 357–60.
Friedman, Stanley. 'Another Possible Source for Dickens' Miss Havisham.' *Victorian Newsletter* 39 (1971): 24–5.
Friedman, Stanley. 'The Complex Origins of Pip and Magwitch.' *Dickens Studies Annual* 15 (1986): 221–31.
Friedman, Stanley. 'Echoes of *Hamlet* in *Great Expectations*.' *Hamlet Studies* 9 (1987): 86–9.
Friedman, Stanley. 'Ridley's *Tales of the Genii* and Dickens's *Great Expectations*.' *Nineteenth-Century Literature* (1989): 215–18.
Frost, Thomas. *In Kent with Charles Dickens*. London: Tinsley, 1890.
Frost, T. 'The Last Gibbet.' In *Bygone Leicestershire*. Ed. W. Andrews 1892.
Fyfe, T. A. *Charles Dickens and the Law*. London: W. Hodge, 1910.
G., T., E. *The Etiquette of Love, Courtship, and Marriage*. London: Simpkin, Marshall, 1847.
Gadd, W. Laurence. *The Great Expectations Country*. London: Cecil Palmer, 1929.
Gadd, W. Laurence. 'The House with the Bow Windows.' *The Dickensian* 33 (1937):

117–21.

Gadd, W. Laurence. 'The Lonely Church on the Marshes.' *The Dickensian* 5 (1909): 68–9.

Gadd, W. Laurence. 'The Topography of *Great Expectations*.' *The Dickensian* 20 (1924): 131–6.

Gadd, W. Laurence. 'The Topography of *Great Expectations*: III. The Beacon and the Gibbet.' *The Dickensian* 22 (1926): 110–11.

Gadd, W. Laurence. 'The Topography of *Great Expectations*: VII. The Forge.' *The Dickensian* 22: (1926): 234–6.

Gadd, W. Laurence. 'The Topography of *Great Expectations*: V. The Hulks.' *The Dickensian* 22 (1926): 182–4.

Gadd, W. Laurence. 'The Topography of *Great Expectations*: VI. The Lime-Kiln and Sluice-House.' *The Dickensian* 22 (1926): 184–6.

Gadd, W. Laurence. 'The Topography of *Great Expectations*: IV. The Old Battery.' *The Dickensian* 22 (1926): 111–13.

Gadd. W. Laurence. 'The Topography of *Great Expectations*: II. The River-side Inn.' *The Dickensian*, 21 (1926): 31–5.

Gadd, W. Laurence. 'The Topography of *Great Expectations*: VIII. The Three Jolly Bargemen.' *The Dickensian* 22 (1926): 236–8.

Gadd, W. Laurence. 'The Topography of *Great Expectations*: IX. The Turnpike Gate.' *The Dickensian* 22 (1926): 234–9.

Gadd, W. Laurence, and T. W. Tyrell. 'Cooling *v.* Higham.' *The Dickensian* 21 (1925): 100–1.

Gager, Valerie L. *Shakespeare and Dickens: The Dynamics of Influence*. Cambridge: Cambridge UP, 1996.

Gatrell, V. A. C. *The Hanging Tree: Execution and the English People, 1770–1868*. Oxford: Oxford UP, 1996.

Gazetteer of the British Isles. Edinburgh: John Bartholomew, 1943.

Gernsheim, Alison. *Fashion and Reality*. London: Faber & Faber, 1963.

Gernsheim, Alison. *Victorian and Edwardian Fashion: A Photographic Survey*. New York: Dover, 1981.

Gernsheim, Helmut and Alison Gernsheim. *A Concise History of Photography*. London: Thames & Hudson, 1965.

Gerson, Stanley. 'Name Creation in Dickens.' *Moderna Sprak* 69 (1975): 299–315.

Gibson, Charles E. *The Story of the Ship from the Earliest Days to the Present*. London: Abelard-Schuman, 1958.

Gilmour, Robin. 'Dickens, Tennyson, and the Past.' *The Dickensian* 75 (1979): 131–42.

Gilmour, Robin. *The Novel in the Victorian Age: A Modern Introduction*. London: Edward Arnold, 1986.

Gissing, George. *Charles Dickens: A Critical Study*. Rev. ed. London: Gresham, 1903.

Gleig, Rev. G. R. *Domestic Economy*. School Series. London: Longman, Brown, Green, Longmans & Roberts, 1856.

Godwin, William. *Caleb Williams*. 1794. Ed. David McCracken. London: Oxford UP, 1970.

Grant, James. *The Great Metropolis*. 2 vols. 1837; rpt New York & London: Garland,

1985.
Grant, James. *Light and Shadows of London Life*. 2 vols. London: George Routledge, 1846.
Grant, James. *Portraits of Public Characters*. London: Saunders & Otley, 1841.
Grant, James. *Sketches in London*. London: W. S. Orr, 1838.
Grant, James. *Travels in Town*. 2 vols. London: Saunders & Otley, 1839.
Greenhill, Basil. Introduction and Notes. *The Coastal Trade*. Paintings by Lionel Willis. London: Phaidon, 1975.
Greenhill, Basil. *The Ship: The Life and Death of the Merchant Sailing Ship, 1815–1965*. London: HMSO, 1980.
Greenhill, Basil and Anne Gifford. *Travelling by Sea in the Nineteenth Century: Interior Design in Victorian Passenger Ships*. London: Adam & Charles Black, 1972.
Gregory, George. *A Dictionary of Arts and Sciences*. 2 vols. London: Richard Phillips, 1806.
Gregory, Henry H. *A Companion to the Medicine Chest*. London: Joseph Butler, 1837.
Gregory, J. W. *The Story of the Road from the Beginning down to A.D. 1931*. London: Alexander Maclehose, 1931.
Griffith, Peter. W. M. *Paddle Steamers*. London: Hugh Evelyn, 1968.
The Groans of the Gallows! Or a Sketch of the Past and Present Life of Wm. Calcraft The English Hangman! Commonly Called Jack Ketch. London: Rial, Monmouth Court, n.d.
Grose, Frances. *1811 Dictionary of the Vulgar Tongue*. Rpt Northfield, Minn.: Digest Books, 1971.
Grosvenor, J. *Trinity House*. London: Staples Press, 1959.
Guiley, Rosemary Ellen. *The Encyclopedia of Ghosts and Spirits*. New York: Facts on File, 1992.
Guiley, Rosemary Ellen. *The Encyclopedia of Witches and Witchcraft*. New York: Facts on File, 1989.
Gwilt, Joseph. *The Encyclopedia of Architecture: Historical, Theoretical and Practical*. 1842; rpt New York: Crown Publishers, 1982.
The Habits of Good Society: A Handbook for Ladies and Gentlemen. New York: Rudd & Carleton, 1860.
Halladay, Eric. *Rowing in England: A Social History*. Manchester: Manchester UP, 1990.
Handbook for Travellers. London: John Murray, 1867.
Hand-Book for Travellers in France: Being a Guide. London: John Murray, 1847.
The Hangman's Record. Revised edn. London: Mrs S. Burgess [1909].
Hanks, Patrick and Flavia Hodges. *A Dictionary of First Names*. Oxford: Oxford UP, 1990.
Harding, Christopher, Bill Hines, Richard Ireland, and Philip Rawlings. *Imprisonment in England and Wales: A Concise History*. London: Croom Helm, 1985.
Hardman, Michael. *Beer Naturally*. London: Bergström & Boyle Books Ltd, 1976.
Hardman, Sir William. *A Mid-Victorian Pepys: The Letters and Memoirs of Sir William Hardman, M.A., F.R.G.S.*. Annotated and edited by S. M. Ellis. New York: George H. Doran, 1923.
Harris, Edwin. 'Reminiscences of Chatham.' The Eastgate Series. No. 25. Rochester, 1916.
Harris, Edwin. *Restoration House; or, Rochester in the Time of the Commonwealth*.

Rochester: Edwin Harris, 1904.

Hartley, Dorothy. *Food in England*. London: Macdonald, 1954.

Hartwell, R. *The London Trades' Directory*. London: Robert Hartwell, 1838.

Harvey, John. *Victorian Novelists and Their Illustrators*. New York: New York UP, 1971.

Hasted, Edward. *The History and Topographical Survey of the County of Kent*. 12 vols. Canterbury: Simmons & Kirby, 1797–1801.

Hayward. J. F. *English Watches*. London: HMSO. Victoria and Albert Museum, 1956.

Heal, Sir Ambrose. *The English Writing-Masters and their Copy-Books, 1570–1800*. Cambridge: Cambridge UP, 1931.

Henney, William. *An Entire New and Improved Edition of Moral and Interesting Epitaphs*. London: J. Tueten, 1829.

Hewett, Edward and W. F. Axton. *Convivial Dickens: The Drinks of Dickens and His Times*. Athens, Ohio: Ohio UP, 1983.

Hill, T. W. 'Notes to *Great Expectations*.' *The Dickensian* 53 (1957): 119–26; 184–6; 54 (1958): 53–60; 123–5; 185; 55 (1959): 57–9; 56 (1960): 121–6.

The Historical Dockyard Chatham, Kent. Norwich: Jarrold Printing, 1989.

Hobbes, R. G. *Reminiscences and Notes of Seventy Years' Life, Travel, and Adventures*. 2 vols. London: Eliot Stock, 1895.

Hoefnagel, Dick. 'An Early Hint of *Great Expectations*.' *The Dickensian* 82 (1986): 83.

Hogan, Charles Beecher, ed. *The London Stage*. Pt 5, Vol. 1, 1660–1800. Carbondale, Ill.: Southern Illinois UP, 1968.

Holdsworth, W. S. *A History of English Law*. London: Methuen, 1923.

Horn, Pamela. *The Rise and Fall of the Victorian Servant*. 1975; rpt Bridgend: Alan Sutton, 1996.

Horn, Pamela *The Victorian Country Child*. Kineton: Hornwood Press, 1974.

House, Humphry. 'G.B.S. on *Great Expectations*.' *The Dickensian* 44 (1948): 63–70; 183–6.

Howard, John. *The State of The Prisons*, 3rd edn, 1792; rpt London: J. M. Dent, 1929.

Hotten, John Camden. *Cant and Vulgar Words: Dictionary of Modern Slang*. 1860. London: John Camden Hotten, 1860.

Howells, William Dean. *Heroines of Fiction*. New York: Harper, 1911.

Hudson, Gilbert. 'Mr. Wopsle.' *The Dickensian* 28 (1932): 243.

Hughes, Robert. *The Fatal Shore: The Epic of Australia's Founding*. New York: Alfred A. Knopf, 1987.

Hughes, William R. *A Week's Tramp in Dickens-Land*. 2nd revised edn. London: Chapman & Hall, 1893.

Humphry, Mrs C. E. *The Book of the Home: A Comprehensive Guide on All Matters Pertaining to the Household*. 6 vols. London: The Gresham Publishing Company, 1914.

Humphry, Mrs C. E. *Manners for Men*. 1897; rpt Kent: Pryor Publications, 1993.

Humphry, Mrs C. E. *Manners for Women*. 1897; rpt Exeter: Webb & Bower, 1979.

Humphry, Mrs C. E. *Manners for Women*. 4th edn. London: James Bowden, 1900.

Hunt, Margaret. 'Wife Beating, Domesticity and Women's Independence in Eighteenth-Century London.' *Gender and History* 4 (1992): 10–33.

Hunter, Herbert. *The Barley Crop*. London: Crosby Lockwood, 1952.

Hutchings, Richard J. 'Dickens at Bonchurch.' *The Dickensian* 61 (1965): 79–100.

Hutton, Laurence. 'A Collection of Death-Masks.' *Harper's Monthly Magazine* 85 (June–November 1892): 619–31; 781–93; 904–16.
Ignatieff, Michael. *A Just Measure of Pain: The Penitentiary in the Industrial Revolution, 1750–1850*. New York: Pantheon Books, 1978.
Imray, J. C. and W. R. Kettle, eds. *The Pilot's Guide for the River Thames and The Strait of Dover*. London: Imray, Laurie, Norie & Wilson, 1905.
Imray, James F. *Pilotage Rates and Regulations of the Principal Ports of the United Kingdom*. London: James Imray, 1858.
Imray, Keith. *The Cyclopaedia of Popular Medicine Intended for Domestic Use*. London: Simpkin, Marshall, 1842.
Ireland, Samuel. *Picturesque Views, on the River Medway, From Nore to the Vicinity of its Source in Sussex*. London: T. & J. Egerton, 1793.
Ireland, Samuel. *Picturesque Views, With An Historical Account of the Inns of Court*. London: R. Faulder, 1800.
Irving, John. *Rivers and Creeks of the Thames Estuary*. The Yachtsman's Pilot. Vol. 1. London: O. M. Watts, 1933.
Irving, Joseph. *The Annals of Our Time: A Diurnal of Events . . . from the Accession of Queen Victoria, June 20, 1837, to February 28, 1871*. London: Macmillan, 1875.
Irving, Washington. *The Sketch Book of Geoffrey Crayon, 1819–20*; rpt in 2 vols. Philadelphia, Pa: Lea & Blanchard, 1842.
Jackson, Peter. *George Scharf's London: Sketches and Water-colours of a Changing City, 1820–50*. London: John Murray, 1987.
Jacobson, Wendy S. *The Companion to 'The Mystery of Edwin Drood'*. London: Allen & Unwin, 1986.
James, Louis. *Fiction for the Working Man, 1830–50*. Harmondsworth: Penguin, 1974.
Jeffs, Julian. *Sherry*. London: Faber & Faber, 1961.
Jerdan, William. *The Autobiography of William Jerdan*. 4 vols. London: Arthur Hall, Virtue & Co., 1852.
Jessup, Frank W. *Kent History Illustrated*. Maidstone: Kent County Council. 1973.
Jones, Barbara. *Design for Death*. London: André Deutsch, 1967.
Jones, Jukes Pritchard. *The Customs Officers' Pocket Index to the Board's General Orders*. Bristol: J. Wright, 1867.
Johnson, Edgar. *Charles Dickens: His Tragedy and Triumph*. 2 vols. New York: Simon & Schuster, 1952.
Johnson, Edgar and Eleanor Johnson, eds. *The Dickens Theatrical Reader*. London: Victor Gollancz, 1964.
Johnson, Frank S. 'Cooling versus Higham.' *The Dickensian* 20 (1924): 216.
Johnson, Paul. *The Birth of the Modern: World Society, 1815–1830*. New York: Harper Collins, 1991.
Kamm, Josephine. *Hope Deferred: Girls' Education in English History*. London: Methuen, 1965.
Kaplan, Fred. *Dickens: A Biography*. New York: William Morrow, 1988.
Kaplan, Fred. *Dickens and Mesmerism: The Hidden Springs of Fiction*. Princeton, NJ: Princeton UP, 1975.
Kaplan, Fred. *Sacred Tears: Sentimentality in Victorian Literature*. Princeton, NJ: Princeton UP, 1987.

Kelly's Directory: Kent. London: Kelly [1882].
Kelly's Directory of Rochester, Strood, Chatham, etc. For 1890. London: Kelly [1890].
Kelly's Directory of Gravesend, Milton, Northfleet, and District for 1901–1902. London: Kelly's Directories, n.d.
Kent, William, ed. *An Encyclopedia of London*. Revised by Godfrey Thompson. London: J. M. Dent, 1970.
The Kentish Traveller's Companion. 2nd edn. Canterbury: Simmons & Kirkby, 1779.
The Kentish Traveller's Companion. 3rd edn. Rochester: Webster Gilman, 1790.
Kerr, Robert. *The Gentleman's House; or, How to Plan English Residences, from the Parsonage to the Palace*. London: John Murray, 1864.
King, Frank A. *Beer Has a History*. London: Hutchinson's Scientific & Technical Publications [1947].
Kingsley, Charles. *Yeast. A Problem*. London: Macmillan, 1888.
Kitchiner, William. *The Housekeeper's Ledger: A Plain and Easy Plan of Keeping Accurate Accounts of the Expenses of Housekeeping and the Elements of Domestic Economy*. London: Hurst Robinson, 1825.
Kitchiner, William. *The Traveller's Oracle; or, Maxims for Locomotion*. London: Henry Colburn, 1827.
Kitton, Frederick G. 'Great Expectations.' In *The Novels of Charles Dickens*. London: Elliot Stock, 1897.
Knight, Charles. *Knight's Cyclopaedia of London 1851*. London: Charles Knight [1851].
Knight, R. J. B., ed. *Guide to the Manuscripts in the National Maritime Museum*. Vol. 2. *Public Records, Business Records and Artificial Collections*. London: Mansell, 1980.
Lamb, Charles. 'On the Tragedies of Shakespeare.' *Miscellaneous Prose*. Ed. E. V. Lucas. London: Methuen, 1912.
Lane, Leonard G. *Down the River to the Sea: An Historical Record of the Thames Pleasure Steamers, 1816 to 1934*. London: British Periodicals Ltd, 1934.
Langbein, John H. 'Shaping the Eighteenth-Century Criminal Trial: A View from the Ryder Sources.' *U of Chicago Law Review*, 50 (1983): 1–136.
Langton, Robert. *The Childhood and Youth of Charles Dickens*. Manchester: the Author, 1883.
Lansbury, Coral. *Arcady in Australia: The Evocation of Australia in Nineteenth-Century English Literature*. Melbourne: Melbourne UP, 1970.
Larwood, Jacob and John Camden Hotten. *The History of Signboards From the Earliest Times*. London: Chatto & Windus, 1898.
Laslett, Peter. *The World We Have Lost: England Before the Industrial Age*. London: Methuen, 1971.
Leach, Martha, ed. *Dictionary of Folklore and Mythology*. 2 vols. New York: Funk & Wagnalls, 1950.
Leavis, Q. D. 'How We Must Read "Great Expectations."' In F. R. Leavis and Q. D. Leavis. *Dickens the Novelist*. London: Chatto & Windus, 1970. Pp 277–331.
Leigh's New Picture of London. London: Samuel Leigh, 1818.
Leigh's New Picture of London; or, A View of the Political, Religious, Medical, Literary, Municipal, Commercial, and Moral State of the British Metropolis. 9th edn. London: Leigh & Co., 1839.
Leigh's New Pocket Road-Book of England and Wales. 4th edn. London: M. A. Leigh,

1833.
Lempriere's Classical Dictionary of Proper Names Mentioned in Ancient Authors. Revised edn. London: Routledge & Kegan Paul, 1963.
Lester, V. Markham. *Victorian Insolvency: Bankruptcy, Imprisonment for Debt, and Company Winding-up in Nineteenth-Century England.* Oxford: Clarendon Press, 1995.
LeVay, John. 'Sidney's Astrophel 21 and Dickens' Great Expectations.' *The Explicator* 45 (1987): 6–7.
Levi, Leone. *Wages and Earnings of the Working Classes.* London: John Murray, 1885.
Lewes, George Henry. 'Macready.' *On Actors and the Art of Acting.* London: Smith, Elder & Co., 1875.
Lewes, Paul. 'What's a Guinea? Money and Coinage in Victorian Britain.' Paul Lewis, 1996. <paul@deadline.demon.co.uk>.
Lewis, Samuel. *A Topographical Dictionary of England.* 4 vols. London: S. Lewis, 1831.
Lightwood, James T. *Charles Dickens and Music.* 1912; rpt New York: Haskell House, 1970.
Lillo, George. *The London Merchant.* Ed. William H. McBurney. Regents Restoration Drama Series. London: Edward Arnold, 1965.
Lister, Margot. *Costumes of Everyday Life: An Illustrated History of Working Clothes.* Boston, Mass.: Plays, Inc., 1972.
Llewellyn, Nigel. *The Art of Death: Visual Culture in the English Death Ritual, c.1500–c.1800.* London: Victoria and Albert Museum, 1991.
Lohman, W. J., Jr. 'The Economic Background of Great Expectations.' *Victorians Institute Journal* 14 (1986): 53–66.
London at Dinner; or, Where to Dine in 1858. Originally published in 1851 as *London at Table; or, How, When and Where to Dine and Order Dinner, and Where to Avoid Dining.* Newton Abbot: David & Charles, 1969.
The London Guide, and Stranger's Safeguard Against the Cheats, Swindlers, and Pickpockets That Abound with the Bills of Mortality; Forming a Picture of London, as Regards Active Life. London: J. Bumpus, 1818.
The London Guide, Describing the Public and Private Buildings of London and Westminster, and Southwark. London: J. Fielding [1818].
Loudon, John Claudius. *An Encyclopaedia of Agriculture.* London: Longman, Brown, Green, Longmans & Roberts, 1857.
Loudon, John Claudius. *An Encyclopaedia of Architecture.* London: Longmans, Green, 1866.
Loudon, John Claudius. *An Encyclopaedia of Gardening.* London: Longman, Rees, Orme, Brown, & Green, 1827.
Lyssons, Daniel. *The Environs of London: Being An Historical Account of the Towns, Villages and Hamlets, Within Twelve Miles of That Capital.* 4 vols. London: T. Cadell & W. Davies, 1792–6.
Lytton, Edward Bulwer. *The Caxtons: A Family Picture.* London: George Routledge, n.d.
Macaulay, Thomas Babington. 'Southey's Colloquies on Society.' In *Critical, Historical, and Miscellaneous Essays. Contributed to the Edinburgh Review.* 3 vols. London: Longman, Brown, Green & Longman, 1843.
McAdam, John Loudon. *Remarks on the Present System of Road-Making.* London: Longman, Hurst, Rees, Orme, & Browne, 1823.

Mackay, Charles. *Memoirs of Extraordinary Popular Delusions.* 3 vols. London: Richard Bentley, 1841.
Mackay, Charles. *The Thames and its Tributaries; or, Rambles Among the Rivers.* 2 vols. London: Richard Bentley, 1840.
McLynn, Frank. *Crime and Punishment in Eighteenth-Century England.* London: Routledge, 1989.
McMaster, Rowland, ed. *Great Expectations.* Toronto: Macmillan, 1965.
Macmorran, Kenneth M. *A Handbook for Churchwardens and Parochial Church Councillors.* New edn. London: A. R. Mowbray, 1968.
McNeil, Ian. Ed. *An Encyclopaedia of the History of Technology.* London & New York: 1990.
Macquarie, Lachlan. *A Letter to the Rt Honourable Viscount Sidmouth, in Refutation of Statements made by the Hon. Henry Grey Bennett, MP in a Pamphlet 'On the Transportation Laws, The State of the Hulks, and of the Colonies in New South Wales.'* London: Richard Rees, 1821.
Major, Gwen. 'The Magwitch Hide-Out.' *The Dickensian* 67 (1971): 31–4.
Margetson, Stella. *Journey by Stages: Some Account of the People who Travelled by Stage-coach and Mail in the Years between 1660 and 1840.* London: Cassell, 1967.
Marlow, James E. 'English Cannibalism: Dickens After 1859.' *Studies in English Literature* 23 (1983): 647–66.
Marsh, Ronald. *Rochester: The Evolution of the City and its Government.* Rochester: Rochester City Council, 1974.
Martineau, Harriet. *Harriet Martineau's Autobiography.* 3 vols. London: Smith, Elder, 1877.
Mason, Oliver. *The Gazetteer of England.* 2 vols. Newton Abbot: David & Charles, 1972.
Mavor, William. *The English Spelling-Book, Accompanied by A Progressive Series of Easy and Familiar Lessons Intended As an Introduction to the English Language.* London: Longmans, Hurst, Rees, Orme, & Brown, 1819.
Mayhew, Augustus and Henry Mayhew. *The Greatest Plague of Life! Or, The Adventures of a Lady in Search of A Good Husband.* London: David Bogue [1848].
Mayhew, Henry. *The Great World of London.* In 9 Parts. London: David Bogue, 1866.
Mayhew, Henry. *London Labour and the London Poor.* 4 vols. Reprinted London: Frank Cass, 1967.
Mayhew, Henry and John Binny. *The Criminal Prisons of London and Scenes of Prison Life.* London: Griffin Bohn, 1862.
Maynard, Margaret. 'A Form of Humiliation: Early Transportation Uniforms in Australia.' *Costume: The Journal of the Costume Society* 21 (1987): 57–66.
'Meat and Murrain.' *Saturday Review*, 12 August 1865, 202–4.
Meckier, Jerome. 'Charles Dickens's *Great Expectations*: A Defense of the Second Ending.' *Studies in the Novel* 25 (1993): 28–58.
Meckier, Jerome. ' "Dashing in Now": *Great Expectations* and Charles Lever's *A Day's Ride.*' *Dickens Studies Annual* (1998): 227–64.
Meckier, Jerome. 'Dating the Action in *Great Expectations*: A New Chronology.' *Dickens Studies Annual* 21 (1992): 157–94.
Meckier, Jerome. 'Dickens, *Great Expectations*, and the Dartmouth College Notes.' *Papers on Language and Literature* 28 (1992): 111–33.

Meckier, Jerome. *Hidden Rivalries in Victorian Fiction: Dickens, Realism, and Revaluation*. Lexington, Ky: Kentucky UP, 1987.
Meisel, Martin. 'Miss Havisham Brought to Book.' *PMLA* 81 (1966): 278–85.
Merchant, Peter. '*Great Expectations* and "Elizabeth Villiers." '. *Dickens Quarterly* 14 (1997): 243–7.
Millingen, J. D. *The History of Duelling*. 2 vols. London: Richard Bentley, 1841.
The Miniature Road-Book of Kent. London: Darton & Clark, 1842.
Moad, M. I. *The Guildhall Rochester: A Brief History*. Rochester: D. A. Printers, n.d.
Morley, John. *Death, Heaven and the Victorians*. London: Studio Vista, 1971.
Morton, Lionel. ' "His Truncheon's Length": A Recurrent Allusion to *Hamlet* in Dickens's Novels.' *Dickens Studies Newsletter* 11 (1980): 47–9.
Morris, Norval and David J. Rothaman, eds. *The Oxford History of the Prison: The Practice of Punishment in Western Society*. New York: Oxford UP, 1995.
Moynahan, Julian. 'The Hero's Guilt: The Case of *Great Expectations*.' *Essays in Criticism* 10 (1960): 60–79.
Mugglestone, Lynda. *'Talking Proper': The Rise of Accent as Social Symbol*. Oxford: Clarendon, 1995.
Muir, Douglas N. *Postal Reform and the Penny Black: A New Appreciation*. London: National Postal Museum, 1990.
Myerly, Scott Hughes. *British Military Spectacle: From the Napoleonic Wars through the Crimea*. Cambridge, Mass.: Harvard UP, 1996.
Nasmyth, James. *James Nasmyth Engineer: An Autobiography*. Ed. Samuel Smiles. London: John Murray, 1883.
Neville, Ralph. *London Clubs: Their History and Treasures*. London, 1911; rpt Chatto & Windus, 1969.
Nevins, Allan, ed. *Diary of John Quincy Adams, 1794–1845*. New York, 1951.
The New Catholic Encyclopedia. New York: McGraw-Hill, 1967.
Newgate: To Which are added some Curious Facts relating to the Prison and Prisoners. London: Henry Vickers, n.d.
Nicholls, Thomas. *The Steam-Boat Companion For Margate, Isle of Thanet, Isle of Sheppy, Southend, Gravesend, and River Thames: Guide, with Biographical Incidents, and Topographical Remarks . . . .* London: Thomas Hughes [1823].
Nineteenth Annual Report of the Registrar-General of Births, Deaths, and Marriages in England. London: HMSO, 1858.
Nisbet, Ada. 'The Autobiographical Matrix of *Great Expectations*.' *Victorian Newsletter* 15 (1959): 10–13.
Oddie, William. *Dickens and Carlyle: The Question of Influence*. London: Centenary Press, 1972.
Old Bailey Experience. London: James Fraser, [1832?].
Opie, Iona and Peter Opie. *The Oxford Dictionary of Nursery Rhymes*. Revised edn. Oxford: Clarendon Press, 1973.
Opie, Iona and Moira Tatem. *A Dictionary of Superstitions*. Oxford: Oxford UP, 1989.
Outler, Albert C., ed. *The Works of John Wesley*. The Bicentennial Edition. Nashville: Abingdon Press, 1984.
Panton, J. E. *Homes of Taste: Economical Hints*. London: Sampson, Low, Marston, Searle & Rivington, 1890.

Paroissien, David. *The Companion to 'Oliver Twist'*. Edinburgh: Edinburgh UP, 1992.
Paroissien, David, ed. *Selected Letters of Charles Dickens*. London: Macmillan, 1985.
Partridge, Eric. *A Dictionary of Slang and Unconventional Modern English*. London: Routledge & Kegan Paul, 1984.
Patterson, Frank Allen, ed. *The Works of John Milton*. Vol. IV. New York: Columbia UP, 1931.
Paz, D. G. *The Politics of Working Class Education in Britain, 1830–1850*. Manchester: Manchester UP, 1980.
Peacock, W. F. 'Charles Dickens's Nomenclature in Two Parts:–Part II.' *Belgravia* 20 (1873): 393–402.
Pearlman, E. 'Inversion in *Great Expectations*.' *Dickens Studies Annual* 7 (1978): 190–202.
Penny, Nicholas. *Mourning*. London: HMSO, 1981.
Perrault, Charles. *Fairy Tales*. Trans. Samuel Robinson Littlewood. London: Herbert & Daniel, 1911.
Peterson, Harold L., ed. *Encyclopedia of Firearms*. New York: E. P. Dutton, 1964.
Peyrouton, Noel. 'Rapping the Rappers.' *The Dickensian* 55 (1959): 19–30.
Peyrouton, Noel. 'Rapping the Rappers: More Grist for the Biographer's Mill.' *The Dickensian* 55 (1959): 75–89.
Philips, R[ichard], Sir. *Reading Exercises for the Use of Schools, on a New and Improved Plan; Being a Sequel to Mavor's Spelling-Book*. Ed. Rev. David Blair. London: Longman, Hurst, Rees, Orme & Brown, 1820.
Phippen, James. *Descriptive Sketches of Rochester, Chatham, and their Vicinities*. Rochester: Pippen, 1862.
Picturesque Tour of the River Thames. [24 Original Drawings by William Westall and Samuel Owen]. London: R. Ackerman, 1828.
Piesse, Septimus. G. W. *The Art of Perfumery*. London: Longman, Brown, Green & Longman, 1855.
Planta, Edward. *A New Picture of Paris; or, The Stranger's Guide to the French Metropolis*. London: Samuel Leigh, 1831.
Plummer, John. 'The Original Miss Havisham.' *The Dickensian* 2 (1906): 298.
Porter, G. R. *The Progress of the Nation, in its Various Social and Economical Relations, From the Beginning of the Nineteenth Century to the Present Time*. 3 vols. London: Charles Knight, 1836.
Porter, G. R. *The Progress of the Nation, in its Various Social and Economical Relations, From the Beginning of the Nineteenth Century to the Present Time*. 3 vols. London: John Murray, 1847.
The Post Office London Directory for 1839, Enumerating, in Alphabetical Order, the Merchants and Traders of London. London: Simpkin & Marshall, [1839].
Pratt, Edwin A. *A History of Inland Transport and Communication in England*. London: Kegan Paul, Trench, Trübner, 1912.
Presnail, James. *Chatham: The Story of a Dockyard Town and the Birthplace of the British Navy*. Chatham: Corporation of Chatham, 1952.
Proposals from Sun-Fire Office. Cornhill, nr the Royal Exchange. 27 April 1786.
Pry, Paul [William Heath]. *Oddities of London Life*. 2 vols. London: Richard Bentley, 1838.
Quillian, W. H. *Hamlet and the New Poetic: James Joyce and T. S. Eliot*. Ann Arbor,

Mich.: UMI Research Press, 1983.

Radzinowicz, Leon. *A History of English Criminal Law and Its Administration from 1750.* 4 vols. London: Stevens, 1948–68.

Reader, W. J. *Macadam: The McAdam Family and the Turnpike Roads, 1798–1861.* London, 1980.

Reed, John R. *Victorian Conventions.* Athens, Ohio: Ohio UP, 1975.

Reeve, Mrs Henry. 'Mistresses and Maids.' *Longman's Magazine* 21 (March 1893): 497–504.

'Revolt of the Convicts at Chatham.' *The Times,* 13 February 1861, 12 cd; 14 February, 12 c; 15 February, 10 f; 16 February, 9 b; 19 February, 9 f; 20 February, 12 c; 22 February, 5 d; 26 March, 11 a; 28 March, 10 Letter from T. Folliot Powell, Governor, Chatham Prison.

Richards, T. Andrew. ' "Joe Gargery" and His Recollections of Dickens.' *Strand Magazine* 45 (April 1913): 464–7.

Richardson, M. T., ed. *Practical Blacksmithing.* 3 vols. New York: Richardson, 1890.

Richardson, Samuel. *The Apprentice's Vade Mecum.* 1734; rpt Los Angeles, Calif.: William Andrews Clark Library, 1975.

Rimmel, Eugene. *The Book of Perfumes.* London: Chapman & Hall, 1865.

Ringler, William. A. *The Poems of Sir Philip Sidney.* Oxford: Clarendon, 1982.

Roberts, Helene E. 'The Exquisite Slave: The Role of Clothes in the Making of the Victorian Woman.' *Signs: Journal of Women in Culture and Society* (1977): 554–69.

Rodes, Robert E. *Law and Modernization in the Church of England: Charles II to the Welfare State.* Notre Dame, Ind.: U of Notre Dame P, 1991.

Rodwell, James. *The Rat: Its History and Destructive Character.* London: G. Routledge, 1858.

Room, Adrian. *Dictionary of Place Names in the British Isles.* London: Bloomsbury Publishing, 1988.

Ronge, John and Bertha. *A Practical Guide to the English Kinder Garten.* London: J. S. Hodson, 1855.

Rosenberg, Edgar. 'A Preface to *Great Expectations*: The Pale Usher Dusts His Lexicons.' *Dickens Studies Annual* 2 (1972): 294–335, 374–8.

Rosenberg, Edgar. 'Small Talk in Hammersmith: Chapter 23 of *Great Expectations.*' *The Dickensian* 69 (1973): 90–101.

Rosenberg, Edgar. 'Wopsle's Consecration.' *Dickens Studies Newsletter* 8 (1977): 6–11.

Ryan, J. S. 'A Possible Australian Source for Miss Havisham.' *Australian Literary Studies* 1 (1963): 134–6.

Sadrin, Anny. *Great Expectations.* Unwin Critical Library. London: Unwin Hyman, 1988.

Schlicke, Paul. *Dickens and Popular Entertainment.* London: Allen & Unwin, 1985.

'The Schoolmaster's Experience in Newgate.' No. 1 June 1832. *Fraser's Magazine* 5 (June 1832): 521–33.

'The Schoolmaster's Experience in Newgate.' 'Hurried Trials.' No. 2 July 1832. *Fraser's Magazine* 5 (July 1832): 736–49.

Scott, P. G. 'Letter to the Editor.' *The Dickensian* 71 (1975): 172.

Scott, George Ryley. *The Story of Baths and Bathing.* London: T. Werner Laurie, 1939.

Shanes, Eric. *Turner's Picturesque Views in England and Wales.* New York, 1979.

Shatto, Susan. *The Companion to 'Bleak House.'* London: Unwin Hyman, 1988.

Shatto, Susan. ' "A complete course, according to question and answer." ' *The Dickensian* 70 (1974): 113–20.

Shatto, Susan. 'Miss Havisham and Mr Mopes the Hermit: Dickens and the Mentally Ill.' *Dickens Quarterly* 2 (1985): 43–50 and 79–84.

Shaw, A. G. L. *Convicts and the Colonies: A Study of Penal Transportation from Great Britain and Ireland to Australia and Other Parts of the British Empire.* London: 1966.

Shaw, George Bernard. 'Introduction.' *Great Expectations.* The Novel Library. London: Hamish Hamilton, 1947. Pp v–20.

Shaw, [George] Bernard. 'Preface.' *Great Expectations.* Edinburgh: R. & R. Clark for the Limited Editions Club [of New York], 1937. Pp v–xxii.

Shepherd, Thomas. *London And its Environs in the Nineteenth Century.* Illustrated by a Series of Views From Original Drawings. London, 1829; rpt Newcastle-upon-Tyne: Frank Graham, 1970.

Sheppard, Francis. *London 1808–1870: The Infernal Wen.* Berkeley & Los Angeles, Calif.: U of California Press, 1971.

Shorter, Edward. *From Paralysis to Fatigue: A History of Psychosomatic Illness in the Modern Era.* New York: Free Press-Macmillan, 1992.

Showalter, Elaine. *The Female Malady: Women, Madness and English Culture 1830–1890.* New York: Pantheon, 1985.

Sichel, Marion. *The Regency.* Costume Reference 5. London: B. T. Batsford, 1978.

Sidney, Samuel. *Gallops and Gossips in the Bush of Australia; or, Passages in the Life of Alfred Barnard.* London: Longman, Brown, Green & Longmans, 1854.

Sidney, Samuel. *The Three Colonies of Australia: New South Wales, Victoria, South Australia: Their Pastures, Copper Mines and Gold Fields.* London: Ingram, Cooke, 1852.

Sidney, Samuel and John Sidney. *Sidney's Australian Hand-book. How to Settle and Succeed in Australia: Comprising Every Information for Intending Emigrants.* By a Bushman. London: Pelham Richardson, 1849.

The Sights of London With Cab Fares. London: Parkins & Gotto [1862].

Simmonds, Peter Lund. *Coffee and Chicory: Their Cultural, Chemical Composition, Preparation for the Market, and Composition.* London: E. and F. N. Spon, 1864.

Simmonds, Peter Lund. *The Curiosities of Food; or, The Dainties . . . and Delicacies of Different Nations Obtained from the Animal . . . Kingdom.* London: Richard Bentley, 1859.

Simmonds, Peter Lund. *A Dictionary of Trade Products, Commercial, Manufacturing and Technical Terms: With a Definition of Moneys, Weights, and Measures of All Countries, Reduced to the British Standard.* London: G. Routledge, 1858.

Simmonds, Peter Lund. *The British Roll of Honour. A Descriptive Account of the Recognized Orders of Chivalry in Various Countries.* London: Dean, 1887.

Simpson, Margaret. *The Companion to 'Hard Times.'* Robertsbridge: Helm Information, 1997.

Singer, Charles, E. J. Holmyard, A. R. Hall, and Trevor I. Williams, eds. *A History of Technology.* 8 vols. Oxford: Clarendon, 1958.

Sinks of London Laid Open: A Pocket Companion for the Uninitiated, To Which is Added a Modern Flash Dictionary. London: J. Duncombe, 1848.

'Sketches of Newgate.' *Illustrated London News* 62 (15 February 1873): 161–2.

Slater, Michael. *Dickens and Women*. London: Dent, 1983.
Smetham, Henry. *Rambles Round Churches in Dickens Land*. 3 vols. Chatham: Parrett & Neves, 1926.
Smiles, Samuel. *Self-Help*. 1859. Abridged by George Bull. Harmondsworth: Penguin Books, 1986.
Smith, Albert. *The English Hotel Nuisance*. London: David Bryce, 1855.
Smith, Bill. *Joe Smith and His Waxworks*. London: Neville Boeman, 1896.
Smith, Charles Manby. *Curiosities of London Life: or, Phases, Physiological and Social, of The Great Metropolis*. London: William and Frederick G. Cash, 1853.
Smith, Charles Manby. *The Little World of London; or, Pictures . . . in Little of London Life*. London: Arthur Hall, Virtue, 1857.
Smith, David. *Victorian Maps of the British Isles*. London: B. T. Batsford, 1985.
Smith, Frederick Francis. *A History of Rochester*. Rochester: John Hallewell Publications, 1976.
Smith, Sydney. *The Works of the Reverend Sydney Smith*. 4 vols. London, 1839.
Smyth, Admiral W. H. *The Sailor's Word-Book: An Alphabetical Digest of Nautical Terms*. London: Blackie, 1867.
Southey, Robert. *Letters from England*. 1807. Ed. Jack Simmons. London: Cresset Press, 1951.
Spence, Gordon. *Charles Dickens as a Familiar Essayist*. Salzburg Studies in English Literature. No. 71. Salzburg: U of Salzburg P, 1977.
Spratt, H. Philip. *The Birth of the Steamboat*. London: Charles Griffin, 1958.
Stanhope, Philip Dormer. *Letters Written . . . by Philip Stanhope Dormer, Earl of Chesterfield to his Son, Philip Stanhope*. 2 vols. London: J. Dodsley, 1774.
Staples, Leslie C. 'Miss Havisham.' *The Dickensian* 54 (1958): 132.
Steig, Michael. *Dickens and Phiz*. Bloomington, Ind.: Indiana UP, 1978.
[Stephen, Fitzjames]. 'Gentlemen.' *Cornhill Magazine* 5 (1862): 327–42.
Stone, Harry. 'An Added Note on Dickens and Miss Havisham.' *Nineteenth-Century Fiction* 10 (1955): 85–6.
Stone, Harry. 'Dickens' Woman in White.' *Victorian Newsletter* 33 (1968): 5–8.
Stone, Harry, ed. *Dickens' Working Notes for his Novels*. Chicago, Ill. London: U of Chicago Press, 1987.
Stone, Harry. 'Fire, Hand, and Gate: Dickens' *Great Expectations*.' *Kenyon Review* 24 (1962): 652–91.
Stone, Harry. 'The Genesis of a Novel: *Great Expectations*.' In *Charles Dickens 1812–1870*. Ed. E. W. F. Tomlin. London: Weidenfeld & Nicolson, 1969. Pp 109–31.
Stone, Harry. '*Great Expectations*: The Fairy-Tale Transfomation.' In *Dickens and the Invisible World: Fairy Tales, Fantasy, and Novel-Making*. Bloomington, Ind.: Indiana UP, 1979. Pp 298–339.
Stone, Harry. *The Night Side of Dickens: Cannibalism, Passion, Necessity*. Columbus, Ohio: Ohio State UP, 1994.
Stone, Laurence. *Sculpture in Britain: The Middle Ages*. Harmondsworth: Penguin, 1955.
Stone, Lawrence, and Jeanne C. Fawtier Stone. *An Open Elite? England 1540–1880*. Oxford: Clarendon Press, 1984.
Storey, Gladys. *All Sorts of People*. London: Methuen, 1929.
Stow, Randolph. 'The Australian Miss Havisham.' *Australian Literary Studies* 6 (1974):

418–19.
Strachan, Charles G. 'The Medical Knowledge of Charles Dickens.' *British Medical Journal* 2 (1924): 780–2.
'Street Ballads.' *National Review* 26 (1861): 397–419.
Strong, Roy. *The Collector's Encyclopedia: Victoriana to Art Deco*. London: Collins, 1974.
Strutt, Joseph. *The Sports and Pastimes of the People of England*. New edn. London: William Reeves, 1830.
Stubblefield, Jay. ' "What Shall I Say I Am—Today?": Subjectivity and Accountability in *Frankenstein* and *Great Expectations*.' *Dickens Quarterly* 14 (1997): 232–42.
Sucksmith, Harvey Peter. *The Narrative Art of Charles Dickens: The Rhetoric of Sympathy and Irony in His Novels*. Oxford: Clarendon, 1970.
Summer Excursions in the County of Kent, Along the Banks of the Rivers Thames and Medway. London: W. S. Orr, 1847.
Sutherland, John. *The Stanford Companion to Victorian Fiction*. Stanford, Calif.: Stanford UP, 1989.
Sutherland, John. *Victorian Fiction: Writers, Publishers, Readers*. New York: St Martin's, 1995.
Swift, Jonathan. *Gulliver's Travels, A Tale of A Tub, The Battle of the Books*. London: Oxford UP, 1956.
Tables of the Rates of Pilotage, to be Demanded and Received by Pilots, Acting Under the Authority of the Corporation of Trinity House. London: Smith & Ebbs, 1862.
Taylor, Anya. 'Devoured Hearts in *Great Expectations*.' *Dickens Studies Newsletter* 13 (1982): 65–71.
Tegg, Thomas. *A Present for an Apprentice. To which is added, Franklin's Way to Wealth*. London: William Tegg, 1848.
Thackeray, William Makepeace. *The Four Georges: Sketches of Manners, Morals, Country and Town Life*. London: Smith & Elder, 1862.
Thackeray, William Makepeace. *Miscellaneous Contributions to Punch, 1843–1854*. Ed. George Saintsbury. London: Oxford UP, n.d.
Thackeray, William Makepeace. *The Works of William Makepeace Thackeray*. 26 vols. New York/London: Harper, 1898, 1910.
'The Thames Embankment.' *The Civil Engineer and Architect's Journal* 7 (April 1842): 158–65.
Thompson, A. G. *The Romance of London*. London: Bradley & Son, 1934.
Thornton, E. C. B. *Thames Coast Pleasure Steamers*. Prescot, Lancs: T. Stephenson, 1972.
Thorpe, J. C. and M. A. Whiteley. *Thorpe's Dictionary of Applied Chemistry*. 12 vols. London: Longmans, Green, 1937–56.
Tillotson, Kathleen. '*Great Expectations* and the Dartmouth College Notes.' *The Dickensian* 83 (1987): 17–18.
Tilt, E. J. *Elements of Health and Principles of Female Hygiene*. Philadelphia, Pa: Lindsay & Blakiston, 1853.
Timbs, John. *Curiosities of London*. London: Virtue & Co., 1867.
Timbs, John, ed. *Manuals of Utility, Practical Information and Universal Knowledge; Manual of Domestic Economy: With a Variety of New Inventions, Hints, Receipts, and*

Improvements in the Domestic Arts. London: David Bogue, 1847.
Timbs, John. *Romance of London: Strange Stories, Scenes and Remarkable Persons of the Great Town*. 3 vols. London: Richard Bentley, 1865.
Tobias, J. J. *Nineteenth-Century Crime: Prevention and Punishment*. Newton Abbott: David & Charles, 1972.
Tomalin, Claire. *The Invisible Woman: The Story of Nelly Ternan and Charles Dickens*. London: Viking, 1990.
Tomlinson, H. Charles and H. M. Tomlinson. *Below London Bridge*. London: Cassell, 1934.
Trades for London Boys And How to Enter Them. Compiled by the Apprenticeship and Skilled Employment Association, 55 Deninson House, Westminster, S.W. London: Longmans, Green & Co., 1908.
Tredgold, Thomas. *Remarks on Steam Navigation, and its Protection, Regulation, and Encouragement in a Letter to the Right Honourable William Huskisson*. London: Longman, Hurst, Rees, Orme, Brown & Green, 1825.
Thurin, Susan Schoenbauer. '*Pictures from Italy*: Pickwick and Podsnap Abroad.' *The Dickensian* 83 (1987): 66–78.
Trustram, Myna. *Women of the Regiment: Marriage and the Victorian Army*. Cambridge: Cambridge UP, 1984.
Turner, J. W. Cecil. *Kenny's Outline of Criminal Law*. 19th edn. Cambridge: Cambridge University Press, 1966.
The Universal Songster. Illus. by George Cruikshank. 3 vols. London: John Fairnburn, 1825.
'A Visit to Messrs. Barclay and Perkin's Brewery.' *Illustrated London News* 60 (6 February 1847): 92–4.
Wakefield, Edward Gibbon. *Facts Relating to the Punishment of Death in the Metropolis.* 1831. In *Collected Works*. Ed. M. F. Lloyd Prichard. London: Collins, 1968.
Walker, David. *The Oxford Companion to Law*. Oxford: Clarendon Press, 1980.
Warlow, Ben. *Shore Establishments of the Royal Navy, Being a List of the Static Ships and Establishments of the Royal Navy*. Liskeard, Cornwall: Maritime Books, 1992.
Warner, John L. 'Dickens Looks at Homer.' *The Dickensian* 60 (1964): 52–4.
Webster, N. W. *The Great North Road*. London, 1974.
Webster, Thomas. *An Encyclopedia of Domestic Economy*. London: Brown, Green, & Longmans, 1844.
Weinreb, Ben and Christopher Hibbert, eds. *London Encyclopaedia*. London: Macmillan, 1983.
West, E. G. *Education and the Industrial Revolution*. London: B. T. Batsford, 1975.
Wilkes, Charles. *Narratives of the United States Exploring Expedition During the Years 1838, 1839, 1840, 1841, 1842*. 5 vols. Philadelphia, Pa: Lea & Blanchard, 1845.
Willis, Frederick. 'The Dickens Road.' *The Dickensian* 25 (1929): 146–7.
Wilson, F. P., ed. *Oxford Dictionary of English Proverbs*.' 3rd edn. London: Oxford UP, 1970.
Wight, John. *Mornings at Bow Street: A Selection of the Most Humorous and Entertaining Reports Which Have Appeared in the Morning Chronicle*. London: Charles Baldwyn, 1824.
Wight, John. *More Mornings at Bow Street. A New Collection of Humorous and Entertaining*

Reports. London: James Robin & Co, 1827.

Wight, John. *Sunday in London. Illustrated in Fourteen Cuts.* By George Cruikshank. And a few words by a Friend of His; With a Copy of Sir Andrew Agnew's Bill. London: Effingham Wilson, 1833.

Wildeblood, Joan. *The Polite World: A Guide to the Deportment of the English in Former Times.* London: Davis-Poynter, 1973.

Wildeblood, Joan and Peter Brinson. *The Polite World: A Guide to English Manners and Deportment from the Thirteenth to the Nineteenth Century.* London: Oxford UP, 1965.

Williman, Daniel. *Legal Terminology: An Historical Guide to the Technical Language of Law.* Peterborough, Canada: Broadview Press, 1986.

Willmot, Frank G. *Cement, Mud and 'Muddies'.* Chatham: Meresborough Books, 1977.

Winters, Warrington. 'Charles Dickens: the Pursuers and the Pursued.' *Victorian Newsletter* 23 (Spring 1963): 23–4.

Withycombe, E. G. *The Oxford Dictionary of English Christian Names.* London: Oxford UP, 1949.

Witt, Richard. 'The Death of Miss Havisham.' *The Dickensian* 80 (1984): 151–6.

Wordsworth, William. *The Prelude, or Growth of a Poet's Mind.* Ed. Ernest de Selincourt. London: Oxford UP, 1960.

Wordsworth, William. *Wordsworth's Guide to the Lakes.* Intro. by Ernest de Sélincourt. London, 1810; 5th edn. 1835. Oxford: Oxford UP, 1977.

Wood, T. *The Oarsman's Guide to the Thames and Other Rivers.* New edn. London: Thomas Day, 1857.

Wootton, A. C. *Chronicles of Pharmacy*, 2 vols in 1. 1910; rpt Boston, Mass.: Milford House, 1910.

Worth, George J. *Great Expectations: An Annotated Bibliography.* New York: Garland Publishing, 1986.

Worth, George J. '*The Uncommercial Traveller* and *Great Expectations*: A Further Note.' *The Dickensian* 83 (1987): 19–21.

Wright, Thomas. *The Life of Charles Dickens.* London: Herbert Jenkins, 1935.

Wright's Topography of Rochester, Chatham, Strood, Brompton, etc. Chatham: I. G. Wright, 1838.

Young, Linda. 'The Experience of Convictism: Five Pieces of Convict Clothing from Western Australia.' *Costume: the Journal of the Costume Society* 22 (1988): 70–84.

INDEX

à Beckett, Gilbert A.: 'Stage Passions', 75, 262, 264, 266, 361, 364
Abel and Cain, 317
Aberdeen, 387
Aberdeen, Lord, 388
Abolition of Slavery Act (1833), 125
abscess, 222
Accessories and Abettors Act (1861), 395
accoucheurs, *see* midwives
accounts, 286-7
Achilles, HMS, 246
Act of Uniformity (1662), 164
Act of Union (1707), 294
actors, 238-9; doubling roles, 263; makeup, 361; pseudonyms, 266; troupes, 329; 'unnatural' diction, 266; *see also* theatre *and* theatres
Acts of Parliament, *see under title of Act*
Adams, John Quincy, 280
Addison, Joseph, 14 n
Adelphi theatre, 85
Admiralty, 80, 362-3, 406
Adventures of Famous Highwaymen, 233
Africa, 35, 125, 205, 294, 296
Agent for Aliens, 378
agricultural unrest, 128
Alcmena, 40
Alderman, John and Mary, 78
Aldersgate Street, 177, 186
Aldgate, 186, 203
Alexandria, 376
All Hallows, 25, 97
'All Night on the Monument', 307
All the Year Round: GE serial instalments, 1-5, 453-5. For contents, *see under individual titles*
Allestree, Richard: *Whole Duty of Man*, 47
Allingham, William: 'Dirty Old Man', 83
allocutus, 334
allusions, literary, *see under author of work referred to*; *for books of the Bible, see under Bible*; *for anonymous works, see title*
Almack's Assembly Rooms, 285
alphabet, 76; dumb/finger, 338
amber, 204
Ambree, Manor of, 95
America, 294; land of opportunity, 285; transportation to, 30, 46, 249; *see also* American Civil War *and* American War of Independence
American Civil War, 376
American Notes, 65

American War of Independence, 46, 249
anaesthesia, 146
anchovy sauce, 279
animals: badgers, 160; bears, 106; buffalo, 285; bulls, 160; cats, 179; deer, 160; dogs, 160, 361; foxes, 160; horses, 101, 137, 178, 185, 318, 329, 361, 366; monkeys, 361; performing, 361; *see also* bestiality
Anne, Queen, 131
Annoncy, 106
Annual Register, 83, 154
Anti-Duelling Association, 300
antiseptics, 146
Anti-Slavery Society, 215
Antwerp, 377
Aphrodite, 296
apoplexy, 79
apothecaries, 42, 89; *see also* chemists *and* druggists
Apothecaries Company, 42
apprentices, 50, 73, 124, 146, 154, 158, 277, 297; binding, 128, 131, 132; holidays, 138; indentures, 124, 172; premium, 127
Apsley House, 230
Arbury Hall, 228
architectural design: *cottage ornée*, 228; Gothic Revival, 228
Arctic: expeditions to, 35, 252, 324
Argus, 341
arithmetic, 105
army, *see* guns; military history; soldiers
articled clerks, 277
Articles of War (1844), 300
Assam, 204
assembly rooms, 301; Almack's, 285
Associate Institute for Improving and Enforcing the Laws for the Protection of Women, 374-5
Athenaeum, 285
Athene, 251
attorneys, 157
Augustus, 62
Austen, Jane: *Northanger Abbey* 210
Australia, 83, 308; Blue Mountains, 320; Botany Bay, 45, 319-20; cattle-farming, 308, 309; colonists, 318-19; emancipists, 319; emigration to, 389; exclusives, 319; first penal colony, 319-20; New South Wales, 45, 249, 308, 313, 320, 321-2, 390; outback, 320, 322; sheep-farming, 114, 308, 309, 311, 318; Tasmania, 34, 204, 308; transportation to, 7,

34, 45, 46, 128, 249, 273, 313, 314, 334, 390; Victoria, 308; Western Australia, 314
Australia; Who Should Go; How to Go; What to Do When There, 309
autobiographical elements, *see under* Dickens, Charles
Aveling, Stephen, 89, 96
Aylesford, 170
Aytoun, W. E.: 'Advice to an Intending Serialist', 317

babies, *see* children
badger-baiting, 160
bagatelle, 398-9
Bagshaw, 95
Bagshot Heath, 38
bailiffs, 288, 408
Baker, John Rose and Sarah Jane, 25
Balcomb Mill, 351
Ball Court, 378
'Ballad of George Barnwell, The', 141-3
ballads, *see* songs
ballad-sellers, 136
Ballarat, 308
ballast-lighters, 391
ballooning, 106
balls, 298-9, 301; *see also* assembly rooms
bandboxes, 392
bankruptcy, 415
banks: Bank of England, 113, 292, 309, 331; banker's parcel, 269; Barings, 202
Banks, Sir Joseph, 261, 319
banns, *see* marriage
Barbados, 205
Barbary, Miss, 61
barbers, *see* hair
Barclay, Robert, 199
Barclay & Perkins brewery, 199
barges, 137, 349, 385, 390
Barkis, 171
Barnaby Rudge, 103, 111, 142, 336
Barnard's Inn, *see* Inns of Court
Barnes, John, 34
Barney, 186
Barnum's Circus, 329
baronets, 211
barrels and casks, wooden, 49, 102, 103, 294
barristers, 157
Bartholomew Close, 186
Bath, 397
Battersea, 217
Battery, the, 36, 65, 66
Bayswater, 184, 191
beacons, 37
Beadnell, Maria Sarah, 98, 141, 254, 255, 298

beam engines, 409-10
bear-baiting, 106
Beard, Thomas: 'Dialogue Concerning Convicts', 273
Bedford Street, 135
beer, 66, 72; 'small', 100; strength, 95; *see also* breweries *and* brewing
beggars, 190; *see also* tramps *and* vagrants
Belgium, 385
benefit of clergy, 334
Bennett, Henry Grey, 185, 245, 270, 271, 274-5, 277, 310
Bentham, Jeremy, 46, 172, 271
Bentley, Nathaniel, 83
Bentley, Richard (publisher), 215
Bentley, Richard (scholar), 215
Bentley's Miscellany. For contents, *see under individual titles*
bereavement, *see* mourning
Berkeley, George, 28; *Siris*, 43
Bermondsey, 349
Bernard, Lionel, 189
bestiality, 311
Bevis Marks, 186
Bexley Heath, 174
Bible: Exodus, 280, 306, 398; Ezekiel, 306; Genesis, 71, 139, 306, 317; Good Samaritan, 76; Hebrews, 317; James, 224; Job, 115, 279, 290; John, 107; Leviticus, 117; Luke, 61, 76, 156, 164, 388, 407, 415; Mark, 164, 388; Matthew, 117, 156, 164, 232, 317, 388; Noah, 71, 250; Prodigal Son, 61; Proverbs, 42, 242; Psalms, 306, 334; Romans, 42, 78, 402; Timothy, 290
Biddy: letter-writing, 236; name, 76; marriage, 414; Pip and, 13 n
Billingsgate Market, 386
'Bill-Sticking', 192
birching, 108
birds: geese, 169; ostriches, 207; parrots, 321; salt on tail, 61; scaring, 73-4
Birmingham, 138
Birnie, Sir Richard, 148
Births and Deaths Registration Act (1836), 155
Black Museum, Scotland Yard, 180
'Black Veil, The', 227
Blackfriars, 293, 306, 307, 334
Blackfriars Bridge, 356, 382
Black's Picturesque Tourist of Scotland, 241-2
blacking warehouses: Day & Martin's, 240-1; Warren's, 48, 100, 135, 148, 241
blacksmiths, 24, 35, 40, 41, 111, 137, 139-40, 251; anvil, 139-40; clothes, 54-5; coal, 134; dentistry, 321; horseshoes, 137; patron saint, 124

Blackstone, Sir William, 46, 335; *Commentaries*, 155
Blackwall, 38, 350, 383
blade (gallant), 223
Blake, William: 'To the Muses', 208
Bleak House, 8 n, 22, 35, 61, 78, 100, 132, 140, 155, 179, 216, 258, 261, 306, 314, 351, 408, 409
blinds, wire, 188
blocks (pulleys), 349
bloodletting, 352
'Bloody Code', 332
blue bags, 258
Blue Blazes, 111
Blue Boar inn, 132, 244, 250, 258
Blyth, 385
Blythe Sands, 393
Board of Trade, 203
boarding schools, *see* education
boats, *see* ships and boats
boatswain, 362
bogey tales, 139
Boley Hill, 95
Bologna, 26
Bonifacio, Giovanni, 338
Book of Common Prayer, The, 59, 77; Apostles' Creed, 28; banns, 55; Catechism, 73, 295; Holy Communion, 414; Lent, 400; Order for Burial of the Dead, 290; prayer for the Church Militant, 287; Solemnization of Matrimony, 55, 398; Table of Kindred and Affinity, 111; Table of Lessons, 164
Book of Memoranda, 5, 21, 23, 35, 55-6, 80, 99, 102, 116, 121, 138, 139, 200, 226, 235, 294-5, 297, 317, 330, 350
book-keeping, 286-7
bookshops, 141
bootmakers, 167-8
boots, *see* shoes and boots
Boots (servant), 251
Borough High Street, 227
Bosworth Field, 145
Botany Bay, 45, 319-20
Bottles: corks, 296; glass, 49, 296; stone, 49
Boulogne, 377
'bounceable', 223
'Bound for the Great Salt Lake', 321
Bow Street: police station, 123; police-court, 148, 149
Bow Street Runners, 123, 148, 149, 224
boxing, *see* sport
box-tree, 115
Bradbury & Evans, 1 n
Braham, John, 267
brandy, 49, 66

brass, 137-8, 205
Brassy's, 260-1
bread: rolls, 166; unleavened, 220-1
breakfast, 54
breast feeding, 39
Brentford, 191, 192, 332
Breweries: Barclay & Perkins, 199; Calvert, 199; Charrington, 199; Courage, 199; Hope, 199; Meux, 199; Moss, 199; Murray, 199; Parson, 199; Thrale, 199; Truman, 199; Woodham's, 90-5, 200
brewing, 72, 90-5, 104, 198-200; liquorice water, 49; 'mashing', 102; scents, 102; utensils, 103
brick buildings: replace timber, 40
brickmakers, 78
Bridewell Palace, 334
Bridge Street, 340
Bridgeman, Laura, 338
brightsmiths, 243
Bristol, 138, 397
Britannia metal, 226, 233
British and Foreign School Society, 290
Brittany, Dukes of, 177
broadsides, 233
Brodie, Sir Benjamin, 119
Brontë, Charlotte, 314; *Jane Eyre*, 370
Brontë, Emily, 314
Brooke's, 285
brothels, *see* prostitutes
Broughton, Jack, 121, 122
Brown, Mrs, 36
Browne, Sir Thomas: *Hydriotaphia*, 150
Browning, Robert: *Dramatis Personae*, 63; 'Mr Sludge, the Medium', 63
Brunel, Mark Isambard, 349
Buckle, Henry Thomas, 110-11
Bucklersbury, 175
buffalo, 285
Bugsby's Hole, 349
Bull Inn, Rochester, 133, 250, 413
bull-baiting, 160
bullfighting, 60
'Bulls and Bears', 74, 208
Bulwer, John, 338
Bulwer-Lytton, Edward, 84, 154, 417; *Caxtons*, 220; ending of GE, 4-5; *Eugene Aram*, 421-2; *Strange Story*, 1 and n, 5 n
Bung, 237
Bunyan, John: *Pilgrim's Progress*, 172, 381
buoys, 390
Burke, John: *Burke's Peerage*, 215
burletta, 239
Burlington Gardens, 167
Burma, 204
burns, 370, 372

Burton, Sir Richard, 376
Butcher, J. & T., 88
butchers, 42, 62; Cag-mag, 186, 187
Bute, Earl of, 261
Byron, Henry James: *Maid and the Magpie*, 24, 126
Byron, Lord: *Childe Harold's Pilgrimage*, 217-18

cabriolets, *see* carriages and coaches
'Cag-mag', 186, 187
Cain and Abel, 139, 317
'Cain in the Fields', 78
Cairo, 376, 397
'Cairo', 376
Calais, 281, 371, 377
calamander, 204
Calcraft, John, 186
'calling', 298
Calvert brewery, 199
Camberwell, 145, 397
Cambridge Giant, The, 329
Cambridge University, 213
Cambridgeshire, 67
Camden Town, 101
Camilla, Queen of the Volscians, 116
Campbell, Lord, 157
Canada, 126
canals, 367
candles, 47, 109, 307, 352, 365; snuffers, 109; tallow, 281; tax, 340; wax, 96
caning, 40
cannibalism, 34-5, 48, 120
Canon Law, 155
Canterbury, 174, 248
Canvey Island, 384, 392, 393; inn, 391
Cape Town, 313
capital punishment, 226, 312-13, 403; death sentence, 404; declining use, 41, 405-6; *see also* hanging Capital Punishment Amendment Act (1868), 321
capitalists, 202
Capitoline Museum, Rome, 218
Capper, John, 376; 'Bulls and Bears', 74, 208
Captain Murderer, 34, 48
carbolic acid, 232
card games, 100, 365; all-fours, 100; beggar my neighbour, 99; French cards, 299; patience/solitaire, 323; piquet, 299; quinze, 299; vingt-et-un, 299; whist, 256-7; *see also* sport
Carlton Club, 285
Carlton House Terrace, 406
Carlyle, Thomas, 160; *Latter-Day Pamphlets*, 128, 273; *Past and Present*, 420; *Sartor Resartus*, 28
Carolingians, 340
carols, 53

carriages and coaches, 88; box, 177; cabriolets, 175, 285; chaises, 56, 81; chariots, 88, 178; coach-founders, 88; coachmakers, 88; coachmen, 177; fares, 179; gigs, 88, 217; hackney-coaches, 160-2, 175, 177, 178, 190, 207; hammercloth, 177; hansom cabs, 162; Hind Standard, 178; hired, 162, 382; increase in, 56; landaus, 88; mail-coaches, 162, 168-9, 397; post-chaises, 88, 382; stagecoaches, 162, 168-9, 174, 244, 247, 250; steps, 177; straw in, 178, 379; tilburies, 88; unauthorized riders, 178; wheels, 56
Carter, George, 351
carters, 169
Cashman, 275
casks, *see* barrels and casks
Castle Museum, Norwich, 180
cat fur, 179
catarrh, 51
Catnach, 136
cattle-farming, Australian, 308, 309
Catullus, 298
Cavendish cakes, 318
Cavendish Square, 378
Cayford, John: 'Recollections', 40, 138-9
Celsus, Cornelius: *Re Medicina*, 146
Central Criminal Court, *see* ; Old Bailey
Cerjat, W. F. de, 8
cestus, 296
Ceylon, 204, 205
Chadwick, Edwin, 79
chairs, high-backed, 181
chaises, *see* carriages and coaches
chalk, 291, 380-1
Chalk, 40, 56, 97, 111, 174; forge, 49, 65, 165
'Chambers', 192, 312, 316
Chambers, Robert: *Vestiges*, 27
Chancellor of the Exchequer, 80
chandlers, 352
Chandos Street, 135
chapbooks, 233
chaplains, prison, 400
chapmen, 327
characterization in GE, *see under individual characters*
Charing Cross, 362, 406
chariots, *see* carriages and coaches
charity schools, *see* education
Charles I, 206, 251
Charles II, 90, 211
Charlotte, Queen, 199
Charrington brewery, 199
chartered companies, 204
Chatham, 87, 248, 250, 336; *David Copperfield*, 36; Dickens and, 73, 310; dockyard, 38, 47,

245, 249, 350-1; hulks, 44, 45; Mitre Hotel, 379; population, 56, 176; Rome Lane, 108; rope-walk, 350-1; St Mary's Convict Prison, 273; Windmill Field, 350
Chatham and Rochester News, The, 251
'Chatham Dockyard', 123, 246, 250
Chattenden Woods, 110
Chavasse, Pye Henry: *Advice to Mothers on the Management of Their Offspring*, 39
Cheapside, 175, 365, 379
cheats, 329
cheese: Double Gloucester, 352; Single Gloucester, 352
Chelsea, 293
Chelsea Suspension Bridge, 293
chemists, 89; *see also* apothecaries *and* druggists
Chequers Inn, Lower Higham, 109-10
Chesterfield, Lord: *Letters*, 197-8, 238
Chesterton, G. K., 417
'Child's Dream of a Star, A', 98
Child's History of England, A, 37
children: breast-feeding babies, 39; child labour, 73; depravity, 47, 61; dry-nursing, 39; feeding, 62; impressionable nature, 101; introduced after dinner, 215-16; law and, 47; liquorice water, 49; mortality rate, 39; sickness, 62
chimney flounces, 54
China, 204
Chips (shipwright), 48
Chisholm, Caroline, 389
Chiswell Street, 199
chocolate nuts, 205
chop-houses, 361-2
Chops, Mr, 314
Christianity, 155; Apostles' Creed, 73; Baptism, 73; Lord's Prayer, 73, 156; public penance, 126-7; Ten Commandments, 73; Trinity, 73; *see also* Bible
Christmas carols, 53
Christmas pudding, *see* plum-pudding
Christmas Stories: 'Going into Society', 314, 317; 'Schoolboy's Story', 151
chronology of GE, *see* time-scheme
Church Building Act (1818), 398
Church of England: clergymen as tutors, 159
churches: elevated pulpits, (illus.) 58; 'marsh', 97; Rochester Cathedral, 258, 368, (illus.) 161; Rochester Congregational church, 93; St George's, Camberwell, 397; St James's, Cooling, 25, 30, 33, 36, 37, (illus.) 32, (illus.) 57; St Mary's, Higham, 30, 33, 36, 37, 68, (illus.) 32; St Paul's Cathedral, 175, 182, 307; St Paul's, Bedford, 402; St Peter's, Cheapside, 175; Trottiscliffe, (illus.) 58; Westminster Abbey, 206

Chuzzlewit, Martin: 'expectations', 21
cigarettes, *see* smoking
cigars, *see* smoking
cinnamon, 204
circus: Barnum's, 329
City of London, *see* London
'City of London Churches', 86, 164
'City of the Absent, The', 398
civil list, 331
Clapper, John Henry, 46, 313
Clare Market, 186
Clarriker: name, 297, 415
class, *see* social classes
cleaners, 316
Clennam, Mrs, 61, 99, 369
Clerkenwell, 228
clerks, articled, 277
Cliffe, 36, 37, 38, 66, 97, 137, 139, 380, 381
Cliffe Creek, 37, 66, 67, 139, 378, 381
Cliffe Road, 414
clocks: church, 307, 314; 'Dutch', 41; stopped, 151; *see also* watches
clothes, *see* costume and appearance
clover, 327
cloves, 204
clubs, men's, 284, 285, 300; Athenaeum, 285; Brooke's, 285; Carlton, 285; Clunn's, 285; Crockford's, 285; 'Our Club', 285; Reform, 285; Turf, 285
Clunn's, 285
coal: fires, 307; small/slack, 134; sea, 385; smoke, 181
coalmen, 285
coal-whippers, 387
coastguard, 45, 67-8
Cobbe, Frances Power, 419
Cobbett, William, 198, 340
Cobham, 40
cochineal, 204
cockfighting, 160
cod, 259
coffee, 205, 240, 242
coffee-houses, 194, 208, 284, 337
Coiler, Mrs: Catherine Dickens and, 210
coinage, *see* currency
Coinage Offences Act (1832), 276
Colby, Sir Thomas, 131
Colchester, 386
Coldstream Guards, 283
Coleridge, Samuel Taylor, 154
colic, 119
College of Dental Surgery, 321
College of Heralds, 288
college scouts, 316
Collins, Charles Alston, 261

Collins, Wilkie, 113, 201-2, 314; *Frozen Deep*, 98; *Man and Wife*, 78; *Message from the Sea*, 4; *Woman in White*, 1 and n, 2, 3, 25, 85
Collins, William: 'Passions', 75, 133
Collucci, Vincent, 331
colonists: Australia, 318-19
Colquhoun, Patrick, 46, 271
Combe, George, 327
Combrune, Michael: *Essay on Brewing*, 199
Comic Adventures of Old Mother Hubbard and Her Dog, The, 168
commercial travellers, 133
Commercial Treaty, Anglo-French (1860), 305
Common Law, 155
companies, chartered, 204
Compeyson: death, 396-7, 403; 'gentleman' impostor, 153; Magwitch and, 39; Miss Havisham and, 39; name, 330
Comport family, 25-6
concierge, 254
conduct manuals, 44, 196, 197. *See also* etiquette
confessions, criminals', 230-1
confidence tricksters, 244, 366
conjurers, 329
Conolly, John, 160, 369-70
constables, 53
convicts, *see* prisons and prisoners
Cook, Captain James, 319, 351
Cooling, 25-6, 30-3, 38, 46, 68, 97; Castle, 25-6, 33; Court, 25-6; National School, 290
coopers, *see* barrels and casks
copper (metal), 205, 243; mines, 203
copper (tub), 43
Copperfield, David, 36, 61, 171; Dora, 255, 298; Gravesend, 390; name, 317; pawnbrokers, 224; prisons, 272; tinkers, 327
coppersmiths, 243
copy-books, 279
Corder, William, 231
Cork Street, 167
corn: grinding, 67
corn-chandlers, 56, 87
corn-doctors, 321
Cornhill, 207, 378
Cornwall, 4, 391
Cornwallis: *Essays*, 116
coroners, 154-5
corporal punishment: birching, 108; brought up 'by hand', 39; caning, 40; flogging, 132, 184, 327
Corporation of London, 203, 276
cosmetics, *see* costume and appearance
Costello, Dudley: 'Incomplete Letter Writer', 317
costume and appearance

clothing: blacksmiths, 54-5; boat-cloak, 38; cloaks, 289; coat-collars, 242; coat-tails, 187; corduroys, 88; embroidered vests, 282; fob pockets, 190; frock-coats, 275; garters (men's), 282; gloves, 170, 295, 398; gold-laced coats, 282; greatcoats, 68, 370; improvised, 362; Inverness overcoats, 370; khaki, 52; knee-breeches, 179, 320; metal buttons, 216; ruffs (bands), 392; secondhand, 178, 186, 267; shawls, 204; shirt-collars, 242; 'shorts', 320; slops, 321; smock-frocks, 89; socks, 168; stockings (men's), 320; stockings (women's), 168; stocks, 64-5; velveteen, 179; waterproofs, 370
cosmetic preparations: absorbent powders, 232; cold cream, 232; depilatories, 232; emulsion, 232; milk, 232; patches, 282; perfume, 232; perfumed soap, 118, 232; powder, 282
dresses catching fire, 369, 370
hair: dyes, 232; powder, 320; washes, 232
hats: bands, 289; beaver bonnet, 126; etiquette, 237-8; fur cap, 179; low-crowned felt, 50; mourning, 289; muslin cap, 140-1; traveller's, 111; 'weepers', 289
tailoring, 166-7
underclothes, 168; farthingales, 282; hooped petticoats, 282; stays, 120, 295 wearers and purposes: actors, 364; Anglican clergymen, 50; army, 52, 64-5, 68, 167; blacksmiths, 54-5; Bow Street Runners, 149; coachmen, 177; convicts, 30, 248; court dress, 126; dentists, 321; elderly gentlemen, 179; grave-clothes, 99; mourning, 151, 289; sailors, 321; seamen, 321; servants, 237, 284; travelling dress, 278; wedding dress, 201
wholesale manufacture, 166
see also shoes and bootscottage economy, 229
cottage ornée, 228
cotton, 205, 294, 376
cotton-wool, 370
counting-house, 205
County Coroners Act (1860), 155
county gaols, 123
County of Middlesex Sessions, 276
Courage brewery, 199
couriers, 118-19
courts of law: conduct of trials, 155; Court for the Relief of the Insolvent Debtor, 408-9; cross-examination, 155; Doctors' Commons, 78, 296; duration of trials, 401; ecclesiastical, 80; evidence, 155, 233, 401; juries, 155, 156, 401; magistrates' courts, 131, 224; nosegays, 402; Old Bailey, 146, 177, 183, 184, 185, 230, 276, 333, 402-3; *oyer and terminer*, 183; police-courts, 224; 'Sessions', 400

courtship, 79
Courvoisier, F. B., 222
'cousin', 119
Coutts, Angela Burdett, 389, 416
cove (man), 223
Covent Garden, 164, 193-4, 285, 340
Coventry, 227
Cox (convict), 34-5
crash (1857), 205-6
Crayford, 174
credit, 220, 236
cressets, 37
Crewe, Lord, 100
'crib', 325
Cricket on the Hearth, The, 352
crime: children, 47; felony, 224, 332, 394-5; fences, 187; flimpers, 190; housebreakers, 190; hue and cry, 147; jobbers, 190; juveniles, 55, 374; larceny, 41, 46, 184, 226, 316, 374; literature, 233; misdemeanour, 224, 332; pickpockets, 128, 190; plate-receivers, 187; poachers, 221; rape, 185; scuffle hunters, 254; sheep-stealing, 185; smashers, 190; smuggling, 392, 393; thimble-riggers, 329; treason, 394; wife-beating, 419
criminal biographies, 233
'Criminal Courts', 269, 270
Criminal Law Act (1827), 334
Cripplegate, 184
Cristofori, B., 120
Crockford's, 285
Cromwell, Oliver, 186, 204
Cross Keys Inn, London, 175, 379
Crow Lane, 90, 93, 94, 104, 253, 254
Crown Inn, Rochester, 368
Cruelty to Animals Act (1835), 160
Cruikshank, George, 180; *Greatest Plague of Life*, 212
Cruikshank, Robert, 180
Cruncher, Jerry, 290; pronunciation, 242
Crusader monuments, 53
Cubitt, Sir William, 259
cucumbers, 229
Cupid, 286
cuppers, 321
'Curious Dance Round a Curious Tree', 84
'Curious Epitaph', 26
currency
  bank-notes, 112-13, 190, 244, 292, 309, 330-1
  coinage, 113; clipping, 90; farthing, 105-6, 187, 381; half-crown, 244; half-penny, 249; penny, 60, 105; shilling, 60, 62, 105, 112; sixpence, 112
  forgery, 185, 190, 223, 269, 276, 309, 330-1
  gold, 331

  guinea, 113, 127, 159
  'small-note era', 113, 309
  washed silver
curriers, 88
Custom House, 357, 377, 378, (illus.) 354
cutlery, 233
cutting (socially), 336
Cuvier, Baron, 328

Daguerre, Louis Jacques Mandé, 24-5
Daily News, The, 223, 402
Dalgarno, George, 338
dame schools, *see* education
Dance, George, II, 182
Dance, Nathaniel, 180
dancing, 363
Darnay, Charles: 'expectations', 22
Dartford, 174
Darwin, Charles, 247, 276; *Origin of Species*, 9 n, 10, 26, 247
David Copperfield, 7 n, 21, 33, 36, 61, 76, 105, 121, 165, 171, 179, 192, 203-4, 224, 244, 255, 258, 259, 272, 295, 296, 298, 302, 317, 327, 369, 370, 389, 390, 413, 415
Davis, Eliza, 187, 266
Day & Martin's blacking warehouse, 240-1
'Day at Day and Martin's, A', 241
Day, C. W.: *Hints on Etiquette*, 196, 318
De Quincey, Thomas: 'On Murder Considered as One of the Fine Arts', 154, 180
Dead Man's Point, 394
deafness, 48
deans, 321
death masks, 180, 222, 271
death sentence, 404
Debrett, John: *Debrett's Peerage*, 215; *New Peerage*, 215
debt, 408; imprisonment for, 220, 326
Debtors Act (1869), 409
Decoy House, 25-6
'Decoying a Young Girl into a Brothel', 374
deer stalking, 208
defaulters, 208
delirium tremens, 331-2
demi-swearing, 117
Denmark Hill, 398
dentists, 232, 321
depilatories, 232
depression (1857), 205-6
Deptford, 349; dockyard, 245; hulks, 45
Derby, 12th Earl of, 329
Descartes, René, 28
'Detective Police Party, A', 149
Devil, 106-7, 156
Deville, Mr, 328

Devon, 4
'Dialogue Concerning Convicts, A', 273
Dibdin, Charles, 362
Dick, Mr, 370
Dickens, Alfred Lamert, 26, 116
Dickens, Catherine, 210, 213, 216, 261
Dickens, Charles, Jr, 101, 186, 202-3, 261, 305, 416, 417
Dickens, Charles: abstinence, 242; *All the Year Round*, 1-2, 5; Autobiographical Fragment, 48, 148; birth, 310; Bow Street Runners, 149; Bradbury & Evans, 1 n; British Museum, 220; burial, 206; and cannibalism, 48; Chatham, 7 n, 27, 45, 73, 202, 245-6, 310; childhood innocence, 171; childhood poverty, 148; childhood recollections, 27, 29, 73, 101; children's names, 100-1; coach travel, 175, 178, 193; *David Copperfield*, 7 n; dependants, 116, 213; disintegration of corpses, 99-100; Doctors' Commons, 78; dogs, 111; Durham, 8; education, 76-7, 108; emigrants, 389; evolution, 26-7, 247; father, 134, 255; fear of being watched, 135; France, 324; and funeral practices, 288; Gad's Hill, 27, 83, 339; *Household Words*, 1, 5; Jews, 178, 186, 187, 266, 267; journeys into the past, 253; Kate's marriage, 261; library, 83, 233; London, 165; Maria Beadnell, 254, 255, 298; marital problems, 1 n; and mentally ill, 369; Mercy, 47-8; mesmerism, 22; neuralgia, 4; Newgate visits, 269-77; opening of GE, 39-40; pantomime, 363; Paris Morgue, 392; pawnbrokers, 224; phrenology, 327; Portsmouth, 309-10; public readings, 4; repeater watch, 227; reporter, 162; Restoration House, 151, 253-4; Rochester bridge, 259; seaside reading, 296; self-determination, 310; sense of social inadequacy, 100; sentimental ethics, 297; shorthand, 76; spiritualism, 63; and spitting, 65; Staplehurst train crash, 281; Switzerland, 101; Tavistock House, 339; Thames excursion, 4, 8, 383; tramps, 111; 'vulgar' taste in clothes, 100; walks, 27, 40, 253, 328, 338-9; Warren's blacking warehouse, 48, 100, 135, 148, 241
Dickens, John, 101, 224, 245, 255, 309-10, 409
Dickens, Kate, 261
Dieppe, 377
diet 352
dikes, 28
dinner, 56, 234, 255; dress, 232; etiquette, 213, 256
'Dirty Old Man, The', 83
disinfectant, 232
Disraeli, Benjamin: *Sybil*, 211, 247

Divine Right of Kings, 340
divorce, 78, 80
Divorce and Matrimonial Causes Act (1857), 80
Dixon, Hepworth, 335
Doctors' Commons, *see* courts of law
dog fighting, 160
dogs, performing, 361
dolls: Dutch, 216; 'peg', 216
Dombey, Florence, 36
Dombey and Son, 36, 101, 8181, 203-4, 366, 369
domestic economy, 282
'Doom of English Wills, The', 253
Dorset, 386
Dorset County Chronicle, The 404
Doubledick, Richard, 171
dovecots, 102
Dover, 248, 281, 343
Dover Road, 40, 111, 343
'Down with the Tide', 217, 392
drainage, 51; marshes, 67
drama, *see* actors; theatre; theatres
drapers, 166
drawing-room, 54
dress, *see* costume and appearance
dressing-room, 96
dressing-table, 97
drink and drinking, *see* food and drink
dripping, 261
drowning, 67
druggists, 89; *see also* apothecaries *and* chemists
Drummle, Bentley: name, 212; nickname, 214-15, 234; wife-beater, 419
dry-nursing, 39
ducking-stool, 140
duelling, 300
'Dullborough Town', 27, 80, 88, 171, 174, 175, 193, 258, 263, 268, 379
dumb alphabet, 338
dumb waiters, 233
Dundee Art Gallery and Museum, 180
Dunkirk, 377
Durham, 8 n
dustmen, 260
Dusty Hill, 414
Dutch clocks, 41
Dutch dolls, 2
Dyes: cochineal, 204; fustic, 204; indigo, 204, 205; lac, 204; logwood, 204; madder, 204; safflower, 204; shumac, 204; yellow berries, 204
'Dying Gaul, The' (sculture), 218-19

ear-trumpet, 48
East Row, 90
east wind, 306

Eastgate House, 87
Eastland Company, 204
Eatanswill, 133
ebony, 204
ecclesiastical courts, 80
Eddystone Lighthouse, 391
Edgeworth, Maria: *Belinda*, 210; *Moral Tales*, 197
Edgware Road, 184
Edinburgh University: Anatomy Department, 180
education, 220, 330; 'barren blooming', 211; boarding schools, 352; British and Foreign School Society, 290; charity schools, 352; cramming, 213; dame schools, 74, 108; evening schools, 74; finishing schools, 9, 141, 255; governesses, 352; grinders, 213; Industrial Schools, 47; learning by heart, 75; National Schools, 290; National Society for Promoting the Education of the Poor in the Principles of the Established Church, 290; nurseries, 136; oral examination, 75; poor and, 81; pupil-teachers, 290; reading primers, 108; recitation, 75; Reformatory Schools, 47; Report (1858), 74; resistance to, 81; social mobility and, 152-3; Sunday school, 106-7; teaching professionalized, 290; tutors, 159, 352; women, 211, 352-5
Education Act (1870), 74
Edward III, 362
Edward IV, 132
Edward VI, 334
eels, 386
Egan, Pierce, 238
Egypt Bay, 45, 67-8, 250
elections: canvassing, 162; election cry, 162
electricity, 307
Eliot, George: *Scenes of Clerical Life*, 86
Elizabeth I, 95
Elizabethan Poor Law, 330
Ellis, Mrs: *Daughters of England*, 209
Elmwood House, 84
emancipists: Australia, 319
embezzlement, 331
emigration, 389
emulsion (cosmetic), 232
Enfield, William: *Speaker*, 75
English Channel: steam-ships, 281, 371, 384
épergnes, 118
'Epsom', 329
Erie, Lake, 285
Erie Canal, 285
Erith, 357
Essex, 174, 327, 380, 384, 386, 390, 392
'Essex Gang', 337
Essex Street, 321, 325

Estella: age, 93, 96; education, 9, 141; name, 23, 98; remarriage, 21
'Eternal Lamps', 100
etiquette, 192, 210, 213, 216, 218; calling, 298; eating, 318; escorting a lady, 278; gloves, 295, 398; hand-shaking, 255; hats, 237-8; ostentatious display, 239; walking, 259; *see also* conduct manuals
Euryalus 47
Evangelicals, 61, 128, 171, 270
Evans, Bessie, 261
Evans, Frederick, 261
Evans, John: *Excursion to Windsor*, 71
evening schools, *see* education
evolution, 26-7
examinations, 59
Examiner, The, 27, 35
exclusives: Australia, 319
Execution Dock, Wapping, 38
Fagin, 186, 187, 266
Fagin, Bob, 134, 135
fainting, 119
Fairbairn, John Bye, 67
Fairborne, Sir Stafford, 131
fairy-tales, *see* nursery tales
'Familiar Epistle from a Parent to a Child', 174
Faringdon Street, 340
Faringdon Without, 157
Farren, William, 238
fashion, *see* costume and appearance
fences, 187
fever, intermittent, *see* ague
Fielding, Henry, 148, 269, 314; *Tom Jones* 116, 262, 411
Fielding, John, 148
figureheads (maritime), 388
finger alphabet, 338
finger-posts, 50
finishing schools, *see* education
'First Fruits', 86
'First of May, The', 362
Fitzball, Edward, 362
flaming spirits, 234-5
flatulence, 119
Fleet Street, 340, 341
Fleet Valley, 191
flimpers, 190
flip, 170
flogging, *see* corporal punishment
flounce, chimney, 54
Folkestone, 281
folk-lore, 120; east wind, 306; old man, 29
Fonblanque, 231
food and drink: anchovy sauce, 279; bread rolls, 166

children's diet, 39, 62; eels, 386; flip, 170; fowl, 53-4, 60, 169, 197; gin, 242; gluttony, 62; hardbake, 132; hares, 49; marriage breakfast, 398; oysters, 259-60, 386; paunching, 49; plum-pudding, 43; pork, 42, 53; prisons, 271, 272, 273; punch, 63, 216, 230; rotten meat, 186; rum, 111, 205, 248; sea biscuit, 221; small salad, 393; stewed steak, 226; suet puddings, 362; sugar, 109, 205, 294; tongue, 169; wine, 100, 200; wine: boiled, 60; brandy, 49, 66; fortified, 59-60, 188; port, 59-60, 256; sherry, 59-60, 188
Foot Guards, 282-3
forensic medicine, 233
Forfeiture Act (1870), 394
forgery, *see* currency
forks, 138
Forster, John: *Arrest of the Five Members*, 251; Dickens's education, 220; Dickens's reading, 296; GE, 3, 14, 21, 29, 82-3, 383, 417; *Life*, 415
Fort Pitt, 253
fortified wines, 59-60
fortune-tellers, 327
fowl, 53-4, 60, 169, 197
Fowler, Charles, 194
fox hunting, 160
France, 385; naval power, 202
franchise, 152; *see also* elections
Franklin, Sir John, 35, 252
free trade, 203, 305
Freemasonry, 42
French Giant, The, 329
Frindsbury, 253-4
Froebel, Friedrich, 97-8
'From the Raven in the Happy Family', 288
Fry, Elizabeth, 271
funerals, 117; cost, 79; disintegration of corpses, 99-100; grave-clothes, 99; health risks, 79; mutes, 288; pallbearers, 290; undertakers, 79; women's role, 289
Furies (Erinyes), 141
Furnival's Inn, *see* Inns of Court
fustic, 204

Gadd, W. Laurence, 7, 26, 87
Gad's Hill, 174
Gad's Hill Place, 27, 110, 131, 199, 253, 254, 259, 339
Gall, Franz Joseph, 327
gallows, *see* hanging
Galt, John: *Annals of the Parish*, 355
gambling: buttons, 216
'game', *see* prostitutes
games: bagatelle, 398-9; flaming spirits, 234-5; *see also* card games *and* sport
Gantlet Creek, 27
gardens, 208; landscape gardeners, 229; topiary, 115
Gargery, Joe: Biddy, 414; dog, 52, 158; name, 35; origins, 40; pronunciation, 76; weeping, 172
Gargery, Mrs Joe: false gentility, 41; injury, 150; 'on the rampage', 41
gas lighting, 142, 186, 207, 280-1
Gaskell, Elizabeth: *Mary Barton*, 230
gatekeepers, 254
Gay, John, 269
geese, 169
general shops, 75
General Steam Navigation, 377
General Theatrical Fund, 263
General and True History of the Most Famous Highwaymen, A, 233
Geneva, 101
gentility, 204
gentleman: defined, 152-3, 165-6
Gentleman's Herald, The, 370
gentry, 167
George I, 25
George III, 385George III, 64, 199, 238, 331, 351
George IV, 25, 65
George Hotel, Nailsworth, 117
Germany, 385Gerrard Street, 232-3
'Ghost of the Cock Lane Ghost, The', 63
'Ghost of the Cock Lane Ghost Wrong Again, The', 63
ghosts, 29, 60
giants, 329, 381
gibbets, 37-8
Giddy, David, 81
gigs, *see* carriages and coaches
Giltspur Street, 374
gin, 242
ginger, 119, 204, 205
Gissing, George, 417
Glasgow, 387
Glastonbury, 145
gluttony, 62
Godwin, William: *Caleb Williams*, 342
'Going into Society', 201, 314, 317
gold mines, 203
Golden Cross Inn, 413
Goldsmith, Oliver: *She Stoops to Conquer*, 44
Good Samaritan, 76
goods-waggons, 175
gooseberries, 193
Gore Green, 73, 414
Gothic Revival, 228
gout, 352

governesses, *see* education
Gowan, Mrs: 'expectations', 21
Gradgrind, Mrs, 110
Grant, Captain James Augustus, 376
grapes, 121
graves, *see* tombstones
Gravesend, 27, 33, 38, 110, 170, 174, 248, 343, 378, 380, 383, 384, 389, 390, 393, 413, (illus.) 360
Gray, Thomas: 'Elegy Written in a Country Churchyard', 13, 164
Gray's Inn, *see* Inns of Court
Great Fire of London (1666), 182, 207
Great Plague (1665), 386
Great Plains, 285
Great Remonstrance, 251
Great Seal of England, 126
Great West Road, 332
Great Yarmouth, 388
Green Park, 206
greengrocers, 89
Greenwich, 174, 228, 342, 358, 385, 392
Greenwich: Royal Observatory, 228
Grenadier Guards, 283
Gresham, Sir Thomas, 207
gridirons, 138
Grimaldi, 363
grinders, 213
grocers, 89
Gruffandgrim, 352
guide-posts, 50
Gundulf, Bishop, 121
Guns: brass-bound stock, 254-5; flintlock, 63; matchlock, 63; musket, 63, 64; muzzle-loading, 255; percussion lock, 63; signal, 144
gypsies, 111, 327, 366

'Hackney Coach Stands', 162, 178
hackney-coaches, *see* carriages and coaches
hair: dyes, 232; powder, 320; washes, 232; wigs, 320
hairdressers, 320: dentistry, 321
Hale, Robert, 329
Hamburg, 384
Hammersmith, 191, 208
Hammersmith Suspension Bridge, 293
Hampden, John, 251
Hampshire, 386Hampstead, 192
Handel, George Frederick, 196; 'Harmonious Blacksmith', 196
Handel Festival (1859), 196
handkerchiefs, 256
hand-kissing, 170
hand-shaking, 189, 192, 193, 244
hanging, 183, 320-1; 'Calcraft's cord', 65;

commercialization of, 183; dissection of victims, 146; 'dying dunghill', 51; gallows, 183-4; Newgate's 'new drop', 1185; public hangings ended, 183, 184, 321; Tyburn, 184
Hanging Sword Alley, 339
hangman, 271; initiation, 185-6; perquisites, 185
Hanseatic Consul, 378
hansom cabs, *see* carriages and coaches
Hanway, Jonas, 328
Hanworth, 367
Hard Times, 98, 361
Hardman, Sir William, 63, 79, 207, 240, 285
Hardwick's Act for the Better Prevention of Clandestine Marriages (1753), 200
Hardy, Thomas: *Woodlanders*, 221
Harmer, James, 157-8, 222
Harper's, 420
harpsichord, 120
Harris, Edward, 222
Harrow School, 213
Harrow-on-the-Hill, 213
Hartley, David: *Observations on Man*, 171
hats, *see* costume and appearance
hatters, 167-8
Havisham, Arthur: name, 331
Havisham, Miss: character, 81-5; Compeyson, 39; Estella, 21; father, 198; 'feast', 35; name, 81; Pip, 29, 170; reclusive, 201; Weird Sisters, 299
hawkers, 328
hay-making, 328
Hazlitt, William, 154
health, 51; abscess, 222; apoplexy, 79; bloodletting, 352; burns, 370, 372; catarrh, 51; cathartics, 392; colic, 119; convicts, 30, 400, 402-3, 406; corpses a danger to, 79; deafness, 48; *delirium tremens*, 331-2; fainting, 119; flatulence, 119; fresh air, 410, 411; gout, 352; hysteria, 119, 140; indigestion, 119; infants, 62; inflammation, 51; jail-fever, 402-3; languors, 119; malaria, 51; melancholia, 98; mental breakdown, 408; nosebleeds, 122; ophthalmia, 112; plaster, 42; poultices, 217, 221-2, 248; prisons, 271, 272; purgation, 352, 392; rheumatism, 51; sal volatile, 119; washing, 86; watercress, 413; whitlow, 217; *see also* mental illness
'Hear the Postman!', 410
Heep, Uriah: 'expectations', 21
Henry I, 41
Henry III, 206, 334
Henry VI, 199
Henry VIII, 36, 334, 339, 390
Hera, 341

Herald, The, 377
heraldry, 288, 289
Hercules, 40
Hermes, 341
Hermit of Hertfordshire, 84
High Halstow, 25-6, 97
Higham, 33, 131
Higham Creek, 36
Higham Upshire, 73
highway robbery, 185
Hill, Rowland: *Post Office Reform*, 191
'hob and nob', 66
Hogarth, Mrs, 210, 213
Hogarth, William: *Industry and Idleness*, 135, 172-3
Hogg, James, 176
Holborn, 191, 241, 281
Holborn Bar, 203
Holborn Hill, 191
Holborn Viaduct, 191
Hole Haven, 384, 390, 391, 393, 394
Hole Haven Creek, 392, (map) 452
Holland, 385, 386
Hollingshead, John: 'All Night on the Monument', 307
home, as source of virtue and emotion, 134
Home, Daniel Dunglas, 63
Home Office: petitions to, 404-5
Homer, 296; *Odyssey*, 251
homosexuality, 276, 311
Hong Kong, 202, 261
Hoo peninsula, 25, 27, 51, 97, 110, 148, 253, 378, 380, 435-7, (map) 449
Hook, Theodore, 154
Hooke, Robert, 89
Hope brewery, 199
hops, 94, 102
Horace: *Odes*, 298
Horne, R. H.: 'One Man in a Dockyard', 249, 253; 'True Story of a Coal Fire', 387, 388
horror-stories, 47
Horse Ferry Pier, 349
Horse Guards, 406
Horse Patrol, 149
horse racing, 329
Horsemonger Lane prison, 320
horse-stealing, 185, 366
horses, 318; Irish hunter, 101; nose-bags, 178; performing, 361; shoes, 137
hosiers, 167-8
'Hospital Patient, The', 78
Houndsditch, 186
Hounslow, 332
Hounslow Heath, 38, 367
House of Commons: brewers as MPs, 199

House of Lords, 211, 215, 388; divorce, 80
'House to Let', 201
housebreakers, 190
Household Narrative of Current Events, 82
Household Words, 1 and n, 182; rates of pay, 127. For contents, see under individual titles. See also *Household Narrative of Current Events*
Howard, John, 46, 184, 271, 272, 328, 330, 335, 402; *State of the Prisons in England and Wales*, 271-2
Howe, Samuel Gridley, 338
Howells, William Dean, 417
Hubble, Mr: name, 55-6
Hudson River, 285
Hudson's Bay, 126
hue and cry, 147
Hugo, Victor: *Hunchback of Notre Dame*, 100
hulks, see prisons and prisoners
Hulks Act (1776), 245
humbug, 116
Hummums, 340, 341, 365
Hungerford Stairs, 135
Hungerford Suspension Bridge, 293
Hunt, Robert: *Poetry of Science*, 27
Hunton, Joseph, 223
Huskisson, William, 203
Hyde Park, 83, 206-7, 281, 314, 325
Hyde Park Corner, 174, 206, 260
Hymen, 398
hysteria, 119, 140

Ibrahim Pasha, 199
Illustrated London News, The, 180, 199
immigrants, Irish, 178
'In and Out of Jail', 326
income, 113, 295
'Incomplete Letter Writer, The', 317
India, 205; army in, 52, 134-5, 323; Civil Service, 59; punch, 63
indigestion, 119
indigo, 204
Indus River, 204
Industrial Schools, 47
'Infallible Physic', 43
Infant Felon Act (1840), 374
'Infant Gardens', 98
infant mortality rate, 39
Infanticide Act (1922), 372
inflammation, 51
informers, 336, 396
inheritance, 21, 152, 314
Inner Temple Lane, 341
Inns of Court, 157, 177, 189, 281
 Barnard's Inn, 188-9, 191, 207, 236, 260, (illus.) 195

door seals, 316
Furnival's Inn, 189
gatekeepers, 207
Gray's Inn, 192
Inns of Chancery, 188-9
porters, 207
Temple, 281, 305, 306, 325, 438-40, (illus.) 303, (illus.) 304; Devereux Court, 341; Garden Court, 356; Gardens, 412; gates, 339, 341; Inner Temple Lane, 341; Middle Temple, 321, 355, (map) 441; Middle Temple Lane, 341; Mitre Court, 341; Palsgrave Place, 341; porters, 316, 339; Ram Alley, 341; Rules and Orders, 316; staircase lamps, 307; Stairs, 341, 355, 356, 358-61; warders, 316; watchmen, 316; Water Gate, 341
inns, *see* public houses
insanity, *see* mental illness
insurance, 202, 203, 267; life assurance, 203; marine, 202, 208, 286, 296; underwriters, 202, 208
interior decorators, 236
intermittent fever, *see* ague
inventions: anaesthesia, 146; antiseptics, 146; beam engines, 409-10; disinfectant, 232; locomotives, 77; matches, 48, 381; pillar boxes, 191; pulleys, 349; sacchrometer, 199; sewing machines, 166; steam power, 50, 77, 159, 409-10; tarmacadam, 145; walking beam engines, 410
Io, 341
Irish immigrants, 178
iron, wrought, 205
irons: box, 264; flat (sad), 264; self-heating, 264
Irving, Washington: 'Little Britain', 176
Isle of Dogs, 217
Isle of Grain, 27
Isle of Wight, 83
Islington, 192
'It is Not Generally Known', 24
Ives, James, 320
ivory, 205

jack-knife, 323
jack-towel, 41
Jackson, John, 121
Jacobites, 336
Jaggers, Mr: hand-washing, 41, 232; immunity from thieves, 233; name, 157; original, 157-8; 'salt and pepper', 366-7; success, 155
jail-fever, 402-3
Jamaica, 205
James I, 67, 80, 294
Jarndyce, Mr, 351
Jefferson, Thomas: First Inaugural Address, 78

Jellyby, Mrs, 216
Jennings, Sir John, 131
Jerrold, Douglas William, 285, 362
jewellery, mourning, 190, 223, 276
Jews, 139, 178, 186, 187, 266, 267
Jingle, Alfred, 200
Joachim, Martha, 82
jobbers, 190
John, King, 402
Johnson, Samuel: *Dictionary*, 317
Johnstone, Frederica, 331
joint-stock companies, 203
Jones, Samuel, 48
jorum, 295
journeymen, 138, 166
Juno, 40
juries, *see* courts of law
juvenile crime, 55, 374
Juvenile Offenders Act (1847), 184, 374

Karr, James, 409
Kean's Prize Wherry, 217
Keats, John: 'To Autumn', 71
Kennington Park Road, 224
Kensington, 191
Kent, 67, 174, 384, 392
Kent, William, 137, 406
Kent Road, 295
kerosene, 307
Kew, 261; Palace, 261; Royal Botanic Gardens, 261
kilns: draw/perpetual, 380
King Edward Street, 177
Kingsgate Street, 241
Kingsley, Charles: *Yeast*, 21
Kingston-upon-Thames: prison, 330
kissing hands, 170
knacker's yard, 181, 279
Kneller, Sir Godfrey, 131
Knight, Charles, 402
knighthoods, 211
Knowlys, Newman, 277
Krook, Mr, 179

lac, 204
Laindon Hills, 384
Laing, David, 358
Lake District, 137, 230
Lamarck, 27
Lamb, Charles, 154
Lamb, Mary: 'Elizabeth Villiers', 25
Lambert, William, 341
landaus, *see* carriages and coaches
landscape gardeners, 229
languors, 119

larceny, see crime
Lares and Penates, 134
laundresses, 316
law: benefit of clergy, 334; Common Law, 155; see also courts of law
lay figures, 136
'Lazy Tour of Two Idle Apprentices, The', 83, 223
lead mines, 203
Leadenhall Market, 186
Leake, Sir John, 131
legacies, see inheritance
Leicester, 37
Leigh, 392
Leith, 387
letter-boxes, 191
letter-writing, 236; etiquette, 287; mourning, 287; seals, 287; wafers, 267; see also penny postage and postboys
Lettsom, Dr 145
Lever, Charles: *Day's Ride*, 1 and n, 2-3, 14 n, 21, 22, 25, 158, 159, 327, 366, 417-18
Lewes, George Henry, 265
Lewis, M. G. M.: *Timour the Tartar*, 361
life assurance, 203
life masks, 180
lighters, 217, 349, 388-9
lighthouses, 37, 307, 391
'Lighthouses and Light-Boats', 307
lightships, 393
Lillo, George: *London Merchant*, 141-3, 145, 147, 416
Lilly Church farm, 414
lime, 110, 378, 380; kilns, 380
lime trees, 414
Limehouse, 342
limestone, 291
limewash, 68
Lincolnshire, 67, 259
linden trees, 414
Linton, Mrs Lynn, 63
liquorice, Spanish, 49
liquorice water, 49
Lister, Joseph, 232
literacy, 77, 312
Little Britain, 176-7, 186, 374, 438-40, (map) 442-3
Little Dorrit, 21, 61, 77, 99, 186, 305, 369, 408
Little Swills, 132
Liverpool, 294
Lloyd's, 202, 286
Lobster Smack Inn, Canvey Island, 392
Locke, John, 28, 171
locksmiths: patron saint, 124
lock-ups, see prisons and prisoners

logwood, 204
London, 371, 397; Admiralty, 406; Aldersgate Street, 177, 186; Aldgate, 186, 203; Apsley House, 230; Balcomb Mill, 351; Ball Court, 378; Bartholomew Close, 186; Battersea, 217; Bayswater, 184, 191; Bedford Street, 135; Bermondsey, 349; Bevis Marks, 186; Billingsgate Market, 386; Blackfriars, 38, 293, 306, 307, 334, 350, 383; Blackfriars Bridge, 356, 382; Borough High Street, 227; Bow Street police-court, 148, 149; Bow Street police station, 123; Brentford, 191, 192, 332; Bridewell Palace, 334; Bridge Street, 340; Bucklersbury, 175; Bugsby's Hole, 349; Burlington Gardens, 167; Camden Town, 101; Carlton House Terrace, 406; Cavendish Square, 378; Chandos Street, 135; Charing Cross, 362, 406; Cheapside, 175, 365, 379; Chelsea, 293; Chelsea Suspension Bridge, 293; Chiswell Street, 199; City, 186, 276, 281, 334, 361, 374, 388; Clare Market, 186; Clerkenwell, 228; clocks, 307, 314; Convent of Westminster, 193; Cork Street, 167; Cornhill, 207, 378; Covent Garden, 164, 193-4, 285, 340; Cripplegate, 184; Cross Keys Inn, 175, 379; Custom House, 357, 377, 378, 384, 393, (illus.) 354; Day & Martin, 240-1; Deptford, 349; 'dissolute city', 190; Edgware Road, 184; Essex Street, 321, 325; Execution Dock, 38; Faringdon Street, 340; Faringdon Without, 157; Fleet Street, 340, 341; Fleet Valley, 191; gas-lighting, 186; General Post Office, 191; Gerrard Street, 232-3; Giltspur Street, 374; Great Fire (1666), 182, 207; Great Plague (1665), 386; Green Park, 206; Greenwich, 174, 228, 342, 358, 385, 392; Hammersmith, 191, 208; Hammersmith Suspension Bridge, 293; Hampstead, 192; Hanging Sword Alley, 339; Hanseatic Consul, 378; Holborn, 191, 241, 281; Holborn Bar, 203; Holborn Hill, 191; Holborn Viaduct, 191; Horse Ferry Pier, 349; Horse Guards, 406; horse-drawn traffic, 174-5; Horsemonger Lane, 320; Houndsditch, 186; Hounslow, 38, 332, 367; Hummums, 340, 341, 365; Hungerford Stairs, 135; Hungerford Suspension Bridge, 293; Hyde Park, 83, 206-7, 281, 314, 325; Hyde Park Corner, 174, 206, 260; Isle of Dogs, 217; Islington, 192; Kennington Park Road, 224; Kensington, 191; Kent Road, 295; King Edward Street, 177; Kingsgate Street, 241; Leadenhall Market, 186; Limehouse, 342; Little Britain, 176-7, 186, 374, 438-40, (map) 442-3; London Bridge, 174, 227, 339, 342, 343, 349,

350, 355, 356-7, 358, 382, 383, 384, 385, 386, (illus.) 353; Long Acre, 193; Lower Thames Street, 357, 386; Madame Tussaud's, 97; Mansion House, 280; Marshalsea, 101; Mayfair, 206, 281; metropolitan, 174, 176; Mill Pond, 349-50; Millbank prison, 328; Minories, 186; Moorfields, 203; New Exchange, 207-8; New Oxford Street, 191; Newgate Market, 186; Newgate Street, 175, 191; Newington, 170; Notting Hill, 191; Old Bailey (street), 182, 183, 270; Old Bond Street, 121; Old Kent Road, 174, 224, 227, 343; Old London Bridge, 293, 307, 356, 386; Oxford Street, 184, 233; Pall Mall, 206, 280, 284, 285, 314, 406; parks, 206; Parliament Street, 362; Paternoster Row, 177; Petticoat Lane, 186; Piccadilly, 206, 233, 281; pollution, 181; Poplar, 174, 349; population, 176; Portland Place, 371; Poultry, 175; Ratcliff, 349; Red Lion Street, 241; Regent's Street, 233; Rotherhithe, 349; Rotten Row, 206-7; Royal Exchange, 203, 207, 208, 286; Royal Hospital, 361; Royal Naval College, 361; Russell Street, 340; Sackville Street, 167; St Bartholomew Priory, 186; St Bridget's Well, 334; St James's Hall, 4; St James's Palace, 406; St James's Park, 206, 406; St James's Street, 285; St John's Wood, 83; St Luke's Hospital for the Insane, 83-4; St Martin's Lane, 157; 'Season', 206-7, 269; Sessions House, 400, 402, 403; Shaftesbury Avenue, 281; Shepherd's Bush, 191; size, 174, 176; Smithfield Market, 175, 177, 181-2, 203, 374; Soho, 232-3, 281; Somerset House, 80; Southwark, 174, 199, 293, 307, 320, 343, 349; Southwark Bridge, 134, 382; Stock Exchange, 208; Strand, 193, 285; street-dirt, 305-6; Tavistock House, 339; Temple Bar, 203, 340; Threadneedle Street, 207; Tottenham Court Road, 233; Tower, 80, 326, 357, 386-7; Treasury, 406; Trinity Street (Rotherhithe Street), 351; Tyburn, 184; Union Hole, 349; Uxbridge, 191; Vauxhall, 293, 307; Walworth, 224, 227, 295, 397; Wapping, 38, 349; Wapping New Stairs, 349; Warren, 80; Warren's blacking warehouse, 48, 100, 135, 148, 241; Waterloo Bridge, 293, 306, 356, 382; Westminster, 174, 307; Westminster Bridge, 293, 356, 385, 392; Westminster Hall, 355; Whitechapel, 186; Whitechapel Market, 186; Whitecross Prison, 184; Whitecross Street, 184; Whitefriars, 339, 341; Whitehall, 362, 406; Wood Street, 175, 177, 244, 270, 379; Woolwich Dockyard, 80; *see also* churches *and* Inns of Court

London, Chatham and Dover Railway, 174
London Gas, Light and Coke Company, 280
London Hackney Carriage Act (1831), 179
London Stone, 27
Long Acre, 193
Lord Chancellor, 126, 183, 211
Lord High Admiral, 80, 363
Lord High Treasurer, 80
Lord Lyndhurst's Act (1835), 112
Lord Mayor of London, 203, 277, 361; banquet, 197
Lord Redesdale's Act (1813), 408
Lords of the Admiralty, 80
Lorraine, Claude, 137
Lorraine, Paul: *Ordinary of Newgate*, 233
Loughton, 337
Louis Napoleon, Prince, *see* Napoleon III
Lowe, Edward, 276
Lower Higham, 25, 26, 30-3, 68, 73, 97, 144, 380; Chequers Inn, 109-10
Lower Hope Point, 36
Lower Thames Street, 357, 386
Lucas, James ('Mad') 84
'Lucifer' matches, 48, 381
Lumpers, 221
lunar caustic, 217
'Lying Awake', 29, 106, 340-1, 392
Lyly, John: *Euphues*, 61
Lyndhurst, Lord, 112

mac mud, 306
Macadam, John Loudon, 145
Macarthur, John, 308
Macaulay, Thomas Babington, 74; 'Southey's Colloquies', 176
mace, 204
Mackintosh, Charles, 370
Mackworth, Dr John, 189
Macquarie, Lachlan, 310
Macquarie Harbour, 34, 35
Macready, William Charles, 4, 146, 238, 265
Macrone, John, 176
Madame Tussaud's, 97
madder, 204
magistrates, *see* courts of law
Magwitch, Abel: age, 308; character, 309; clicking, 51; coarseness, 322; and Compeyson, 39; death, 396; disguise, 388; man of feeling, 51-2; name, 317; origins, 29; Pip and, 407; speech, 33-4, 36; tears, 51, 172
Maidstone, 40, 169-70
Maidstone county gaol, 411
Maidstone Road, 90
mail-coaches, *see* carriages and coaches
makeup, *see* cosmetic preparations

malaria, 51
Malefactors' Register, 233
malt, 102, 104
'Malvern Water', 120
mangles, 68
Mansion House, 280
man-traps, 221
Margate, 385
marine insurance, *see* insurance
marine stores, 260-1
markets, 81
marriage, 55, 111-12; banns, 79; breakfast, 398; common-law, 367; legal status of wives, 201; private, 200; wedding dress, 201; wedding tour, 201; wife-beating, 78, 365-6, 419
Marriage Acts: (1823), 200; (1886), 398
Married Women's Property Act (1870), 201
Marryat, Frederick: *Dog Fiend*, 153
Marseilles, 305, 324
'marsh' churches, 97
Marshalsea, 101
marshes, 33, 37, 45, 51, 66, 390
Martin, Maria, 231
Martin, Richard, 160
Martin Chuzzlewit, 21, 24, 113, 142, 265, 288, 314, 356, 408
Martineau, Harriet: 'Malvern Water', 120; penny postage, 191
Marwood, Alice, 366
Mary II, 131
Massachusetts School for the Blind, Boston, 338
matches, 48
Matrimonial Causes Act (1884), 419
Matsys, Quentin, 251
Matthews, Charles: 'Next Door Neighbours', 84-5
Mavor, William: *English Spelling-Book*, 61, 139-40, 196
Mayfair, 206, 281
Mayhew, August: *Greatest Plague of Life*, 212, 236, 258; *Whom to Marry?*, 22
Mayhew, Henry: *Greatest Plague of Life*, 212, 236, 258; *London Labour and the London Poor*, 261, 78, 305-6; *Whom to Marry?* 22
Maynard, Thomas, 276
Maypole Inn, 111
Measor, C. P., 273
meat, *see* food and drink
Mechanics Institute, Rochester, 268
Medical Act (1858), 321
medical jurisprudence, 233
medicines: bogus, 43; tar-water, 43
mediums, *see* spiritualism
Medusa, 34
Medway River, 27, 45, 47, 87, 95, 110, 169, 172, 174, 246, 250, 258, 259, 393, (illus.) 161

melancholia, 98
Melbourne, Lord, 419
melodrama, 239; nautical, 363
memorial (document), 396
mental illness, 160, 369-70
Mentor, 251
merchants, 208
Mercury, 286
Mercy, 47-8
mesmerism, 22
Message from the Sea, A, 4
Metropolitan Board of Works, 306
Metropolitan Police Act (1829), 53, 149, 336
Meux brewery, 199
Mexico, 205
Micawber, Mr, 224; emigration, 389
Micawber, Mrs: gloves, 295
Middle Temple, *see* Temple
Middlesex, 174, 392
Middlesex Justices Act (1792), 148, 396
midwives, 55
military history
  Articles of War (1844), 300
  battles: Bosworth Field, 145; Trafalgar (1805), 202, 203; Waterloo (1815), 174, 203
milk (cosmetic), 232
Mill, John Stuart: *Essay on the Subjection of Women*, 78
Mill Pond, 349-50
Millbank prison, 328
mills: post mills, 67; windmills, 67
Milton, 174
Milton, John: *Areopagitica*, 107; *Paradise Lost*, 13, 21; 172, 420-1
Minerva House, 141
miniatures: photography replaces, 25
mining, 203, 367
Minories, 186
mirrors, 97; diminishing, 279
misdemeanour, *see* crime
Misnar, the Sultan of India, 301
Mitre Hotel, Chatham, 379
Mockbeggar House, 290
Mogg's map of the Thames, 217
Mogul, 81
Molesworth Committee, 34, 46, 311
Molly, 299, 366, 372; age, 234
money, *see* currency
monkeys, performing, 361
Montgolfier, Etienne and Joseph, 106
monuments: cross-legged knights, 53
mooncalf, 85
Moore, Thomas: 'Fill the bumper fair!', 362; *Irish Melodies*, 352; 'Oh, Lady fair!', 133
Moorfields, 203

Morell, Sir Charles, 301
Morley, Henry: 'Ghost of the Cock Lane Ghost', 63; 'In and Out of Jail', 326; 'Infant Gardens', 98; 'Photography', 24-5
Morning Chronicle, The, 162, 269, 377
Morris, William, 230
Moss brewery, 199
Mould, Mr, 288
mourning, 117; dress, 151; hats, 289; jewellery, 190, 223, 276; letters, 287
Mucking Creek, 391
Mucking Flat, 383
Mucking Flat Lighthouse, 391
mud, 305-6
Mullender, Mr, 40
Mulready, William, 180
mundus inversus, 33
Murdstone, Edward and Jane, 61, 105
Murray brewery, 199
Museum of Comparative Anatomy, Paris, 328
musical parties, 298-9
musk, 204
Myrmidons, 123
Mystery of Edwin Drood, The, 100, 107, 254, 436

Nailsworth: George Hotel, 117
Nancy, 78
Napier, David, 281
Napoleon III, 128, 199
Napoleonic Wars, 44, 74, 106, 113, 174, 253
Nasmyth, James, 50, 159
National Debt, 74
National Society for Promoting the Education of the Poor in the Principles of the Established Church, 290
National Trust, 230
'Natural Selection', 26, 247
Nature, 369
nautical melodrama, 363
navvies, 367
navy, *see* Royal Navy
Navy Board, 80
'neck verse', *see* benefit of clergy
negroes, 361
New Exchange, 207-8
New Guinea, 204
New Holland, 204
New Oxford Street, 191
New South Wales, *see* Australia
'New Year's Day', 29
Newcastle, 385
Newgate Calendar, The, 233, 323
Newgate Market, 186
Newgate Prison, 177, 180, 182, 183, 184, 269-77, 320-1, 325, 326, 400; condemned cells, 270; Debtors' Door, 184-5, 270; diet, 271, 272; 'new drop', 185; overcrowding, 271; sanitation, 271; sickness, 271, 272; windows, 275
Newgate Street, 175, 191
Newington, 170
newspapers, 109, 154, 233, 251
Nicholas Nickleby, 59, 307, 369
Niépce, Nicéphore, 24-5
'Niger Expedition, The', 35
'Night Walks', 330
night-lights, 340-1
Nile River, 376, 377
Noah, 71, 250
nobility: titles, 167
noodle, 140
Nore, the, 383, 384, 393
Norfolk, 67, 259
Normanby, Lord, 312
North Northamptonshire by-election, 162
Northfleet, 38, 174
Norton, Caroline, 419; *Stuart of Dunleath*, 419
Norton, Sir George Chapple, 419
Norwich: Castle Museum, 180
nosegays (court), 402-3
noses: bleeding, 122; Roman, 59
Notting Hill, 191
Nuremberg, 216
nurseries, *see* education
nursery rhymes: 'Fee, fo, fi, fum', 381; 'Old Mother Hubbard', 168; 'Who Killed Cock Robin?', 187-8
nursery tales, 34; 'Jack and the Beanstalk', 120; Mother Hubbard, 168; 'Sleeping Beauty', 253
'Nurse's Stories', 34, 47-8, 139
nutmeg, 204
nuts: throwing, 240

oaths, 33-4, 36
Odysseus, 25
ogres, 34
oil-lamps, 142, 281, 307
oils, 232
Old Bailey, *see* courts of law
Old Bailey (street), 182, 183, 270
Old Bailey Experience, 320
Old Bond Street, 121
Old Curiosity Shop, The, 41, 314, 408
Old English lettering, 109
Old Kent Road, 174, 224, 227, 343
Old London Bridge, 293, 307, 356, 386
'Old Stage-Coaching House, An', 174, 279
olive oil, 118
Oliver Twist, 27, 39, 78, 131, 149, 179, 186, 266, 270, 330, 336
Ollier, Edmund: 'Eternal Lamps', 100

omnibuses, horse-drawn, 162, 175
Once a Week, 1 n
'One Man in the Dockyard', 182, 249, 253
operetta, 239
ophthalmia, 112
opium, 204
orange peel: thrown, 240
orange-flower water, 210
Order of the Bath, 362
Ordnance Board, 80
Orlick: alibi, 147; mouth, 35; name, 138-9; origins, 138-9; sentry box, 254
Ostend, 377
Ottoman Empire, 376
'Our Club', 285
Our Mutual Friend, 35, 132, 152, 179, 186, 211, 226, 260, 266, 314, 317, 319, 349, 352, 408, 410
'Our Next-Door Neighbour', 327
'Our School', 108
'Our Vestry', 317
Oxford Street, 184, 233
Oxford University, 213
oyer and terminer, 183
oysters, 259-60, 386
packet-boats, 281, 342, 371, 377
paddle steamers, 394
pages, 215, 255
Pall Mall, 206, 280, 284, 285, 314, 406
Palmer, John, 397
Palmer, Sir Thomas, 131
Palmer, William, 154
Palmerston, Lord, 388
pannikins, 323
pantomime, 363
'Pantomime of Life, The', 363
pantry, 48-9
paper: foxing, 109; ironmould, 109; machine-made, 108-9; silver, 54; tissue, 54, 292
paraffin, 307
Paris, 86, 106, 371; finishing schools, 9, 141, 255; Morgue, 392; Museum of Comparative Anatomy, 328
parish clerk, 56, 75, 111, 240
Parker, Archbishop, 111
Parkhouse Model Prison, 273
Parliament Street, 362
parlour, 54
Parramatta, 319-20
parrots, 321
Parson brewery, 199
partners in business, 415
'passions', 75
passports, 378
Paternoster Row, 177

patron saints, 123-4
pavements, wooden, 182
pawnbrokers, 224
Peacock Inn, 133
Peacock, James, 207
Pearce. Alexander, 34-5
peas, 89
pedlars, 327
Peel, Sir Robert, 149, 198, 222, 223, 336, 405
peerage: titles, 167
'peg' dolls, 216
Peggotty, Clara, 171
Peggotty, Mr: emigration, 389, 390
Penal Servitude Act (1857), 46
Penitentiary Act (1779), 45
penny dreadfuls, 233
penny postage, 191
Pentonville Prison, 46, 328
pepper, 204
performing animals, see under types of animal
perfume, 232
Perils of Certain English Prisoners, The, 5-6
Perrault, Charles: 'Sleeping Beauty', 253
Peru, 203-4
'Pet Prisoners', 272
Peter of Ponce, 338
petitions, 404-5
Petticoat Lane, 186
pew openers, 398
Pewsey, Dorset, 26
pewter, 205
Pharmaceutical Society, 89
Pharmacy Act (1852), 89
Philippine Islands, 204
Philips, Sir Richard: *Reading Exercises for the Use of Schools*, 196
Phillip, Captain Arthur, 319
phonetic spelling, 76
photography, 8, 24-5
phrenology, 327-8
physicians, 89, 146
piano, 120; tuners, 120
Piccadilly, 206, 233, 281
pickpockets, 128, 190
Pickwick Papers, 24, 41, 79, 133, 136, 142, 177, 200, 224, 259, 307, 308, 332, 375, 419
Pictures from Italy, 26, 305
'picturesque', 137
piemen, 188
pigeon clubs, 276
pigs, 53, 61; squeaker, 62; stuck, 42
pillar boxes, 191
pilots (maritime), 388
pimento, 204, 205
Pip: age, 39, 96, 292; Cairo, 414; Darwin, 27;

'greatly instructed', 21; hand-shaking, 189; Magwitch and, 407; Miss Havisham, 29, 170; name, 23-4, 196; rise in society, 152; Telemachus, 251
Pipchin, Mrs, 203-4
pipes, *see* smoking
Piracy Acts: (1717-18), 46; (1719-20), 46
pirates, 38
Pitt, William, 1st Earl of Chatham, 206
Pitts, 136
plaster, 42
plate-receivers, 187
playbills, 239
plumbing, 85-6, 140
plum-pudding, 43
poachers, 221
Pocket, Herbert: age, 292; Cairo, 414; China, 203; mercantile ambitions, 204; name, 117; partnership, 297; Pip's name, 23
Pocket, Mrs: aristocratic pretensions, 210; Catherine Dickens, 210; character, 209
point-of-view, 7 n
police force, *see* Metropolitan Police
police-courts, *see* courts of law
police-offices, 224, 366
pollution, 181
pomades, 232
Pontius Pilate, 232
Pool of London, *see* Thames River'Poor Mercantile Jack', 294
Pope, Alexander: *Rape of the Lock*, 210, 306
Poplar, 174, 349
port, 59-60, 256
Port of London, 27, 393
portable property, 224
porters, 316, 339
Portfolio, 34
Portland Place, 371
portraits, photographic, 25
Portsmouth, 309-10; dockyard, 245; hulks, 45, 46
Post, The, 377
post mills, 67
postage, 191
postboys, 119, 162, 289
post-chaises, *see* carriages and coaches
posting inns, 160, 169, 172
postmen, 410
post-mortem examinations, 396-7
pottles, 183
poultices, 42, 217, 221-2, 248
Poultry, 175
Poussin, Nicholas, 137
powder mills, 296
Pratt, John, 276

Pretender, *see* Jacobites
Priestley, Joseph, 171
primogeniture, 152
prisons and prisoners, 326 Bridewells, 326, 334 chaplains, 400 convicts: beer, 274; conditional pardon, 311; dockyard labour, 249, 334; escapes, 43-4, 64; health, 30; irons, 29-30, 248, 270; money, 248; numbered, 30, 52, 246; pardons, 322; sexual immorality, 274; stagecoach travel, 244; uniforms, 248; women, 274
 county gaols, 123
 dark cells, 335 debtors, 326, 408-9 diet, 271, 272, 273 health, 400, 402-3, 406
 hulks, 30, 43-6, 47, 64, 71, 147, 246, 248, 249, 313, 319, 335, (illus.) 69, (illus.) 70
 lock-ups, 334
 military, 326
 sexual immorality, 274
 sponging-houses, 409
 suicides, 406 Victorian penal philosophy, 328
 warders, 316
 see also under names of individual prisons
privacy, 228
'Private Theatres', 266, 267, 361
privy, *see* water-closet
prizefighting, 121, 122
Prodigal Son, 61
Promontory Point, Utah, 285
pronunciation, 241-2, 243
property, portable, 224
prostitutes, 184, 190, 223, 374-5; brothels, 375; 'game', 223
proverbs and proverbial phrases, 54, 158, 200, 212, 242, 260, 279, 295, 355, 382
Pry, Paul: *Oddities of London Life*, 318
public houses, 133, 146, 194, 208, 246; Angel, Strood, 144; Blue Boar, 132, 244, 250, 258; Bull, Rochester, 133, 250, 413; Chequers, Lower Higham, 109-10; Cross Keys, Cheapside, 175, 244, 379; Crown, Rochester, 368; Guy, Earl of Warwick, Welling, 248; Lobster Smack, Canvey Island, 392; posting inns, 160, 169, 172, 337; Stonehouse, Rochester, 290, 414; Three Boys, Lower Higham, 110; Three Crutches, 110; Three Daws, Gravesend, 110; Three Gardeners, Strood, 110; Three Merry Boys, 110
public offices, 224
publicans, 221
pulleys, 349
pulpits: three-decker, 59
Pumblechook, Uncle: name, 55-6; Pip's fate, 35
pumps (domestic), *see* water-supply
pumps (maritime), 388

punch, 63, 216, 230
Punch, 1 n, 63
Punch (puppet), 230
punts, 349
pupil-teachers, *see* education
puppets: Punch, 230
Purfleet, 386
purgation, 352, 392
purse, long, 159
purser, 261
Pym, John, 251
Quakers, 128, 223
quarantine, 393
Quarter Sessions, 277
Queensberry, Sir John Sholto Douglas, Marquis of, 121
Queensberry Rules, 121
quill pens, 76, 286, 375

rag-and-bottle shops, 178, 261
railway, 56, 175, 383, 394; American, 285; London, Brighton and South Coast, 281; London, Chatham and Dover and South Eastern, 174, 281; Lower Higham, 37; North Kent, 357; Staplehurst crash, 281; Stockton and Darlington, 77
Ramsgate, 385
rantipole, 128
rape, 185
raspberries, 193
rat-catchers, 221
Ratcliff, 349
Ratcliff Highway murders (1811), 154, 180
reaches (Thames), 383
recitation books, 266
recluses, 83, 103, 201
Recorder of London, 185, 276-7, 404-5
Red Lion Street, 241
Red Sea, 376
redcoats, 52
Reform Bill (1832), 387
Reform Club, 285
Reformation, 206
reformatories, 55
Reformatory Schools, *see* education
Regent's Street, 233
Relief Act (1813), 409
Repton, Humphry, 137
Restoration House, 90-6, 103, 115, 118, 121, 123, 151, 199-200, 253-4, (illus.) 91, (illus.) 92
revisions of GE: chapters 23 and 24, 210-25; ending, 4-5, 12-14, 416-18, 420-2
rheumatism, 51
Riah, 186, 187

Richard II, 37
Richards, John: *Philosophical Principles of the Science of Brewing*, 199
Richmond, Surrey, 261, 278, 281
Richmond, Yorkshire, 278
Richmond Green, 281-2
rick-burning, 128
Riderhood, Rogue, 179, 226
Ridley, Reverend Sir James: *Tales of the Genii*, 301-2
Rio de Janeiro, 313
'River, The', 77
roads: badly maintained, 145, 174; improved, 56; straw on, 182; turnpike, 143-4, 169; wooden pavements, 182
roasting-jack, 231
Rochester, 27, 171, 248, 435-7; Benedictine priory, 121; bookshops, 141; boundaries, 250; bridge, 143-4, 259; Bull Inn, 133, 250, 413; Castle, (illus.) 161; Crow Lane, 90, 93, 94, 104, 253, 254; Crown Inn, 368; East Row, 90; Eastgate House, 87; gaol, 411; Guildhall, 81, 131, (illus.) 129, (illus.) 130; High Street, 87, 88, 90, 93, 128, 131, 141, 166, 167, 250, 253, 258, 259, 368, 379; Maidstone Road, 90; maps, 450, 451; market, 81; Mechanics Institute, 268; Mockbeggar House, 290; population, 56, 176; post office, 259; Restoration House, 90-6, 103, 115, 118, 121, 123, 151, 199-200, 253-4, (illus.) 91, (illus.) 92; Satis House, 95, 131, (illus.) 92; schoolhouse, 290; Stonehouse Inn, 290; Theatre Royal, 263; timber houses, 40; Town Hall, 128, 411; Victoria Street, 103; Vines, 90, 115, 121, 253, 254; Woodham's brewery, 90-5, 200; *see also* churches
Rochester and Chatham Journal, The, 251
Rochester Gazette, The, 251
Roebuck, John, 409
rogues, 329
rolls, hot, 166
Roman Empire, 62, 169, 180
Romanticism, 369
Rome: Capitoline Museum, 218
Romilly, Samuel, 271
Ronge, John and Bertha, 98
Rosa, Salvator, 137
Roscius, 239
Rosenberg, Charles, 351
Rosenberg, Edgar, 5 and n, 267, 366
rose-wood, 204
Rotherhithe, 349
Rotten Row, 206-7
Rotterdam, 377, 378, 384
Rousseau, Jean-Jacques: *Social Contract*, 286

routs, 298-9
rowing, *see* sport
Royal Commission on Education (1858), 108
Royal Exchange, 203, 207, 208, 286
Royal Geographical Society, 376
Royal Hospital, 361
Royal Naval College, 361
Royal Navy, 202, 204, 221; deserters, 329; enlistment, 134-5; signal guns, 44
Royal Observatory, Greenwich, 228
Royal Society, 106
Rudge, Mr, 111
Rugeley poisoner, 154
rum, 111, 205, 248
rushlights, 281, 340-1, 411
Russell, Lord John, 388
Russell, Lord William, 222
Russell Street, 340
Russia Company, 204

Sackville Street, 167
'Sacred to the Memory', 26
saddlers, 88
safflower, 204
sailing colliers, 385, 387
sailing vessels, 349, 385, 387
sailors, *see* seamen
St Albans, 154
St Andrew, cross of, 294
St Andrew's Priory, 95
St Bartholomew Priory, 186
St Bridget's Well, 334
St Clement I, Pope, 123
St Dunstan, 123-4
St George, cross of, 294
St James's Hall, 4
St James's Palace, 406
St James's Park, 206, 406
St James's Street, 285
St John the Baptist, 388
St John's Wood, 83
St Luke's Hospital for the Insane, 83-4
St Martin's Lane, 157
St Mary's, 97
St Mary's Convict Prison, Chatham, 273
St Mary's Island, 246
St Patrick, cross of, 294
saints, 123-4
sal volatile, 119
Salisbury assizes, 404
salt, 204; mines, 203; on bird's tail, 61
sanitation, 51
sapan-wood, 204
Sapsea, Mr, 79, 107
satin-wood, 204

Satis House, 101, 103, 115; originals, 89-96, 117, 131, (illus.) 92
sauce: anchovy, 279
Savoy military prison, 326
'Schoolboy's Story, The', 151
schools, *see* education
schoolteachers, *see* education
scolds, 140
Scotland, 137, 386
Scotland Yard: Black Museum, 180
Scots Fusilier Guards, 283
Scott, Sir Walter, 154, 314; *Guy Mannering*, 242
screws, 137
scuffle hunters, 254
sea biscuit, 221
sea captains, 208
seals (door), 316
seals (jewellery), 190
sea-marks, 37
seamen, 367; clothes, 321; parrots, 321; sea captains, 208; *see also* Royal Navy
'Season', the, 206-7, 269
Security from Violence Act (1863), 184
sedan chairs, 106, 162
sensibility, culture of, 171
servants, 212, 218, 237, 256, 284
Sessions House, 400, 402, 403
Seven Poor Travellers, The, 87, 171
sewing machines, 166
Shaftesbury Avenue, 281
shake-down, 325
Shakespeare, William: *Antony and Cleopatra*, 127; *As You Like It*, 103; *Coriolanus*, 155; *Cymbeline*, 200; *Hamlet*, 24, 60, 84, 103, 142, 239, 240, 262-4, 265, 323, 361, 364; *1 Henry IV*, 107; *2 Henry IV*, 338; *Henry V*, 158; *2 Henry VI*, 41; *Julius Caesar*, 75; *King John*, 146; *King Lear*, 120-1; *Macbeth*, 71, 114, 118, 232, 234, 263, 299; *Merchant of Venice*, 299, 401; *Midsummer Night's Dream*, 334; *Richard III*, 60, 112, 145; *Timon of Athens*, 155
sheep-farming, Australia, 114, 308, 309, 311, 318
sheep-stealing, 185
Sheerness, 393
Sheerness: dockyard, 245; hulks, 45
Shelley, Mary: *Frankenstein*, 106, 237, 324
Shepherd's Bush, 191
Sheridan, Richard Brinsley: *Critic*, 284; *School for Scandal*, 21, 300
sheriffs, 86, 402
sherry, 59-60, 188; 'doctored', 60
ship-brokers, 296
ships and boats: ballast-lighters, 391; barges, 137, 349, 385, 390; coal fires, 307; emigrant

ships, 389; figureheads, 388; gigs, 217; lighters, 217, 349, 388-9; paddle steamers, 394; provisioning, 261; punts, 349; sailing colliers, 385, 387; sailing vessels, 137, 349, 385, 387; skiffs, 217, 386; steam power, 77; troop transports, 389-90; wherries, 349, 386
shoes and boots clogs, 126; pattens, 126; throwing, 126; top-boots, 236-7; Wellington boots, 412
Shooter's Hill, 174
shooting, 160
'Short-timers', 374
Shovel, Admiral Cloudesley, 131
Shrewsbury, 145
Shropshire, 336
shumac, 204
shutters, 65
'Shy Neighbourhoods', 339
Sidney, Sir Philip: *Astrophil and Stella*, 13, 21, 23, 98, 254, 260
Sidney's Australian Hand-book, 309, 310, 311, 312, 318, 319, 322-3
Sidney's Emigrant Journal, 309, 312
signal guns, 144
Sikes, Bill, 78
silhouettes: photography replaces, 25
silver, 205; household, 326; mines, 203; paper, 54
Silvester, Sir John, 277
Singlewell, 40
Sittingbourne, 170
Sketches by Boz: 'Black Veil', 227; 'Criminal Courts', 269, 270; 'First of May', 362; 'Hackney Coach Stands', 162, 178; 'Hospital Patient', 78; 'Our Next-Door Neighbour', 327; 'Private Theatres', 266, 267, 361; 'River', 77; 'Sentiment', 141; 'Tuggs of Ramsgate', 56; 'Vauxhall Gardens by Day', 106; 'Visit to Newgate', 270
Skiffins, Miss: age, 295; and Aphrodite, 296; gloves, 170; name, 294-5
skiffs, 217, 386
slang, underworld, 325
slate tablets, 76
slaughter-houses, 181-2, 305, 381, 387
slave trade, 125, 294, 332
slop sellers, 349
slop-basins, 242
sluice-houses, 139, 378
smashers, 190
Smiles, Samuel, 7; *Self-Help*, 9 n, 10, 309, 420
Smith, Albert, 279
Smith, Captain Alexander: *Lives of the Most Noted Highwaymen*, 233
Smith, Charles Manby, 237, 385

Smith, Charlotte: *Old Manor House*, 85
Smith, Joe, 97
Smith, John, 276
Smith, Reverend Sydney, 272, 312
Smithfield Market, 175, 177, 181-2, 203, 374
Smithson, Harriet, 84
smoking: cigarettes, 163; cigars, 131, 321; pipes, 131, 162-3, 231, 318
Smollett, Tobias, 269, 314; *Humphry Clinker*, 411; *Peregrine Pickle*, 62-3, 227, 362; *Roderick Random*, 362
smuggling, 392, 393
Snagsby, Mrs, 140
snuff, 131, 163
soap, perfumed, 118, 232
social classes, 152
  bias among judges and jurors, 333
  craftsmen, 77
  lower classes, 77; cottage economy, 229; scuffle hunters, 254; Tag and Rag and Bobtail, 254; wife-beating, 78
social mobility, 152-3, 202
Society for Protecting Ancient Buildings, 230
Society for the Prevention of Cruelty to Animals, 160
Soho, 232-3, 281
Soldiers: barracks, 68; billeting, 64; buying discharge, 276; Coldstream Guards, 283; deserters, 329; drill, 64; enlistment, 134-5; Foot Guards, 282-3; forced march, 54; Grenadier Guards, 283; redcoats, 52; Scots Fusilier Guards, 283; uniform, 167
Somerset, 67, 226, 336
Somerset House, 80
songs, 136; 'Astonished Countryman', 136; 'Auld Lang Syne', 136; carols, 53; comic, 136; 'Fill the bumper fair!', 362; 'Oh, Lady fair!', 133; 'Old Clem', 123; 'Rule Britannia', 264; street-ballads, 136, 326; 'When I arrived in London Town', 136; 'When I to London first came in', 136; 'Yorkshire Man in London', 136
Songs of the Present, 78
South Benfleet, 392
South-East Asia, 204
Southend, 383, 384; pier, 27
Southey, Robert, 294
Southwark, 174, 199, 293, 307, 320, 343, 349
Southwark Bridge, 134, 382
Spain: naval power, 202
speaking-trumpet, 48
'Species', 26
Spectator, The, 14 n
Speke, John Hanning, 376
spelling, phonetic, 76

Spenlow, Dora, 255
Spices: cinnamon, 204; cloves, 204; ginger, 119, 204, 205; mace, 204; nutmeg, 204; pepper, 204; pimento, 204, 205
spiritualism, 63
spit, roasting, 231
spitting: Dickens's aversion to, 65
splitting (informing), 324
sponging-houses, 409
sport: boxing, 59, 121, 122; cricket, 242; prizefighting, 121, 122; ratting, 221; rowing, 217, 358; sculling, 217; shooting, 160; wrestling, 81; see also card games and games
Spurzheim, Johann Kaspar, 327, 328
stagecoaches, see carriages and coaches
Staines, 367
staircases, crumbling, 192
Staplehurst train crash, 281
Startop, 212
state trials, 233
stays, see costume and appearance: underclothes
steak, stewed, 226
steam, 77, 281, 371, 377, 387, 409-10
steam-hammers, 50, 159
steam-ships, 77, 281, 371, 377, 384, 385
Steele, Sir Richard, 39
Stephen, Fitzjames, 165
Stephenson, George, 77
Stevens, Alderman Thomas, 131, 199
Stevenson, Robert Louis: *Wrong Box*, 181
sticking plaster, 132
Stock Exchange, 208
stocks, 132, 140, 326-7
Stockton and Darlington Railway, 77
Stoke, 97
Stonehouse Inn, Rochester, 290, 414
storms (1860-1), 306
Strand, The, 193, 285
Strand Theatre, 24
straw: imported, 390; in coaches, 178, 379; on roads, 182; straw-yards, 178
strawberries, 164, 193
Strawberry Hill, 228
streets: cleaners, 260; mud and dirt, 305-6
Strood, 169, 253, 258; Angel Inn, 144; bridge, 259; Frindsbury Road, 144; High Street, 144; Hill, 143, 174; Three Gardeners Inn, 110
stuck pig, 42
Sudbury, Suffolk, 133
suet puddings, 362
sugar, 205, 294; moist, 109
suicides, prison, 406
sulphur mines, 203
Summerson, Esther, 409
Sun Fire Office, 267

Sunderland, 385
supernatural tales, 47
surgeons, 146, 232
Surrey, 174, 392; Downs, 329
Surtees, Robert, 247
Sussex, 380
swab, 362
Swan, Robert, 276
swearing, demi-, 117
sweating-baths, 340
Swift, Jonathan: *Battle of the Books*, 214-15
Swinstead Abbey, Lincolnshire, 145-6
Switzerland, 101
Sydney, 83
Syncretic Society, 268

table-rapping, see spiritualism
Tag and Rag and Bobtail, 254
tailoring, 166-7, 287
Talbot, William Henry Fox, 25
Tale of Two Cities, A, 1, 2, 22, 100, 183, 242, 290, 336, 453
tar-water, 43, 62-3, 72
Tasmania, see Australia
Tatler, The, 39
taverns, see public houses
Tavistock House, 339
tax, 331; Customs, 358, 393; hair powder, 320
tea, 42, 240, 242, 248; twig, 280
teachers, see education
teak, 204
Tegg, Thomas: 'Manual', 238, 259
Telemachus, 251
Telford, Thomas, 145
Temple Bar, 203, 340
Temple, see Inns of Court
Tennyson, Alfred, Lord: 'Aylmer's Field', 100; 'Lady of Shalott', 84; 'Mariana', 84, 85, 103, 118; 'Maud', 84
Ternan, Ellen Lawless, 98, 298
Terrific Register, 34
Thackeray, William Makepeace, 314; *Book of Snobs*, 113-14, 165, 167, 260; *Four Georges*, 165, 257, 299, 301, 351; *Sketches and Travels*, 239, 284
Thames River, 27-8, 174, 203, 208, 221, 258, 332, 343, (illus.) 353, (illus.) 354, 438-40; beacons, 37; bridges, 293, 382; Chelsea Reach, 293; collisions on, 394; customs officers, 389; Deptford Reach, 387; drownings, 394; embankment, 306-7, 341, 355, 358; gibbets, 38; Gravesend Reach, 384; Greenwich time signal, 228; Hope Reach, 383; Limehouse Reach, 355, 387; Lower Hope Reach, 383, 390; maps, 444-8, 452; Mogg's

map, 217; Pool of London, 342, 343, 357, 388-9, 390; reaches, 383; Sea Reach, 383, 390; 'shooting the bridge', 356; steamers on, 377, 385; tides, 137, 356, 383, 384, 389, 390, 391, 393; Tower Pier, 377; Upnor Reach, 250; Upper Pool, 293
Thames River Police, 392
Theatre Royal, Covent Garden, 24
theatre: burletta, 239; extravaganza, 239; farce, 239; 'legitimate', 239; melodrama, 239, 363; nautical melodrama, 363; pantomime, 363; Stage Negro, 361
theatres: audience, 263; bill-posting, 285; Drury Lane, 239, 240; Haymarket, 206; Opera, 206; orange peel and nuts thrown, 240; patent, 268; playbills, 239; Strand, 24; Theatre Royal, Covent Garden, 24, 239; Theatre Royal, Rochester, 263; unlicensed, 361
Theatres Act (1843), 239
thimble-riggers, 329
Thirty-Nine Articles, 59
Thomson, James: *Alfred*, 264; 'Rule Britannia', 264; *Seasons*, 286
Thornbury, George, 149
Thornhill, Sir James, 180
Thousand and One Nights, 376
Thrale brewery, 199
Threadneedle Street, 207
Three Boys Inn, 110
Three Crutches Inn, 110
Three Daws Inn, Gravesend, 110
Three Jolly Bargemen: originals, 109-10
Three Merry Boys Inn, 110
Thurtell, John, 154
Tibullus, 298
tick (credit), 110
ticket-of-leave men, 313
tilburies, *see* carriages and coaches
Tilt, Dr E. J., 120
timber buildings: brick replaces, 40
Timbs, John, 209
Times, The, 162, 273, 317, 341, 377
time-scheme of GE, 8-12, 25, 28, 39, 47, 65, 76, 99, 124, 144, 147-8, 275, 308, 329, 373, 423-34
tin, 243; mines, 203
Tindale, 124
tinder-boxes, 48, 381
tinkers, 327
tinsmiths, 243
tissue-paper, 292
Tite, William, 208
title, 3, 21
toadies, 116, 213
toasters, 138

toasting, 66, 300
tobacco, 192, 205, 248, 294, 318; Cavendish cakes, 318; Negro-head, 318; Oroonoko, 318; Pigtail, 318; Roll, 318; shag, 318; *see also* smoking
tobacco-stoppers, 231
Tobago, 205
'Tom Tiddler's Ground', 84, 103
tombstones, 26; Baker and Comport, 25-6, 28, 36; inscriptions, 79
Tompion, Thomas, 89
tongue, 169
tooth powders, 232
tooth washes, 232
toothache, 222
top-boots, *see* shoes and boots
topography, 6-9, 435-7, 438-40, 441-52; *see also under individual place-names*
Tottenham Court Road, 233
Tower of London, 80, 326, 357, 386-7
Towns Improvement Clauses Act (1847), 181
Townshend, Chauncy Hare, 22
toys: dolls, 216
Trabb's boy, 259
tracts, 128-31, 328
'Trading in Death', 288
Trafalgar, battle of (1805), 202, 203
tramps, 111, 328, 329
'Tramps', 328
'Transmutation of the Species', 26
transportation, 187; America, 30, 46, 249; Australia, 7, 34, 45, 46, 128, 249, 273, 313, 314, 334, 390; children, 374; hanging commuted to, 312; sentence, 335
travel: coach, 126, 174, 179, 193; railway, 175; sedan chair, 106, 162; walking, 126, 259, 339
Travellers' Rests, 329
'Travelling Abroad', 101, 174
Treasury, 80, 406
trespassers, 221
trials, *see* courts of law
Trinity House Company, 37, 388, 390
Trinity Street (Rotherhithe Street), 351
Trollope, Anthony: *Orley Farm*, 234-5
Trottiscliffe parish church, 59
Trotwood, Betsey, 203-4, 296, 370
'True Story of a Coal Fire, The', 387, 388
Truman brewery, 199
'Tuggs of Ramsgate', 56
Turkey Company, 204
Turner, J. M. W., 37, 385
Turner's Cerate, 372
turnips, 327
turnpike houses, 143, 144
turnpike roads, 143-4, 169

turpentine, 372
Turpin, Dick, 337
Tussaud, Madame, 97, 180
tutors, *see* education
Twist, Oliver, 39
'Two Chapters on Bank Note Forgeries', 112, 309, 330, 331, 423
'Two View of a Cheap Theatre', 363-4
Tyburn, 184
Tyler, Wat, 37
Ullathorne, Reverend William, 311
Uncle John, 98
Uncommercial Traveller, The, 2, 7 n, 27, 29, 86, 101, 164, 171, 192, 245-6, 258, 263, 268, 379
undertakers, 79, 287, 288, 289. *See also* funerals
underworld slang, 325
underwriters, *see* insurance
Uniform Penny Postage (1840), 191
Union Hole, 349
Union Jack, 294, 363
Universal Songster, The, 136
unleavened bread, 220-1
upholstery, 236
Upnor, 97; Castle, 38; hulks, 45
Uxbridge, 191

Vagrancy Act (1824), 184
vagrants, 111, 184, 327, 330
Van Diemen's Land, *see* Tasmania
Vanbrugh, Sir John: *Provok'd Wife*, 210
vats, copper, 102
Vauxhall, 293, 307
'Vauxhall Gardens by Day', 106
Veneering, Mr, 132
Venetian turpentine, 372
Venn, Henry: *Complete Duty of Man*, 47
Venus, 286
Vernon, Admiral Edward, 355
Victoria, *see* Australia
Victoria, Queen, 176, 329, 406
Victoria Nyanza, Lake, 376
Victoria Street, 90, 93, 94, 103
Vines, The, 90, 115, 121, 253, 254
Virgil: *Aeneid*, 116
'Visit to Newgate, A', 270
Vulcan, 35

Wade, John: *Treatise on the Police*, 29-30, 45
wafers (documents), 267
waggons, 175, 328
waiters: behaviour, 279
Wakefield, Edward Gibbon, 222, 406
Waldegrave family, 267
Waldengarver, 266-7
Wales, 385

Wales, Edward, Prince of, 307
Wales, Frederick Lewis, Prince of, 261
Walker, John, 48
walking, *see* travel
walking beam engines, 410
Walpole, Horace, 228
Walworth, 224, 227, 295, 397
Wandering Jew, 139
Wapping, 349; Execution Dock, 38
Wapping New Stairs, 349
Ward, John, 45, 246
warders, 316
Wardle, Rachel, 200
Warren, Robert, 136
Warren, The, 80
Warren's blacking warehouse, 48, 100, 135, 148, 241
washing, 86
watches, 97, 205; chains, 190; pocket, 190; repeater, 227
watchmakers, 89
watchmen, 316
water, 85-6
water-closet, 229
water-supply, 85-6; pumps, 140, 237
watercress, 413
Waterloo, battle of (1815), 174, 203
Waterloo Bridge, 293, 306, 356, 382
Watling Street, 110, 174, 343
Watson, Richard, 2
Watt, James, 77, 159, 409-10
Watts, Isaac: *Divine Songs*, 413
Watts, Richard, 95, 131
waxworks, 97
'wealth, aristocracy of', 198
Weare, William, 154, 231
weatherboarding, Dutch, 40
Webber, James, 351
Webster, Professor J. W., 234
Webster's Royal Red Book, 215
Weekly Dispatch, The, 222
weeping, 171-2, 406
Wegg, Silas, 319
'Well-Authenticated Rappings', 63
Welling, 174, 248
Wellington, Sir Arthur Wellesley, 1st Duke of, 65, 134, 230, 387, 412
Wellington boots, 412
Wemmick: age, 295
Wesley, John, 131; 'Great Assize', 402; 'On Dress', 54
West Indies, 205, 294
Western Australia, *see* Australia
Westminster, 174, 307
Westminster Bridge, 293, 356, 385, 392

Westminster Convent, 193
Westminster Hall, 355
wheels, carriage, 56
wheelwrights, 56
'Where We Stopped Growing', 81
wherries, 349, 386
whipping, see flogging
Whitbread, Samuel, 81, 199
Whitechapel, 186; Market, 186
Whitecross Prison, 184
Whitecross Street, 184
Whitefriars, 339, 341
Whitehall, 362, 406
whitesmiths, 243
whitewash, 68
whitlow, 217
Whittington, Dick, 136
Wight, John: *Mornings at Bow*, 78; *More Mornings at Bow*, 78
wigs, see hair
William III, 74, 131
William IV, 74
William the Conqueror, 334
Williams, John, 180
Williamson, Sir Joseph, 131
wills, 314
Wills, W. H., 112, 113, 202; 'Epsom', 329; *Household Words* 1 n; 'Photography', 24-5; 'Two Chapters on Bank Note Forgeries', 309, 330, 331, 423
Wimbledon Common, 38
wind: east, 306
windmills, 67, 350
windows: blinds, 188; blocking up, 90; bow and bay, 351; shutters, 65; tax, 90
wine, see food and drink
Winzer (Winsor), Friedrich Albrecht, 280
witches, 34
Wollstonecraft, Mary: *Vindication of the Rights of Women*, 211
women: cigarettes, 163; cleaners, 316; convicts, 274; funeral practices, 289; governesses, 352; humanizing influence, 311; laundresses, 316; legal status, 201; public whipping, 184; rape, 185; scolds, 140; wife-beating, 78, 365-6, 419; see also prostitutes
wood, 205; calamander, 204; ebony, 204; rosewood, 204; sapan-wood, 204; satin-wood, 204; teak, 204
Wood Street, 175, 177, 244, 270, 379
Woodham's brewery, 90-5, 200
wool, 205; Great Custom, 358
Woolsack, 211
Woolwich, 38; dockyard, 80, 245; hulks, 45
Wopsle, Mr: name, 55-6

Wordsworth, William, 230, 328, 338; 'Immortality' ode, 338; *Prelude*, 172
World Upside Down, The, 33
Wren, Sir Christopher, 182, 228
wrestling, see sport
Wright's Topography of Rochester, Chatham . . ., 88, 89, 141, 166, 251, 259
writing-tablet, 368-9
wrought iron, 205

Yates, Edmund, 83
Yates, Frederick: 'Next Door Neighbours', 84-5
yellow berries, 204
York, 45
York, Richard, Duke of, 132
Yorkshire Youth, The, 329

Zeus, 341

MAP OF DICKENS' LONDON

HOLBORN
HOLBORN HILL
West Smithfield
SNOW HILL
FETTER LANE
NEWGATE STREET
FLEET STREET
OLD BAILEY
St. Paul's
The Temple
Temple Stairs
Blackfriar's Bridge

KEY
- Parks and Gardens
- Buildings
- Important Buidings
- Buildings significant to Book